VW Automotive Repair Manual

by AK Legg, Larry Warren, Robert Maddox and John H Haynes
Member of the Guild of Motoring Writers

Models covered:
All Volkswagen Rabbit, Golf, Jetta, Scirocco and Pick-up models with a gasoline engine
1975 through 1992

(10Y11 – 96016)
(884)

ABCDE
FGHIJ
KLMNO
PQ   2

Haynes Publishing Group
Sparkford Nr Yeovil
Somerset BA22 7JJ England

Haynes North America, Inc
861 Lawrence Drive
Newbury Park
California 91320 USA

Acknowledgements

We are grateful for the help and cooperation of Volkswagen of America, Inc., for assistance with technical information, certain illustrations and vehicle photos.

© Haynes North America 1990, 1991, 1993

A book in the **Haynes Automotive Repair Manual Series**

Printed in the USA

ISBN 1 56392 061 1

Library of Congress Catalog Card Number 93-77334

While every attempt is made to ensure that the information in this manual is correct, no liability can be accepted by the authors or publishers for loss, damage or injury caused by any errors in, or omissions from, the information given.

Contents

Introductory pages

About this manual 6
Introduction to the Volkswagen Rabbit, Golf, Jetta,
  Scirocco and Pick-up 6
Vehicle identification numbers 7
Buying parts 9
Maintenance techniques, tools and working facilities 9
Booster battery (jump) starting 16
Jacking and towing 16
Automotive chemicals and lubricants 18
Safety first! 19
Conversion factors 20
Troubleshooting 21

Chapter 1
Tune-up and routine maintenance 1–1

Chapter 2 Part A
Engine 2A–1

Chapter 2 Part B
General engine overhaul procedures 2B–1

Chapter 3
Cooling, heating and air conditioning systems 3–1

Chapter 4
Fuel and exhaust systems 4–1

Chapter 5
Engine electrical systems 5–1

Chapter 6
Emissions control systems 6–1

Chapter 7 Part A
Manual transaxle 7A–1

Chapter 7 Part B
Automatic transaxle 7B–1

Chapter 8
Clutch and driveaxles 8–1

Chapter 9
Brakes 9–1

Chapter 10
Suspension and steering systems 10–1

Chapter 11
Body 11–1

Chapter 12
Chassis electrical system 12–1

Wiring diagrams 12–14

Index IND–1

1

2A

2B

3

4

5

6

7A

7B

8

9

10

11

12

VW Rabbit "L"

VW Scirocco

VW Jetta

VW Pick-up

About this manual

Its purpose

The purpose of this manual is to help you get the best value from your vehicle. It can do so in several ways. It can help you decide what work must be done, even if you choose to have it done by a dealer service department or a repair shop; it provides information and procedures for routine maintenance and servicing; and it offers diagnostic and repair procedures to follow when trouble occurs.

We hope you use the manual to tackle the work yourself. For many simpler jobs, doing it yourself may be quicker than arranging an appointment to get the vehicle into a shop and making the trips to leave it and pick it up. More importantly, a lot of money can be saved by avoiding the expense the shop must pass on to you to cover its labor and overhead costs. An added benefit is the sense of satisfaction and accomplishment that you feel after doing the job yourself.

Using the manual

The manual is divided into Chapters. Each Chapter is divided into numbered Sections, which are headed in bold type between horizontal lines. Each Section consists of consecutively numbered paragraphs.

At the beginning of each numbered section you will be referred to any illustrations which apply to the procedures in that section. The reference numbers used in illustration captions pinpoint the pertinent Section and the Step within that section. That is, illustration 3.2 means the illustration refers to Section 3 and Step (or paragraph) 2 within that Section.

Procedures, once described in the text, are not normally repeated. When it's necessary to refer to another Chapter, the reference will be given as Chapter and Section number. Cross references given without use of the word "Chapter" apply to Sections and/or paragraphs in the same Chapter. For example, "see Section 8" means in the same Chapter.

References to the left or right side of the vehicle assume you are sitting in the driver's seat, facing forward.

Even though we have prepared this manual with extreme care, neither the publisher nor the author can accept responsibility for any errors in, or omissions from, the information given.

NOTE

A **Note** provides information necessary to properly complete a procedure or information which will make the procedure easier to understand.

CAUTION

A **Caution** provides a special procedure or special steps which must be taken while completing the procedure where the **Caution** is found. Not heeding a **Caution** can result in damage to the assembly being worked on.

WARNING

A **Warning** provides a special procedure or special steps which must be taken while completing the procedure where the **Warning** is found. Not heeding a **Warning** can result in personal injury.

Introduction to the Volkswagen Rabbit, Golf, Jetta, Scirocco and Pick-up

The Volkswagen front wheel drive models covered by this manual are all very similar in design, with a variety of body styles offered. The Rabbit, Golf and Jetta models are available in 2-door coupe or 4-door sedan arrangements, while the Scirocco and Pick-up models are available in 2-door styles only.

The transversely mounted, inline four-cylinder engine used in these models is equipped with either a carburetor, mechanical fuel injection or electronic fuel injection. Early models utilized a breaker points-type ignition system, while later models are equipped with a breakerless electronic ignition system.

The engine drives the front wheels through either a 4 or 5-speed manual or 3-speed automatic transaxle via independent driveaxles.

Independent suspension, featuring coil spring/strut damper units, is used on the front wheels. The rack and pinion steering unit is mounted behind the engine.

The rear suspension on all models but the pick-up is semi-independent, using a torsion-type axle beam, coil springs and separate shock absorbers. The pick-up uses a solid beam axle, leaf springs and shock absorbers.

Early models came equipped with drum brakes on all four wheels. Disc brakes replaced the drum brakes on the front axles of later models, but retained the drum brakes on the rear wheels. Certain later models employed disc brakes on all four wheels.

Vehicle identification numbers

Modifications are a continuing and unpublicized process in vehicle manufacturing. Since spare parts manuals and lists are compiled on a numerical basis, the individual vehicle numbers are essential to correctly identify the component required.

Vehicle Identification Number (VIN)

This very important identification number is found in different locations, depending on model and year **(see illustration)**. The VIN also appears on the Vehicle Certificate of Title and Registration. It contains information such as where and when the vehicle was manufactured, the model year and the body style.

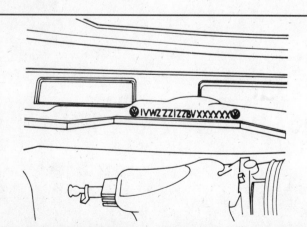

On some models, the chassis number is stamped on the firewall – on other models this number can be found on the right front strut tower, on the top of the frame by the radiator, on the instrument panel (visible through the window), on the floor panel in the luggage compartment near the spare tire, and on the driver's door jamb

The engine serial number is stamped on the cylinder block, behind the distributor

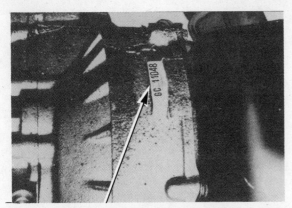

The manual transaxle code letters and numbers are located
on the bellhousing

Locations of the type numbers (A) and code numbers (B) on
automatic transaxles

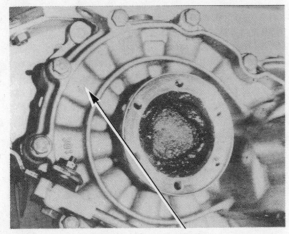

The manual transaxle type number is located on the side of
the transaxle case

Vehicle identification plate

The vehicle identification plate is attached to the left front door jamb. The plate contains the name of the manufacturer, the month and year of production, the Gross Vehicle Weight Rating (GVWR), the Gross Axle Weight Rating (GAWR) and the certification statement.

Engine number

The engine serial number is located on the left (driver's) end of the cylinder block **(see illustration)**.

Transaxle numbers

Manual transaxles are identified by code letters and numbers on the bellhousing, and also a type number cast into the side of the transaxle case **(see illustrations)**. On automatic transaxles, the type and code numbers are located on the top of the bellhousing **(see illustration)**.

Buying parts

Replacement parts are available from many sources, which generally fall into one of two categories – authorized dealer parts departments and independent retail auto parts stores. Our advice concerning these parts is as follows:

Retail auto parts stores: Good auto parts stores will stock frequently needed components which wear out relatively fast, such as clutch components, exhaust systems, brake parts, tune-up parts, etc. These stores often supply new or reconditioned parts on an exchange basis, which can save a considerable amount of money. Discount auto parts stores are often very good places to buy materials and parts needed for general vehicle maintenance such as oil, grease, filters, spark plugs, belts, touch-up paint, bulbs, etc. They also usually sell tools and general accessories, have con-

venient hours, charge lower prices and can often be found not far from home.

Authorized dealer parts department: This is the best source for parts which are unique to the vehicle and not generally available elsewhere (such as major engine parts, transmission parts, trim pieces, etc.).

Warranty information: *If the vehicle is still covered under warranty, be sure that any replacement parts purchased – regardless of the source – do not invalidate the warranty!*

To be sure of obtaining the correct parts, have engine and chassis numbers available and, if possible, take the old parts along for positive identification.

Maintenance techniques, tools and working facilities

Maintenance techniques

There are a number of techniques involved in maintenance and repair that will be referred to throughout this manual. Application of these techniques will enable the home mechanic to be more efficient, better organized and capable of performing the various tasks properly, which will ensure that the repair job is thorough and complete.

Fasteners

Fasteners are nuts, bolts, studs and screws used to hold two or more parts together. There are a few things to keep in mind when working with fasteners. Almost all of them use a locking device of some type, either a lockwasher, locknut, locking tab or thread adhesive. All threaded fasteners should be clean and straight, with undamaged threads and undamaged corners on the hex head where the wrench fits. Develop the habit of replacing all damaged nuts and bolts with new ones. Special locknuts

with nylon or fiber inserts can only be used once. If they are removed, they lose their locking ability and must be replaced with new ones.

Rusted nuts and bolts should be treated with a penetrating fluid to ease removal and prevent breakage. Some mechanics use turpentine in a spout-type oil can, which works quite well. After applying the rust penetrant, let it work for a few minutes before trying to loosen the nut or bolt. Badly rusted fasteners may have to be chiseled or sawed off or removed with a special nut breaker, available at tool stores.

If a bolt or stud breaks off in an assembly, it can be drilled and removed with a special tool commonly available for this purpose. Most automotive machine shops can perform this task, as well as other repair procedures, such as the repair of threaded holes that have been stripped out.

Flat washers and lockwashers, when removed from an assembly, should always be replaced exactly as removed. Replace any damaged washers with new ones. Never use a lockwasher on any soft metal surface (such as aluminum), thin sheet metal or plastic.

Fastener sizes

For a number of reasons, automobile manufacturers are making wider and wider use of metric fasteners. Therefore, it is important to be able to tell the difference between standard (sometimes called U.S. or SAE) and metric hardware, since they cannot be interchanged.

All bolts, whether standard or metric, are sized according to diameter, thread pitch and length. For example, a standard 1/2 – 13 x 1 bolt is 1/2 inch in diameter, has 13 threads per inch and is 1 inch long. An M12 – 1.75 x 25 metric bolt is 12 mm in diameter, has a thread pitch of 1.75 mm (the distance between threads) and is 25 mm long. The two bolts are nearly identical, and easily confused, but they are not interchangeable.

In addition to the differences in diameter, thread pitch and length, metric and standard bolts can also be distinguished by examining the bolt heads. To begin with, the distance across the flats on a standard bolt head is measured in inches, while the same dimension on a metric bolt is sized in millimeters (the same is true for nuts). As a result, a standard wrench should not be used on a metric bolt and a metric wrench should not be used on a standard bolt. Also, most standard bolts have slashes radiating out from the center of the head to denote the grade or strength of the bolt, which is an indication of the amount of torque that can be applied to it. The greater the number of slashes, the greater the strength of the bolt. Grades 0 through 5 are commonly used on automobiles. Metric bolts have a property class (grade) number, rather than a slash, molded into their heads to indicate bolt strength. In this case, the higher the number, the stronger the bolt. Property class numbers 8.8, 9.8 and 10.9 are commonly used on automobiles.

Strength markings can also be used to distinguish standard hex nuts from metric hex nuts. Many standard nuts have dots stamped into one side, while metric nuts are marked with a number. The greater the number of dots, or the higher the number, the greater the strength of the nut.

Metric studs are also marked on their ends according to property class (grade). Larger studs are numbered (the same as metric bolts), while smaller studs carry a geometric code to denote grade.

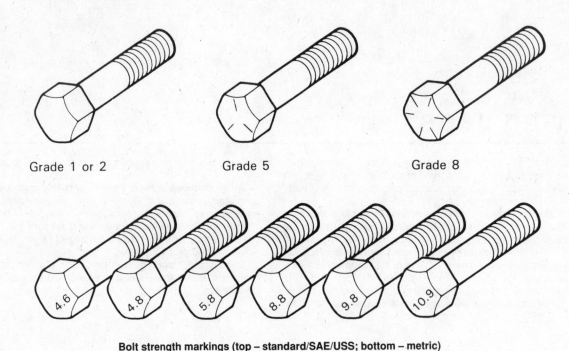

Grade 1 or 2   Grade 5   Grade 8

Bolt strength markings (top – standard/SAE/USS; bottom – metric)

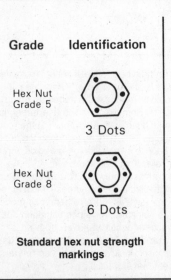

Grade	Identification
Hex Nut Grade 5	3 Dots
Hex Nut Grade 8	6 Dots

Standard hex nut strength markings

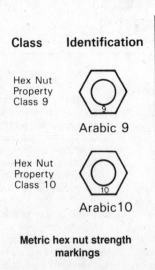

Class	Identification
Hex Nut Property Class 9	Arabic 9
Hex Nut Property Class 10	Arabic 10

Metric hex nut strength markings

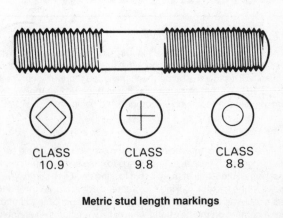

CLASS 10.9   CLASS 9.8   CLASS 8.8

Metric stud length markings

It should be noted that many fasteners, especially Grades 0 through 2, have no distinguishing marks on them. When such is the case, the only way to determine whether it is standard or metric is to measure the thread pitch or compare it to a known fastener of the same size.

Standard fasteners are often referred to as SAE, as opposed to metric. However, it should be noted that SAE technically refers to a non-metric *fine thread* fastener only. Coarse thread non-metric fasteners are referred to as USS sizes.

Since fasteners of the same size (both standard and metric) may have different strength ratings, be sure to reinstall any bolts, studs or nuts removed from your vehicle in their original locations. Also, when replacing a fastener with a new one, make sure that the new one has a strength rating equal to or greater than the original.

Tightening sequences and procedures

Most threaded fasteners should be tightened to a specific torque value (torque is the twisting force applied to a threaded component such as a nut or bolt). Overtightening the fastener can weaken it and cause it to break, while undertightening can cause it to eventually come loose. Bolts, screws and studs, depending on the material they are made of and their thread diameters, have specific torque values, many of which are noted in the Specifications at the beginning of each Chapter. Be sure to follow the torque recommendations closely. For fasteners not assigned a specific torque, a general torque value chart is presented here as a guide. These torque values are for dry (unlubricated) fasteners threaded into steel or cast iron (not aluminum). As was previously mentioned, the size and grade of a fastener determine the amount of torque that can safely

Metric thread sizes	Ft-lbs	Nm
M-6	6 to 9	9 to 12
M-8	14 to 21	19 to 28
M-10	28 to 40	38 to 54
M-12	50 to 71	68 to 96
M-14	80 to 140	109 to 154

Pipe thread sizes		
1/8	5 to 8	7 to 10
1/4	12 to 18	17 to 24
3/8	22 to 33	30 to 44
1/2	25 to 35	34 to 47

U.S. thread sizes		
1/4 – 20	6 to 9	9 to 12
5/16 – 18	12 to 18	17 to 24
5/16 – 24	14 to 20	19 to 27
3/8 – 16	22 to 32	30 to 43
3/8 – 24	27 to 38	37 to 51
7/16 – 14	40 to 55	55 to 74
7/16 – 20	40 to 60	55 to 81
1/2 – 13	55 to 80	75 to 108

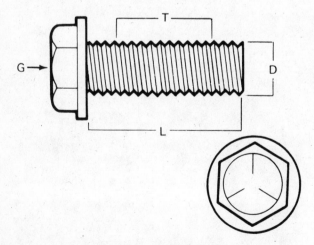

Standard (SAE and USS) bolt dimensions/grade marks

G	Grade marks (bolt length)
L	Length (in inches)
T	Thread pitch (number of threads per inch)
D	Nominal diameter (in inches)

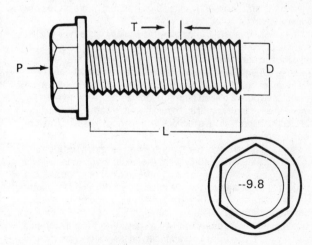

Metric bolt dimensions/grade marks

P	Property class (bolt strength)
L	Length (in millimeters)
T	Thread pitch (distance between threads in millimeters)
D	Diameter

be applied to it. The figures listed here are approximate for Grade 2 and Grade 3 fasteners. Higher grades can tolerate higher torque values.

Fasteners laid out in a pattern, such as cylinder head bolts, oil pan bolts, differential cover bolts, etc., must be loosened or tightened in sequence to avoid warping the component. This sequence will normally be shown in the appropriate Chapter. If a specific pattern is not given, the following procedures can be used to prevent warping.

Initially, the bolts or nuts should be assembled finger-tight only. Next, they should be tightened one full turn each, in a criss-cross or diagonal pattern. After each one has been tightened one full turn, return to the first one and tighten them all one-half turn, following the same pattern. Finally, tighten each of them one-quarter turn at a time until each fastener has been tightened to the proper torque. To loosen and remove the fasteners, the procedure would be reversed.

Component disassembly

Component disassembly should be done with care and purpose to help ensure that the parts go back together properly. Always keep track of the sequence in which parts are removed. Make note of special characteristics or marks on parts that can be installed more than one way, such as a grooved thrust washer on a shaft. It is a good idea to lay the disassembled parts out on a clean surface in the order that they were removed. It may also be helpful to make sketches or take instant photos of components before removal.

When removing fasteners from a component, keep track of their locations. Sometimes threading a bolt back in a part, or putting the washers and nut back on a stud, can prevent mix-ups later. If nuts and bolts cannot be returned to their original locations, they should be kept in a compartmented box or a series of small boxes. A cupcake or muffin tin is ideal for this purpose, since each cavity can hold the bolts and nuts from a particular area (i.e. oil pan bolts, valve cover bolts, engine mount bolts, etc.). A pan of this type is especially helpful when working on assemblies with very small parts, such as the carburetor, alternator, valve train or interior dash and trim pieces. The cavities can be marked with paint or tape to identify the contents.

Whenever wiring looms, harnesses or connectors are separated, it is a good idea to identify the two halves with numbered pieces of masking tape so they can be easily reconnected.

Gasket sealing surfaces

Throughout any vehicle, gaskets are used to seal the mating surfaces between two parts and keep lubricants, fluids, vacuum or pressure contained in an assembly.

Many times these gaskets are coated with a liquid or paste-type gasket sealing compound before assembly. Age, heat and pressure can sometimes cause the two parts to stick together so tightly that they are very difficult to separate. Often, the assembly can be loosened by striking it with a soft-face hammer near the mating surfaces. A regular hammer can be used if a block of wood is placed between the hammer and the part. Do not hammer on cast parts or parts that could be easily damaged. With any particularly stubborn part, always recheck to make sure that every fastener has been removed.

Avoid using a screwdriver or bar to pry apart an assembly, as they can easily mar the gasket sealing surfaces of the parts, which must remain smooth. If prying is absolutely necessary, use an old broom handle, but keep in mind that extra clean up will be necessary if the wood splinters.

After the parts are separated, the old gasket must be carefully scraped off and the gasket surfaces cleaned. Stubborn gasket material can be soaked with rust penetrant or treated with a special chemical to soften it so it can be easily scraped off. A scraper can be fashioned from a piece of copper tubing by flattening and sharpening one end. Copper is recommended because it is usually softer than the surfaces to be scraped, which reduces the chance of gouging the part. Some gaskets can be removed with a wire brush, but regardless of the method used, the mating surfaces must be left clean and smooth. If for some reason the gasket surface is gouged, then a gasket sealer thick enough to fill scratches will have to be used during reassembly of the components. For most applications, a non-drying (or semi-drying) gasket sealer should be used.

Hose removal tips

Warning: *If the vehicle is equipped with air conditioning, do not disconnect any of the A/C hoses without first having the system depressurized by a dealer service department or a service station.*

Hose removal precautions closely parallel gasket removal precautions. Avoid scratching or gouging the surface that the hose mates against or the connection may leak. This is especially true for radiator hoses. Because of various chemical reactions, the rubber in hoses can bond itself to the metal spigot that the hose fits over. To remove a hose, first loosen the hose clamps that secure it to the spigot. Then, with slip-joint pliers, grab the hose at the clamp and rotate it around the spigot. Work it back and forth until it is completely free, then pull it off. Silicone or other lubricants will ease removal if they can be applied between the hose and the outside of the spigot. Apply the same lubricant to the inside of the hose and the outside of the spigot to simplify installation.

As a last resort (and if the hose is to be replaced with a new one anyway), the rubber can be slit with a knife and the hose peeled from the spigot. If this must be done, be careful that the metal connection is not damaged.

If a hose clamp is broken or damaged, do not reuse it. Wire-type clamps usually weaken with age, so it is a good idea to replace them with screw-type clamps whenever a hose is removed.

Tools

A selection of good tools is a basic requirement for anyone who plans to maintain and repair his or her own vehicle. For the owner who has few tools, the initial investment might seem high, but when compared to the spiraling costs of professional auto maintenance and repair, it is a wise one.

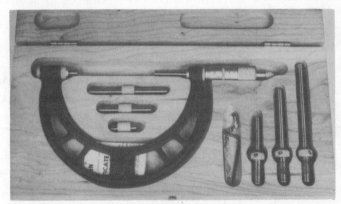

Micrometer set

Dial indicator set

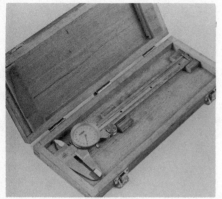

Dial caliper

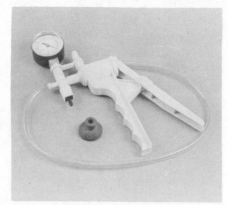

Hand-operated vacuum pump

Timing light

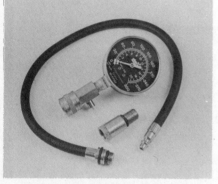

Compression gauge with spark plug hole adapter

Damper/steering wheel puller

General purpose puller

Hydraulic lifter removal tool

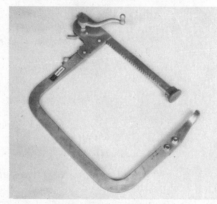

Valve spring compressor

Valve spring compressor

Ridge reamer

Piston ring groove cleaning tool

Ring removal/installation tool

Ring compressor

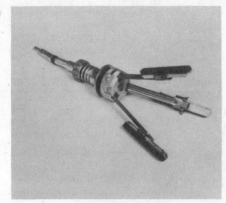

Cylinder hone

Brake hold-down spring tool

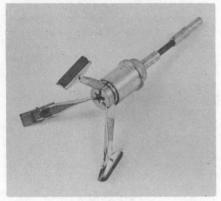

Brake cylinder hone

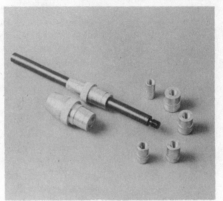

Clutch plate alignment tool

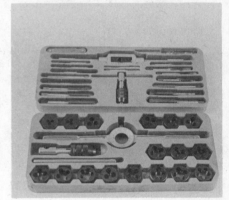

Tap and die set

To help the owner decide which tools are needed to perform the tasks detailed in this manual, the following tool lists are offered: *Maintenance and minor repair, Repair/overhaul and Special*.

The newcomer to practical mechanics should start off with the maintenance and minor repair tool kit, which is adequate for the simpler jobs performed on a vehicle. Then, as confidence and experience grow, the owner can tackle more difficult tasks, buying additional tools as they are needed. Eventually the basic kit will be expanded into the repair and overhaul tool set. Over a period of time, the experienced do-it-yourselfer will assemble a tool set complete enough for most repair and overhaul procedures and will add tools from the special category when it is felt that the expense is justified by the frequency of use.

Maintenance and minor repair tool kit

The tools in this list should be considered the minimum required for performance of routine maintenance, servicing and minor repair work. We recommend the purchase of combination wrenches (box-end and open-end combined in one wrench). While more expensive than open end wrenches, they offer the advantages of both types of wrench.

Combination wrench set (1/4-inch to 1 inch or 6 mm to 19 mm)
Adjustable wrench, 8 inch
Spark plug wrench with rubber insert
Spark plug gap adjusting tool
Feeler gauge set
Brake bleeder wrench
Standard screwdriver (5/16-inch x 6 inch)
Phillips screwdriver (No. 2 x 6 inch)
Combination pliers – 6 inch
Hacksaw and assortment of blades
Tire pressure gauge
Grease gun
Oil can
Fine emery cloth
Wire brush

Battery post and cable cleaning tool
Oil filter wrench
Funnel (medium size)
Safety goggles
Jackstands(2)
Drain pan

Note: *If basic tune-ups are going to be part of routine maintenance, it will be necessary to purchase a good quality stroboscopic timing light and combination tachometer/dwell meter. Although they are included in the list of special tools, it is mentioned here because they are absolutely necessary for tuning most vehicles properly.*

Repair and overhaul tool set

These tools are essential for anyone who plans to perform major repairs and are in addition to those in the maintenance and minor repair tool kit. Included is a comprehensive set of sockets which, though expensive, are invaluable because of their versatility, especially when various extensions and drives are available. We recommend the 1/2-inch drive over the 3/8-inch drive. Although the larger drive is bulky and more expensive, it has the capacity of accepting a very wide range of large sockets. Ideally, however, the mechanic should have a 3/8-inch drive set and a 1/2-inch drive set.

Socket set(s)
Reversible ratchet
Extension – 10 inch
Universal joint
Torque wrench (same size drive as sockets)
Ball peen hammer – 8 ounce
Soft-face hammer (plastic/rubber)
Standard screwdriver (1/4-inch x 6 inch)
Standard screwdriver (stubby – 5/16-inch)
Phillips screwdriver (No. 3 x 8 inch)
Phillips screwdriver (stubby – No. 2)

Pliers – vise grip
Pliers – lineman's
Pliers – needle nose
Pliers – snap-ring (internal and external)
Cold chisel – 1/2-inch
Scribe
Scraper (made from flattened copper tubing)
Centerpunch
Pin punches (1/16, 1/8, 3/16-inch)
Steel rule/straightedge – 12 inch
Allen wrench set (1/8 to 3/8-inch or 4 mm to 10 mm)
A selection of files
Wire brush (large)
Jackstands (second set)
Jack (scissor or hydraulic type)

Note: Another tool which is often useful is an electric drill motor with a chuck capacity of 3/8-inch and a set of good quality drill bits.

Special tools

The tools in this list include those which are not used regularly, are expensive to buy, or which need to be used in accordance with their manufacturer's instructions. Unless these tools will be used frequently, it is not very economical to purchase many of them. A consideration would be to split the cost and use between yourself and a friend or friends. In addition, most of these tools can be obtained from a tool rental shop on a temporary basis.

This list primarily contains only those tools and instruments widely available to the public, and not those special tools produced by the vehicle manufacturer for distribution to dealer service departments. Occasionally, references to the manufacturer's special tools are included in the text of this manual. Generally, an alternative method of doing the job without the special tool is offered. However, sometimes there is no alternative to their use. Where this is the case, and the tool cannot be purchased or borrowed, the work should be turned over to the dealer service department or an automotive repair shop.

Valve spring compressor
Piston ring groove cleaning tool
Piston ring compressor
Piston ring installation tool
Cylinder compression gauge
Cylinder ridge reamer
Cylinder surfacing hone
Cylinder bore gauge
Micrometers and/or dial calipers
Hydraulic lifter removal tool
Balljoint separator
Universal-type puller
Impact screwdriver
Dial indicator set
Stroboscopic timing light (inductive pick-up)
Hand operated vacuum/pressure pump
Tachometer/dwell meter
Universal electrical multimeter
Cable hoist
Brake spring removal and installation tools
Floor jack

Buying tools

For the do-it-yourselfer who is just starting to get involved in vehicle maintenance and repair, there are a number of options available when purchasing tools. If maintenance and minor repair is the extent of the work to be done, the purchase of individual tools is satisfactory. If, on the other hand, extensive work is planned, it would be a good idea to purchase a modest tool set from one of the large retail chain stores. A set can usually be bought at a substantial savings over the individual tool prices, and they often come with a tool box. As additional tools are needed, add–on sets, individual tools and a larger tool box can be purchased to expand the tool selection. Building a tool set gradually allows the cost of the tools to be spread over a longer period of time and gives the mechanic the freedom to choose only those tools that will actually be used.

Tool stores will often be the only source of some of the special tools that are needed, but regardless of where tools are bought, try to avoid cheap ones, especially when buying screwdrivers and sockets, because they won't last very long. The expense involved in replacing cheap tools will eventually be greater than the initial cost of quality tools.

Care and maintenance of tools

Good tools are expensive, so it makes sense to treat them with respect. Keep them clean and in usable condition and store them properly when not in use. Always wipe off any dirt, grease or metal chips before putting them away. Never leave tools lying around in the work area. Upon completion of a job, always check closely under the hood for tools that may have been left there so they won't get lost during a test drive.

Some tools, such as screwdrivers, pliers, wrenches and sockets, can be hung on a panel mounted on the garage or workshop wall, while others should be kept in a tool box or tray. Measuring instruments, gauges, meters, etc. must be carefully stored where they cannot be damaged by weather or impact from other tools.

When tools are used with care and stored properly, they will last a very long time. Even with the best of care, though, tools will wear out if used frequently. When a tool is damaged or worn out, replace it. Subsequent jobs will be safer and more enjoyable if you do.

Working facilities

Not to be overlooked when discussing tools is the workshop. If anything more than routine maintenance is to be carried out, some sort of suitable work area is essential.

It is understood, and appreciated, that many home mechanics do not have a good workshop or garage available, and end up removing an engine or doing major repairs outside. It is recommended, however, that the overhaul or repair be completed under the cover of a roof.

A clean, flat workbench or table of comfortable working height is an absolute necessity. The workbench should be equipped with a vise that has a jaw opening of at least four inches.

As mentioned previously, some clean, dry storage space is also required for tools, as well as the lubricants, fluids, cleaning solvents, etc. which soon become necessary.

Sometimes waste oil and fluids, drained from the engine or cooling system during normal maintenance or repairs, present a disposal problem. To avoid pouring them on the ground or into a sewage system, pour the used fluids into large containers, seal them with caps and take them to an authorized disposal site or recycling center. Plastic jugs, such as old antifreeze containers, are ideal for this purpose.

Always keep a supply of old newspapers and clean rags available. Old towels are excellent for mopping up spills. Many mechanics use rolls of paper towels for most work because they are readily available and disposable. To help keep the area under the vehicle clean, a large cardboard box can be cut open and flattened to protect the garage or shop floor.

Whenever working over a painted surface, such as when leaning over a fender to service something under the hood, always cover it with an old blanket or bedspread to protect the finish. Vinyl covered pads, made especially for this purpose, are available at auto parts stores.

Booster battery (jump) starting

Observe these precautions when using a booster battery to start a vehicle:

a) Before connecting the booster battery, make sure the ignition switch is in the Off position.

b) Turn off the lights, heater and other electrical loads.

c) Your eyes should be shielded. Safety goggles are a good idea.

d) Make sure the booster battery is the same voltage as the dead one in the vehicle.

e) The two vehicles MUST NOT TOUCH each other!

f) Make sure the transmission is in Neutral (manual) or Park (automatic).

g) If the booster battery is not a maintenance-free type, remove the vent caps and lay a cloth over the vent holes.

Connect the red jumper cable to the positive (+) terminals of each battery.

Connect one end of the black jumper cable to the negative (–) terminal of the booster battery. The other end of this cable should be connected to a good ground on the vehicle to be started, such as a bolt or bracket on the engine block **(see illustration)**. Make sure the cable will not come into contact with the fan, drivebelts or other moving parts of the engine.

Start the engine using the booster battery, then, with the engine running at idle speed, disconnect the jumper cables in the reverse order of connection.

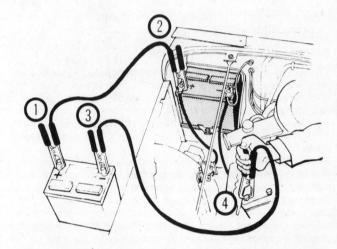

Make the booster battery cable connections in the numerical order shown (note that the negative cable of the booster battery is NOT attached to the negative terminal of the dead battery)

Jacking and towing

Jacking

Warning: *The jack supplied with the vehicle should only be used for changing a tire or placing jackstands under the frame. Never work under the vehicle or start the engine while this jack is being used as the only means of support.*

The vehicle should be on level ground. Place the shift lever in Park, if you have an automatic, or Reverse if you have a manual transaxle. Block the wheel diagonally opposite the wheel being changed. Set the parking brake.

Remove the spare tire and jack from stowage. Remove the wheel cover and trim ring (if so equipped) with the tapered end of the lug nut wrench by inserting and twisting the handle and then prying against the back of the wheel cover. Loosen, but do not remove, the lug bolts (one-half turn is sufficient).

Place the scissors-type jack under the side of the vehicle and adjust the jack height until it fits between the notches in the vertical rocker panel flange nearest the wheel to be changed. There is a front and rear jacking point on each side of the vehicle **(see illustrations)**.

Turn the jack handle clockwise until the tire clears the ground. Remove the lug bolts and pull the wheel off. Replace it with the spare.

Replace the lug bolts and tighten them snugly. Don't attempt to tighten

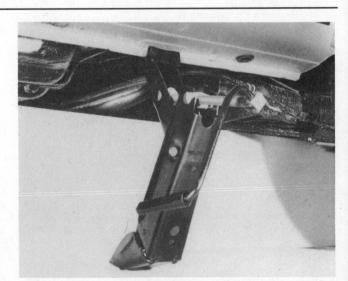

The vehicle jack engages with the flange on the body, directly below the depression in the rocker panel (there are two jacking points on each side of the vehicle)

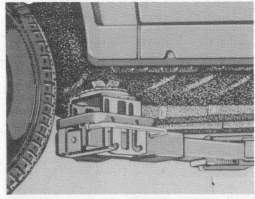

Front jacking point (for floor jack or vehicle hoist)

Rear jacking point (for floor jack or vehicle hoist)

Typical front towing hook

Typical rear towing hook

them completely until the vehicle is lowered or it could slip off the jack. Turn the jack handle counterclockwise to lower the vehicle. Remove the jack and tighten the lug bolts in a criss-cross pattern.

Stow the tire, jack and wrench. Unblock the wheels.

Towing

As a general rule, the vehicle should be towed with the front (drive) wheels off the ground. If they can't be raised, place them on a dolly. The ignition key must be in the ACC position, since the steering lock mechanism isn't strong enough to hold the front wheels straight while towing.

Vehicles equipped with an automatic transaxle should be towed with the front wheels off the ground, but they can be towed from the front with all four wheels on the ground, provided that speeds don't exceed 30 mph and the distance is not over 40 miles. Before towing, check the transmission fluid level (see Chapter 1). If the level is below the HOT line on the dipstick, add fluid or use a towing dolly. Release the parking brake, put the transaxle in Neutral and place the ignition key in the ACC position. **Caution:** *Never tow a vehicle with an automatic transaxle from the rear with the front wheels on the ground.*

Equipment specifically designed for towing should be used. It should be attached to the tow hooks of the vehicle **(see illustrations)**, not the tie-down hooks, bumpers or brackets.

Safety is a major consideration when towing and all applicable state and local laws must be obeyed. A safety chain system must be used at all times. Remember that power steering and power brakes will not work with the engine off.

Automotive chemicals and lubricants

A number of automotive chemicals and lubricants are available for use during vehicle maintenance and repair. They include a wide variety of products ranging from cleaning solvents and degreasers to lubricants and protective sprays for rubber, plastic and vinyl.

Cleaners

Carburetor cleaner and choke cleaner is a strong solvent for gum, varnish and carbon. Most carburetor cleaners leave a dry-type lubricant film which will not harden or gum up. Because of this film it is not recommended for use on electrical components.

Brake system cleaner is used to remove grease and brake fluid from the brake system, where clean surfaces are absolutely necessary. It leaves no residue and often eliminates brake squeal caused by contaminants.

Electrical cleaner removes oxidation, corrosion and carbon deposits from electrical contacts, restoring full current flow. It can also be used to clean spark plugs, carburetor jets, voltage regulators and other parts where an oil-free surface is desired.

Demoisturants remove water and moisture from electrical components such as alternators, voltage regulators, electrical connectors and fuse blocks. They are non-conductive, non-corrosive and non-flammable.

Degreasers are heavy-duty solvents used to remove grease from the outside of the engine and from chassis components. They can be sprayed or brushed on and, depending on the type, are rinsed off either with water or solvent.

Lubricants

Motor oil is the lubricant formulated for use in engines. It normally contains a wide variety of additives to prevent corrosion and reduce foaming and wear. Motor oil comes in various weights (viscosity ratings) from 5 to 80. The recommended weight of the oil depends on the season, temperature and the demands on the engine. Light oil is used in cold climates and under light load conditions. Heavy oil is used in hot climates and where high loads are encountered. Multi-viscosity oils are designed to have characteristics of both light and heavy oils and are available in a number of weights from 5W-20 to 20W-50.

Gear oil is designed to be used in differentials, manual transmissions and other areas where high-temperature lubrication is required.

Chassis and wheel bearing grease is a heavy grease used where increased loads and friction are encountered, such as for wheel bearings, balljoints, tie-rod ends and universal joints.

High-temperature wheel bearing grease is designed to withstand the extreme temperatures encountered by wheel bearings in disc brake equipped vehicles. It usually contains molybdenum disulfide (moly), which is a dry-type lubricant.

White grease is a heavy grease for metal-to-metal applications where water is a problem. White grease stays soft under both low and high temperatures (usually from –100 to +190-degrees F), and will not wash off or dilute in the presence of water.

Assembly lube is a special extreme pressure lubricant, usually containing moly, used to lubricate high-load parts (such as main and rod bearings and cam lobes) for initial start-up of a new engine. The assembly lube lubricates the parts without being squeezed out or washed away until the engine oiling system begins to function.

Silicone lubricants are used to protect rubber, plastic, vinyl and nylon parts.

Graphite lubricants are used where oils cannot be used due to contamination problems, such as in locks. The dry graphite will lubricate metal parts while remaining uncontaminated by dirt, water, oil or acids. It is electrically conductive and will not foul electrical contacts in locks such as the ignition switch.

Moly penetrants loosen and lubricate frozen, rusted and corroded fasteners and prevent future rusting or freezing.

Heat-sink grease is a special electrically non-conductive grease that is used for mounting electronic ignition modules where it is essential that heat is transferred away from the module.

Sealants

RTV sealant is one of the most widely used gasket compounds. Made from silicone, RTV is air curing, it seals, bonds, waterproofs, fills surface irregularities, remains flexible, doesn't shrink, is relatively easy to remove, and is used as a supplementary sealer with almost all low and medium temperature gaskets.

Anaerobic sealant is much like RTV in that it can be used either to seal gaskets or to form gaskets by itself. It remains flexible, is solvent resistant and fills surface imperfections. The difference between an anaerobic sealant and an RTV-type sealant is in the curing. RTV cures when exposed to air, while an anaerobic sealant cures only in the absence of air. This means that an anaerobic sealant cures only after the assembly of parts, sealing them together.

Thread and pipe sealant is used for sealing hydraulic and pneumatic fittings and vacuum lines. It is usually made from a teflon compound, and comes in a spray, a paint-on liquid and as a wrap-around tape.

Chemicals

Anti–seize compound prevents seizing, galling, cold welding, rust and corrosion in fasteners. High-temperature anti-seize, usually made with copper and graphite lubricants, is used for exhaust system and exhaust manifold bolts.

Anaerobic locking compounds are used to keep fasteners from vibrating or working loose and cure only after installation, in the absence of air. Medium strength locking compound is used for small nuts, bolts and screws that may be removed later. High-strength locking compound is for large nuts, bolts and studs which aren't removed on a regular basis.

Oil additives range from viscosity index improvers to chemical treatments that claim to reduce internal engine friction. It should be noted that most oil manufacturers caution against using additives with their oils.

Gas additives perform several functions, depending on their chemical makeup. They usually contain solvents that help dissolve gum and varnish that build up on carburetor, fuel injection and intake parts. They also serve to break down carbon deposits that form on the inside surfaces of the combustion chambers. Some additives contain upper cylinder lubricants for valves and piston rings, and others contain chemicals to remove condensation from the gas tank.

Miscellaneous

Brake fluid is specially formulated hydraulic fluid that can withstand the heat and pressure encountered in brake systems. Care must be taken so this fluid does not come in contact with painted surfaces or plastics. An opened container should always be resealed to prevent contamination by water or dirt.

Weatherstrip adhesive is used to bond weatherstripping around doors, windows and trunk lids. It is sometimes used to attach trim pieces.

Undercoating is a petroleum-based, tar-like substance that is designed to protect metal surfaces on the underside of the vehicle from corrosion. It also acts as a sound-deadening agent by insulating the bottom of the vehicle.

Waxes and polishes are used to help protect painted and plated surfaces from the weather. Different types of paint may require the use of different types of wax and polish. Some polishes utilize a chemical or abrasive cleaner to help remove the top layer of oxidized (dull) paint on older vehicles. In recent years many non-wax polishes that contain a wide variety of chemicals such as polymers and silicones have been introduced. These non-wax polishes are usually easier to apply and last longer than conventional waxes and polishes.

Safety first!

Regardless of how enthusiastic you may be about getting on with the job at hand, take the time to ensure that your safety is not jeopardized. A moment's lack of attention can result in an accident, as can failure to observe certain simple safety precautions. The possibility of an accident will always exist, and the following points should not be considered a comprehensive list of all dangers. Rather, they are intended to make you aware of the risks and to encourage a safety conscious approach to all work you carry out on your vehicle.

Essential DOs and DON'Ts

DON'T rely on a jack when working under the vehicle. Always use approved jackstands to support the weight of the vehicle and place them under the recommended lift or support points.

DON'T attempt to loosen extremely tight fasteners (i.e. wheel lug nuts) while the vehicle is on a jack – it may fall.

DON'T start the engine without first making sure that the transmission is in Neutral (or Park where applicable) and the parking brake is set.

DON'T remove the radiator cap from a hot cooling system – let it cool or cover it with a cloth and release the pressure gradually.

DON'T attempt to drain the engine oil until you are sure it has cooled to the point that it will not burn you.

DON'T touch any part of the engine or exhaust system until it has cooled sufficiently to avoid burns.

DON'T siphon toxic liquids such as gasoline, antifreeze and brake fluid by mouth, or allow them to remain on your skin.

DON'T inhale brake lining dust – it is potentially hazardous (see Asbestos below)

DON'T allow spilled oil or grease to remain on the floor – wipe it up before someone slips on it.

DON'T use loose fitting wrenches or other tools which may slip and cause injury.

DON'T push on wrenches when loosening or tightening nuts or bolts. Always try to pull the wrench toward you. If the situation calls for pushing the wrench away, push with an open hand to avoid scraped knuckles if the wrench should slip.

DON'T attempt to lift a heavy component alone – get someone to help you.

DON'T rush or take unsafe shortcuts to finish a job.

DON'T allow children or animals in or around the vehicle while you are working on it.

DO wear eye protection when using power tools such as a drill, sander, bench grinder, etc. and when working under a vehicle.

DO keep loose clothing and long hair well out of the way of moving parts.

DO make sure that any hoist used has a safe working load rating adequate for the job.

DO get someone to check on you periodically when working alone on a vehicle.

DO carry out work in a logical sequence and make sure that everything is correctly assembled and tightened.

DO keep chemicals and fluids tightly capped and out of the reach of children and pets.

DO remember that your vehicle's safety affects that of yourself and others. If in doubt on any point, get professional advice.

Asbestos

Certain friction, insulating, sealing, and other products – such as brake linings, brake bands, clutch linings, torque converters, gaskets, etc. – contain asbestos. *Extreme care must be taken to avoid inhalation of dust from such products since it is hazardous to health.* If in doubt, assume that they *do* contain asbestos.

Fire

Remember at all times that gasoline is highly flammable. Never smoke or have any kind of open flame around when working on a vehicle. But the risk does not end there. A spark caused by an electrical short circuit, by two metal surfaces contacting each other, or even by static electricity built up in your body under certain conditions, can ignite gasoline vapors, which in a confined space are highly explosive. Do not, under any circumstances, use gasoline for cleaning parts. Use an approved safety solvent.

Always disconnect the battery ground (–) cable *at the battery* before working on any part of the fuel system or electrical system. Never risk spilling fuel on a hot engine or exhaust component.

It is strongly recommended that a fire extinguisher suitable for use on fuel and electrical fires be kept handy in the garage or workshop at all times. Never try to extinguish a fuel or electrical fire with water.

Fumes

Certain fumes are highly toxic and can quickly cause unconsciousness and even death if inhaled to any extent. Gasoline vapor falls into this category, as do the vapors from some cleaning solvents. Any draining or pouring of such volatile fluids should be done in a well ventilated area.

When using cleaning fluids and solvents, read the instructions on the container carefully. Never use materials from unmarked containers.

Never run the engine in an enclosed space, such as a garage. Exhaust fumes contain carbon monoxide, which is extremely poisonous. If you need to run the engine, always do so in the open air, or at least have the rear of the vehicle outside the work area.

If you are fortunate enough to have the use of an inspection pit, never drain or pour gasoline and never run the engine while the vehicle is over the pit. The fumes, being heavier than air, will concentrate in the pit with possibly lethal results.

The battery

Never create a spark or allow a bare light bulb near a battery. They normally give off a certain amount of hydrogen gas, which is highly explosive.

Always disconnect the battery ground (–) cable *at the battery* before working on the fuel or electrical systems.

If possible, loosen the filler caps or cover when charging the battery from an external source (this does not apply to sealed or maintenancefree batteries). Do not charge at an excessive rate or the battery may burst.

Take care when adding water to a non maintenance–free battery and when carrying a battery. The electrolyte, even when diluted, is very corrosive and should not be allowed to contact clothing or skin.

Always wear eye protection when cleaning the battery to prevent the caustic deposits from entering your eyes.

Household current

When using an electric power tool, inspection light, etc., which operates on household current, always make sure that the tool is correctly connected to its plug and that, where necessary, it is properly grounded. Do not use such items in damp conditions and, again, do not create a spark or apply excessive heat in the vicinity of fuel or fuel vapor.

Secondary ignition system voltage

A severe electric shock can result from touching certain parts of the ignition system (such as the spark plug wires) when the engine is running or being cranked, particularly if components are damp or the insulation is defective. In the case of an electronic ignition system, the secondary system voltage is much higher and could prove fatal.

Conversion factors

Length (distance)
Inches (in)	X	25.4	= Millimetres (mm)	X 0.0394	= Inches (in)
Feet (ft)	X	0.305	= Metres (m)	X 3.281	= Feet (ft)
Miles	X	1.609	= Kilometres (km)	X 0.621	= Miles

Volume (capacity)
Cubic inches (cu in; in³)	X	16.387	= Cubic centimetres (cc; cm³)	X 0.061	= Cubic inches (cu in; in³)
Imperial pints (Imp pt)	X	0.568	= Litres (l)	X 1.76	= Imperial pints (Imp pt)
Imperial quarts (Imp qt)	X	1.137	= Litres (l)	X 0.88	= Imperial quarts (Imp qt)
Imperial quarts (Imp qt)	X	1.201	= US quarts (US qt)	X 0.833	= Imperial quarts (Imp qt)
US quarts (US qt)	X	0.946	= Litres (l)	X 1.057	= US quarts (US qt)
Imperial gallons (Imp gal)	X	4.546	= Litres (l)	X 0.22	= Imperial gallons (Imp gal)
Imperial gallons (Imp gal)	X	1.201	= US gallons (US gal)	X 0.833	= Imperial gallons (Imp gal)
US gallons (US gal)	X	3.785	= Litres (l)	X 0.264	= US gallons (US gal)

Mass (weight)
Ounces (oz)	X	28.35	= Grams (g)	X 0.035	= Ounces (oz)
Pounds (lb)	X	0.454	= Kilograms (kg)	X 2.205	= Pounds (lb)

Force
Ounces-force (ozf; oz)	X	0.278	= Newtons (N)	X 3.6	= Ounces-force (ozf; oz)
Pounds-force (lbf; lb)	X	4.448	= Newtons (N)	X 0.225	= Pounds-force (lbf; lb)
Newtons (N)	X	0.1	= Kilograms-force (kgf; kg)	X 9.81	= Newtons (N)

Pressure
Pounds-force per square inch (psi; lbf/in²; lb/in²)	X	0.070	= Kilograms-force per square centimetre (kgf/cm²; kg/cm²)	X 14.223	= Pounds-force per square inch (psi; lbf/in²; lb/in²)
Pounds-force per square inch (psi; lbf/in²; lb/in²)	X	0.068	= Atmospheres (atm)	X 14.696	= Pounds-force per square inch (psi; lbf/in²; lb/in²)
Pounds-force per square inch (psi; lbf/in²; lb/in²)	X	0.069	= Bars	X 14.5	= Pounds-force per square inch (psi; lbf/in²; lb/in²)
Pounds-force per square inch (psi; lbf/in²; lb/in²)	X	6.895	= Kilopascals (kPa)	X 0.145	= Pounds-force per square inch (psi; lbf/in²; lb/in²)
Kilopascals (kPa)	X	0.01	= Kilograms-force per square centimetre (kgf/cm²; kg/cm²)	X 98.1	= Kilopascals (kPa)

Torque (moment of force)
Pounds-force inches (lbf in; lb in)	X	1.152	= Kilograms-force centimetre (kgf cm; kg cm)	X 0.868	= Pounds-force inches (lbf in; lb in)
Pounds-force inches (lbf in; lb in)	X	0.113	= Newton metres (Nm)	X 8.85	= Pounds-force inches (lbf in; lb in)
Pounds-force inches (lbf in; lb in)	X	0.083	= Pounds-force feet (lbf ft; lb ft)	X 12	= Pounds-force inches (lbf in; lb in)
Pounds-force feet (lbf ft; lb ft)	X	0.138	= Kilograms-force metres (kgf m; kg m)	X 7.233	= Pounds-force feet (lbf ft; lb ft)
Pounds-force feet (lbf ft; lb ft)	X	1.356	= Newton metres (Nm)	X 0.738	= Pounds-force feet (lbf ft; lb ft)
Newton metres (Nm)	X	0.102	= Kilograms-force metres (kgf m; kg m)	X 9.804	= Newton metres (Nm)

Power
Horsepower (hp)	X	745.7	= Watts (W)	X 0.0013	= Horsepower (hp)

Velocity (speed)
Miles per hour (miles/hr; mph)	X	1.609	= Kilometres per hour (km/hr; kph)	X 0.621	= Miles per hour (miles/hr; mph)

Fuel consumption*
Miles per gallon, Imperial (mpg)	X	0.354	= Kilometres per litre (km/l)	X 2.825	= Miles per gallon, Imperial (mpg)
Miles per gallon, US (mpg)	X	0.425	= Kilometres per litre (km/l)	X 2.352	= Miles per gallon, US (mpg)

Temperature
Degrees Fahrenheit = ($°C \times 1.8$) + 32   Degrees Celsius (Degrees Centigrade; °C) = ($°F - 32$) x 0.56

*It is common practice to convert from miles per gallon (mpg) to litres/100 kilometres (l/100km), where mpg (Imperial) x l/100 km = 282 and mpg (US) x l/100 km = 235

Troubleshooting

Contents

Symptom	Section

Engine and performance

Engine backfires 15
Engine diesels (continues to run) after switching off 18
Engine hard to start when cold 3
Engine hard to start when hot 4
Engine lacks power 14
Engine lopes while idling or idles erratically 8
Engine misses at idle speed 9
Engine misses throughout driving speed range 10
Engine rotates but will not start 2
Engine runs with oil pressure light on 17
Engine stalls 13
Engine starts but stops immediately 6
Engine stumbles on acceleration 11
Engine surges while holding accelerator steady 12
Engine will not rotate when attempting to start 1
Oil puddle under engine 7
Pinging or knocking engine sounds during acceleration or uphill . 16
Starter motor noisy or excessively rough in engagement 5

Engine electrical system

Alternator light fails to go out 20
Battery will not hold a charge 19
Alternator light fails to come on when key is turned on 21

Fuel system

Excessive fuel consumption 22
Fuel leakage and/or fuel odor 23

Cooling system

Coolant loss 28
External coolant leakage 26
Internal coolant leakage 27
Overcooling 25
Overheating 24
Poor coolant circulation 29

Clutch

Clutch pedal stays on floor 37
Clutch slips (engine speed increases
   with no increase in vehicle speed) 33
Grabbing (chattering) as clutch is engaged 34
High pedal effort 31
Noise in clutch area 36
Pedal travels to floor – no pressure or very little resistance 30
Transaxle rattling (clicking) 35
Unable to select gears 32

Manual transaxle

Clicking noise in turns 41
Clunk on acceleration or deceleration 40
Knocking noise at low speeds 38
Leaks lubricant 47
Locked in gear 48

Symptom	Section

Noise most pronounced when turning 39
Noisy in all gears 45
Noisy in neutral with engine running 43
Noisy in one particular gear 44
Slips out of gear 46
Vibration 42

Automatic transaxle

Engine will start in gears other than Park or Neutral 53
Fluid leakage 49
General shift mechanism problems 51
Transaxle fluid brown or has burned smell 50
Transaxle slips, shifts roughly, is noisy or
   has no drive in forward or reverse gears 54
Transaxle will not downshift with accelerator pedal
   pressed to the floor 52

Driveaxles

Clicking noise in turns 55
Shudder or vibration during acceleration 56
Vibration at highway speeds 57

Brakes

Brake pedal feels spongy when depressed 65
Brake pedal travels to the floor with little resistance 66
Brake roughness or chatter (pedal pulsates) 60
Dragging brakes 63
Excessive brake pedal travel 62
Excessive pedal effort required to stop vehicle 61
Grabbing or uneven braking action 64
Noise (high-pitched squeal when the brakes are applied) 59
Parking brake does not hold 67
Vehicle pulls to one side during braking 58

Suspension and steering systems

Abnormal or excessive tire wear 69
Abnormal noise at the front end 74
Cupped tires 79
Erratic steering when braking 76
Excessive pitching and/or rolling around corners or during braking 77
Excessive play or looseness in steering system 83
Excessive tire wear on inside edge 81
Excessive tire wear on outside edge 80
Hard steering 72
Poor returnability of steering to center 73
Rattling or clicking noise in rack and pinion 84
Shimmy, shake or vibration 71
Suspension bottoms 78
Tire tread worn in one place 82
Vehicle pulls to one side 68
Wander or poor steering stability 75
Wheel makes a thumping noise 70

This section provides an easy reference guide to the more common problems which may occur during the operation of your vehicle. These problems and their possible causes are grouped under headings denoting various components or systems, such as Engine, Cooling system, etc. They also refer you to the chapter and/or section which deals with the problem.

Remember that successful troubleshooting is not a mysterious black art practiced only by professional mechanics. It is simply the result of the right knowledge combined with an intelligent, systematic approach to the problem. Always work by a process of elimination, starting with the simplest solution and working through to the most complex – and never overlook the obvious. Anyone can run the gas tank dry or leave the lights on overnight, so don't assume that you are exempt from such oversights.

Finally, always establish a clear idea of why a problem has occurred and take steps to ensure that it doesn't happen again. If the electrical system fails because of a poor connection, check the other connections in the system to make sure that they don't fail as well. If a particular fuse continues to blow, find out why – don't just replace one fuse after another. Remember, failure of a small component can often be indicative of potential failure or incorrect functioning of a more important component or system.

Engine

1   Engine will not rotate when attempting to start

1   Battery terminal connections loose or corroded (Chapter 1).
2   Battery discharged or faulty (Chapter 1).
3   Automatic transmission not completely engaged in Park (Chapter 7) or clutch not completely depressed (Chapter 8).
4   Broken, loose or disconnected wiring in the starting circuit (Chapters 5 and 12).
5   Starter motor pinion jammed in flywheel ring gear (Chapter 5).
6   Starter solenoid faulty (Chapter 5).
7   Starter motor faulty (Chapter 5).
8   Ignition switch faulty (Chapter 12).
9   Starter pinion or flywheel teeth worn or broken (Chapter 5).

2   Engine rotates but will not start

1   Fuel tank empty.
2   Battery discharged (engine rotates slowly) (Chapter 5).
3   Battery terminal connections loose or corroded (Chapter 1).
4   Leaking fuel injector(s), faulty cold start valve, fuel pump, pressure regulator, etc. (Chapter 4).
5   Fuel not reaching fuel distributor or rail, or other fuel injection problem (Chapter 4).
6   Ignition components damp or damaged (Chapter 5).
7   Worn, faulty or incorrectly gapped spark plugs (Chapter 1).
8   Broken, loose or disconnected wiring in the starting circuit (Chapter 5).
9   Ignition points incorrectly gapped (Chapter 5).
10   Broken, loose or disconnected wires at the ignition coil or faulty coil (Chapter 5).
11   Defective timing belt (Chapter 2).

3   Engine hard to start when cold

1   Battery discharged or low (Chapter 1).
2   Malfunctioning fuel system (Chapter 4).
3   Faulty cold start injector (Chapter 4).
4   Injector(s) leaking (Chapter 4).
5   Faulty ignition system (Chapter 5).

4   Engine hard to start when hot

1   Air filter clogged (Chapter 1).
2   Fuel not reaching the fuel injection system (Chapter 4).
3   Corroded battery connections, especially ground (Chapter 1).
4   Worn starter motor (Chapter 5).
5   Leaking injector(s)
6   Defective thermo-time switch (Chapter 4)

5   Starter motor noisy or excessively rough in engagement

1   Pinion or flywheel gear teeth worn or broken (Chapter 5).
2   Starter motor mounting bolts loose or missing (Chapter 5).

6   Engine starts but stops immediately

1   Loose or faulty electrical connections at coil or distributor (Chapter 5).
2   Defective coil (Chapter 5)
3   Insufficient fuel reaching the fuel injector(s) (Chapters 1 and 4).
4   Vacuum leak at the gasket between the intake manifold/plenum and throttle body (Chapter 4).

7   Oil puddle under engine

1   Oil pan gasket and/or oil pan drain bolt washer leaking (Chapter 2).
2   Oil pressure sending unit leaking (Chapter 2).
3   Camshaft cover leaking (Chapter 2).
4   Engine oil seals leaking (Chapter 2).

8   Engine lopes while idling or idles erratically

1   Vacuum leakage (Chapters 2 and 4).
2   Leaking EGR valve (Chapter 6).
3   Air filter clogged (Chapter 1).
4   Fuel pump not delivering sufficient fuel to the fuel injection system (Chapter 4).
5   Leaking head gasket (Chapter 2).
6   Timing belt and/or pulleys worn (Chapter 2).
7   Camshaft lobes worn (Chapter 2).
8   Throttle body ports clogged (Chapter 4).
9   Carburetor misadjusted or worn (Chapter 4).

9   Engine misses at idle speed

1   Spark plugs worn or not gapped properly (Chapter 1).
2   Faulty spark plug wires (Chapter 1).
3   Vacuum leaks (Chapter 1).
4   Incorrect ignition timing (Chapter 1).
5   Uneven or low compression (Chapter 2).

10   Engine misses throughout driving speed range

1   Fuel filter/carburetor/injectors clogged and/or impurities in the fuel system (Chapter 1).
2   Low fuel output at the injector(s) (Chapter 4).
3   Faulty or incorrectly gapped spark plugs (Chapter 1).
4   Incorrect ignition timing (Chapter 5).

5 Cracked distributor cap or rotor (Chapters 1 and 5).
6 Leaking spark plug wires (Chapters 1 or 5).
7 Faulty emission system components (Chapter 6).
8 Low or uneven cylinder compression pressures (Chapter 2).
9 Weak or faulty ignition system (Chapter 5).
10 Vacuum leak in fuel injection system, intake manifold, air regulator valve or vacuum hoses (Chapter 4).

11 Engine stumbles on acceleration

1 Spark plugs fouled (Chapter 1).
2 Carburetor/fuel injection system needs adjustment or repair (Chapter 4).
3 Fuel filter clogged (Chapters 1 and 4).
4 Incorrect ignition timing (Chapter 5).
5 Intake manifold air leak (Chapters 2 and 4).

12 Engine surges while holding accelerator steady

1 Intake air leak (Chapter 4).
2 Fuel pump faulty (Chapter 4).
3 Loose fuel injector wire harness connectors (Chapter 4).
4 Defective ECU (Chapter 6).
5 Damaged air flow sensor (Chapter 4).

13 Engine stalls

1 Idle speed incorrect (Chapter 1).
2 Fuel filter clogged and/or water and impurities in the fuel system (Chapters 1 and 4).
3 Distributor components damp or damaged (Chapter 5).
4 Faulty emissions system components (Chapter 6).
5 Faulty or incorrectly gapped spark plugs (Chapter 1).
6 Faulty spark plug wires (Chapter 1).
7 Vacuum leak in the fuel injection system, intake manifold or vacuum hoses (Chapters 2 and 4).
8 Valve clearances incorrectly set (Chapter 1).

14 Engine lacks power

1 Incorrect ignition timing (Chapter 5).
2 Excessive play in distributor shaft (Chapter 5).
3 Worn rotor, distributor cap, points or wires (Chapters 1 and 5).
4 Faulty or incorrectly gapped spark plugs (Chapter 1).
5 Fuel injection system out of adjustment or excessively worn (Chapter 4).
6 Faulty coil (Chapter 5).
7 Brakes binding (Chapter 9).
8 Automatic transaxle fluid level incorrect (Chapter 1).
9 Clutch slipping (Chapter 8).
10 Fuel filter clogged and/or impurities in the fuel system (Chapters 1 and 4).
11 Emission control system not functioning properly (Chapter 6).
12 Low or uneven cylinder compression pressures (Chapter 2).
13 Exhaust system plugged (Chapter 4).

15 Engine backfires

1 Emission control system not functioning properly (Chapter 6).
2 Ignition timing incorrect (Chapter 5).
3 Faulty secondary ignition system (cracked spark plug insulator, faulty plug wires, distributor cap and/or rotor) (Chapters 1 and 5).

4 Carburetor/fuel injection system in need of adjustment or worn excessively (Chapter 4).
5 Vacuum leak at fuel injector(s), intake manifold, air regulator valve or vacuum hoses (Chapters 2 and 4).
6 Valve clearances incorrectly set and/or valves sticking (Chapter 1).

16 Pinging or knocking engine sounds during acceleration or uphill

1 Incorrect grade of fuel.
2 Ignition timing incorrect (Chapter 5).
3 Carburetor/fuel injection system in need of adjustment (Chapter 4).
4 Improper or damaged spark plugs or wires (Chapter 1).
5 Worn or damaged ignition components (Chapter 5).
6 Faulty emission system (Chapter 6).
7 Vacuum leak (Chapters 2 and 4).

17 Engine runs with oil pressure light on

1 Low oil level (Chapter 1).
2 Idle rpm below specification (Chapter 1).
3 Short in wiring circuit (Chapter 12).
4 Faulty oil pressure sender (Chapter 2).
5 Worn engine bearings and/or oil pump (Chapter 2).

18 Engine diesels (continues to run) after switching off

1 Idle speed too high (Chapter 1).
2 Excessive engine operating temperature (Chapter 3).

Engine electrical system

19 Battery will not hold a charge

1 Alternator drivebelt defective or not adjusted properly (Chapter 1).
2 Battery electrolyte level low (Chapter 1).
3 Battery terminals loose or corroded (Chapter 1).
4 Alternator not charging properly (Chapter 5).
5 Loose, broken or faulty wiring in the charging circuit (Chapter 5).
6 Short in vehicle wiring (Chapter 12).
7 Internally defective battery (Chapters 1 and 5).

20 Alternator light fails to go out

1 Faulty alternator or charging circuit (Chapter 5).
2 Alternator drivebelt defective or out of adjustment (Chapter 1).
3 Alternator voltage regulator inoperative (Chapter 5).

21 Alternator light fails to come on when key is turned on

1 Warning light bulb defective (Chapter 12).
2 Fault in the printed circuit, dash wiring or bulb holder (Chapter 12).

Fuel system

22 Excessive fuel consumption

1 Dirty or clogged air filter element (Chapter 1).
2 Incorrectly set ignition timing (Chapter 5).

3 Emissions system not functioning properly (Chapter 6).
4 Carburetor/fuel injection internal parts excessively worn or damaged (Chapter 4).
5 Low tire pressure or incorrect tire size (Chapter 1).

23 Fuel leakage and/or fuel odor

1 Leaking fuel feed or return line (Chapters 1 and 4).
2 Tank overfilled.
3 Evaporative canister filter clogged (Chapters 1 and 6).
4 Fuel injector internal parts excessively worn (Chapter 4).
5 Leaking fuel injector(s) (Chapter 4).
6 Carburetor worn (Chapter 4).

Cooling system

24 Overheating

1 Insufficient coolant in system (Chapter 1).
2 Water pump drivebelt defective or out of adjustment (Chapter 1).
3 Radiator core blocked or grille restricted (Chapter 3).
4 Thermostat faulty (Chapter 3).
5 Electric coolant fan blades broken or cracked (Chapter 3).
6 Radiator cap not maintaining proper pressure (Chapter 3).
7 Ignition timing incorrect (Chapter 5).
8 Defective cylinder head gasket (Chapter 2).

25 Overcooling

1 Faulty thermostat (Chapter 3).
2 Inaccurate temperature gauge sending unit (Chapter 3)

26 External coolant leakage

1 Deteriorated/damaged hoses; loose clamps (Chapters 1 and 3).
2 Water pump seal defective (Chapter 3).
3 Leakage from radiator core or coolant reservoir bottle (Chapter 3).
4 Engine drain or water jacket core plugs leaking (Chapter 2).

27 Internal coolant leakage

1 Leaking cylinder head gasket (Chapter 2).
2 Cracked cylinder bore or cylinder head (Chapter 2).

28 Coolant loss

1 Too much coolant in system (Chapter 1).
2 Coolant boiling away because of overheating (Chapter 3).
3 Internal or external leakage (Chapter 3).
4 Faulty radiator cap (Chapter 3).

29 Poor coolant circulation

1 Inoperative water pump (Chapter 3).
2 Restriction in cooling system (Chapters 1 and 3).
3 Water pump drivebelt defective/out of adjustment (Chapter 1).

4 Thermostat sticking (Chapter 3).

Clutch

30 Pedal travels to floor – no pressure or very little resistance

1 Broken release bearing or fork (Chapter 8).
2 Collapsed diaphragm spring in clutch pressure plate (Chapter 8).

31 High pedal effort

1 Clutch cable worn (Chapter 8).
2 Clutch release shaft/housing worn (Chapter 8).

32 Unable to select gears

1 Faulty transaxle (Chapter 7).
2 Faulty clutch disc (Chapter 8).
3 Faulty pressure plate (Chapter 8).
4 Pressure plate-to-flywheel bolts loose (Chapter 8).

33 Clutch slips (engine speed increases with no increase in vehicle speed)

1 Clutch plate worn (Chapter 8).
2 Clutch plate is oil soaked by leaking rear main seal (Chapter 8).
3 Clutch plate not seated. It may take 30 or 40 normal starts for a new one to seat.
4 Warped pressure plate or flywheel (Chapter 8).
5 Weak diaphragm spring (Chapter 8).
6 Clutch plate overheated. Allow to cool.

34 Grabbing (chattering) as clutch is engaged

1 Oil on clutch plate lining, burned or glazed facings (Chapter 8).
2 Worn or loose engine or transaxle mounts (Chapters 2 and 7).
3 Worn splines on clutch plate hub (Chapter 8).
4 Warped pressure plate or flywheel (Chapter 8).
5 Burned or smeared resin on flywheel or pressure plate (Chapter 8).

35 Transaxle rattling (clicking)

1 Clutch plate damper spring failure (Chapter 8).
2 Low engine idle speed (Chapter 1).

36 Noise in clutch area

1 Release shaft improperly installed (Chapter 8).
2 Faulty bearing (Chapter 8).

37 Clutch pedal stays on floor

1 Binding release cable (Chapter 8).
2 Broken release bearing or fork (Chapter 8).

Manual transaxle

38 Knocking noise at low speeds

Worn driveaxle constant velocity (CV) joint(s) (Chapter 8).

39 Noise most pronounced when turning

1 Differential gear noise (Chapter 7A).*
2 Worn outer constant velocity (CV) joint(s)

40 Clunk on acceleration or deceleration

1 Loose engine or transaxle mounts (Chapters 2 and 7A).
2 Worn differential pinion shaft in case.*
3 Worn or damaged driveaxle inboard CV joints (Chapter 8).

41 Clicking noise in turns

Worn or damaged outer CV joint (Chapter 8).

42 Vibration

1 Rough wheel bearing (Chapters 1 and 10).
2 Damaged driveaxle (Chapter 8).
3 Out of round tires (Chapter 1).
4 Tire out of balance (Chapters 1 and 10).
5 Worn CV joint (Chapter 8).

43 Noisy in neutral with engine running

1 Damaged input gear bearing (Chapter 7A).*
2 Damaged clutch release bearing (Chapter 8).

44 Noisy in one particular gear

1 Damaged or worn constant mesh gears (Chapter 7A).*
2 Damaged or worn synchronizers (Chapter 7A).*
3 Bent reverse fork (Chapter 7A).*
4 Damaged fourth speed gear or output gear (Chapter 7A).*
5 Worn or damaged reverse idler gear or idler bushing (Chapter 7A).*

45 Noisy in all gears

1 Insufficient lubricant (Chapter 7A).
2 Damaged or worn bearings (Chapter 7A).*
3 Worn or damaged input gear shaft (Chapter 7A).*

46 Slips out of gear

1 Worn or improperly adjusted linkage (Chapter 7A).
2 Transaxle loose on engine (Chapter 7A).
3 Shift linkage does not work freely, binds (Chapter 7A).
4 Input gear bearing retainer broken or loose (Chapter 7A).*
5 Worn shift fork (Chapter 7A).*

47 Leaks lubricant

1 Side gear shaft seals worn (Chapter 8).
2 Excessive amount of lubricant in transaxle (Chapters 1 and 7A).
3 Loose or broken input gear shaft bearing retainer (Chapter 7A).*
4 Input gear bearing retainer O-ring and/or lip seal damaged (Chapter 7A).*

48 Locked in gear

Lock pin or interlock pin missing (Chapter 7A).*

* Although the corrective action necessary to remedy the symptoms described is beyond the scope of the home mechanic, the above information should be helpful in isolating the cause of the condition so the owner can communicate clearly with a professional mechanic.

Automatic transaxle

Note: *Due to the complexity of the automatic transaxle, it is difficult for the home mechanic to properly diagnose and service this component. For problems other than the following, the vehicle should be taken to a dealer or transmission shop.*

49 Fluid leakage

1 Automatic transmission fluid is a deep red color. Fluid leaks should not be confused with engine oil, which can easily be blown onto the transaxle by air flow.
2 To pinpoint a leak, first remove all built-up dirt and grime from the transaxle housing with degreasing agents and/or steam cleaning. Then drive the vehicle at low speeds so air flow will not blow the leak far from its source. Raise the vehicle and determine where the leak is coming from. Common areas of leakage are:
   a) Control valve cover (Chapters 1 and 7)
   b) Dipstick tube (Chapters 1 and 7)
   c) Transaxle oil lines (Chapter 7)
   d) Speed sensor (Chapter 7)

50 Transaxle fluid brown or has a burned smell

Transaxle fluid burned (Chapter 1).

51 General shift mechanism problems

1 Chapter 7, Part B, deals with checking and adjusting the shift linkage on automatic transaxles. Common problems which may be attributed to poorly adjusted linkage are:
   a) Engine starting in gears other than Park or Neutral.
   b) Indicator on shifter pointing to a gear other than the one actually being used.
   c) Vehicle moves when in Park.
2 Refer to Chapter 7B for the shift linkage adjustment procedure.

52 Transaxle will not downshift with accelerator pedal pressed to the floor

Throttle valve cable out of adjustment (Chapter 7B).

53 Engine will start in gears other than Park or Neutral

Neutral start switch malfunctioning (Chapter 7B).

54   Transaxle slips, shifts roughly, is noisy or has no drive in forward or reverse gears

There are many probable causes for the above problems, but the home mechanic should be concerned with only one possibility – fluid level. Before taking the vehicle to a repair shop, check the level and condition of the fluid as described in Chapter 1. Correct the fluid level as necessary or change the fluid and filter if needed. If the problem persists, have a professional diagnose the cause.

Driveaxles

55   Clicking noise in turns

Worn or damaged outer CV joint (Chapter 8).

56   Shudder or vibration during acceleration

1   Excessive toe-in (Chapter 10).
2   Incorrect spring heights (Chapter 10).
3   Worn or damaged inboard or outboard CV joints (Chapter 8).
4   Sticking inboard CV joint assembly (Chapter 8).

57   Vibration at highway speeds

1   Out of balance front wheels and/or tires (Chapters 1 and 10).
2   Out of round front tires (Chapters 1 and 10).
3   Worn CV joint(s) (Chapter 8).

Brakes

Note: Before assuming that a brake problem exists, make sure that:
   a)   The tires are in good condition and properly inflated (Chapter 1).
   b)   The front end alignment is correct (Chapter 10).
   c)   The vehicle is not loaded with weight in an unequal manner.

58   Vehicle pulls to one side during braking

1   Incorrect tire pressures (Chapter 1).
2   Front end out of line (have the front end aligned).
3   Front, or rear, tires not matched to one another.
4   Restricted brake lines or hoses (Chapter 9).
5   Malfunctioning drum brake or caliper assembly (Chapter 9).
6   Loose suspension parts (Chapter 10).
7   Loose calipers (Chapter 9).
8   Excessive wear of brake shoe or pad material or disc/drum on one side.

59   Noise (high-pitched squeal when the brakes are applied)

Brake pads or shoes worn out. Replace pads/shoes with new ones immediately (Chapter 9). Be sure to check the disc/drums for damage as well.

60   Brake roughness or chatter (pedal pulsates)

1   Excessive disc lateral runout (Chapter 9).
2   Uneven pad wear (Chapter 9).
3   Defective disc (Chapter 9).
4   Drum out-of-round (Chapter 9).

61   Excessive brake pedal effort required to stop vehicle

1   Malfunctioning power brake booster (Chapter 9).
2   Partial system failure (Chapter 9).
3   Excessively worn pads or shoes (Chapter 9).
4   Piston in caliper or wheel cylinder stuck or sluggish (Chapter 9).
5   Brake pads or shoes contaminated with oil or grease (Chapter 9).
6   New pads or shoes installed and not yet seated. It will take a while for the new material to seat against the rotor or drum.

62   Excessive brake pedal travel

1   Partial brake system failure (Chapter 9).
2   Insufficient fluid in master cylinder (Chapters 1 and 9).
3   Air trapped in system (Chapters 1 and 9).
4   Brakes in need of adjustment (Chapter 9).

63   Dragging brakes

1   Master cylinder pistons not returning correctly (Chapter 9).
2   Restricted brake lines or hoses (Chapters 1 and 9).
3   Incorrect parking brake adjustment (Chapter 9).

64   Grabbing or uneven braking action

1   Malfunction of pressure regulator/proportioning valve (Chapter 9).
2   Malfunction of power brake booster unit (Chapter 9).
3   Binding brake pedal mechanism (Chapter 9).
4   Grease or oil on brake lining (Chapter 9).

65   Brake pedal feels spongy when depressed

1   Air in hydraulic lines (Chapter 9).
2   Master cylinder mounting bolts loose (Chapter 9).
3   Master cylinder defective (Chapter 9).

66   Brake pedal travels to the floor with little resistance

1   Little or no fluid in the master cylinder reservoir caused by leaking caliper or wheel cylinder piston(s) (Chapter 9).
2   Loose, damaged or disconnected brake lines (Chapter 9).

67   Parking brake does not hold

Parking brake linkage improperly adjusted (Chapters 1 and 9).

Suspension and steering systems

Note: Before attempting to diagnose the suspension and steering systems, perform the following preliminary checks:
   a)   Tires for wrong pressure and uneven wear.
   b)   Steering universal joints from the column to the rack and pinion for loose connectors or wear.
   c)   Front and rear suspension and the rack and pinion assembly for loose or damaged parts.
   d)   Out-of-round or out-of-balance tires, bent rims and loose and/or rough wheel bearings.

68 Vehicle pulls to one side

1 Mismatched or uneven tires (Chapter 10).
2 Broken or sagging springs (Chapter 10).
3 Wheel alignment (Chapter 10).
4 Front brake dragging (Chapter 9).

69 Abnormal or excessive tire wear

1 Wheel alignment (Chapter 10).
2 Sagging or broken springs (Chapter 10).
3 Tire out of balance (Chapter 10).
4 Worn strut damper (Chapter 10).
5 Overloaded vehicle.
6 Tires not rotated regularly.

70 Wheel makes a thumping noise

1 Blister or bump on tire (Chapter 10).
2 Improper strut damper action (Chapter 10).

71 Shimmy, shake or vibration

1 Tire or wheel out-of-balance or out-of-round (Chapter 10).
2 Loose or worn wheel bearings (Chapters 1 and 10).
3 Worn tie-rod ends (Chapter 10).
4 Worn balljoints (Chapters 1 and 10).
5 Excessive wheel runout (Chapter 10).
6 Blister or bump on tire (Chapter 10).

72 Hard steering

1 Lack of lubrication at balljoints, tie-rod ends and rack and pinion assembly (Chapter 10).
2 Front wheel alignment (Chapter 10).
3 Low tire pressure(s) (Chapters 1 and 10).

73 Poor returnability of steering to center

1 Lack of lubrication at balljoints and tie-rod ends (Chapter 10).
2 Binding in balljoints (Chapter 10).
3 Binding in steering column (Chapter 10).
4 Lack of lubricant in rack and pinion assembly (Chapter 10).
5 Front wheel alignment (Chapter 10).

74 Abnormal noise at the front end

1 Lack of lubrication at balljoints and tie-rod ends (Chapters 1 and 10).
2 Damaged strut mounting (Chapter 10).
3 Worn control arm bushings or tie-rod ends (Chapter 10).
4 Loose stabilizer bar (Chapter 10).
5 Loose wheel nuts (Chapters 1 and 10).
6 Loose suspension bolts (Chapter 10).

75 Wander or poor steering stability

1 Mismatched or uneven tires (Chapter 10).

2 Lack of lubrication at balljoints and tie-rod ends (Chapters 1 and 10).
3 Worn strut assemblies (Chapter 10).
4 Loose stabilizer bar (Chapter 10).
5 Broken or sagging springs (Chapter 10).
6 Wheel alignment (Chapter 10).

76 Erratic steering when braking

1 Wheel bearings worn (Chapter 10).
2 Broken or sagging springs (Chapter 10).
3 Leaking wheel cylinder or caliper (Chapter 10).
4 Warped discs or drums (Chapter 10).

77 Excessive pitching and/or rolling around corners or during braking

1 Loose stabilizer bar (Chapter 10).
2 Worn strut dampers or mountings (Chapter 10).
3 Broken or sagging springs (Chapter 10).
4 Overloaded vehicle.

78 Suspension bottoms

1 Overloaded vehicle.
2 Worn strut dampers (Chapter 10).
3 Incorrect, broken or sagging springs (Chapter 10).

79 Cupped tires

1 Front wheel or rear wheel alignment (Chapter 10).
2 Worn strut dampers or shock absorbers (Chapter 10).
3 Wheel bearings worn (Chapter 10).
4 Excessive tire or wheel runout (Chapter 10).
5 Worn balljoints (Chapter 10).

80 Excessive tire wear on outside edge

1 Inflation pressures incorrect (Chapter 1).
2 Excessive speed in turns.
3 Front end alignment incorrect (excessive toe-in). Have professionally aligned.
4 Suspension arm bent or twisted (Chapter 10).

81 Excessive tire wear on inside edge

1 Inflation pressures incorrect (Chapter 1).
2 Front end alignment incorrect (toe-out). Have professionally aligned.
3 Loose or damaged steering components (Chapter 10).

82 Tire tread worn in one place

1 Tires out of balance.
2 Damaged or buckled wheel. Inspect and replace if necessary.
3 Defective tire (Chapter 1).

83   Excessive play or looseness in steering system

1   Wheel bearing(s) worn (Chapter 10).
2   Tie-rod end loose (Chapter 10).
3   Rack and pinion loose (Chapter 10).
4   Worn or loose steering intermediate shaft (Chapter 10).

84   Rattling or clicking noise in steering gear

1   Insufficient or improper lubricant in steering gear (Chapter 10).
2   Steering gear attachment loose (Chapter 10).
3   Internal steering gear problem (Chapter 10).

Chapter 1   Tune-up and routine maintenance

Contents

Air filter replacement	15
Air injection pump filter replacement	16
Automatic transaxle differential lubricant change	41
Automatic transaxle differential lubricant level check	33
Automatic transaxle fluid and filter change	39
Automatic transaxle fluid level check	7
Battery check and maintenance	10
Brake fluid replacement	38
Brake system check	28
Carburetor choke check	34
Clutch freeplay check and adjustment	18
Cooling system check	13
Cooling system servicing (draining, flushing and refilling)	36
Driveaxle boot check	30
Drivebelt check, adjustment and replacement	11
Drum brake adjustment (1975 through 1978 models only)	27
Engine oil and filter change	8
Evaporative emissions control system check and canister replacement	42
Exhaust Gas Recirculation (EGR) system check and service light resetting	17
Exhaust system check	31
Fluid level checks	4
Fuel filter replacement	25
Fuel system check	26
Idle speed check and adjustment	20
Ignition points replacement	22
Ignition timing check and adjustment	21
Introduction	1
Maintenance schedule	2
Manual transaxle lubricant change	40
Manual transaxle lubricant level check	32
Oxygen sensor replacement and service light resetting	44
Power steering fluid level check	6
Positive crankcase Ventilation (PCV) system check	43
Rear wheel bearing check, repack and adjustment	37
Spark plug replacement	23
Spark plug wire, distributor cap and rotor check and replacement	24
Steering and suspension checks	29
Thermostatically-controlled air cleaner check (carbureted models)	35
Tire and tire pressure checks	5
Tire rotation	14
Tune-up general information	3
Underhood hose check and replacement	12
Valve clearance check and adjustment (1975 through 1984 models only)	19
Windshield wiper blade inspection and replacement	9

1

Specifications

Recommended lubricants and fluids

Engine oil type	API grade SF or SF/CC multigrade and fuel efficient oil
Viscosity	See accompanying chart
Fuel	Unleaded gasoline, 87 octane or higher
Automatic transaxle fluid type	Dexron II automatic transmission fluid
Automatic transaxle differential lubricant	API GL-5 SAE 90W hypoid gear oil
Manual transaxle lubricant type	API GL-5 SAE 80W90W gear oil
Brake fluid type	DOT 3 brake fluid
Power steering system fluid	
1980 through 1984	VW Part No. ZVW 239 902 or equivalent
1985 on	Dexron II automatic transmission fluid
Rear wheel bearing grease	NLGI No. 2 EP moly-base wheel bearing grease

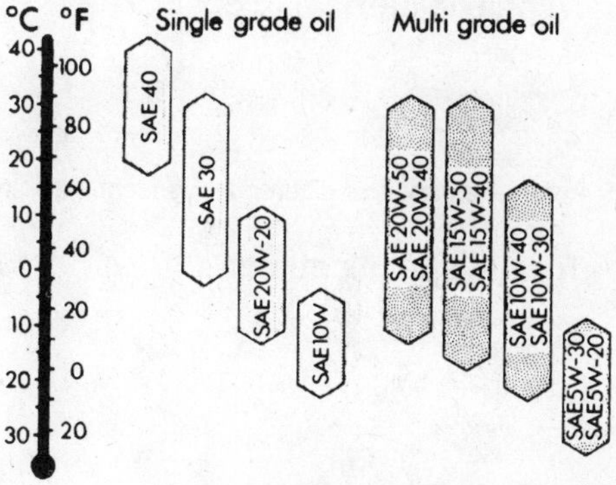

OIL VISCOSITY CHART

Ignition system

Distributor point gap	0.016 in (0.40 mm)
Dwell angle	
New points	44-degrees to 59-degrees
Service limit	42-degrees to 58-degrees
Spark plug type and gap	Refer to the *Emission Control Information label* in the engine compartment
Ignition timing	Refer to the *Emission Control Information label* in the engine compartment
Engine firing order	1-3-4-2

Cooling system

Coolant capacity	
1975 through 1979	
With coolant reservoir	6.8 qt (5.7 liters)
Without coolant reservoir	4.9 qt (4.6 liters)
1980 on	2.7 gal (6.5 liters)
Radiator cap pressure rating	17 to 19 psi (13 to 15 if cap no. 171 121 321 is installed)
Accessory drivebelt deflection	
1975 through 1984	
Air conditioned models	
New	2/5 in (10 mm)
Used	3/5 in (15 mm)

Accessory drivebelt deflection (continued)
  Non-air conditioned models ....
    New .... 1/8 in (2 mm)
    Used .... 1/4 in (5 mm)
  1985 on
    Alternator .... 5/64 to 3/16 in (2 to 5 mm)
    Power steering and air conditioning .... 3/8 in (10 mm)

Clutch

Clutch pedal free play .... 5/8 in (15 mm)
Clutch cable free play
  1975 through 1980 .... 1/8 in (3 mm)
  1981 through 1984 .... 1/4 in (6 mm)
  1985 on .... 15/32 in (12 mm)

Brakes

Disc brake backing plate and pad lining thickness (minimum) ... 1/4 in (6 mm)
Drum brake shoe lining thickness (minimum)
  Riveted .... 7/64 in (2.5 mm)
  Bonded .... 5/64 in (2 mm)

Suspension and steering

Steering wheel freeplay limit .... 1 in (26 mm)

Engine

Oil capacity (with filter)
  1975 through 1980 .... 3.7 qt (3.5 liters)
  1981 on .... 4.2 qt (4.0 liters)
Valve clearances (engine hot)
  Intake valve .... 0.008 to 0.012 in (0.20 to 0.30 mm)
  Exhaust valve .... 0.016 to 0.020 in (0.40 to 0.50 mm)
Firing order .... 1 – 3 – 4 – 2

Transaxle lubricant capacity

Automatic .... 3.2 qt (3.0 liters)
Manual
  4-speed .... 1.3 qt (1.25 liters)
  5-speed .... 2.0 qt (1.9 liters)
Automatic transaxle differential lubricant capacity .... 0.79 qt (0.75 liters)

Torque specifications

Ft-lb (unless otherwise indicated)

Automatic transaxle
  Pan bolts 15
  Fluid filter bolt 3
  Drain plug 25
Driveaxle flange bolt 33
Engine oil pan drain plug 22
Fuel filter bolt 18
Camshaft cover bolt/nut .... 84 in-lbs
Spark plug .... 18 to 22
Wheel lug bolts
  1975 through 1984 66
  1985 and on 81

0799H

1990 and later 2.0L engine

0800H

1989 and later 1.8L engine

0801H

All other engines

Cylinder location and distributor rotation

1   Introduction

This Chapter is designed to help the home mechanic maintain Volkswagen front wheel drive models covered by this manual with the goals of maximum performance, economy, safety and reliability in mind.

Included is a master maintenance schedule, followed by procedures dealing specifically with each item on the schedule. Visual checks, adjustments, component replacement and other helpful items are included. Refer to the accompanying illustrations of the engine compartment and the underside of the vehicle for the locations of various components.

Adhering to the mileage/time maintenance schedule and following the step-by-step procedures, which is simply a preventive maintenance program, will result in maximum reliability and vehicle service life. Keep in mind that it is a comprehensive program – maintaining some items but not others at the specified intervals will not produce the same results.

As you service the vehicle, you will discover that many of the procedures can – and should – be grouped together because of the nature of the particular procedure you're performing or because of the close proximity of two otherwise unrelated components to one another.

For example, if the vehicle is raised for chassis lubrication, you should inspect the exhaust, suspension, steering and fuel systems while you're under the vehicle. When you're rotating the tires, it makes good sense to check the brakes, since the wheels are already removed. Finally, let's suppose you have to borrow or rent a torque wrench. Even if you only need it to tighten the spark plugs, you might as well check the torque of as many critical fasteners as time allows.

1.1a Typical Golf/Jetta engine compartment component checking points

1	Oil filler cap	6	Clutch cable adjuster	11	Alternator drivebelt
2	Brake fluid reservoir	7	Radiator	12	Air cleaner assembly
3	Coolant reservoir	8	Distributor	13	Fuel lines
4	Windshield washer fluid tank	9	Spark plug		
5	Battery	10	Radiator hose		

1

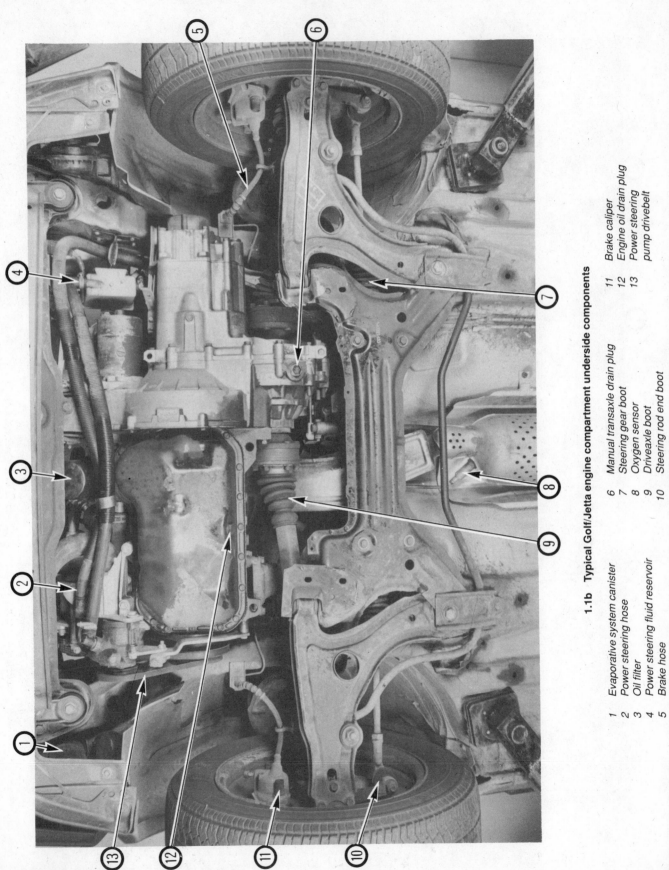

1.1b   Typical Golf/Jetta engine compartment underside components

1   Evaporative system canister
2   Power steering hose
3   Oil filter
4   Power steering fluid reservoir
5   Brake hose

6   Manual transaxle drain plug
7   Steering gear boot
8   Oxygen sensor
9   Driveaxle boot
10 Steering rod end boot

11 Brake caliper
12 Engine oil drain plug
13 Power steering
    pump drivebelt

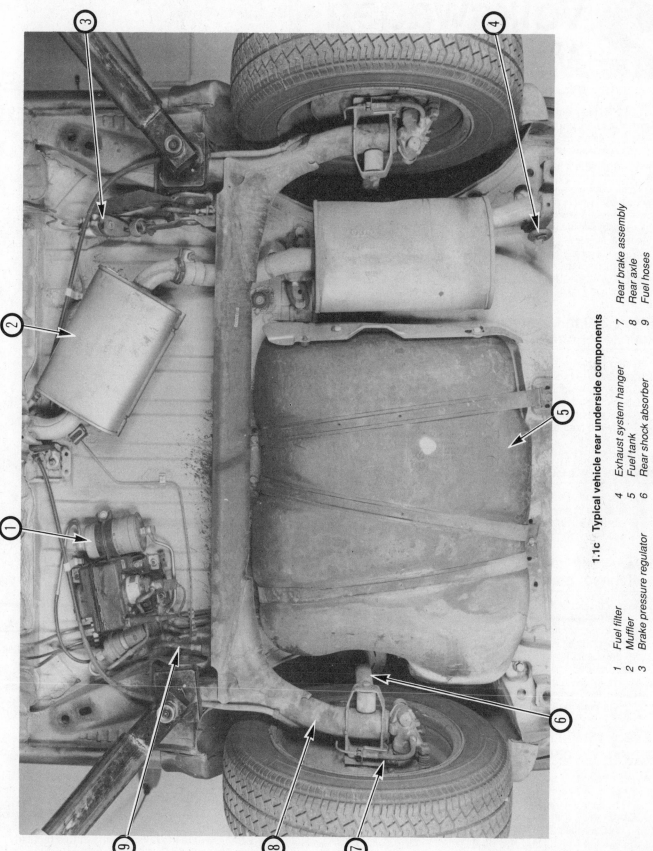

1.1c   Typical vehicle rear underside components

1	Fuel filter	4	Exhaust system hanger	7	Rear brake assembly
2	Muffler	5	Fuel tank	8	Rear axle
3	Brake pressure regulator	6	Rear shock absorber	9	Fuel hoses

1

2 Volkswagen Maintenance schedule

The following maintenance intervals are based on the assumption that the vehicle owner will be doing the maintenance or service work, as opposed to having a dealer service department do the work. Although the time/mileage intervals are loosely based on factory recommendations, most have been shortened to ensure, for example, that such items as filters, lubricants and fluids are checked/changed at intervals that promote maximum engine/driveline service life. Also, subject to the preference of the individual owner interested in keeping his or her vehicle in peak condition at all times, and with the vehicle's ultimate resale in mind, many of the maintenance procedures may be performed more often than recommended in the following schedule. We encourage such owner initiative.

When the vehicle is new it should be serviced initially by a factory authorized dealer service department to protect the factory warranty. In many cases the initial maintenance check is done at no cost to the owner (check with your dealer service department for more information).

Every 250 miles or weekly, whichever comes first

Check the engine oil level (Section 4)
Check the engine coolant level (Section 4)
Check the windshield washer fluid level (Section 4)
Check the water (electrolyte) in the battery (Section 4)
Check the brake fluid level (Section 4)
Check the tires and tire pressures (Section 5)

Every 3500 miles or 3 months, whichever comes first

All items listed above plus . . .
Check the power steering fluid level (Section 6)
Check the automatic transaxle fluid level (Section 7)
Change the engine oil and oil filter (Section 8)

Every 7500 miles or 6 months, whichever comes first

Inspect/replace if necessary the windshield wiper blades (Section 9)
Check and service the battery (Section 10)
Check and adjust if necessary, the engine drivebelts (Section 11)
Inspect and, if necessary, replace all underhood hoses (Section 12)
Check the cooling system (Section 13)
Rotate the tires (Section 14)

Every 15,000 miles or 12 months, whichever comes first

All items listed above plus . . .
Replace the air and PCV filter (Section 15)
Replace the air injection system filter (Section 16)
Check the Exhaust Gas Recirculation (EGR) system (Section 17)
Check the clutch for proper freeplay (Section 18)
Check the cylinder compression (Chapter 2)
Check and adjust, if necessary, the valve clearances (1975 through 1984 models) (Section 19)

Check and adjust, if necessary, the idle speed (Section 20)
Check and adjust, if necessary, the ignition timing (Section 21)
Replace the ignition points (Section 22)
Check and replace, if necessary, the spark plugs (Section 23)
Inspect, and replace if necessary, the spark plug wires, distributor cap and rotor (Section 24)
Replace the fuel filter (Section 25)
Inspect the fuel system (Section 26)
Adjust the drum brakes (1975 through 1978 models only) (Section 27)
Inspect the brake system (Section 28)
Inspect the suspension and steering components (Section 29)
Check the driveaxle boots (Section 30)
Inspect the exhaust system (Section 31)
Check the manual transaxle lubricant level (Section 32)
Check the automatic transaxle differential lubricant level (Section 33)

Every 30,000 miles or 24 months, whichever comes first

Check the carburetor choke operation (Section 34)
Check the thermostatic air cleaner operation (Section 35)
Service the cooling system (drain, flush and refill) (Section 36)
Check and repack, if necessary, the rear wheel bearings (Section 37)
Replace the brake fluid (Section 38)
Change the automatic transaxle fluid and filter (Section 39)
Change the manual transaxle lubricant (Section 40)
Change the automatic transaxle differential lubricant (Section 41)
Inspect the evaporative emissions control system and, if necessary, replace the canister (Section 42)
Check the PCV system (Section 43)
Replace the oxygen sensor (1985 through 1987 SOHC engines) (Section 44)

Every 60,000 miles or 48 months, whichever comes first

Replace the oxygen sensor (1987 DOHC engines and all 1988 and later models) (Section 44)
Replace the timing belt (Chapter 2)
* This item is affected by "severe" operating conditions as described below. If your vehicle is operated under "severe" conditions, perform all maintenance indicated with an asterisk (*) at 7500 mile/6 month intervals.
Consider the conditions "severe" if most driving is done . . .
In dusty areas
When towing a trailer
At low speeds or with extended periods of engine idling
When outside temperatures remain below freezing and most trips are less than 4 miles
** If most driving is done under one or more of the following conditions, change the automatic transaxle fluid every 15,000 miles:
In heavy traffic where the outside temperature regularly reaches 90-degrees F (32-degrees C) or higher
In hilly or mountainous terrain
Frequent trailer pulling

The first step in this maintenance program is to prepare yourself before the actual work begins. Read through all the procedures you're planning to do, then gather up all the parts and tools needed. If it looks like you might run into problems during a particular job, seek advice from a mechanic or an experienced do-it-yourselfer.

3 Tune-up general information

The term tune-up is used in this manual to represent a combination of individual operations rather than one specific procedure.

If, from the time the vehicle is new, the routine maintenance schedule is followed closely and frequent checks are made of fluid levels and high wear items, as suggested throughout this manual, the engine will be kept in relatively good running condition and the need for additional work will be minimized.

More likely than not, however, there will be times when the engine is running poorly due to lack of regular maintenance. This is even more likely if a used vehicle, which has not received regular and frequent maintenance checks, is purchased. In such cases, an engine tune-up will be needed outside of the regular routine maintenance intervals.

The first step in any tune-up or diagnostic procedure to help correct a poor running engine is a cylinder compression check (see Chapter 2). This check will help determine the condition of internal engine components and should be used as a guide for tune-up and repair procedures. For instance, if a compression check indicates serious internal engine wear, a conventional tune-up will not improve the performance of the engine and would be a waste of time and money. Because of its importance, the compression check should be done by someone with the right equipment and the knowledge to use it properly.

The following procedures are those most often needed to bring a generally poor running engine back into a proper state of tune.

Minor tune-up

Clean, inspect and test the battery (Section 10)
Check all engine related fluids (Section 4)
Check and adjust the drivebelts (Section 11)
Replace the spark plugs (Section 23)
Inspect the distributor cap and rotor (Section 24)
Inspect the spark plug and coil wires (Section 24)
Check and adjust the ignition timing (Section 21)
Check and adjust the idle speed (Section 20)
Check the PCV system (Section 43)
Check the air filter (Section 15)
Check the cooling system (Section 13)
Check all underhood hoses (Section 12)

Major tune-up

All items listed under Minor tune-up, plus . . .
Check the EGR system (Section 17)
Check the ignition system (Chapter 5)
Check the charging system (Chapter 5)
Check the fuel system (Chapter 4)
Replace the air filter (Section 15)
Replace the distributor cap and rotor (Section 24)
Replace the spark plug wires (Section 24)
Replace the ignition points (if equipped) (Section 22)

4 Fluid level checks

Note: *The following fluid level checks should be done on a 250 mile or weekly basis. Additional fluid level checks can be found in specific maintenance procedures which follow. Regardless of intervals, be alert for fluid leaks under the vehicle which would indicate a leak to be fixed immediately.*

Warning: *The electric cooling fan can activate at any time, even when the ignition is in the Off position. Disconnect the fan motor or negative battery cable when working in the vicinity of the fan.*

1   Fluids are an essential part of the lubrication, cooling, brake and windshield washer systems. Because the fluids gradually become depleted and/or contaminated during normal operation of the vehicle, they must be periodically replenished. See *Recommended lubricants and fluids* at the beginning of this Chapter before adding fluid to any of the following components. **Note:** *The vehicle must be on level ground when fluid levels are checked.*

Engine oil

Refer to illustrations 4.2, 4.4 and 4.6

2   The engine oil level is checked with a dipstick located at the front (radiator) side of the engine **(see illustration)**. It extends through a tube and into the oil pan at the bottom of the engine.

3   The oil level should be checked before the vehicle has been driven, or about 15 minutes after the engine has been shut off. If the oil is checked immediately after driving the vehicle, some of the oil will remain in the upper engine components, resulting in an inaccurate reading on the dipstick.

4   Pull the dipstick out and wipe all the oil off the end with a clean rag or paper towel. Insert the clean dipstick all the way back into the tube, then pull it out again. Note the oil at the end of the dipstick. Add oil as necessary to keep the level within the acceptable range on the dipstick **(see illustration)**.

4.2   The engine oil dipstick (arrow) is located on the front side of the engine, behind the radiator

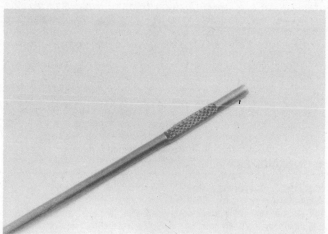

4.4   The oil level should be kept within the cross-hatched area on the dipstick – if it isn't, add enough oil to bring the level to or near the top of the cross-hatched area (it takes one full quart to raise the level from the bottom to the top)

4.6   The oil filler cap is located at the front of the camshaft cover – always make sure that the area around this opening is clean before unscrewing the cap to prevent dirt from contaminating the engine

4.8   Make sure that the coolant level in the reservoir is between the MIN and MAX marks – if it's below the Min mark, add a sufficient quantity of the prescribed mixture of antifreeze and water

5   Don't overfill the engine by adding too much oil, since it may result in oil fouled spark plugs, oil leaks or oil seal failures.

6   Oil is added to the engine after removing the cap from the camshaft cover **(see illustration)**. An oil can spout or funnel may help to reduce spills.

7   Checking the oil level is an important preventive maintenance step. A consistently low oil level indicates oil leakage through damaged seals, defective gaskets or past worn rings or valve guides. If the oil looks milky in color or has water droplets in it, the cylinder head gasket may be blown or the head or block may be cracked. The engine should be checked immediately. The condition of the oil should also be noted. Whenever you check the oil level, slide your thumb and index finger up the dipstick before wiping off the oil. If you see small dirt or metal particles clinging to the dipstick, the oil should be changed (see Section 8).

Engine coolant

Refer to illustration 4.8

Warning: *Do not allow antifreeze to come in contact with your skin or painted surfaces of the vehicle. Flush contaminated areas immediately with plenty of water. Don't store new coolant or leave old coolant lying around where it's accessible to children or pets – they're attracted by its sweet taste. Ingestion of even a small amount of coolant can be fatal! Wipe up garage floor and drip pan coolant spills immediately. Keep antifreeze containers covered and repair leaks in your cooling system as soon as they are noted.*

8   All later model vehicles covered by this manual are equipped with a pressurized coolant recovery system. A white plastic coolant reservoir located near the brake master cylinder in the engine compartment is connected by a hose to the radiator filler neck **(see illustration)**. If the engine overheats, coolant escapes through a valve in the radiator cap and travels through the hose into the reservoir. As the engine cools, the coolant is automatically drawn back into the cooling system to maintain the correct level.

9   The coolant level in the reservoir should be checked regularly. **Warning:** *Do not remove the radiator cap to check the coolant level when the engine is warm.* The level in the reservoir varies with the temperature of the engine. When the engine is cold, the coolant level should be at or slightly above the LOW mark on the reservoir **(see illustration 4.8)**. Once the engine has warmed up, the level should be at or near the FULL mark. If it isn't, allow the engine to cool, then remove the cap from the reservoir and add a 50/50 mixture of ethylene glycol-based antifreeze and water.

10   Drive the vehicle and recheck the coolant level. If only a small amount of coolant is required to bring the system up to the proper level, water can be used. However, repeated additions of water will dilute the antifreeze and water solution. In order to maintain the proper ratio of antifreeze and water, always top up the coolant level with the correct mixture. An empty plastic milk jug or bleach bottle makes an excellent container for mixing coolant. Do not use rust inhibitors or additives.

11   If the coolant level drops consistently, there may be a leak in the system. Inspect the radiator, hoses, filler cap, drain plugs and water pump (see Section 13). If no leaks are noted, have the radiator cap pressure tested by a service station.

12   If you have to remove the radiator cap, wait until the engine has cooled, then wrap a thick cloth around the cap and turn it to the first stop. If coolant or steam escapes, let the engine cool down longer, then remove the cap. On models which do not have a coolant reservoir, fill the radiator until the level reaches the protrusion in the filler neck.

13   Check the condition of the coolant as well. It should be relatively clear. If it's brown or rust colored, the system should be drained, flushed and refilled. Even if the coolant appears to be normal, the corrosion inhibitors wear out, so it must be replaced at the specified intervals.

Windshield washer fluid

Refer to illustration 4.14

14   Fluid for the windshield washer system is located in a plastic reservoir in the engine compartment **(see illustration)**.

15   In milder climates, plain water can be used in the reservoir, but it should be kept no more than 2/3 full to allow for expansion if the water freezes. In colder climates, use windshield washer system antifreeze, available at any auto parts store, to lower the freezing point of the fluid. Mix the antifreeze with water in accordance with the manufacturer's directions on the container. **Caution:** *Don't use cooling system antifreeze – it will damage the vehicle's paint.*

16   To help prevent icing in cold weather, warm the windshield with the defroster before using the washer.

Battery electrolyte

Refer to illustration 4.17

17   Most later model vehicles with which this manual is concerned are equipped with a battery which is permanently sealed (except for vent holes) and has no filler caps. Water doesn't have to be added to these batteries at any time. If a maintenance-type battery is installed, the caps on top of the battery should be removed periodically to check for a low water level **(see illustration)**. This check is most critical during the warm summer months.

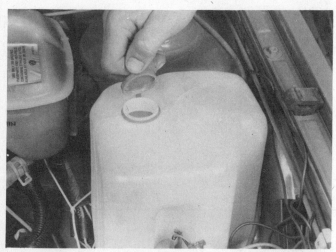

4.14   The windshield washer fluid reservoir is located in the left rear corner of the engine compartment – fluid can be added after flipping up the cap

4.17   Remove the cell caps to check the water level in the battery – if the level is low, add distilled water only

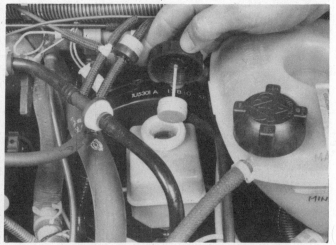

4.19   The brake fluid level should be kept between the Min and Max marks on the translucent plastic reservoir – unscrew the cap to add fluid

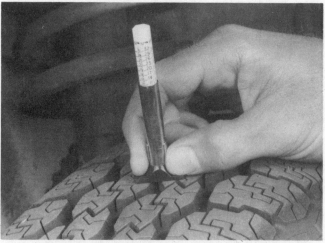

5.2   A tire tread depth indicator should be used to monitor tire wear – they are available at auto parts stores and service station and cost very little

Brake fluid

Refer to illustration 4.19

18   The brake master cylinder is mounted on the firewall or the front of the power booster unit in the engine compartment.

19   The fluid inside is readily visible. The level should be between the MIN and MAX marks on the reservoir **(see illustration)**. If a low level is indicated, be sure to wipe the top of the reservoir cover with a clean rag to prevent contamination of the brake system before removing the cover.

20   When adding fluid, pour it carefully into the reservoir to avoid spilling it onto surrounding painted surfaces. Be sure the specified fluid is used, since mixing different types of brake fluid can cause damage to the system. See *Recommended lubricants and fluids* at the front of this Chapter or your owner's manual. **Warning:** *Brake fluid can harm your eyes and damage painted surfaces, so use extreme caution when handling or pouring it. Do not use brake fluid that has been standing open or is more than one year old. Brake fluid absorbs moisture from the air. Excess moisture can cause a dangerous loss of braking effectiveness.*

21   At this time the fluid and master cylinder can be inspected for contamination. The system should be drained and refilled if deposits, dirt particles or water droplets are seen in the fluid (see Section 38).

22   After filling the reservoir to the proper level, make sure the cover is on tight to prevent fluid leakage.

23   The brake fluid level in the master cylinder will drop slightly as the pads and the brake shoes at each wheel wear down during normal operation. If the master cylinder requires repeated additions to keep it at the proper level, it's an indication of leakage in the brake system, which should be corrected immediately. Check all brake lines and connections (see Section 28 for more information).

24   If, upon checking the master cylinder fluid level, you discover the reservoir empty or nearly empty, the brake system should be bled (see Chapter 9).

---

5   Tire and tire pressure checks

Refer to illustrations 5.2, 5.3, 5.4a, 5.4b and 5.8

1   Periodic inspection of the tires may spare you the inconvenience of being stranded with a flat tire. It can also provide you with vital information regarding possible problems in the steering and suspension systems before major damage occurs.

2   The original tires on this vehicle are equipped with 1/2-inch side bands that will appear when tread depth reaches 1/16-inch, but they don't appear until the tires are worn out. Tread wear can be monitored with a simple, inexpensive device known as a tread depth indicator **(see illustration)**.

Condition	Probable cause	Corrective action	Condition	Probable cause	Corrective action
Shoulder wear	• Underinflation (both sides wear) • Incorrect wheel camber (one side wear) • Hard cornering • Lack of rotation	• Measure and adjust pressure. • Repair or replace axle and suspension parts. • Reduce speed. • Rotate tires.	Feathered edge Toe wear	• Incorrect toe	• Adjust toe-in.
Center wear	• Overinflation • Lack of rotation	• Measure and adjust pressure. • Rotate tires.	Uneven wear	• Incorrect camber or caster • Malfunctioning suspension • Unbalanced wheel • Out-of-round brake drum • Lack of rotation	• Repair or replace axle and suspension parts. • Repair or replace suspension parts. • Balance or replace. • Turn or replace. • Rotate tires.

5.3   This chart will help you determine the condition of the tires, the probable cause(s) of abnormal wear and the corrective action necessary

3   Note any abnormal tread wear **(see illustration)**. Tread pattern irregularities such as cupping, flat spots and more wear on one side than the other are indications of front end alignment and/or balance problems. If any of these conditions are noted, take the vehicle to a tire shop or service station to correct the problem.

4   Look closely for cuts, punctures and embedded nails or tacks. Sometimes a tire will hold air pressure for a short time or leak down very slowly after a nail has embedded itself in the tread. If a slow leak persists, check the valve stem core to make sure it's tight **(see illustration)**. Examine the tread for an object that may have embedded itself in the tire or for a "plug" that may have begun to leak (radial tire punctures are repaired with a plug that's installed in a puncture). If a puncture is suspected, it can be easily verified by spraying a solution of soapy water onto the suspected area **(see illustration)**. The soapy solution will bubble if there's a leak. Unless the puncture is unusually large, a tire shop or service station can usually repair the tire.

5.4a   If a tire loses air on a steady basis, check the valve core first to make sure it's snug (special inexpensive wrenches are commonly available at auto parts stores)

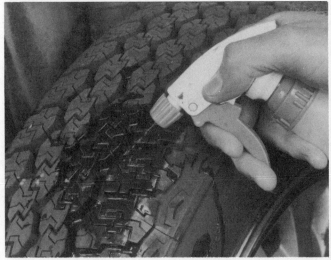

5.4b   If the valve core is tight, raise the corner of the vehicle with the low tire and spray a water soapy solution onto the tread as the tire is turned slowly – leaks will cause small bubbles to appear

5.8 To extend the life of the tires, check the air pressure at least once a week with an accurate gauge (don't forget the spare!)

5 Carefully inspect the inner sidewall of each tire for evidence of brake fluid. If you see any, inspect the brakes immediately.
6 Correct air pressure adds miles to the lifespan of the tires, improves mileage and enhances overall ride quality. Tire pressure cannot be accurately estimated by looking at a tire, especially if it's a radial. A tire pressure gauge is essential. Keep an accurate gauge in the vehicle. The pressure gauges attached to the nozzles of air hoses at gas stations are often inaccurate.
7 Always check tire pressure when the tires are cold. Cold, in this case, means the vehicle has not been driven over a mile in the three hours preceding a tire pressure check. A pressure rise of four to eight pounds is not uncommon once the tires are warm.
8 Unscrew the valve cap protruding from the wheel or hubcap and push the gauge firmly onto the valve stem (see illustration). Note the reading on the gauge and compare the figure to the recommended tire pressure shown on the label attached to the inside of the glove compartment door. Be sure to reinstall the valve cap to keep dirt and moisture out of the valve

stem mechanism. Check all four tires and, if necessary, add enough air to bring them up to the recommended pressure.
9 Don't forget to keep the spare tire inflated to the specified pressure (refer to your owner's manual or the tire sidewall).

---

6 Power steering fluid level check

Refer to illustrations 6.6 and 6.7
Warning: *The electric cooling fan can activate at any time, even when the ignition is in the Off position. Disconnect the fan motor or negative battery cable when working in the vicinity of the fan.*
1 Unlike manual steering, the power steering system relies on fluid which may, over a period of time, require replenishing.
2 The fluid reservoir for the power steering pump is located in the engine compartment near the battery.
3 For the check, the front wheels should be pointed straight ahead and the engine should be off.

1980 through 1984 models

4 Use a clean rag to wipe off the reservoir cap and the area around the cap. This will help prevent any foreign matter from entering the reservoir during the check.
5 Remove the cap and note the dipstick attached to it.
6 Wipe off the fluid with a clean rag, reinsert the dipstick, then withdraw it and read the fluid level. The level should be within the FULL COLD and FULL HOT marks, depending on the temperature of the fluid (see illustration).

1985 and later models

7 On these models, the fluid in the translucent plastic reservoir can be checked visually. The fluid level should be between the MIN and MAX marks on the side of the reservoir (see illustration). Never allow the fluid to drop below the MIN mark.

All models

8 If additional fluid is required, pour the specified type directly into the reservoir, using a funnel to prevent spills.
9 If the reservoir requires frequent fluid additions, all power steering hoses, hose connections and the power steering pump should be carefully checked for leaks.

6.6 On earlier models the power steering fluid is checked with a dipstick which is part of the cap – the fluid level varies with temperature so the dipstick is marked accordingly

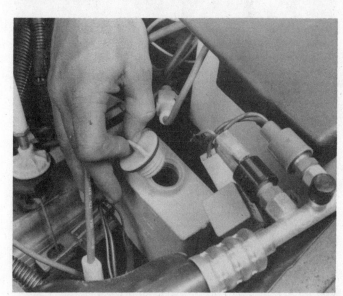

6.7 On later models, the power steering fluid reservoir is translucent so the fluid level can be checked without removing the cap – unscrew the cap to add fluid

7.4a   On earlier models, the automatic transaxle dipstick (arrow) is located in a long tube which extends from the transaxle toward the battery

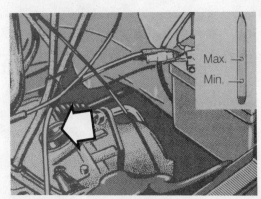

Max.
Min.

7.4b   On later models the automatic transaxle dipstick (arrow) is located in the housing – the fluid level should be between the two marks

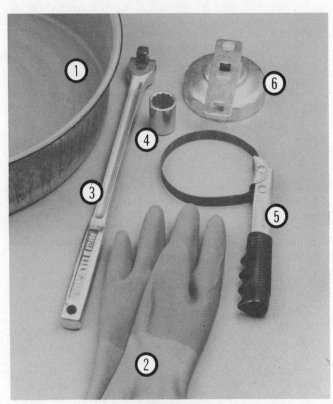

8.3   These tools are required when changing the engine oil and filter

1   *Drain pan* – *It should be fairly shallow in depth, but wide to prevent spills*
2   *Rubber gloves* – *When removing the drain plug and filter, you will get oil on your hands (the gloves will prevent burns)*
3   *Breaker bar* – *Sometimes the oil drain plug is tight and a long breaker bar is needed to loosen it*
4   *Socket* – *To be used with the breaker bar or a ratchet (must be the correct size to fit the drain plug – 6-point preferred)*
5   *Filter wrench* – *This is a metal band-type wrench, which requires clearance around the filter to be effective*
6   *Filter wrench* – *This type fits on the bottom of the filter and can be turned with a ratchet or breaker bar (different size wrenches are available for different types of filters)*

7   Automatic transaxle fluid level check

Refer to illustrations 7.4a and 7.4b
Warning: *The electric cooling fan can activate at any time, even when the ignition is in the Off position. Disconnect the fan motor or negative battery cable when working in the vicinity of the fan.*

1   The level of the automatic transaxle fluid should be carefully maintained. Low fluid level can lead to slipping or loss of drive, while overfilling can cause foaming, loss of fluid and transaxle damage.
2   The transaxle fluid level should only be checked when the engine is at normal operating temperature. **Caution:** *If the vehicle has just been driven for a long time at high speed or in city traffic in hot weather, or if it has been pulling a trailer, an accurate fluid level reading cannot be obtained. Allow the fluid to cool down for about 30 minutes.*
3   Park on level ground, apply the parking brake and start the engine. While the engine is idling, depress the brake pedal and move the selector lever through all the gear ranges, beginning and ending in Park.
4   With the engine still idling, remove the dipstick **(see illustrations)**.
5   Wipe the fluid off the dipstick with a clean rag and reinsert it until the cap seats.
6   Pull the dipstick out again. The fluid level should be between the two marks. If the level is at the low side of the range, add the specified automatic transmission fluid through the dipstick tube with a funnel.
7   Add the fluid a little at a time and keep checking the level until it's correct.
8   The condition of the fluid should also be checked along with the level. If the fluid at the end of the dipstick is black or a dark reddishbrown color, or if it smells burned, the fluid should be changed (see Section 39). If you're in doubt about the condition of the fluid, purchase some new fluid and compare the two for color and odor.

8   Engine oil and filter change

Refer to illustrations 8.3, 8.9, 8.14 and 8.18

1   Frequent oil changes are the most important preventive maintenance procedures that can be done by the home mechanic. As engine oil ages, it becomes diluted and contaminated, which leads to premature engine wear.
2   Although some sources recommend oil filter changes every other oil change, a new filter should be installed every time the oil is changed.
3   Gather together all necessary tools and materials before beginning this procedure **(see illustration)**.
4   You should have plenty of clean rags and newspapers handy to mop up any spills. Access to the underside of the vehicle is greatly improved if the vehicle can be lifted on a hoist, driven onto ramps or supported by jack

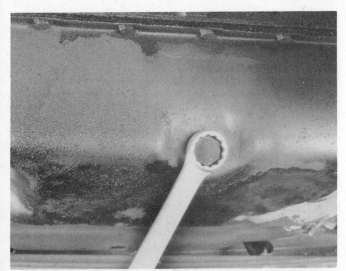

8.9   Use the proper size box end wrench or six-point socket to remove the oil drain plug without rounding it off

8.14   The oil filter is usually on very tight and will require a special wrench for removal – DO NOT use the wrench to tighten the new filter

stands. **Warning:** *Do not work under a vehicle which is supported only by a bumper, hydraulic or scissors-type jack.*

5   If this is your first oil change, get under the vehicle and familiarize yourself with the locations of the oil drain plug and the oil filter. The engine and exhaust components will be warm during the actual work, so note how they are situated to avoid touching them when working under the vehicle.

6   Warm the engine to normal operating temperature. If the new oil or any tools are needed, use this warm-up time to gather everything necessary for the job. Refer to Recommended lubricants and fluids at the beginning of this Chapter for the type of oil required.

7   With the engine oil warm (warm engine oil will drain better and more built-up sludge will be removed with it), raise and support the vehicle. Make sure it's safely supported!

8   Move all necessary tools, rags and newspapers under the vehicle. Set the drain pan under the drain plug. Keep in mind that the oil will initially flow from the pan with some force; position the pan accordingly.

9   Being careful not to touch any of the hot exhaust components, use a wrench to remove the drain plug near the bottom of the oil pan **(see illustration)**. Depending on how hot the oil is, you may want to wear gloves while unscrewing the plug the final few turns.

10   Allow the old oil to drain into the pan. It may be necessary to move the pan as the oil flow slows to a trickle.

11   After all the oil has drained, wipe off the drain plug with a clean rag. Small metal particles may cling to the plug and would immediately contaminate the new oil.

12   Clean the area around the drain plug opening and reinstall the plug. Tighten it securely with the wrench. If a torque wrench is available, use it to tighten the plug.

13   Move the drain pan into position under the oil filter.

14   Use the filter wrench to loosen the oil filter **(see illustration)**. Chain or metal band filter wrenches may distort the filter canister, but it doesn't matter since the filter will be discarded anyway.

15   Completely unscrew the old filter. Be careful; it's full of oil. Empty the oil inside the filter into the drain pan.

16   Compare the old filter with the new one to make sure they're the same type.

17   Use a clean rag to remove all oil, dirt and sludge from the area where the oil filter mounts to the engine.

18   Apply a light coat of clean oil to the rubber gasket on the new oil filter **(see illustration)**.

19   Attach the new filter to the engine, following the tightening directions printed on the filter canister or packing box. Most filter manufacturers recommend against using a wrench due to the possibility of overtightening the filter and damaging the seal.

20   Remove all tools, rags, etc. from under the vehicle, being careful not

8.18   Lubricate the oil filter gasket with clean engine oil before installing the filter on the engine

to spill the oil in the drain pan, then lower the vehicle.

21   Move to the engine compartment and locate the oil filler cap.

22   Pour the fresh oil through the filler opening into the engine. A funnel should be used to prevent spills.

23   Pour four quarts of fresh oil into the engine. Wait a few minutes to allow the oil to drain into the pan, then check the level on the oil dipstick (see Section 4 if necessary). If the oil level is above the MIN mark, start the engine and allow the new oil to circulate.

24   Run the engine for only about a minute and then shut it off. Immediately look under the vehicle and check for leaks at the oil pan drain plug and around the oil filter. If either is leaking, tighten with a bit more force.

25   With the new oil circulated and the filter now completely full, recheck the level on the dipstick and add more oil as necessary.

26   During the first few trips after an oil change, make it a point to check frequently for leaks and proper oil level.

27   The old oil drained from the engine cannot be reused in its present state and should be disposed of. Oil reclamation centers, auto repair shops and gas stations will normally accept the oil, which can be refined and used again. After the oil has cooled it can be drained into a container (capped plastic jugs, topped bottles, milk cartons, etc.) for transport to a disposal site.

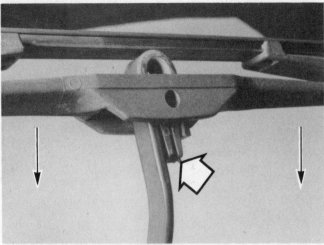

9.5   To detach the wiper blade element from the arm, swing the assembly around, depress the tab (arrow) and slide the assembly down the arm until it is clear of the hooked end

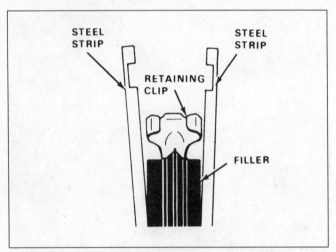

9.6   Squeeze the end of the element (filler), twist it to disengage it from the retaining clip, then remove the steel strips and slide the element from the frame

9   Windshield wiper blade inspection and replacement

Refer to illustrations 9.5 and 9.6

1   The windshield wiper and blade assembly should be inspected periodically for damage, loose components and cracked or worn blade elements.

2   Road film can build up on the wiper blades and affect their efficiency, so they should be washed regularly with a mild detergent solution.

3   The action of the wiping mechanism can loosen bolts, nuts and fasteners, so they should be checked and tightened, as necessary, at the same time the wiper blades are checked.

4   If the wiper blade elements are cracked, worn or warped, or no longer clean adequately, they should be replaced with new ones.

5   Lift the arm assembly away from the glass for clearance, lift up on the release lever and detach the blade assembly from the arm **(see illustration).**

6   Squeeze the end of the element (filler), twist it to detach it from the retaining clip, then pull the two steel strips out **(see illustration).** Remove the element.

7   Insert the new element and then insert the steel strips into it. Make sure the notches in the ends of the strips face each other, then squeeze the

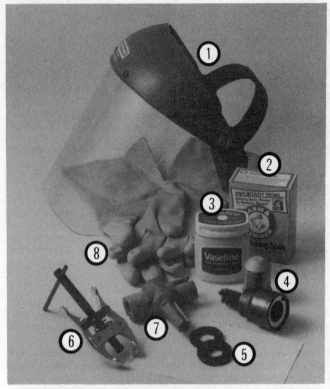

10.1   Tools and materials required for battery maintenance

1   *Face shield/safety goggles* – When removing corrosion with a brush, the acidic particles can easily fly up into your eyes
2   *Baking soda* – A solution of baking soda and water can be used to neutralize corrosion
3   *Petroleum jelly* – A layer of this on the battery posts will help prevent corrosion
4   *Battery post/cable cleaner* – This wire brush cleaning tool will remove all traces of corrosion from the battery posts and cable clamps
5   *Treated felt washers* – Placing one of these on each post, directly under the cable clamps, will help prevent corrosion
6   *Puller* – Sometimes the cable clamps are very difficult to pull off the posts, even after the nut/bolt has been completely loosened. This tool pulls the clamp straight up and off the post without damage.
7   *Battery post/cable cleaner* – Here is another cleaning tool which is a slightly different version of number 4 above, but it does the same thing
8   *Rubber gloves* – Another safety item to consider when servicing the battery; remember that's acid inside the battery!

end of the element and insert the element into the retaining clip. Release the end of the element, allowing the retaining clip to lock it in place.

8   On some models the element is not removable, in which case the entire blade assembly must be replaced.

10   Battery check and maintenance

Refer to illustrations 10.1, 10.6, 10.7a, 10.7b, and 10.7c

Warning: *Several precautions must be followed when checking and servicing the battery. Hydrogen gas, which is highly flammable, is always present in the battery cells, so keep lighted tobacco and all other open flames and sparks away from the battery. The electrolyte in the cells is actually dilute sulfuric acid, which will cause injury if splashed on your skin or in your eyes. It'll also ruin clothes and painted surfaces. When removing the battery cables, always detach the negative cable first and hook it up last!*

10.6   Removing a cable from the battery post with a wrench – sometimes a special battery pliers is required for this procedure if corrosion has caused deterioration of the nut hex (always remove the ground cable first and hook it up last!)

10.7a   Battery terminal corrosion usually appears as light, fluffy powder

1

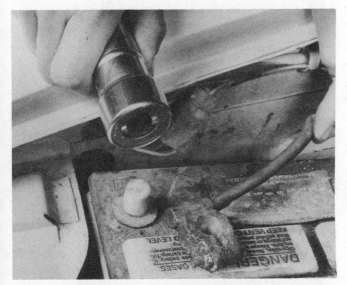

10.7b   Regardless of the type of tool used to clean the battery post, a clean, shiny surface should be the result

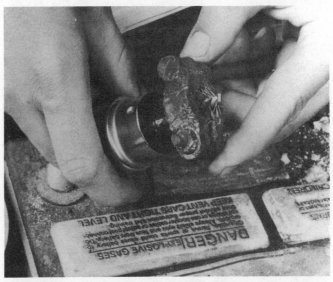

10.7c   When cleaning the cable clamps, all corrosion must be removed (the inside of the clamp is tapered to match the taper on the post, so don't remove too much material)

Check

1   Battery maintenance is an important procedure which will help ensure that you aren't stranded because of a dead battery. Several tools are required for this procedure (see illustration).
2   On vehicles equipped with a conventional battery, the electrolyte level should be checked every week (see Section 4).
3   If the vehicle is equipped with a battery electrolyte level warning light, the electrolyte should still be visually checked on a regular basis to make sure all cells are full.
4   On some models a sealed maintenance-free battery is used. Unlike a conventional battery, it has no removable cell caps and is completely sealed except for a small vent hole. Because of its sealed design, water cannot be added to the cells.
5   Periodically clean the top and sides of the battery. Remove all dirt and moisture. This will help prevent corrosion and ensure that the battery doesn't become partially discharged by leakage through moisture and dirt. Check the case for cracks and distortion.

6   Check the tightness of the battery cable bolts (see illustration) to ensure good electrical connections. Inspect the entire length of each cable, looking for cracked or abraded insulation and frayed conductors.
7   If corrosion, which usually appears as white, fluffy deposits, is evident, remove the cables from the terminals, clean them with a battery brush and reinstall them (see illustrations). Corrosion can be kept to a minimum by applying a layer of petroleum jelly to the terminals after the cables are in place.
8   Make sure the battery carrier is in good condition and the hold-down clamp is tight. If the battery is removed, make sure that nothing is in the bottom of the carrier when it's reinstalled and don't overtighten the clamp nuts.
9   A temperature-compensated hydrometer is built into the top of some maintenance-free batteries. It gives an indication of the electrolyte level and the battery's state of charge. If a blue dot is seen in the indicator window on top of the battery, the battery is properly charged. If the indicator is

transparent, the battery should be recharged from an external source and the charging system should be checked (see Chapter 5).

10 The freezing point of electrolyte depends on its specific gravity. Since freezing can ruin a battery, it should be kept in a fully charged state to protect against freezing.

11 If you frequently have to add water to a conventional battery and the case has been inspected for cracks that could cause leakage, but none are found, the battery is being overcharged; the charging system should be checked as described in Chapter 5.

12 If any doubt exists about the battery state of charge, a hydrometer should be used to test it by withdrawing a little electrolyte from each cell, one at a time.

13 The specific gravity of the electrolyte at 80-degrees F will be approximately 1.270 for a fully charged battery. For every 10-degrees F that the electrolyte temperature is above 80-degrees F, add 0.04 to the specific gravity. Subtract 0.04 if the temperature is below 80-degrees F.

14 A specific gravity reading of 1.240 with an electrolyte temperature of 80-degrees F indicates a half-charged battery.

15 Some of the common causes of battery failure are:
   a) Accessories, especially headlights, left on overnight or for several hours.
   b) Slow average driving speeds for short intervals.
   c) The electrical load of the vehicle being more than the alternator output. This is very common when several high draw accessories are being used simultaneously (such as radio/stereo, air conditioning, window defoggers, lights, etc.).
   d) Charging system problems such as short circuits, slipping drivebelt, defective alternator or faulty voltage regulator.
   e) Battery neglect, such as loose or corroded terminals or loose battery hold-down clamp.

Battery charging

16 In winter when heavy demand is placed upon the battery, it's a good idea to occasionally have it charged from an external source.

17 When charging the battery, the negative cable should be disconnected. The charger leads should be connected to the battery before the charger is plugged in or turned on. If the leads are connected to the battery terminals after the charger is on, a spark could occur and the hydrogen gas given off by the battery could explode!

18 The battery should be charged at a low rate of about 4 to 6 amps, and should be left on for at least three or four hours. A trickle charger charging at the rate of 1.5 amps can be safely used overnight.

19 Special rapid boost charges which are claimed to restore the power of the battery in a short time can cause serious damage to the battery plates and should only be used in an emergency situation.

20 The battery should be left on the charger only until the specific gravity is brought up to a normal level. On maintenance-free batteries, continue to charge only until the blue dot is seen in the indicator window. Don't overcharge the battery! **Note:** *Some battery chargers will automatically shut off after the battery is fully charged, making it unnecessary to keep a close watch on the state of charge.*

21 When disconnecting the charger, unplug it before disconnecting the charger leads from the battery.

---

11   Drivebelt check, adjustment and replacement

Refer to illustrations 11.3, 11.5, 11.6 and 11.7

Warning: *The electric cooling fan can activate at any time, even when the ignition is in the Off position. Disconnect the fan motor or negative battery cable when working in the vicinity of the fan.*

Check

1 The alternator and air conditioning compressor drivebelts, also referred to as V-belts or simply "fan" belts, are located at the right (passenger's) side of the engine compartment. The condition and proper adjustment of the drivebelts is critical to the operation of the engine. Since they stretch and deteriorate as they get older, they must be inspected periodically.

2 The number of belts used on a particular vehicle depends on the accessories installed. One belt transmits power from the crankshaft to the alternator and water pump. If the vehicle is equipped with air conditioning, the air conditioning compressor is driven by another belt.

3 With the engine off, open the hood and locate the drivebelts at the left end of the engine. With a flashlight, check each belt for separation of the adhesive rubber on both sides of the core, core separation from the belt side, a severed core, separation of the ribs from the adhesive rubber, cracking or separation of the ribs, and torn or worn ribs or cracks in the inner ridges of the ribs **(see illustration)**. Also check for fraying and glazing, which gives the belt a shiny appearance. Both sides of the belt should be inspected, which means you will have to twist the belt to check the underside. Use your fingers to feel the belt where you can't see it. If any of the above conditions are evident, replace the belt (go to Step 8).

4 To check the tension of each belt in accordance with factory specifications, follow the procedure in Step 5. Measure the tension and compare your measurement to the specified drivebelt tension for either a used or new belt. **Note:** *A "used" belt is defined as any belt which has been operated more than five minutes on the engine; a "new" belt is one that has been used for less than five minutes.*

5 The following rule of thumb method is recommended: Push firmly on the belt with your thumb at a distance halfway between the pulleys and note how far the belt can be moved (deflected). Measure the deflection with a ruler **(see illustration)**. Compare the measurements to this Chapter's Specifications.

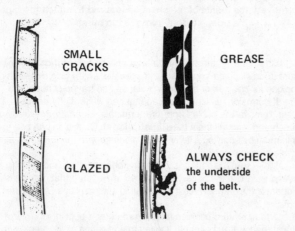

SMALL CRACKS

GREASE

GLAZED

ALWAYS CHECK
the underside
of the belt.

11.3   Check the V-ribbed belt for signs of wear like these – if it looks worn, replace it

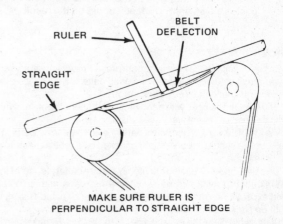

RULER

BELT DEFLECTION

STRAIGHT EDGE

MAKE SURE RULER IS
PERPENDICULAR TO STRAIGHT EDGE

11.5   Measuring drivebelt deflection with a straightedge and ruler

11.6   On later models, loosen the alternator adjuster locknut (A), then use a larger wrench to turn the toothed adjusting bolt (B) to tighten or loosen the belt tension

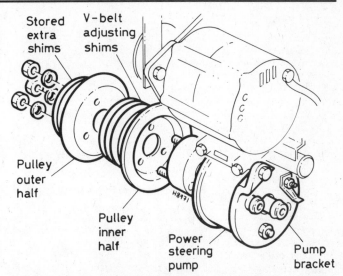

11.7   On early models, the power steering pump pulley will have to be disassembled and shims installed or removed from the pulley to adjust belt tension

Adjustment

6   If the alternator belt must be adjusted, loosen the pivot bolt followed by the adjusting bolt, then pivot the alternator away from the engine to tighten the belt. Some later models have a tensioner built into the adjuster **(see illustration)**.

7   The power steering pump and air conditioning compressor can be adjusted using tensioning bolts which are a part of their respective brackets. On some 1980 through 1984 model power steering pumps, it will be necessary to remove the pulley bolts and nuts, separate the pulley halves and then install or remove adjusting shims to adjust the belt tension **(see illustration)**.

Replacement

8   To replace a belt, follow the above procedures for drivebelt adjustment but slip the belt off the crankshaft pulley and remove it. If you're replacing the alternator belt, you'll have to remove the air conditioning compressor belt first because of the way they're arranged. Because of this and because belts tend to wear out more or less together, it's a good idea to replace both belts at the same time. Mark each belt and its appropriate pulley groove so the replacement belts can be installed in the proper positions.

9   Take the old belts to the parts store in order to make a direct comparison for length, width and design.

10   After replacing a belt, make sure it fits properly in the grooves in the pulleys.

11   Adjust the belt(s) as described above.

12   Underhood hose check and replacement

Caution: *Replacement of air conditioning hoses must be left to a dealer service department or air conditioning shop that has the equipment to depressurize the system safely. Never remove air conditioning components or hoses until the system has been depressurized.*

General

1   High temperatures in the engine compartment can cause the deterioration of the rubber and plastic hoses used for engine, accessory and emission systems operation. Periodic inspection should be made for cracks, loose clamps, material hardening and leaks.

2   Information specific to the cooling system hoses can be found in Section 13.

3   Some, but not all, hoses are secured to the fittings with clamps. Where clamps are used, check to be sure they haven't lost their tension, allowing the hose to leak. If clamps aren't used, make sure the hose has not expanded and/or hardened where it slips over the fitting, allowing it to leak.

Vacuum hoses

4   It's quite common for vacuum hoses, especially those in the emissions system, to be color coded or identified by colored stripes molded into them. Various systems require hoses with different wall thicknesses, collapse resistance and temperature resistance. When replacing hoses, be sure the new ones are made of the same material.

5   Often the only effective way to check a hose is to remove it completely from the vehicle. If more than one hose is removed, be sure to label the hoses and fittings to ensure correct installation.

6   When checking vacuum hoses, be sure to include any plastic T-fittings in the check. Inspect the fittings for cracks and the hose where it fits over the fitting for distortion, which could cause leakage.

7   A small piece of vacuum hose (1/4-inch inside diameter) can be used as a stethoscope to detect vacuum leaks. Hold one end of the hose to your ear and probe around vacuum hoses and fittings, listening for the "hissing" sound characteristic of a vacuum leak. **Warning:** *When probing with the vacuum hose stethoscope, be very careful not to come into contact with moving engine components such as the drivebelts, cooling fan, etc.*

Fuel hose

Warning: *There are certain precautions which must be taken when inspecting or servicing fuel system components. Work in a well ventilated area and do not allow open flames (cigarettes, appliance pilot lights, etc.) or bare light bulbs near the work area. Mop up any spills immediately and do not store fuel soaked rags where they could ignite.*

8   Check all rubber fuel lines for deterioration and chafing. Check especially for cracks in areas where the hose bends and just before fittings, such as where a hose attaches to the fuel filter.

9   High quality fuel line, usually identified by the word Fluroelastomer printed on the hose, should be used for fuel line replacement. Never, under any circumstances, use unreinforced vacuum line, clear plastic tubing or water hose for fuel lines.

10   Spring-type clamps are commonly used on fuel lines. These clamps often lose their tension over a period of time, and can be "sprung" during removal. Replace all spring-type clamps with screw clamps whenever a hose is replaced.

Metal lines

11   Sections of metal line are often used for fuel line between the fuel pump and carburetor. Check carefully to be sure the line has not been bent or crimped and that cracks have not started in the line.

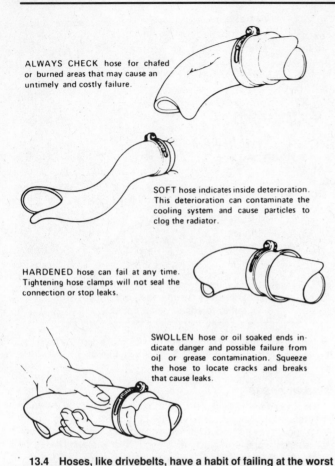

ALWAYS CHECK hose for chafed or burned areas that may cause an untimely and costly failure.

SOFT hose indicates inside deterioration. This deterioration can contaminate the cooling system and cause particles to clog the radiator.

HARDENED hose can fail at any time. Tightening hose clamps will not seal the connection or stop leaks.

SWOLLEN hose or oil soaked ends indicate danger and possible failure from oil or grease contamination. Squeeze the hose to locate cracks and breaks that cause leaks.

13.4　Hoses, like drivebelts, have a habit of failing at the worst possible time – to prevent the inconvenience of a blown radiator or heater hose, inspect them carefully as shown here

12　If a section of metal fuel line must be replaced, only seamless steel tubing should be used, since copper and aluminum tubing don't have the strength necessary to withstand normal engine vibration.

13　Check the metal brake lines where they enter the master cylinder and brake proportioning unit (if used) for cracks in the lines or loose fittings. Any sign of brake fluid leakage calls for an immediate thorough inspection of the brake system

13　Cooling system check

Refer to illustration 13.4

1　Many major engine failures can be attributed to a faulty cooling system. If the vehicle is equipped with an automatic transmission, the cooling system also cools the transmission fluid and thus plays an important role in prolonging transmission life.

2　The cooling system should be checked with the engine cold. Do this before the vehicle is driven for the day or after the engine has been shut off for at least three hours.

3　Remove the radiator cap by turning it to the left until it reaches a stop. If you hear a hissing sound (indicating there is still pressure in the system), wait until it stops. Now press down on the cap with the palm of your hand and continue turning to the left until the cap can be removed. Thoroughly clean the cap, inside and out, with clean water. Also clean the filler neck on the radiator. All traces of corrosion should be removed. The coolant inside the radiator should be relatively transparent. If it's rust colored, the system should be drained and refilled (see Section 36). If the coolant level isn't up to the top, add additional antifreeze/coolant mixture (see Section 4).

4　Carefully check the large upper and lower radiator hoses along with the smaller diameter heater hoses which run from the engine to the fire-

FRONT

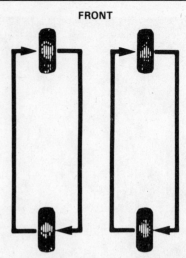

14.2　The recommended tire rotation pattern for these models

wall. Inspect each hose along its entire length, replacing any hose which is cracked, swollen or shows signs of deterioration. Cracks may become more apparent if the hose is squeezed **(see illustration)**. Regardless of condition, it's a good idea to replace hoses with new ones every two years.

5　Make sure that all hose connections are tight. A leak in the cooling system will usually show up as white or rust colored deposits on the areas adjoining the leak. If wire-type clamps are used at the ends of the hoses, it may be a good idea to replace them with more secure screw-type clamps.

6　Use compressed air or a soft brush to remove bugs, leaves, etc. from the front of the radiator or air conditioning condenser. Be careful not to damage the delicate cooling fins or cut yourself on them.

7　Every other inspection, or at the first indication of cooling system problems, have the cap and system pressure tested. If you don't have a pressure tester, most gas stations and repair shops will do this for a minimal charge.

14　Tire rotation

Refer to illustration 14.2

1　The tires should be rotated at the specified intervals and whenever uneven wear is noticed. Since the vehicle will be raised and the tires removed anyway, check the brakes (see Section 28) at this time.

2　Radial tires must be rotated in a specific pattern **(see illustration)**.

3　Refer to the information in *Jacking and towing* at the front of this manual for the proper procedures to follow when raising the vehicle and changing a tire. If the brakes are to be checked, do not apply the parking brake as stated. Make sure the tires are blocked to prevent the vehicle from rolling.

4　Preferably, the entire vehicle should be raised at the same time. This can be done on a hoist or by jacking up each corner and then lowering the vehicle onto jackstands placed under the frame rails. Always use four jackstands and make sure the vehicle is firmly supported.

5　After rotation, check and adjust the tire pressures as necessary and be sure to check the lug bolt tightness.

6　For further information on the wheels and tires, refer to Chapter 10.

15　Air filter replacement

Refer to illustrations 15.2 and 15.3

Warning: *The electric cooling fan on these models can activate at any time, even when the ignition is in the Off position. Disconnect the fan motor or negative battery cable when working in the vicinity of the fan.*

1　At the specified intervals, the air cleaner element should be replaced with a new one.

2　On carbureted models, disengage the air cleaner housing clips, rotate the cover up and remove the element **(see illustration)**.

15.2   On carbureted models, detach the air cleaner housing clips and rotate the top of the housing up for access to the filter element

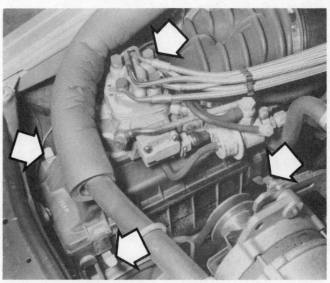

15.3   On fuel injected models, release the clips at the corners of the housing (arrows) and lift up the cover and fuel metering unit for access to the element (1985 model shown, others similar)

1

3   On fuel injected models, release the housing clips, separate the upper half of the air cleaner complete with the fuel mixture assembly from the bottom half of the housing and remove the filter element (see illustration).
4   On all models, be careful not to drop anything into the air cleaner housing. Wipe out the inside of the housing with a clean rag.
5   Place the new element in the air cleaner housing. On later models the upper side of the element is marked UP and this marking must face toward the front of the vehicle.
6   Place the top cover or half of the air cleaner assembly in position and secure it with the clips.

2   Remove the wingnut and washer and extract the filter element from the housing (see illustration).
3   Place the new element in the housing and install the washer and wingnut.
4   Connect the hose to the filter housing and secure it with the clamp.

17   Exhaust Gas Recirculation (EGR) system check and service light resetting

Refer to illustrations 17.1, 17.6 and 17.7
Warning: *The electric cooling fan on these models can activate at any time, even when the ignition is in the Off position. Disconnect the fan motor or negative battery cable when working in the vicinity of the fan.*

16   Air injection pump filter replacement

Refer to illustration 16.2
Warning: *The electric cooling fan on these models can activate at any time, even when the ignition is in the Off position. Disconnect the fan motor or negative battery cable when working in the vicinity of the fan.*
1   Remove the hose clamp and detach the air filter housing from the pump.

Check

1   On models so equipped, check the EGR system at the specified interval, when the EGR light goes on, or when driveability problems, such as hard starting, rough idle, stalling and hesitation when the engine is cold occur. The EGR valve is located on the intake manifold and most of the time when a problem develops in this emissions system it is due to a stuck or corroded EGR valve (see illustration).

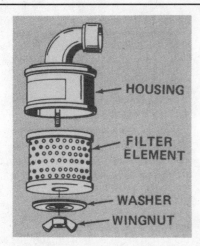

16.2   Air injection pump filter replacement details

17.1   The EGR valve is located on the manifold on these models (arrow)

17.6   Push the white button on the counter (arrow) to reset it

17.7   On 1981 through 1984 U.S.-built models, use a wire hook to pull back the EGR reset lever in the instrument cluster

2   Check the hoses connected to the EGR for damage and leaks.

3   With the engine idling, apply vacuum by connecting a hand vacuum pump or by disconnecting the vacuum hose from the EGR valve and, using a T-fitting, connecting the power brake servo vacuum hose. With vacuum is applied, the idle speed should drop or the engine should stall, indicating that the valve is operating properly.

4   If the idle speed does not drop, the EGR valve or feed hose are clogged or the valve is faulty.

Service light resetting

5   After completing the valve checking procedure, reset the EGR light. On all but 1981 through 1984 U.S.-built models, this is located in the speedometer cable adjacent to the brake master cylinder reservoir. On some later models it may be necessary to detach the coolant reservoir and move it out of the way for access to the counter.

6   Push the white reset button on the counter (**see illustration**). Turn the ignition key On to verify that the EGR light is now out. It may be necessary to push the reset button several times to reset the counter.

7   On 1981 through 1984 U.S.-built models, remove the instrument cluster bezel for access to the bezel (see Chapter 12). Fabricate a six inch long piece of coat hanger with a hook at the end, reach through the opening in the cluster and pull the lever on the left side toward you to reset the EGR counter (**see illustration**).

8   Refer to Chapter 6 for more information on the EGR system.

18   Clutch freeplay check and adjustment

Refer to illustrations 18.2 and 18.3

1   While some later models are equipped with self-adjusting clutch cables, most models require clutch adjustment at the specified intervals to compensate for clutch disc wear. Clutch cables which require adjustment can be identified by the white plastic adjuster and locknut located at the transaxle bracket.

2   Push down on the clutch pedal and use a small steel ruler to measure the distance that it moves freely before clutch resistance is felt (**see illustration**). The freeplay should be within the specified limits. If it isn't, it must be adjusted.

3   Prior to adjustment, operate the clutch pedal several times. Working in the engine compartment, loosen the adjusting nut and turn the adjuster until the cable can be pulled the specified distance (freeplay) up out of the bracket (**see illustration**).

4   Adjust as necessary to achieve the specified freeplay at the clutch pedal and the bracket, then tighten the locknut. On 1985 and on models, pull the clutch release lever up until resistance is felt, loosen the locknut and insert VW tool US-5043 or a 15/32 inch (12 mm) gauge between the large plastic flange and the transaxle housing. Turn the adjuster counterclockwise until the flange is snug against the tool and tighten the locknut.

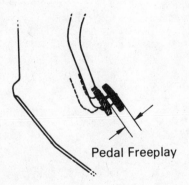

18.2   To check clutch pedal free play, measure the distance between the natural resting place of the pedal and the point at which you encounter resistance

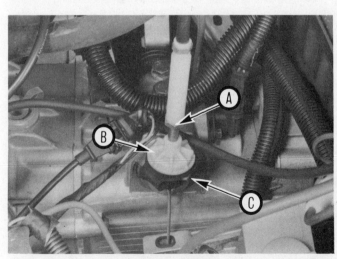

18.3   Loosen the clutch cable locknut (A), turn the adjuster (B), then measure the freeplay (C) between the adjuster and the bracket

19.4   Insert a feeler gauge between the heel of the cam lobe and the adjusting disk (number 1 exhaust valve shown)

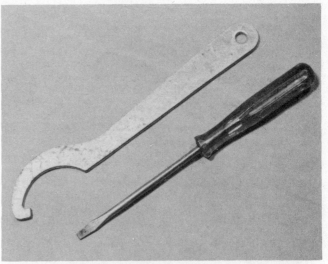

19.7a   A tool for depressing the cam follower and a magnetic screwdriver can be used to remove the adjusting disk

19   Valve clearance check and adjustment (1975 through 1984 models only)

Refer to illustrations 19.4, 19.7a and 19.7b

Warning: *The electric cooling fan on some models can activate at any time, even when the ignition is in the Off position. Disconnect the fan motor or negative battery cable when working in the vicinity of the fan.*

1   The valve clearances are checked and adjusted with the engine at normal operating temperature.
2   Disconnect the cable from the negative terminal of the battery.
3   Remove the camshaft cover (see Chapter 2).
4   Rotate the engine using a socket and extension on the crankshaft pulley bolt until the number 1 cylinder camshaft lobe is positioned as shown and insert the appropriate size feeler gauge between the number 1 cylinder (next to the camshaft pulley) exhaust valve camshaft lobe and adjusting disc **(see illustration)**. Don't turn the camshaft pulley to rotate the engine because this will damage the timing belt.
5   Check the valve clearances following the firing order (1-3-4-2) and compare these clearances with those in this Chapter's Specifications or on the vehicle emission control label in the engine compartment.
6   If the clearances are not as specified, the valve adjusting disc will have to be removed and replaced with one which will achieve the specified clearance. The adjusting discs are available from your dealer in 0.002 inch (0.05 mm) increments. To determine the thickness of the disc(s) you will need, refer to the following example:

	Intake valve	Exhaust valve
Specified clearance	0.010 in (0.25 mm)	0.018 in (0.45 mm)
Measured clearance	0.012 in (0.31 mm)	0.011 in (0.28 mm)
Insert a disc that is	0.002 in (0.05 mm) thicker	0.006 in (0.15 mm) thinner

7   To remove a disc, use factory tool VW-546 or equivalent to depress the cam follower, then remove the disc with tool 10-208 or a thin screwdriver or needle nose pliers **(see illustrations)**.
8   Install the new disc with the numbered side facing down and recheck the clearance if necessary.
9   After checking/adjusting the number one cylinder valves, rotate the engine 180-degrees clockwise and check/adjust the valves on the number 3 cylinder. Rotate the engine another 180-degrees and check/adjust cylinder number 4. Finally, rotate the engine 180-degrees and carry out the checking and adjustment procedure on the number 2 cylinder.
10   Install the rocker arm cover and the air cleaner assembly.

19.7b   With the cam follower depressed, the adjusting disk can be extracted

20   Idle speed check and adjustment

Warning: *The electric cooling fan on some models can activate at any time, even when the ignition is in the Off position. Disconnect the fan motor or negative battery cable when working in the vicinity of the fan.*

1   Engine idle speed is the speed at which the engine operates when no accelerator pedal pressure is applied, as when stopped at a traffic light. This speed is critical to the performance of the engine itself, as well as many engine subsystems.
2   Set the parking brake firmly and block the wheels to prevent the vehicle from rolling. Place the transaxle in Neutral.
3   Start the engine and allow it to reach normal operating temperature (the cooling fan will come on).
4   Check and adjust, if necessary, the ignition timing (Section 21).
5   Turn off the engine and connect a hand held tachometer.

Carbureted models

Refer to illustrations 20.6, 20.8a and 20.8b

6   On 1980 through 1984 models, disconnect the vacuum advance and retard hoses from the distributor vacuum unit and plug them. If equipped

20.6 It will be necessary to unplug the digital idle stabilizer connectors and connect them together (arrow) when adjusting the idle speed on some models

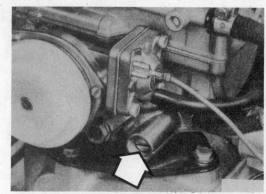

20.8a On carburetor equipped models, turn the bypass screw on the carburetor body (arrow) to adjust the idle speed (early models)

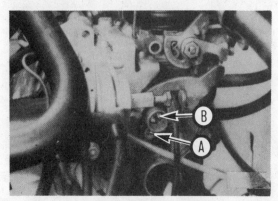

20.8b Later model carburetor bypass screw location (B) – Don't turn the mixture screw (A)

20.15 The bypass screw used for adjusting idle speed on CIS fuel injected models is located on the throttle valve housing (arrow)

with a digital idle stabilizer (located next to the windshield wiper motor), detach the two electrical connectors from the stabilzer and connect them to each other **(see illustration)**.

7　Start the engine and check the idle speed.

8　If the idle speed is not as specified on the Emissions Control Label in the engine compartment, turn the bypass screw on the carburetor **(see illustrations)**. Turn the screw counterclockwise to increase the idle speed, clockwise to decrease it.

9　On 1980 through 1984 models, connect the vacuum advance and retard hoses to the distributor vacuum unit. The idle speed should drop to the specified range.

10　Shut off the engine, disconnect the tachometer and reconnect the digital idle stabilizer electrical connectors (1980 through 1984 models).

Fuel injected models

Refer to illustration 20.15

Note: *The idle speed on CIS-E, CIS-E Motronic and Digifant II fuel injection systems cannot be adjusted without special equipment. Take the vehicle to a dealer service department.*

11　On 1975 through 1979 models, the headlights must be on high beam during the check and adjustment procedure.

12　On 1980 through 1984 models, make sure all lights and accessories, including the cooling fan, are off during the procedure.

13　On 1980 through 1982 models equipped with a digital idle stabilizer (located next to the windshield wiper motor), detach the two electrical connectors from the stabilizer and connect them to each other **(see illustration 20.6)**.

14　Start the engine and check the idle speed.

15　If the idle speed is not as specified on the Emissions Control Label in the engine compartment, turn the bypass screw on the throttle valve housing **(see illustration)**. Turn the screw counterclockwise to increase the idle speed, clockwise to decrease it.

16　Shut off the engine, disconnect the tachometer and reconnect the digital idle stabilizer electrical connectors (1980 through 1982 models).

21　Ignition timing check and adjustment

Refer to illustrations 21.1, 21.5, 21.8a and 21.8b

Warning: *The electric cooling fan on these models can activate at any time, even when the ignition is in the Off position. Disconnect the fan motor or negative battery cable when working in the vicinity of the fan.*

Note: *If the information in this Section differs from the Vehicle Emission Control Information label in the engine compartment of your vehicle, the label should be considered correct.*

1　Some special tools are required for this procedure **(see illustration)**. The engine must be at normal operating temperature and the air conditioner must be Off. Make sure the idle speed is correct (see Section 20).

2　Apply the parking brake and block the wheels to prevent movement of the vehicle. The transmission must be in Park (automatic) or Neutral (manual).

3　The timing marks on these models are located on the engine flywheel and are viewed through the timing check hole in the bellhousing.

4　On some very early models, it will be necessary to disconnect the wire from the computer analysis TDC sensor on the bellhousing and use a special tool VW-4463 to unscrew the TDC sensor so the timing marks can be seen.

5　On later models, remove the plastic cover and use a 27 mm hex end tool to unscrew the plastic plug from the timing check hole **(see illustration)**. This plug is used for the computer engine analysis probe and unless it is removed you won't be able to see the timing marks.

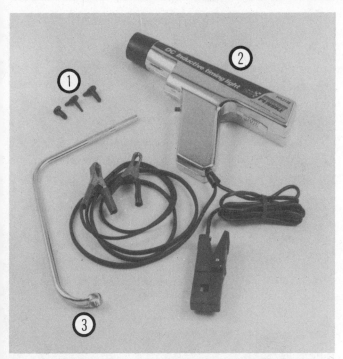

21.1 Tools needed to check and adjust the ignition timing

1 **Vacuum plugs** – *Vacuum hoses will, in most cases, have to be disconnected and plugged. Molded plugs in various shapes and sizes are available for this.*
2 **Inductive pick-up timing light** – *Flashes a bright concentrated beam of light when the number one spark plug fires. Connect the leads according to the instructions supplied with the light.*
3 **Distributor wrench** – *On some models, the hold-down bolt for the distributor is difficult to reach and turn with conventional wrenches or sockets. A special wrench like this must be used.*

6   Hook up the timing light by following the manufacturer's instructions (an inductive pick-up timing light is preferred). Generally, the power leads are attached to the battery terminals and the pick-up lead is attached to the number one spark plug wire. The number one spark plug is the one closest to the drivebelt end of the engine. **Caution:** *If an inductive pick-up timing light isn't available, don't puncture the spark plug wire to attach the timing light pick-up lead. Instead, use an adapter between the spark plug and plug wire. If the insulation on the plug wire is damaged, the secondary voltage will jump to ground at the damaged point and the engine will misfire.*
7   On carbureted 1980 through 1984 models with breakerless ignition, disconnect and plug the distributor vacuum retard hose. If equipped with a digital idle stabilizer (located next to the windshield wiper motor) detach the two electrical connectors from the stabilizer and connect them together **(see illustration 20.6)**. On 1984 models, clamp the idle bypass hose shut.
8   On 1985 and later models with Digifant fuel injection, unplug the coolant temperature sensor and disconnect and plug the evaporative system crankcase hose **(see illustrations)**.
9   Make sure the timing light wires are routed away from the drivebelts and fan, then start the engine. On 1985 and later models with Digifant fuel injection, briefly raise the engine speed over 3000 rpm three or four times before checking the timing.
10   Allow the idle speed to stabilize, then point the flashing timing light at the timing marks – be very careful of moving engine components.
11   The mark on the flywheel will appear stationary. If it's aligned with the specified point on the bellhousing, the ignition timing is correct.
12   If the marks aren't aligned, adjustment is required. Loosen the distributor mounting nut and turn the distributor very slowly until the marks are aligned.

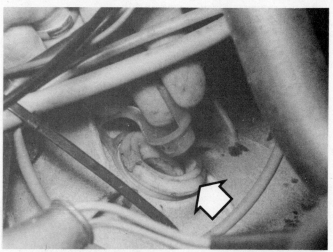

21.5   Pull out the smaller plastic plug, then use a 27 mm hex tool to unscrew the white plastic plug (arrow) so the timing marks on the flywheel will be visible

21.8a   Unplug the Digifant system coolant sensor electrical connector (arrow) during the ignition timing procedure – it's located on the front side of the cylinder head

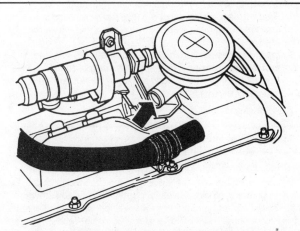

21.8b   Disconnect the Digifant evaporative system hose from the connector (arrow)

13   Tighten the nut and recheck the timing.
14   Turn off the engine and remove the timing light (and adapter, if used). Reconnect and install any components which were disconnected or removed.

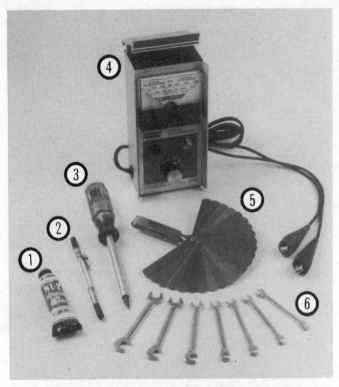

22.1   Tools and materials needed for contact point replacement and dwell angle adjustment

1 **Distributor cam lube** – *Sometimes this special lubricant comes with the new points; however, it's a good idea to buy a tube and have it on hand*

2 **Screw starter** – *This tool has special claws which hold the screw securely as it's started, which helps prevent accidental dropping of the screw*

3 **Magnetic screwdriver** – *Serves the same purpose as 2 above. If you don't have one of these special screwdrivers, you risk dropping the point mounting screws down into the distributor body.*

4 **Dwell meter** – *A dwell meter is the only accurate way to determine the point setting (gap). Connect the meter according to the instructions supplied with it.*

5 **Blade-type feeler gauges** – *These are required to set the initial point gap (space between the points when they are open)*

6 **Ignition wrenches** – *These special wrenches are made to work within the tight confines of the distributor. Specifically, they are needed to loosen the nut/bolt which secures the leads to the points.*

22   Ignition point replacement

Refer to illustrations 22.1, 22.4, 22.5, 22.12a and 22.12b

1   The ignition points must be replaced at the specified intervals. Occasionally the rubbing block will wear enough to require adjustment of the points. While it is possible to clean and dress them with a fine file, replacement is recommended since they are fairly accessible and very inexpensive. Several special tools are required for this procedure **(see illustration)**. **Caution:** *This procedure requires the removal of a small screw which can easily fall down into the distributor. Retrieval would require disassembly of the distributor so use a magnetic or spring-loaded screwdriver and be very careful during removal and installation.*

Point replacement

2   Use a screwdriver to release the two spring clips, remove the distribu-

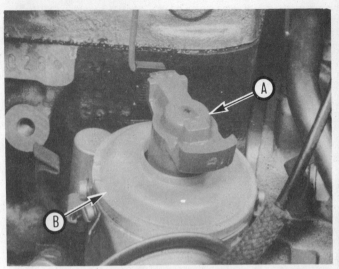

22.4   Lift off the rotor (A) and dust shield (B) for access to the ignition points

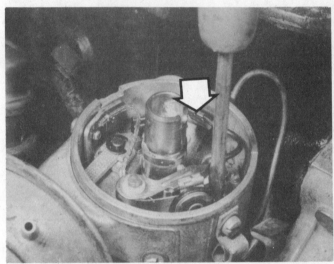

22.5   Unplug the points electrical connector (arrow) and remove the retaining screw

tor cap, then position it out of the way with the wires attached.

3   The condenser can now be removed from the outside of the distributor housing by removing the clamp screw, unplugging the connector and detaching the condenser from the clamp.

4   Remove the distributor rotor and dust shield **(see illustration)**.

5   Unplug the electrical connector, remove the screw and lift the points assembly from the distributor **(see illustration)**.

6   Before installing the new points, clean the breaker plate and the cam on the distributor shaft to remove all dirt, dust and oil.

7   Place the point set in position, install the screw and plug in the connector. Make sure the points meet squarely, bending the stationary (not the movable) contact as necessary.

8   Install the new condenser and plug in the connector.

9   Apply a small amount of distributor cam lube (usually supplied with new points, but also available separately at auto parts stores) to the cam lobes. Lubricate the point rubbing block and the breaker plate ball with multi-purpose grease. Use clean engine oil to lubricate the wick in the center of the distributor shaft and then apply one drop to the breaker plate pivot.

10   Although the gap between the contact points (dwell angle) will be adjusted later, make the initial adjustment now, which will allow the engine to be started.

22.12a With the points open, insert the feeler gauge between the point contacts

22.12b Turning the screwdriver very slightly will change the point gap – increasing the point gap decreases the dwell and vice versa

11 Make sure the point rubbing block is resting on one of the high points of the cam. If it isn't turn the ignition switch to the Start position in short bursts to reposition the cam. You can also turn the crankshaft with a breaker bar and socket attached to the crankshaft pulley bolt.

12 With the points mounting screw loosened and the rubbing block on a cam high point (points open), insert a 0.016 inch (0.40 mm) feeler gauge between the contact surfaces of the points **(see illustration)**. Use a screwdriver engaged in the slot in the breaker plate and between the dimples **(see illustration)** to adjust the position of the fixed contact until the point gap is equal to the feeler gauge thickness. The gap is correct when a slight amount of drag is felt as the feeler gauge is withdrawn. Tighten the points mounting screw.

13 Install the shield plate.

14 Before installing the rotor, check it as described in Section 24.

15 Install the the rotor. The rotor is indexed so that it will fit only one way.

16 Before installing the distributor cap, inspect it as described in Section 24.

17 Install the distributor cap and lock it in place with the clips.

18 Start the engine and check the dwell angle and ignition timing, in that order.

Dwell angle adjustment

19 Whenever new ignition points are installed or the original points are cleaned, the dwell angle must be checked and adjusted.

20 Precise adjustment of the dwell angle requires a dwell meter. Combination tach/dwell meters are available at auto parts stores.

21 Connect the dwell meter, following the manufacturer's instructions.

22 With the engine at normal operating temperature, switch the dwell meter to the tachometer position and allow it to idle at 1000 rpm.

23 Switch the dwell meter to the dwell position and read the dwell, comparing your reading to this Chapter's Specifications. **Note:** *When adjusting dwell, aim for the lower end of the dwell specification range. Then, as the points wear, the dwell will remain within the specified range over a longer period of time.*

24 If it is necessary to adjust the dwell, turn off the engine and remove the distributor cap, shield plate and rotor.

25 Disconnect the coil high tension wire from the distributor cap and connect it to a good ground. Loosen the points screw, insert the screwdriver in the slot in the breaker plate and between the dimples **(see illustration 22.12b)**.

26 While turning the engine over with the starter, adjust the position of the stationary ignition point contact to widen the gap (decreasing the dwell) or narrowing it (increasing the dwell).

27 After adjustment, tighten the points mounting screw and install the dust shield, rotor and distributor cap.

28 Start the engine and recheck the dwell, adjusting as necessary.

29 Check the ignition timing.

23 Spark plug replacement

Refer to illustrations 23.1, 23.4a, 23.4b, 23.6 and 23.10

1 Spark plug replacement requires a spark plug socket which fits onto a ratchet wrench. This socket is lined with a rubber grommet to protect the porcelain insulator of the spark plug and to hold the plug while you insert it into the spark plug hole. You will also need a wire-type feeler gauge to check and adjust the spark plug gap and a torque wrench to tighten the new plugs to the specified torque **(see illustration)**.

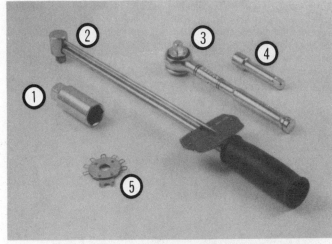

23.1 Tools required for changing spark plugs

1 ***Spark plug socket*** – This will have special padding inside to protect the spark plug's porcelain insulator

2 ***Torque wrench*** – Although not mandatory, using this tool is the best way to ensure the plugs are tightened properly

3 ***Ratchet*** – Standard hand tool to fit the spark plug socket

4 ***Extension*** – Depending on model and accessories, you may need special extensions and universal joints to reach one or more of the plugs

5 ***Spark plug gap gauge*** – This gauge for checking the gap comes in a variety of styles. Make sure the gap for your engine is included

23.4a   Spark plug manufacturers recommend using a wire-type gauge when checking the gap – if the wire does not slide between the electrodes with a slight drag, adjustment is required

23.4b   To change the gap, bend the side electrode only, as indicated by the arrows, and be very careful not to crack or chip the porcelain insulator surrounding the center electrode

2   When replacing the plugs, purchase the new plugs in advance, adjust them to the proper gap and then replace each plug one at a time. **Note:** *When buying new spark plugs, it's essential that you obtain the correct plugs for your specific vehicle. This information can be found on the Vehicle Emissions Control Information (VECI) label located on the underside of the hood or in the owner's manual. If these two sources specify different plugs, purchase the spark plug type specified on the VECI label because that information is provided specifically for your engine.*

3   Inspect each of the new plugs for defects. If there are any signs of cracks in the porcelain insulator of a plug, don't use it.

4   Check the electrode gaps of the new plugs. Check the gap by inserting the wire gauge of the proper thickness between the electrodes at the tip of the plug **(see illustration)**. The gap between the electrodes should be identical to that specified on the VECI label. If the gap is incorrect, use the notched adjuster on the feeler gauge body to bend the curved side electrode slightly **(see illustration)**.

5   If the side electrode is not exactly over the center electrode, use the notched adjuster to align them. **Caution:** *If the gap of a new plug must be*

adjusted, bend only the base of the ground electrode do not touch the tip.

Removal

6   To prevent the possibility of mixing up spark plug wires, work on one spark plug at a time. Remove the wire and boot from one spark plug. Grasp the boot – not the cable – as shown, give it a half twisting motion and pull it off **(see illustration)**.

7   If compressed air is available, blow any dirt or foreign material away from the spark plug area before proceeding (a common bicycle pump will also work).

8   Remove the spark plug.

9   Compare each old spark plug with those shown in the accompanying photos to determine the overall running condition of the engine.

Installation

10   It's often difficult to insert spark plugs into their holes without cross-threading them. To avoid this possibility, fit a short piece of 5/16-inch ID rubber hose over the end of the spark plug **(see illustration)**. The flexible

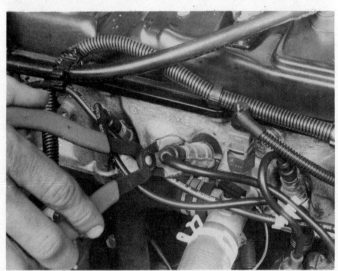

23.6   When removing the spark plug wires, pull only on the boot and use a twisting/pulling motion

23.10   A length of 5/16-inch ID rubber hose will save time and prevent damaged threads when installing the spark plugs

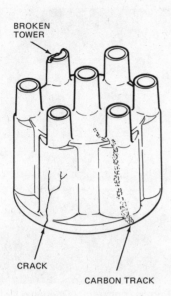

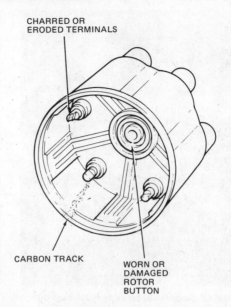

24.11 Shown here are some of the common defects to look for when inspecting the distributor cap (if in doubt about its condition, install a new one)

hose acts as a universal joint to help align the plug with the plug hole. Should the plug begin to cross-thread, the hose will slip on the spark plug, preventing thread damage. Tighten the plug securely.

11 Attach the plug wire to the new spark plug, again using a twisting motion on the boot until it is firmly seated on the end of the spark plug.

12 Follow the above procedure for the remaining spark plugs, replacing them one at a time to prevent mixing up the spark plug wires.

24 Spark plug wire, distributor cap and rotor check and replacement

Refer to illustrations 24.11 and 24.12

1 The spark plug wires should be checked whenever new spark plugs are installed.

2 Begin this procedure by making a visual check of the spark plug wires while the engine is running. In a darkened garage (make sure there is ventilation) start the engine and observe each plug wire. Be careful not to come into contact with any moving engine parts. If there is a break in the wire, you will see arcing or a small spark at the damaged area. If arcing is noticed, make a note to obtain new wires, then allow the engine to cool and check the distributor cap and rotor.

3 The spark plug wires should be inspected one at a time to prevent mixing up the order, which is essential for proper engine operation. Each original plug wire should be numbered to help identify its location. If the number is illegible, a piece of tape can be marked with the correct number and wrapped around the plug wire.

4 Disconnect the plug wire from the spark plug. A removal tool can be used for this purpose or you can grasp the rubber boot, twist the boot half a turn and pull the boot free. Do not pull on the wire itself **(see illustration 23.6)**.

5 Check inside the boot for corrosion, which will look like a white crusty powder.

6 Push the wire and boot back onto the end of the spark plug. It should fit tightly onto the end of the plug. If it doesn't, remove the wire and use pliers to carefully crimp the metal connector inside the wire boot until the fit is snug.

7 Using a clean rag, wipe the entire length of the wire to remove built-up dirt and grease. Once the wire is clean, check for burns, cracks and other damage. Do not bend the wire sharply, because the conductor within the wire might break.

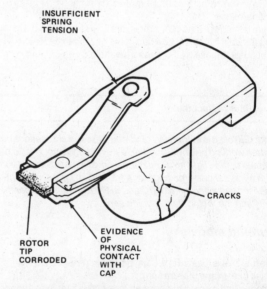

24.12 The ignition rotor should be checked for wear and corrosion as indicated here (if in doubt about its condition, buy a new one)

8 Disconnect the wire from the distributor. Again, pull only on the rubber boot. Check for corrosion and a tight fit. Press the wire back into the distributor.

9 Inspect the remaining spark plug wires, making sure that each one is securely fastened at the distributor and spark plug when the check is complete.

10 If new spark plug wires are required, purchase a set for your specific engine model. Pre-cut wire sets with the boots already installed are available. Remove and replace the wires one at a time to avoid mix-ups in the firing order.

11 Detach the distributor cap by prying off the two cap retaining clips. Look inside it for cracks, carbon tracks and worn, burned or loose contacts **(see illustration)**.

12 Pull the rotor off the distributor shaft and examine it for cracks and carbon tracks **(see illustration)**. Replace the cap and rotor if any damage or defects are noted.

25.1   The fuel filter used on carbureted engines is located near the timing belt end of the cylinder head

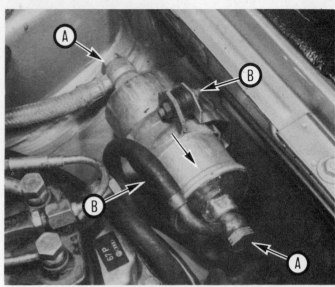

25.6a   Engine compartment mounted fuel injection system fuel filter installation details – the arrow on the filter denotes the direction of fuel flow

A   Union bolts   *B   Mounting clamp bolts (lower one hidden under filter)*

13   It is common practice to install a new cap and rotor whenever new spark plug wires are installed, but if you wish to continue using the old cap, clean the terminals first.
14   When installing a new cap, remove the wires from the old cap one at a time and attach them to the new cap in the exact same location – do not simultaneously remove all the wires from the old cap or firing order mix-ups may occur.

25   Fuel filter replacement

Warning: *Gasoline is extremely flammable, so extra precautions must be taken when working on any part of the fuel system. Do not smoke or allow open flames or bare light bulbs near the work area. Also, do not work in a garage if a natural gas-type appliance with a pilot light is present. It is a good idea to keep a dry chemical (Class B) fire extinguisher near the work area any time the fuel system is being serviced.*

Carbureted models

Refer to illustration 25.1

1   The fuel filter is located in the engine compartment in the vicinity of the timing belt cover **(see illustration)**.
2   Release and discard the hose clamps at the filter inlet and outlet.
3   Disconnect the hoses and remove the filter.
4   Making sure the arrow on the new filter faces in the direction of fuel flow (toward the carburetor), push the hoses onto the filter and install new screw type clamps approximately 1/4-inch back from the ends.
5   Start the vehicle and check for leaks.

Fuel injected models

Refer to illustrations 25.6a and 25.6b

6   On these models the fuel filter is mounted in the engine compartment to the rear of the battery or under the vehicle adjacent to the fuel tank **(see illustrations)**.
7   Depressurize the fuel system (see Chapter 4).
8   Place a container or newspapers and rags under the fuel filter, depending on location. Clamp the fuel lines with locking pliers if necessary to keep them from leaking, then use a wrench to remove the union bolts.
9   Loosen the fuel filter clamp nuts and detach the filter from the bracket.
10   Install a new filter reversing the removal procedure. Make sure the arrow on the filter faces in the direction of flow **(see illustrations 25.6a and 25.6b)**. Tighten the union bolts to the torque listed in this Chapter's Specifications.

25.6b   Under vehicle mounted fuel filter details (arrow shows direction of fuel flow)

26   Fuel system check

Warning: *Certain precautions should be observed when inspecting or servicing the fuel system components. Work in a well ventilated area and do not allow open flames (cigarettes, appliance pilot lights, etc.) near the work area. Mop up spills immediately and do not store fuel soaked rags where they could ignite. It is a good idea to keep a dry chemical (Class B) fire extinguisher near the work area any time the fuel system is being serviced.*

1   If you smell gasoline while driving or after the vehicle has been sitting in the sun, inspect the fuel system immediately.
2   Remove the gas filler cap and inspect if for damage and corrosion. The gasket should have an unbroken sealing imprint. If the gasket is damaged or corroded, replace the cap.
3   Inspect the fuel feed and return lines for cracks. Check the metal fuel line connections to make sure they are tight.

Common spark plug conditions

NORMAL

Symptoms: Brown to grayish-tan color and slight electrode wear. Correct heat range for engine and operating conditions.

Recommendation: When new spark plugs are installed, replace with plugs of the same heat range.

WORN

Symptoms: Rounded electrodes with a small amount of deposits on the firing end. Normal color. Causes hard starting in damp or cold weather and poor fuel economy.

Recommendation: Plugs have been left in the engine too long. Replace with new plugs of the same heat range. Follow the recommended maintenance schedule.

CARBON DEPOSITS

Symptoms: Dry sooty deposits indicate a rich mixture or weak ignition. Causes misfiring, hard starting and hesitation.

Recommendation: Make sure the plug has the correct heat range. Check for a clogged air filter or problem in the fuel system or engine management system. Also check for ignition system problems.

ASH DEPOSITS

Symptoms: Light brown deposits encrusted on the side or center electrodes or both. Derived from oil and/or fuel additives. Excessive amounts may mask the spark, causing misfiring and hesitation during acceleration.

Recommendation: If excessive deposits accumulate over a short time or low mileage, install new valve guide seals to prevent seepage of oil into the combustion chambers. Also try changing gasoline brands.

OIL DEPOSITS

Symptoms: Oily coating caused by poor oil control. Oil is leaking past worn valve guides or piston rings into the combustion chamber. Causes hard starting, misfiring and hesitation.

Recommendation: Correct the mechanical condition with necessary repairs and install new plugs.

GAP BRIDGING

Symptoms: Combustion deposits lodge between the electrodes. Heavy deposits accumulate and bridge the electrode gap. The plug ceases to fire, resulting in a dead cylinder.

Recommendation: Locate the faulty plug and remove the deposits from between the electrodes.

TOO HOT

Symptoms: Blistered, white insulator, eroded electrode and absence of deposits. Results in shortened plug life.

Recommendation: Check for the correct plug heat range, over-advanced ignition timing, lean fuel mixture, intake manifold vacuum leaks, sticking valves and insufficient engine cooling.

PREIGNITION

Symptoms: Melted electrodes. Insulators are white, but may be dirty due to misfiring or flying debris in the combustion chamber. Can lead to engine damage.

Recommendation: Check for the correct plug heat range, over-advanced ignition timing, lean fuel mixture, insufficient engine cooling and lack of lubrication.

HIGH SPEED GLAZING

Symptoms: Insulator has yellowish, glazed appearance. Indicates that combustion chamber temperatures have risen suddenly during hard acceleration. Normal deposits melt to form a conductive coating. Causes misfiring at high speeds.

Recommendation: Install new plugs. Consider using a colder plug if driving habits warrant.

DETONATION

Symptoms: Insulators may be cracked or chipped. Improper gap setting techniques can also result in a fractured insulator tip. Can lead to piston damage.

Recommendation: Make sure the fuel anti-knock values meet engine requirements. Use care when setting the gaps on new plugs. Avoid lugging the engine.

MECHANICAL DAMAGE

Symptoms: May be caused by a foreign object in the combustion chamber or the piston striking an incorrect reach (too long) plug. Causes a dead cylinder and could result in piston damage.

Recommendation: Repair the mechanical damage. Remove the foreign object from the engine and/or install the correct reach plug.

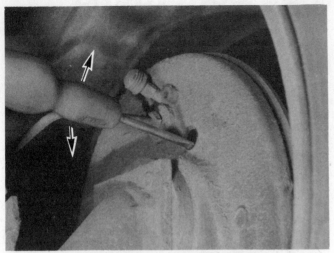

27.5   Insert a screwdriver through the access hole in the backing plate and turn the adjuster to compensate for shoe wear

4   Since some components of the fuel system – the fuel tank and part of the fuel feed and return lines, for example – are underneath the vehicle, they can be inspected more easily with the vehicle raised on a hoist. If that's not possible, raise the vehicle and secure it on jackstands.

5   With the vehicle raised and safely supported, inspect the gas tank and filler neck for punctures, cracks and other damage. The connection between the filler neck and the tank is particularly critical. Sometimes a rubber filler neck will leak because of loose clamps or deteriorated rubber. These are problems a home mechanic can usually rectify. **Warning:** *Do not, under any circumstances, try to repair a fuel tank (except rubber components). A welding torch or any open flame can easily cause fuel vapors inside the tank to explode.*

6   Carefully check all rubber hoses and metal lines leading away from the fuel tank. Check for loose connections, deteriorated hoses, crimped lines and other damage. Carefully inspect the lines from the tank to the carburetor. Repair or replace damaged sections as necessary.

---

27   Drum brake adjustment (1975 through 1978 models only)

Refer to illustration 27.5

1   The non-self adjusting drum brakes used on some 1975 through 1978 models must be adjusted to compensate for shoe wear at the specified intervals or when the brake pedal travel becomes excessive.

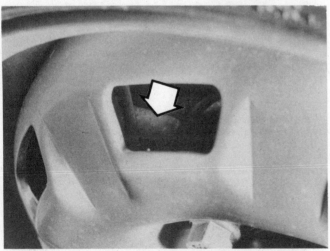

28.5a   On some models the disc brake pad (arrow) can be checked for wear by shining a small flashlight through the wheel slot

2   Raise the vehicle and support it securely on jackstands.

3   On models equipped with a brake pressure regulator, push the regulator lever toward the rear axle to release any brake pressure. The pressure regulator is located underneath the vehicle, mounted on the floorpan just ahead of the rear axle.

4   Pry the rubber plug out of the adjuster hole in the backing plate.

5   Insert a screwdriver into the hole and turn the adjuster star wheel teeth down until the brake binds and the wheel will no longer turn freely, then back off on the adjuster until the wheel just turns **(see illustration)**.

6   Install the rubber plug and adjust the remaining wheels.

---

28   Brake system check

Warning: *Brake dust produced by lining wear and deposited on brake components may contain asbestos, which is hazardous to your health. DO NOT blow it out with compressed air and DO NOT inhale it! DO NOT use gasoline or solvents to remove the dust. Brake system cleaner should be used to flush the dust into a drain pan. After the brake components are wiped clean with a damp rag, dispose of the contaminated rag(s) and solvent in a covered and labelled container. Try to use non-asbestos replacement parts whenever possible.*

Note: *For detailed photographs of the brake system, refer to Chapter 9.*

1   In addition to the specified intervals, the brakes should be inspected every time the wheels are removed or whenever a defect is suspected. Any of the following symptoms could indicate a potential brake system defect: The vehicle pulls to one side when the brake pedal is depressed; the brakes make squealing or dragging noises when applied; brake travel is excessive; the pedal pulsates; brake fluid leaks, usually onto the inside of the tire or wheel.

2   Loosen the wheel lug bolts.

3   Raise the vehicle and place it securely on jackstands.

4   Remove the wheels (see *Jacking and towing* at the front of this book, or your owner's manual, if necessary).

Disc brakes

Refer to illustrations 28.5a, 28.5b and 28.10

5   There are two pads – an outer and an inner – in each caliper. On some models, the brake pad thickness can be checked without removing the wheels, by looking through the wheel slots using a small flashlight **(see illustration)**. On other models it is necessary to remove the wheels. The pads are then visible through small inspection holes in each caliper **(see illustration)**. A vernier caliper can be used to measure the thickness of the backing plate and pad material.

28.5b   You will find an inspection hole like this in each caliper on most models – placing a steel ruler across the hole should enable you to determine the thickness of remaining pad material for both inner and outer pads

28.10   Always inspect the brake hoses before installing the wheels – look for cracks, leaks and damage of any kind

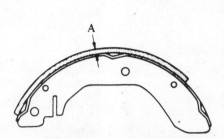

28.12   The brake shoe lining thickness is measured from the outer surface of the lining to the metal shoe

28.14   Peel the wheel cylinder boot back carefully and check for leaking fluid indicating that the cylinder must be replaced or rebuilt

6   Check the pad thickness by looking at each end of the caliper and through the inspection hole in the caliper body. If the lining material is less than the specified thickness, replace the pads. **Note:** *Keep in mind that the lining material is riveted or bonded to a metal backing plate and the metal portion on these models is included in this measurement.*

7   If it is difficult to determine the exact thickness of the remaining pad material by the above method, or if you are at all concerned about the condition of the pads, remove the caliper(s), then remove the pads from the calipers for further inspection (refer to Chapter 9).

8   Once the pads are removed from the calipers, clean them with brake cleaner and remeasure them with a small steel pocket ruler or a vernier caliper.

9   Check the disc. Look for score marks, deep scratches and burned spots. If these conditions exist, the hub/disc assembly will have to be removed (see Chapter 9).

10   Before installing the wheels, check all brake lines and hoses for damage, wear, deformation, cracks, corrosion, leakage, bends and twists, particularly in the vicinity of the rubber hoses at the calipers **(see illustration)**. Check the clamps for tightness and the connections for leakage. Make sure that all hoses and lines are clear of sharp edges, moving parts and the exhaust system. If any of the above conditions are noted, repair, reroute or replace the lines and/or fittings as necessary (see Chapter 9).

Drum brakes

Refer to illustrations 28.12 and 28.14

11   Refer to Chapter 9 and remove the brake drums. **Note:** *On some models the remaining lining thickness can be checked without removing the brake drums, by removing a rubber plug from the backing plate.*

12   Note the thickness of the lining material on the brake shoes **(see illustration)** and look for signs of contamination by brake fluid and grease. If the lining material is within 1/16-inch of the recessed rivets or metal shoes, replace the brake shoes with new ones. The shoes should also be replaced if they are cracked, glazed (shiny lining surfaces) or contaminated with brake fluid or grease. See Chapter 9 for the replacement procedure.

13   Check the shoe return and hold-down springs and the adjusting mechanism to make sure they're installed correctly and in good condition. Deteriorated or distorted springs, if not replaced, could allow the linings to drag and wear prematurely.

14   Check the wheel cylinders for leakage by carefully peeling back the rubber boots **(see illustration)**. If brake fluid is noted behind the boots, the wheel cylinders must be replaced (see Chapter 9).

15   Check the drums for cracks, score marks, deep scratches and hard spots, which will appear as small discolored areas. If imperfections cannot be removed with emery cloth, the drums must be resurfaced by an automotive machine shop (see Chapter 9 for more detailed information).

16   Refer to Chapter 9 and install the brake drums.

17   Install the wheels and tighten the wheel lug bolts finger tight.

18   Remove the jackstands and lower the vehicle.

19   Tighten the wheel lug bolts to the torque listed in this Chapter's Specifications.

Parking brake

20   A simple method of checking the parking brake is to park the vehicle on a steep hill with the parking brake set and the transmission in Neutral. If the parking brake cannot prevent the vehicle from rolling, it is in need of adjustment (see Chapter 9).

---

29   Steering and suspension checks

Note: *For detailed illustrations of the steering and suspension components, refer to Chapter 10.*

With the wheels on the ground

1   With the vehicle stopped and the front wheels pointed straight ahead, rock the steering wheel gently back and forth. If free play is excessive, a front wheel bearing, main shaft yoke, intermediate shaft yoke, lower arm balljoint or steering system joint is worn or the steering gear is out of adjustment or broken. Refer to Chapter 10 for the appropriate repair procedure.

2   Other symptoms, such as excessive vehicle body movement over rough roads, swaying (leaning) around corners and binding as the steering wheel is turned, may indicate faulty steering and/or suspension components.

3   Check the shock absorbers by pushing down and releasing the vehicle several times at each corner. If the vehicle does not come back to a level position within one or two bounces, the shocks/struts are worn and must be replaced. When bouncing the vehicle up and down, listen for squeaks and noises from the suspension components. Additional information on suspension components can be found in Chapter 10.

With the vehicle raised

4   Raise the vehicle and support it securely on jackstands. See Jacking and towing at the front of this book for the proper jacking points.

5   Check the tires for irregular wear patterns (see Section 5) and proper inflation. See Section 5 in this Chapter for information regarding tire wear and Section 37 for the rear wheel bearing maintenance procedures.

6   Inspect the universal joint between the steering shaft and the steering gear housing. Check the steering gear housing for grease leakage or ooz-

30.2   Flex the driveaxle boots by hand to check for cracks and leaking grease

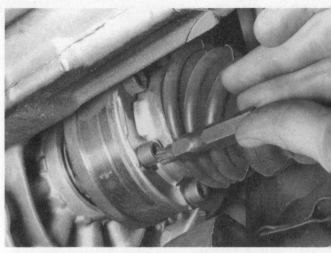

30.3   Check the driveaxle flange bolt tightness when you check the CV joints – a special internal socket tool will be required

ing. Make sure that the dust seals and boots are not damaged and that the boot clamps are not loose. Check the steering linkage for looseness or damage. Check the tie-rod ends for excessive play. Look for loose bolts, broken or disconnected parts and deteriorated rubber bushings on all suspension and steering components. While an assistant turns the steering wheel from side to side, check the steering components for free movement, chafing and binding. If the steering components do not seem to be reacting with the movement of the steering wheel, try to determine where the slack is located

7   Inspect the balljoint boots for damage and leaking grease. Replace the balljoints with new ones if they are damaged (see Chapter 10).

30   Driveaxle boot check

Refer to illustrations 30.2 and 30.3

1   The driveaxle boots are very important because they prevent dirt, water and foreign material from entering and damaging the constant velocity (CV) joints. Oil and grease can cause the boot material to deteriorate prematurely, so it's a good idea to wash the boots with soap and water.

2   Inspect the boots for tears and cracks as well as loose clamps **(see illustration)**. If there is any evidence of cracks or leaking lubricant, they must be replaced as described in Chapter 8.

3   It's a good idea to check the tightness of the driveaxle flange bolts dur-

ing boot inspection. A special 12-point internal socket tool will be required for these bolts **(see illustration)**

31   Exhaust system check

Refer to illustrations 31.2a and 31.2b

1   With the engine cold (at least three hours after the vehicle has been driven), check the complete exhaust system from its starting point at the engine to the end of the tailpipe. This should be done on a hoist where unrestricted access is available.

2   Check the pipes and connections for evidence of leaks, severe corrosion or damage. Make sure that all brackets and hangers are in good condition and tight **(see illustrations)**.

3   At the same time, inspect the underside of the body for holes, corrosion, open seams, etc. which may allow exhaust gases to enter the passenger compartment. Seal all body openings with silicone or body putty

4   Rattles and other noises can often be traced to the exhaust system, especially the mounts and hangers. Try to move the pipes, muffler and catalytic converter. If the components can come in contact with the body or suspension parts, secure the exhaust system with new mounts.

5   Check the running condition of the engine by inspecting inside the end of the tailpipe. The exhaust deposits here are an indication of engine state-

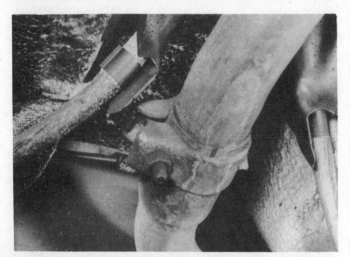

31.2a   Check the clamp bolts for damage and corrosion

31.2b   Make sure the rubber exhaust hangers aren't deteriorated

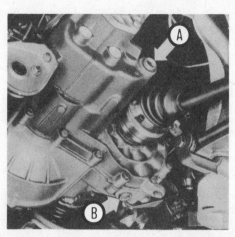

32.1   The manual transaxle filler (A) and drain (B) plug locations – remove them with an Allen wrench

33.3   Automatic transaxle differential fill plug location

of-tune. If the pipe is black and sooty or coated with white deposits, the engine is in need of a tune-up, including a thorough fuel system inspection and adjustment.

32   Manual transaxle lubricant level check

Refer to illustration 32.1
1   The manual transaxle does not have a dipstick. To check the lubricant level, raise the vehicle and support it securely on jackstands. On the lower rear side of the transaxle housing, you will see a plug **(see illustration)**. Remove it. Most models require a 17 mm Allen wrench for the removal of the drain and fill plugs. If the lubricant level is correct, it should be up to the lower edge of the hole.
2   If the transaxle needs more lubricant (if the level is not up to the hole), use a syringe to add more. Stop filling the transaxle when the lubricant begins to run out the hole.
3   On some 1985 and later models, the correct lubricant level is actually above the fill hole, so some lubricant may be lost during the checking procedure. On these models, remove the speedometer drive gear bolt, lift out the gear and add 0.53-quarts (0.5 L) of the specified lubricant through the hole, to replace what was lost during the checking procedure. On models built after September 8, 1987 (transaxle number 08097 and higher), the hole has been relocated and the lubricant level should be up to the lower edge of the hole, as described in Step 2.

34.3   The choke plate (arrow) is located in the carburetor opening

4   Install the plug and tighten it securely. Drive the vehicle a short distance, then check for leaks.

33   Automatic transaxle differential lubricant level check

Refer to illustration 33.3
1   On these models the differential lubricant supply is separate from that of the transaxle so the level must be checked separately at the specified intervals.
2   Raise the vehicle and support it securely on jackstands.
3   Remove the differential fill plug (17mm) on the side of the transaxle **(see illustration)**.
4   The differential (final drive) lubricant level should be even with the lower edge of the fill hole. If it is not, use a syringe to add the specified lubricant until the lubricant begins to run out of the hole.
5   Install the plug and tighten it securely. Drive the vehicle a short distance, then check for leaks.

34   Carburetor choke check

Refer to illustration 34.3
Warning: *The electric cooling fan can activate at any time, even when the ignition is in the Off position. Disconnect the fan motor or negative battery cable when working in the vicinity of the fan.*
1   The choke operates only when the engine is cold, so this check should be performed before the engine has been started for the day.
2   Take off the air intake elbow. It's held in place by a hose clamp. If any vacuum hoses must be disconnected, make sure you tag the hoses for reinstallation in their original positions. Place the elbow aside, out of the way of moving engine components.
3   Look at the center of the carburetor. You will notice a flat plate at the carburetor opening **(see illustration)**.
4   Press the accelerator pedal to the floor. The plate should close completely. Start the engine while you watch the plate at the carburetor. Don't position your face near the carburetor, as the engine could backfire, causing serious burns. When the engine starts, the choke plate should open slightly.
5   Allow the engine to continue running at an idle speed. As the engine warms up to operating temperature, the plate should slowly open, allowing more air to enter through the top of the carburetor.
6   After a few minutes, the choke plate should be fully open to the vertical position. Blip the throttle to make sure the fast idle cam disengages.
7   You'll notice that the engine speed corresponds with the plate opening. With the plate fully closed, the engine should run at a fast idle speed. As the plate opens and the throttle is moved to disengage the fast idle cam, the engine speed will decrease.

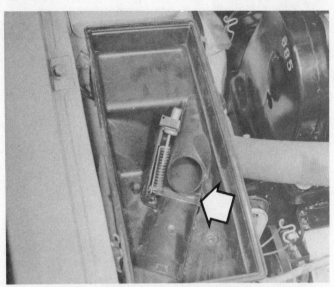

35.3   The thermostatically-controlled air cleaner valve (arrow) is in the Up position when the engine is cold, allowing heated air to enter from the bottom of the housing

8   Refer to Chapter 4 for specific information on adjusting and servicing the choke components.

---

35   Thermostatically – controlled air cleaner check (carbureted models)

Refer to illustration 35.3
Warning: *The electric cooling fan can activate at any time, even when the ignition is in the Off position. Disconnect the fan motor or negative battery cable when working in the vicinity of the fan.*

1   All engines are equipped with a thermostatically controlled air cleaner which draws air to the carburetor or fuel injection system from different locations, depending on engine temperature.
2   This is a visual check, requiring the removal of the air filter element (see Section 15).
3   When the engine is cold, locate the air control valve inside the air cleaner assembly. It's at the bottom of the air cleaner housing **(see illustration)**.
4   Install the air filter element.
5   Start the engine and allow it to warm up. The valve should move up to block off the opening at the front of the air cleaner. With the valve closed, air cannot enter through the end of the air cleaner, but instead enters the air cleaner through the flexible duct at the bottom, attached to the exhaust manifold and the heat stove passage.
6   As the engine warms up to operating temperature, the valve should move down to allow air to be drawn through the front of the housing. Depending on outside temperature, this may take 10-to-15 minutes. To speed up this check you can drive the vehicle, then check to see if the valve is completely open.
7   Shut off the engine. Remove the filter housing and make sure the flap has now closed, allowing air to enter through the opening at the front of the housing.
8   If the thermostatically controlled air cleaner isn't operating properly, see Chapter 6 for more information.

---

36   Cooling system servicing (draining, flushing and refilling)

Warning: *Do not allow antifreeze to come in contact with your skin or painted surfaces of the vehicle. Flush contaminated areas immediately with plenty of water. Don't store new coolant or leave old coolant lying around where it's accessible to children or pets – they're attracted by its sweet taste. Ingestion of even a small amount of coolant can be fatal! Wipe up garage floor and drip pan spills immediately. In many areas, reclamation centers have been established to collect used oil and coolant mixtures. Also, the electric cooling fan can activate at any time, even when the ignition is in the Off position. Disconnect the fan motor or negative battery cable when working in the vicinity of the fan.*

1   Periodically, the cooling system should be drained, flushed and refilled to replenish the antifreeze mixture and prevent formation of rust and corrosion, which can impair the performance of the cooling system and cause engine damage. When the cooling system is serviced, all hoses and the radiator cap should be checked and replaced if necessary.

Draining

2   Apply the parking brake and block the wheels. If the vehicle has just been driven, wait several hours to allow the engine to cool down before beginning this procedure.
3   Once the engine is completely cool, remove the radiator cap or coolant recovery bottle cap.
4   Remove the splash cover located beneath the radiator. Then move a large container under the radiator to catch the coolant. Loosen the hose clamps and detach the lower radiator hose, the coolant recovery hose and the lower end of the hose between the water pump and the upper inlet from the water pump.
5   While the coolant is draining, check the condition of the radiator hoses, heater hoses and clamps (refer to Section 13 if necessary).
6   Replace any damaged clamps or hoses (refer to Chapter 3 for detailed replacement procedures).

Flushing

7   Once the system is completely drained, flush the radiator with fresh water from a garden hose until water runs clear at the drain. The flushing action of the water will remove sediments from the radiator but will not remove rust and scale from the engine and cooling tube surfaces.
8   These deposits can be removed by the chemical action of a cleaner. Follow the procedure outlined in the manufacturer's instructions. If the radiator is severely corroded, damaged or leaking, it should be removed (see Chapter 3) and taken to a radiator repair shop.
9   Remove the overflow hose from the coolant recovery reservoir. Drain the reservoir and flush it with clean water, then reconnect the hose.

Refilling

10   Connect the radiator hose.
11   Place the heater temperature control in the maximum heat position.
12   Slowly add new coolant (a 50/50 mixture of water and antifreeze) to the radiator until it's full. Add coolant to the reservoir up to the lower mark.
13   Leave the radiator cap or coolant recovery bottle cap off and run the engine in a well-ventilated area until the thermostat opens (coolant will begin flowing through the radiator and the upper radiator hose will become hot).
14   Turn the engine off and let it cool. Add more coolant mixture to bring the level back up to the lip on the radiator filler neck.
15   Squeeze the upper radiator hose to expel air, then add more coolant mixture if necessary. Install the radiator or coolant recovery bottle cap.
16   Start the engine, allow it to reach normal operating temperature and check for leaks.

---

37   Rear wheel bearing check, repack and adjustment

Check

Refer to illustration 37.1
1   In most cases the rear wheel bearings will not need servicing until the brake shoes are changed. However, the bearings should be checked whenever the rear of the vehicle is raised for any reason. Several items, including a torque wrench and special grease, are required for this procedure **(see illustration)**.
2   With the vehicle securely supported on jackstands, spin each wheel and check for noise, rolling resistance and free play.

3   Grasp the top of each tire with one hand and the bottom with the other. Move the wheel in-and-out on the spindle. If there's any noticeable movement, the bearings should be checked and then repacked with grease or replaced if necessary.

Repack

Refer to illustrations 37.9, 37.11 and 37.15

4   Remove the wheel.
5   If necessary, back off the parking brake adjuster (see Chapter 9).
6   Pry the dust cap out of the drum/hub assembly using a screwdriver or hammer and chisel.
7   Straighten the bent ends of the cotter pin, then pull the cotter pin out of the nut lock. Discard the cotter pin and use a new one during reassembly. Remove the nut lock.
8   Remove the spindle nut and washer from the end of the spindle.
9   Pull the drum/hub assembly out slightly, then push it back into its original position. This should force the outer bearing off the spindle enough so it can be removed **(see illustration)**.
10   Pull the drum/hub off the spindle.
11   Use a seal puller or screwdriver to pry the seal out of the rear of the drum/hub **(see illustration)**. As this is done, note how the seal is installed.
12   Remove the inner wheel bearing from the drum/hub.
13   Use solvent to remove all traces of the old grease from the bearings, hub and spindle. A small brush may prove helpful; however make sure no bristles from the brush embed themselves inside the bearing rollers. Allow the parts to air dry.
14   Carefully inspect the bearings for cracks, heat discoloration, worn rollers, etc. Check the bearing races inside the hub for wear and damage. If the bearing races are defective, the hubs should be taken to a machine shop with the facilities to remove the old races and press new ones in. Note that the bearings and races come as matched sets and old bearings should never be installed on new races.
15   Use wheel bearing grease to pack the bearings. Work the grease completely into the bearings, forcing it between the rollers, cone and cage from the back side **(see illustration)**.
16   Apply a thin coat of grease to the spindle at the outer bearing seat, inner bearing seat, shoulder and seal seat.
17   Put a small quantity of grease inboard of each bearing race inside the hub. Using your finger, form a dam at these points to provide extra grease availability and to keep thinned grease from flowing out of the bearing.
18   Place the grease-packed inner bearing into the rear of the drum/hub and put a little more grease outboard of the bearing.
19   Place a new seal over the inner bearing and tap the seal evenly into place with a hammer and block of wood until it's flush with the hub.
20   Carefully place the drum/hub assembly onto the spindle and push the grease-packed outer bearing into position.

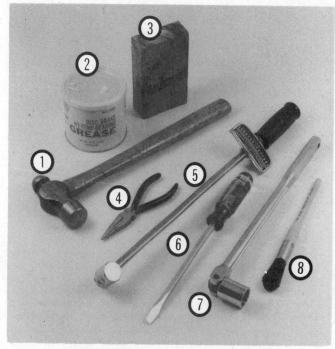

37.1   Tools and materials needed for rear wheel bearing maintenance

1   *Hammer* – *A common hammer will do just fine*
2   *Grease* – *High-temperature grease which is formulated specially for wheel bearings should be used*
3   *Wood block* – *If you have a scrap piece of 2x4, it can be used to drive the new seal into the hub*
4   *Needle-nose pliers* – *Used to straighten and remove the cotter pin in the spindle*
5   *Torque wrench* – *This is very important in this procedure; if the bearing is too tight, the wheel won't turn freely – if it's too loose, the wheel will "wobble" on the spindle. Either way, it could mean extensive damage.*
6   *Screwdriver* – *Used to remove the seal from the hub (a long screwdriver would be preferred)*
7   *Socket/breaker bar* – *Needed to loosen the nut on the spindle if it's extremely tight*
8   *Brush* – *Together with some clean solvent, this will be used to remove old grease from the hub and spindle*

37.9   Pull the drum/hub out slightly to dislodge the outer bearing and the washer

37.11   Pry the seal out of the hub with a screwdriver or seal puller tool

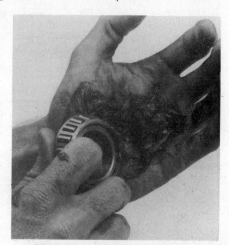

37.15   Work the grease into each bearing from the large diameter side until grease oozes out the small diameter side

37.25a   The wheel bearing is properly adjusted when the washer can be moved by applying moderate pressure with the tip of the screwdriver

37.25b   After adjustment, install the nut lock and insert a new cotter pin

Adjustment

Refer to illustrations 37.25a and 37.25b

21   Install the washer and spindle nut. Tighten the nut only slightly (no more than 7 ft-lbs of torque).

22   Spin the drum/hub in a forward direction to seat the bearings and remove any grease or burrs which could cause excessive bearing play later.

23   Check to see that the tightness of the spindle nut is still approximately 7 ft-lbs.

24   Loosen the spindle nut until it's just loose, no more.

25   Tighten the nut until you can just move the thrust washer back and forth with the tip of a screwdriver **(see illustration)**. Install the nut lock, then install a new cotter pin through the hole in the spindle and the slots in the nut lock **(see illustration)**. If the slots don't line up, loosen the nut slightly until they do. From the hand-tight position, the nut should not be loosened more than one-half flat to install the cotter pin.

26   Bend the ends of the cotter pin until they're flat against the nut. Cut off any extra length which could interfere with the dust cap.

27   Install the dust cap, tapping it into place with a hammer and a large punch.

28   Install the tire and tighten the lug bolts to the torque listed in this Chapter's Specifications.

29   Grasp the top and bottom of the tire and check the bearings in the manner described earlier in this Section.

30   Lower the vehicle.

38   Brake fluid replacement

1   Because brake fluid absorbs moisture which could ultimately cause corrosion of the brake components, and air which could make the braking system less effective, the fluid should be replaced at the specified intervals. This job can be accomplished for a nominal fee by a properly equipped brake shop using a pressure bleeder. The task can also be done by the home mechanic with the help of an assistant. To bleed the air and old fluid and replace it with fresh fluid from sealed containers, refer to the brake bleeding procedure in Chapter 9.

2   If there is any possibility that incorrect fluid has been used in the system, drain all the fluid and flush the system with methylated spirits. Replace all piston seals and cups, as they will be affected and could possibly fail under pressure.

39   Automatic transaxle fluid and filter change

Refer to illustration 39.9

1   At the specified time intervals, the automatic transaxle fluid should be drained and replaced.

2   Before beginning work, purchase the specified transmission fluid (see *Recommended lubricants and fluids* at the front of this chapter).

3   Other tools necessary for this job include jackstands to support the vehicle in a raised position, a drain pan capable of holding at least eight pints, newspapers and clean rags.

4   The fluid should be drained immediately after the vehicle has been driven. Hot fluid is more effective than cold fluid at removing built up sediment. **Warning:** *Fluid temperature can exceed 350-degrees in a hot transaxle. Wear protective gloves.*

5   After the vehicle has been driven to warm up the fluid, raise it and place it on jackstands for access to the transaxle drain plug.

6   Move the necessary equipment under the vehicle, being careful not to touch any of the hot exhaust components.

7   Place the drain pan under the drain plug in the transaxle and remove the drain plug (if equipped). Be sure the drain pan is in position, as fluid will come out with some force. Once the fluid is drained, reinstall the drain plug securely. On models without drain plugs, loosen the front and side transaxle pan bolts, lower the front of the pan and allow the fluid to drain.

8   Remove the transaxle pan bolts, carefully pry the pan loose with a screwdriver and remove it.

9   Remove the filter retaining screws and detach the filter and cover from the transaxle **(see illustration)**. Be careful when lowering the filter as it contains residual fluid.

10   Place the new filter in position and install the screws. Tighten the screws securely.

11   Carefully clean the gasket surfaces of the fluid pan, removing all traces of old gasket material. Wash the pan in clean solvent and dry it with compressed air.

12   Install a new gasket, place the fluid pan in position and install the bolts. Tighten the bolts to the specified torque.

13   Lower the vehicle.

14   With the engine off, add new fluid to the transaxle through the dipstick tube (see *Recommended lubricants and fluids* for the recommended fluid type and capacity). Use a funnel to prevent spills. It is best to add a little fluid at a time, continually checking the level with the dipstick (see Section 7). Allow the fluid time to drain into the pan.

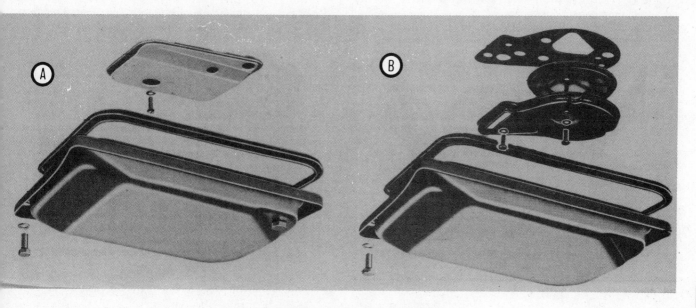

39.9   Automatic transaxle pan and filter details

A   Early model   *B   Later model*

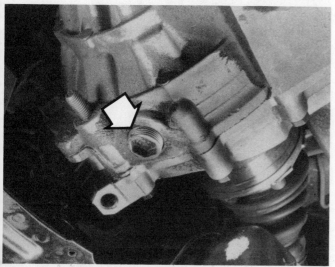

40.3   The manual transaxle drain plug is located at the bottom of the housing and a 17 mm Allen wrench is required for removal on most models

15   Start the engine and shift the selector into all positions from Park through Low, then shift into Park and apply the parking brake.
16   With the engine idling, check the fluid level. Add fluid to bring the level between the two marks on the dipstick.

40   Manual transaxle lubricant change

Refer to illustration 40.3

1   Raise the vehicle and support it securely on jackstands.
2   Move a drain pan, rags, newspapers and wrenches under the vehicle. Most models require a 17 mm Allen wrench for the removal of the drain and fill plugs.
3   Remove the drain and filler plugs and drain the lubricant **(see illustration)**.
4   Reinstall the drain plug. Tighten it securely.

5   Add new lubricant until it begins to run out of the filler hole (see Section 32). See *Recommended lubricants and fluids* for the specified lubricant type.

41   Automatic transaxle differential lubricant change

1   Raise the vehicle and support it securely on jackstands.
2   Move a drain pan, rags, newspapers and wrenches under the vehicle. Most models require a 17 mm Allen wrench for removal of the drain and fill plugs.
3   Remove the differential drain plug at the bottom of the transaxle housing, followed by the fill plug and allow the lubricant to drain completely (see Section 33). If there is no drain plug, use a suction pump to pump the lubricant out of the housing.
4   Reinstall the drain plug. Tighten it securely.
5   Use a syringe to add the specified lubricant until it begins to run out of the fill hole.
6   Install the fill plug and tighten it securely. Drive the vehicle a short distance, then check for leaks.

42   Evaporative emissions control system check and canister replacement

1   The function of the evaporative emissions control system is to draw fuel vapors from the gas tank and fuel system, store them in a charcoal canister and route them to the intake manifold during normal engine operation.
2   The most common symptom of a fault in the evaporative emissions system is a strong fuel odor in the engine compartment. If a fuel odor is detected, inspect the charcoal canister, located in the engine compartment. Check the canister and all hoses for damage and deterioration.
3   If it is clogged or damaged, the charcoal canister must be replaced with a new one. Disconnect the hoses, remove the screws or bolts and lift the canister from the engine compartment. Installation is the reverse of removal.
4   The evaporative emissions control system is explained in more detail in Chapter 6.

43.1   The PCV system hose (arrow) connects the camshaft cover to the intake system

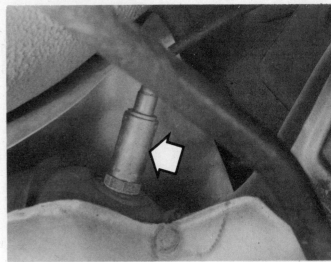

44.1   The oxygen sensor (arrow) is screwed into the exhaust manifold – follow the wire and disconnect the electrical connector

43   Positive Crankcase Ventilation (PCV) system check

Refer to illustration 43.1

1   The Positive Crankcase Ventilation (PCV) system on these models consists of a hose connected between the camshaft cover and the carburetor or fuel injection air intake assembly **(see illustration)**. On some early models a PCV valve is installed in the hose.
2   At the specified intervals, check the PCV valve (if equipped) and hose.

PCV valve

3   With the engine idling at normal operating temperature, disconnect the hose from the camshaft cover and place your hand over the end. If there is no vacuum, check for a plugged hose (see below) or valve.
4   Check the valve by noting the direction in which it is installed and then removing it from the hose. Blow through the from the side that faces the camshaft cover. If air will not pass through the valve in this direction, replace it with a new one.
5   When purchasing a replacement PCV valve, make sure it's for your particular vehicle and engine. Compare the old valve with a new one to make sure they're the same.

Hose

6   Remove the hose and inspect it for cracks, deterioration and clogging. If compressed air is available, blow through the hose to remove any sludge or contaminants.
7   To further clean the hose, soak it in solvent and scrub it out with a long, thin brush. Blow out the hose with compressed air.

44   Oxygen sensor replacement and service light resetting

Refer to illustrations 44.1 and 44.5
Warning: *The electric cooling fan can activate at any time, even when the ignition is in the Off position. Disconnect the fan motor or negative battery cable when working in the vicinity of the fan.*
Note: *Each type of fuel injection system has a different oxygen sensor system – see Chapter 6 for oxygen sessor location.*

44.5   Use a screwdriver to push the oxygen sensor reset button in and turn out the service light

1   Unplug the oxygen sensor wire after tracing the wire from the sensor to the nearest electrical connector **(see illustration)**.
2   Unscrew the oxygen sensor.
3   Screw the new oxygen sensor into the exhaust manifold. Tighten the sensor securely.
4   Plug in the electrical connector.
5   After replacing the oxygen sensor, reset the counter located on the firewall (follow the speedometer cable). On later models, detach the coolant reservoir for access. Push the white reset button in to reset the counter **(see illustration)**. turn the ignition On to verify that the service light is out. It may be necessary to push the button several times to reset the counter.
6   On 1981 through 1984 U.S. built models, it will be necessary to remove the instrument cluster bezel and use a hooked piece of wire to pull back the reset lever located at the right corner of the cluster, similar to the EGR counter reset procedure described in Section 17.

Chapter 2 Part A   Engine

Contents

Camshaft and cam followers – removal,
  inspection and installation 10
Crankshaft front oil seal – replacement 9
Crankshaft rear oil seal – replacement 15
Cylinder compression check . . . . See Chapter 2B
Cylinder head – removal and installation 11
Drivebelt check, adjustment and replacement . . . . See Chapter 1
Driveplate – removal and installation 14
Engine mounts – check and replacement 16
Engine oil and filter change . . . . See Chapter 1
Engine overhaul – general information . . . . See Chapter 2B
Engine – removal and installation . . . . See Chapter 2B
General information 1
Intake/exhaust manifold – removal and installation 5

Camshaft cover – removal and installation 4
Camshaft oil seal – replacement 7
Intermediate shaft oil seal – replacement 8
Oil pan – removal and installation 12
Oil pump – removal, inspection and installation 13
Repair operations possible with the engine in the vehicle 2
Spark plug replacement . . . . See Chapter 1
Timing belt and sprockets – removal, inspection and installation . . 6
Top Dead Center (TDC) for number one piston – locating 3
Valve clearance check and adjustment
  (1975 through 1984 models only) . . . . See Chapter 1
Valves – servicing . . . . See Chapter 2B
Water pump – removal and installation . . . . See Chapter 3

Specifications

General
Firing order 1-3-4-2
Cylinder numbers (drivebelt end-to-transaxle end) 1-2-3-4

Camshaft
Endplay (except 16-valve engines) . . . . 0.006 in (0.15 mm)
Bearing oil clearance
   DOHC engine . . . . 0.0043 in. (0.11 mm) with Plastigage

Cylinder head
Warpage limit . . . . 0.004 in (0.1 mm)

Intake/exhaust manifolds
Warpage limit . . . . 0.008 in (0.2 mm) per foot of manifold length

Oil pump gears
Backlash (clearance between gear teeth) . . . . 0.002 to 0.008 in (0.105 to 0.20 mm)
Endplay . . . . 0.006 in (0.15 mm) max
Driveplate-to-engine block clearance . . . . 1.20 to 1.26 in

0799H

1990 and later 2.0L engine

0800H

1989 and later 1.8L engine

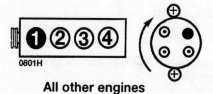

0801H

All other engines

Cylinder location and distributor rotation

Torque specifications

	Ft-lbs (unless otherwise indicated)
Camshaft bearing cap nuts	
SOHC engine	14
DOHC engine	11
Camshaft cover bolts	
SOHC engine	87 in-lbs
DOHC engine	87 in-lbs
Manifold support bolt	15
Manifold nuts	15
Camshaft sprocket bolt	
SOHC engine	58
DOHC engine	48
Crankshaft pulley Allen head bolts	14
Crankshaft sprocket bolt	58
Crankshaft sprocket bolt (12-point)	148
Crankshaft rear oil seal housing	
Top two bolts	15
All others	87 in-lbs
Crankshaft front oil seal housing bolts	14
Cylinder head bolts (engine cold)	
1975 through 1977 models – hex socket bolts	
Step 1	22
Step 2	43
Step 3	54
1978 and 1979 models – 12-point socket bolts	
Step 1	29
Step 2	43
Step 3	54
Step 4	Tighten an additional 1/2-turn
1980 through 1984 models – hex socket bolts	
Step 1	30
Step 2	44
Step 3	55
Step 4	Tighten an additional 1/4-turn without hesitating
1980 through 1992 models – 12-point socket bolts	
Step 1	30
Step 2	44
Step 3	Tighten an additional 1/2-turn
Driveplate-to-crankshaft bolts	50
Flywheel-to-crankshaft bolts	60
Intake/exhaust manifold nuts/bolts	
SOHC engine	18
DOHC engine	15
Intermediate shaft oil seal housing bolts	18
Intermediate shaft sprocket bolt	58
Oil pan-to-engine block fasteners	
Allen screws	7
6 mm bolt	14
Oil pick-up tube-to-oil pump housing bolt	7
Oil pump mounting bolts	14
Timing belt tensioner locknut	32
Timing belt cover bolts	
SOHC engine	7.5
DOHC engine	
Top cover	53 in-lbs
Lower cover	87 in-lbs

1   General information

This Part of Chapter 2 is devoted to in-vehicle repair procedures for the engine. All information concerning engine removal and installation and engine block and cylinder head overhaul can be found in Part B of this Chapter.

The following repair procedures are based on the assumption that the engine is installed in the vehicle. If the engine has been removed from the vehicle and mounted on a stand, many of the steps outlined in this Part of Chapter 2 will not apply.

The Specifications included in this Part of Chapter 2 apply only to the procedures contained in this Part. Part B of Chapter 2 contains the Specifications necessary for cylinder head and engine block rebuilding.

Two different types of cylinder heads were used on the engines covered by this manual. A single overhead camshaft design with two valves per cylinder (referred to in this Chapter as the SOHC engine) and a high-performance, double overhead camshaft design with four valves per cylinder (referred to in this Chapter as the DOHC engine).

3.6 Use paint, a felt-tip permanent marker or chalk to mark the distributor housing directly under the number one spark plug wire terminal (the housing probably has a notch at this point anyway) (SOHC engine shown)

3.8 When you're bringing the number one piston to TDC, look at the timing marks on the edge of the flywheel/driveplate through the opening in the bellhousing – the pointer will align with the notch on the flywheel at TDC

2 Repair operations possible with the engine in the vehicle

Many major repair operations can be accomplished without removing the engine from the vehicle.

Clean the engine compartment and the exterior of the engine with some type of degreaser before any work is done. It'll make the job easier and help keep dirt out of the internal areas of the engine.

Depending on the components involved, it may be helpful to remove the hood to improve access to the engine as repairs are performed (refer to Chapter 11 if necessary). Cover the fenders to prevent damage to the paint. Special pads are available, but an old bedspread or blanket will also work.

If vacuum, exhaust, oil or coolant leaks develop, indicating a need for gasket or seal replacement, the repairs can generally be made with the engine in the vehicle. The intake and exhaust manifold gaskets, oil pan gasket, crankshaft oil seals and cylinder head gasket are all accessible with the engine in place.

Exterior engine components, such as the intake and exhaust manifolds, the oil pan (and the oil pump), the water pump, the starter motor, the alternator, the distributor and the fuel system components can be removed for repair with the engine in place.

Since the cylinder head can be removed without pulling the engine, camshaft and valve component servicing can also be accomplished with the engine in the vehicle. Replacement of the timing belt on both engines and the timing chain on DOHC engines is also possible with the engine in the vehicle.

In extreme cases caused by a lack of necessary equipment, repair or replacement of piston rings, pistons, connecting rods and rod bearings is possible with the engine in the vehicle. However, this practice isn't recommended because of the cleaning and preparation work that must be done to the components involved.

3 Top Dead Center (TDC) for number one piston – locating

Refer to illustrations 3.6 and 3.8

Note: *The following procedure is based on the assumption that the spark plug wires and distributor are correctly installed. If you're trying to locate TDC to install the distributor correctly, piston position must be determined by feeling for compression at the number one spark plug hole, then aligning the ignition timing marks as described in Step 8.*

1   Top Dead Center (TDC) is the highest point in the cylinder each piston reaches as it travels up-and-down when the crankshaft turns. Each piston reaches TDC on the compression stroke and again on the exhaust stroke, but TDC generally refers to piston position on the compression stroke.

2   Positioning the piston(s) at TDC is an essential part of many procedures such as camshaft and timing belt/chain removal and distributor removal.

3   Before beginning this procedure, be sure to place the transmission in Neutral and apply the parking brake or block the rear wheels. Also, disable the ignition system by detaching the coil wire from the center terminal of the distributor cap and grounding it on the block with a jumper wire. Remove the spark plugs (see Chapter 1).

4   In order to bring any piston to TDC, the crankshaft must be turned using one of the methods outlined below. When looking at the front of the engine, normal crankshaft rotation is clockwise.

   a)   The preferred method is to turn the crankshaft with a socket and ratchet attached to the bolt threaded into the front of the crankshaft.

   b)   A remote starter switch, which may save some time, can also be used. Follow the instructions included with the switch. Once the piston is close to TDC, use a socket and ratchet as described in the previous Paragraph.

   c)   If an assistant is available to turn the ignition switch to the Start position in short bursts, you can get the piston close to TDC without a remote starter switch. Make sure your assistant is out of the vehicle, away from the ignition switch, then use a socket and ratchet as described in Paragraph a) to complete the procedure.

5   Note the position of the terminal for the number one spark plug wire on the distributor cap. If the terminal isn't marked, follow the plug wire from the number one cylinder spark plug to the cap.

6   Use a felt-tip pen or chalk to make a mark on the distributor body directly under the terminal **(see illustration)**.

7   Detach the cap from the distributor and set it aside (see Chapter 1 if necessary).

8   Locate the round window in the bellhousing (located under the inspection plug on the transaxle). You'll see a stationary pointer at the edge of the window. Turn the crankshaft (see Paragraph 3 above) until the TDC mark (zero) on the edge of the flywheel/driveplate is aligned with the stationary pointer **(see illustration)**.

9   Look at the distributor rotor – it should be pointing directly at the mark you made on the distributor body. If the rotor is pointing at the mark, go to Step 12. If it isn't, go to Step 10.

10   If the rotor is 180-degrees off, the number one piston is at TDC on the exhaust stroke.

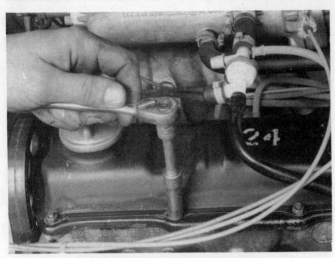

4.5   Remove the camshaft cover bolts

4.16a   Be sure to tuck the ends of the front cover seal into the corners of the cam bearing cap and cylinder head surfaces (arrow) – a little dab of RTV will help keep it in place and ensure an oil-tight seal

11   To get the piston to TDC on the compression stroke, turn the crankshaft one complete turn (360-degrees) clockwise. The rotor should now be pointing at the mark on the distributor. When the rotor is pointing at the number one spark plug wire terminal in the distributor cap and the ignition timing marks are aligned, the number one piston is at TDC on the compression stroke.

12   After the number one piston has been positioned at TDC on the compression stroke, TDC for any of the remaining pistons can be located by turning the crankshaft and following the firing order. Mark the remaining spark plug wire terminal locations on the distributor body just like you did for the number one terminal, then number the marks to correspond with the cylinder numbers. As you turn the crankshaft, the rotor will also turn. When it's pointing directly at one of the marks on the distributor, the piston for that particular cylinder is at TDC on the compression stroke.

4   Camshaft cover – removal and installation

Removal

SOHC Engine
Refer to illustration 4.5

1   Detach the cable from the negative battery terminal.
2   Detach the accelerator cable from the cable bracket.
3   Wipe off the camshaft cover to prevent debris from falling into the exposed cylinder head or camshaft/valve train assembly.
4   Detach the PCV hose assembly from the camshaft cover (see Chapter 1). **Note:** *Except for 1975 models, Rabbits don't have a PCV valve – just a hose.*
5   Remove the camshaft cover bolts and, if equipped, the "doubles" strips which reinforce the cover flanges **(see illustration)**.
6   Carefully lift off the camshaft cover and gasket. If the gasket is stuck to the cylinder head, use a putty knife to remove it. Set the cover aside.
7   Remove and discard the front and rear rubber seals.

DOHC engine
8   Follow Steps 1 through 3 of the procedure for the SOHC engine, then remove the intake air boot from the throttle housing and detach the small rubber hose between the intake air boot and the idle air valve.
9   Disconnect the electrical connector for the charcoal canister control valve and the large vacuum hose from the back of the upper intake manifold.
10   Remove the support bolt and nuts that attach the upper intake manifold to the lower intake manifold.

11   Mark the wires and vacuum hoses and move the upper manifold up and away from the engine.
12   Remove the eight camshaft cover bolts and lift the cover off the cylinder head.
13   Clean the camshaft cover and remove all traces of the old gasket material.

Installation

SOHC engine
Refer to illustrations 4.16a, 4.16b and 4.17

14   Make sure the gasket mating surfaces of the cylinder head and camshaft cover are clean.
15   If the engine is equipped with a curtain (baffle for enhancing air/oil separation, and its been removed), install it now, manifold side first, with the cutouts over the cam towers and contacting the cylinder head floor, then press the opposite (distributor) side into position below the gasket mating surface. Be sure to install the rubber bumpers on top of the curtain.
16   Install new front and rear seals **(see illustrations)**. Tack them in place with gasket sealant.
17   Carefully lay the new gasket in place **(see illustration)** and install the cam cover, "doubles" strips (if equipped) and bolts. Tighten the bolts to the torque listed in this Chapter's Specifications.
18   The remainder of installation is the reverse of removal. Be sure to check the PCV hose (see Chapter 1) before you install it.

DOHC engine
19   Apply a thin layer of RTV sealant to the new gasket, then position it on the head and install the cover and bolts.
20   First tighten the eight cover bolts, then the five manifold nuts to the torque listed in this Chapter's Specifications. Finally, tighten the manifold support bolt.
21   The remaining steps are the reverse of removal.

5   Intake/exhaust manifold – removal and installation

Warning: *Gasoline is extremely flammable, so take extra precautions when working on any part of the fuel system. Don't smoke or allow open flames or bare light bulbs in or near the work area. And don't work in a garage where a natural gas-type appliance (such as a water heater or clothes dryer) with a pilot light is present. Have a fire extinguisher handy and know how to use it! If you spill fuel on your skin, wash it off immediately with soap and plenty of water.*

4.16b Install a new rear seal in the cylinder head recess

4.17 Carefully lay a new gasket on the cylinder head – make sure the ends are engaged with the cover seal

SOHC engine with carburetor

Removal

Refer to illustrations 5.9 and 5.11

1 Detach the cable from the negative battery terminal.

2 Clearly label, then remove the fuel lines from the carburetor and plug them to avoid any fuel from spilling onto the engine.

3 Remove the air cleaner (see Chapter 4).

4 Clearly label, then detach all vacuum lines and electrical wires.

5 Detach the accelerator cable from the throttle linkage (see Chapter 4).

6 Detach the power brake vacuum hose from the intake manifold.

7 Raise the front of the vehicle and support it securely on jackstands. Apply the parking brake and block the rear wheels to keep the vehicle from rolling off the jackstands. Detach the exhaust pipe from the exhaust manifold (see Chapter 4).

8 If the vehicle is equipped with an EGR valve, remove the intake manifold support bracket and detach the EGR tube from the exhaust manifold.

9 Remove the intake and exhaust manifold fasteners **(see illustration)**.

10 Lower the vehicle.

11 Remove the carburetor and intake/exhaust manifold as a single as-sembly **(see illustration)**.

12 Detach the carburetor and gasket from the intake manifold (see Chapter 4).

13 Remove the nuts, then separate the intake and exhaust manifolds.

14 Discard the old gaskets and clean all gasket mating surfaces.

15 Clean the manifolds with solvent and dry them with compressed air.

16 Check the mating surfaces of the manifolds for flatness with a precision straightedge and feeler gauges. Refer to this Chapter's Specifications for the warpage limit.

17 Inspect the manifolds for cracks and distortion.

18 If the manifolds are cracked or warped, replace them or see if they can be resurfaced/repaired at an automotive machine shop.

Installation

19 If you're replacing either manifold, transfer the studs from the old manifold to the new one. Clean all mating surfaces with lacquer thinner or acetone.

20 Attach the intake manifold to the exhaust manifold. DO NOT tighten the nuts at this time.

21 Install the carburetor on the manifold (see Chapter 4) and attach the manifold (with a new gasket) to the cylinder head.

22 Tighten all intake and exhaust manifold nuts and bolts until they're just snug (about 10 to 15 in-lbs).

5.9 Remove the fasteners that retain the intake and exhaust manifolds (arrows)

5.11 Remove the bolts and detach the carburetor and intake manifold as a unit

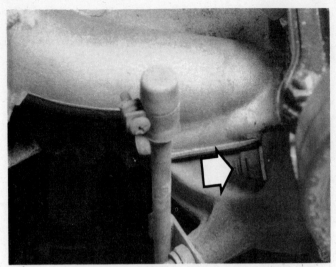

5.39 Apply penetrating oil and let it soak in, then remove the nuts that retain the exhaust manifold to the cylinder head (arrow)

23 Gradually tighten the inner and outer intake manifold-to-exhaust manifold nuts. Alternate between the inner and outer nuts until the torque listed in this Chapter's Specifications is reached. Don't overtighten them.

24 Starting at the center and working out in both directions, gradually tighten the intake and exhaust manifold-to-cylinder head nuts and bolts to the torque listed in this Chapter's Specifications.

25 The remainder of the installation procedure is the reverse of removal.

SOHC engine with fuel-injection/DOHC engine

Removal
Refer to illustration 5.39

26 Disconnect the negative cable from the battery.

27 Drain the cooling system (see Chapter 1).

28 Raise the front of the vehicle and support it securely on jackstands. Apply the parking brake and block the rear wheels to keep the vehicle from rolling off the jackstands.

29 Working under the vehicle, disconnect the exhaust pipe from the manifold (if equipped, unplug the oxygen sensor wire harness connector). **Note:** *Soak the exhaust flange nuts with penetrating oil to help prevent stripping any rusty threads.*

30 Remove the four Allen-head bolts that hold the intake manifold to the cylinder head.

31 Lower the vehicle.

32 Working in the engine compartment, remove the rubber and plastic ducts that connect the throttle valve housing to the mixture control unit.

33 Disconnect all the hoses from the intake manifold and the throttle valve housing. Carefully mark each hose as you remove it so you'll be able to install it in its original location.

34 Disconnect the EGR pipe and the vacuum hose from the EGR valve. Remove the bolts and take the EGR valve off the intake manifold.

35 Remove the fuel injectors (see Chapter 4).

36 Disconnect the accelerator cable from the throttle valve lever connector.

37 Remove the cold-start valve (see Chapter 4).

38 For more working clearance, remove the decel valve (see Chapter 6).

39 Remove the nuts and bolts and detach the intake and exhaust manifolds **(see illustration)**.

40 Discard the gasket and clean the cylinder head and manifold gasket surfaces.

41 Check the gasket mating surfaces of the manifolds for flatness with a precision straightedge and feeler gauges. Refer to this Chapter's Specifications for the warpage limit.

42 Inspect the manifolds for cracks, corrosion and damage. If they're warped or cracked, an automotive machine shop may be able to resurface/repair them.

Installation

43 Clean the manifold and head surfaces with lacquer thinner or acetone. Install a new gasket. **Note:** *Don't use sealant on the manifold gasket.*

44 Place the exhaust manifold in position. Apply anti-seize compound to the threads and install the mounting nuts. Working from the center out in both directions, tighten the nuts in 1/4-turn increments to the torque listed in this Chapter's Specifications.

45 Place the intake manifold in position and install the bolts and washers. Working from the center out in both directions, tighten the bolts in 1/4-turn increments until all bolts are at the torque listed in this Chapter's specifications.

46 Reconnect the throttle linkage, wires and vacuum hoses.

47 Install the fuel injectors (see Chapter 4).

48 Reconnect the exhaust pipe.

49 Install the cold start valve (use a new gasket).

50 Fill the cooling system (see Chapter 1).

51 Connect the negative battery cable.

---

6   Timing belt and sprockets – removal, inspection and installation

Timing belt removal
Refer to illustrations 6.6 and 6.7
Note: *This procedure applies to both SOHC and DOHC engines.*

1 Detach the cable from the negative battery terminal.

2 On carburetor-equipped vehicles, remove the air cleaner assembly and air ducts (see Chapter 4) (this step is unnecessary on vehicles with fuel injection).

3 Remove the air injection pump drivebelt, if equipped (see Chapter 1).

4 Loosen the upper and lower alternator mounting bolts and remove the alternator drivebelt (see Chapter 1).

5 Remove the water pump pulley (see Chapter 3).

6 Remove the nuts and bolts and detach the timing belt cover **(see illustration)**.

7 Loosen the tensioner locknut. To remove tension from the belt, turn the tensioner counterclockwise with a wrench **(see illustration)**. Slide the timing belt off the sprockets.

Timing belt, tensioner and sprocket inspection
Refer to illustration 6.9

8 Rotate the tensioner pulley by hand and move it side-to-side to detect roughness and excessive play. Replace it if it doesn't turn smoothly or if play is noted.

9 Inspect the timing belt for cracks, wear, signs of stretching, ply separation and damaged or missing teeth. Look for contamination by oil, gasoline, coolant and other liquids, which could damage the belt **(see illustration)**. Replace the belt if it's worn or damaged. **Note:** *Unless the engine has very low mileage, it's common practice to replace the timing belt with a new one every time it's removed. Don't reinstall the original belt unless it's in like-new condition. Never reinstall a belt in questionable condition.*

10 Visually inspect the sprockets for wear and damage. If any of the sprockets are damaged or worn, replace them.

11 Inspect the area directly below each sprocket for leaking engine oil. If there's oil below a sprocket, the seal behind it is leaking and must be replaced (see Sections 7, 8 and 9).

Sprocket removal and installation
Refer to illustrations 6.13 and 6.14

12 The camshaft, intermediate shaft and crankshaft sprockets are aligned with each shaft by a Woodruff key and retained by a center bolt and washer. The following procedure applies to all three sprockets.

13 If the factory special tool is available, immobilize the sprocket and loosen the center bolt with a socket and ratchet or breaker bar. If you don't

6.6 Timing belt and related components – exploded view (SOHC engine)

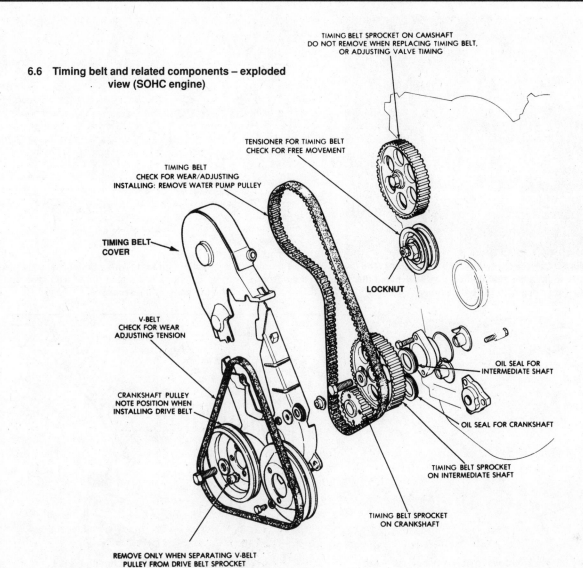

TIMING BELT SPROCKET ON CAMSHAFT
DO NOT REMOVE WHEN REPLACING TIMING BELT,
OR ADJUSTING VALVE TIMING

TENSIONER FOR TIMING BELT
CHECK FOR FREE MOVEMENT

TIMING BELT
CHECK FOR WEAR/ADJUSTING
INSTALLING: REMOVE WATER PUMP PULLEY

TIMING BELT COVER

LOCKNUT

V-BELT
CHECK FOR WEAR
ADJUSTING TENSION

OIL SEAL FOR
INTERMEDIATE SHAFT

CRANKSHAFT PULLEY
NOTE POSITION WHEN
INSTALLING DRIVE BELT

OIL SEAL FOR CRANKSHAFT

TIMING BELT SPROCKET
ON INTERMEDIATE SHAFT

TIMING BELT SPROCKET
ON CRANKSHAFT

REMOVE ONLY WHEN SEPARATING V-BELT
PULLEY FROM DRIVE BELT SPROCKET

6.7 Loosen the locknut and turn the tensioner counterclockwise to release the tension on the timing belt

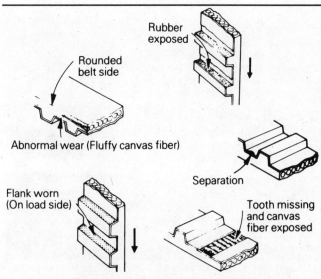

Rubber exposed

Rounded belt side

Abnormal wear (Fluffy canvas fiber)

Separation

Flank worn (On load side)

Tooth missing and canvas fiber exposed

6.9 Carefully inspect the timing belt for the conditions shown here

6.13   Insert a punch or large screwdriver through one of the holes and wedge it against the manifold or head to prevent the sprocket from turning as the bolt is loosened

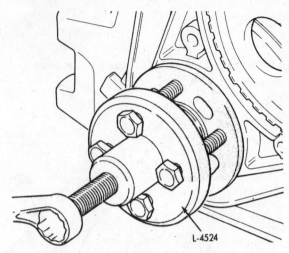

6.14   Remove the crankshaft sprocket with a puller that attaches to the sprocket with bolts – don't use a gear puller with jaws that grip the edge of the sprocket

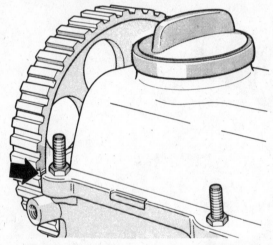

6.16a   Align the dimple or groove in the camshaft sprocket (arrow) with the upper surface of the cylinder head, where the cover mounts (on the front [spark plug] side) of the engine

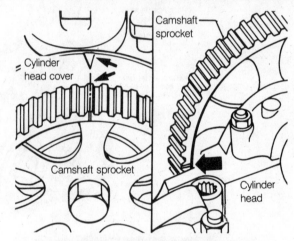

6.16b   DOHC engine camshaft timing marks

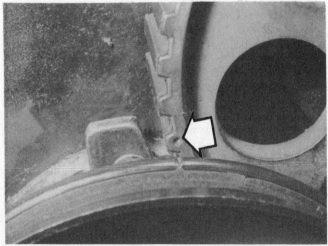

6.17   Align the dimple (arrow) on the intermediate shaft sprocket with the V-notch in the crankshaft pulley

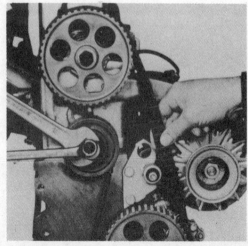

6.19   Using one wrench on the locknut and another on the tension adjuster, turn the tension adjuster until the belt is tight – when the belt is properly adjusted, you should be able to turn it 90-degrees with your thumb and index finger

have the special tool, you can prevent the sprocket from turning by inserting a large drift punch through a hole in the sprocket **(see illustration)**.

14   Pull off the sprocket **(see illustration)**. Don't lose the Woodruff key.

15   To install a sprocket, place the Woodruff key in the slot, align the slot in the sprocket bore with the key, push the sprocket onto the shaft, install the bolt and washer and tighten the bolt to the torque listed in this Chapter's Specifications.

Timing belt installation

Refer to illustrations 6.16a, 6.16b, 6.17 and 6.19

16   Turn the camshaft sprocket by hand until the dimple or groove in the back side is aligned with the cylinder head-to-camshaft cover mounting surface **(see illustrations)**. Note: *The DOHC engine has a groove instead of a dimple in the back side of the sprocket. It also has a groove in the front side that must be aligned with the mark on the cylinder head cover* **(see illustration 6.16b)**.

17   Turn the crankshaft and intermediate shaft by hand until the dimple on the intermediate shaft sprocket is aligned with the V-notch in the crankshaft pulley **(see illustration)**. Note: *The intermediate shaft on the DOHC engine doesn't have to be timed.*

18   Install the timing belt on the crankshaft sprocket first, then on the camshaft sprocket. Don't allow any slack between the crankshaft and intermediate shaft sprockets or between the intermediate shaft and camshaft sprockets. In other words, make sure all the slack in the timing belt is at the tensioner, between the crankshaft and the camshaft sprockets.

19   Using a wrench on the tensioner, tighten the belt until you can just barely twist it 90-degrees with your thumb and finger at a point halfway between the camshaft and intermediate shaft sprockets **(see illustration)**.

20   Tighten the tensioner locknut securely, then check the timing marks on the crankshaft pulley and the intermediate shaft sprocket. If they have moved out of alignment, remove the timing belt and repeat the installation procedure.

21   The remainder of installation is the reverse of removal. Be sure to adjust the drivebelt tension when reassembly is complete (see Chapter 1).

7   Camshaft oil seal – replacement

Refer to illustration 7.6

Note: *The following procedure applies to the camshaft oil seal on both SOHC and DOHC engines.*

1   Remove the timing belt and camshaft sprocket (see Section 6).

2   On DOHC engines, remove the ignition distributor from the cylinder head (see Chapter 5).

3   Wrap the tip of a small screwdriver with tape and use it to carefully pry out the seal. Don't nick or scratch the camshaft journal or the new seal will leak.

4   Thoroughly clean and inspect the seal bore and the seal journal on the camshaft. Both must be clean and smooth. Use emery cloth or 400-grit sandpaper to remove small burrs.

5   If a groove has been worn into the journal on the camshaft (from contact with the seal lip), installing a new seal probably won't stop the leak. Such wear normally indicates the camshaft or the bearing surfaces in the caps are worn. It's probably time to overhaul the cylinder head (see Chapter 2, Part B) or replace the head or camshaft.

6   Coat the lip of the new seal with clean engine oil or moly-base grease and carefully tap the seal into place with a large socket or piece of pipe and a hammer **(see illustration)**. If you don't have a socket as large in diameter as the seal, tap around the outer edge of the seal with the large end of a punch.

7   Install the camshaft sprocket and timing belt (see Section 6).

8   Start the engine and check for oil leaks.

8   Intermediate shaft oil seal – replacement

Refer to illustrations 8.3 and 8.8

Note: *The following procedure applies to the intermediate shaft oil seal on both SOHC and DOHC engines*

1   Drain the engine oil (see Chapter 1).

2   Remove the timing belt and intermediate shaft sprocket (Section 6).

3   Remove the oil seal housing **(see illustration)**.

4   Pry the old seal out of the housing with a screwdriver (wrap the tip of the screwdriver with tape). Make sure you don't scratch the seal bore.

5   Thoroughly clean and inspect the seal bore and the seal journal on the intermediate shaft. Both must be clean and smooth. Remove small burrs with emery cloth or 400 grit sandpaper.

6   If a groove has been worn in the seal journal (from contact with the seal lip), installing a new seal probably won't stop the leak. Such wear normally indicates the intermediate shaft or shaft bearing surfaces in the engine block are worn. It's probably time to overhaul the engine (see Chapter 2, Part B).

7   Using a soft-face hammer, carefully tap the new seal into the housing.

8   Coat the lip of the seal with clean engine oil or moly-base grease and install the housing and seal on the front of the engine block. Make sure the O-ring is in place and in good condition **(see illustration)** and don't damage the seal lip. Install the housing bolts and tighten them to the torque listed in this Chapter's specifications.

9   Install the intermediate shaft sprocket and the timing belt (Section 6).

10   Check the engine oil level and add oil, if necessary (see Chapter 1).

11   Start the engine and check for oil leaks.

7.6   Carefully tap the seal into place with a large socket and hammer

8.3   The intermediate shaft oil seal housing is attached to the block with two bolts (arrows)

8.8   Make sure the O-ring (arrow) at the rear of the housing is in place

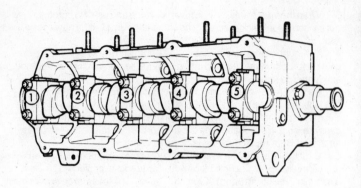

10.3a   The camshaft bearing caps are numbered beginning from the drivebelt end of the engine – they must be reinstalled in their original locations

10.3b   Note that the bearing cap numbers are offset to one side – make sure they're reinstalled the exact same way!

9   Crankshaft front oil seal – replacement

Note: *The following procedure applies to the crankshaft oil seal on both SOHC and DOHC engines.*

1   Drain the engine oil (see Chapter 1).
2   Remove the timing belt and crankshaft sprocket (see Section 6).
3   Raise the front of the vehicle and support it securely on jackstands. Apply the parking brake and block the rear wheels to keep the vehicle from rolling off the jackstands.
4   Working underneath the vehicle, remove the bolts and detach the oil seal housing.
5   Use a punch and hammer to drive the old seal out of the housing. Make sure you don't damage the seal bore.
6   Thoroughly clean the seal bore in the housing and the seal journal on the end of the crankshaft. Remove small burrs with emery cloth or 400-grit sandpaper. Clean the housing and block mating surfaces with lacquer thinner or acetone to remove all traces of oil and old sealant.
7   If a groove has been worn in the seal journal on the crankshaft (from contact with the seal lip), installing a new seal probably won't stop the leak. Such wear normally indicates the crankshaft and/or the main bearings are excessively worn. It's probably time to overhaul the engine (see Chapter 2, Part B).
8   Apply a thin coat of RTV sealant to the surface of the seal bore, lay the housing on a clean, flat work surface, position the new seal in the bore and tap it into place with a large socket and a hammer.
9   Lubricate the seal lip with moly-base grease and apply a 1 mm wide bead of anaerobic gasket sealant to the engine block mating surface of the seal housing. Position the housing on the engine. Install the retaining bolts and tighten them to the torque listed in this Chapter's specifications.
10   Reinstall the crankshaft sprocket, timing belt and related components.
11   Check the engine oil level and add oil, if necessary (see Chapter 1).
12   Start the engine, let it warm up and check for leaks.

10   Camshaft and cam followers – removal, inspection and installation

Note: *If the valvetrain is making noise, and you suspect the hydraulic cam followers are causing it, before removing them for inspection, make sure the engine oil level is correct and allow some time after a cold start for the followers to quiet down. If the noise is still excessive, check the followers – just make sure the engine is warmed up completely (be careful not to burn yourself when working on a hot engine). Refer to Section 4 and remove the camshaft cover. Turn the crankshaft until all cam lobes for the first cylinder are pointing away from the followers, then try to push the followers down with a wood or plastic tool. If a follower can be depressed more than*

10.7   Remove the cam followers and shims (if used) and keep them together – store hydraulic followers with the camshaft surface down

0.004-inch (0.1 mm) with hand pressure only (which isn't very much movement), it's defective and should be replaced. Repeat the check for all followers (make sure the cam lobes are pointing up when the check is done). Hydraulic followers are not adjustable or repairable – if they're defective, they must be discarded and new ones must be installed.

SOHC engine

Removal
Refer to illustrations 10.3a, 10.3b and 10.7

1   Remove the camshaft cover, if not already done (Section 4).
2   Remove the timing belt cover, timing belt and camshaft sprocket (see Section 6). **Note:** *If you want to save time by not removing and installing the timing belt, you can unfasten the camshaft sprocket and suspend it out of the way – with the belt still attached – on a piece of wire. Be sure the wire maintains tension on the belt so it won't disengage any of the sprockets.*
3   The camshaft rides on five bearings. Each bearing cap is held by two fasteners. On some engines, the bearing caps are numbered from 1 to 5, beginning at the drivebelt end of the engine **(see illustrations)**. **Note:** *All numbers face either the spark plug or manifold side of the engine. This is to ensure you install the caps facing the right direction.*

10.8   To check camshaft endplay, set up a dial indicator like this, with the gauge stem touching the nose of the camshaft

10.9   A dial indicator and V-blocks are needed to measure camshaft runout

4   On some engines, the bearing caps aren't numbered. If this is the case, you must mark them before removal. Be sure to put the marks on the same ends of all the caps to prevent incorrect orientation of the caps during installation.

5   Remove the nuts and washers from all bearing caps except numbers 2 and 4. Next, loosen each of the four fasteners on 2 and 4 a little at a time to relieve valve spring tension evenly until the caps are loose. If any of the caps stick, gently tap them with a soft-face hammer. **Caution:** *Failure to follow this procedure exactly as described could tilt the camshaft in the bearings, which could damage the bearings or bend the camshaft.*

6   Lift out the camshaft, wipe it off with a clean shop towel and set it aside.

7   If equipped, wipe off each valve adjustment shim with a clean shop towel and number it with a felt-tip marker. Remove each cam follower/valve adjustment shim set and set them aside in labelled plastic bags or an egg carton to keep them from getting mixed up **(see illustration)**. **Note:** *Hydraulic cam followers should be removed, placed on a clean surface with the camshaft contact surface facing DOWN (to prevent bleed-down) and covered with a clean shop towel.*

Inspection

Refer to illustrations 10.8 and 10.9

Note: *The following procedure applies to both SOHC and DOHC engines.*

8   To check camshaft endplay:
   a) Install the camshaft and secure it with caps 1 and 5.
   b) Mount a dial indicator on the head **(see illustration)**.
   c) Using a large screwdriver as a lever at the opposite end, move the camshaft forward-and-backward and note the dial indicator reading.
   d) Compare the reading with the endplay listed in this Chapter's Specifications.
   e) If the indicated reading is excessive, either the camshaft or the head is worn. Replace parts as necessary.

9   To check camshaft runout:
   a) Mount the camshaft between a pair of V-blocks and attach a dial indicator with the stem resting against the center bearing journal on the camshaft.
   b) Rotate the camshaft and note the indicated runout **(see illustration)**.
   c) Compare the results to the camshaft runout listed in this Chapter's Specifications.
   d) If the indicated runout exceeds the specified runout, replace the camshaft.

10   To check the camshaft bearing oil clearance, refer to Section 22 in Part B of Chapter 2. If the clearance at any of the journals exceeds the specified limit, replace the head.

11   Check the cam lobes for wear:
   a) Check the toe and ramp areas of each cam lobe for score marks and uneven wear. Also check for flaking and pitting.

   b) If there's wear on the toe or the ramp, replace the camshaft, but first try to find the cause of the wear. Check the valve clearances (see Chapter 1), look for abrasive substances in the oil and inspect the oil pump and oil passages for blockage. Lobe wear is usually caused by inadequate lubrication or dirty oil.

12   Check the valve adjustment shims. They're usually worn too if the camshaft lobes are worn. If the shims are worn, replace them.

13   Inspect the cam followers for galling and signs of seizure. If aluminum from the cylinder head is adhering to cam followers, replace them. If any of the cam follower bores are rough, scored or worn, replace the cylinder head.

14   If any of the conditions described above are noted, the cylinder head is probably getting insufficient lubrication or dirty oil, so make sure you track down the cause of this problem (low oil level, low oil pump capacity, clogged oil passage, etc.) before installing a new head, camshaft or followers.

Installation

Refer to illustration 10.17

Note: *If new hydraulic cam followers are installed, the engine must be allowed to sit without starting it for at least 30 minutes after reassembly. If the engine is started before the followers have bled down, the valves may contact the pistons and cause extensive engine damage.*

15   Thoroughly clean the camshaft, the bearing surfaces in the head and caps, the cam followers and shims (if used). Remove all sludge and dirt. Wipe off all components with a clean, lint-free cloth.

16   Lightly lubricate the cam follower bores with assembly lube or moly-base grease. Refer to the numbers marked on the shims and install the cam followers and valve adjustment shims in the head. Lubricate the upper side of the shims with assembly lube or moly-base grease.

17   Lubricate the camshaft bearing surfaces in the head and the bearing journals and lobes on the camshaft with assembly lube or moly-base grease. Slide a new oil seal onto the front of the camshaft, then carefully lower the camshaft into position with the lobes for the number one cylinder pointing away from the cam followers **(see illustration)**. **Caution:** *Failure to adequately lubricate the camshaft and related components can cause serious damage to bearing and friction surfaces during the first few seconds after engine start-up, when the oil pressure is low or nonexistent.*

18   Apply a thin coat of assembly lube or moly-base grease to the bearing surfaces of the camshaft bearing caps and install the caps in their original locations.

19   Install the nuts/bolts for bearing caps 2 and 5. Gradually tighten all four fasteners – 1/4-turn at a time – until the camshaft is drawn down and seated in the bearing saddles. Don't tighten the fasteners completely at this time.

20   Install bearing caps 3 and 4 and tighten the fasteners the same way you did for caps 2 and 5.

2A

21 Next, install bearing cap 1. Don't tighten the fasteners completely at this time.

22 Working in a criss-cross pattern, tighten the fasteners for bearing caps 2 and 4 to the torque listed in this Chapter's Specifications. Then torque the fasteners for bearing caps 3 and 5 the same way. Finally, tighten the fasteners for bearing cap 1.

23 Install the camshaft sprocket, timing belt, timing belt cover and related components (see Section 6). If you suspended the camshaft sprocket out of the way and didn't disturb the timing belt or sprockets, the valve timing should still be correct. Rotate the camshaft as necessary to reattach the sprocket to the camshaft. If the valve timing was disturbed, align the sprockets and install the belt as described in Section 6.

24 Remove the spark plugs and rotate the crankshaft by hand to make sure the valve timing is correct. After two revolutions, the timing marks on the sprockets should still be aligned. If they're not, reindex the timing belt to the sprockets (see Section 6). **Note:** *If you feel resistance while rotating the crankshaft, stop immediately and check the valve timing by referring to Section 6.*

DOHC engine

Removal

Refer to illustration 10.28

Note: *The DOHC engine is equipped with a separate timing chain that connects the two camshafts.*

25 Turn the engine over by hand until the no. 1 piston is at Top Dead Center (TDC) and remove the timing belt from the camshaft sprocket (see Section 6).

26 Remove the camshaft cover and gasket, if not already done (see Section 4).

27 Remove the distributor from the rear of the cylinder head (see Chapter 5).

28 Remove the nuts and detach the two very end bearing caps on the exhaust side as well as the single end bearing cap on the intake side (nearest to the chain connecting the camshafts). Next, remove the nuts and detach bearing caps 1, 3, 5 and 7 **(see illustration)**.

29 Loosen each of the nuts for bearing caps 2, 4, 6 and 8 in 1/4-turn increments so valve spring pressure and cam chain tension are relieved evenly. **Caution:** *Follow this procedure exactly – removal of the camshaft bearing caps by any other method may damage the camshafts, the camshaft chain or the bearing caps.*

30 Lift the camshafts out of the cylinder head and separate them from the timing chain.

Inspection

31 Refer to the inspection procedure for the SOHC engine. In addition, check the cam chain and sprockets for wear and damage.

Installation

Refer to illustration 10.35

Note: *If new hydraulic cam followers are installed, the engine must be allowed to sit without starting it for at least 30 minutes. If the engine is started before the followers have bled down, the valves may contact the pistons and cause extensive engine damage.*

32 Thoroughly clean the camshaft, the bearing surfaces in the head and caps and the cam followers. Remove all sludge and dirt. Wipe off all components with a clean, lint-free cloth.

33 Lightly lubricate the cam follower bores with assembly lube or moly-base grease. Install the cam followers in the head. Lubricate the upper side of the followers with assembly lube or moly-base grease.

34 Lubricate the camshaft bearing surfaces in the head and the bearing journals and lobes on the camshaft with assembly lube or moly-base grease. **Caution:** *Failure to adequately lubricate the camshaft and related components can cause serious damage to bearing and friction surfaces during the first few seconds after engine start-up, when the oil pressure is low or nonexistent.*

10.17   Slide the new seal onto the camshaft nose, then position the camshaft in the head – turn it until the lobes for the number one cylinder are pointing away from the followers

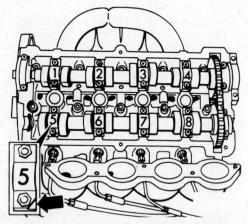

10.28   Top view of the DOHC engine cylinder head showing the camshaft bearing cap locations – the inset shows the bearing cap bevelled corner that must face the intake side of the engine

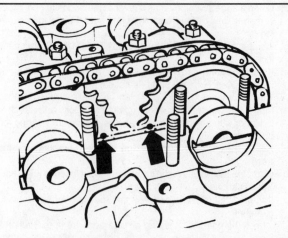

10.35   Align the camshaft drive chain sprocket dimples with the cylinder head surface (DOHC engine)

35   Install the camshafts and chain so the marks on the sprockets face each other and align with the top of the cylinder head **(see illustration)**.

36   Install the bearing caps in their original locations with the bevelled corners facing the intake manifold side of the engine.

37   Install the nuts for bearing caps 2, 4, 6 and 8. Gradually tighten all fasteners – 1/4-turn at a time – until the camshafts are drawn down and seated in the bearing saddles. Don't tighten the fasteners completely at this time.

38   Install bearing caps 1, 3, 5 and 7 and tighten the fasteners the same way you did for the other caps.

39   Install a new oil seal on the front of the camshaft, then position the end bearing cap and install the nuts – don't tighten the nuts completely at this time. Position the bearing caps on the other end of the head (nearest the cam chain) and install the nuts.

40   Working in a criss-cross pattern, tighten the nuts for bearing caps 2, 4, 6 and 8 to the torque listed in this Chapter's Specifications. Then torque the fasteners for bearing caps 1, 3, 5 and 7 the same way. Finally, tighten the fasteners for the three end bearing caps.

41   Refer to Steps 23 and 24 in the SOHC engine procedure.

42   Install the ignition distributor and adjust the ignition timing (see Chapter 1).

11   Cylinder head – removal and installation

Caution: *Allow the engine to cool completely before beginning this procedure.*

Removal

Refer to illustration 11.10

1   Position the number one piston at Top Dead Center (Section 3).

2   Disconnect the negative cable from the battery.

3   Drain the cooling system and remove the spark plugs (Chapter 1).

4   Remove the intake/exhaust manifold (see Section 5). **Note:** *If you're only replacing the cylinder head gasket, it's not absolutely necessary to remove the manifold. If you leave the manifold attached, you may need an assistant to help lift the head off the engine.*

5   Remove the distributor (see Chapter 5), including the cap and wires.

6   If the engine is equipped with a carburetor, remove the fuel pump (see Chapter 4).

7   If the engine is equipped with fuel injection, pull out the fuel injectors and remove the cold start valve from the intake manifold (leave the fuel lines attached). Be sure to cover the cold start valve and injectors to keep dirt from entering.

8   Remove the timing belt (see Section 6).

9   Remove the camshaft cover (see Section 4).

10   Loosen the head bolts in 1/4-turn increments until they can be removed by hand **(see illustration)**. Reverse the tightening sequence to avoid warping the head **(see illustration 11.18)**.

11   Lift the head off the engine. If resistance is felt, don't pry between the head and block – damage to the mating surfaces will result. To dislodge the head, place a block of wood against the end and strike the wood block with a hammer. Store the head on blocks of wood to prevent damage to the gasket sealing surfaces.

12   Cylinder head disassembly and inspection procedures are covered in detail in Chapter 2, Part B. It's a good idea to have the head checked for warpage, even if you're just replacing the gasket.

Installation

Refer to illustrations 11.17a, 11.17b and 11.18

13   The mating surfaces of the cylinder head and block must be perfectly clean when the head is installed.

14   Use a gasket scraper to remove all traces of carbon and old gasket material, then clean the mating surfaces with lacquer thinner or acetone. If there's oil on the mating surfaces when the head is installed, the gasket may not seal correctly and leaks may develop. When working on the block, stuff the cylinders with clean shop rags to keep out debris. Use a vacuum cleaner to remove material that falls into the cylinders. Since the head is made of aluminum, aggressive scraping can cause damage. Be extra careful not to nick or gouge the mating surfaces with the scraper.

15   Check the block and head mating surfaces for nicks, deep scratches and other damage. If damage is slight, it can be removed with a file; if it's excessive, machining may be the only alternative.

16   Use a tap of the correct size to chase the threads in the head bolt holes. Mount each bolt in a vise and run a die down the threads to remove corrosion and restore the threads. Dirt, corrosion, sealant and damaged threads will affect torque readings.

17   Place a new gasket on the block. The word "OBEN" (TOP), imprinted on the gasket near the part number, should face up **(see illustrations)**. Set the cylinder head in position.

11.10   Loosen the head bolts 1/4-turn at a time until they can be removed by hand – some head bolts require a 12-point internal socket driver (shown here), while others require a hex socket (Allen-head) tool

11.17a   When you put the new head gasket in position on the engine block, be sure the "OBEN" (TOP) mark is facing up . . .

11.17b . . . and on the correct side of the block – the holes in the gasket must match the passages in the block for coolant and oil to circulate properly

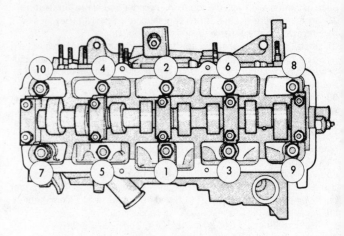

11.18   Cylinder head bolt TIGHTENING sequence – reverse the sequence for removal

18   Install the bolts. They must be tightened in several steps, following a specific sequence **(see illustration)**, to the torque listed in this Chapter's Specifications.
19   Reinstall the timing belt (see Section 6).
20   Reinstall the remaining parts in the reverse order of removal.
21   Be sure to refill the cooling system and check all fluid levels.
22   Rotate the crankshaft clockwise slowly by hand through two complete revolutions. Recheck the camshaft timing marks (see Section 6).
23   Start the engine and check the ignition timing (see Chapter 1).
24   Run the engine until normal operating temperature is reached. Check for leaks and proper operation.

12   Oil pan – removal and installation

Refer to illustration 12.4
Note: *The following procedure is based on the assumption the engine is in the vehicle. If you're working on an engine that's out of the vehicle, mounted on a stand, it's not necessary to use sealant to hold the gasket in place on the engine block. Just turn the engine upside-down.*

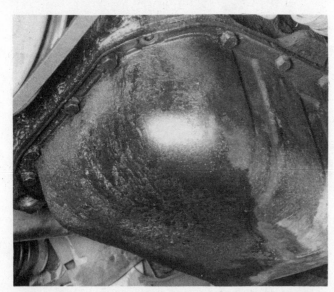

12.4   Remove the bolts that retain the oil pan to the block

1   Warm up the engine, then drain the oil and replace the oil filter (see Chapter 1).
2   Detach the cable from the negative battery terminal.
3   Raise the vehicle and support it securely on jackstands.
4   Remove the bolts securing the oil pan to the engine block **(see illustration)**.
5   Tap on the pan with a soft-face hammer to break the gasket seal, then detach the oil pan from the engine.
6   Using a gasket scraper, remove all traces of old gasket and/or sealant from the engine block and oil pan. Clean the mating surfaces with lacquer thinner or acetone. Make sure the threaded bolt holes in the block are clean.
7   Clean the oil pan with solvent and dry it thoroughly. Check the gasket flanges for distortion, particularly around the bolt holes. If necessary, place the pan on a block of wood and use a hammer to flatten and restore the gasket surfaces.
8   Attach the new gasket to the engine block with a few dabs of sealant to hold it in place.
9   Apply a 1/8-inch wide bead of RTV sealant to the oil pan gasket surfaces. Continue the bead across the end seals. Make sure the sealant is applied to the inside of the bolt holes.
10   Carefully place the oil pan in position.
11   Install the bolts and tighten them in 1/4-turn increments to the torque listed in this Chapter's Specifications. Start with the bolts closest to the center of the pan and work out in a spiral pattern. Don't overtighten them or leakage may occur.
12   Add oil, run the engine and check for oil leaks.

13   Oil pump – removal, inspection and installation

Removal
Refer to illustration 13.2
1   Remove the oil pan (see Section 12).
2   Remove the oil pump mounting bolts **(see illustration)**.
3   Detach the oil pump assembly.

Inspection
Refer to illustrations 13.4, 13.7 and 13.8
4   Pry off the oil deflector plate with a screwdriver and set the plate aside. Remove the strainer. Wash the plate and strainer in clean solvent. Unbolt the oil pump cover and wash it in clean solvent. Check the face of the pump cover for score marks **(see illustration)**. If it's worn or damaged, replace the pump.

13.2   Remove the oil pump mounting bolts and detach the pump from the engine block

13.4   Check the face of the oil pump cover for score marks

2A

13.7   To check gear backlash, insert feeler gauge(s) between the gear teeth

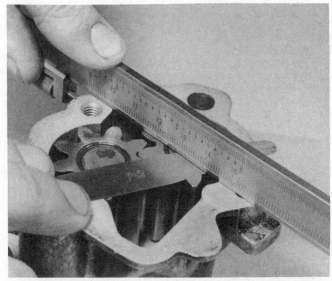

13.8   Check the gear endplay by placing a precision straightedge across the pump housing like this and inserting feeler gauges between the gear faces and the straightedge

5   Look inside the pump body at the two gears. If any of the gear teeth are broken, replace the pump. You should consider an engine overhaul too, because metal particles have probably caused damage elsewhere in the engine.

6   Turn the pump main shaft and see if the gears rotate smoothly inside the pump body. If they don't, replace the pump.

7   To measure gear backlash, remove the gears, clean them and the inside of the pump body, reinstall them and try to slide various size feeler gauges between the gear teeth **(see illustration)**. The feeler gauge that slides between the gears with a slight drag should be within the range listed in this Chapter's Specifications. If it isn't, replace the pump.

8   To measure gear endplay, place a straightedge across the gear faces and try to stick a 0.006-inch feeler gauge between the gear faces and the straightedge **(see illustration)**. It shouldn't fit. If it does, try a 0.007-inch gauge. If it fits, replace the pump.

9   If you replace the pump, swap the strainer and deflector plate from the old pump to the new one.

10   Reassemble the pump and tighten the housing bolts (the shorter ones) securely. Make sure the deflector plate and strainer are properly assembled.

Installation

11   Put a small dab of assembly lube or moly-base grease on the tip of the oil pump driveshaft. Install the pump and tighten the mounting bolts to the torque listed in this Chapter's specifications. If the oil pick-up has been removed from the pump cover, replace the O-ring when installing the pick-up. Check the strainer one more time to make sure it's properly seated in the end of the oil pump cover. If it's loose, use a pair of locking pliers to crimp the edges tighter.

12   Install the oil pan (see Section 12).

14.3   Driveplate and related components – exploded view (the notch in the washer faces the driveplate; the shim is used to achieve correct driveplate-to-engine block clearance)

14   Driveplate – removal and installation

Refer to illustrations 14.3 and 14.8
Note: *This procedure doesn't apply to manual transaxle models. Removing the flywheel on these models is part of the clutch removal procedure (see Chapter 8).*

Removal

1   Raise the vehicle and support it securely on jackstands, then refer to Chapter 7 and remove the transaxle. If it's leaking, now would be a very good time to replace the front pump seal/O-ring.
2   Use a center punch to make alignment marks on the driveplate and crankshaft to ensure correct alignment during reinstallation.
3   Remove the bolts that secure the driveplate to the crankshaft **(see illustration)**. If the crankshaft turns, wedge a screwdriver through the starter opening to jam the driveplate teeth.
4   Detach the driveplate from the crankshaft.

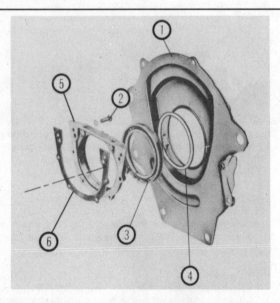

15.5   Typical crankshaft rear oil seal and housing – exploded view

1	Intermediate plate	4	Sealing ring (not used on all models)
2	Bolt	5	Seal housing
3	Oil seal	6	Gasket

14.8   Use a depth gauge to measure the driveplate-to-engine block clearance

5   Clean the driveplate to remove grease and oil. Check for cracked and broken ring gear teeth.
6   Clean and inspect the mating surfaces of the driveplate and crankshaft. If the crankshaft rear seal is leaking, replace it before reinstalling the driveplate.

Installation

7   Position the driveplate against the crankshaft. Be sure to align the marks made during removal. Note that some engines have an alignment dowel or staggered bolt holes to ensure correct installation. Before installing the bolts, apply thread locking compound to the threads.
8   Check the driveplate-to-engine block clearance **(see illustration)**. If necessary, use a shim to achieve the dimension listed in this Chapter's Specifications.
9   Wedge a screwdriver through the starter motor opening to keep the driveplate from turning as you tighten the bolts to the torque listed in this Chapter's Specifications.
10   The remainder of installation is the reverse of the removal procedure.

15   Crankshaft rear oil seal – replacement

Refer to illustrations 15.5, 15.8a, 15.8b and 15.9
1   Remove the transaxle (See Chapter 7).
2   If the vehicle has a manual transaxle, remove the clutch and flywheel (see Chapter 8).

15.8a   Use a soft-face hammer to tap the new seal into the housing

15.8b Be sure to lubricate the seal lips (arrows) before slipping it over the end of the crankshaft

15.9 Make sure the new gasket is correctly positioned on the block before installing the seal housing assembly

2A

3   If the vehicle has an automatic transaxle, remove the driveplate (see Section 14).
4   Remove the oil pan (see Section 12).
5   Remove the rear oil seal housing and gasket **(see illustration)**.
6   Support the housing on wood blocks and drive the seal out with a hammer and punch.
7   Thoroughly clean the seal bore in the housing with a shop towel. Remove all traces of oil and dirt.
8   Apply a small amount of grease or oil to the outer edge of the new seal, then carefully tap it into the housing with a soft-face hammer **(see illustration)**. Coat the seal lip with moly-base grease so it'll slide onto the crankshaft easily **(see illustration)**.
9   Install a new gasket **(see illustration)** (the dowel pins will hold it in place). Install the housing/seal assembly and tighten the bolts to the torque listed in this Chapter's Specifications.
10   Install the driveplate or flywheel and clutch (if equipped).
11   Install the transaxle.

16   Engine mounts – check and replacement

Refer to illustrations 16.4a, 16.4b, 16.4c and 16.5
1   Engine mounts seldom require attention, but broken or deteriorated mounts should be replaced immediately or the added strain placed on the driveline components may cause damage or wear.

Check

2   During the check, the engine must be raised slightly to remove the weight from the mounts.
3   Raise the vehicle and support it securely on jackstands, then position a jack under the engine oil pan. Place a large block of wood between the jack head and the oil pan, then carefully raise the engine just enough to take the weight off the mounts.
4   Check the mount insulators **(see illustrations)** to see if the rubber is

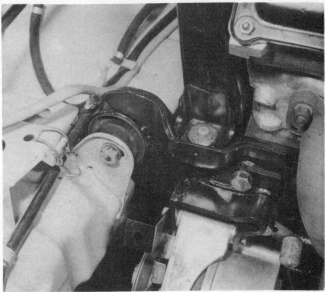

16.4a Typical rear engine-to-frame mount

16.4b Typical front engine-to-frame mount

16.4c   Typical front transaxle mount

16.5   Use a large prybar to try to move the mount (if there's play between the two mount brackets, replace the mount)

cracked, hardened or separated from the metal plates. Sometimes the rubber will split right down the center.

5   Check for relative movement between the mount plates and the engine or frame (use a large screwdriver or prybar to attempt to move the mounts) **(see illustration)**. If movement is noted, lower the engine and tighten the mount fasteners.

6   Rubber preservative should be applied to the insulators to slow deterioration.

Replacement

7   Disconnect the negative battery cable from the battery, then raise the vehicle and support it securely on jackstands (if not already done).

8   Remove the frame-to-mount bracket fasteners.

9   Raise the engine slightly with a jack or hoist. Remove the mount-to-engine or transaxle nuts and/or bolts and detach the mount.

10   Installation is the reverse of removal. Use thread locking compound on all fasteners and be sure to tighten them securely.

Chapter 2 Part B
General engine overhaul procedures

Contents

Crankshaft – inspection 18
Crankshaft – installation and main bearing oil clearance check . . 22
Cylinder compression check 3
Cylinder head – cleaning and inspection 9
Cylinder head – disassembly 8
Cylinder head – reassembly 11
Cylinder honing 16
Engine block – cleaning 14
Engine block – inspection 15
Engine overhaul – disassembly sequence 7
Engine overhaul – general information 2
Engine overhaul – reassembly sequence 20
Engine rebuilding alternatives 6
Engine – removal and installation 5

Crankshaft – removal 13

Engine removal – methods and precautions 4
General information 1
Initial start-up and break-in after overhaul 25
Main and connecting rod bearings – inspection 19
Pistons/connecting rods – inspection 17
Pistons/connecting rods – installation and rod bearing
    oil clearance check 24
Pistons/connecting rods – removal 12
Piston rings – installation 21
Rear main oil seal – installation 23
Valves – servicing 10

2B

Specifications

General

Engine code letter

1975	
Manual transaxle	FC
Automatic transaxle	FG
1976 and 1977	
Carbureted	FN
Fuel-injected	
Manual transaxle	EE
Automatic transaxle	EF
1978 (fuel-injected)	EH
1979 (fuel-injected)	
Rabbit	EH
Scirocco	EJ
1980	
1.5 liter engine (carbureted)	FX
1.6 liter engine (fuel-injected)	EJ
1981 through 1984 (1.7 liter engine)	EN
1983 and 1984 (1.8 liter engine)	JH
1985 on (GTI, Golf and Jetta)	
GTI and Jetta GLI only (CIS-E)	
1985 only	HT
1986 on	RD
CIS/CIS-E	GX
CIS (Canada only)	MZ
Digifant II	RV/PF
DOHC engine	
CIS-E	PL
CIS-E Motronic	9A

Displacement

Engine code FX, EH and FH	88.9 cu in
Engine code FC and FG	89.7 cu in
Engine code EJ, EF and EE	96.9 cu in
Engine code EN	105.0 cu in
Engine code JH, GX, MZ, HT, RD, RV, PF and PL	109.0 cu in
Engine code 9A	121 cu in

Oil pressure (at 2000 rpm) .... 28 psi

Cylinder compression pressure

Engine code GX	131 to 174 psi
Engine code HT, RD, PL, RV and PF	145 to 189 psi
All others	Not available

Cylinder head

Warpage limit .... 0.004 in (0.10 mm)

Valves

Stem diameter	
Intake	
SOHC engine	0.314 in (7.97 mm)
DOHC engine	0.2744 in (6.97 mm)
Exhaust	
SOHC engine	0.3130 in (7.95 mm)
DOHC engine	0.2732 in (6.94 mm)
Stem-to-guide clearance	
Intake	0.039 in (1.0 mm)
Exhaust	0.059 in (1.3 mm)
Valve margin width (minimum)	0.020 in (0.5 mm)
Seat angle	45-degrees
Spring	
Free length	Not available
Installed height	Not available

Camshaft

Maximum endplay (except 16-valve) .... 0.006 in (0.15 mm)

Crankshaft

Maximum endplay	0.010 in (0.25 mm)
Main bearing journal diameter	2.124 to 2.125 in (53.96 to 53.98 mm)
Connecting rod journal diameter	
Engine codes JH, GX, M2, HT, RD, RV, PF and PL	1.880 to 1.881 in (47.76 to 47.78 mm)
Engine codes FX, EJ, and EN	1.809 to 1.810 in (45.96 to 45.98 mm)
Engine code 9A	1.881 to 1.882 in (47.78 to 47.80 mm)
Journal out-of-round/taper limits	0.0012 in (0.03 mm)
Main bearing oil clearance	
Standard	0.0012 to 0.003 in (0.03 to 0.08 mm)
Service limit	0.007 in (0.17 mm)
Connecting rod bearing oil clearance through 1984	0.001 to 0.004 in (0.028 to 0.088 mm)
1985 on	0.005 (0.12 mm)
Connecting rod endplay (side clearance) limit	0.014 in (0.37 mm)
Intermediate shaft side clearance	0.010 in (0.25 mm)

Engine block

Cylinder taper limit	0.002 in (0.050 mm)
Block deck warpage limit	0.004 in (0.10 mm)

Pistons and piston rings

Piston-to-bore clearance	
Standard	0.0012 in (0.030 mm)
Service limit	0.0030 in (0.08 mm)
Piston ring side clearance limit	0.0008 to 0.0019 in (0.02 to 0.05 mm)
Piston ring end gap	
Compression ring	0.012 to 0.017 in (0.30 to 0.45 mm)
Oil ring	0.010 to 0.016 in (0.25 to 0.40 mm)

Torque specifications*   Ft-lbs

Main bearing cap bolts	48
Connecting rod bearing cap nuts	
Engine code JH	22 plus an additional 1/2-turn
Engine code GX, MZ, HT, RD, RV and PF	22 plus an additional 1/4-turn
All others	32
Bellhousing bolts	59

***Note:** *Refer to Part A for additional torque specifications.*

---

1   General information

Included in this portion of Chapter 2 are the general overhaul procedures for the cylinder head and internal engine components.

The information ranges from advice concerning preparation for an overhaul and the purchase of replacement parts to detailed, step-by-step procedures covering removal and installation of internal engine components and the inspection of parts.

The following Sections have been written based on the assumption that the engine has been removed from the vehicle. For information concerning in-vehicle engine repair, as well as removal and installation of the external components necessary for the overhaul, see Part A of this Chapter and Section 7 of this Part.

The Specifications included in this Part are only those necessary for the inspection and overhaul procedures which follow. Refer to Part A for additional Specifications.

2   Engine overhaul – general information

Refer to illustration 2.4

It's not always easy to determine when, or if, an engine should be completely overhauled, as a number of factors must be considered.

High mileage is not necessarily an indication that an overhaul is needed, while low mileage doesn't preclude the need for an overhaul. Frequency of servicing is probably the most important consideration. An engine that's had regular and frequent oil and filter changes, as well as other required maintenance, will most likely give many thousands of miles of reliable service. Conversely, a neglected engine may require an overhaul very early in its life.

Excessive oil consumption is an indication that piston rings, valve seals and/or valve guides are in need of attention. Make sure that oil leaks aren't responsible before deciding the rings and/or guides are bad. Perform a cylinder compression check to determine the extent of the work required (see Section 3).

Check the oil pressure with a gauge installed in place of the oil pressure sending unit **(see illustration)** and compare it to this Chapter's Specifications. If it's extremely low, the bearings and/or oil pump are probably worn out.

Loss of power, rough running, knocking or metallic engine noises, excessive valve train noise and high fuel consumption rates may also point to the need for an overhaul, especially if they're all present at the same time. If a complete tune-up doesn't remedy the situation, major mechanical work is the only solution.

An engine overhaul involves restoring the internal parts to the specifications of a new engine. During an overhaul, the piston rings are replaced and the cylinder walls are reconditioned (rebored and/or honed). If a rebore is done by an automotive machine shop, new oversize pistons will also be installed. The main bearings and connecting rod bearings are generally replaced with new ones and, if necessary, the crankshaft may be reground to restore the journals. Generally, the valves are serviced as well, since they're usually in less-than-perfect condition at this point. While the engine is being overhauled, other components, such as the distributor, starter and alternator, can be rebuilt as well. The end result should be a like new engine that will give many trouble free miles. **Note:** *Critical cooling system components such as the hoses, drivebelts, thermostat and water pump MUST be replaced with new parts when an engine is overhauled.* The radiator should be checked carefully to ensure that it isn't clogged or leaking (see Chapter 3). Also, we don't recommend overhauling the oil pump – always install a new one when an engine is rebuilt.

Before beginning the engine overhaul, read through the entire procedure to familiarize yourself with the scope and requirements of the job. Overhauling an engine isn't difficult, if you follow all of the instructions carefully, have the necessary tools and equipment and pay close attention to all specifications; however, it can be time consuming. Plan on the vehicle being tied up for a minimum of two weeks, especially if parts must be taken to an automotive machine shop for repair or reconditioning. Check on availability of parts and make sure any necessary special tools and equipment are obtained in advance. Most work can be done with typical hand tools, although a number of precision measuring tools are required for inspecting parts to determine if they must be replaced. Often an automotive machine shop will handle the inspection of parts and offer advice concerning reconditioning and replacement. **Note:** *Always wait until the engine has been completely disassembled and all components, especially the engine block, have been inspected before deciding what service and repair operations must be performed by an automotive machine shop.* Since the block's condition will be the major factor to consider when determining whether to overhaul the original engine or buy a rebuilt one, never purchase parts or have machine work done on other components until the block has been thoroughly inspected. As a general rule, time is the primary cost of an overhaul, so it doesn't pay to install worn or substandard parts.

As a final note, to ensure maximum life and minimum trouble from a rebuilt engine, everything must be assembled with care in a spotlessly clean environment.

2.4   Remove the oil pressure sending unit and install a pressure gauge in its place

3.6   A compression gauge with a threaded fitting for the plug hole is preferred over the type that requires hand pressure to maintain the seal

3   Cylinder compression check

Refer to illustration 3.6

1   A compression check will tell you what mechanical condition the upper end (pistons, rings, valves, head gasket) of an engine is in. Specifically, it can tell you if the compression is down due to leakage caused by worn piston rings, defective valves and seats or a blown head gasket. **Note:** *The engine must be at normal operating temperature and the battery must be fully charged for this check. Also, if the engine is equipped with a carburetor, the choke valve must be all the way open to get an accurate compression reading (if the engine's warm, the choke should be open).*

2   Begin by cleaning the area around the spark plugs before you remove them (compressed air should be used, if available, otherwise a small brush or even a bicycle tire pump will work). The idea is to prevent dirt from getting into the cylinders as the compression check is being done.

3   Remove all of the spark plugs from the engine (see Chapter 1).

4   Block the throttle wide open.

5   Detach the coil wire from the center of the distributor cap and ground it on the engine block. Use a jumper wire with alligator clips on each end to ensure a good ground. On fuel-injected vehicles, the fuel pump circuit should also be disabled (see Chapter 4).

6   Install the compression gauge in the number one spark plug hole **(see illustration)**.

7   Crank the engine over at least seven compression strokes and watch the gauge. The compression should build up quickly in a healthy engine. Low compression on the first stroke, followed by gradually increasing pressure on successive strokes, indicates worn piston rings. A low compression reading on the first stroke, which doesn't build up during successive strokes, indicates leaking valves or a blown head gasket (a cracked head could also be the cause). Deposits on the undersides of the valve heads can also cause low compression. Record the highest gauge reading obtained.

8   Repeat the procedure for the remaining cylinders and compare the results to this Chapter's Specifications.

9   Add some engine oil (about three squirts from a plunger-type oil can) to each cylinder, through the spark plug hole, and repeat the test.

10   If the compression increases after the oil is added, the piston rings are definitely worn. If the compression doesn't increase significantly, the leakage is occurring at the valves or head gasket. Leakage past the valves may be caused by burned valve seats and/or faces or warped, cracked or bent valves.

11   If two adjacent cylinders have equally low compression, there's a strong possibility the head gasket between them is blown. The ap-

pearance of coolant in the combustion chambers or the crankcase would verify this condition.

12   If one cylinder is 20 percent lower than the others, and the engine has a slightly rough idle, a worn exhaust lobe on the camshaft could be the cause.

13   If the compression is unusually high, the combustion chambers are probably coated with carbon deposits. If that's the case, the cylinder head should be removed and decarbonized.

14   If compression is way down or varies greatly between cylinders, it would be a good idea to have a leak-down test performed by an automotive repair shop. This test will pinpoint exactly where the leakage is occurring and how severe it is.

4   Engine removal – methods and precautions

If you've decided an engine must be removed for overhaul or major repair work, several preliminary steps should be taken.

Locating a suitable place to work is extremely important. Adequate work space, along with storage space for the vehicle, will be needed. If a shop or garage isn't available, at the very least a flat, level, clean work surface made of concrete or asphalt is required.

Cleaning the engine compartment and engine before beginning the removal procedure will help keep tools clean and organized.

An engine hoist or A-frame will also be necessary. Make sure the equipment is rated in excess of the combined weight of the engine and transaxle. Safety is of primary importance, considering the potential hazards involved in lifting the engine out of the vehicle.

If the engine is being removed by a novice, a helper should be available. Advice and aid from someone more experienced would also be helpful. There are many instances when one person cannot simultaneously perform all of the operations required when lifting the engine out of the vehicle.

Plan the operation ahead of time. Arrange for or obtain all of the tools and equipment you'll need prior to beginning the job. Some of the equipment necessary to perform engine removal and installation safely and with relative ease are (in addition to an engine hoist) a heavy duty floor jack, complete sets of wrenches and sockets as described in the front of this manual, wooden blocks and plenty of rags and cleaning solvent for mopping up spilled oil, coolant and gasoline. If the hoist must be rented, make sure you arrange for it in advance and perform all of the operations possible without it beforehand. This will save you money and time.

Plan for the vehicle to be out of use for quite a while. A machine shop will be required to perform some of the work which the do-it-yourselfer can't accomplish without special equipment. These shops often have a busy schedule, so it would be a good idea to consult them before removing the engine in order to accurately estimate the amount of time required to rebuild or repair components that may need work.

Always be extremely careful when removing and installing the engine. Serious injury can result from careless actions. Plan ahead, take your time and a job of this nature, although major, can be accomplished successfully.

5   Engine – removal and installation

Warning: *Gasoline is extremely flammable, so take extra precautions when working on any part of the fuel system. Don't smoke or allow open flames or bare light bulbs near the work area, and don't work in a garage where a natural gas-type appliance (such as a water heater or clothes dryer) with a pilot light is present. If you spill gas on your skin, rinse it off immediately with soap and water. Also, when disconnecting fuel system components, wear safety glasses and have a Class B fire extinguisher on hand.*

Note: *Read through the entire Section before you attempt to remove the engine. The engine and transaxle must be removed as a single assembly then separated after removal.*

5.9 One way to ensure proper reattachment of connectors is to label each side of the connection with bits of masking tape and number them with a felt-tip pen – another way is to use matching colors of electrical tape

Removal

Vehicles with a manual transaxle

Refer to illustrations 5.9 and 5.23

1　If the vehicle is air conditioned, have the system discharged by a dealer service department or a service station.
2　Start the engine, warm it up, turn it off, allow it to cool for awhile, drain the oil and remove the oil filter (see Chapter 1).
3　If the vehicle is fuel-injected, relieve the fuel system pressure (see Chapter 4).
4　Place protective covers on the fenders.
5　Remove the battery (see Chapter 5).
6　Remove the hood (see Chapter 11).
7　Remove the air cleaner assembly (see Chapter 4).
8　Drain the cooling system (see Chapter 1).
9　Carefully label, then disconnect all vacuum lines, coolant and emission hoses, heater hoses and electrical wiring harness connectors. Disconnect the oxygen sensor connector behind the cylinder head. **Note:** *Not all the coolant and emissions hoses can be detached from above. Some can only be reached from underneath the vehicle, after you raise it.* Masking tape and felt-tip pens work well for marking items **(see illustration)**. If necessary, take instant photos or sketch the locations to ensure correct reinstallation.
10　Detach the fuel lines from the carburetor and fuel injection components (separate them from any clamps and brackets as well) (Chapter 4).
11　Remove the accessory drivebelts (see Chapter 1).
12　Remove the radiator and cooling fan assembly (see Chapter 3).
13　Remove the alternator (see Chapter 5).
14　If the vehicle is air conditioned, remove the air conditioning compressor mounting bolts and set the compressor aside (see Chapter 3). **Note:** *It may be necessary to restrain the compressor with a piece of wire to make sure it remains clear of the engine during removal.*
15　If the vehicle is equipped with power steering, remove the power steering pump mounting bolts and set the pump aside (see Chapter 10).
16　Disconnect the clutch cable and speedometer cable from the transaxle (see Chapter 7, Part A).
17　Raise the vehicle and place it securely on jackstands.
18　Detach the exhaust pipe from the exhaust manifold (see Chapter 4).
19　Label, then detach, any remaining air pump hoses and lines, if equipped. Remove the air pump (see Chapter 6).
20　Detach the transaxle linkage (see Chapter 7, Part A).
21　Detach the driveaxles (see Chapter 8).
22　Lower the vehicle.
23　Attach a short length of heavy duty chain to the engine lifting brackets and hook up an engine hoist **(see illustration)**.

5.23 To lift the engine out of the engine compartment, attach a short section of heavy chain to the lifting brackets on the head, then hook up the engine hoist to the chain

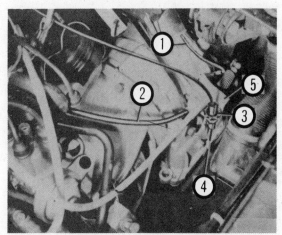

5.31 Items to be disconnected from the transaxle

1	ground strap	4	operating rod
2	selector cable	5	selector cable conduit
3	accelerator cable		mounting bracket

24　Raise the engine/transaxle assembly slightly and remove the front engine mounting bolt (see Chapter 2, Part A).
25　Remove the right engine mounting bolt.
26　Remove the left engine mounting bolt.
27　Lift the engine and transmission assembly out of the vehicle.
28　Remove the engine-to-transaxle bolts and separate the engine from the transaxle.

Vehicles with an automatic transaxle

Refer to illustrations 5.31, 5.44 and 5.46

29　Follow Steps 1 through 15 of the manual transaxle removal procedure (they're the same for the automatic).
30　Drain the automatic transaxle fluid (see Chapter 1) and detach the transaxle cooler lines (see Chapter 7, Part B).
31　Detach the ground strap from the transaxle left mount **(see illustration)**.

2B

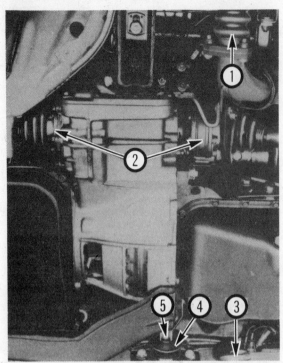

5.44   Items to be disconnected from under the vehicle on automatic transaxle models

1	exhaust flex pipe	3	horn
2	drive shafts and flange shafts	4	outer front transaxle mount
		5	rubber core and bracket

32   Detach the selector cable and housing from the lever on the transaxle and from the bracket **(see illustration 5.31)**.

33   Disconnect the accelerator cable from the operating rod on the transmission. Then detach the cable housing from the bracket on the side of the transaxle **(see illustration 5.31)**.

34   Raise the vehicle and place it securely on jackstands.

35   Detach the exhaust pipe from the exhaust manifold (see Chapter 4).

36   Label, then detach, any remaining air pump hoses and lines, if equipped. Remove the air pump (see Chapter 6).

37   Remove the left wheel.

38   If equipped, remove the left inner splash shield.

39   Remove the right wheel.

40   If equipped, remove the right inner splash shield.

41   Remove the starter cover plate and disconnect the starter.

42   Detach the lower radiator hose from the water pump (see Chapter 3).

43   Remove the water pump pulley (see Chapter 3) and crankshaft pulley (see Chapter 2, Part A).

44   Disconnect both driveshafts from the flanged shafts on the transaxle **(see illustration)**.

45   Remove the front engine mount bolts **(see illustration 5.44)**.

46   Detach the inspection cover from the transaxle and remove the driveplate bolts **(see illustration)**.

47   Lower the vehicle.

48   Attach a short length of heavy duty chain to the engine lifting brackets and hook up an engine hoist **(see illustration 5.23)**.

49   Remove the right engine mount (see Chapter 2, Part A).

50   Lift the engine/transaxle out of the vehicle. Carefully lower the engine/transaxle unit onto the floor or a dolly.

51   Separate the engine from the transaxle. **Caution:** *Don't let the torque converter fall out of the bellhousing after the engine is lifted out. Have an assistant hold it in place until you can secure it with a piece of wire or rope.*

Installation

52   Check the engine/transaxle mounts. If they're worn or damaged, replace them.

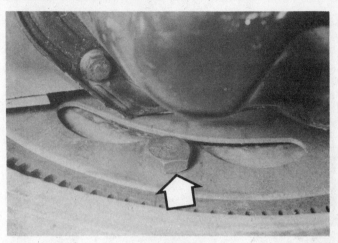

5.46   Remove the three bolts that attach the driveplate to the torque converter

53   On manual transaxle equipped vehicles, inspect the clutch components (see Chapter 8) and apply a very small amount of high-temperature grease to the transaxle input shaft splines.

54   Carefully rejoin the transaxle and engine following the procedure outlined in Chapter 7. **Caution:** *Do not use the bolts to force the engine and transaxle into alignment. It may crack or damage major components.*

55   Install the transaxle-to-engine bolts and tighten them securely. On automatic transaxle equipped vehicles, install the driveplate-to-torque converter bolts (see Chapter 7, Part B).

56   Attach the hoist to the engine and carefully lower the engine/transaxle assembly into the vehicle.

57   Install the mount bolts and tighten them securely. **Note:** *Don't tighten any bolts until you've installed all of them.*

58   Reinstall the remaining components and fasteners in the reverse order of removal.

59   Add coolant, oil, power steering and transmission fluid/lubricant as needed (see Chapter 1).

60   Run the engine and check for proper operation and leaks. Shut off the engine and recheck the fluid levels.

---

6   Engine rebuilding alternatives

The do-it-yourselfer is faced with a number of options when performing an engine overhaul. The decision to replace the engine block, piston/connecting rod assemblies and crankshaft depends on a number of factors, with the number one consideration being the condition of the block. Other considerations are cost, access to machine shop facilities, parts availability, time required to complete the project and the extent of prior mechanical experience on the part of the do-it-yourselfer.

Some of the rebuilding alternatives include:

Individual parts – If the inspection procedures reveal the engine block and most engine components are in reusable condition, purchasing individual parts may be the most economical alternative. The block, crankshaft and piston/connecting rod assemblies should all be inspected carefully. Even if the block shows little wear, the cylinder bores should be surface honed.

Short block – A short block consists of an engine block with a crankshaft and piston/connecting rod assemblies already installed. All new bearings are incorporated and all clearances will be correct. The existing camshaft(s), cylinder head, manifolds and external parts can be bolted to the short block with little or no machine shop work necessary.

Long block – A long block consists of a short block plus an oil pump, oil pan, cylinder head, camshaft cover, camshaft and valve train components, timing sprockets and belt and timing belt cover. All components are installed with new bearings, seals and gaskets incorporated throughout. The installation of manifolds and external parts is all that's necessary.

Give careful thought to which alternative is best for you and discuss the situation with local automotive machine shops, auto parts dealers and experienced rebuilders before ordering or purchasing replacement parts.

7   Engine overhaul – disassembly sequence

Refer to illustrations 7.5a and 7.5b

1   It's much easier to disassemble and work on the engine if it's mounted on a portable engine stand. A stand can often be rented quite cheaply from an equipment rental yard. Before the engine is mounted on a stand, the driveplate should be removed from the engine.

2   If a stand isn't available, it's possible to disassemble the engine with it blocked up on the floor. Be extra careful not to tip or drop the engine when working without a stand.

3   If you're going to obtain a rebuilt engine, all external components must come off first, to be transferred to the replacement engine, just as they will if you're doing a complete engine overhaul yourself. These include:

Alternator and brackets
Emissions control components
Distributor, spark plug wires and spark plugs
Thermostat and housing cover
Water pump
EFI components or carburetor
Intake/exhaust manifolds
Oil filter
Engine mounts
Driveplate
Engine intermediate (rear) plate

Note: *When removing the external components from the engine, pay close attention to details that may be helpful or important during installation. Note the installed position of gaskets, seals, spacers, pins, brackets, washers, bolts and other small items.*

4   If you're obtaining a short block, which consists of the engine block, crankshaft, pistons and connecting rods all assembled, then the cylinder head, oil pan and oil pump will have to be removed as well. See Engine rebuilding alternatives for additional information regarding the different possibilities to be considered.

5   If you're planning a complete overhaul, the engine must be disassembled and the internal components removed in the following order (**see illustrations**):

Camshaft cover
Timing belt cover
Timing belt and sprockets
Intake and exhaust manifolds
Camshaft
Cam followers
Cylinder head
Oil pan
Oil pump
Piston/connecting rod assemblies
Crankshaft rear main oil seal housing
Crankshaft and main bearings

2B

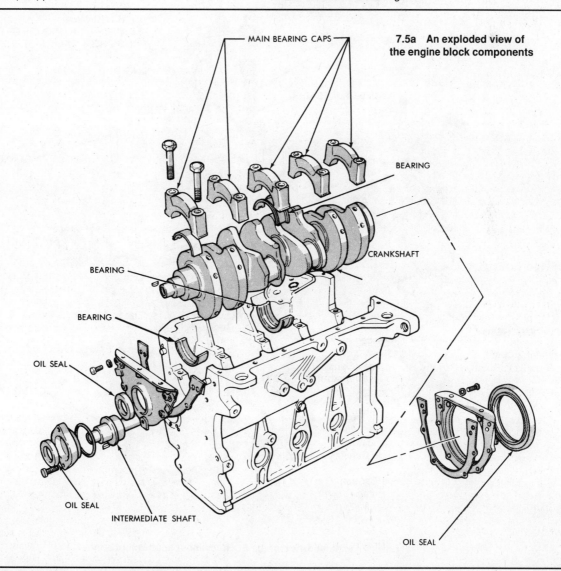

7.5a   An exploded view of the engine block components

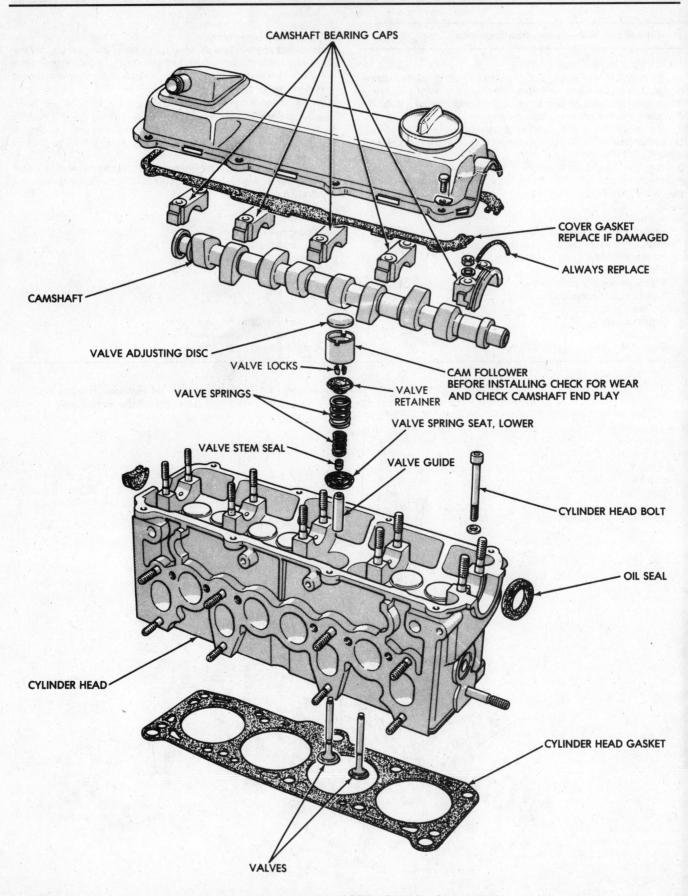

CAMSHAFT BEARING CAPS

COVER GASKET
REPLACE IF DAMAGED

ALWAYS REPLACE

CAMSHAFT

VALVE ADJUSTING DISC

VALVE LOCKS

CAM FOLLOWER
BEFORE INSTALLING CHECK FOR WEAR
AND CHECK CAMSHAFT END PLAY

VALVE SPRINGS

VALVE
RETAINER

VALVE SPRING SEAT, LOWER

VALVE STEM SEAL

VALVE GUIDE

CYLINDER HEAD BOLT

OIL SEAL

CYLINDER HEAD

CYLINDER HEAD GASKET

VALVES

7.5b   An exploded view of the SOHC cylinder head components

6   Before beginning the disassembly and overhaul procedures, make sure the following items are available. Also, refer to *Engine overhaul – reassembly sequence* for a list of tools and materials needed for engine reassembly.

Common hand tools
Small cardboard boxes or plastic bags for storing parts
Gasket scraper
Ridge reamer
Vibration damper puller
Micrometers
Telescoping gauges
Dial indicator set
Valve spring compressor
Cylinder surfacing hone
Piston ring groove cleaning tool
Electric drill motor
Tap and die set
Wire brushes
Oil gallery brushes
Cleaning solvent

8   Cylinder head – disassembly

Refer to illustrations 8.2, 8.3a, 8.3b and 8.3c
Note: *New and rebuilt cylinder heads are commonly available for most engines at dealerships and auto parts stores. Due to the fact that some specialized tools are necessary for the disassembly and inspection procedures, and replacement parts may not be readily available, it may be more practical and economical for the home mechanic to purchase a replacement head rather than taking the time to disassemble, inspect and recondition the original.*

1   Cylinder head disassembly involves removal of the intake and exhaust valves and related components. If they're still in place, remove the camshaft, cam followers and shims (if equipped) from the cylinder head (see Chapter 2, Part A). Label the parts or store them separately so they can be reinstalled in their original locations.

2   Before the valves are removed, arrange to label and store them, along with their related components, so they can be kept separate and reinstalled in the same valve guides they are removed from **(see illustration)**.
3   Compress the springs on the first valve with a spring compressor and remove the keepers **(see illustration)**. Carefully release the valve spring compressor and remove the retainer, the spring and the spring seat (if used) **(see illustrations)**. **Caution:** *Be very careful not to nick or otherwise damage the cam follower bore when compressing the valve springs.*
4   Pull the valve out of the head, then remove the oil seal from the guide.
5   Repeat the procedure for the remaining valves. Remember to keep all the parts for each valve together so they can be reinstalled in the same locations.

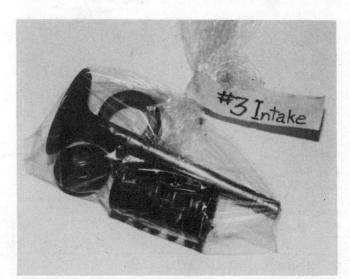

8.2   Have eight plastic bags – one for each intake and exhaust valve – ready before you start disassembling the head; label each bag as shown and put the entire contents of each valve assembly in one bag

8.3a   You'll need a valve spring compressor to strip the head – valve spring compressors come in a wide variety of sizes and configurations, so if you've never bought or borrowed one of these tools before, take the head with you, if possible, to make sure the compressor fits

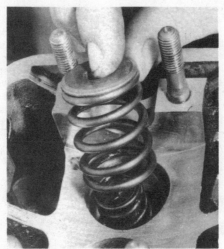

8.3b   Carefully remove the valve springs and don't nick or gouge the cam follower bores

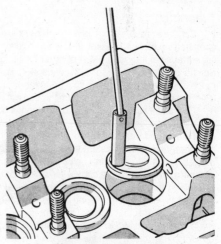

8.3c   Use a magnet to remove the spring seats from the cam follower bores

2B

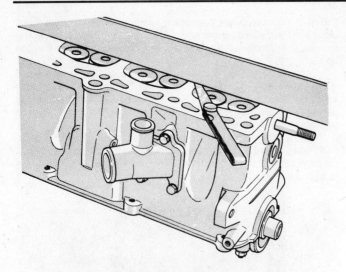

9.11   Check the cylinder head gasket surface for warpage by trying to slip a feeler gauge (of the thickness listed in this Chapter's Specifications) under the straightedge

9.13   To determine the valve stem-to-guide clearance, set up a dial indicator touching the valve head, move the valve from side to side as shown and note the gauge reading

6   Once the valves and related components have been removed and stored in an organized manner, the head should be thoroughly cleaned and inspected. If a complete engine overhaul is being done, finish the engine disassembly procedures before beginning the cylinder head cleaning and inspection process.

9   Cylinder head – cleaning and inspection

Refer to illustrations 9.11, 9.13, 9.16 and 9.18

1   Thorough cleaning of the cylinder head and related valve train components, followed by a detailed inspection, will enable you to decide how much valve service work must be done during the engine overhaul. **Note:** *If the engine was severely overheated, the cylinder head is probably warped (see Step 11).*

Cleaning

2   Scrape all traces of old gasket material and sealing compound off the camshaft cover, head gasket, intake manifold and exhaust manifold sealing surfaces of the head. Be very careful not to gouge the cylinder head. Special gasket removal solvents that soften gaskets and make removal much easier are available at auto parts stores.

3   Remove all built up scale from the coolant passages.

4   Run a stiff wire brush through the various holes to remove deposits that may have formed in them.

5   Run an appropriate size tap into each of the threaded holes to remove corrosion and thread sealant that may be present. If compressed air is available, use it to clear the holes of debris produced by this operation. **Warning:** *Wear eye protection when using compressed air!*

6   Clean the cylinder head with solvent and dry it thoroughly. Compressed air will speed the drying process and ensure that all holes and recessed areas are clean. **Note:** *Decarbonizing chemicals are available and may prove very useful when cleaning cylinder heads and valve train components. They're very caustic and should be used with caution. Be sure to follow the instructions on the container.*

7   Clean the mechanical cam followers and shims with solvent and dry them thoroughly (don't mix them up during the cleaning process). Compressed air will speed the drying process and can be used to clean out any oil passages. Don't submerge hydraulic cam followers in solvent – just make sure they're not contaminated with grit or dirt.

8   Clean all the valve springs, spring seats, keepers and retainers with solvent and dry them thoroughly. Do the components from one valve at a time to avoid mixing up the parts.

9   Scrape off any heavy deposits that may have formed on the valves, then use a motorized wire brush to remove deposits from the valve heads and stems. Again, make sure the valves don't get mixed up.

Inspection

Note: *Be sure to perform all of the following inspection procedures before concluding that machine shop work is required. Make a list of the items that need attention.*

Cylinder head

10   Inspect the head very carefully for cracks, evidence of coolant leakage and other damage. If cracks are found, check with an automotive machine shop concerning repair. If repair isn't possible, a new cylinder head should be obtained. **Note:** *Small, fine cracks between the valve seats and plug threads are permissible, as long as they're no more than 0.020-inch wide and don't extend into more than the first few threads.*

11   Using a straightedge and feeler gauge, check the head gasket mating surface for warpage **(see illustration)**. If the warpage exceeds the limit listed in this Chapter's Specifications, the head can be resurfaced at an automotive machine shop.

12   Examine the valve seats in each of the combustion chambers. If they're pitted, cracked or burned, the head will require valve service that's beyond the scope of the home mechanic.

13   Check the valve stem-to-guide clearance by measuring the lateral movement of the valve stem with a dial indicator attached securely to the head **(see illustration)**. The valve must be in the guide and raised off the seat. The total valve stem movement indicated by the gauge needle must be divided by two to obtain the actual clearance. After this is done, if there's still some doubt regarding the condition of the valve guides, they should be checked by an automotive machine shop (the cost should be minimal).

Valves

14   Carefully inspect each valve face for uneven wear, deformation, cracks, pits and burned areas.

15   Check the valve stem for scuffing and galling and the neck for cracks. Rotate the valve and check for any obvious indication that it's bent. Look for pits and excessive wear on the end of the stem. The presence of any of these conditions indicates the need for valve service by an automotive machine shop.

16   Measure the margin width on each valve **(see illustration)**. Any valve with a margin narrower than specified will have to be replaced with a new one.

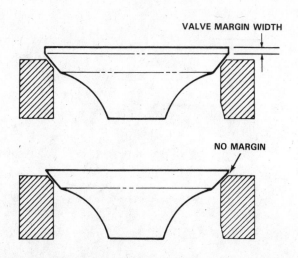

9.16   Measure the margin width of each valve and compare your measurement to this Chapter's Specifications – if the margin is too narrow, or no margin remains, discard the valve and install a new one

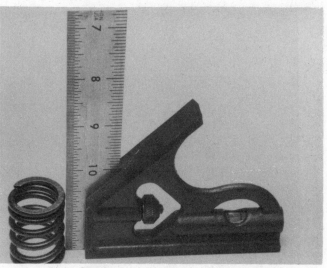

9.18   Check each valve spring for squareness

2B

Valve components

17   Check each valve spring for wear (on the ends) and pits. The tension of all springs should be checked with a special fixture before deciding that they're suitable for use in a rebuilt engine (take the springs to an automotive machine shop for this check).

18   Stand each spring on a flat surface and check it for squareness **(see illustration)**. If any of the springs are distorted or sagged, replace all of them with new parts.

19   Check the spring retainers and keepers for obvious wear and cracks. Any questionable parts should be replaced with new ones, as extensive damage will occur if they fail during engine operation.

Camshaft and camshaft followers

20   Refer to Part A for the inspection procedures for these components.

All components

21   If the inspection process indicates the valve components are in generally poor condition and worn beyond the limits specified, which is usually the case in an engine that's being overhauled, reassemble the valves in the cylinder head and refer to Section 10 for valve servicing recommendations.

10   Valves – servicing

1   Because of the complex nature of the job and the special tools and equipment needed, servicing of the valves, the valve seats and the valve guides, commonly known as a valve job, should be done by a professional.

2   The home mechanic can remove and disassemble the head, do the initial cleaning and inspection, then reassemble and deliver it to a dealer service department or an automotive machine shop for the actual service work. Doing the inspection will enable you to see what condition the head and valvetrain components are in and will ensure that you know what work and new parts are required when dealing with an automotive machine shop.

3   The dealer service department, or automotive machine shop, will remove the valves and springs, recondition or replace the valves and valve seats, recondition the valve guides, check and replace the valve springs, spring retainers and keepers (as necessary), replace the valve seals with new ones, reassemble the valve components and make sure the installed spring height is correct. The cylinder head gasket surface will also be restored if it's warped.

4   After the valve job has been performed by a professional, the head will be in like new condition. When the head is returned, be sure to clean it

again before installation on the engine to remove any metal particles and abrasive grit that may still be present from the valve service or head resurfacing operations. Use compressed air, if available, to blow out all the oil holes and passages.

11   Cylinder head – reassembly

Refer to illustrations 11.3 and 11.6

1   Regardless of whether or not the head was sent to an automotive repair shop for valve servicing, make sure it's clean before beginning reassembly.

2   If the head was sent out for valve servicing, the valves and related components will already be in place. Begin the reassembly procedure with Step 8.

3   Install new seals on each of the intake valve guides. Using a hammer and a deep socket or seal installation tool, gently tap each seal into place until it's completely seated on the guide **(see illustration)**. Don't twist or cock the seals during installation or they won't seal properly on the valve stems.

4   Beginning at one end of the head, lubricate and install the first valve – apply moly-based grease or clean engine oil to the valve stem.

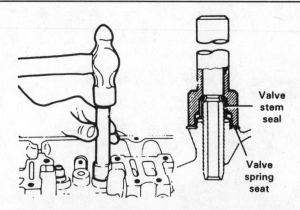

11.3   Using a hammer and a deep socket (or this special seal installation tool, if you've got one), gently tap each seal into place until it's completely seated on the guide – don't twist or cock the seal during installation or it won't seal properly

11.6   Apply a small dab of grease to each keeper, as shown here, before installation – this will hold the keeper in place on the valve stem as the spring is released

5   Drop the spring seat over the valve guide and set the valve spring and retainer in place.
6   Compress the springs with a valve spring compressor and carefully install the keepers in the groove, then slowly release the compressor and make sure the keepers seat properly. Apply a small dab of grease to each keeper to hold it in place if necessary **(see illustration)**.
7   Repeat the procedure for the remaining valves. Be sure to return the components to their original locations – don't mix them up!
8   Refer to Part A and install the cam followers and shims.

12   Pistons/connecting rods – removal

Refer to illustrations 12.1, 12.3 and 12.6
Note: *Prior to removing the piston/connecting rod assemblies, remove the cylinder head, the oil pan and the oil pump by referring to the appropriate Sections in Chapter 2, Part A.*
1   Use your fingernail to feel if a ridge has formed at the upper limit of ring travel (about 1/4-inch down from the top of each cylinder). If carbon deposits or cylinder wear have produced ridges, they must be completely removed with a special tool **(see illustration)**. Follow the manufacturer's instructions provided with the tool. Failure to remove the ridges before attempting to remove the piston/connecting rod assemblies may result in piston breakage.

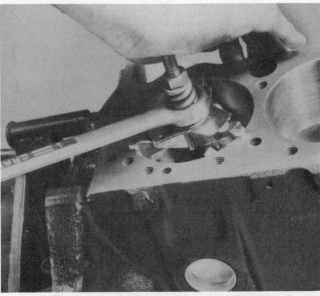

12.1   You'll need a ridge reamer to remove the ridge from the top of the cylinder before removing the pistons

2   After the cylinder ridges have been removed, turn the engine upside-down so the crankshaft is facing up.
3   Before the connecting rods are removed, check the endplay with feeler gauges. Slide them between the first connecting rod and the crankshaft throw until the play is removed **(see illustration)**. The endplay is equal to the thickness of the feeler gauge(s). If the endplay exceeds the limit listed in this Chapter's Specifications, new connecting rods will be required. If new rods (or a new crankshaft) are installed, the endplay may fall under the specified minimum (if it does, the rods will have to be machined to restore it – consult an automotive machine shop for advice if necessary). Repeat the procedure for the remaining connecting rods.
4   Check the connecting rods and caps for identification marks. If they aren't plainly marked, use a small center punch to make the appropriate number of indentations on each rod and cap (1, 2, 3 or 4, depending on the cylinder they're associated with).
5   Loosen each of the connecting rod cap nuts 1/2-turn at a time until they can be removed by hand. Remove the number one connecting rod cap and bearing insert. Don't drop the bearing insert out of the cap.
6   Slip a short length of plastic or rubber hose over each connecting rod cap bolt to protect the crankshaft journal and cylinder wall as the piston is removed **(see illustration)**.

12.3   Check the connecting rod side clearance with a feeler gauge as shown

12.6   To prevent damage to the crankshaft journals and cylinder walls, slip sections of hose over the rod bolts before removing the pistons

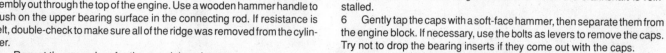

7   Remove the bearing insert and push the connecting rod/piston assembly out through the top of the engine. Use a wooden hammer handle to push on the upper bearing surface in the connecting rod. If resistance is felt, double-check to make sure all of the ridge was removed from the cylinder.

8   Repeat the procedure for the remaining pistons.

9   After removal, reassemble the connecting rod caps and bearing inserts in their respective connecting rods and install the cap nuts finger-tight. Leaving the old bearing inserts in place until reassembly will help prevent the connecting rod bearing surfaces from being accidentally nicked or gouged.

10   Don't separate the pistons from the connecting rods (see Section 17 for additional information).

13   Crankshaft – removal

Refer to illustrations 13.1, 13.3 and 13.4

Note: *The crankshaft can be removed only after the engine has been removed from the vehicle. It's assumed the driveplate, timing belt, oil pan, oil pump and piston/connecting rod assemblies have already been removed. Since the engine is equipped with a one-piece rear main oil seal, the seal housing must also be unbolted and separated from the block before proceeding with crankshaft removal.*

1   Before the crankshaft is removed, check the endplay. Mount a dial indicator with the stem in line with the crankshaft and just touching one of the crank throws **(see illustration)**.

2   Push the crankshaft all the way to the rear and zero the dial indicator. Next, pry the crankshaft to the front as far as possible and check the reading on the dial indicator. The distance that it moves is the endplay. If it's greater than specified, check the crankshaft thrust surfaces for wear. If no wear is evident, new main bearings should correct the endplay.

3   If a dial indicator isn't available, feeler gauges can be used. Gently pry or push the crankshaft all the way to the front of the engine. Slip feeler gauges between the crankshaft and the front face of the thrust main bearing to determine the clearance **(see illustration)**.

4   Check the main bearing caps to see if they're marked to indicate their locations **(see illustration)**. They should be numbered consecutively from the front of the engine to the rear. If they aren't, mark them with number stamping dies or a center punch. Each cap should have a cast-in number, which must be positioned opposite the oil pump when the caps are reinstalled.

5   Loosen the main bearing cap bolts 1/4-turn at a time each, until they can be removed by hand. Note if any stud bolts are used and make sure

they're returned to their original locations when the crankshaft is reinstalled.

6   Gently tap the caps with a soft-face hammer, then separate them from the engine block. If necessary, use the bolts as levers to remove the caps. Try not to drop the bearing inserts if they come out with the caps.

7   Carefully lift the crankshaft out of the engine. It may be a good idea to have an assistant available, since the crankshaft is quite heavy. With the bearing inserts in place in the engine block and main bearing caps, return the caps to their respective locations on the engine block and tighten the bolts finger-tight.

14   Engine block – cleaning

Refer to illustrations 14.1, 14.8 and 14.10
Caution: *The core plugs (also known as freeze or soft plugs) may be difficult or impossible to retrieve if they're driven into the block coolant passages.*

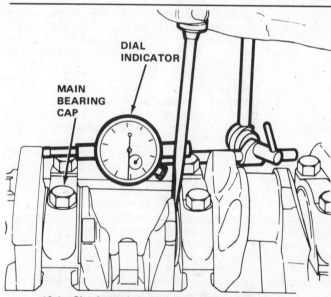

13.1   Check crankshaft endplay with a dial indicator

13.3   If you don't have a dial indicator to measure endplay, use feeler gauges instead

13.4   If there are offset numbers already stamped on the bearing caps, make sure the number is on the side opposite the oil pump

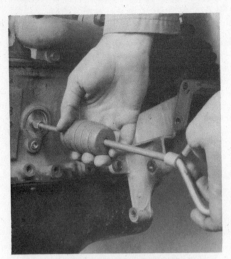

14.1   Remove the engine block core plugs with a puller – if you drive them into the block, they might be impossible to retrieve

14.8   Clean and restore all bolt holes in the block – especially the main bearing cap and head bolt holes – with a tap (and be sure you remove the debris from the holes after you're finished!)

14.10   Use a large socket on an extension to drive the new core plugs into the bores

1   Drill a small hole in the center of each core plug and pull them out with an auto body type dent puller **(see illustration).**

2   Using a gasket scraper, remove all traces of gasket material from the engine block. Be very careful not to nick or gouge the gasket sealing surfaces.

3   Remove the main bearing caps and separate the bearing inserts from the caps and the engine block. Tag the bearings, indicating which location they were removed from and whether they were in the cap or the block, then set them aside.

4   Remove all of the threaded oil gallery plugs from the block. The plugs are usually very tight – they may have to be drilled out and the holes re-tapped. Use new plugs when the engine is reassembled.

5   If the engine is extremely dirty it should be taken to an automotive machine shop to be steam cleaned or hot tanked.

6   After the block is returned, clean all oil holes and oil galleries one more time. Brushes specifically designed for this purpose are available at most auto parts stores. Flush the passages with warm water until the water runs clear, dry the block thoroughly and wipe all machined surfaces with a light, rust preventive oil. If you have access to compressed air, use it to speed the drying process and to blow out all the oil holes and galleries. **Warning:** *Wear eye protection when using compressed air!*

7   If the block isn't extremely dirty or sludged up, you can do an adequate cleaning job with hot soapy water and a stiff brush. Take plenty of time and do a thorough job. Regardless of the cleaning method used, be sure to clean all oil holes and galleries very thoroughly, dry the block completely and coat all machined surfaces with light oil.

8   The threaded holes in the block must be clean to ensure accurate torque readings during reassembly. Run the proper size tap into each of the holes to remove rust, corrosion, thread sealant or sludge and restore damaged threads **(see illustration).** If possible, use compressed air to clear the holes of debris produced by this operation. Now is a good time to clean the threads on the head bolts and the main bearing cap bolts as well.

9   Reinstall the main bearing caps and tighten the bolts finger tight.

10   After coating the sealing surfaces of the new core plugs with Permatex no. 2 sealant, install them in the engine block **(see illustration).** Make sure they're driven in straight and seated properly or leakage could result. Special tools are available for this purpose, but a large socket, with an outside diameter that will just slip into the core plug, a 1/2-inch drive extension and a hammer will work just as well.

11   Apply non-hardening sealant (such as Permatex no. 2 or Teflon pipe sealant) to the new oil gallery plugs and thread them into the holes in the block. Make sure they're tightened securely.

12   If the engine isn't going to be reassembled right away, cover it with a large plastic trash bag to keep it clean.

15   Engine block – inspection

Refer to illustrations 15.4a, 15.4b and 15.4c

1   Before the block is inspected, it should be cleaned as described in Section 14.

2   Visually check the block for cracks, rust and corrosion. Look for stripped threads in the threaded holes. It's also a good idea to have the block checked for hidden cracks by an automotive machine shop that has the special equipment to do this type of work. If defects are found, have the block repaired, if possible, or replaced.

3   Check the cylinder bores for scuffing and scoring.

4   Measure the diameter of each cylinder at the top (just under the ridge area), center and bottom of the cylinder bore, parallel to the crankshaft axis **(see illustrations). Note:** *These measurements should not be made with the bare block mounted on an engine stand – the cylinders will be distorted and the measurements will be inaccurate.*

5   Next, measure each cylinder's diameter at the same three locations across the crankshaft axis. Compare the results to the figures listed in this Chapter's Specifications.

6   If the required precision measuring tools aren't available, the piston-to-cylinder clearances can be obtained, though not quite as accurately, using feeler gauge stock. Feeler gauge stock comes in 12-inch lengths and various thicknesses and is generally available at auto parts stores.

7   To check the clearance, select a feeler gauge and slip it into the cylinder along with the matching piston. The piston must be positioned exactly as it normally would be. The feeler gauge must be between the piston and cylinder on one of the thrust faces (90-degrees to the piston pin bore).

8   The piston should slip through the cylinder (with the feeler gauge in place) with moderate pressure.

9   If it falls through or slides through easily, the clearance is excessive and a new piston will be required. If the piston binds at the lower end of the cylinder and is loose toward the top, the cylinder is tapered. If tight spots are encountered as the piston/feeler gauge is rotated in the cylinder, the cylinder is out-of-round.

10   Repeat the procedure for the remaining pistons and cylinders.

11   If the cylinder walls are badly scuffed or scored, or if they're out-of-round or tapered beyond the limits given in this Chapter's Specifications, have the engine block rebored and honed at an automotive machine shop. If a rebore is done, oversize pistons and rings will be required.

12   If the cylinders are in reasonably good condition and not worn to the outside of the limits, and if the piston-to-cylinder clearances can be maintained properly, then they don't have to be rebored. Honing is all that's necessary (see Section 16).

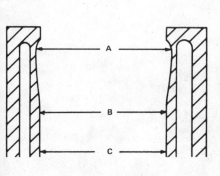

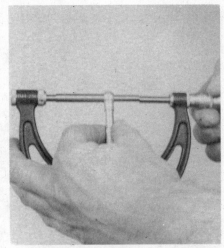

15.4a Measure the diameter of each cylinder just under the wear ridge (A), at the center (B) and at the bottom (C)

15.4b To obtain accurate bore measurements, you need to develop an ability to "feel" when the telescoping bore gauge is aligned with the axis of the cylinder – and this takes a little practice – so work slowly and repeat the check until you're satisfied that the bore measurement is correct

15.4c Measure the bore gauge with a micrometer to determine the bore size

16 Cylinder honing

Refer to illustrations 16.3a and 16.3b

1   Prior to engine reassembly, the cylinder bores must be honed so the new piston rings will seat correctly and provide the best possible combustion chamber seal. **Note:** *If you don't have the tools or don't want to tackle the honing operation, most automotive machine shops will do it for a reasonable fee.*

2   Before honing the cylinders, install the main bearing caps and tighten the bolts to the specified torque.

3   Two types of cylinder hones are commonly available – the flex hone or "bottle brush" type and the more traditional surfacing hone with spring-loaded stones. Both will do the job, but for the less experienced mechanic the "bottle brush" hone will probably be easier to use. You'll also need some kerosene or honing oil, rags and an electric drill motor. Proceed as follows:

a) Mount the hone in the drill motor, compress the stones and slip it into the first cylinder **(see illustration)**. Be sure to wear safety goggles or a face shield!

b) Lubricate the cylinder with plenty of honing oil, turn on the drill and move the hone up-and-down in the cylinder at a pace that will produce a fine crosshatch pattern on the cylinder walls. Ideally, the crosshatch lines should intersect at approximately a 60-degree angle **(see illustration)**. Be sure to use plenty of lubricant and don't take off any more material than absolutely necessary to produce the desired finish. **Note:** *Piston ring manufacturers may specify a smaller crosshatch angle than the traditional 60-degrees – read and follow any instructions included with the new rings.*

c) Don't withdraw the hone from the cylinder while it's running. Instead, shut off the drill and continue moving the hone up-and-down in the cylinder until it comes to a complete stop, then compress the stones and withdraw the hone. If you're using a "bottle brush" type hone, stop the drill motor, then turn the chuck in the normal direction of rotation while withdrawing the hone from the cylinder.

d) Wipe the oil out of the cylinder and repeat the procedure for the remaining cylinders.

16.3a If this is the first time you've ever honed cylinders, you'll get better results with a "bottle brush" type hone than you would with a traditional spring-loaded hone

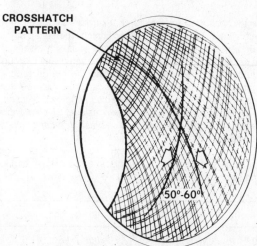

CROSSHATCH PATTERN

50°-60°

16.3b Your hone job should have a smooth, crosshatch pattern, like this, with the lines intersecting at about a 60-degree angle

2B

17.4a   Clean the piston rings with a special groove
cleaning tool . . .

17.4b   . . . or use a piece of broken piston ring

17.10   Check the side clearance with a feeler gauge at several
points around the groove

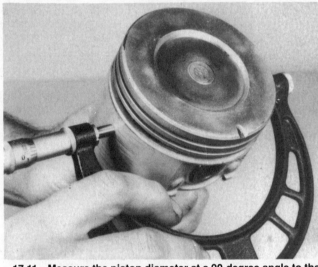

17.11   Measure the piston diameter at a 90-degree angle to the
piston pin and in line with it

4   After the honing job is complete, chamfer the top edges of the cylinder bores with a small file so the rings won't catch when the pistons are installed. Be very careful not to nick the cylinder walls with the end of the file.

5   The entire engine block must be washed again very thoroughly with warm, soapy water to remove all traces of the abrasive grit produced during the honing operation. **Note:** *The bores can be considered clean when a lint-free white cloth – dampened with clean engine oil – used to wipe them out doesn't pick up any more honing residue, which will show up as gray areas on the cloth. Be sure to run a brush through all oil holes and galleries and flush them with running water.*

6   After rinsing, dry the block and apply a coat of light rust preventive oil to all machined surfaces. Wrap the block in a plastic trash bag to keep it clean and set it aside until reassembly.

17   Pistons/connecting rods – inspection

Refer to illustrations 17.4a, 17.4b, 17.10 and 17.11

1   Before the inspection process can be carried out, the piston/connecting rod assemblies must be cleaned and the original piston rings removed from the pistons. **Note:** *Always use new piston rings when the engine is reassembled.*

2   Using a piston ring installation tool, carefully remove the rings from the pistons. Be careful not to nick or gouge the pistons in the process.

3   Scrape all traces of carbon from the top of the piston. A hand-held wire brush or a piece of fine emery cloth can be used once the majority of the deposits have been scraped away. Do not, under any circumstances, use a wire brush mounted in a drill motor to remove deposits from the pistons. The piston material is soft and may be eroded away by the wire brush.

4   Use a piston ring groove cleaning tool to remove carbon deposits from the ring grooves. If a tool isn't available, a piece broken off the old ring will do the job. Be very careful to remove only the carbon deposits – don't remove any metal and don't nick or scratch the sides of the ring grooves **(see illustrations)**.

5   Once the deposits have been removed, clean the piston/rod assemblies with solvent and dry them with compressed air (if available). Make sure the oil return holes in the back sides of the ring grooves are clear.

6   If the pistons and cylinder walls aren't damaged or worn excessively, and if the engine block isn't rebored, new pistons won't be necessary. Normal piston wear appears as even vertical wear on the piston thrust surfaces and slight looseness of the top ring in its groove. New piston rings, however, should always be used when an engine is rebuilt.

7   Carefully inspect each piston for cracks around the skirt, at the pin bosses and at the ring lands.

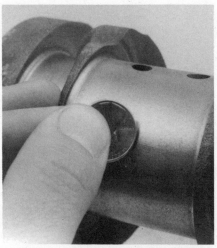

18.1   Clean the crankshaft journal lubrication passages with a stiff brush and flush them out with solvent

18.3   Rubbing a penny across each journal will give you a quick idea of its condition – if copper rubs off the penny and adheres to the crankshaft, have the crankshaft journals reground

18.4   Chamfer the oil holes to remove sharp edges that might gouge or scratch the new bearings

8   Look for scoring and scuffing on the thrust faces of the skirt, holes in the piston crown and burned areas at the edge of the crown. If the skirt is scored or scuffed, the engine may have been suffering from overheating and/or abnormal combustion, which caused excessively high operating temperatures. The cooling and lubrication systems should be checked thoroughly. A hole in the piston crown is an indication that abnormal combustion (preignition) was occurring. Burned areas at the edge of the piston crown are usually evidence of spark knock (detonation). If any of the above problems exist, the causes must be corrected or the damage will occur again. The causes may include intake air leaks, incorrect fuel/air mixture, incorrect ignition timing and EGR system malfunctions.

9   Corrosion of the piston, in the form of small pits, indicates that coolant is leaking into the combustion chamber and/or the crankcase. Again, the cause must be corrected or the problem may persist in the rebuilt engine.

10   Measure the piston ring side clearance by laying a new piston ring in each ring groove and slipping a feeler gauge in beside it **(see illustration)**. Check the clearance at three or four locations around each groove. Be sure to use the correct ring for each groove – they are different. If the side clearance is greater than the limit listed in this Chapter's Specifications, new pistons will have to be used.

11   Check the piston-to-bore clearance by measuring the bore (see Section 15) and the piston diameter. Make sure the pistons and bores are correctly matched. Measure the piston across the skirt, at a 90-degree angle to and in-line with the piston pin **(see illustration)**. Subtract the piston diameter from the bore diameter to obtain the clearance. If it's greater than the limit listed in this Chapter's Specifications, the block will have to be rebored and new pistons and rings installed.

12   Check the piston-to-rod clearance by twisting the piston and rod in opposite directions. Any noticeable play indicates excessive wear, which must be corrected. The piston/connecting rod assemblies should be taken to an automotive machine shop to have the pistons and rods resized and new pins installed.

13   If the pistons must be removed from the connecting rods for any reason, they should be taken to an automotive machine shop. While they are there, have the connecting rods checked for bend and twist, since automotive machine shops have special equipment for this purpose. **Note:** *Unless new pistons and/or connecting rods must be installed, do not disassemble the pistons and connecting rods.*

14   Check the connecting rods for cracks and other damage. Temporarily remove the rod caps, lift out the old bearing inserts, wipe the rod and cap bearing surfaces clean and inspect them for nicks, gouges and scratches. After checking the rods, replace the old bearings, slip the caps into place and tighten the nuts finger tight. **Note:** *If the engine is being rebuilt because of a connecting rod knock, be sure to install new rods.*

18   Crankshaft – inspection

Refer to illustrations 18.1, 18.3, 18.4, 18.6 and 18.8

1   Clean the crankshaft with solvent and dry it with compressed air (if available). Be sure to clean the oil holes with a stiff brush **(see illustration)** and flush them out with solvent.

2   Check the main and connecting rod bearing journals for uneven wear, scoring, pits and cracks.

3   Rub a penny across each journal several times **(see illustration)**. If a journal picks up copper from the penny, it's too rough and must be reground.

4   Remove all burrs from the crankshaft oil holes with a stone, file or scraper **(see illustration)**.

5   Check the rest of the crankshaft for cracks and other damage. It should be magnafluxed to reveal hidden cracks – an automotive machine shop will handle the procedure.

6   Using a micrometer, measure the diameter of the main and connecting rod journals and compare the results to the figures listed in this Chapter's Specifications **(see illustration)**. By measuring the diameter at a

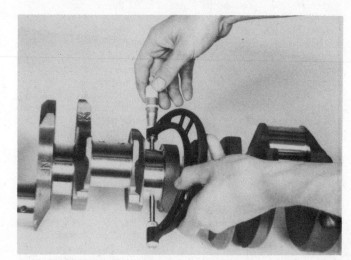

18.6   Measure the diameter of each crankshaft journal at several points to detect taper and out-of-round conditions

2B

18.8   If the seals have worn grooves in the crankshaft journals, or if the seal contact surfaces are nicked or scratched, the new seals will leak

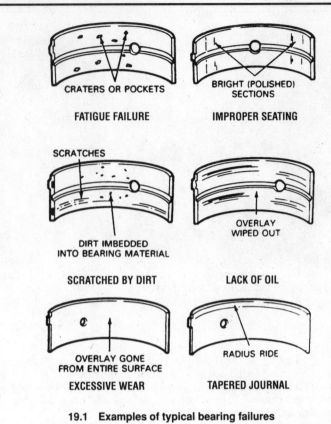

19.1   Examples of typical bearing failures

number of points around each journal's circumference, you'll be able to determine whether or not the journal is out-of-round. Take the measurement at each end of the journal, near the crank throws, to determine if the journal is tapered.

7   If the crankshaft journals are damaged, tapered, out-of-round or worn beyond the limits given in the Specifications, have the crankshaft reground by an automotive machine shop. Be sure to use the correct size bearing inserts if the crankshaft is reconditioned.

8   Check the oil seal journals at each end of the crankshaft for wear and damage. If the seal has worn a groove in the journal, or if it's nicked or scratched **(see illustration)**, the new seal may leak when the engine is reassembled. In some cases, an automotive machine shop may be able to repair the journal by pressing on a thin sleeve. If repair isn't feasible, a new or different crankshaft should be installed.

9   Refer to Section 19 and examine the main and rod bearing inserts.

19   Main and connecting rod bearings – inspection

Refer to illustration 19.1

1   Even though the main and connecting rod bearings should be replaced with new ones during the engine overhaul, the old bearings should be retained for close examination, as they may reveal valuable information about the condition of the engine **(see illustration)**.

2   Bearing failure occurs because of lack of lubrication, the presence of dirt or other foreign particles, overloading the engine and corrosion. Regardless of the cause of bearing failure, it must be corrected before the engine is reassembled to prevent it from happening again.

3   When examining the bearings, remove them from the engine block, the main bearing caps, the connecting rods and the rod caps and lay them out on a clean surface in the same general position as their location in the engine. This will enable you to match any bearing problems with the corresponding crankshaft journal.

4   Dirt and other foreign particles get into the engine in a variety of ways. It may be left in the engine during assembly, or it may pass through filters or the PCV system. It may get into the oil, and from there into the bearings. Metal chips from machining operations and normal engine wear are often present. Abrasives are sometimes left in engine components after reconditioning, especially when parts are not thoroughly cleaned using the proper cleaning methods. Whatever the source, these foreign objects often end up embedded in the soft bearing material and are easily recognized. Large particles will not embed in the bearing and will score or gouge the bearing and journal. The best prevention for this cause of bearing failure is to clean all parts thoroughly and keep everything spotlessly clean during

engine assembly. Frequent and regular engine oil and filter changes are also recommended.

5   Lack of lubrication (or lubrication breakdown) has a number of interrelated causes. Excessive heat (which thins the oil), overloading (which squeezes the oil from the bearing face) and oil leakage or throw off (from excessive bearing clearances, worn oil pump or high engine speeds) all contribute to lubrication breakdown. Blocked oil passages, which usually are the result of misaligned oil holes in a bearing shell, will also oil starve a bearing and destroy it. When lack of lubrication is the cause of bearing failure, the bearing material is wiped or extruded from the steel backing of the bearing. Temperatures may increase to the point where the steel backing turns blue from overheating.

6   Driving habits can have a definite effect on bearing life. Full throttle, low speed operation (lugging the engine) puts very high loads on bearings, which tends to squeeze out the oil film. These loads cause the bearings to flex, which produces fine cracks in the bearing face (fatigue failure). Eventually the bearing material will loosen in pieces and tear away from the steel backing. Short trip driving leads to corrosion of bearings because insufficient engine heat is produced to drive off the condensed water and corrosive gases. These products collect in the engine oil, forming acid and sludge. As the oil is carried to the engine bearings, the acid attacks and corrodes the bearing material.

7   Incorrect bearing installation during engine assembly will lead to bearing failure as well. Tight fitting bearings leave insufficient bearing oil clearance and will result in oil starvation. Dirt or foreign particles trapped behind a bearing insert result in high spots on the bearing which lead to failure.

20   Engine overhaul – reassembly sequence

1   Before beginning engine reassembly, make sure you have all the necessary new parts, gaskets and seals as well as the following items on hand:

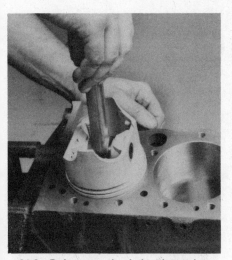

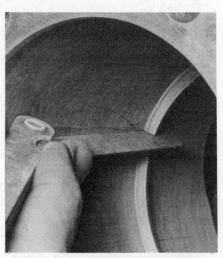

21.3 Before you check the piston ring end gap, square the ring in the cylinder by pushing the ring down with the top of the piston

21.4 Once the ring is square in the cylinder, measure the end gap with a feeler gauge

21.5 If the end gap is too small, clamp a file in a vise and file the ring ends (from the outside in only) to enlarge the gap slightly

Common hand tools
A 1/2-inch drive torque wrench
Piston ring installation tool
Piston ring compressor
Vibration damper installation tool
Short lengths of rubber or plastic hose to fit over connecting rod bolts
Plastigage
Feeler gauges
A fine-tooth file
New engine oil
Engine assembly lube or moly-base grease
Gasket sealant
Thread locking compound

2   In order to save time and avoid problems, engine reassembly must be done in the following general order:

Piston rings
Crankshaft and main bearings
Piston/connecting rod assemblies
Oil pump
Rear main oil seal/housing
Cam followers and shims
Camshaft
Cylinder head
Oil pan
Timing belt and sprockets
Timing cover
Intake and exhaust manifolds
Camshaft cover
Flywheel/driveplate

---

21 Piston rings – installation

Refer to illustrations 21.3, 21.4, 21.5, 21.9a, 21.9b and 21.12

1   Before installing the new piston rings, the ring end gaps must be checked. It's assumed the piston ring side clearance has been checked and verified correct (see Section 17).
2   Lay out the piston/connecting rod assemblies and the new ring sets so the ring sets will be matched with the same piston and cylinder during the end gap measurement and engine assembly.
3   Insert the top (number one) ring into the first cylinder and square it up with the cylinder walls by pushing it in with the top of the piston **(see illustration)**. The ring should be near the bottom of the cylinder, at the lower limit of ring travel.

4   To measure the end gap, slip feeler gauges between the ends of the ring until a gauge equal to the gap width is found **(see illustration)**. The feeler gauge should slide between the ring ends with a slight amount of drag. Compare the measurement to this Chapter's Specifications. If the gap is larger or smaller than specified, double-check to make sure you have the correct rings before proceeding.
5   If the gap is too small, it must be enlarged or the ring ends may come in contact with each other during engine operation, which can cause serious damage to the engine. The end gap can be increased by filing the ring ends very carefully with a fine file. Mount the file in a vise equipped with soft jaws, slip the ring over the file with the ends contacting the file face and slowly move the ring to remove material from the ends. When performing this operation, file only from the outside in **(see illustration)**.
6   Excess end gap isn't critical unless it's greater than 0.040-inch. Again, double-check to make sure you have the correct rings for the engine.
7   Repeat the procedure for each ring that will be installed in the first cylinder and for each ring in the remaining cylinders. Remember to keep rings, pistons and cylinders matched up.
8   Once the ring end gaps have been checked/corrected, the rings can be installed on the pistons.
9   The oil control ring (lowest one on the piston) is usually installed first. It's composed of three separate components. Slip the spacer/expander into the groove **(see illustration)**. If an anti-rotation tang is used, make

21.9a Install the three-piece oil control ring first, one part at a time, beginning with the spacer/expander ring . . .

21.9b ... followed by the oil ring side rails – DON'T use a piston ring installation tool to install the side rails

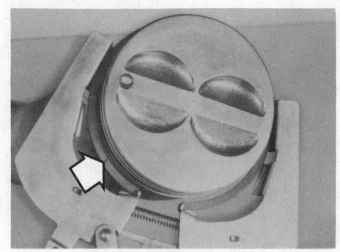

21.12 Install the piston rings with a ring expander – make sure that the mark (arrow) faces up

sure it's inserted into the drilled hole in the ring groove. Next, install the lower side rail. Don't use a piston ring installation tool on the oil ring side rails, as they may be damaged. Instead, place one end of the side rail into the groove between the spacer/expander and the ring land, hold it firmly in place and slide a finger around the piston while pushing the rail into the groove **(see illustration)**. Next, install the upper side rail in the same manner.

10   After the three oil ring components have been installed, check to make sure both the upper and lower side rails can be turned smoothly in the ring groove.

11   The number two (middle) ring is installed next. It's usually stamped with a mark which must face up, toward the top of the piston. **Note:** *Always follow the instructions printed on the ring package or box – different manufacturers may require different approaches. Do not mix up the top and middle rings, as they have different cross sections.*

12   Use a piston ring installation tool and make sure the identification mark is facing the top of the piston, then slip the ring into the middle groove on the piston **(see illustration)**. Don't expand the ring any more than necessary to slide it over the piston.

13   Install the number one (top) ring in the same manner. Make sure the mark is facing up. Be careful not to confuse the number one and number two rings.

14   Repeat the procedure for the remaining pistons and rings.

22   Crankshaft – installation and main bearing oil clearance check

Refer to illustrations 22.5, 22.6, 22.11 and 22.15

1   Crankshaft installation is the first step in engine reassembly. It's assumed at this point that the engine block and crankshaft have been cleaned, inspected and repaired or reconditioned.

2   Position the engine with the bottom facing up.

3   Remove the main bearing cap bolts and lift out the caps. Lay them out in the proper order to ensure correct installation.

4   If they're still in place, remove the original bearing inserts from the block and the main bearing caps. Wipe the bearing surfaces of the block and caps with a clean, lint-free cloth. They must be kept spotlessly clean.

Main bearing oil clearance check

5   Clean the back sides of the new main bearing inserts and lay one in each main bearing saddle in the block. If one of the bearing inserts from each set has a large groove in it, make sure the grooved insert is installed in the block. Lay the other bearing from each set in the corresponding main bearing cap. Make sure the tab on the bearing insert fits into the recess in the block or cap. **Caution:** *The oil holes in the block must line up with the oil holes in the bearing insert* **(see illustration)**. Do not hammer the bearing

22.5 Make sure that the tab on the bearing insert (arrow) fits into the recess in the block and that the oil hole lines up with the oil passage in the block

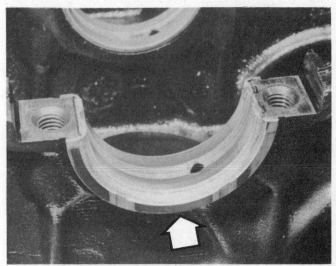

22.6 The thrust bearing (identified by the flange on each side – arrow) must be installed in the number three (center) cap and saddle

22.11 Lay a Plastigage strip (arrow) on each main bearing journal, parallel to the crankshaft centerline

22.15 Compare the width of the crushed Plastigage to the scale printed on the container (always take your measurement where the crushed Plastigage is widest); be sure you're using the right scale too – standard and metric scales are printed on the container

2B

into place and don't nick or gouge the bearing faces. No lubrication should be used at this time.

6   The thrust washers must be installed in the center cap and saddle with the tabs engaged in the cap. Early engines and replacement bearings have a flange that's integral with the bearing insert **(see illustration)**.

7   Clean the faces of the bearings in the block and the crankshaft main bearing journals with a clean, lint-free cloth.

8   Check or clean the oil holes in the crankshaft, as any dirt here can only go one way – straight through the new bearings. Also check the rear seal contact surface very carefully for scratches and nicks that could damage the new seal lip and cause oil leaks. If the crankshaft is damaged, the only alternative is a new or different crankshaft.

9   Once you're certain the crankshaft is clean, carefully lay it in position in the main bearings.

10   Before the crankshaft can be permanently installed, the main bearing oil clearance must be checked.

11   Cut several pieces of the appropriate size Plastigage (they must be slightly shorter than the width of the main bearings) and place one piece on each crankshaft main bearing journal, parallel with the journal axis **(see illustration)**.

12   Clean the faces of the bearings in the caps and install the caps in their respective positions (don't mix them up) with the arrows pointing toward the front of the engine. Don't disturb the Plastigage.

13   Starting with the center main and working out toward the ends, tighten the main bearing cap bolts, in three steps, to the torque listed in this Chapter's Specifications. Don't rotate the crankshaft at any time during this operation.

14   Remove the bolts and carefully lift off the main bearing caps. Keep them in order. Don't disturb the Plastigage or rotate the crankshaft. If any of the main bearing caps are difficult to remove, tap them gently from side-to-side with a soft-face hammer to loosen them.

15   Compare the width of the crushed Plastigage on each journal to the scale printed on the Plastigage envelope to obtain the main bearing oil clearance **(see illustration)**. Check the Specifications to make sure it's correct.

16   If the clearance is not as specified, the bearing inserts may be the wrong size (which means different ones will be required). Before deciding that different inserts are needed, make sure no dirt or oil was between the bearing inserts and the caps or block when the clearance was measured. If the Plastigage was wider at one end than the other, the journal may be tapered (refer to Section 18).

17   Carefully scrape all traces of the Plastigage material off the main bearing journals and/or the bearing faces. Use your fingernail or the edge of a credit card – don't nick or scratch the bearing faces.

Final crankshaft installation

18   Carefully lift the crankshaft out of the engine.

19   Clean the bearing faces in the block, then apply a thin, uniform layer of moly-base grease or engine assembly lube to each of the bearing surfaces. Be sure to coat the thrust faces as well as the journal face of the thrust bearing(s).

20   Make sure the crankshaft journals are clean, then lay the crankshaft back in place in the block.

21   Clean the faces of the bearings in the caps, then apply lubricant to them.

22   Install the caps in their respective positions with the arrows pointing toward the front of the engine or with the bearing cap numbers aligned with each other (all on the side opposite the oil pump).

23   Install the bolts.

24   Tighten all but the center main bearing cap bolts to the torque listed in this Chapter's Specifications. Work from the center out and approach the final torque in three steps. Tighten the center cap bolts to 10 ft-lbs.

25   Tap the ends of the crankshaft forward and backward with a lead or brass hammer to line up the main bearing and crankshaft thrust surfaces.

26   Retighten all main bearing cap bolts to the specified torque, starting with the center main and working out toward the ends.

27   Rotate the crankshaft a number of times by hand to check for any obvious binding.

28   Check the crankshaft endplay with a feeler gauge or a dial indicator as described in Section 13. The endplay should be correct if the crankshaft thrust faces aren't worn or damaged and new bearings have been installed.

29   Refer to Section 23 and install the new crankshaft rear seal, then bolt the housing to the block.

23   Rear main oil seal – installation

Refer to illustrations 23.1, 23.2 and 23.3
Note: *The crankshaft must be installed and the main bearing caps bolted in place before the new seal and housing assembly can be bolted to the block.*

1   Remove the old seal from the housing with a hammer and punch **(see illustration)** by driving it out from the back side. Be sure to note how far it's recessed into the housing bore before removing it; the new seal will have to be recessed an equal amount. Be very careful not to scratch or otherwise damage the bore in the housing or oil leaks could develop.

2   Make sure the housing is clean, then apply a thin coat of engine oil to the outer edge of the new seal. The seal must be pressed squarely into the housing bore, so hammering it into place is not recommended. If you don't have access to a press, sandwich the housing and seal between two

23.1   To remove the old crankshaft rear seal, support the housing on a pair of wood blocks and drive out the seal with a punch or screwdriver and hammer – make sure you don't damage the seal bore

23.2   To install the new crankshaft rear seal in the housing, protect the seal and housing with a block of wood on each side and press the seal into place with a large vise (not shown) – if you don't have a vise, simply lay the housing on a clean, flat workbench, lay a block of wood on the seal and carefully tap it into place with a hammer

23.3   Align the dowel pins with the holes (arrows) and gently push the seal onto the end of the crankshaft

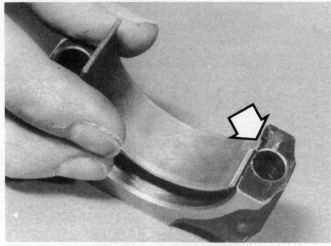

24.4   The tab on the bearing (arrow) must fit into the cap recess so the bearing will seat properly

smooth pieces of wood and press the seal into place with the jaws of a large vise. The pieces of wood must be thick enough to distribute the force evenly around the entire circumference of the seal. If you don't have a vise big enough, lay the housing on a workbench and drive the seal into place with a block of wood and a hammer **(see illustration)**. Work slowly and make sure the seal enters the bore squarely.

3   Lubricate the seal lips with moly-based grease or engine assembly lube before you slip the seal/housing over the crankshaft and bolt it to the block. Use a new gasket – no sealant is required – and make sure the dowel pins are in place before installing the housing **(see illustration)**.

4   Tighten the housing bolts a little at a time until they're all snug.

24   Pistons/connecting rods – installation and rod bearing oil clearance check

Refer to illustrations 24.4, 24.5, 24.9, 24.11, 24.13, 24.14a, 24.14b and 24.17

1   Before installing the piston/connecting rod assemblies, the cylinder walls must be perfectly clean, the top edge of each cylinder must be

chamfered, and the crankshaft must be in place.

2   Remove the cap from the end of the number one connecting rod (refer to the marks made during removal). Remove the original bearing inserts and wipe the bearing surfaces of the connecting rod and cap with a clean, lint-free cloth. They must be kept spotlessly clean.

Connecting rod bearing oil clearance check

3   Clean the back side of the new upper bearing insert, then lay it in place in the connecting rod. Make sure the tab on the bearing fits into the recess in the rod. Don't hammer the bearing insert into place and be very careful not to nick or gouge the bearing face. Don't lubricate the bearing at this time.

4   Clean the back side of the other bearing insert and install it in the rod cap. Again, make sure the tab on the bearing fits into the recess in the cap **(see illustration)**, and don't apply any lubricant. It's critically important that the mating surfaces of the bearing and connecting rod are perfectly clean and oil free when they're assembled.

5   Position the piston ring gaps at the proper locations around the piston **(see illustration)**.

6   Slip a section of plastic or rubber hose over each connecting rod cap bolt.

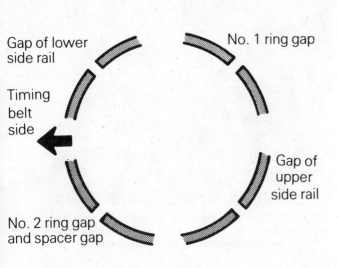

24.5   Position the ring gaps as shown here before you install the piston/connecting rod assemblies in the engine

Gap of lower side rail

No. 1 ring gap

Timing belt side

Gap of upper side rail

No. 2 ring gap and spacer gap

24.9   The arrow on the top of the piston must point to the front (timing belt) end of the engine

2B

24.11   Gently tap the piston into the cylinder bore with the end of a wooden hammer handle

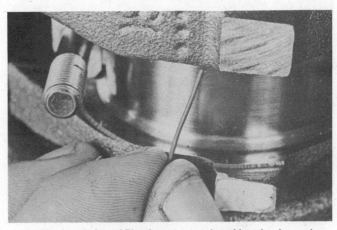

24.13   Lay strips of Plastigage on each rod bearing journal, parallel to the crankshaft centerline

7   Lubricate the piston and rings with clean engine oil and attach a piston ring compressor to the piston. Leave the skirt protruding about 1/4-inch to guide the piston into the cylinder. The rings must be compressed until they're flush with the piston.

8   Rotate the crankshaft until the number one connecting rod journal is at BDC (bottom dead center) and apply a coat of engine oil to the cylinder walls.

9   Gently insert the piston/connecting rod assembly into the number one cylinder bore and rest the bottom edge of the ring compressor on the engine block. Make sure the mark (arrow) on top of the piston points to the front of the engine (see illustration).

10   Tap the top edge of the ring compressor to make sure it's contacting the block around its entire circumference.

11   Gently tap on the top of the piston with the end of a wooden hammer handle (see illustration) while guiding the end of the connecting rod into place on the crankshaft journal. The piston rings may try to pop out of the ring compressor just before entering the cylinder bore, so keep some downward pressure on the ring compressor. Work slowly, and if any resistance is felt as the piston enters the cylinder, stop immediately. Find out what's hanging up and fix it before proceeding. Do not, for any reason, force the piston into the cylinder – you might break a ring and/or the piston.

12   Once the piston/connecting rod assembly is installed, the connecting rod bearing oil clearance must be checked before the rod cap is permanently bolted in place.

13   Cut a piece of the appropriate size Plastigage slightly shorter than the width of the connecting rod bearing and lay it in place on the number one connecting rod journal, parallel with the journal axis (see illustration).

14   Clean the connecting rod cap bearing face, remove the protective hoses from the connecting rod bolts and install the rod cap. Make sure the mating mark on the cap is on the same side as the mark on the connecting rod (see illustrations).

15   Install the nuts and tighten them to the torque listed in this Chapter's Specifications, working up to it in three steps. **Note:** *Use a thin-wall socket to avoid erroneous torque readings that can result if the socket is wedged between the rod cap and nut. If the socket tends to wedge itself between the nut and the cap, lift up on it slightly until it no longer contacts the cap. Do not rotate the crankshaft at any time during this operation.*

16   Remove the nuts and detach the rod cap, being very careful not to disturb the Plastigage.

17   Compare the width of the crushed Plastigage to the scale printed on the Plastigage envelope to obtain the oil clearance (see illustration). Compare it to the Specifications to make sure the clearance is correct.

24.14a   Install the rod bearing cap

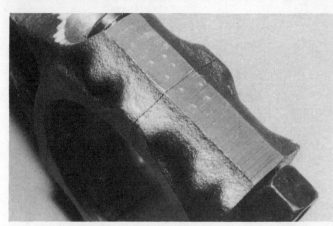

24.14b   Make sure the marks on the rod and cap are matched up when the cap is installed (the marks shown here are center punch indentations made when the rod cap was removed)

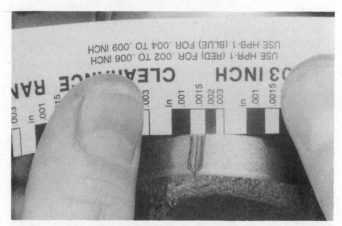

24.17   To determine rod bearing oil clearance, compare the width of the crushed Plastigage to the correct scale printed on the container (be sure you use the right scale – there are standard and metric scales included)

18   If the clearance is not as specified, the bearing inserts may be the wrong size (which means different ones will be required). Before deciding different inserts are needed, make sure no dirt or oil was between the bearing inserts and the connecting rod or cap when the clearance was measured. Also, recheck the journal diameter. If the Plastigage was wider at one end than the other, the journal may be tapered (refer to Section 18).

Final connecting rod installation

19   Carefully scrape all traces of the Plastigage material off the rod journal and/or bearing face. Be very careful not to scratch the bearing – use your fingernail or the edge of a credit card.
20   Make sure the bearing faces are perfectly clean, then apply a uniform layer of clean moly-base grease or engine assembly lube to both of them. You'll have to push the piston into the cylinder to expose the face of the bearing insert in the connecting rod – be sure to slip the protective hoses over the rod bolts first.
21   Slide the connecting rod back into place on the journal, remove the protective hoses from the rod cap bolts, install the rod cap and tighten the nuts to the specified torque. Again, work up to the torque in three steps.
22   Repeat the entire procedure for the remaining pistons/connecting rods.
23   The important points to remember are . . .
   a) Keep the back sides of the bearing inserts and the insides of the connecting rods and caps perfectly clean when assembling them.
   b) Make sure you have the correct piston/rod assembly for each cylinder.
   c) The marks on the top of the piston and the oil holes in the rods must face the appropriate directions **(see illustration 24.9).**

   d) Lubricate the cylinder walls with clean oil.
   e) Lubricate the bearing faces when installing the rod caps after the oil clearance has been checked.
24   After all the piston/connecting rod assemblies have been properly installed, rotate the crankshaft a number of times by hand to check for any obvious binding.
25   As a final step, the connecting rod endplay must be checked. Refer to Section 12 for this procedure.
26   Compare the measured endplay to this Chapter's Specifications to make sure it's correct. If it was correct before disassembly and the original crankshaft and rods were reinstalled, it should still be right. If new rods or a new crankshaft were installed, the endplay may be inadequate. If so, the rods will have to be removed and taken to an automotive machine shop for resizing.

25   Initial start-up and break-in after overhaul

Warning: *Have a fire extinguisher handy when starting the engine for the first time.*

1   Once the engine has been installed in the vehicle, double-check the engine oil and coolant levels.
2   With the spark plugs out of the engine and the ignition system disabled (see Section 3), crank the engine until oil pressure registers on the gauge or the light goes out.
3   Install the spark plugs, hook up the plug wires and restore the ignition system functions (see Section 3).
4   Start the engine. It may take a few moments for the fuel system to build up pressure, but the engine should start without a great deal of effort. **Note:** *If backfiring occurs through the carburetor or throttle body, recheck the valve timing and ignition timing.*
5   After the engine starts, it should be allowed to warm up to normal operating temperature. While the engine is warming up, make a thorough check for fuel, oil and coolant leaks.
6   Shut the engine off and recheck the engine oil and coolant levels.
7   Drive the vehicle to an area with minimum traffic, accelerate at full throttle from 30 to 50 mph, then allow the vehicle to slow to 30 mph with the throttle closed. Repeat the procedure 10 or 12 times. This will load the piston rings and cause them to seat properly against the cylinder walls. Check again for oil and coolant leaks.
8   Drive the vehicle gently for the first 500 miles (no sustained high speeds) and keep a constant check on the oil level. It's not unusual for an engine to use oil during the break-in period.
9   At approximately 500 to 600 miles, change the oil and filter.
10 For the next few hundred miles, drive the vehicle normally. Don't pamper it or abuse it.
11 After 2000 miles, change the oil and filter again and consider the engine broken in.

Chapter 3   Cooling, heating and air conditioning systems

Contents

Air conditioning compressor – removal and installation	15	
Air conditioning condenser – removal and installation	16	
Air conditioning receiver–drier – removal and installation	14	
Air conditioning system – check and maintenance	13	
Antifreeze – general information	2	
Coolant level check	See Chapter 1	
Coolant reservoir – removal and installation	6	
Coolant temperature sending unit – check and replacement	9	
Cooling system check	See Chapter 1	
Cooling system servicing (draining, flushing and refilling)	See Chapter 1	
Drivebelt check, adjustment and replacement	See Chapter 1	

Engine cooling fan and thermoswitch – check and replacement	4	
General information	1	
Heater and air conditioner blower motor – removal and installation	10	
Heater core – replacement	11	
Heater or heater/air conditioner control assembly – removal, installation and cable adjustment	12	
Radiator – removal and installation	5	
Thermostat – check and replacement	3	
Underhood hose check and replacement	See Chapter 1	
Water pump – check	7	
Water pump – replacement	8	

3

Specifications

General

Radiator cap pressure rating	See Chapter 1
Thermostat rating (opening temperature)	
1975 through 1978	176-degrees F (80-degrees C)
1979	185-degrees F (85-degrees C)
1980 through 1984	176-degrees F (80-degrees C)
1985 on	185-degrees F (85-degrees C)
Cooling system capacity	See Chapter 1
Refrigerant capacity	33 to 34 ounces

Torque specifications

Ft-lbs (unless otherwise indicated)

Thermostat housing-to-water pump bolts	90 in-lbs
Water pump pulley bolts	15
Water pump-to-housing bolts	90 in-lbs
Water pump housing-to-block	15

---

1   General information

Engine cooling system

All vehicles covered by this manual employ a pressurized engine cooling system with thermostatically controlled coolant circulation. An impeller type water pump mounted on the front of the block pumps coolant through the engine. The coolant flows around the combustion chambers and toward the rear of the engine. Cast-in coolant passages direct coolant near the intake ports, exhaust ports, and spark plug areas.

A wax pellet type thermostat is located in a housing near the water pump. During warm-up, the closed thermostat prevents coolant from circulating through the radiator. As the engine nears normal operating temperature, the thermostat opens and allows hot coolant to travel through the radiator, where it's cooled before returning to the engine.

The cooling system is sealed by a pressure type radiator cap, which raises the boiling point of the coolant and increases the cooling efficiency of the radiator. If the system pressure exceeds the cap pressure relief value, the excess pressure in the system forces the spring-loaded valve inside the cap off its seat and on early models, allows the coolant to escape through the overflow tube into a coolant reservoir. When the system cools the excess coolant is automatically drawn from the reservoir back into the radiator. On later models the coolant reservoir is pressurized and there is enough room in the reservoir for expansion.

The coolant reservoir also serves as the point at which fresh coolant is added to the cooling system to maintain the proper fluid level.

This type of cooling system is known as a closed design because coolant that escapes past the pressure cap is saved and reused.

Heating system

The heating system consists of a blower fan and heater core located in the heater box, the hoses connecting the heater core to the engine cooling system and the heater/air conditioning control head on the dashboard. Hot engine coolant is circulated through the heater core. When the heater mode is activated, a flap door opens to expose the heater box to the passenger compartment. A fan switch on the control head activates the blower motor, which forces air through the core, heating the air.

Air conditioning system

The air conditioning system consists of a condenser mounted in front of the radiator, an evaporator mounted adjacent to the heater core, a compressor mounted on the engine, a filter-drier or receiver-drier (accumulator) which contains a high pressure relief valve and the plumbing connecting all of the above components.

A blower fan forces the warmer air of the passenger compartment through the evaporator core (sort of a radiator-in-reverse), transferring the heat from the air to the refrigerant. The liquid refrigerant boils off into low pressure vapor, taking the heat with it when it leaves the evaporator.

---

2   Antifreeze – general information

Warning: *Do not allow antifreeze to come in contact with your skin or painted surfaces of the vehicle. Rinse off spills immediately with plenty of water. Never leave antifreeze lying around in an open container or in a puddle in the driveway or on the garage floor. Children and animals are attracted by it's sweet smell. Antifreeze is toxic, so use common sense when disposing of it. Some communities maintain toxic material disposal sites and/or offer regular pick-up of hazardous materials. Antifreeze is also flammable, so don't store or use it near open flames.*

The cooling system should be filled with a water/ethylene glycol based antifreeze solution, which will prevent freezing down to at least -20 degrees F, or lower if local climate requires it. It also provides protection against corrosion and increases the coolant boiling point.

The cooling system should be drained, flushed and refilled at the specified intervals (see Chapter 1). Old or contaminated antifreeze solutions are likely to cause damage and encourage the formation of rust and scale in the system. Use distilled water with the antifreeze.

Before adding antifreeze, check all hose connections, because antifreeze tends to leak through very minute openings. Engines don't normally consume coolant, so if the level goes down, find the cause and correct it.

The exact mixture of antifreeze-to-water which you should use depends on the relative weather conditions. The mixture should contain at least 50 percent antifreeze, but should never contain more than 70 percent antifreeze. Consult the mixture ratio chart on the antifreeze container before adding coolant. Hydrometers are available at most auto parts stores to test the coolant. Use antifreeze which meets the vehicle manufacturer's specifications.

---

3   Thermostat – check and replacement

Warning: *Do not remove the radiator cap, drain the coolant or replace the thermostat until the engine has cooled completely.*

Check

1   Before assuming the thermostat is to blame for a cooling system problem, check the coolant level, drivebelt tension (see Chapter 1) and temperature gauge operation.

2   If the engine seems to be taking a long time to warm up (based on heater output or temperature gauge operation), the thermostat is probably stuck open. Replace the thermostat with a new one.

3   If the engine runs hot, use your hand to check the temperature of the upper radiator hose. If the hose isn't hot, but the engine is, the thermostat is probably stuck closed, preventing the coolant inside the engine from escaping to the radiator. Replace the thermostat. **Caution:** *Don't drive the vehicle without a thermostat. The computer may stay in open loop and emissions and fuel economy will suffer.*

4   If the upper radiator hose is hot, it means that the coolant is flowing and the thermostat is open. Consult the Troubleshooting Section at the front of this manual for cooling system diagnosis.

Replacement

Refer to illustrations 3.10a, 3.10b and 3.13

5   Disconnect the negative battery cable from the battery.

6   Drain the cooling system (see Chapter 1). If the coolant is relatively new or in good condition, save it and reuse it.

7   Follow the lower radiator hose to the engine to locate the thermostat housing.

8   Loosen the hose clamp, then detach the hose from the fitting. If it's stuck, grasp it near the end with a pair of adjustable pliers and twist it to break the seal, then pull it off. If the hose is old or deteriorated, cut it off and install a new one.

9   If the outer surface of the large fitting that mates with the hose is deteriorated (corroded, pitted, etc.) it may be damaged further by hose removal. If it is, the thermostat housing cover will have to be replaced.

10   Remove the bolts and detach the housing cover (see illustrations). If the cover is stuck, tap it with a soft-face hammer to jar it loose. Be prepared for some coolant to spill as the gasket seal is broken.

3.10a   The thermostat housing is bolted to the water pump housing

3.10b   The thermostat is accessible after removing the bolts and
detaching the housing cover

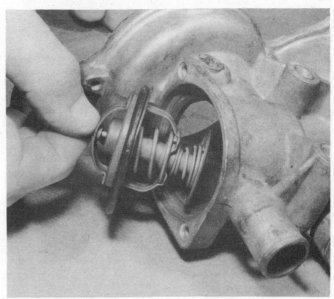

3.13   Make sure the thermostat is installed correctly – the spring
end must be directed toward the engine

11   Note how it's installed (which end is facing up), then remove the thermostat **(see illustration 3.10b)**.
12   Stuff a rag into the engine opening, then remove all traces of old gasket material and sealant from the housing and cover with a gasket scraper. Remove the rag from the opening and clean the gasket mating surfaces with lacquer thinner or acetone.
13   Install the new thermostat in the housing. Make sure the correct end faces up (the spring end should be directed toward the engine) **(see illustration)**. Apply a thin, uniform layer of RTV sealant to both sides of the new gasket and position it on the housing.
14   Install the cover and bolts. Tighten the bolts to the torque listed in this Chapter's Specifications.
15   Reattach the hose to the fitting and tighten the hose clamp securely.
16   Refill the cooling system (see Chapter 1).
17   Start the engine and allow it to reach normal operating temperature, then check for leaks and proper thermostat operation (as described in Steps 2 through 4).

**4   Engine cooling fan and thermoswitch – check
and replacement**

Warning: *To avoid possible injury or damage, DO NOT operate the engine with a damaged fan. Do not attempt to repair fan blades – replace a damaged fan with a new one.*

Check
Refer to Illustrations 4.1, 4.2a and 4.2b

1   If the engine is overheating and the cooling fan is not coming on, unplug the electrical connector at the motor **(see illustration)** and use jumper wires to connect the fan directly to the battery. If the fan still doesn't work, replace the motor.
2   If the motor is OK, but the cooling fan still doesn't come on when the engine gets hot, the fault lies in the radiator thermoswitch **(see illustrations)** or the wiring which connects the components. Bridge the terminals

4.1   Disconnect the harness from the fan motor and apply
battery voltage directly to the motor terminals

4.2a   On some models, the radiator fan switch is located in the
lower tank of the radiator

3

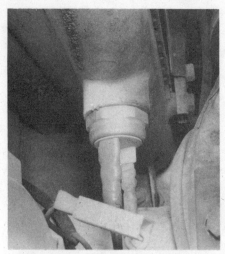

4.2b   On other models, the radiator fan switch is located on the side of the radiator, near the bottom

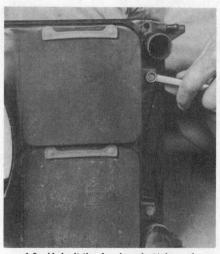

4.6   Unbolt the fan bracket/shroud assembly from the radiator

4.7   Remove the small circlip on the fan motor shaft and slide the fan out

on the switch. If the fan operates, the switch is defective. If the fan still doesn't come on, use a voltmeter or test light to check the fan circuit (wiring diagrams are included at the end of Chapter 12). Carefully check all wiring and connections. If no obvious problems are found, further diagnosis should be done by a dealer service department or repair shop.

Replacement

Fan

Refer to illustrations 4.6, 4.7, 4.8 and 4.9

3   Disconnect the negative battery cable from the battery.

4   Remove the fan wire harness from the clips.

5   Insert a small screwdriver into the connector to lift the lock tab and unplug the fan wire harness.

6   Unbolt the fan bracket and shroud assembly **(see illustration)** and carefully lift it up.

7   To detach the fan from the motor, remove the clip from the motor shaft **(see illustration)**.

8   To remove the fan motor from the shroud, remove the mounting nuts **(see illustration)**.

9   Installation is the reverse of removal. Be sure to line up the pin with the notch in the fan blade **(see illustration)**.

Thermoswitch

10   Drain the coolant.

11   Unplug the electrical connector from the switch.

12   Unscrew the switch from the radiator **(see illustrations 4.2a and 4.2b)**.

13   Wrap the threads of the new switch with teflon tape to prevent leaks.

14   Install the switch and tighten it securely.

15   Plug in the electrical connector.

16   Fill the cooling system (see Chapter 1).

17   Start the engine and check for leaks.

---

5   Radiator – removal and installation

Warning: *Wait until the engine is completely cool before beginning this procedure.*

Removal

Refer to illustrations 5.5, 5.7a and 5.7b

1   Disconnect the negative battery cable from the battery.

4.8   Remove the nuts on the fan bracket to detach the motor

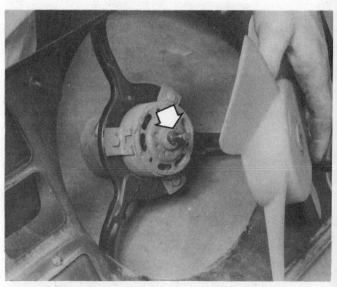

4.9   Be sure to line up the pin (arrow) with the notch in the fan blade

5.5   Remove the clip that retains the radiator to the body

5.7a   Remove the radiator mounting bolts at the bottom of the radiator (some models use nuts and rubber insulators)

2   Drain the cooling system (see Chapter 1). If the coolant is relatively new and in good condition, save it and reuse it.

3   Loosen the hose clamps, then detach the radiator hoses from the fittings. If they're stuck, grasp each hose near the end with a pair of adjustable pliers and twist it to break the seal, then pull it off – be careful not to distort the radiator fittings! If the hoses are old or deteriorated, cut them off and install new ones.

4   Disconnect the reservoir hose from the radiator.

5   Remove the clip that attaches the radiator to the vehicle body **(see illustration)**.

6   Unplug the electrical connector from the radiator thermoswitch (see Section 4).

7   Remove the radiator mounting bolts **(see illustrations)**.

8   Carefully lift out the radiator. Don't spill coolant on the vehicle or scratch the paint.

9   Check the radiator for leaks and damage. If it needs repair, have a radiator shop or dealer service department perform the work as special techniques are required.

3

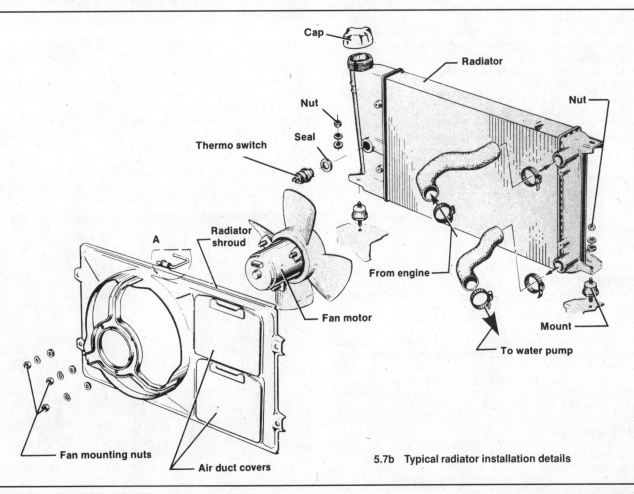

Cap

Radiator

Nut

Nut

Seal

Thermo switch

Radiator shroud

A

Fan motor

From engine

Mount

To water pump

Fan mounting nuts

Air duct covers

5.7b   Typical radiator installation details

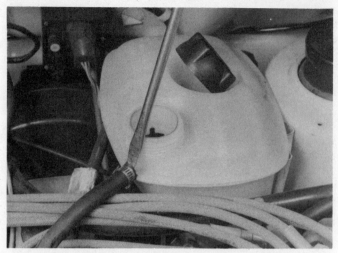

6.1   On models that have a pressurized coolant reservoir, detach the small upper hose and the large lower hose

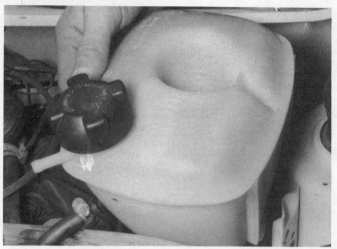

6.2   Remove the coolant reservoir from the bracket by lifting it up

10 Remove bugs and dirt from the radiator with compressed air and a soft brush (don't bend the cooling fins).

11 Inspect the radiator mounts for deterioration and make sure there's no dirt or gravel in them when the radiator is installed.

Installation

12 Installation is the reverse of the removal procedure. Make sure the radiator seats properly in the bottom mounting brackets before fastening the top brackets.

13 After installation, fill the cooling system with the proper mixture of antifreeze and water. See Chapter 1 if necessary.

14 Start the engine and check for leaks. Allow the engine to reach normal operating temperature, indicated by the upper radiator hose becoming hot. Recheck the coolant level and add more if required.

15 If you're working on an automatic transmission equipped vehicle, check and add fluid as needed.

---

6   Coolant reservoir – removal and installation

Refer to illustrations 6.1 and 6.2

1   Remove the coolant from the reservoir with a suction gun. Detach the hose(s) from the coolant reservoir **(see illustration)**. Plug the hose(s) to prevent coolant loss and contamination.

2   Lift the reservoir straight up out of its bracket **(see illustration)**.

3   Installation is the reverse of removal.

---

7   Water pump – check

1   A failure in the water pump can cause serious engine damage due to overheating.

2   There are three ways to check the operation of the water pump while it's installed on the engine. If the pump is defective, it should be replaced with a new or rebuilt unit.

3   With the engine running at normal operating temperature, squeeze the upper radiator hose. If the water pump is working properly, a pressure surge should be felt as the hose is released. **Warning:** *Keep your hands away from the fan blades!*

4   Water pumps are equipped with "weep" or vent holes. If a failure occurs in the pump seal, coolant will leak from the hole. In most cases you'll need a flashlight to find the hole on the water pump from underneath to check for leaks.

5   If the water pump shaft bearings fail there may be a howling sound at the front of the engine while it's running. Shaft wear can be felt if the water pump pulley is rocked up-and-down. Don't mistake drivebelt slippage, which causes a squealing sound, for water pump bearing failure.

---

8   Water pump – replacement

Refer to illustrations 8.6, 8.8, 8.9a, 8.9b and 8.12

Warning: *Wait until the engine is completely cool before beginning this procedure.*

1   Disconnect the negative battery cable from the battery.

2   Drain the cooling system (see Chapter 1). If the coolant is relatively new or in good condition, save and reuse it.

3   Remove the drivebelts (see Chapter 1) and the pulley at the end of the water pump shaft.

4   If it's in the way, remove the alternator (see Chapter 5).

5   Loosen the clamps and detach the hoses from the water pump. If they're stuck, grasp each hose near the end with a pair of adjustable pliers and twist it to break the seal, then pull it off. If the hoses are deteriorated, cut them off and install new ones.

6   Remove the bolts **(see illustration)** and detach the water pump housing. Note the locations of the various lengths and different types of bolts as they're removed to ensure correct installation.

8.6   Water pump housing mounting bolt locations (arrows)

8.8   Scrape the old sealant material off the engine block and the water pump housing

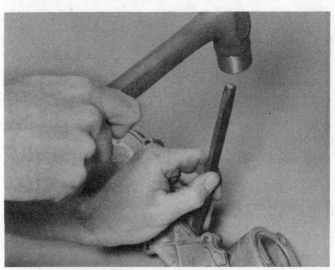

8.9a   You may have to use a hammer and chisel to separate the water pump from the housing, but be extremely careful – don't damage the mating surface of the housing

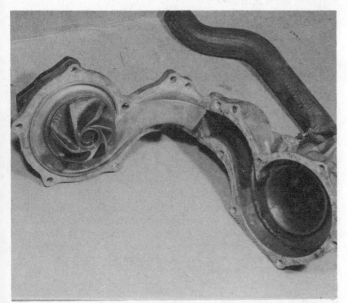

8.9b   Once the bond has been broken, separate the pump from the housing

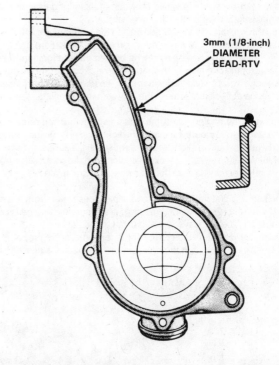

3mm (1/8-inch) DIAMETER BEAD-RTV

8.12   Apply a continuous bead of RTV sealant between the bolt holes and the inner edge of the housing

7   Clean the bolt threads and the threaded holes in the engine to remove corrosion and sealant.
8   Remove all traces of old gasket material from the engine and pump housing with a gasket scraper (see illustration).
9   Remove the bolts and separate the water pump from the housing (see illustrations).
10   If you're installing a new pump, compare the new pump to the old pump to make sure they're identical.
11   Clean the mating surfaces of the housing. Remove all old sealant material. Remove the old O-ring from the housing groove.
12   Apply a bead of RTV sealant to the mating surface of the housing (see illustration). Install a new O-ring in the housing groove.
13   Attach the new pump to the housing and tighten the bolts to the torque listed in this Chapter's Specifications.
14   Install the pump/housing assembly on the engine (make sure a new gasket is used) and tighten the bolts to the torque listed in this Chapter's Specifications.
15   Reinstall all parts removed for access to the pump.

16   Refill the cooling system and check the drivebelt tension (see Chapter 1). Run the engine and check for leaks.

9   Coolant temperature sending unit – check and replacement

Refer to illustration 9.1
Warning: Wait until the engine is completely cool before beginning this procedure.
1   The coolant temperature indicator system is composed of a light or temperature gauge mounted in the instrument panel and a coolant tem-

9.1   Coolant temperature sending unit location (typical)

perature sending unit mounted on the thermostat housing or water box **(see illustration)**. Most of the vehicles covered by this book have more than one sending unit on the housing, but only one is used for the indicator system. **Warning:** *If the vehicle is equipped with an electric cooling fan, stay clear of the fan blades, which can come on at any time.*

2   If an overheating indication occurs, check the coolant level in the system and then make sure the wiring between the light or gauge and the sending unit is secure and all fuses are intact.

3   When the ignition switch is turned on and the starter motor is turning, the indicator light should be on (overheated engine indication).

4   If the light is not on, the bulb may be burned out, the ignition switch may be faulty or the circuit may be open. Test the circuit by grounding the wire to the sending unit while the ignition is on (engine not running for safety). If the gauge deflects full scale or the light comes on, replace the sending unit.

5   As soon as the engine starts, the light should go out and remain out unless the engine overheats. Failure of the light to go out may be due to a grounded wire between the light and the sending unit, a defective sending unit or a faulty ignition switch. Check the coolant to make sure it's the proper type. Plain water may have too low a boiling point to activate the sending unit.

6   If the sending unit must be replaced, simply unscrew it from the engine and install the replacement. **Warning:** *Make sure the engine is cool before removing the defective sending unit.* Use sealant on the threads. There will be some coolant loss as the unit is removed, so be prepared to catch it. Check the level after the replacement has been installed.

10   Heater and air conditioner blower motor – removal and installation

1975 and 1976 models

1   Disconnect the cable from the negative terminal of the battery. Working in the engine compartment, remove the heater cover and cut-off flap from the fresh air housing.

2   Remove the clips retaining the fan motor assembly and remove the fan and motor.

3   If the motor is defective, the motor and fan should be replaced as a unit.

4   Installation is the reverse of removal.

1977 through 1984 models

Refer to illustrations 10.8, 10.9, 10.10, 10.11a, 10.11b and 10.12

5   Detach the cable from the negative terminal of the battery.

6   Drain the engine coolant (see Chapter 1).

7   Remove the screws from the heater outlet duct and disconnect the duct from the housing.

8   Pry the cable clamp off the control flap arm **(see illustration)**.

9   Use a pair of needle nose pliers and remove the cable from the control flap arm **(see illustration)**.

10   Loosen the clamps that hold the heater core hoses and detach the hoses **(see illustration)**.

11   Remove the bolts and screws that retain the blower assembly to the dash and firewall **(see illustrations)**. Lower the assembly from under the dash.

12   Remove the screws retaining the blower motor to the heater assembly **(see illustration)**.

13   Detach the blower assembly and lift it out of the housing.

14   Installation is the reverse of removal.

1985 and later models

Refer to illustrations 10.15 and 10.16

15   Disconnect the cable from the negative terminal of the battery. Remove the glove compartment and the lower right instrument panel tray to gain access to the blower **(see illustration)**.

16   On vehicles without air-conditioning, remove the blower assembly by depressing the retaining tab and rotating the motor clockwise **(see illustration)**.

17   On vehicles with air-conditioning, remove the three retaining screws and remove the blower motor from the evaporator case.

18   Installation is the reverse of removal.

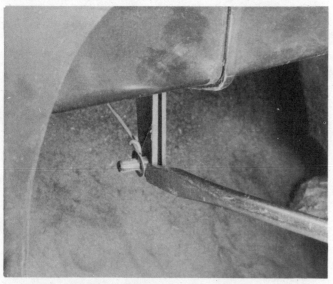

10.8   Carefully pry the clamp off the control flap arm

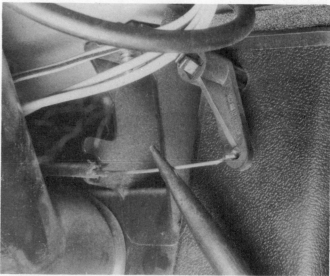

10.9   Use pliers to remove the cable from the control arm

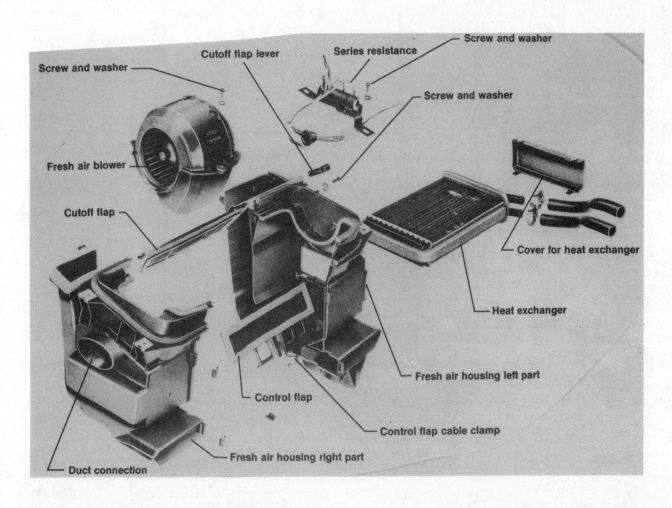

Screw and washer

Cutoff flap lever

Series resistance

Screw and washer

Fresh air blower

Screw and washer

Cutoff flap

Cover for heat exchanger

Heat exchanger

Fresh air housing left part

Control flap

Control flap cable clamp

Duct connection

Fresh air housing right part

3

10.10 Exploded view of heating and ventilation system on vehicles without air conditioning (1977 through 1984 models)

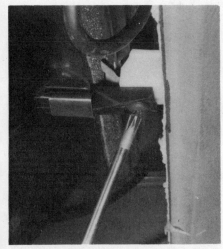

10.11a Remove the panel screw that retains the heater assembly to the upper dash frame

10.11b Remove the bolts that retain the blower assembly to the firewall – the bolts are accessible in the engine compartment

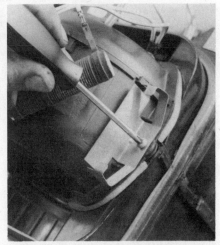

10.12 Remove the screws that retain the blower motor to the housing

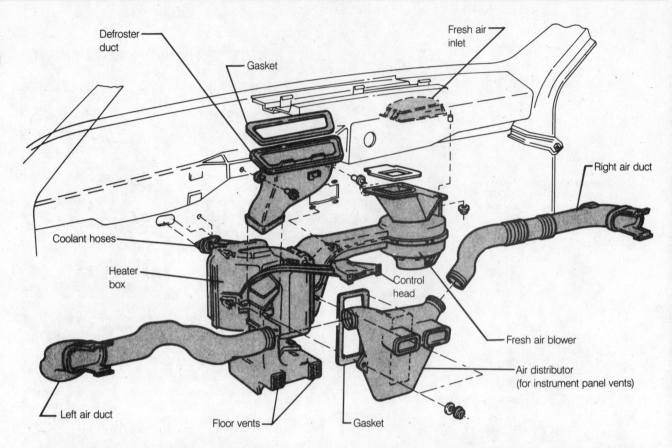

10.15   Exploded view of heating and ventilation system on vehicles without air conditioning (1985 and later models)

10.16   Push the retaining tab (A) and rotate the motor clockwise for removal

11.5   Remove the cover that retains the heater core

---

11   Heater core – replacement

Heater core only

Refer to illustrations 11.2 and 11.3

Warning: *Removal of the heater core on vehicles with A/C requires that the air conditioning system be discharged. Because special tools are required, any work on the A/C system should be performed by a dealership service department or other repair shop.*

1   Detach the cable from the negative terminal of the battery.

2   Drain the engine coolant.

3   Loosen the clamps retaining the heater hoses to the heater core and remove the hoses.

4   On 1977 and later models, working in the passenger compartment, remove the heater unit. **Note:** *On 1984 and later models, it is necessary to remove the instrument panel (see Chapter 12) before removing the heater unit.*

5   Remove the screws that retain the heater core cover to the heater unit and lift the cover up **(see illustration)**.

11.6   Lift the heater core up and out of the heater assembly

6   Lift the heater core up and out of the heater unit **(see illustration)**.
7   Installation is the reverse of removal. Be sure to install the gasket onto the bottom of the heater unit when the new heater core is installed.

Heater/evaporator assembly (air conditioned vehicles)

8   Have the air conditioning system discharged by a service station before beginning this procedure.
9   Remove the heater unit.
10   Remove the evaporator retaining screws and remove the evaporator from the evaporator housing.
11   Installation is the reverse of removal.
12   Take the vehicle back to the shop that discharged the air conditioning system to have it recharged.

12   Heater or heater/air conditioner control assembly – removal, installation and cable adjustment

Removal and installation

Refer to illustrations 12.3a and 12.3b

1   Detach the cable from the negative terminal of the battery.
2   Pull the knobs straight out and off the heater controls.
3   Carefully pry off the cover plate, starting on the right hand side **(see illustrations)**. Remove the under dash panels for access to the heater controls.
4   Disconnect the wires from the fan harness and the cables from the heater.
5   Remove the screws that hold the heater controls to the dashboard frame. Remove the heater controls, detaching them from the flap cables only if necessary.
6   Installation is the reverse of removal.

3

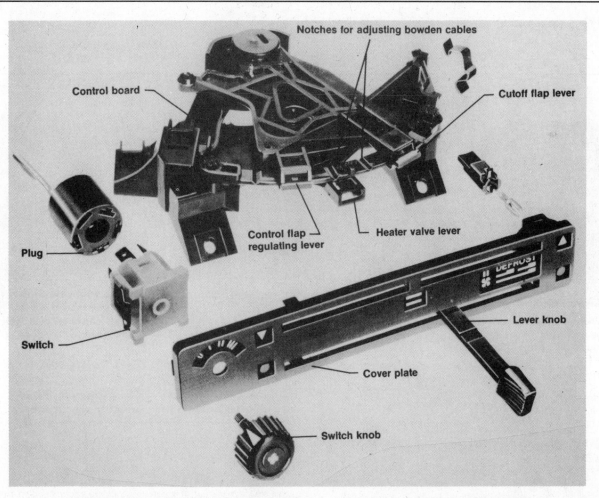

12.3a   Heater controls used on vehicles without air conditioning (1980 through 1984 models)

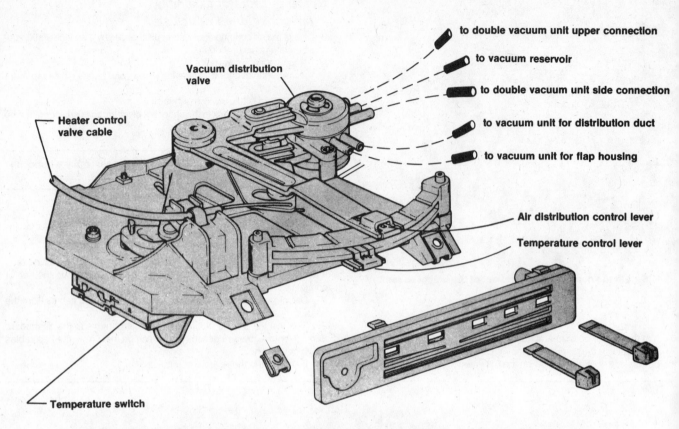

12.3b   Heater controls used on pickup truck models with air conditioning (1980 through 1984 models)

12.8a   Adjust the short black cable for the heater/defroster door by pushing down on the lever (arrow) (1984 and later models)

12.8b   Adjust the blue cable for the blend door by pushing on the lever (arrow) (1984 and later models)

12.8c   Adjust the long black cable for the instrument panel vent door (arrow) (1984 and later models)

Cable adjustment

Refer to illustrations 12.8a, 12.8b and 12.8c

7   To adjust the control cables, remove all of the cable housing retaining clips on the heater blower unit. Push the levers on the control head all the way to the left.

8   Push the heater unit door levers to the farthest closed position **(see illustrations)**. Hold the levers in these positions and install the cable housing retaining clips.

9   Move the levers to test for smooth opening and closing of the doors.

13   Air conditioning system – check and maintenance

Refer to illustrations 13.3 and 13.7

Warning: *The air conditioning system is under high pressure. Do not loosen any hose fittings or remove any components until after the system has been discharged by a dealer service department or service station. Always wear eye protection when disconnecting air conditioning system fittings.*

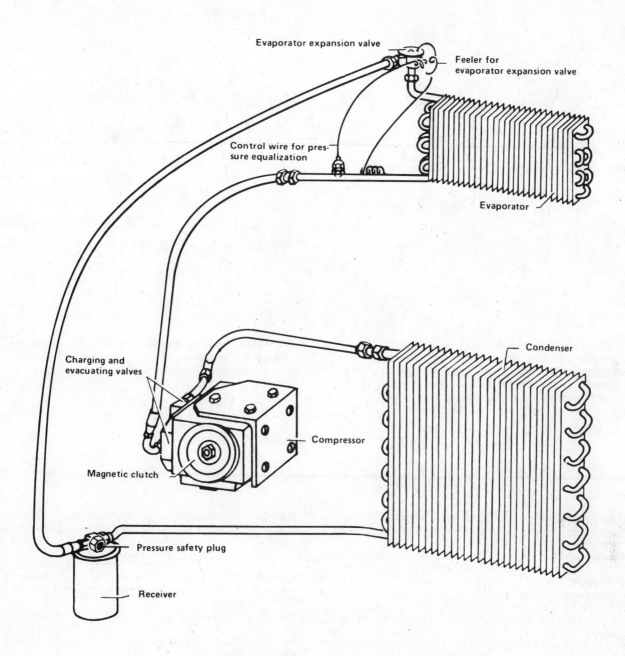

13.3   Schematic view of the air conditioning system

Check

1   The following maintenance checks should be performed on a regular basis to ensure the air conditioner continues to operate at peak efficiency.

   a) Check the compressor drivebelt. If it's worn or deteriorated, replace it (see Chapter 1).
   b) Check the drivebelt tension and, if necessary, adjust it (see Chapter 1).
   c) Check the system hoses. Look for cracks, bubbles, hard spots and deterioration. Inspect the hoses and all fittings for oil bubbles and seepage. If there's any evidence of wear, damage or leaks, replace the hose(s).
   d) Inspect the condenser fins for leaves, bugs and other debris. Use a "fin comb" or compressed air to clean the condenser.
   e) Make sure the system has the correct refrigerant charge.

2   It's a good idea to operate the system for about 10 minutes at least once a month, particularly during the winter. Long term non-use can cause hardening, and subsequent failure, of the seals.

3   Because of the complexity of the air conditioning system (**see illustration**) and the special equipment necessary to service it, in-depth troubleshooting and repairs are not included in this manual (refer to the *Haynes Automotive Heating and Air Conditioning Repair Manual*). However, simple checks and component replacement procedures are provided in this Chapter.

4   The most common cause of poor cooling is simply a low system refrigerant charge. If a noticeable drop in cool air output occurs, the following quick check will help you determine if the refrigerant level is low.

5   Warm the engine up to normal operating temperature.

6   Place the air conditioning temperature selector at the coldest setting

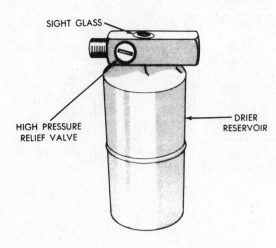

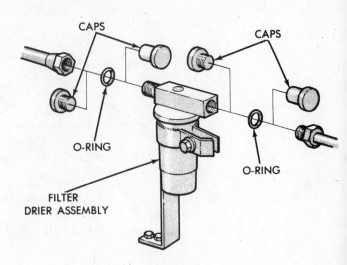

13.7   The sight glass on top of the receiver-drier assembly enables you to view the condition of the refrigerant in a air conditioning system while the system is opening – if the refrigerant looks foamy, the charge is low (on some models the sight glass is located elsewhere in the high pressure line)

14.5   Typical receiver-drier installation details – if you plan to reinstall the same unit, be sure to plug the openings immediately after detaching the refrigerant lines

and put the blower at the highest setting. Open the doors (to make sure the air conditioning system doesn't cycle off as soon as it cools the passenger compartment).

7   With the compressor engaged – the clutch will make an audible click and the center of the clutch will rotate – inspect the sight glass, if equipped **(see illustration)**. If the refrigerant looks foamy, it's low. Charge the system as described later in this Section.

8   If there's no sight glass, feel the inlet and outlet pipes at the compressor. One side should be cold and one hot. If there's no perceptible difference between the two pipes, there's something wrong with the compressor or the system. It might be a low charge – it might be something else. Take the vehicle to a dealer service department or an automotive air conditioning shop.

Adding refrigerant

9   Buy an automotive air conditioning charging kit at an auto parts store. A charging kit includes a 14-ounce can of refrigerant, a tap valve and a short section of hose that can be attached between the tap valve and the system low side service valve. Because one can of refrigerant may not be sufficient to bring the system charge up to the proper level, it's a good idea to buy a few additional cans. Make sure that one of the cans contains red refrigerant dye. If the system is leaking, the red dye will leak out with the refrigerant and help you pinpoint the location of the leak. **Warning:** *Never add more than three cans of refrigerant to the system.*

10   Connect the charging kit by following the manufacturer's instructions. **Warning:** *DO NOT hook the charging kit hose to the system high side!*

11   Warm up the engine and turn on the air conditioner. Keep the charging kit hose away from the fan and other moving parts.

12   Add refrigerant to the low side of the system until the refrigerant visible in the sight glass has no more bubbles in it.

13   Place a thermometer in the dashboard vent nearest the evaporator and add refrigerant until the indicated temperature is around 40 to 45-degrees F.

---

14   Air conditioning receiver-drier – removal and installation

Refer to illustration 14.5

Warning: *The air conditioning system is under high pressure. DO NOT disassemble any part of the system (hose, compressor, line fittings, etc.) until after the system has been depressurized by a dealer service department or service station.*

Caution: *Replacement receiver-drier units are so effective at absorbing moisture that they can quickly saturate upon exposure to the atmosphere. When installing a new unit, have all tools and supplies ready for quick reassembly to avoid having the system open any longer than necessary.*

1   The receiver-drier, of filter-drier, acts as a reservoir for the system refrigerant. It's located near the radiator.

2   Have the system discharged (see **Warning** above).

3   Disconnect the cable from the negative terminal of the battery.

4   Unplug any electrical connectors from the receiver-drier.

5   Disconnect the refrigerant lines from receiver drier **(see illustration)**. Use a back-up wrench to prevent twisting the tubing.

6   Plug the open fittings to prevent entry of dirt and moisture.

7   Loosen the mounting bracket bolts and lift the filter drier-receiver drier out.

8   Installation is the reverse of removal

9   Take the vehicle back to the shop that discharged it. Have the system evacuated, recharged and leak tested.

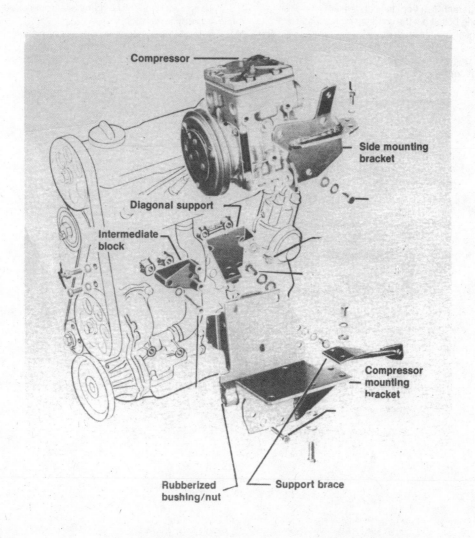

15.6   Air conditioning compressor and mounting brackets (typical)

Labels on illustration:
- Compressor
- Side mounting bracket
- Diagonal support
- Intermediate block
- Compressor mounting bracket
- Rubberized bushing/nut
- Support brace

15   Air conditioning compressor – removal and installation

Refer to illustration 15.6

Warning: *The air conditioning system is under high pressure. DO NOT disassemble any part of the system (hoses, compressor, line fittings, etc.) until after the system has been depressurized by a dealer service department or service station.*

Note: *The filter-drier/receiver-drier (see Section 14) should be replaced whenever the compressor is replaced.*

1   Have the system discharged (see **Warning** above).
2   Disconnect the negative cable from the battery.
3   Disconnect the compressor clutch wiring harness.
4   Remove the drivebelt (see Chapter 1).
5   Disconnect the refrigerant lines from the rear of the compressor. Plug the open fittings to prevent entry of dirt and moisture.
6   Unbolt the compressor from the mounting brackets **(see illustration)** and lift it out of the vehicle.
7   If a new compressor is being installed, follow the directions with the compressor regarding the draining of excess oil prior to installation.

8   The clutch may have to be transferred from the original to the new compressor.
9   Installation is the reverse of removal. Replace all O-rings with new ones specifically made for A/C system use and lubricate them with refrigerant oil.
10   Have the system evacuated, recharged and leak tested by the shop that discharged it.

16   Air conditioning condenser – removal and installation

Warning: *The air conditioning system is under high pressure. DO NOT disassemble any part of the system (hoses, compressor, line fittings, etc.) until after the system has been depressurized by a dealer service department or service station.*

Note: *The filter-drier/receiver-drier should be replaced whenever the condenser is replaced (see Section 14).*

1   Have the system discharged (see **Warning** above).
2   Remove the battery (see Chapter 5).
3   Drain the cooling system (see Chapter 1).
4   Remove the radiator (see Section 5).

5   Disconnect the refrigerant lines from the condenser.

6   Remove the mounting bolts from the condenser brackets.

7   Lift the condenser out of the vehicle and plug the lines to keep dirt and moisture out.

8   If the original condenser will be reinstalled, store it with the line fittings on top to prevent oil from draining out.

9   If a new condenser is being installed, pour one ounce of refrigerant oil into it prior to installation.

10   Reinstall the components in the reverse order of removal. Be sure the rubber pads are in place under the condenser.

11   Have the system evacuated, recharged and leak tested by the shop that discharged it.

Chapter 4   Fuel and exhaust systems

Contents

Air cleaner housing – removal and installation 4
Air filter replacement . . . . See Chapter 1
Airflow sensor – description, check and adjustment 17
Auxiliary air regulator – check and replacement 22
Carburetor diagnosis and overhaul – general information 7
Carburetor – general information 6
Carburetor – removal and installation 8
Carburetor (Solex/Zenith 2B2 and 2B5 models) – adjustments . . . 10
Carburetor (Solex/Zenith 2B2 and 2B5 models) – overhaul
 and initial adjustment 9
Carburetor (Solex 34 PICT-5) – adjustments 12
Carburetor (Solex 34 PICT-5) – overhaul 11
Catalytic converter . . . . See Chapter 6
Cold start valve – check and replacement 21
Control pressure regulator – check and replacement 19
Coolant temperature sensor – check and replacement 28
Differential pressure regulator – description and replacement 27
Engine idle speed check and adjustment . . . . See Chapter 1
Exhaust manifold – removal and installation . . . . See Chapter 2A
Exhaust system check . . . . See Chapter 1
Exhaust system servicing – general information 33
Fuel distributor – check and adjustment 18

Fuel filter replacement . . . . See Chapter 1
Fuel gauge sending unit – removal and installation 30
Fuel injection systems – general checks and adjustments 16
Fuel injection systems – general information 13
Fuel injection system – troubleshooting and fault diagnosis 14
Fuel injectors – check and replacement 25
Fuel pressure regulator – check and replacement 29
Fuel pressure relief procedure (fuel-injected models) 15
Fuel pump – check 2
Fuel pump – replacement 3
Fuel system check . . . . See Chapter 1
Fuel tank cleaning and repair – general information 32
Fuel tank – removal and installation 31
General information 1
Idle air stabilizer system – check and replacement 23
Idle speed boost valve – check 24
Oxygen sensor replacement . . . . See Chapter 1
Thermo-time switch – check and replacement 20
Throttle cable – removal, installation and adjustment 5
Throttle switches and throttle valve – check and adjustment 26
Underhood hose check and replacement . . . . See Chapter 1

Specifications

Carbureted engines

Fuel pump operating pressure .... 2.9 to 3.6 psi

Carburetor specifications

Solex/Zenith 2B2
Engine codes FC and FG

Carburetor number .... 055 129 017 C (automatic)

Jets and settings	1st stage	2nd stage
Main jet	115	115
Air correction jet	140	92.5
Pilot fuel/air jet	52.5/135	70/100
Auxiliary fuel/air jet	42.5/127.5	–
Enrichment with ball	1.0	–
Accelerator pump delivery (cc/stroke)	0.75 to 1.05	–
Float height	1.1 in (28 mm)	1.18 in (30 mm)
Needle valve diameter	0.08 in (2 mm)	
Choke plate-to-wall clearance	0.15 to 0.17 in (3.8 to 4.2 mm)	
Idle speed	850 ± 50 rpm	
Fast idle speed	3400 ± 50 rpm	

Engine code FN

Carburetor number .... 055 129 021, 021 B, 021 D (manual), 055 129 021 A, 021 C, 021 E (automatic)

Jets and settings	1st stage	2nd stage
Main jet (except Canada)	117.5 (112.5 without converter)	110 (120 without converter)
Main jet (Canada)	115	110
Air correction jet (except Canada)	130	92.5
Air correction jet (Canada)	140	92.5
Pilot fuel/air jet	52.5/135 (140 without converter)	65/140
Auxiliary fuel/air jet	42.5/127.5	–
Enrichment without ball	–	1.1
Accelerator pump delivery (cc/stroke)		
Cold	1.3 to 1.7	–
Warm	0.6 to 0.9	–
Needle valve diameter	0.08 in (2 mm)	
Float height	1.1 in (28 mm)	1.18 in (30 mm)
Choke plate-to-wall clearance	0.14 in (3.5 mm)	0.20 in (5.0 mm)
Throttle valve gap	0.02 in (0.45 mm)	–
Idle speed	950 ± 50 rpm	
Fast idle speed	3400 ± 50 rpm	

Solex 34 PICT-5
Engine code FH

Carburetor number .... 055 129 015 D or K (manual), 055 129 015 E or L (automatic)

Jets and settings
Main jet x135
Air correction jet with emulsion tube 115z
Pilot jet .... 52.5 or 60
Pilot air jet .... 100 or 95
Auxiliary fuel jet 40
Auxiliary air jet 140
Enrichment without ball 0.7
Accelerator pump delivery (cc/stroke) 1.1
Float needle valve 1.5
Choke plate-to-wall clearance .... 0.13 in (3.2 mm)
Choke cover mark
   Suffix D or K 106
   Suffix E or L 130
Fast idle speed .... 2400 ± 50 rpm
Idle speed .... 950 ± 50 rpm

Engine code FP

Carburetor number .... 055 129 015 S (manual) or T (automatic)

Jets and settings
Main jet x142.5
Air correction jet with emulsion tube 115z
Pilot jet 52.5
Pilot air jet 140

Auxiliary fuel jet	40
Auxiliary air jet	160
Enrichment with/without ball	85/85
Accelerator pump delivery (cc/stroke)	1.1
Float needle valve	1.5
Choke plate-to-wall clearance	
Suffix S	0.17 in (4.4 mm)
Suffix T	0.16 in (4.0 mm)
Choke cover mark	
Suffix S	137
Suffix T	133
Fast idle speed	2400 ± 50 rpm
Idle speed	950 ± 50 rpm

Engine code JB

Carburetor number	055 129 022 S or 023 D (manual), 055 129 022 T or 023 J (automatic)	
Jets and settings	022 s/023D	022 T/023 J
Main jet	x135	x132.5
Air correction jet with emulsion tube	100z	100z
Pilot jet	50	50
Pilot air jet	120 (S), 130 (D)	135
Auxiliary fuel jet	40	40
Auxiliary air jet	120	120
Enrichment without ball	0.9	0.9 (T), 0.95 (J)
Float needle valve	1.5	1.5
Accelerator pump delivery (cc/stroke)	1.1	1.1
Choke plate-to-wall clearance	0.19 in (4.8 mm) (S) 0.18 in (4.6 mm) (D)	0.15 in (3.8 mm)
Choke cover mark	162	162
Fast idle speed	2400 ± 50 rpm	2400 ± 50 rpm
Idle speed	950 ± 50 rpm	950 ± 50 rpm

Engine code FX (1980 Rabbit, except California)

Carburetor number	055 129 024 D
Jets and settings	
Main jet	x127.5
Air correction jet	120z
Idle fuel jet (stamped on float chamber)	50.0/52.5/55.0/57.5
Idle air jet	120
Auxiliary fuel jet	45
Auxiliary air jet	155
Accelerator pump delivery (cc/stroke)	0.8 to 1.2
Float needle valve	1.5
Choke plate-to-wall clearance	0.13 to 0.15 in (3.3 to 3.7 mm)
Fast idle speed	2350 to 2450 rpm
Idle speed	900 ± 50 rpm

Continuous Injection System (CIS)

Fuel pump delivery @ 12-volts	
Electrical connectors with screws	900 cc/30 seconds
Push-on electrical connectors	750 cc/30 seconds
System pressures	
Control pressure, warm	49 to 57 psi
System pressure	65 to 75 psi
Residual pressure	
After 10 minutes	37.7 psi
After 20 minutes	34.8 psi

Continuous Injection System – Electronic (CIS-E and CIS-E) Motronic

Fuel pump delivery @ 12-volts	760 cc/30 seconds
System pressures	
System pressure	
CIS-E	75 to 82 psi
CIS-E Motronic	89 to 95 psi
Differential pressure (regulator harness disconnected)	
CIS-E	2.9 to 7.0 psi less than system pressure
CIS-E Motronic	4.4 to 7.3 psi less than system pressure
Residual pressure after 10 minutes	
CIS-E	38 psi
CIS-E Motronic	48 psi (after 20 minutes, 46 psi)

4

Digifant II fuel injection system

Fuel pump delivery	500 cc/30 seconds
System pressure	36 psi
Residual pressure after 10 minutes	29 psi
Fuel injector resistance	15 to 20 ohms

Torque specifications

Ft-lbs (unless otherwise indicated)

Fuel pump mounting bolts (mechanical)	14
Carburetor mounting bolts/nuts	12
Fuel hose union bolts (CIS)	18
Cold start valve fitting (CIS)	84 in-lbs
Throttle body bolts (CIS)	14
Thermo-time switch (CIS)	22
Fuel distributor bolts (CIS)	25
Fuel distributor return line (CIS)	15
Fuel distributor fuel lines (CIS)	84 in-lbs
Fuel distributor supply line (CIS)	15
Fuel distributor return line banjo bolt (CIS-E/CIS-E Motronic	87 in-lbs

1   General information

Each of the vehicles covered in this chapter is equipped with one of four different types of fuel systems. Each has its own unique features and service methods, but all achieve the same result. At first they might appear complicated, but they operate on simple principles and can easily be understood. This chapter provides separate and thorough descriptions of each system. Test procedures for individual components also explain their function so the purpose and result of each test can be understood.

2   Fuel pump – check

Warning: *Gasoline is extremely flammable, so take extra precautions when you work on any part of the fuel system. Don't smoke or allow open flames or bare light bulbs near the work area, and don't work in a garage where a natural gas-type appliance (such as a water heater or clothes dryer) with a pilot light is present. If you spill any fuel on your skin, rinse it off immediately with soap and water. When you perform any kind of work on the fuel system, wear safety glasses and have a Class B type fire extinguisher on hand.*

Mechanical fuel pump

Refer to illustration 2.3

1   If you suspect insufficient fuel delivery, first inspect all fuel lines to ensure that the problem is not simply a leak in a line.

2   If there are no leaks evident in the fuel lines, inspect the fuel pump itself. The following checks will tell you if the fuel pump is leaking and whether it is pumping fuel.

3   Locate the fuel pump, on the front side of the engine adjacent to the distributor. Note whether there is any fuel or oil leaking from the breather hole **(see illustration)**. If there is, either the oil seal or the diaphragm in the fuel pump is defective. Replace the fuel pump if leakage is noted (see Section 3).

Fuel pump output check

4   Hook up a remote starter switch in accordance with the manufacturer's instructions. If you don't have a remote starter switch, you will need an assistant to help you with this and the following procedure.

5   Trace the fuel outlet hose from the pump to the carburetor and detach it at the carburetor (see Section 8).

6   Detach the wires from the ignition coil primary terminals (see Chapter 5).

2.3   Carefully check the fuel pump for any fuel or oil leaking from the breather hole (arrow)

7   Place an approved gasoline container under the open end of the fuel pump outlet hose.

8   Direct the fuel pump outlet hose into the container while cranking the engine for a few seconds with the remote starter (or while an assistant cranks the engine with the ignition key).

9   If fuel is emitted in well defined spurts, the pump is operating satisfactorily. If fuel dribbles or trickles out the hose, the pump is defective. Replace it (see Section 3).

Inlet valve check

10   Detach the inlet hose from the fuel pump.

11   Attach a vacuum gauge to the inlet fitting.

12   Crank the engine with a remote starter switch (or have an assistant crank it with the ignition key).

13   A fairly steady vacuum, uninterrupted by alternating blowback pulses (sudden pulses of pressure), should be evident.

14   If blowback is evident, the fuel pump inlet valve is not seating properly. Replace the pump (see Section 3).

15   Connect the wires to the ignition coil primary terminals.

2.19 On fuel injected models, the fuel pump is mounted next to the fuel tank

Electric fuel pump

Refer to illustration 2.19

16 If you suspect a problem with the fuel pump, verify the pump actually runs. Remove the fuel filler cap and have an assistant turn the ignition switch to On – you should hear a brief whirring noise at the filler neck as the pump comes on and pressurizes the system. Have the assistant start the engine. This time you should hear a constant whirring sound from the pump (but it's more difficult to hear with the engine running).

17 If the pump does not come on (makes no sound), check the fuses. If the fuses are all good, proceed to the next step.

18 Raise the rear of the vehicle and place it securely on jackstands.

19 Remove the fuel pump cover **(see illustration)** .

20 Disconnect the fuel pump electrical connector (make sure the ignition switch is turned off before disconnecting the wires).

21 Connect a voltmeter across the terminals, then turn on the ignition switch and verify there is voltage available.

22 If voltage is available, replace the fuel pump (see Section 3).

23 If no voltage is available, check the fuel pump relay (see below).

Fuel pump relay check

Refer to illustrations 2.24a, 2.24b, 2.24c, 2.24d and 2.24e

Note: *If you don't see the fuse/relay panel on your vehicle amongst the illustrations included here, refer to your owner's manual.*

24 To test the fuel pump relay, first remove it from the relay panel **(see illustrations)**.

25 Using a jumper wire, connect the proper terminals to activate the fuel pump (see the illustrations referred to in the previous Step). If the pump did not run previously with the relay installed but runs when the terminals are bridged, the relay is faulty and must be replaced. If the fuse blows or the fuel pump fails to run correctly, there is a problem in the fuel pump or the wiring harness.

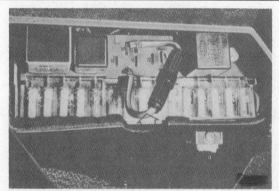

2.24a On 1980 and earlier U.S. built models (1981 and earlier German models) remove the fuel pump relay and bridge terminals L13 and L14 to activate the fuel pump

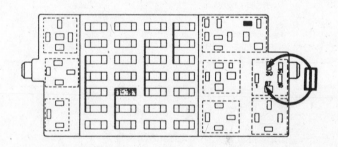

2.24b On Pickups and 1981 to 1984 car models, bridge terminals 30 and 87 to activate the fuel pump

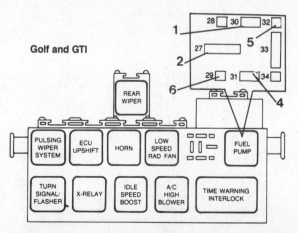

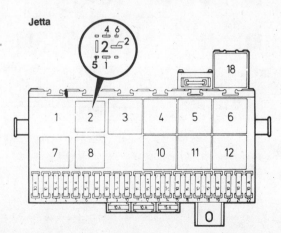

2.24c Fuel pump relay locations on 1985 through December 1988 Golf, GTI and Jetta models – to activate the fuel pump on Golf and GTI models, bridge terminals 27 and 33 on the relay panel – on Jetta models bridge the terminals on the relay panel which correspond to terminals 30 and 87 on the fuel pump relay

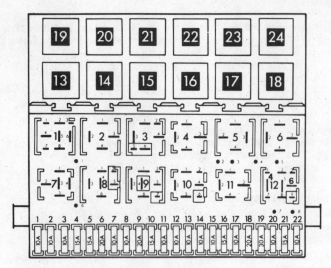

Fuses

Fuse No.	Description	Ampere Rating
1	Headlight, low beam, left	10
2	Headlight, low beam, right	10
3	Instrument panel lights, license plate lights	10
4	Glove box light	15
5	Wiper/washer	15
6	Fresh air blower	20
7	Taillights, side marker light, right	10
8	Taillights, side marker light, left	10
9	Rear window defogger	20
10	Open, or fog lights (2.0 16-valve)	15
11	Headlight, high beam, left	10
12	Headlight, high beam, right	10
13	Horn, radiator cooling fan	10
14	Backup lights, washer nozzle heaters	10
15	Open, or engine electronics (2.0 16-valve)	10
16	Dash warning lights	15
17	Emergency flasher switch	10
18	Fuel pump, OXS heater (gasoline engines)	20
19	Radiator cooling fan, A/C	30
20	Brake lights, cruise control	10
21	Interior lights, digital clock	15
22	Radio, cigarette lighter	10

Relays

Relay No.	Description		
1	A/C	14	Automatic transmission, coolant temperature
2	Open		indicator, or radiator cooling fan after run (2.0
3	Digifant control unit, or open		16-valve), or starter interlock relay
4	Load reduction relay	15	ABS pump relay
5	Low coolant level control unit	16	ABS relay
6	Emergency flasher	17	Open, or heated seat control unit, driver
7	Open	18	Heated seat control unit, passenger, or power
8	Intermittent wiper		seat circuit breaker
9	Seat belt warning system	19	Automatic transmission
10	Open	20	Open
11	Horn	21	Power window relay/ABS pump fuse
12	Fuel pump	22	ABS valves fuse
13	Radiator cooling fan after run, or	23	A/C, power seat fuse
	starter interlock relay (2.0 16-valve)	24	Power window fuse

2.24d   Location of the fuel pump relay on January 1989 through 1990 Jetta fuse panel – to activate the fuel pump, bridge terminals 4 and 6

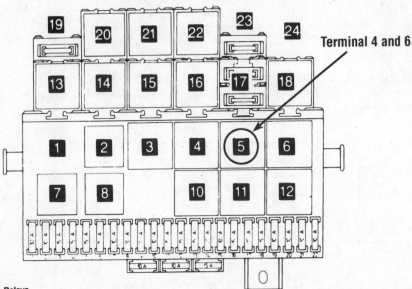

Terminal 4 and 6

Fuses

Fuse No.	Description	Ampere Rating
1	Radiator fan	30
2	Brake lights	10
3	Cigarette lighter, radio, clock, interior lights, central locking	10
4	Emergency flashers	15
5	Fuel pump	15
6	Open	
7	Taillights, side marker lights, left	10
8	Taillights, side marker lights, right	10
9	High beam, right, high beam indicator	10
10	High beam, left	10
11	Windshield wiper/washer	15
12	Heated seats, electric mirrors	15
13	Rear window defogger, heated rear view mirrors, rear wiper	15
14	Fresh air blower, glove box light	20
15	Backup lights, shift console light	10
16	Horn	15
17	Knock sensor control unit	10
18	Horn relay, coolant level and temperature warning light	10
19	Turn signals, brake warning light	10
20	License plate lights	10
21	Low beam, left	10
22	Low beam, right	10

Relays

Relay No.	Description		
1	Open	13	Power window
2	Fuel pump or glow plug	14	Open, or brake lights (16-valve)
3	Seat belt warning system	15	Open
4	Open	16	Idle stabilizer
5	A/C	17	A/C thermofuse
6	Dual horn	18	Coolant level indicator
7	Open	19	Power window
8	Load reduction	20	Heated seat
9	Open	21	Heated seat
10	Intermittent wipers	22	Open
11	Rear wiper/washer	23	Power window fuse
12	Emergency flasher	24	Open

2.24e   Location of the fuel pump relay on 1989 (Mexican production) Golf and GTI fuse/relay panel – to activate the fuel pump, bridge terminals 4 and 6

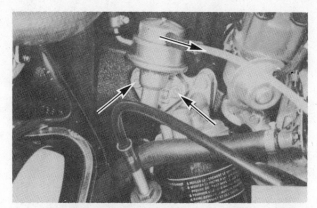

3.2   Detach the hoses, remove the mounting bolts and lift the fuel pump from the engine

26   To verify that the fuel pump works, use jumper wires and apply battery voltage to the fuel pump positive terminal and ground the other terminal. If the pump now runs, the problem is in the wiring harness. Check for power to the relay panel and check the fuel pump wiring harness for an open circuit or short-to-ground condition. If it doesn't run, replace it.

3   Fuel pump – replacement

Warning: *Gasoline is extremely flammable, so take extra precautions when you work on any part of the fuel system. Don't smoke or allow open flames or bare light bulbs near the work area, and don't work in a garage where a natural gas-type appliance (such as a water heater or clothes dryer) with a pilot light is present. If you spill any fuel on your skin, rinse it off immediately with soap and water. When you perform any kind of work on the fuel system, wear safety glasses and have a Class B type fire extinguisher on hand.*

Mechanical fuel pump

Refer to illustration 3.2

1   Detach the cable from the negative battery terminal.
2   Loosen the hose clamps, detach the hoses and remove the fuel pump mounting bolts **(see illustration)**.
3   Carefully break the fuel pump loose with your hand – do not use a pry bar – and remove the pump, gaskets and insulator. Note that the insulator is sandwiched between the two gaskets.
4   Using a scraper, remove the old gasket material from the insulator, the pump (if it will be reused), and the pump mating surface on the engine block.
5   Inspect the condition of the fuel inlet, outlet and return hoses. If they're damaged or worn, replace them.
6   Installation is the reverse of removal. Be sure to use new gaskets. Tighten the mounting bolts to the torque listed in this Chapter's Specifications.

Electric fuel pump

7   Relieve the fuel pressure (see Section 15).
8   Detach the cable from the negative battery terminal.
9   Raise the vehicle and support it securely on jackstands.
10   Disconnect the electrical connectors on the fuel pump **(see illustration 2.19)**.
11   Clamp shut the fuel hoses with line clamps or locking pliers. If locking pliers are used, wrap the hoses with rags to prevent damage. Clean the fuel hose connections, loosen the hose clamps and disconnect both of them from the fuel pump. If the hoses are deteriorated, replace them.
12   Remove the bolts that retain the pump box assembly and remove the assembly from the vehicle. Loosen the clamp and slide the pump out.
13   Installation is the reverse of removal.

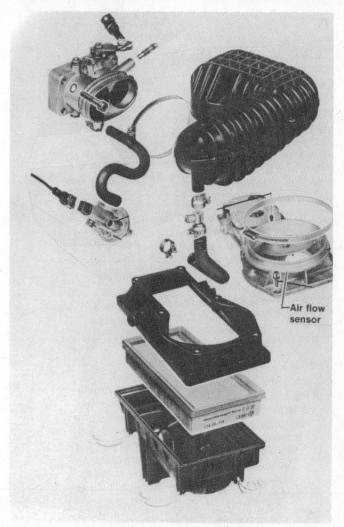

Air flow sensor

4.3   Air cleaner installation details

4   Air cleaner housing – removal and installation

Refer to illustration 4.3

1   Remove the air filter element (see Chapter 1).
2   Detach the heated air inlet hose and the fresh air inlet hose from the lower portion of the air cleaner housing.
3   On CIS fuel injected models, loosen the hose clamps on the throttle body and the air flow sensor and remove the air intake duct **(see illustration)**. On some models it may be necessary to disconnect the smaller hose from the auxiliary air regulator.
4   Remove the bolts that secure the air flow sensor to the upper portion of the air cleaner housing and reposition the air flow sensor out of the way.
5   Remove the bolts or nuts that secure the lower portion of the air cleaner housing to the vehicle, then remove the housing.
6   Installation is the reverse of the removal procedure.

5   Throttle cable – removal, installation and adjustment

Refer to illustrations 5.1a, 5.1b, 5.1c and 5.2
Note: *Vehicles with an automatic transaxle have two cables which connect the accelerator pedal to both the throttle valve and the kickdown mechanism. The adjustment of the kickdown cable affects the operation of the automatic transaxle and is covered in Chapter 7B.*

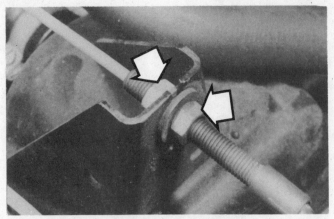

5.1a   To adjust the throttle cable on CIS models, change the position of the nuts (arrows) on the cable casing

5.1b   To adjust the throttle cable on the 2B2 carburetor, loosen the clamp nut and pull the cable taut with the throttle lever 0.040 in (1 mm) from the stop

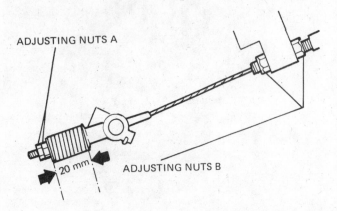

5.1c   Throttle cable adjustment details on the PICT carburetor

5.2   Remove the clip that retains the cable end onto the throttle lever (typical CIS-type fuel injection throttle lever)

Removal and installation

1   Loosen the inside adjuster nut **(see illustrations)**, remove it from the cable and slide the nut out of the way.

2   Remove the end clip from the top of the throttle cable and lift the cable off the throttle valve **(see illustration)**.

3   Slide the cable forward and out of the cable guide.

4   Disconnect the throttle cable from the accelerator pedal inside the driver's compartment and remove the throttle cable.

5   Installation is the reverse of removal.

Adjustment

6   Before adjusting the cable, check that it is correctly aligned over its full length.

7   Have an assistant fully depress the accelerator pedal to the floor.

8   Check that the clearance between the throttle lever at the carburetor or throttle body and the fully open stop is a maximum of 0.040 in (1.0 mm). Note that the throttle lever must not be resting against the fully open stop (there must be a small clearance).

9   There are three different cable adjustment arrangements. Where locknuts are provided at the engine end of the cable casing, loosen them, then adjust the cable position and tighten the locknuts. Where a grooved section and circlip are provided, remove the clip, adjust the cable position then install the circlip so it snaps over the cable. On some models it is necessary to adjust the inner cable by loosening the clamp screw, repositioning the lever while holding the cable taut, then tightening the screw (see illustrations 5.1a, 5.1b and 5.1c).

6   Carburetor – general information

The carburetor is basically a tube through which air is drawn into the engine by action of the pistons. Fuel is introduced into the air stream in the tube due to the fact that vacuum is created by the downward travel of the pistons on the intake stroke.

The main fuel discharge point is situated in the carburetor between two butterfly valves. One is operated by the accelerator pedal and positioned at the engine end of the carburetor. The other is the choke, which is operated by an electric device.

When the engine is warm and running normally the choke is wide open and the throttle open partially or fully, the amount of fuel/air mixture being controlled according to the required speed.

When cold, the choke is closed, partially or fully, and the suction therefore draws more fuel and less air (a richer mixture) to aid starting a cold engine.

At idle, the throttle butterfly is shut so that no air and fuel can get to the engine in the regular way. For this there are separate routes leading to small holes in the side of the carburetor on the engine side of the throttle butterfly. These "bleed" the required amounts of fuel and air to the engine for slow speeds only.

The fuel is held in a separate chamber alongside the choke and its level is governed by a float so that it is not too high or low. If too high, the engine would run too rich. If too low, it would run too lean.

The main jet, which is simply an orifice of a particular size through which the fuel passes, is designed to let so much fuel flow at particular conditions of suction (properly called depression) in the carburetor. At idle, the depression draws fuel from orifices below the throttle which has passed through the main jet and after that a pilot jet to reduce the quantity further. Both main and pilot jets have air bleed jets also which let in air to assist emulsification of the eventual fuel/air mixture.

The choke is controlled by an electrically operated bi-metal strip. This consists of a coiled bi-metal strip connected to the choke flap spindle. When the ignition is switched off the coiled metal strip is cool and the flap is shut. When the ignition is switched on, current flows through a heater which causes the strip to uncoil, opening the choke flap after a few minutes.

On carburetors from model year 1976 the automatic choke is controlled by engine coolant as well as the electric element. The electric element is controlled by one or two thermo-switches (depending on model) in the coolant circuit, and in this arrangement the electric element is used to open the choke valve during the initial warm-up period, afer which the coolant temperature controls the choke valve.

The fuel in the float chamber is regulated at the correct height by a float which operates a needle valve. When the level drops the needle is lowered away from the entry orifice and fuel under pressure from the fuel pump enters. When the level rises the flow is shut off. The pump delivery is always greater than the maximum requirement from the carburetor.

Another device fitted is an electro-magnetic cut-off valve. This is a feature which is designed to positively stop the fuel flow when the engine is stopped. Otherwise the engine tends to run on – even with the ignition switched off – when the engine is hot.

---

7   Carburetor diagnosis and overhaul – general information

Refer to illustration 7.6
Warning: *Gasoline is extremely flammable, so take extra precautions when you work on any part of the fuel system. Don't smoke or allow open flames or bare light bulbs near the work area, and don't work in a garage where a natural gas-type appliance (such as a water heater or clothes dryer) with a pilot light is present. If you spill any fuel on your skin, rinse it off immediately with soap and water. When you perform any kind of work on the fuel system, wear safety glasses and have a Class B type fire extinguisher on hand.*

Diagnosis

1   A thorough road test and check of carburetor adjustments should be done before any major carburetor service work. Specifications for some adjustments are listed on the Vehicle Emissions Control Information (VECI) label found in the engine compartment.

2   Carburetor problems usually show up as flooding, hard starting, stalling, severe backfiring and poor acceleration. A carburetor that's leaking fuel and/or covered with wet looking deposits definitely needs attention.

3   Some performance complaints directed at the carburetor are actually a result of loose, out-of-adjustment or malfunctioning engine or electrical components. Others develop when vacuum hoses leak, are disconnected or are incorrectly routed. The proper approach to analyzing carburetor problems should include the following items:

- a)   Inspect all vacuum hoses and actuators for leaks and correct installation (see Chapters 1 and 6).
- b)   Tighten the intake manifold and carburetor mounting nuts/bolts evenly and securely.
- c)   Perform a cylinder compression test (see Chapter 2).
- d)   Clean or replace the spark plugs as necessary (see Chapter 1).
- e)   Check the spark plug wires (see Chapter 1).
- f)   Inspect the ignition primary wires.
- g)   Check the ignition timing (follow the instructions printed on the Emissions Control Information label).
- h)   Check the fuel pump pressure/volume.
- i)   Check the heat control valve in the air cleaner for proper operation (see Chapter 1).
- j)   Check/replace the air filter element (see Chapter 1).
- k)   Check the PCV system (see Chapter 6).
- l)   Check/replace the fuel filter (see Chapter 1). Also, the strainer in the tank could be restricted.
- m)   Check for a plugged exhaust system.
- n)   Check EGR valve operation (see Chapter 6).
- o)   Check the choke. It should be completely open at normal engine operating temperature (see Chapter 1).
- p)   Check for fuel leaks and kinked or dented fuel lines (see Chapters 1 and 4)
- q)   Check accelerator pump operation with the engine off (remove the air cleaner cover and operate the throttle as you look into the carburetor throat – you should see a stream of gasoline enter the carburetor).
- r)   Check for incorrect fuel or bad gasoline.
- s)   Check the valve clearances (if applicable) and camshaft lobe lift (see Chapters 1 and 2)
- t)   Have a dealer service department or repair shop check the electronic engine and carburetor controls.

4   Diagnosing carburetor problems may require that the engine be started and run with the air cleaner off. While running the engine without the air cleaner, backfires are possible. This situation is likely to occur if the carburetor is malfunctioning, but just the removal of the air cleaner can lean the fuel/air mixture enough to produce an engine backfire. **Warning:** *Do not position any part of your body, especially your face, directly over the carburetor during inspection and servicing procedures. Wear eye protection!*

Overhaul

5   Once it's determined that the carburetor needs an overhaul, several options are available. If you're going to attempt to overhaul the carburetor yourself, first obtain a good quality carburetor rebuild kit (which will include all necessary gaskets, internal parts, instructions and a parts list). You'll also need some special solvent and a means of blowing out the internal passages of the carburetor with air.

6   An alternative is to obtain a new or rebuilt carburetor. They are readily available from dealers and auto parts stores. Make absolutely sure the exchange carburetor is identical to the original. A tag is usually attached to the top of the carburetor or a number is stamped on the float bowl **(see illustration)**. It will help determine the exact type of carburetor you have.

7.6   Carburetor number tag (arrow)

When obtaining a rebuilt carburetor or a rebuild kit, make sure the kit or carburetor matches your application exactly. Seemingly insignificant differences can make a large difference in engine performance.

7   If you choose to overhaul your own carburetor, allow enough time to disassemble it carefully, soak the necessary parts in the cleaning solvent (usually for at least one-half day or according to the instructions listed on the carburetor cleaner) and reassemble it, which will usually take much longer than disassembly. When disassembling the carburetor, match each part with the illustration in the carburetor kit and lay the parts out in order on a clean work surface. Overhauls by inexperienced mechanics can result in an engine which runs poorly or not at all. To avoid this, use care and patience when disassembling the carburetor so you can reassemble it correctly.

---

8   Carburetor – removal and installation

Warning: *Gasoline is extremely flammable, so take extra precautions when you work on any part of the fuel system. Don't smoke or allow open flames or bare light bulbs near the work area, and don't work in a garage where a natural gas-type appliance (such as a water heater or clothes dryer) with a pilot light is present. If you spill any fuel on your skin, rinse it off immediately with soap and water. When you perform any kind of work on the fuel system, wear safety glasses and have a Class B type fire extinguisher on hand.*

Removal

1   Remove the fuel filler cap to relieve fuel tank pressure.
2   Remove the air cleaner duct from the carburetor.
3   Disconnect the throttle cable from the throttle lever (see Section 5).
4   If the vehicle is equipped with an automatic transmission, disconnect the kickdown cable from the throttle lever.
5   Clearly label all vacuum hoses and fittings, then disconnect the hoses.
6   Disconnect the fuel line from the carburetor. Plug the line to prevent fuel spillage.
7   Label the wires and terminals, then disconnect all of the electrical connectors.
8   Remove the mounting fasteners and detach the carburetor from the intake manifold. Remove the carburetor mounting gasket. Cover the intake manifold openings with a rag to prevent the entry of foreign objects.

Installation

9   Use a gasket scraper to remove all traces of gasket material and sealant from the intake manifold (and the carburetor, if it's being reinstalled). Clean the mating surfaces with lacquer thinner or acetone.
10   Place a new gasket on the intake manifold.
11   Position the carburetor on the gasket and install the mounting fasteners.
12   To prevent carburetor distortion or damage, tighten the fasteners to the torque listed in this Chapter's Specifications, in a criss-cross pattern, 1/4-turn at a time.
13   The remaining installation steps are the reverse of removal.
14   Check and, if necessary, adjust the idle speed.
15   If the vehicle is equipped with an automatic transmission, refer to Chapter 7B for the kickdown cable adjustment procedure.
16   Start the engine and check carefully for fuel leaks.

---

9   Carburetor (Solex/Zenith 2B2 and 2B5 models) – overhaul and initial adjustments

---

Warning: *Gasoline is extremely flammable, so take extra precautions when you work on any part of the fuel system. Don't smoke or allow open flames or bare light bulbs near the work area, and don't work in a garage where a natural gas-type appliance (such as a water heater or clothes dry-*

er) with a pilot light is present. If you spill any fuel on your skin, rinse it off immediately with soap and water. When you perform any kind of work on the fuel system, wear safety glasses and have a Class B type fire extinguisher on hand.

Overhaul

Refer to illustrations 9.2, 9.3a, 9.3b, 9.3c and 9.3d

1   Apart from cleaning the jets, setting the choke and throttle butterfly and checking the accelerator pump injection capacity, the only other repair possible is the adjustment of the float level. These tests are included in this Section because they must be done with the carburetor off the car. Running tests are described in Section 10.
2   Remove the carburetor (see Section 8). Look into the throat of the carburetor **(see illustration)**. The various air jets, except the air correction jets and emulsion tubes, may be located, removed and blown out with compressed air. Do not clean them with a wire or a pin. If they are so blocked that the compressed air will not remove the obstruction, then install a new jet.

9.2   Jet locations in top of Solex 2B2/2B5 carburetor

3   Remove the screws holding the carburetor top to the carburetor body **(see illustrations)** and turn the head upside down. The main jets are now accessible and may be serviced **(see illustrations)**.
4   Remove all plastic parts and parts which contain rubber diaphragms or electrical solenoids. Immerse the remaining components in a carburetor cleaning solution and allow them to soak for awhile (read the instructions on the can).
5   Remove the components from the solution, rinse them with water then blow them dry with compressed air.
6   Reassemble the carburetor, except for the top portion of the carburetor body, using the exploded views for guidance, then perform the initial adjustments described below.

Initial adjustments

Refer to illustrations 9.11, 9.12 and 9.14

7   The automatic choke is identical with that of the 34 PICT 5 carburetor (see Section 11) except that the choke heater resistance element has a different value. The method of setting the choke valve gap is identical to that described in Section 12, however, make sure that the gap is measured against the carburetor outer wall.
8   The stage 1 throttle valve basic setting is made at the factory; however, if it is found necessary to adjust it, proceed as follows.
9   Remove the tamperproof cap and turn out the screw until there is a gap between it and the stop.
10   Open and close the throttle valve quickly, then turn in the screw until it just touches the stop. From this point turn it in a further quarter of a turn.

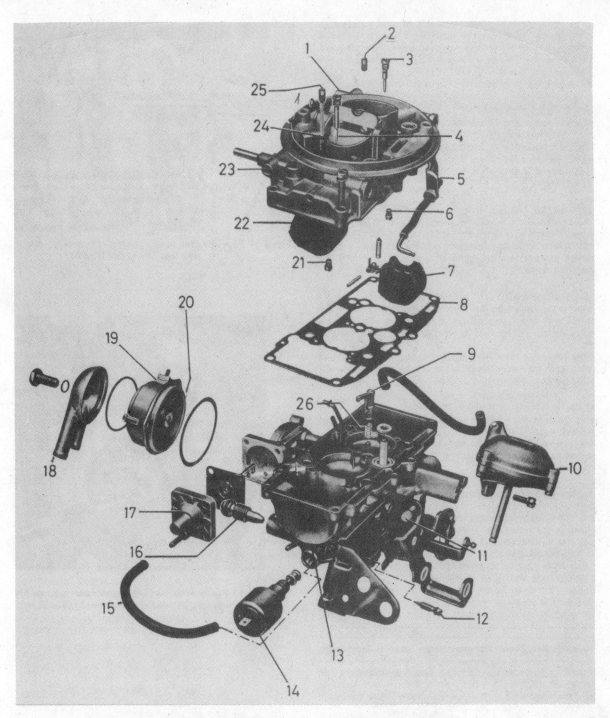

9.3a   Exploded view of an early Solex 2B2 carburetor

1	Pilot fuel and air jet (1st stage)	14	Magnetic cut-off valve
2	Progression air jet	15	Hose
3	Pilot fuel and air jet (2nd stage)	16	Idle adjustment screw
4	Choke valve flap	17	Choke valve cover and adjustment screw
5	Injection quantity control screw	18	Choke valve cover coolant supply cover
6	Main jet (2nd stage)	19	Choke valve control body
7	Float (2nd stage)	20	Choke valve electric element
8	Gasket	21	Main jet (1st stage)
9	Injection tube	22	Float (1st stage)
10	Vacuum capsule for control (2nd stage)	23	Upper part of carburetor body
11	Basic throttle setting adjustment screw	24	Bypass air fuel jet
12	Mixture adjustment screw	25	Bypass air jet
13	Carburetor body	26	Progression fuel jet

4

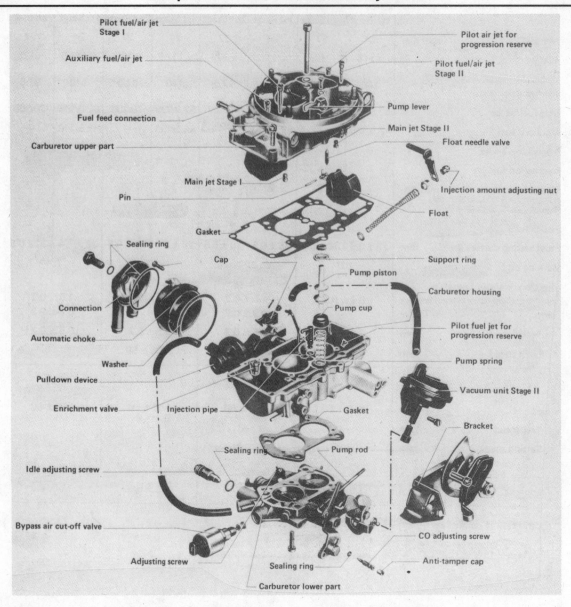

Pilot fuel/air jet Stage I

Auxiliary fuel/air jet

Fuel feed connection

Carburetor upper part

Main jet Stage I

Pin

Gasket

Sealing ring

Cap

Connection

Automatic choke

Washer

Pulldown device

Enrichment valve

Injection pipe

Idle adjusting screw

Bypass air cut-off valve

Adjusting screw

Sealing ring

Carburetor lower part

Pilot air jet for progression reserve

Pilot fuel/air jet Stage II

Pump lever

Main jet Stage II

Float needle valve

Injection amount adjusting nut

Float

Support ring

Pump piston

Carburetor housing

Pump cup

Pilot fuel jet for progression reserve

Pump spring

Vacuum unit Stage II

Bracket

Gasket

Pump rod

CO adjusting screw

Anti-tamper cap

9.3b   Exploded view of a later Solex 2B2/2B5 carburetor

9.3c   Location of progression fuel jet (10) and enrichment valve (11) on Solex 2B2/2B5 carburetor

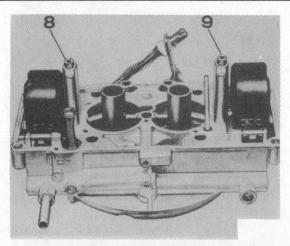

9.3d   Location of main jets stage 1 (8) and 2 (9) on Solex 2B2/2B5 carburetor

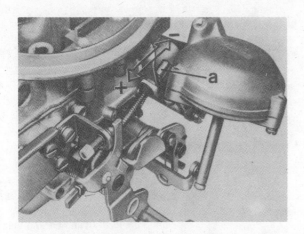

9.11 Accelerator pump discharge adjustment nut (a) on Solex 2B2/2B5 carburetor (Sec 11)

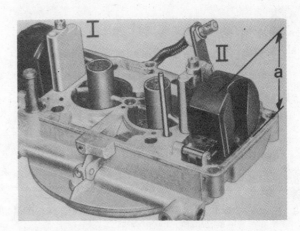

9.12 Measure dimension (a) to determine the float level (Solex 2B2/2B5 carburetors)

9.14 Stage 2 throttle valve basic setting adjusting screw (arrow) on Solex 2B2/2B5 carburetor

11   To adjust the accelerator pump output, first make sure the float chambers are full and that a supply of fuel to the carburetor is available. A piece of hose and a funnel connected to the carburetor inlet will do. Hold the carburetor over a container and operate the throttle lever until fuel begins to run from the carburetor into the funnel. Hold the choke valve in its fully open position. Now hold a measuring glass under the carburetor and operate the throttle fully ten times. Allow the fuel to run into the glass and divide the quantity by ten. The correct amount is given in this Chapter's Specifications. If necessary adjust the nut on the accelerator pump rod **(see illustration)**. After adjustment, recheck the pump's output.

12   While the top is separated from the carburetor body the float position may be checked. Turn the top of the carburetor body upside down and measure the float level **(see illustration)**, comparing your measurement with the Specifications. If it isn't as specified, bend the bracket until the correct level is obtained. Attach the top of the carburetor to main portion and install the screws.

13   The stage 2 throttle valve basic setting is made at the factory; however, if it is found necessary to adjust it, proceed as follows.

14   With the stage 1 throttle valve in the idling position and the automatic choke fast idle cam set to its hot position, turn the adjusting screw **(see illustration)** to give a gap between the screw and the stop.

15   Disconnect the vacuum unit pullrod and lightly press the throttle valve lever to the closed position to eliminate any play.

16   Turn in the adjusting screw until it just contacts the stop, then on the 2B2 carburetor turn it a further half turn, or on the 2B5 carburetor turn it a further quarter turn. Lock the screw with sealing paint and reconnect the vacuum unit pullrod.

17   Install the carburetor (see Section 8) and perform the on-vehicle carburetor adjustments described in the next Section.

10 Carburetor (Solex/Zenith 2B2 and 2B5 models) – adjustments

Warning: *Gasoline is extremely flammable, so take extra precautions when you work on any part of the fuel system. Don't smoke or allow open flames or bare light bulbs near the work area, and don't work in a garage where a natural gas-type appliance (such as a water heater or clothes dryer) with a pilot light is present. If you spill any fuel on your skin, rinse it off immediately with soap and water. When you perform any kind of work on the fuel system, wear safety glasses and have a Class B type fire extinguisher on hand.*

Idle speed

Models with conventional (breaker points) ignition

1   Connect a tachometer to the engine in accordance with the manufacturer's instructions.

2   Disconnect the crankcase ventilation hose from the air cleaner or intake and plug the exposed hole (not the hose).

3   Run the engine at a fast idling speed until it reaches its normal operating temperature. Switch off all electrical components and only make an adjustment when the radiator fan is stopped.

4   Check that the fast idle screw is not touching the cam, then allow the engine to idle and if necessary adjust the idle speed screw **(see illustrations 9.3a and 9.3b)** until the engine runs at the specified speed.

5   Stop the engine, remove the instruments, and reconnect the crankcase ventilation hose.

Models with electronic ignition

Refer to illustration 10.9

6   Carry out the procedure described in Steps 1 and 2.

7   To check the idle speed, run the engine at a fast idle until it reaches its normal operating temperature. Switch off all electrical components and only make the check when the radiator fan is stopped.

8   Check that the fast idle screw is not touching the cam, then allow the engine to idle and check that the idle speed is as given in the Specifications.

9   To adjust the idle speed, stop the engine, then disconnect the electrical connectors from the digital idle stabilizer and connect them together

10.9   Remove the electrical connectors for the digital idle stabilizer and connect them together (arrow)

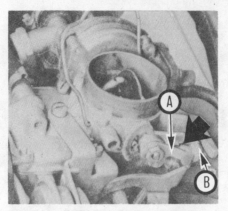

10.12   Fast idle adjustment details

A   Choke valve lever
B   Fast idle adjusting screw

10.13   Adjust the vacuum pullrod by loosening the locknut and turning the rod – dimension (a) should be 0.04 to 0.08-inch (1 to 2 mm)

11.3a   Automatic choke alignment mark (arrow)

(see illustration). Adjust the idle speed to the speed listed in this Chapter's Specifications. Stop the engine and reconnect the digital idle stabilizer plugs, then start the engine again and accelerate the engine briefly. The idling speed should now be as given in this Chapters Specifications.

10   Stop the engine, remove the instruments, and reconnect the crankcase ventilation hose.

Fast idle (cold idling) speed

Refer to illustration 10.12

11   Run the engine until it reaches normal operating temperature. Connect a tachometer to the engine.

12   Set the fast idle adjusting screw on the highest step of the fast idle cam, then without touching the throttle, start the engine and check that the fast idle speed is as given in this Chapters Specifications. If not, turn the adjusting screw as necessary – due to its location, access to the screw is difficult and therefore it is necessary to operate the throttle to release the screw from the cam. The screw must be set up again as previously described in order to check the adjustment **(see illustration)**.

Vacuum pullrod

Refer to illustration 10.13

13   Disconnect the pullrod, loosen the locknut and adjust the rod so that the dimension shown in Fig. 3.26 is 1 to 2 mm (0.04 to 0.08 in).

---

11   Carburetor (Solex 34 PICT-5) – overhaul

Refer to illustrations 11.3a, 11.3b, 11.4a, 11.4b, 11.4c, 11.7 and 11.10
Warning: *Gasoline is extremely flammable, so take extra precautions when you work on any part of the fuel system. Don't smoke or allow open flames or bare light bulbs near the work area, and don't work in a garage where a natural gas-type appliance (such as a water heater or clothes dryer) with a pilot light is present. If you spill any fuel on your skin, rinse it off immediately with soap and water. When you perform any kind of work on the fuel system, wear safety glasses and have a Class B type fire extinguisher on hand.*

1   The carburetor should not be dismantled without a very good reason. Any alterations of the settings will alter the CO content of the exhaust gas and may violate the emission control regulations. However, the top may be separated from the body to check the level of fuel in the float chamber and the jets may be cleaned without altering any vital settings.

2   Remove the carburetor (see Section 8).

3   If equipped, remove the plastic cover from the automatic choke. Note the relationship of the alignment marks on the automatic choke **(see illustration)** then remove the retaining ring (three screws) or water chamber (one bolt), and withdraw the heater body and bi-metal spring together with the gasket or cover. Note how the operating lever locates in the spring **(see illustration)**.

11.3b   Separate the automatic choke cover from the carburetor top

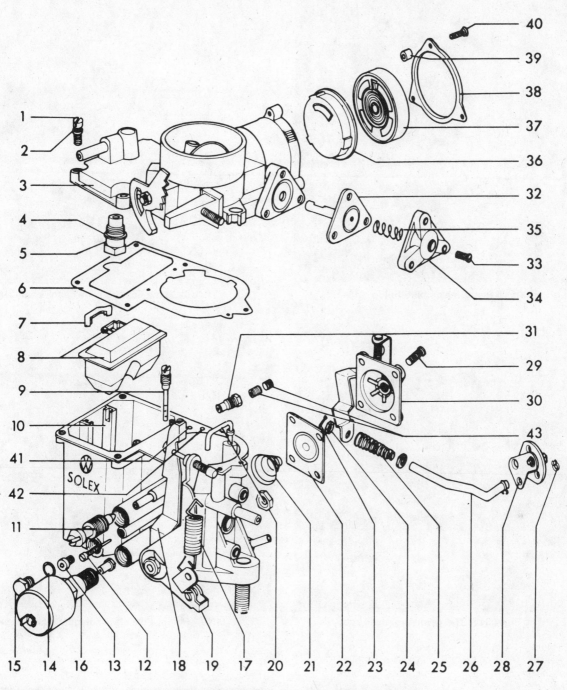

11.4a   Exploded view of an early Solex PICT-5 carburetor

1	Cover screw	12	Idle mixture control screw	22	Accelerator pump diaphragm	33	Countersunk screw
2	Spring washer					34	Diaphragm cover
3	Top cover	13	Main jet	23	Split pin	35	Spring
4	Needle valve washer	14	Washer	24	Washer	36	Choke cover
5	Needle valve	15	Plug	25	Spring	37	Heater coil and insert
6	Gasket	16	Electromagnetic cutoff valve	26	Connecting link	38	Retaining ring
7	Float pin bracket			27	Circlip	39	Spacer
8	Float and pin	17	Return spring	28	Bellcrank lever (adjustable)	40	Screw
9	Air correction jet and emulsion tube	18	Fast idle lever			41	Pilot air jet
		19	Throttle lever	29	Countersunk screw	42	Auxiliary air jet
10	Carburetor low housing	20	Injection pipe from accelerator pump	30	Pump cover	43	Auxiliary fuel jet and plug
				31	Pilot jet		
11	Bypass air screw	21	Diaphragm spring	32	Vacuum diaphragm		

11.4b   Remove the carburetor top

11.4c   Lift the float from inside the chamber

11.7   The Solex 34 PICT-5 carburetor main body

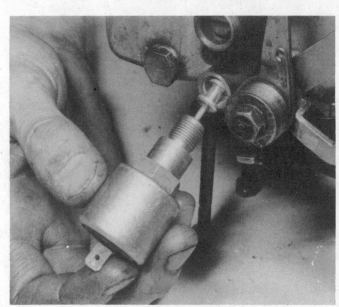

11.10   Remove the electromagnetic cutoff valve

A	Main jet plug	E	Auxiliary air jet
B	Main jet	F	Injection pipe from
C	Air jet and emulsion tube		accelerator pump
D	Pilot air jet	G	Main fuel/air delivery tube

4   Unhook the return spring and remove the five screws holding the top of the carburetor to the body **(see illustration)**. Lift the top away **(see illustration)**. Be careful not to damage the gasket. The float may be removed from the float chamber **(see illustration)** and checked for leaks. A simple way to do this is to immerse it in warm, not hot, water. Any pin holes will be detected by bubbles as the air inside the float expands. Dry the float thoroughly. It may not be repaired, only replaced by a new one.

5   The needle valve may be unscrewed from the top of the carburetor and checked. Clean out the float chamber, removing any sediment with a soft brush.

6   Remove the plug from the outside at the base of the float chamber and then through this hole unscrew the main jet and check that it is clear. Jets must not be cleaned with wires or pins. Use compressed air to blow out

any obstruction. If wire is pushed in the jet will be enlarged and the delicate balance of fuel mixture upset. If in doubt install a new jet (see this Chapter's Specifications).

7   On the top rim of the body are two more jets and the air correction jet with the emulsion tube. Unscrew the air correction jet, take it out and clean the emulsion tube. The jet next to it is the pilot air jet and the one on the outside is the auxiliary air jet. These may be removed and cleaned **(see illustration)**.

8   There are two more jets to find: the pilot jet and the auxiliary fuel jet. The pilot jet is alongside the accelerator pump cover; the auxiliary fuel jet is approached from the same side as the pilot jet but hides behind a plug, and is not easily accessible.

9   With all the removable jets taken out, blow out all the holes with compressed air.

10   The electro-magnetic cut-off valve may be removed **(see illustration)** and its action tested by supplying 12 volts to the tag terminal and

grounding the case. The plunger should first be depressed 3 to 4 mm (0.118 to 0.157 in).

11   The accelerator pump may be disassembled and the diaphragm inspected for cracks or damage. Do not remove the screw on the end of the operating rod or the pump will have to be recalibrated. Take the rod off the lever at the other end. Remove the four screws holding the pump cover and extract the diaphragm. Be careful not to lose the spring. When installing the cover tighten the screws with the diaphragm center pushed in. This means holding the operating lever out while the screws are tightened.

12   The choke vacuum diaphragm may be inspected in a similar way. Do not alter the setting of the center screw or the choke opening will need to be reset.

13   There is one other check to be made. If the bushings of the throttle shaft are worn and the spindle is loose in its bearings then air may leak past and affect the air/fuel ratio. The remedy is, unfortunately, a replacement carburetor.

12.3   Push the choke pull-off rod toward the diaphragm, measure the distance between the choke plate and carburetor wall and turn the diaphragm adjusting screw if necessary

14   Assemble all the parts methodically. Put a sealant on the main jet plug. The carburetor should not need recalibration as you have not moved any of the adjusting screws.

15   Install the carburetor and perform the adjustments described in Section 12.

---

12   Carburetor (Solex 34 PICT-5) – adjustments

Warning: *Gasoline is extremely flammable, so take extra precautions when you work on any part of the fuel system. Don't smoke or allow open flames or bare light bulbs near the work area, and don't work in a garage where a natural gas-type appliance (such as a water heater or clothes dryer) with a pilot light is present. If you spill any fuel on your skin, rinse it off immediately with soap and water. When you perform any kind of work on the fuel system, wear safety glasses and have a Class B type fire extinguisher on hand.*

Choke valve gap

Refer to illustration 12.3

1   Remove the air cleaner or intake duct. Remove the automatic choke cover (see Section 11).

2   Close the choke valve and at the same time where applicable position the fast idle speed adjusting screw in the upper notch.

3   Push the choke pull-off rod fully toward the diaphragm, then check that the distance between the choke plate and the carburetor wall is as given in this Chapters Specifications. If not, turn the diaphragm adjusting screw as necessary **(see illustration)**.

4   Install the cover and air cleaner or intake duct.

Throttle valve stop screw

Refer to illustrations 12.5a, 12.5b and 12.7

5   This screw determines the basic throttle valve opening **(see illustrations)** – on some models the screw is non-adjustable.

4

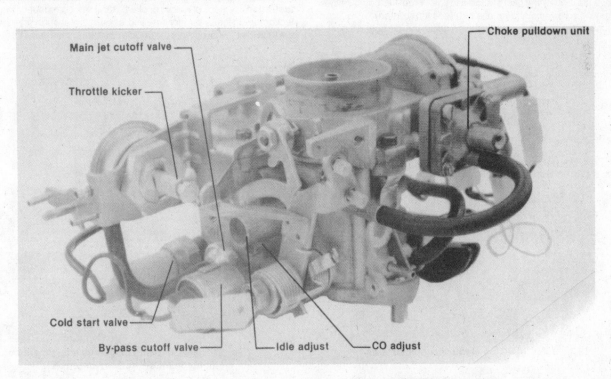

12.5a   Locations of the various components on the Solex 34 PICT-5 carburetor

Main jet cutoff valve

Throttle kicker

Choke pulldown unit

Cold start valve

By-pass cutoff valve

Idle adjust

CO adjust

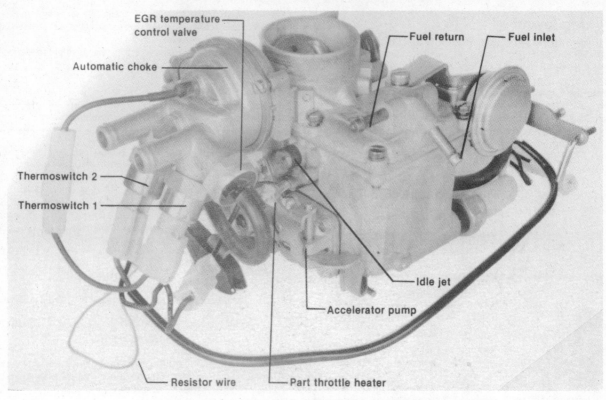

12.5b   Rear view of the Solex 34 PICT-5 carburetor

6   With the engine idling at normal operating temperature, remove the vacuum advance hose and connect a vacuum gauge to the outlet on the carburetor.

7   Turn the stop screw clockwise until the gauge registers vacuum, then unscrew it slowly until the gauge returns to zero. From this point unscrew the adjusting screw one quarter of a turn **(see illustration)**.

8   Install the vacuum advance hose and adjust the idle speed if necessary.

Accelerator pump discharge

Refer to illustrations 12.9a and 12.9b

9   The accelerator pump may be adjusted to give the correct quantity of fuel per stroke by turning the nut on the end of the connecting rod **(see illustration)**. A piece of rubber or plastic tube must be clipped over the injection pipe in the carburetor bore and led out to a measuring cylinder. With the tube in position, operate the throttle until fuel comes out of the tube into

12.7   Solex 34 PICT-5 carburetor adjustments

A   Choke valve gap   B   Throttle valve stop screw
     adjusting screw   C   Fast idle screw

12.9a   Accelerator pump discharge adjustment on Solex 34 PICT-5 carburetor (arrow)

12.9b Early type accelerator pump discharge adjustment

12.18 Solex 34 PICT-5 carburetor

A   Fast idle cam   C   Mixture screw
B   Idle speed screw

the glass. Empty the glass and then operate the throttle five times catching the fuel in the measuring glass. Divide the amount in the glass by five and compare the result with the amount given in this Chapters Specifications. To adjust the stroke, alter the setting of the nut and repeat the test. Lengthen the rod by screwing the nut out to decrease the amount injected. On some early models the arrangement may be a little different **(see illustration)**. Screw the adjusting screw out to increase the amount injected.

Vacuum valve (float chamber)

10   Some 1.5 liter automatic transmission models equipped with carburetor number 055 129 015 L have an electrically-controlled vacuum valve which channels manifold depression to the float chamber in order to improve take-off performance up to 1800 rpm.
11   To test the system connect a test lamp into the vacuum valve circuit, then start the engine and allow it to idle – the test lamp should light up. Now increase the engine speed to between 1700 and 1900 rpm – the test lamp should go out.
12   The same carburetor also incorporates an automatic cold idle valve which effectively varies the opening of the cold idle valve according to the coolant temperature. The valve is operated by manifold vacuum.

Idle speed
Refer to illustration 12.18

13   Connect a tachometer to the engine in accordance with the manufacturer's instructions.
14   Disconnect the crankcase ventilation hose from the air cleaner or intake manifold and plug the exposed hole.
15   On 1980 North American models, similarly disconnect the charcoal filter hose at the intake and seal the intake hole. Also disconnect the hoses from the air injection valves and plug the valves.
16   On all models run the engine at a fast idle until it reaches its normal operating temperature. Switch off all electrical components and only make an adjustment when the radiator fan is stopped.
17   On models equipped with electronic ignition, briefly accelerate the engine in order to operate the idle stabilizer.

All except North American models with electronic ignition

18   Make sure that the choke valve is fully open, then allow the engine to idle and if necessary adjust the idle speed screw until the engine runs at the specified speed **(see illustration)**.

North American models with electronic ignition

19   If adjustment of the idle speed is necessary on North America models equipped with electronic ignition, the procedure is different. First disconnect the plugs from the idle stabilizer and connect them together, then disconnect and plug the vacuum advance and retard hoses. Adjust the idle speed to the specified adjusting value, then reconnect the vacuum advance and retard hoses. Now readjust the idle speed if necessary to regain

the specified value. Reconnect the idle stabilizer plugs, accelerate the engine briefly, then check that the idle speed is within the specified checking values.

All models
20   Finally check the idling speed and make any small adjustment as necessary. Stop the engine, remove the instruments, and reconnect all the hoses as necessary. If the vehicle has been used under frequent stop/start conditions, the CO content may rise after reconnecting the crankcase breather hose, however this is due to the presence of fuel in the engine oil. A long fast drive or an oil change will solve the problem.

Fast idle (cold idling) speed
Refer to illustration 12.22

21   Adjust the idle speed as described in steps 13 to 20.
22   Set the fast idle stop screw on the third step **(see illustration)**.
23   Hold the choke valve fully open, then run the engine and check that the fast idle speed is as given in this Chapters Specifications. If not, adjust the screw as necessary.

Part throttle heater (North American models)
Refer to illustration 12.24

24   1980 North American models are equipped with a heating element for

12.22 Fast idle stop screw position (arrow) when adjusting the fast idle speed

4

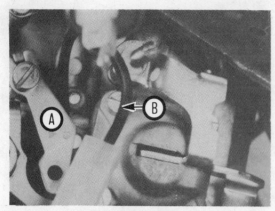

**12.24   Location of the part throttle heating element (A)
and supply wire (B)**

**12.28   Location of the main jet shut-off valve (A) and the cold
start enrichment valve (B)**

part throttle channel heating up to 167-degrees F (75-degrees C) **(see illustration)**.

25   To test the heater, connect a test lamp into the supply wire direct from the battery positive terminal – the lamp should light up if the heater is operating correctly.

Main jet shut-off valve (North America models)

26   This valve is controlled by an electro-pneumatic relay in the vacuum control unit, and it cuts off fuel flow through the main jet when the relay voltage is less than five volts or when the ignition is switched off.

27   To test the valve, run the engine at idling speed, then disconnect the wiring plug from the vacuum control unit. If the engine does not stall, either the valve or the vacuum system is faulty.

Cold start valve (North American models)

Refer to illustration 12.28

28   This valve supplies extra fuel for up to two minutes for starting at temperatures below 60-degrees F (16-degrees C) **(see illustration)**.

29   To test the valve, disconnect the supply wire and connect a test lamp and battery to the terminal. At temperatures below 60-degrees F (16-degrees C) the test lamp should light up.

Throttle kicker (North American models)

Refer to illustration 12.30

30   The throttle kicker increases the idle speed when the air conditioner is operating, in order to prevent the engine from stalling **(see illustration)**.

31   Before testing the kicker the ignition timing, idle speed and CO content must first be checked and adjusted if necessary. An ignition timing lamp (strobe) will be required.

32   Briefly accelerate the engine, then switch on the air conditioner to the coldest temperature and highest blower speed. The ignition timing should not alter – if it does, loosen the locknut on the throttle kicker and turn the adjusting screw as necessary. Tighten the locknut, using a liquid locking agent, when adjustment is correct.

13   Fuel injection systems – general information

Refer to illustrations 13.2a, 13.2b and 13.6

Warning: *Gasoline is extremely flammable, so take extra precautions when you work on any part of the fuel system. Don't smoke or allow open flames or bare light bulbs near the work area, and don't work in a garage where a natural gas-type appliance (such as a water heater or clothes dryer) with a pilot light is present. If you spill any fuel on your skin, rinse it off immediately with soap and water. When you perform any kind of work on the fuel system, wear safety glasses and have a Class B type fire extinguisher on hand.*

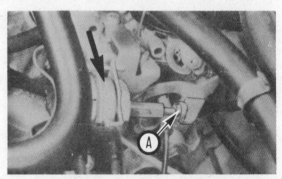

**12.30   Location of the throttle kicker (arrow) and
adjusting screw**

Continuous Injection System (CIS)

The Continuous Injection System is found on most of the models covered by this manual. It is a well-proven system, with little to go wrong and no black boxes to worry about. As the name implies, fuel injection takes place continuously while the engine is running. The rate of injection is varied to suit the prevailing speed and load.

Fuel is drawn from the tank by an electric fuel pump. The pump pressurizes the system to approximately 75 psi. An accumulator next to the pump provides a reservoir of pressure to improve hot starting and to dampen the pulses from the pump. From the accumulator the fuel passes through a filter and then to the fuel distributor on top of the intake manifold **(see illustrations)**.

The fuel distributor looks a little like an ignition distributor, but it has fuel lines instead of spark plug wires. There is one fuel line per injector, with additional lines for the start injector and the control pressure regulator. The fuel distributor's main function is to regulate the fuel supply to the injectors in proportion to the incoming airflow. Incoming air deflects the airflow sensor plate, which moves the control plunger in the fuel distributor and so varies the supply to the injectors. The airflow sensor and the fuel distributor together are sometimes called the fuel control unit.

The control pressure regulator reduces the control pressure during warm-up and under condition of low manifold vacuum, and so enriches the mixture. A lower control pressure means that the airflow sensor plate is deflected further, and the quantity of fuel injected is increased.

An electrically-controlled cold start injector provides extra fuel during cold engine starting. A thermal time switch controls the duration of start injector operation when the engine is cold; on a hot engine an impulse relay provides a smaller quantity of extra fuel to be injected. An auxiliary air valve provides the extra air needed to maintain idle speed when the engine is cold.

13.2a CIS fuel injection components (typical)

1 Fuel filter	5 Control pressure regulator
2 Fuel distributor	6 Intake air distributor
3 Air flow sensor	7 Thermo-time switch
4 Throttle chamber	8 Cold start valve

4

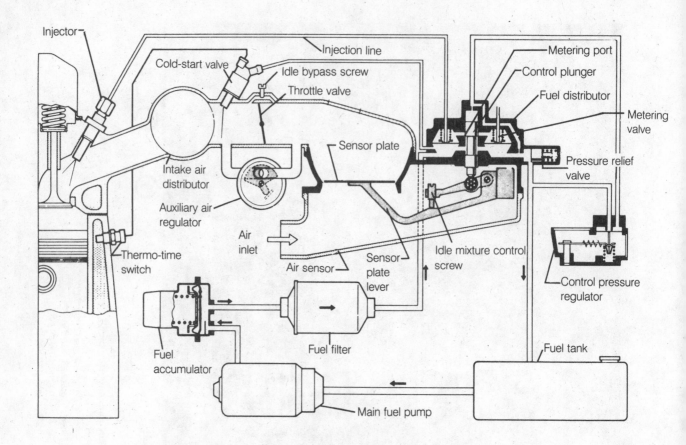

13.2b   Schematic view of the CIS fuel injection system

Continuous Injection System – Electronic (CIS-E) fuel system

The CIS-E fuel injection system **(see illustration)** is much like the simpler CIS fuel injection described earlier. The basic part of CIS-E is mechanical. However, electronic control regulates a large part of the fuel pressures and fuel mixture and consequently the running condition.

The differential pressure regulator is controlled by a fluctuating signal from the oxygen sensor control unit based on the input data received from various sensors. By regulating the electric current flow in the differential pressure regulator circuit, fuel pressure in the lower chamber of the fuel distributor is used to control the volume of fuel delivered to the injectors by the metering valves.

The CIS-E system is designed so that all the components can be tested by using a simple multimeter and test light. The basic fuel metering system is dependent on fuel pressure and must be tested by using the basic fuel pressure tests similar to that of the CIS fuel injection system.

CIS-E Motronic engine management system

The CIS-E Motronic engine management system is used on vehicles equipped with the 2.0L 16-valve engine (engine code 9A). The Motronic system combines the fuel control of the CIS-E fuel injection system with the control of ignition timing, idle speed and emissions into one control unit.

The fuel injection and idle speed control functions of CIS-E Motronic are similar to those used on the CIS-E system described above. Where the Motronic differs from CIS-E is its "adaptive circuitry" in the oxygen sensor system. Adaptive circuitry enables the oxygen sensor system to adjust the operating range of fuel metering in accordance with subtle changes in operating conditions caused by such things as normal engine wear, vacuum leaks, changes in altitude, etc. For more information on the CIS-E Motronic system, see Chapter 6.

Digifant II fuel-injection system

Refer to illustration 13.9

The Bosch Digifant II fuel injection system **(see illustration)** is used on some later model engines. It is an electronically controlled fuel injection system that utilizes one solenoid operated fuel injector per cylinder. The system is governed by an Electronic Control Unit (ECU) which processes information sent by various sensors, and in turn precisely meters the fuel to the cylinders by adjusting the amount of time that the injectors are open.

An electric fuel pump delivers fuel under high pressure to the injectors through the fuel feed line and an in-line filter. A pressure regulator keeps fuel available at an optimum pressure, allowing pressure to rise or fall depending on engine speed and load. Fuel in excess of injector needs is returned to the fuel tank by a separate line.

A sensor in the air intake duct constantly measures the mass of the incoming air, and through the ECU adjusts the fuel mixture to provide an optimum air/fuel ratio.

Another device, called the oxygen sensor, is mounted on the exhaust manifold and continually reads the oxygen content of the exhaust gas. This information is also used by the ECU to adjust the duration of injection, making it possible to meter the fuel very accurately to comply with strict emission control standards.

Other components incorporated in the system are the throttle valve (which controls airflow to the engine), the coolant temperature sensor, the throttle position switch, idle stabilizer valve (which bypasses air around the throttle plate to control idle speed) and associated relays and fuses.

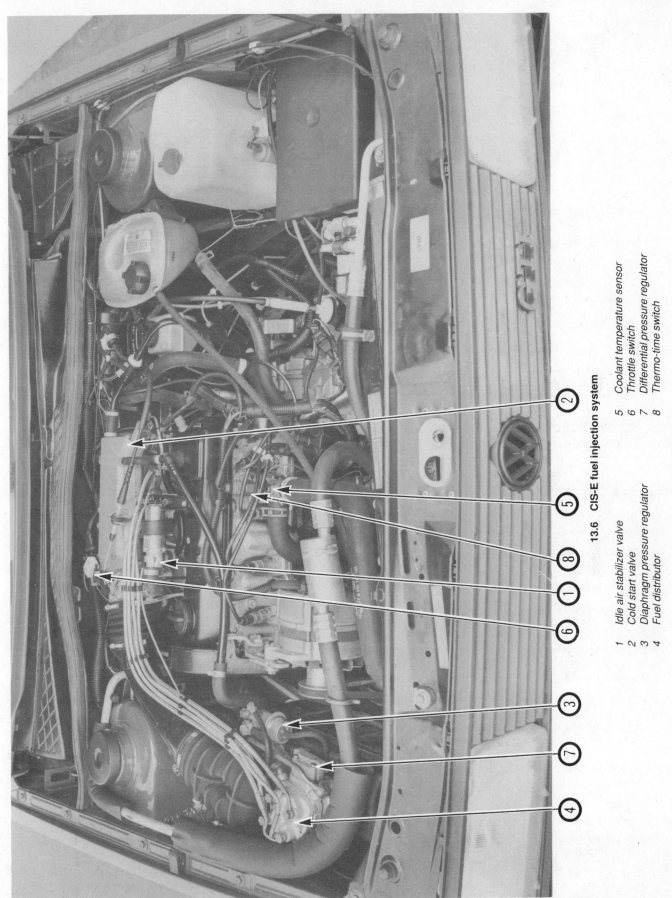

13.6 CIS-E fuel injection system

1 Idle air stabilizer valve
2 Cold start valve
3 Diaphragm pressure regulator
4 Fuel distributor

5 Coolant temperature sensor
6 Throttle switch
7 Differential pressure regulator
8 Thermo-time switch

4

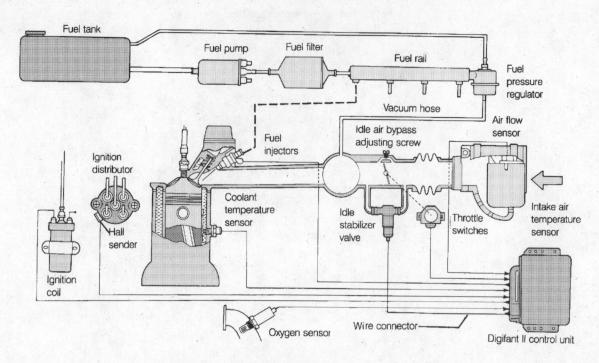

13.9   Schematic view of the Digifant II engine management system

14   Fuel injection system – troubleshooting

CIS fuel injection system

Symptom	Probable cause	Corrective action
Engine starts hard or fails to start when cold	Cold start valve or thermo-time switch faulty	Test cold start valve and thermo-time switch. Replace faulty parts (see Sections 20 and 21)
	Fuel pump not running	Check fuel pump fuse and fuel pump relay (see Section 2)
	Air flow sensor plate rest position incorrect	Inspect air flow sensor plate rest position and adjust if necessary (see Section 17)
	Fuel pressure incorrect	Test system pressure and cold control pressure (see Section 16)
Engine starts hard or fails to start when warm	Cold start valve leaking or operating continuously	Test cold start valve and thermo-time switch (see Sections 20 and 21)
	Fuel pressure incorrect	Test warm control pressure. Replace control pressure regulator if necessary (see Section 16)
	Air flow sensor plate rest position incorrect	Inspect air flow sensor plate rest position and adjust if necessary (see Section 17)
	Insufficient residual fuel pressure	Test residual fuel pressure. Replace fuel pump check valve or fuel accumulator as necessary (see Section 16)
	Fuel leak(s)	Inspect fuel lines and connections. Correct leaks as required (see Chapters 1 and 4)
Engine misses and hesitates under load	Fuel injector clogged	Test fuel injectors. Check for clogged injector lines. Replace faulty injectors (see Section 25)
	Fuel pressure incorrect	Test system pressure and warm control pressure. Adjust system pressure regulator or replace control pressure regulator as necessary (see Section 16)
	Fuel leak(s)	Inspect fuel lines and connections. Correct leaks as required (see Chapter 1)

CIS fuel injection system

Symptom	Probable cause	Corrective action
Engine starts but stalls at idle	Incorrect fuel pressure	Test system pressure and control pressure (see Section 16)
	Cold start valve leaking	Test and, if necessary, replace cold start valve (see Section 21)
	Auxiliary air regulator faulty	Test and, if necessary, replace auxiliary air regulator (see Section 22)
	Vacuum (intake air) leak	Inspect intake air components for leaking hoses, hose connections and cracks or other leaks. Repair as required (see Chapter 1)
Engine idles too fast	Accelerator pedal, cable or throttle valve binding	Inspect for worn or broken parts, kinked cable or other damage. Replace faulty parts (see Section 5)
	Auxiliary air regulator faulty	Test and, if necessary, replace auxiliary air regulator (see Section 22)
	Air leaking past throttle valve	Inspect throttle valve and adjust or replace as required (see Section 13)
Hesitation on acceleration	Vacuum (intake air) leak	Inspect intake air components for leaking hoses, hose connections and cracks or other leaks. Repair as required
	Fuel injectors clogged	Test injector spray pattern and quantity. Replace faulty injectors (see Section 25)
	Cold start valve leaking	Test and, if necessary, replace cold start valve (see Section 21)
	Control plunger in fuel distributor binding or fuel distributor faulty	Check air flow sensor plate movement and, if necessary, replace fuel distributor (see Section 17)
	Air flow sensor plate out of adjustment	Inspect air flow sensor plate position and adjust if necessary (see Section 17)
	Fuel pressure incorrect	Test system pressure and warm control pressure. If necessary, replace control pressure regulator (see Section 19)
Poor fuel mileage	Idle speed, ignition timing and idle mixture	Check and adjust (see Chapter 1) (mixture adjustment must be performed by a dealer service department or other repair shop)
	Cold start valve leaking	Test and, if necessary, replace cold start valve (see Section 21)
	Fuel pressure incorrect	Test system pressure and warm control pressure. If necessary, replace control pressure regulator (see Section 19)
Engine continues to run (diesels) after ignition is turned off	Incorrect ignition timing or faulty ignition system	Check ignition timing (see Chapter 1)
	Engine overheated	Inspect cooling system (see Chapters 1 and 3)

CIS-E and CIS-E Motronic fuel injection systems

Note: *On CIS-E Motronic systems, begin troubleshooting by reading any stored trouble codes (see Chapter 6).*

Symptom	Probable cause	Corrective action
Engine starts hard or fails to start when cold	Cold start valve or thermo-time switch faulty	Test cold start valve and thermo-time switch. Replace faulty parts (see Sections 20 and 21)
	Fuel pump not running	Check fuel pump fuse and relay (see Section 2)
	Air flow sensor plate rest position incorrect	Inspect air flow sensor plate rest position/adjust as necessary (see Section 17)

CIS-E and CIS-E Motronic fuel injection systems (continued)

Symptom	Probable cause	Corrective action
Engine starts hard or fails to start when cold (continued)	Fuel pressure incorrect	Check differential pressure regulator, system pressure and differential pressure (see Section 27)
	Coolant temperature sensor faulty or wire to sensor broken	Test coolant temperature sensor and wiring. Repair wiring or replace sensor as required (see Section 28)
	Poor ignition system ground (PL, 9A engines)	(See Chapter 5)
Engine starts hard or fails to start when warm	Cold start valve leaking or operating continuously	Test cold start valve and thermo-time switch (see Sections 20 and 21)
	Fuel pressure incorrect	Check differential pressure regulator, system pressure and differential pressure (see Section 27)
	Insufficient residual fuel pressure	Test residual fuel pressure. Replace fuel pump check valve or fuel accumulator as necessary (see Section 16)
	Oxygen sensor system faulty	This test requires special tools. Take the vehicle to a dealer service department or other repair shop
	Air flow sensor plate rest position incorrect	Inspect air flow sensor plate rest position and adjust if necessary (see Section 17)
	Fuel injector faulty or clogged	Test injector spray patterns and quantity. Replace faulty injectors (see Section 25)
	Fuel pump delivery inadequate	Check the fuel pump (see Section 2)
	Fuel leak(s)	Inspect fuel lines and connections. Correct leaks as required
	Evaporative emission control system faulty (CIS-E Motronic)	Check carbon canister solenoid valves (see Chapter 6)
Engine stalls or idles rough (cold or warm)	Fuel pressure incorrect	Check differential pressure regulator, system pressure and differential pressure (see Section 27)
	Cold start valve faulty	Test cold start valve. Replace if leaking or otherwise faulty (see Section 21)
	Fuel injector faulty or clogged	Test injector spray patterns and quantity. Replace faulty injectors (see Section 25)
	Coolant temperature sensor faulty or wiring to sensor broken	Test coolant temperature sensor and wiring. Repair wiring or replace sensor as required (see Section 28)
	Vacuum (intake air) leak	Inspect intake air components for leaking hoses, hose connections and cracks or other leaks. Repair as required
	Control plunger in fuel distributor binding or fuel distributor faulty	Check air flow sensor plate movement and, if necessary, replace fuel distributor (see section 17)
	Auxiliary air regulator faulty	Test auxiliary air regulator and replace if faulty (see Section 22)
	Idle air stabilizer valve not operating (HT, RD and PL engines)	Test air stabilizer valve (see Section 23). Test idle switch (see Section 26)
	Airflow sensor plate rest position incorrect	Visually inspect air flow sensor plate rest position and adjust if necessary (see Section 17)
	Inadequate after-start, warm-up or acceleration enrichment.	Perform system electrical checks (see Section 16)
Engine misses and hesitates	Fuel injector clogged under load	Test injector spray patterns and quantity. Replace faulty injectors (see Section 25)
	Fuel pressure incorrect	Check differential pressure regulator, system pressure and differential pressure (see Section 27).

CIS-E and CIS-E Motronic fuel injection systems (continued)

Symptom	Probable cause	Corrective action
Engine misses and hesitates (continued)	Oxygen sensor system faulty	This test requires special tools. Take the vehicle to a dealer service department or other repair shop
	Fuel leak(s)	Inspect fuel lines and connections. Correct leaks as required
	Coolant temperature sensor faulty or wire to sensor broken	Test coolant temperature sensor and wiring. Repair wiring or replace sensor if faulty (see Section 28)
Engine idles too fast	Accelerator pedal, cable or throttle valve binding	Inspect for worn or broken parts, kinked cable or other damage. Replace faulty parts
	Auxiliary air regulator faulty	Test auxiliary air regulator and replace if faulty (see Section 22)
	Idle boost valve faulty	Test idle boost valve system and replace faulty components (see Section 24)
	Idle air stabilizer valve not operating (HT, RD, and PL engines)	Test idle air stabilizer valve (see Section 23). Test idle switch (see Section 26)
	Air leaking past throttle valve	Inspect throttle valve and adjust or replace as required
	Evaporative emission control system faulty (CIS-E Motronic)	Check carbon canister solenoid valves (see Chapter 6)
Hesitation on acceleration	Vacuum (intake air) leak	Inspect intake air components for leaking hoses, hose connections and cracks or other leaks. Repair as required
	Fuel injectors clogged	Test injector spray pattern and quantity. Replace faulty injectors (see Section 25)
	Cold start valve leaking	Test and, if necessary, replace cold start valve (see Section 21)
	Control plunger in fuel distributor binding or fuel distributor faulty	Check air flow sensor plate movement and, if necessary, replace fuel distributor (see Section 17)
	Air flow sensor plate out of adjustment	Inspect air flow sensor plate position and adjust if necessary (see Section 17)
	Fuel pressure incorrect	Check differential regulator, system pressure and differential pressure (see Section 27)
	Air flow sensor plate potentiometer faulty or incorrectly adjusted	Have the air flow sensor potentiometer checked by a dealer service department or other repair shop
	Inadequate after-start, warm-up or acceleration enrichment.	Perform system electrical checks (see Section 16)
Low power	Coolant temperature sensor faulty or wire to sensor broken	Test coolant temperature sensor and wiring. Repair wiring or replace sensor if faulty (see Section 28)
	Fuel pressure incorrect	Check differential pressure regulator, system pressure and differential pressure (see Section 27)
	Throttle plate not opening fully	Check throttle cable adjustment to make sure throttle is opening fully. Adjust cable if necessary (see Section 5)
	Full throttle switch faulty or incorrectly adjusted (HT, RD, PL amd 9A engines)	Check throttle switch and adjust if necessary. Replace a faulty switch (see Section 26)
Poor fuel mileage	Idle speed, ignition timing, idle mixture out of adjustment	Check and adjust (see Chapter 1) (idle mixture must be adjusted by a dealer service department or other repair shop)
	Cold start valve leaking	Test and, if necessary, replace cold start valve (see Section 21)
	Fuel pressure incorrect	Check differential pressure regulator, system pressure and differential pressure (see Section 27)

4

CIS-E and CIS-E Motronic fuel injection systems (continued)

Symptom	Probable cause	Corrective action
Engine continues to run (diesels) after ignition is turned off	Incorrect ignition timing or faulty ignition system	See Chapters 1 and 5
	Carbon canister control valve faulty (CIS-E Motronic)	Check carbon canister solenoid valve II (see Chapter 6)
	Engine overheated	See Chapter 3

Digifant II fuel injection system

Note: *California models with Digifant II are equipped with fault diagnosis capabilities. Begin troubleshooting by displaying any stored trouble codes (see Chapter 6).*

Symptom	Probable cause	Corrective action
Engine starts hard or fails to start when cold	Coolant temperature sensor faulty	Test coolant temperature sensor and replace if necessary (see Section 28)
	Fuel pump not running	Check fuel pump fuse and fuel pump relay (see Section 2)
	Fuel filter clogged	Check fuel filter (see Chapter 1)
	Vacuum (intake air) leak	Inspect intake air components for leaking hoses, hose connections and cracks or other leaks. Repair as required. Check for loose oil fill cap or dipstick
	Low fuel pressure	Test fuel pressure (see Section 16)
	Electronic control unit faulty	Have the system diagnosed by a dealer service department or other repair shop
Engine starts when cold but stalls at idle	Coolant temperature sensor faulty	Test coolant temperature sensor and replace if necessary (see Section 28)
	Electronic control unit faulty	Have the system diagnosed by a dealer service department or other repair shop
Engine idles rough or stalls (cold or warm)	Vacuum (intake air) leak	Inspect intake air components for leaking hoses, hose connections and cracks or other leaks. Repair as required. Check for loose oil fill cap or dipstick
	Air flow sensor flap binding or faulty	Check air flow sensor flap for binding. Have the system diagnosed by a dealer service department or other repair shop
	Inadequate fuel being delivered to engine	Test fuel pump (see Section 2)
	Blocked fuel filter	Replace fuel filter (see Chapter 1)
	Idle air stabilizer valve faulty	Test idle switch. Test idle air stabilizer valve (see Section 23)
	Low fuel pressure	Test fuel pressure (see Section 16)
	Electronic control unit faulty	Have the system diagnosed by a dealer service department or other repair shop
Engine misses, hesitates or stalls under load	Air flow sensor flap binding or faulty	Check air flow sensor flap. Have the system diagnosed by a dealer service department or other repair shop
	Intake air preheating system faulty	Test intake air preheating system and replace faulty components as required
	Vacuum (intake air) leak	Inspect intake air components for leaking hoses, hose connections and cracks or other leaks. Repair as required. Check for loose oil fill cap or dipstick.
	Low fuel pressure	Test fuel pressure (see Section 16)
Engine idles too fast	Accelerator pedal, cable or throttle valve binding	Inspect for worn or broken parts, kinked cable or other damage. Replace faulty parts (see Section 5)

Digifant II fuel injection system (continued)

Symptom	Probable cause	Corrective action
Engine idles too fast (continued)	Coolant temperature sensor wire disconnected or broken	Check wiring between control unit and sensor (see Chapter 12)
	Idle air stabilizer valve faulty	Test idle switch. Test idle air stabilizer valve (see Section 23)
Low power	Air intake restricted	Check air filter element, housing and preheating system (see Chapter 1)
	Air flow sensor flap not opening fully	Check movement of air flow sensor plate. Replace air flow sensor, if necessary (see Section 17)
	Throttle plate not opening fully	Check throttle cable adjustment, to make sure throttle is opening fully. Adjust cable if necessary (see Section 5)
	Full throttle switch faulty or incorrectly adjusted	Check throttle switch and adjust if necessary. Replace a faulty switch (see Section 26)
	Electronic control unit faulty	Have the system diagnosed by a dealer service department or other repair shop
Engine continues to run (diesels) after ignition is turned off	Incorrect timing or faulty ignition system	Check ignition timing (see Chapter 1)
	Engine overheated	See Chapter 3

15   Fuel pressure relief procedure (fuel-injected models)

Warning: *Gasoline is extremely flammable, so take extra precautions when you work on any part of the fuel system. Don't smoke or allow open flames or bare light bulbs near the work area, and don't work in a garage where a natural gas-type appliance (such as a water heater or clothes dryer) with a pilot light is present. If you spill any fuel on your skin, rinse it off immediately with soap and water. When you perform any kind of work on the fuel system, wear safety glasses and have a Class B type fire extinguisher on hand.*

1   Before disconnecting the fuel line, the fuel pressure must be released from the fuel line to eliminate any danger of fire or contamination.
2   Remove the fuel pump relay (see Section 2) to temporarily disable the fuel pump.
3   Allow the engine to run until it stalls.
4   Disconnect the negative battery cable before performing any work on the fuel system.

16   Fuel injection systems – general checks and adjustments

Warning: *Gasoline is extremely flammable, so take extra precautions when you work on any part of the fuel system. Don't smoke or allow open flames or bare light bulbs near the work area, and don't work in a garage where a natural gas-type appliance (such as a water heater or clothes dryer) with a pilot light is present. If you spill any fuel on your skin, rinse it off immediately with soap and water. When you perform any kind of work on the fuel system, wear safety glasses and have a Class B type fire extinguisher on hand.*

Preliminary checks

1   Check the ground wire connections on the intake manifold for tightness. Check all wiring harness connectors that are related to the system.

Loose connectors and poor grounds can cause many problems that resemble more serious malfunctions.
2   Check to see that the battery is fully charged, as the control unit and sensors depend on an accurate supply voltage in order to properly meter the fuel.
3   Check the air filter element – a dirty or partially blocked filter will severely impede performance and economy.
4   Open the fuel filler cap and listen for fuel pump operation while an assistant cranks the engine. If no whirring noise is heard, check the fuel pump (see Section 2).
5   Check the fuses. If a blown fuse is found, replace it and see if it blows again. If it does, search for a grounded wire in the harness to the fuel pumps.
6   Check the air intake duct from the air flow sensor to the intake manifold for leaks, which will result in an excessively lean mixture. Also check the condition of all of the vacuum hoses connected to the intake manifold.
7   Remove the air intake duct from the throttle body and check for dirt, carbon or other residue build-up. If it's dirty, clean it with carburetor cleaner and a toothbrush.

Throttle switch

8   Turn the ignition switch to the On position and open the throttle lever by hand and listen for a click as soon as the throttle comes off its stop. This test will indicate that the idle switch is functioning. If no click is heard, proceed to Section 26 for adjustment (or if necessary, replacement) of the switch.

Fuel pressure checks
CIS, CIS-E and CIS-E Motronic fuel injection systems
Refer to illustrations 16.10, 16.11, 16.15a, 16.15b, and 16.17
Note: *This check requires the use of a special Volkswagen fuel pressure gauge number 1318 or equivalent.*
9   Relieve the fuel pressure (see Section 15)

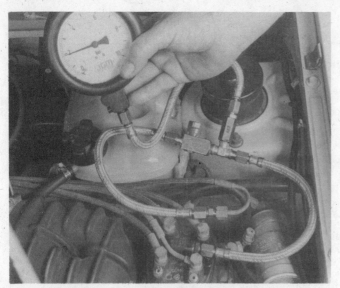

16.10   Be sure to connect the gauge with the valve on the control pressure regulator side on CIS systems

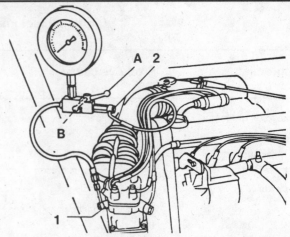

16.11   On CIS-E and CIS-E Motronic systems, connect the gauge to the fuel distributor test port (1) and the cold start valve supply line (2) (removed from the cold-start valve)

| A | Gauge valve in open position | B | Gauge valve in closed position |

10   On CIS systems, connect the fuel pressure gauge between the control pressure regulator and the fuel distributor with the valve side of the gauge toward the control pressure regulator **(see illustration)**.

11   On CIS-E and CIS-E Motronic systems, connect the above mentioned fuel pressure gauge (or equivalent) between the fuel distributor test port and the end of the line that supplies the cold start valve **(see illustration)**.

12   Start the vehicle and observe the pressure reading. There are three significant fuel pressure values:

System pressure – the basic fuel pressure produced by the fuel pump and maintained by the pressure relief valve in the fuel distributor (CIS) or the diaphragm pressure regulator (CIS-E and CIS-E Motronic).

Control pressure – the difference between system pressure and lower chamber pressure in the fuel distributor as determined by the control pressure regulator (CIS) or the differential pressure regulator (CIS-E and CIS-E Motronic). It is used to counter system pressure and regulate the movement of the control plunger.

Residual pressure – the amount of pressure which remains in the closed system after the engine and fuel pump are shut off.

Checking system pressure

13   First check the system pressure. Close the valve on the pressure gauge (this prevents fuel from entering the control pressure regulator) and observe the reading. System pressure should be as listed in this Chapter's Specifications. If the system pressure is too low, look for leaks, a clogged fuel filter or a damaged fuel line blocking the fuel flow. If no other cause can be found, the pressure can be adjusted by adding shims to the pressure relief valve (see Section 18).

14   On CIS systems, if the fuel pressure cannot be accurately adjusted, then the fuel distributor is faulty and must be replaced. On CIS-E and CIS-E Motronic systems, fuel pressure is not adjustable. If the fuel pressure is incorrect, replace the diaphragm pressure regulator.

Checking control pressure (CIS)

15   Next, check the control pressure. Turn the valve on the fuel pressure gauge to the open position. Make sure the vehicle is cold (68-degrees F) in order to obtain an accurate pressure reading. Disconnect the electrical connectors from the control pressure regulator and the auxiliary air valve. Start the vehicle and observe the gauge. The fuel pressure will increase as the temperature of the vehicle warms up **(see illustrations)**. The initial

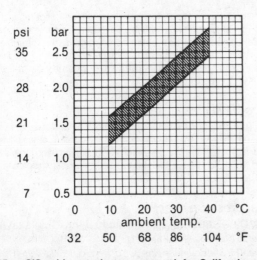

16.15a   CIS cold control pressure graph for California models

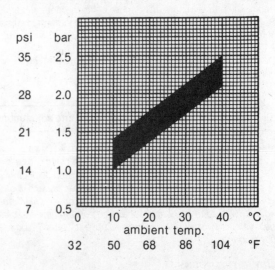

16.15b   CIS cold control pressure graph for North American models except California

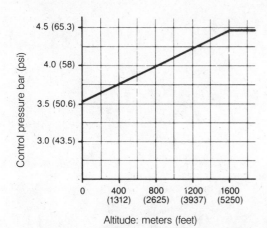

16.17 Graph of warm control pressure, as affected by altitude, for U.S. cars except California - example: at 800 meters (2625 ft.) above sea level, warm control pressure should be approximately 4.5 bar (58 psi)

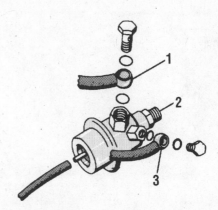

16.23 An exploded view of a typical diaphragm type pressure regulator (CIS-E and CIS-E Motronic systems) – always use new sealing washers when reconnecting the fuel lines

1   *Line from fuel distributor*   3   *Return line to fuel distributor*
2   *Return line to fuel tank*   *(differential pressure)*

---

pressure value is called cold control pressure. The cold control pressure should be accurate according to the climate and altitude of the region.

16   If the cold control pressure is too high, check for a fuel line that is blocked or kinked. Also, check the fuel union at the control pressure regulator for a plugged filter screen. If no problems are found, replace the control pressure regulator. **Warning:** *Be sure to relieve the fuel pressure before disconnecting any fuel lines (see Section 15).*

17   To check the warm control pressure, reconnect the electrical connectors onto the control pressure regulator and the auxiliary air regulator. Run the engine until the control pressure is no longer increasing (approximately 2 minutes) and observe the gauge. The warm control pressure should be as listed in this Chapter's Specifications. **Note:** *US vehicles with engine code GX (except those sold new in California) have control pressure regulators which compensate for changes in altitude. Refer to the chart to convert warm control pressure vs. altitude above sea level* **(see illustration).**

18   If the warm control pressure is too high, check for a blocked or kinked fuel line. Also, check the fuel union at the control pressure regulator for a plugged filter screen. If no problems are found, replace the control pressure regulator.

19   If warm control pressure is low, or takes more than 2 minutes to reach its highest value, test the resistance of the heating element and test for voltage reaching the harness connector at the control pressure regulator.

Checking differential pressure on CIS-E and CIS-E Motronic systems

Refer to illustrations 16.23 and 16.26

20   Differential pressure, which is controlled by the differential pressure regulator, is the difference in pressure between the upper and lower chambers of the fuel distributor. The differential pressure regulator determines the pressure differential at the fuel distributor metering ports, which determines how much fuel flows to the injectors, which in turn determines the air/fuel mixture. Here's how to check it:

21   Hook up the gauge as shown in illustration 16.11, close the valve on the gauge and bypass the fuel pump relay so the fuel pump will run (see Section 2).

22   Disconnect the electrical connector for the differential pressure regulator, note the indicated differential pressure (gauge valve closed) and compare your reading to the fuel pressure listed in this Chapter's Specifications.

23   If the differential pressure is too low, measure the volume of fuel coming from the fuel distributor return line: Disconnect the fuel distributor fuel line from the diaphragm pressure regulator **(see illustration)** and put the

detached line in a measuring container suitable for catching fuel. Plug the open port on the diaphragm pressure regulator and run the fuel pump. After one minute, there should be 130 to 150 cc of fuel in the container. When you reattach the line, use new sealing washers and tighten the banjo fitting to the torque listed in this Chapter's Specifications.

24   If the quantity of fuel is correct, but the differential pressure tested below specifications, the differential pressure regulator is faulty. Replace it (see Section 27).

25   If the quantity of fuel is incorrect, recheck the system pressure (see above). If the system pressure is within specification but the differential pressure and the measured fuel quantity aren't, the fuel distributor is probably faulty.

26   Hook up an ammeter to the differential pressure regulator (see Step 42). On CIS-E (not CIS-E Motronic) systems, disconnect the electrical connector for the coolant temperature sensor and connect a 15 k-ohm resistor across the connector terminals **(see illustration)**.

27   Turn on the ignition and operate the fuel pump. Differential pressure and differential pressure regulator current should be within the specifications listed in this Chapter's Specifications.

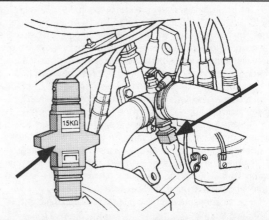

16.26 You'll need to bridge the terminals on the electrical connector for the coolant temperature sensor (right arrow) with a 15 k-ohm resistor before you can complete the differential pressure test for CIS-E systems – VW's special factory tool (VW 1490) is shown (left arrow, but a resistor from an electronics supply store will work

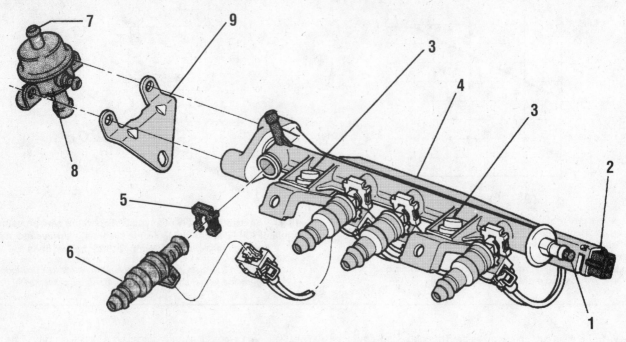

16.35　An exploded view of the fuel rail assembly used on Digifant II systems

1	Service port for fuel pressure testing	3	Fuel rail mounting bolt	7	Vacuum from intake manifold
2	Electrical connector f or fuel injectors	4	Fuel rail	8	Fuel pressure regulator
		5	Fuel injector retaining clip	9	Fuel pressure regulator mounting bracket
		6	Fuel injector		

28   If the differential pressure regulator current is within specifications, but the differential pressure isn't, the differential pressure regulator is faulty and must be replaced (see Section 27). If both the pressure and the regulator current are out of specifications, look for an electrical problem (see Electrical tests below). But first, check all wires and connections. Check for a good ground connection at the cold-start valve. If you can't find any other faults, the electronic control unit is probably faulty.

Checking residual pressure

29   Finally, check the residual pressure. Check the residual pressure with the gauge connected as described in the previous fuel pressure tests.
30   When the engine is warm (control pressure 49 to 55 psi) shut the engine off and leave the gauge connected. Wait ten minutes and observe the gauge. The fuel pressure should not have dropped off below 38 psi.
31   If the pressure drops off excessively, check for leaks in the fuel lines, the fuel distributor, the injectors, the cold start valve and the oxygen sensor frequency valve. Also check residual pressure at the fuel supply line from the fuel pump. Disconnect the gauge from the fuel distributor and the control pressure regulator and reconnect those lines. Next, connect the gauge to the main supply line from the fuel pump and be sure to close the valve. Run the fuel pump with a jumper wire as described in Section 2 and pressurize the system until the gauge reads 49 to 55 psi. Once again, the pressure should not drop off below 38 psi within ten minutes.
32   If the pressure drops off excessively and there are no apparent leaks between the fuel pump and the gauge, pinch closed the fuel line between the tank and the fuel pump and observe the gauge.
33   If residual pressure now remains steady, then the check valve in the fuel pump is faulty.
34   If the residual pressure still drops off quickly, then the fuel accumulator is at fault.

Digifant II fuel injection system

Refer to illustration 16.35
35   Check system pressure and residual pressure by removing the plug on the service port at the end of the fuel rail **(see illustration)**.
36   Connect the fuel pressure gauge to the service port. Start the engine and let the vehicle idle. System pressure should be approximately 36 psi.
37   Disconnect the vacuum hose from the top of the fuel pressure regulator. The fuel pressure should jump to about 44 psi.
38   Turn the engine off and observe the gauge after 10 minutes. The residual pressure should be at least 29 psi.
39   If the system pressure is excessive, the pressure regulator is faulty and should be replaced with a new unit (see Section 29).
40   If the system pressure is too low, run the engine for awhile to build up fuel pressure, then turn the engine off and quickly pinch shut the fuel return line. If pressure holds, then the pressure regulator is defective and should be replaced with a new unit. If the pressure still drops, check for leaks in the fuel system; fuel injectors, O-rings, or a defective fuel pump check valve.

Electrical tests (CIS-E and CIS-E Motronic)

Note: *The following electrical tests are presented in a specific sequence so you can logically isolate the cause of a problem, so it's imperative that you perform them in the order shown.*

Measuring differential pressure regulator current

Refer to illustration 16.42
41   Although the differential pressure regulator itself can't be diagnosed or repaired, the measurement of its current output during some of the following tests is the most important means by which you can check the operation of CIS-E and CIS-E Motronic fuel injection systems.
42   VW dealers use a special test harness **(see illustration)** to hook up a digital ammeter multimeter to the differential pressure regulator. If you don't want to buy this special harness, you can fabricate your own leads and hook up an ammeter or multimeter between the corresponding terminals of the regulator and the harness connector. If you decide to make your own test leads, make sure all connections between the leads and the two sides of the connector, and the ammeter/multimeter itself are

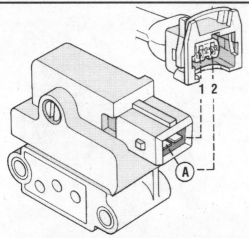

16.42   This convenient test harness (VW 1315A/1) for checking differential pressure regulator current on CIS-E and CIS-E Motronic systems is available at VW Dealers, but you can get along without the factory tool by fabricating your own test leads as described in the text

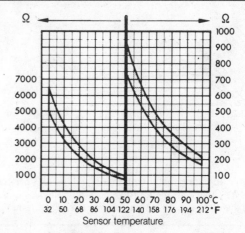

16.45   This graph shows the relationship between the resistance of the coolant temperature sensor (expressed in ohms, on the vertical axis) versus coolant temperature (expressed in degrees Centigrade and Fahrenheit, on the horizontal axis) (CIS-E systems)

secure. Use male spade type terminals of the same dimensions as the terminals on the regulator for the harness end; use female terminals for the regulator ends of the leads. If you don't have good positive connections, you'll get an erroneous current measurement – the current values you'll be measuring are in milliamps (mA), so good connections are essential.

CIS-E

After-start and cold-running enrichment

Refer to illustration 16.45

Note: *If the CIS-E system is functioning properly, it provides extra fuel to the engine when it's cold by increasing differential pressure regulator current for a brief period of time after starting and during warm-up. The control unit gets its information from two sources: When the starter is cranked, it signals the control unit to initiate after-start enrichment, a phase which lasts about 40 seconds. If the engine is still cold, a coolant temperature sensor prolongs this phase. Using the coolant temperature sensor as its monitor, the control unit gradually decreases the cold-running enrichment phase as the engine warms up. Here's how to test these two functions:*

43   Remove the electrical connector from the coolant temperature sensor to simulate an open circuit, i.e. a cold engine. To check cold-running enrichment, turn on the ignition. Hook up a digital ohmmeter to measure the differential pressure regulator current (see Step 21). Indicated current should be 80 to 100 mA on 16-valve engines and 80 to 110 mA on all other engines. **Note:** *Don't disconnect the ohmmeter – you'll need to measure differential regulator current again during some of the following tests.*

44   You must activate the starter to check after-start enrichment, but you don't want the engine to actually start, so disconnect the ignition coil wire from the distributor cap and use a jumper wire to ground it. Actuate the starter for two to three seconds, then leave the ignition turned on. The differential pressure regulator current should increase to more than 120 mA for 20 to 50 seconds, then return to the cold-running value above. On 16-valve engines, the after-start enrichment phase lasts a little longer about 30 to 60 seconds). When the test is completed, turn off the ignition and reconnect the coil wire and the coolant temperature sensor electrical connector.

45   To test the coolant temperature sensor, disconnect the electrical connector and check the resistance across the sensor terminals. The resistance varies with the temperature of the engine coolant **(see illustration)**. If the indicated resistance doesn't match the value shown, replace the sensor.

Cold-acceleration enrichment

Refer to illustrations 16.47 and 16.48

Note: *To maintain good throttle response while the engine is still warming up, the CIS-E system provides extra fuel when the throttle valve is sudden-*

ly opened. How does the control unit "know" when the throttle valve is opened? A potentiometer mounted on the side of the air flow sensor housing sends a voltage signal to the control unit. The strength of this voltage signal varies in accordance with the position of the air sensor plate. The potentiometer is adjusted at the factory and its mounting screws are sealed, so it shouldn't need adjustment. However, if the following test determines that it's faulty and must be replaced, you'll have to adjust the new unit. Here's how to check it:

46   Unplug the electrical connector for the coolant temperature sensor and remove the black rubber boot for the air intake from the air flow sensor plate.

On engines with throttle valve switches (HT, RD and PL), open the throttle so the idle switch is no longer touching the throttle lever. Turn on the ignition and immediately raise the air flow sensor plate to its stop. The differential pressure regulator current should briefly exceed – then return to – the cold-running enrichment value given in the previous test above. Turn off the ignition and plug in the electrical connector for the temperature sensor.

47   If the indicated current isn't as specified above, check the operation of the potentiometer. Unplug the electrical connector for the potentiometer and use an ohmmeter to measure the resistance between the indicated terminals **(see illustration)**. The resistance between terminals 1 and 2

16.47   Hook up an ohmmeter to measure the resistance between the indicated terminals – if you have to replace the potentiometer, leave the four adjustment screws (arrows) loose until the new unit is adjusted (CIS-E systems)

1	Terminal 1 (positive terminal)
2	Terminal 2
3	Terminal 3 (negative terminal)

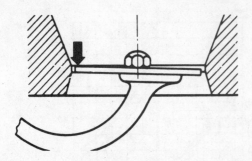

16.48   While adjusting the potentiometer, lift the air flow sensor plate until it's flush with the narrowest point in the air cone and hold the plate steady in this position (CIS-E systems)

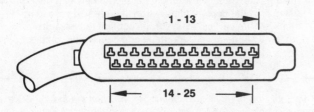

16.60a   Terminal guide for electrical connector for CIS-E oxygen sensor control unit

16.54   When you close the full-throttle switch from 4000 rpm (8-valve engines) or 2500 rpm (16-valve engines), the differential pressure regulator current should increase to about 14 mA (8-valve engines) or 16 mA (16-valve engines) (CIS-E systems)

should be more than 4000 ohms; the resistance between terminals 2 and 3 should be less than 1000 ohms. Check the resistance between terminals 2 and 3 while slowly and evenly lifting the sensor plate. The resistance should steadily increase, without any flat spots, to about 4000 ohms. If the potentiometer doesn't operate within these specifications, replace it.

48   To replace the potentiometer, remove its mounting screws and pull it off the fuel distributor. Install the new potentiometer and mounting screws, but leave the screws just loose enough to permit adjustment of the potentiometer. Lift the air flow sensor plate until it's flush with the narrowest point in the air cone **(see illustration)** and hold the plate steady in this position.

49   On eight-valve engines, adjust the position of the potentiometer until the voltage between the center terminal and ground is 0.2 to 0.3 volts; on 16-valve engines, adjust the position of the potentiometer until the voltage between the center and bottom terminals is 0.02 to 0.2 volts. Carefully tighten the mounting screws and recheck your voltage reading.

50   Raise the sensor plate all the way to its stop. The voltage should increase to about 7.0 volts. If it doesn't, check the resting position of the sensor plate and recheck the initial position setting of the potentiometer.

Full-throttle enrichment (HT, RD and PL engines)
Refer to illustration 16.54

Note: *Full-throttle enrichment can only occur when the engine is warmed up, the engine speed is above 4000 rpm (2500 rpm on 16-valve engines) and the throttle is fully open. When the throttle is opened all the way, a full-throttle switch supplies a signal to the control unit. Here's how to check it:*

51   Unplug the electrical connector from the coolant temperature sensor.

52   Using a jumper wire, bridge the connector terminals.

53   Start the engine and let it warm up.

54   Move the throttle until the engine speed exceeds 4000 rpm (eight-valve engines) or 2500 rpm (16-valve engines) and close the full-throttle switch on top of the throttle valve **(see illustration)**. The differential pressure regulator current should increase to about 14 mA (16 mA on 16-valve engines).

55   If the indicated differential pressure regulator current is high, first verify that your jumper wire at the temperature sensor connector is fully seated into both terminals; if the current doesn't increase when you close the full-throttle switch, either the switch itself is faulty or the rpm signal from the ignition control unit is faulty.

Deceleration fuel shut-off (HT, RD and PL engines)

Note: *During deceleration, fuel flow to the injectors is shut off to enhance fuel economy. At normal operating temperature, fuel flow is cut off when the throttle is closed at engine speeds above 1600 rpm, and resumes when rpm drops below 1300 rpm (these limits are slightly higher when the engine isn't yet warmed up). The signal for a closed throttle is supplied to the control unit by an idle switch mounted under the throttle body. To check it:*

56   Unplug the electrical connector from the coolant temperature sensor and bridge the connector terminals with a jumper wire.

57   Start the engine and let it warm up.

58   Increase engine speed to about 3000 rpm, then release the throttle. The positive differential pressure regulator current should momentarily change to a negative reading (about -45 mA), then return to its normal value.

59   If the current doesn't change to a negative value of about -45 mA, either the idle switch is incorrectly adjusted (see Section 26) or the rpm signal from the control unit is faulty (see below).

Control unit inputs
Refer to illustrations 16.60a and 16.60b

60   Checking the control unit inputs is simply a matter of checking the voltage or continuity at each terminal of the multi-pin electrical connector for the control unit. The accompanying terminal guide **(see illustration)** shows you the terminal numbers; the table **(see illustration)** lists the correct resistance or voltage value for each terminal.

61   Before you try to check the control unit connector, you'll need to make a special pair of test leads. You can fabricate an inexpensive set using a pair of insulated alligator clips, a pair of leads and a couple of flat connectors (VW Part No. N 17 457 2, or equivalent). Use the flat connectors to make contact with the female terminals of the multi-pin connector and attach the meter leads to the insulated alligator clips.

62   Disconnect the coil wire from the center tower of the distributor cap and ground it on the engine block with a jumper wire.

63   The control unit is located in the upper left (driver's) side of the engine compartment, beneath the drip tray. The tray is clipped into place. To remove it, carefully pull it up.

64   Make sure the ignition is turned off, then unplug the 25-pin connector from the oxygen sensor control unit.

65   Using a high-impedance (10 mega-ohm) digital multimeter, check the indicated terminals and compare your readings to the specified values. Don't try to take your readings with the test probes of the meter itself – they're too big and they're the wrong shape, so they'll provide inaccurate or faulty readings and they could damage the connector terminals.

66   If there are discrepancies, refer to the Wiring Diagrams at the end of

All 1985 to 1989 models with CIS-E

Component or circuit	Test terminals	Test conditions	Correct test value
Voltage supply and control unit ground	1 and 2 1 and 2	Ignition on Starter operated	Battery voltage (approximately 12 VDC) 8 volts minimum
Signal from starter to control unit	2 and 24	Starter operated	8 volts minimum
Differential pressure regulator	10 and 12	Ignition off	17-22 ohms
Air flow sensor plate potentiometer	17 and 18 14 and 17 14 and 17	Air flow sensor plate at rest Air flow sensor plate at rest Air flow sensor plate lifted to stop	More than 4000 ohms Less than 1000 ohms More than 4000 ohms
Coolant temperature sensor Wire from oxygen sensor to control unit	2 and 21 2 and 8 2 and 8	Ignition off Green oxygen sensor wire disconnected and touched to ground Green oxygen sensor wire connected to black wire	Resistance per Fig. 6-37 Continuity No continuity
Ground connection to intake manifold for ground cable bridge	2 and 15	Ignition off	Continuity
Ground connection to intake manifold for oxygen sensor cable shiield	2 and 7	Ignition off	Continuity
Ground connection to intake manifold (manual transmission only)	2 and 9	Ignition off	Continutity

Engine codes HT, RD and PL

Component or circuit	Test terminals	Test conditions	Correct test value
Idle air stabilizer valve	2 and 3 2 and 4	Ignition on	Battery voltage (approximately 12 VDC)
Full throttle switch	2 and 5	Ignition on; Throttle fully open (full-throtttle switch closed)	Battery voltage (approximately 12 VDC)
Idle switch	2 and 13	Ignition on; Throttle closed	Battery voltage (approximately 12 VDC)
RPM signal from knock sensor control unit	2 and 25	LED test light connected between terminals 2 and 25; Starter operated	LED must flicker
Ground connection to intake manifold (automatic trans. only)	2 and 22	Ignition off	Continuity
Voltage signal from air conditioning system	2 and 6 2 and 16 2 and 19	Ignition on Ignition on A/C switch on	Continuity Continuity
Battery ground	2 and 20	Ignition off	Continuity

16.60b Electrical test table for CIS-E systems

Chapter 12 and troubleshoot the faulty circuits. **Note:** *As a rule of thumb, an absence of the specified voltage or resistance indicates an open circuit in the wiring harness, but don't automatically assume it's a bad component. First, check for loose or corroded connectors, either one of which is much more likely than a bad component.*

CIS-E Motronic
After-start, warm-up and cold acceleration enrichment
Note: *To enhance driveability, the CIS-E Motronic system supplies extra fuel to the engine when it's cold by momentarily increasing the differential pressure regulator current for a short period after starting and during warm-up. The control unit uses the coolant temperature sensor to monitor engine temperature. The Motronic system also improves the throttle response of a cold engine by supplying extra fuel when the throttle valve is suddenly opened. To test it:*

67 Unplug the electrical connector for the oxygen sensor (it's a four-terminal connector located on the right engine mount).

68 Hook up a digital ohmmeter to measure the differential pressure regulator current.

69 Unplug the electrical connector from the harness for the coolant temperature sensor attach a 25 k-ohm resistor across the connector terminals to simulate a cold engine signal.

70 Start the engine and let it idle. Differential pressure regulator current should adjust itself to between 15 and 25 mA for about six to nine seconds, then gradually drop to between 9 and 15 mA.

71 Open the throttle all the way, then let it close. Differential pressure regulator current should increase momentarily, indicating cold acceleration enrichment. **Note:** *Don't disconnect the ohmmeter – you'll need to measure differential pressure regulator current again during some of the following tests.*

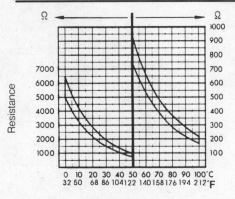

Coolant temperature

16.72   This graph shows the relationship between the resistance of the coolant temperature sensor (expressed in Ohms, on the vertical axis) versus coolant temperature (expressed in degrees Centigrade and Fahrenheit, on the horizontal axis) (CIS-E Motronic systems)

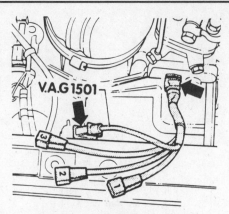

16.77   You'll need this special adapter (VW no. VAG 1501) to check the terminals on the air flow sensor potentiometer on CIS-E Motronic systems

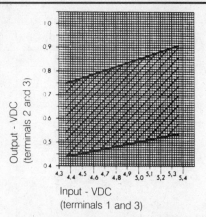

Input - VDC
(terminals 1 and 3)

16.78   This graph shows the relationship between the voltage input at terminals 1 and 3 (horizontal axis) and the output voltage at terminals 2 and 3 (vertical axis) of the air flow sensor potentiometer on CIS-E Motronic systems

Coolant temperature sensor

Refer to illustration 16.72

72   To test the coolant temperature sensor, detach its harness connector and check the resistance across the sensor terminals. The resistance varies with the engine coolant temperature **(see illustration)**. A sensor with resistance that doesn't correlate to the values shown is faulty. Drain the cooling system (see Chapter 3) and replace it. Be sure to coat the threads of the new sensor with thread sealant.

Deceleration fuel shut-off

Note: *When the throttle is closed and engine rpm is significantly above idle, the control unit shuts off the fuel supply to reduce exhaust emissions and conserve fuel consumption. To verify that this control is functioning correctly, you must measure the differential pressure regulator current while simulating deceleration conditions.*

73   Hook up an ohmmeter to measure the differential pressure regulator current (see Step 41).

74   Unplug the harness connector from the coolant temperature sensor.

75   Turn on the ignition. The differential pressure regulator current should be between 90 and 110 mA (if the indicated current is negative, reverse the leads).

76   Start the engine. Open the throttle to raise the engine speed to at least 3000 rpm, then close it abruptly. Differential pressure regulator current should briefly read in the negative range.

Air flow sensor potentiometer

Refer to illustrations 16.77, 16.78 and 16.79

Note: *On CIS-E Motronic systems, the air flow sensor plate potentiometer sends an engine load signal to the control unit which it uses to control ignition timing, acceleration, full-throttle enrichment and several other functions. To check the operation of the potentiometer, measure its output for a given voltage input.*

77   You'll need a special VW adapter **(see illustration)** to do this procedure. Hook up the tool as shown and measure the input (supply) voltage between terminals 1 and 3 with the ignition on. It should be 4.35 to 5.35 volts.

78   Switch off the ignition and connect the voltmeter to terminals 2 and 3. Start the engine and let it idle. The output voltage measured between terminals 2 and 3 should fall within the specified range for the supply voltage you measured in the previous step **(see illustration)**.

79   If the output value doesn't fall within the range specified on the graph for the supply voltage measured in Step 75, you can adjust it by turning the small trim screw located on the side near the electrical connector **(see illustration)**. Remove the sealing compound covering the screw, rotate the trim screw until the indicated output voltage falls within the specified range for the input voltage you measured in Step 75, then reseal the screw with

silicone sealer. If you can't adjust the potentiometer using this method, replace the entire air flow sensor assembly (with potentiometer).

Control unit inputs

Refer to illustration 16.80

80   The procedure for checking the multi-pin connector for a CIS-E Motronic control unit is the same as that used on a CIS-E control unit (see Steps 40 through 46). But refer to the accompanying electrical resistance and voltage table for the Motronic system **(see illustration)** instead of the the CIS-E table. You'll also need to fabricate an inexpensive and simple pair of test leads.

Cold-start and cold-running enrichment tests (Digifant II)

81   The Digifant II system provides extra fuel to the engine, when it's still cold, to ensure good starts and smooth running until the engine warms up. The coolant temperature sensor monitors the coolant as it warms up and sends a signal to the control unit, which adjusts injector opening time to provide a richer mixture.

82   To test the coolant temperature sensor, refer to Section 28.

83   In cold weather, an intake air preheat system warms the air entering the intake. The preheat system operates a regulator flap in the lower part of the air filter housing. During cold weather, the regulator flap opens so the engine can draw in air heated by the exhaust manifold. Vacuum from the throttle valve which opens or closes the regulator flap is controlled by a temperature regulator valve in the side of the upper air filter housing.

84   To test the temperature regulator valve, apply vacuum to its upper

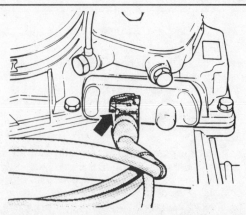

16.79   Location of the trim screw (arrow) for adjusting the air flow sensor potentiometer on CIS-E Motronic systems

CIS-E Motronic Electrical tests

Component or circuit	Test terminals	Test conditions (if any)	Correct test value
Voltage supply and control unit ground	18 and 19		Battery voltage (approximately 12 VDC)
Voltage supply	14 and 35	Ignition on	Battery voltage (approximately 12 VDC)
Idle stabilizer valve	17 and 35	Ignition on	Battery voltage (approximately 12 VDC)
Speed sensor signal	2 and 35	Ignition on; Raise car and rotate one front wheel	0 to 4 VDC minimum
Differential pressure regular	4 and 5		15 to 25 ohms
Coolant temperature sensor	3 and 35		Resistance (ohms) per Fig. 6-45
Idle switch	28 and 35 28 and 35	Throttle closed Throttle open	0.5 ohms maximum No continuity (infinite ohms)
Cold-start valve	14 and 16		10 ohms (approx.)
Solenoid valve I (for evaporative emissions control EVAP system)	14 and 15		30 to 60 ohms
Wiring to Hall sender	30 and 35 30 and 21	Hall sender disconnected; Harness connector terminals 1 and 2 jumpered Hall sender disconnected; Harness connector terminals 2 and 3 jumpered	0.5 ohms maximum 0.5 ohms maximum
Ignition coil power output stage wiring	11 and 35	Disconnect coil power output stage; Ground center terminal of harness connector	0.5 ohms maximum
Knock sensor I (left side) wiring	6 and 8 6 and 8	Separate knock sensor connector near ignition distributor Connect terminals 1 and 2 of harness connector	No continuity (infinite ohms) 0.5 ohms maximum
Knock sensor II (right side wiring)	8 and 24 8 and 24	Separate knock sensor connector near ignition distibutor Connect terminals 1 and 2 of harness connector	No continuity (infinite ohms) 0.5 ohms maximum
Oxygen sensor wiring	7 and 35 7 and 35	 Disconnect harness connector (on right engine mount) and connect terminals 2 and 4 of connector	No continuity (infinite ohms) 0.5 ohms maximum
Ignition reference sensor	27 and 29		1.5 ohms
Air flow sensor potentiometer	23 and 26 26 and 35	Sensor plate at rest position	5000 ohms (approx.) 4000 ohms (approx.)
Ground connection	34 and 35		0.5 ohms maximum
Fuel pump relay and wiring	12 and 35	Ignition on	Fuel pump must run
Wiring to diagnostic connectors	1 and 22 13 and 22	Jumper terminals of white connector Jumper left terminal of white connector to blue connector terminal	0.5 ohms maximum 0.5 ohms maximum

16.80   Electrical test table for CIS-E Motronic systems

4

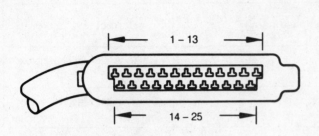

16.91a   Terminal guide for 25-pin Digifant control unit electrical connector

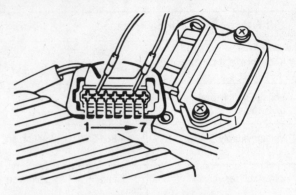

16.91b   Terminal guide for 7-pin Digifant ignition control unit connector

port. When the engine is still cold, the valve should be open and air should easily pass through. When the engine compartment is warm, the valve should be closed and no air should pass through. If the temperature regulator valve is bad, replace it.

85   To test the regulator flap, detach the vacuum hose from the lower port on the temperature regulator valve and separate the upper half of the air filter housing from the lower half and remove the air filter so the regulator flap is visible. Apply vacuum to the disconnected vacuum hose and verify that the flap moves smoothly. If it doesn't, replace the lower half of the air filter housing.

Digifant II Electrical tests			
Component or circuit	**Test terminals (at Digifant connector unless otherwise specified)**	**Test conditions**	**Correct test value**
Voltage supply to control unit	13 and 14 14 and 19	Ignition on Ignition on	Battery voltage (approximately 12 VDC) Battery voltage (approximately 12 VDC)
Wire from starter solenoid (terminal 50)	1 and 13	Actuate starter	8 VDC (minimum)
Fuel injectors	12 and 14		3.7 to 5.0 ohms
Ignition control unit	25 (Digifant control unit) and 6 (ignition control unit)	Ignition off	Continuity
Throttle switches	6 and 11	Throttle closed Open throttle slowly to half-open position Full-throttle	Continuity No continuity Continuity
Air flow sensor	6 and 17 17 and 21	Move sensor flap or actuate starter	500 to 1000 ohms Resistance must fluctuate
Fuel pumps and fuel pump relay	3 and 13	Bridge termianls with jumper wire; Switch ignition on	Fuel pumps run (audibly)
Ignition (Hall sender)	6 and 8 6 and 18	Remove connector at distributor and bridge all three wires with jumper wire	Continuity
Knock sensor	4 and 5 4 and 7	Disconnect knock sensor harness connector and bridge all three wires with jumper wire	Continuity
Idle air stabilizer valve	22 and 23		Continuity
Oxygen sensor	2 and 13	Separate connector and connect green wire to ground Green wire connected	Continuity No continuity

16.91c   Electrical testing table for Digifant II system

Electrical tests (Digifant II)

Refer to illustrations 16.91a, 16.91b and 16.91c

Caution: *Use only a high impedance multimeter, ohmmeter or voltmeter for the following tests to avoid inaccurate measurements or damage to components.*

86   The voltage and continuity tests described here will help you determine whether there are faults in the components which provide information to the control unit, or in the wires which connect them to the control unit. If all control unit inputs are correct, but the system still doesn't perform as it should, the control unit may be bad.

87   Before you begin, here are a few tips: Usually, a total absence of the specified voltage or continuity indicates an open in the circuit. Test results which differ from the specified values don't automatically mean that a component is bad. Look for contaminated, corroded or loose connections before you assume that a component must be replaced. "Floating" (intermittent) ground connections will damage the control unit. Make sure all grounds are clean and tight at the intake manifold, the cylinder block coolant outlet and the battery negative terminal.

88   To prevent damage to the delicate connector terminals, fabricate a set of test leads with insulated alligator clips on one end and flat connectors on the other.

89   Detach the coil high tension cable from the center terminal of the distributor cap and ground it with a jumper wire.

90   With the ignition turned off, unplug the 25-pin electrical connector from the Digifant II control unit and the 7-pin connector from the ignition control unit. The Digifant control unit and the ignition control unit are mounted together in the upper left side of the engine compartment, under the drip tray. You'll have to remove the drip tray to get at the connectors. You'll also have to remove the control unit from its mounting bracket to unplug the connector.

91   Perform the following sequence of electrical tests, in the order shown, using the accompanying table and terminal guides **(see illustrations)**.

92   If a component fails to check out, replace it, but only after you have verified that the wires and connections for that circuit are in good condition.

---

17   Airflow sensor – discription, check and adjustment

Warning: *Gasoline is extremely flammable, so take extra precautions when you work on any part of the fuel system. Don't smoke or allow open flames or bare light bulbs near the work area, and don't work in a garage where a natural gas-type appliance (such as a water heater or clothes dryer) with a pilot light is present. If you spill any fuel on your skin, rinse it off immediately with soap and water. When you perform any kind of work on the fuel system, wear safety glasses and have a Class B type fire extinguisher on hand.*

CIS, CIS-E and CIS-E Motronic systems

Refer to illustrations 17.2a, 17.2b, 17.3a, 17.3b, 17.3c, 17.5a, 17.5b, 17.5c, 17.5d, 17.5e and 17.5f

Description

1   The air flow sensor measures the air drawn in by the engine. As air flows past the air flow sensor plate, the plate is lifted, which lifts the control plunger in the fuel distributor to meter the fuel (see Section 18). The air flow sensor plate and its conical venturi are carefully machined to achieve an optimal ratio between air and fuel for every operating condition, from idle to full throttle. If the sensor plate is binding, or off-center, or the lever has too much resistance, the fuel distributor won't respond correctly to the air flow sensor plate.

Check

2   To check the position of the sensor plate it is necessary to remove the air intake casing, but before doing this run the engine for a few minutes to build up pressure in the fuel lines. Loosen the clamp and take off the air intake duct. The sensor plate may now be seen **(see illustration)**. Check the position of the plate relative to the venturi **(see illustration)**. There must be a gap of 0.004 in (0.10 mm) all around, between it and the venturi. The plate surface must also be even with the bottom of the air cone with the fuel line residual pressure is removed.

3   If the level is not correct then the plate should be lifted with a magnet or pliers, being careful not to scratch the bore. The clip underneath may be bent to adjust the level, using small pliers **(see illustrations)**. Pull the plate up as far as it will come and the job can be done without dismantling anything else. The tolerance is 0.020 in (0.5 mm) on 1977 through 1984 models; on 1985 and later models, it's 0.075 in (1.9 mm) (and can be as much as 0.083 in [2.1 mm]). On CIS-E Motronic systems, up to 0.118 in (3.0 mm) is acceptable. On these systems an adjustable screw **(see illustration)** is used instead of a clip.

17.2a   The sensor plate is located at the bottom of the venturi (arrow)

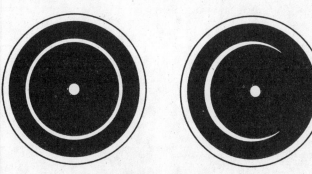

17.2b   The airflow sensor plate must be centered in the venturi

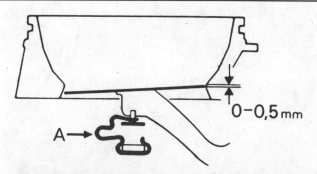

17.3a   When the sensor plate is at rest (ignition off), the plate should be within 0.019 in (0.5 mm) of the lower edge of the venturi on 1977 through 1984 vehicles and within 0.075 in (1.9 mm) on 1985 and later models)

17.3b   Airflow sensor plate adjusting clip (arrow)

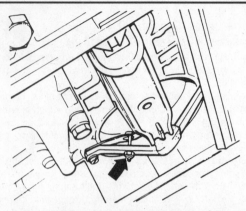

17.3c   On CIS-E Motronic systems, the height of the air flow sensor plate is adjusted with this adjustment screw (arrow) located under the sensor housing

4   Centering the plate can be easy or difficult. Try the easy way first. Remove the center bolt – it is fairly stiff as it is held by thread locking compound. Take the bolt out and clean the threads. Now try to center the plate with the bolt loosely in position. If this can be done then remove the bolt, put a drop of thread locking compound on the threads and reinstall it holding the plate central. Tighten the bolt securely.

5   If the plate will not center then the sensor unit must be removed from the vehicle (**see illustrations**). It is probably easier to remove the mixture control unit from the sensor unit than to remove all the fuel lines, but be careful that the plunger doesn't drop out when you separate the units. Disconnect the sensor unit from the top of the air cleaner. Take the sensor unit out and turn it upside down. Now check that the sensor beam is central in

17.5a   Fuel distributor fuel line connections

17.5b   Note the direction of the arrow on the fuel inlet – when reconnecting the lines, make sure the feed line goes here

17.5c   Disconnect the air inlet hose from the air cleaner

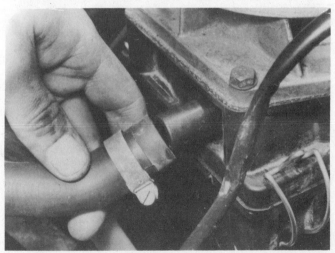

17.5d   Crankcase ventilation hose location on the air cleaner

17.5e   Removing the airflow sensor/air cleaner unit

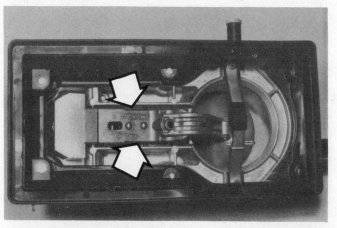

17.5f   Bottom view of the airflow sensor unit – the clearance on either side of the sensor beam (arrows) should be even

its bearings **(see illustration)**. If it is not, loosen the clamp bolt on the counterweight and it may be possible to center the beam in its bearings and at the same time center the sensor plate in the cone. If this is possible, remove the bolt, clean the threads, put a drop of thread locking compound on them and reinstall the bolt with the beam and plate in the correct positions. If this doesn't work, a new sensor unit must be purchased, because if the plate is not central you will have major problems.

6   Once the plate is centralized and level, the unit reassembled, the mixture control unit installed and the system recharged with fuel by turning the ignition on for a few seconds, it is possible to check the action of the airflow sensor. Turn the ignition off and, using a small magnet, lift the plate to the top of its movement. There must be a slight, but even, resistance, but no hard spots. Now depress the plate quickly. This time there should be no resistance to movement.

7   If there is resistance to movement, or hard spots in both directions then the plate may not be centralized, so check it again. If the resistance or hard spot happens only when lifting the plate, then the problem is with the plunger of the fuel mixture unit. Remove the mixture unit from the sensor casing and carefully remove the plunger. Wash it with carburetor cleaner to remove any residue, reinstall it and try again. If this does not cure the problem then it is probable that a new mixture control unit is needed. DO NOT try to remove the hard spot with abrasives; this will only make matters worse. A visit to the dealer service department or other repair shop is indi-

cated. They may be able to cure the problems but be prepared to purchase a new mixture control unit.

8   On CIS-E and CIS-E Motronic systems, a sensor plate potentiometer provides the control unit with information on the position of the sensor plate. On CIS-E systems, this signal is used for cold acceleration enrichment (see CIS-E electrical tests in Section 16); on CIS-E Motronic systems, the potentiometer's signal to the control unit is used to indicate load (see CIS-E Motronic electrical tests in Section 16).

Digifant II systems
Description
9   As intake air is drawn past a spring-loaded "flap" inside the air flow sensor housing, the flap swings open, which actuates a potentiometer. The variable resistance of this potentiometer provides a signal to the control unit that's proportional to air flow. The air flow sensor also has an intake air temperature sensor which measures the the temperature of the incoming air.

Check
Refer to illustration 17.10 and 17.12
10   Free movement of the flap inside the air flow sensor housing is vital to the proper measurement of air flow. To check the movement of the flap, loosen the clamps **(see illustration)**, remove the rubber intake air duct,

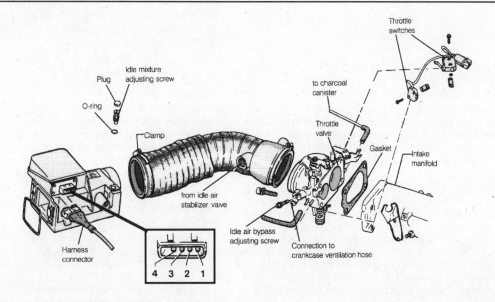

17.10   An exploded view of the air flow sensor, throttle valve and intake air duct assemblies (Digifant II systems)

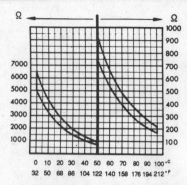

17.12   This graph shows the relationship between the resistance of the intake air temperature sensor and the ambient temperature of incoming air (Digifant II systems)

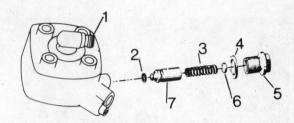

18.1   **Exploded view of the pressure regulating valve on the fuel distributor body**

1	Fuel distributor body	5	Plug
2	Rubber ring	6	Shims for pressure
3	Spring		adjustment
4	Copper washer	7	Valve piston

and move the flap through its range of travel. If the flap binds at any point, remove the air flow sensor housing (see below), and look for foreign material that might be interfering with the flap's movement. If the flap moves freely, proceed to the next test; if it doesn't, replace the air flow sensor unit.

11   To check the air flow sensor potentiometer, unplug the electrical connector from the sensor, hook up an ohmmeter and measure the resistance across the terminals of its electrical connector **(see illustration 17.10** for terminal identification). The resistance between terminals 3 and 4 should be 500 to 1000 ohms; the resistance between terminals 2 and 3 should vary as you move the flap. If the resistance is as specified, proceed to the next test; if it isn't, replace the air flow sensor unit.

12   To check the intake air temperature sensor, measure the resistance between terminals 1 and 4 **(see illustration 17.10** for terminal identification). The resistance value depends on the temperature of the air entering the air flow sensor housing **(see illustration)**. If the resistance is as specified, the air temperature sensor is good; if it isn't, replace the air flow sensor unit.

Replacement

13   Unplug the electrical connector.
14   Loosen the large hose clamp and detach the intake air duct.
15   Separate the upper half of the air filter housing from the lower half.
16   Working from inside the upper air filter housing, remove the air flow sensor mounting bolts and remove the sensor and its gasket.
17   Installation is the reverse of removal. Use a new gasket if the old one is damaged. Don't overtighten the mounting bolts (no more than 44 in-lbs).

18   Fuel distributor – check and adjustment

Refer to illustration 18.1
Warning: *Gasoline is extremely flammable, so take extra precautions when you work on any part of the fuel system. Don't smoke or allow open flames or bare light bulbs near the work area, and don't work in a garage where a natural gas-type appliance (such as a water heater or clothes dryer) with a pilot light is present. If you spill any fuel on your skin, rinse it off immediately with soap and water. When you perform any kind of work on the fuel system, wear safety glasses and have a Class B type fire extinguisher on hand.*

1   The pressure regulating valve for the system pressure is included in the fuel distributor body **(see illustration)**. A hexagonal plug on the corner of the fuel distributor casing may be unscrewed and inside will be found a copper ring, shims for adjusting the pressure on the spring, the spring, a piston and a rubber ring. Be careful not to scratch the bore or the piston since these are mated on assembly and a new piston means a new distributor body. If the piston is stuck either blow it out with compressed air or work it out using a piece of soft wood. Do not attempt to adjust the system pressure by altering the shims. Always use new seals when refitting the plug.
2   Pressure can be adjusted by adding shims to the pressure relief

valve. An additional 0.020-inch shim will increase system pressure by about 4 psi. A 0.040-inch shim will increase system pressure by about 8 psi.
3   If system pressure is too high, check for a blocked or damaged fuel return line. If the return line is good, the pressure can be lowered by reducing the thickness of the shims on the pressure relief valve. A reduction of a 0.020-inch shim thickness will decrease system pressure by about 4 psi. A reduction of 0.040-inch total shim thickness will decrease system pressure by 8 psi.
4   From the tests on the air sensor plate movement, the operation of the plunger will have been checked. If it is suspect then the fuel distributor body must be disconnected from the airflow sensor plate and lifted clear. Be careful that the plunger does not fall out and get damaged. Carefully extract the plunger and wash it in carburetor cleaner. When installing it, the small shoulder goes in first. Do not attempt to cure any hard spots by rubbing with abrasive. If washing it in carburetor cleaner does not cure the problem then a new assembly is required.

19   Control pressure regulator – check and replacement

Warning: *Gasoline is extremely flammable, so take extra precautions when you work on any part of the fuel system. Don't smoke or allow open flames or bare light bulbs near the work area, and don't work in a garage where a natural gas-type appliance (such as a water heater or clothes dryer) with a pilot light is present. If you spill any fuel on your skin, rinse it off immediately with soap and water. When you perform any kind of work on the fuel system, wear safety glasses and have a Class B type fire extinguisher on hand.*
Note: *This section applies to CIS systems only.*

Check

Refer to illustration 19.1
1   Disconnect the wiring from the control pressure (warm up) regulator and auxiliary air valve **(see illustration)**.
2   Connect a voltmeter across the electrical connectors and operate the starter briefly – there should be a minimum of 11.5 volts.
3   Connect an ohmmeter across the regulator heater element terminals – the resistance should be between 16 and 22 ohms.
4   Replace the regulator if necessary and reconnect the wiring.

Replacement

Refer to illustration 19.8
5   Relieve the fuel pressure (see Section 15).
6   Disconnect the electrical connector from the regulator.
7   Use a box end or socket wrench and disconnect the fuel lines from the regulator.
8   Use a 6 mm Allen wrench and remove the two bolts that retain the regulator to the block **(see illustration)**.
9   Installation is the reverse of removal.

19.1   The control pressure regulator is located on the front side of the engine block

19.8   Use a 6 mm Allen wrench and remove the control pressure regulator mounting bolts

20.2a   Thermotime switch location – CIS fuel injection

20.2b   Thermotime switch location – CIS-E fuel injection (arrow)

4

---

20   Thermo-time switch – check and replacement

Note: *This section applies to CIS and CIS-E systems only.*

Check

Refer to illustrations 20.2a and 20.2b

1   To test the switch, remove the plug from the cold start valve and bridge the contacts with a test light or a voltmeter. The test must be done with a cold (coolant below 95-degrees F, 35-degrees C) engine.

2   Remove the coil wire from the center of the distributor and ground it with a jumper wire. Have an assistant operate the starter for ten seconds. Depending on the coolant temperature the bulb should light or the voltmeter register for a period of between three and ten seconds and then cease to register. If the circuit is not broken in ten seconds the thermo-time switch must be replaced **(see illustrations)**. If the bulb does not light at all and you are sure the engine is cold, then check that there is voltage supplied to the switch. If there is no voltage then the fuel pump relay must be checked.

Replacement

3   Drain the coolant from the radiator (see Chapter 1).

4   Disconnect the electrical connector from the thermo-time switch.

5   Unscrew the thermo-time switch.

6   Installation is the reverse of removal, but wrap the threads of the switch with teflon tape before installing it.

---

21   Cold start valve – check and replacement

Warning: *Gasoline is extremely flammable, so take extra precautions when you work on any part of the fuel system. Don't smoke or allow open flames or bare light bulbs near the work area, and don't work in a garage where a natural gas-type appliance (such as a water heater or clothes dryer) with a pilot light is present. If you spill any fuel on your skin, rinse it off immediately with soap and water. When you perform any kind of work on the fuel system, wear safety glasses and have a Class B type fire extinguisher on hand.*

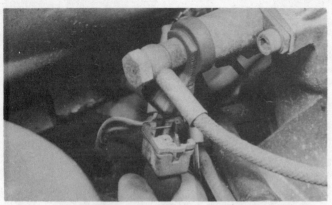

21.1   Disconnect the cold start valve electrical connector

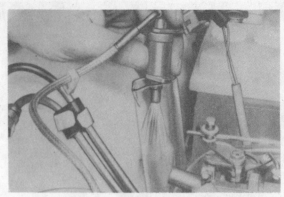

21.2   Check for proper cold start valve operation

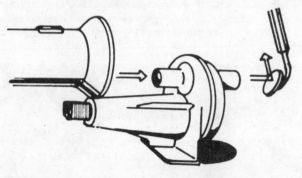

22.2   Shine a flashlight into the port of the regulator – when the regulator is cold, it should be open and light will pass through

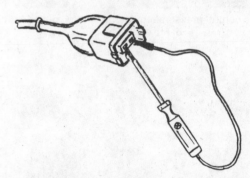

22.3   Use a test light to check for current at the auxiliary air regulator electrical connector while the engine is running

Check

Refer to illustrations 21.1 and 21.2

1   Make sure engine coolant is below 86-degrees F. Preferably the engine should sit for several hours. Disconnect the electrical connector from the cold start valve **(see illustration)** and move it aside, away from the work area – there will be fuel vapor present. Remove the two screws holding the valve to the intake chamber and take the valve out. The fuel line must be left connected to the valve. Wipe the nozzle of the valve. Pull the coil wire out of the center of the distributor and connect it to a good ground. Turn the ignition On and operate the fuel pump for one minute. There must be no fuel dripping from the nozzle. If there is, the valve is faulty and must be replaced. Switch off the ignition.

2   Now put the stem of the valve in a glass jar. Reconnect the plug to the valve. Unplug the electrical connector from the thermotime switch and connect a jumper lead over the plug terminals. Have an assistant turn the ignition On and operate the starter. The valve should squirt a conical shaped spray into the jar **(see illustration)**. If the spray is correct the valve is working properly. If the spray pattern is irregular the valve is damaged and should be replaced.

Replacement

3   Relieve the fuel pressure (see Section 15).

4   Use a box end or socket wrench and remove the fuel line connected to the cold start valve.

5   Remove the Allen bolts that retain the cold start valve to the air intake distributor and remove the valve.

6   Installation is the reverse of removal, but be sure to clean the mating surfaces and use a new gasket.

22   Auxiliary air regulator – check and replacement

Refer to illustrations 22.2 and 22.3

Check

1   The auxiliary air regulator allows air to bypass the throttle plate while the engine is cold. When the ignition is switched On the heater resistance causes a bi-metallic strip within the regulator to deform, slowly turning the rotating valve until the air passage is closed. It remains in this position during normal operation.

2   To check the operation of the regulator, remove it from the engine (see Step 4), disconnect the hoses and shine a flashlight into the port **(see illustration)**. If the unit is cold there must be a clear passage. Connect it to a 12-volt supply for five minutes and watch the operation through the inlet. At the end of the five minutes the valve should be closed. If it does not operate correctly check the resistance of the heater unit. This should be 30 ohms.

3   If the auxiliary air regulator resistance is in the correct range, disconnect the electrical connector from the control pressure regulator. Use a test light to determine whether the battery voltage is reaching the heating element while the engine is running **(see illustration)**. If it is not, test the fuel pump relay.

Replacement

4   Disconnect both air hoses from the auxiliary air regulator to the intake air chamber.

5   Disconnect the electrical connector from the auxiliary air regulator.

23.1   Location of idle air stabilizer valve on CIS-E fuel injection systems – on CIS systems it is located on the right strut tower, with hoses leading to the intake air chamber

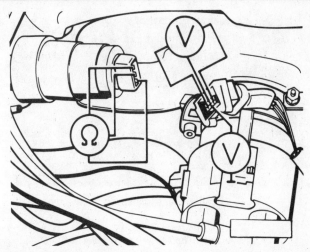

23.10   Check the resistance of the valve with an ohmmeter – also check the voltage signal to ground and across the terminals in the electrical connector

6   Remove the mounting screws that retain the auxiliary air regulator to the intake air chamber.

7   Installation is the reverse of removal.

---

23   Idle air stabilizer system – check and replacement

Note: *This section applies to 1984 CIS systems, all CIS-E systems (except those with GX engines), all CIS-E Motronic systems and all Digifant II systems).*

Refer to illustrations 23.1

1   The idle air stabilizer system works to maintain engine idle speed within a 200 rpm range regardless of varying engine loads at idle. An electrically operated valve **(see illustration)** allows a small amount of air to flow past the throttle plate to raise the idle speed whenever the idle speed drops below 750 rpm. If the idle speed rises above 1050 rpm, the idle air stabilizer valve closes and stops extra air from bypassing the throttle plate, consequently reducing the idle speed. A second valve is used on air conditioned vehicles to boost the idle speed when the system is ON.

Check
CIS fuel injection systems

2   The idle air stabilizer valve is governed by an electronic control relay that senses engine speed from the no. 1 terminal of the ignition coil. On U.S. built vehicles the electronic control relay is attached to the steering column brace next to the fuse panel. On German built vehicles, the electronic control relay is located above the fuse/relay panel.

3   Clamp shut the hose from the valve to the air intake chamber.

4   Connect a tachometer to the engine (see Chapter 1).

5   Start the engine and warm it up to normal operating temperature and disconnect the oxygen sensor electrical connector.

6   Adjust the idle speed to less than 750 rpm and listen for a clicking sound from the valve. Remove the clamp from the air supply hose and check to make sure the idle speed raises slightly.

7   If the system is faulty, take the vehicle to a dealer service department or other repair shop for further diagnosis.

CIS-E fuel injection systems

Refer to illustration 23.10

Note: *The idle air stabilizer valve is used on CIS-E fuel injection systems only with engines coded HT, RD and PL.*

8   Whenever the throttle valve idle switch is closed, the idle air stabilizer valve receives a cycled voltage signal from the oxygen sensor control unit based on the engine rpm and other inputs. The voltage signal cycles on and off to incrementally open or close the the valve to adjust idle speed. This on/off signal is referred to as the valve duty cycle and is measured with a duty cycle meter or a dwell meter.

9   Start the engine and make sure the valve is vibrating and humming slightly. If not, check for a voltage signal reaching the valve and check the valve's resistance.

10   With the ignition On, the voltage at the harness connector should be approximately 12 volts (battery voltage) between the center terminal and ground and 10 volts between the center terminal and the outer two terminals **(see illustration)**.

11   Check the resistance on the connector terminals of the idle air stabilizer valve **(see illustration 23.10)**. There should be continuity between the center terminal and each of the outer terminals. If the readings are incorrect, replace the valve.

Note: *If the resistance of the idle air stabilizer valve is correct and the voltage is correct then have the oxygen sensor control unit tested by a dealer service department or other repair shop.*

CIS-E Motronic engine management system

12   Idle speed control on CIS-E Motronic systems is completely electronic. The idle air stabilizer system can't be adjusted. The idle air adjusting screw should always be turned all the way in until it stops. VW dealer service departments check the idle air stabilizer as part of an electronic diagnostic check.

Digifant II fuel injection system

13   Start the engine and make sure the valve is vibrating and humming slightly. If it is not, check that the idle switch on the throttle valve is closed and functioning correctly.

14   If the idle switch is not faulty, then turn the engine off and disconnect the harness connector from the valve. Check for continuity on the terminals of the valve. If there is no continuity, replace the valve.

15   If the idle switch is OK, connect an ammeter to the harness connector. Start the engine and briefly raise the engine speed over 3000 rpm three times and then let the engine return to idle. With the engine running, the current reading should be between 390 and 450 mA. **NOTE:** *The idle air stabilizer current will fluctuate between 400 and 1100 mA if the engine is too cold, if the coolant temperature sensor is faulty , if the idle speed needs to be adjusted, if there is an engine vacuum leak or if electrical accessories are on.*

Replacement

16   Remove the harness connector and the bracket from the idle air stabilizer valve and remove the valve.

17   Installation is the reverse of removal.

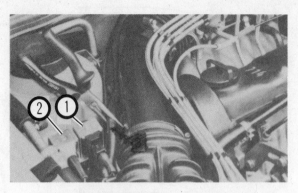

24.1　Location of the idle speed boost valve

1　Idle speed boost valve
2　Additional boost valve for vehicles with A/C

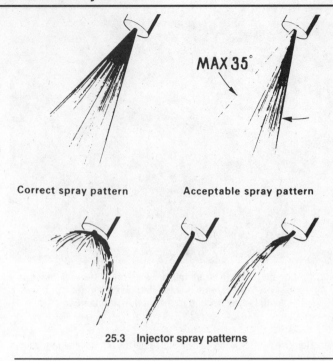

Correct spray pattern　　　Acceptable spray pattern

25.3　Injector spray patterns

24　Idle speed boost valve – check

Note: *This section applies to CIS systems and CIS-E systems on GX engines).*
Refer to illustration 24.1

1　The idle speed boost valve maintains the idle speed within a 300 rpm range. Vehicles with air conditioning have an extra boost valve. The electrically operated valves **(see illustration)** allow additional air to bypass the throttle plate and increase idle speed whenever the idle speed drops below 750 rpm. The idle speed boost valve is a solenoid valve that is controlled by an electronic control unit on the fuse/relay panel that turns the valve on and off according to an engine speed signal from the coil.
2　If the valve does not respond properly, check the voltage signal to the valve at the harness connector using a voltmeter. If the valve is receiving a voltage signal below 750 rpm and still does not open then the valve is faulty. If the valve is not receiving voltage below 750 rpm, take the vehicle to a dealer service department or other repair shop for further diagnosis.

25　Fuel injectors – check and replacement

Warning: *Gasoline is extremely flammable, so take extra precautions when you work on any part of the fuel system. Don't smoke or allow open flames or bare light bulbs near the work area, and don't work in a garage where a natural gas-type appliance (such as a water heater or clothes dryer) with a pilot light is present. If you spill any fuel on your skin, rinse it off immediately with soap and water. When you perform any kind of work on the fuel system, wear safety glasses and have a Class B type fire extinguisher on hand.*

CIS, CIS-E and CIS-E Motronic fuel injectors
Refer to illustration 25.3

1　Each cylinder is equipped with one injector. They are pushed into bushings in the intake manifold. At first sight this seems odd, but these injectors spray onto the back of the inlet valve ports so they are working in a lower pressure than atmospheric pressure and the tendency is for them to be pulled in rather than blown out at high speeds. They are pulled out quite easily. Inspect the rubber seal in the intake manifold. If it is cracked remove it and install a new one. Moisten the new seal with fuel before installing it and likewise moisten the injector before pushing it into the seal.
2　The injector may give trouble for one of four reasons. The spray pattern may be irregular in shape; the nozzle may not close when the engine is shut down, causing flooding when restarting; the nozzle filter may be clogged, giving less than the required ration of fuel, or the seal may be damaged allowing an air leak.
3　If the engine is running roughly and missing on one cylinder, allow it to idle and pull each spark plug wire off (use a pair of insulated pliers) and

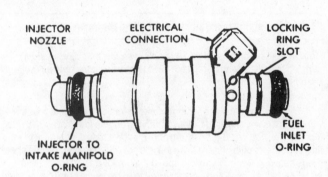

25.5　Details of a Digifant II fuel injector

install it – one cylinder at a time (don't perform this check on electronic ignition models). If that cylinder is working properly this will have an even more adverse effect on the idle speed, when the wire is pulled off, which will promptly improve once the wire is reinstalled. If there is little difference when the spark plug lead is removed, then that is the cylinder giving trouble. Stop the engine and check and service the spark plug. Now have a look at the injector. Pull it our of the seal and hold over a container. Start the engine and look at the shape of the spray. It should be of a symmetrical cone shape **(see illustration)**. If it is not, the injector must be changed because the vibrator pin is damaged or the spring is broken. Shut off the engine and wait for 15 seconds. There must be no leak from the nozzle. If there is, the injector must be replaced as leaking will cause flooding and difficult starting. If the spray is cone shaped and no leak occurs then the fuel output should be checked.
4　The injector can't be disassembled for cleaning. If an injector is removed from the line the new one should be installed and the union tightened to the torque listed in this Chapter's Specifications.

Digifant II fuel injectors
Refer to illustrations 25.5 and 25.8

5　The injectors used on the Digifant II System are electrically operated solenoid valves which are turned on and off by the Digifant II control unit **(see illustration)**.

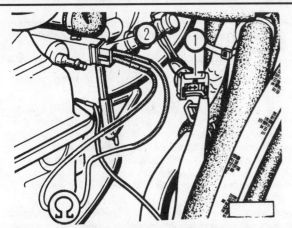

25.8   Check the resistance of the Digifant II fuel injectors at the main electrical connector on the fuel rail

1   *Electrical connector disconnected*
2   *Terminals of the ohmmeter connected across main electrical connector*

6   The four injectors are connected to a common fuel supply which is called the fuel rail. The injectors are switched off and on (open or closed) by the control unit. Each injector opens the needle valve with a solenoid to spray fuel into the intake ports.

7   All four injectors open simultaneously and are synchronized to the engine RPM. The control unit regulates the amount of fuel by controlling the length of time the injectors are open. The injectors are not serviceable and must be replaced as a unit.

8   The injectors can be tested by checking resistance at the main electrical connector at the end of the fuel rail **(see illustration)**. The resistance should be between 3.7 to 5.0 ohms. If the resistance is greater – at least one injector is faulty.

9   To isolate a faulty injector, one at a time – disconnect each injector harness connector from the injector and observe the resistance. The resistance should INCREASE each time one is disconnected: When one injector electrical connector is disconnected, the resistance should be approximately 5.0 to 6.7 ohms. When two are disconnected, the resistance should be about 7.5 to 10 ohms. When three are disconnected, the resistance should be about 15 to 20 ohms.

10   If the resistance does not increase each time, check the resistance directly on the injectors. The resistance should be 15 to 20 ohms. If the resistance value is incorrect, replace the injector.

11   To check for battery voltage at the injector, connect an LED test light to the wiring harness connector (any other kind of test light may damage the ECU). Put the transmission in neutral and the parking brake on and activate the starter. Observe the test light for flickering. If it doesn't, take the vehicle to a dealer service department or other repair shop for further diagnosis.

---

26   Throttle switches and throttle valve – check and adjustment

Note: *This section applies to CIS-E and CIS-E Motronic systems.*
Refer to illustration 26.1

1   On CIS-E systems, the idle switch supplies the control unit with a signal when the throttle is fully closed (used for idle air stabilizing and deceleration fuel shut off). It also supplies the control unit with a signal when the throttle valve is fully open, used for full throttle enrichment **(see illustration)**. On CIS-E Motronic systems, a single idle switch is mounted on the throttle valve housing. It signals the control unit when the throttle is closed. This signal is used for controlling idle speed and deceleration fuel shut-off.

2   Check to see if voltage is reaching the switch(es) when the ignition is in the On position. Check for voltage between the center terminal of the electrical connector and ground. With the ignition On, there should be battery voltage. If not, check for a blown fuse.

26.1   The full throttle switch is activated when the throttle is fully open – when this happens, a signal is sent to the ECM and the mixture is enriched

3   Next, check the switch(es). Check at the switch connector for continuity between the center terminal and each of the outer terminals to indicate when a switch is open or closed.

4   To check the idle switch on CIS-E and CIS-E Motronic systems, and on Digifant II systems, open the throttle valve about half way and slowly let it close. The idle switch should close, completing the circuit and indicating continuity. When the throttle valve lever gets to within .006-.016 in. of its stop, check the gap at which the switch closes with a feeler gauge and if necessary, the switch can be repositioned by loosening the switch mounting screws.

5   To check the full throttle switch on CIS-E and Digifant II systems, slowly open the valve to the maximum position (full throttle). The full throttle switch should close indicating continuity when the throttle is 10-degrees ± 2-degrees from its fully open position (you'll need a protractor to check it. If necessary, the switch can be adjusted by loosening the screws and repositioning the switch.

Throttle valve basic adjustment

6   The throttle valve adjustment screw provides a positive stop for the linkage and prevents the throttle plate from closing so far that it becomes worn or damaged. Do NOT use it to adjust idle speed!

CIS, CIS-E and CIS-E Motronic systems

Refer to illustration 26.7a and 26.7b

7   To readjust the throttle valve, loosen the locknut and back off the throttle valve adjustment screw until there's clearance between its tip and the throttle valve lever **(see illustrations)**.

26.7a   Adjustment screw (arrow) for basic adjustment of the throttle valve on CIS, CIS-E and CIS-E Motronic throttle body – to adjust the throttle valve, back off this screw until there's clearance between its tip and the throttle valve lever, insert a strip of paper between the lever and the screw, turn in the screw until it's just touching the paper, remove the paper and tighten the locknut

4

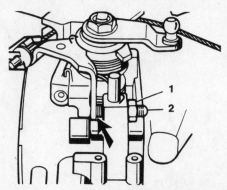

26.7b   Throttle valve adjusting screw (2) and locknut (1) on a Digifant II type throttle body – to adjust the valve, insert a piece of paper between the screw and the lever and turn the adjusting screw (2) until it's just barely pinching the paper, remove the paper and turn the screw an extra 1/2-turn and tighten the locknut (1)

8   Place a thin strip of paper between the throttle valve adjustment screw and the throttle valve lever. With the throttle valve closed, turn the screw in until it just touches the paper, then remove the paper and turn the screw in an extra 1/2-turn.

Digifant II systems

9   To check the adjustment, detach the vacuum line from the carbon canister control valve, and hook up a vacuum gauge in its place. There should be zero – or very close to zero – vacuum at idle (up to one inch of vacuum is acceptable). If the gauge indicates more than one inch of vacuum at idle, readjust the throttle valve basic adjustment (see Steps 7 and 8 above).

27   Differential pressure regulator (CIS-E) – description and replacement

Note: *This section applies to CIS-E and CIS-E Motronic systems. Refer to illustrations 27.1a and 27.1b*

Warning: *Gasoline is extremely flammable, so take extra precautions when you work on any part of the fuel system. Don't smoke or allow open flames or bare light bulbs near the work area, and don't work in a garage where a natural gas-type appliance (such as a water heater or clothes dryer) with a pilot light is present. If you spill any fuel on your skin, rinse it off immediately with soap and water. When you perform any kind of work on the fuel system, wear safety glasses and have a Class B type fire extinguisher on hand.*

Note: *Due to the sensitive nature of the differential pressure regulator circuit and the need for special tools, diagnosis should be left to a dealer service department or other repair shop. Once determined faulty, however, the regulator can be replaced using the following procedure.*

Description

1   The differential pressure regulator controls pressure in the lower chamber of the fuel distributor, consequently controlling the pressure difference across the metering valves and the volume of fuel that is delivered to the injectors. It is operated by the control unit which continuously makes adjustments based on the signal received from the oxygen sensor and other inputs **(see illustrations)**. The differential pressure regulator is the single most important device for controlling and changing the fuel mixture.

Replacement

2   Relieve the fuel pressure (see Section 15).
3   Remove the electrical connector and the two mounting screws. Re-

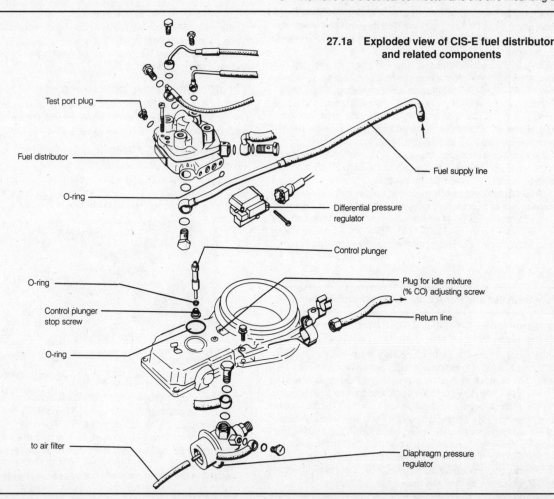

27.1a   Exploded view of CIS-E fuel distributor and related components

Test port plug

Fuel distributor

O-ring

O-ring

Control plunger stop screw

O-ring

to air filter

Fuel supply line

Differential pressure regulator

Control plunger

Plug for idle mixture (% CO) adjusting screw

Return line

Diaphragm pressure regulator

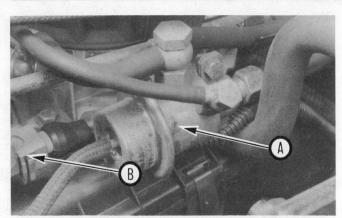

27.1b   Location of diaphragm pressure regulator (A) and differential pressure regulator (B)

move the regulator and the O-rings from the fuel distributor.
4   Installation is the reverse of removal, but be sure to use new O-rings.

28   Coolant temperature sensor – check and replacement

Note: *This section applies to CIS-E, CIS-E Motronic, and Digifant II systems.*
Refer to illustrations 28.1a and 28.1b

Check

1   The coolant temperature sensor is located in the cylinder head **(see illustration)**. To test the sensor, disconnect the electrical connector and measure the resistance across the sensor terminals. The proper resistance value depends on the temperature of the coolant. Check the graph for proper values **(see illustration)**. If the readings are incorrect, replace the sensor.

Replacement

Warning: *Wait until the engine is completely cool before beginning this procedure.*

2   Prepare the new sensor for installation by wrapping the threads with teflon tape. Unscrew the sensor from the cylinder head (or water outlet). Install the new sensor as quickly as possible to minimize coolant loss.
3   Screw the new sensor into its hole and tighten it securely. Plug in the electrical connector.
4   Check the coolant level and top it up if necessary (see Chapter 1).

29   Fuel pressure regulator – check and replacement

Refer to illustration 29.2 and 29.3
Warning: *Gasoline is extremely flammable, so take extra precautions when you work on any part of the fuel system. Don't smoke or allow open flames or bare light bulbs near the work area, and don't work in a garage where a natural gas-type appliance (such as a water heater or clothes dryer) with a pilot light is present. If you spill any fuel on your skin, rinse it off immediately with soap and water. When you perform any kind of work on the fuel system, wear safety glasses and have a Class B type fire extinguisher on hand.*

Check

1   Each of the different types of fuel injection systems covered in this section employ a different type of fuel pressure regulator to maintain a constant system pressure. All three recirculate excess fuel back to the fuel reservoir near the main fuel pump. Perform the fuel pressure tests described in Section 16, and if the readings are incorrect, replace the fuel pressure regulator.

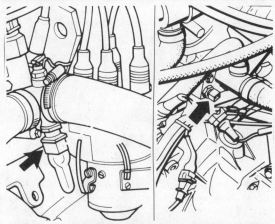

28.1a   On all but 16-valve engines (left) the coolant temperature sensor is screwed into the bottom or the top of the water outlet – on 16-valve engines it's threaded into the left end of the cylinder head

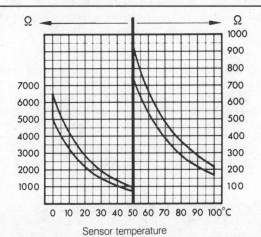

28.1b   Coolant temperature sensor graph – as the coolant temperature increases, the resistance of the sensor decreases

Replacement

CIS pressure relief valve

2   Fuel pressure in this system is determined by the pressure relief valve mounted in the fuel distributor **(see illustration)**. Fuel pressure can be adjusted by removing the plug and adding or subtracting the shims.

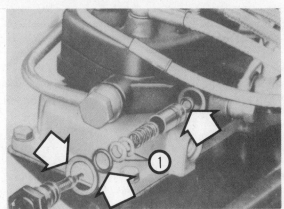

29.2   Exploded view of the CIS pressure relief valve – always replace the sealing washer and O-rings when reassembling the valve

1   *Adjusting shims*

29.3   The diaphragm pressure regulator is mounted on the side of the fuel distributor (arrow)

30.3   Remove the rear seat cushion for access to the fuel gauge sending unit (Jetta shown, others similar)

CIS-E and CIS-E Motronic diaphragm pressure regulator

3   The CIS-E diaphragm pressure regulator is mounted on the side of the fuel distributor **(see illustration)**. It can control system pressure as well as act as a one way check valve to control residual pressure. The diaphragm pressure regulator cannot be adjusted and it should be replaced if the pressure is incorrect.

4   To replace the regulator, first relieve the fuel pressure (see Section 15). Unscrew the union bolts from the fuel lines, disconnect the vacuum hose and remove the regulator mounting bolts. When installing the regulator, be sure to use new sealing washers on the fuel line fittings.

Digifant II fuel pressure regulator

5   The Digifant pressure regulator is a diaphragm type, similar to the CIS-E regulator. The Digifant II system operates at a much lower pressure than the CIS-E system.

6   Relieve the fuel pressure (see Section 15).

7   Loosen the hose clamp and disconnect the fuel return hose from the regulator.

8   Disconnect the vacuum hose from the regulator. Remove the two screws holding the regulator to the fuel rail and pull the regulator out, using a twisting motion.

9   Installation is the reverse of removal, but be sure to use a new O-ring and hose clamp.

---

30   Fuel gauge sending unit – removal and installation

Refer to illustration 30.3

Warning: *Gasoline is extremely flammable, so take extra precautions when you work on any part of the fuel system. Don't smoke or allow open flames or bare light bulbs near the work area, and don't work in a garage where a natural gas-type appliance (such as a water heater or clothes dryer) with a pilot light is present. If you spill any fuel on your skin, rinse it off immediately with soap and water. When you perform any kind of work on the fuel system, wear safety glasses and have a Class B type fire extinguisher on hand.*

Note: *For safety reasons the fuel gauge sending unit must always be removed in a well-ventilated area.*

1   Disconnect the battery negative cable.

2   On pre-January 1976 models, drain the fuel tank by using a siphon or by disconnecting the bottom filler hose.

3   On January 1976 and later models (except Pickup), remove the rear seat cushion (see Chapter 11) and remove the sending unit cover **(see il-lustration).**

4   On Pick-up models, remove the fuel tank as described in Section 31.

5   On all models, disconnect the wiring and, where applicable, disconnect the supply and return hoses after noting their positions. Also note the position of the wiring for installation purposes .

6   Using two crossed screwdrivers, turn the locking ring to release it from the tank.

7   Remove the sending unit and sealing ring.

8   Installation is the reverse of removal. Always install a new O-ring.

---

31   Fuel tank – removal and installation

Refer to illustrations 31.1 and 31.9

Warning: *Gasoline is extremely flammable, so take extra precautions when you work on any part of the fuel system. Don't smoke or allow open flames or bare light bulbs near the work area, and don't work in a garage where a natural gas-type appliance (such as a water heater or clothes dryer) with a pilot light is present. If you spill any fuel on your skin, rinse it off immediately with soap and water. When you perform any kind of work on the fuel system, wear safety glasses and have a Class B type fire extinguisher on hand.*

Note: *The following procedure is much easier to perform if the fuel tank is empty. Some tanks have a drain plug for this purpose. If the tank does not have a drain plug, use a siphon hose and pump to drain the fuel into an approved fuel container. DO NOT start the siphoning action by mouth!*

1   Remove the fuel tank filler cap **(see illustration)** to relieve fuel tank pressure.

2   If the vehicle is fuel-injected, relieve the fuel system pressure (see Section 15).

3   Detach the cable from the negative terminal of the battery.

4   If the tank still has fuel in it, you can drain it at the fuel feed line after raising the vehicle. If the tank has a drain plug, remove it and allow the fuel to drain into an approved gasoline container.

5   Raise the vehicle and place it securely on jackstands.

6   Disconnect the fuel lines, the vapor return line and the fuel filler neck.

Note: *The fuel feed and return lines and the vapor return line are three different diameters, so reattachment is simplified. If you have any doubts, however, clearly label the three lines and the fittings. Be sure to plug the hoses to prevent leakage and contamination of the fuel system.*

7   Siphon the fuel from the tank at the fuel feed – not the return -line.

8   Support the fuel tank with a floor jack. Position a piece of wood between the jack head and the fuel tank to protect the tank.

31.1 Typical fuel supply components on late North American models with CIS

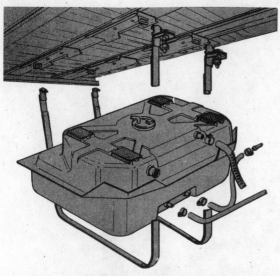

31.9   Fuel tank installation details (pick-up shown)

9   Disconnect both fuel tank retaining straps and pivot them down until they are hanging out of the way **(see illustration)**.
10   Lower the tank enough to disconnect the electrical connectors and ground strap from the fuel pump/fuel gauge sending unit, if you have not already done so.
11   Remove the tank from the vehicle.
12   Installation is the reverse of removal, but be sure the rubber insulators are in place on top of the fuel tank before raising it into position.

32   Fuel tank cleaning and repair – general information

1   All repairs to the fuel tank or filler neck should be carried out by a professional who has experience in this critical and potentially dangerous work. Even after cleaning and flushing of the fuel system, explosive fumes can remain and ignite during repair of the tank.
2   If the fuel tank is removed from the vehicle, it should not be placed in an area where sparks or open flames could ignite the fumes coming out of the tank. Be especially careful inside garages where a natural gas-type appliance is located, because the pilot light could cause an explosion.

33   Exhaust system servicing – general information

Warning: *Inspection and repair of exhaust system components should be done only after enough time has elapsed after driving the vehicle to allow the system components to cool completely. Also, when working under the vehicle, make sure it is securely supported on jackstands.*

1   The exhaust system consists of the exhaust manifold(s), the catalytic converter, the muffler, the tailpipe and all connecting pipes, brackets, hangers and clamps. The exhaust system is attached to the body with mounting brackets and rubber hangers. If any of the parts are improperly installed, excessive noise and vibration will be transmitted to the body.
2   Conduct regular inspections of the exhaust system to keep it safe and quiet. Look for any damaged or bent parts, open seams, holes, loose connections, excessive corrosion or other defects which could allow exhaust fumes to enter the vehicle. Deteriorated exhaust system components should not be repaired; they should be replaced with new parts.
3   If the exhaust system components are extremely corroded or rusted together, welding equipment will probably be required to remove them. The convenient way to accomplish this is to have a muffler repair shop remove the corroded sections with a cutting torch. If, however, you want to save money by doing it yourself (and you don't have a welding outfit with a cutting torch), simply cut off the old components with a hacksaw. If you have compressed air, special pneumatic cutting chisels can also be used. If you do decide to tackle the job at home, be sure to wear safety goggles to protect your eyes from metal chips and work gloves to protect your hands.
4   Here are some simple guidelines to follow when repairing the exhaust system:
   a) Work from the back to the front when removing exhaust system components.
   b) Apply penetrating oil to the exhaust system component fasteners to make them easier to remove.
   c) Use new gaskets, hangers and clamps when installing exhaust systems components.
   d) Apply anti-seize compound to the threads of all exhaust system fasteners during reassembly.
   e) Be sure to allow sufficient clearance between newly installed parts and all points on the underbody to avoid overheating the floor pan and possibly damaging the interior carpet and insulation. Pay particularly close attention to the catalytic converter and heat shield.

Chapter 5   Engine electrical systems

Contents

Alternator brushes – replacement	14
Alternator – removal and installation	13
Battery cables – check and replacement	4
Battery check and maintenance	See Chapter 1
Battery – emergency jump starting	2
Battery – removal and installation	3
Charging system – general information, precautions and check	12
Distributor – overhaul	9
Distributor – removal and installation	8
General information	1
Hall sender and ignition control unit – check and replacement	10
Ignition coil and resistance wire – check and replacement	7
Ignition point replacement	See Chapter 1
Ignition system – check	6
Ignition system – general information	5
Ignition timing check and adjustment	See Chapter 1
Knock sensor system – check and replacement	11
Spark plug replacement	See Chapter 1
Spark plug wire, distributor cap and rotor check and replacement	See Chapter 1
Starter motor – in-vehicle check	17
Starter motor – removal and installation	18
Starter solenoid – removal and installation	19
Starting system – general information and precautions	16
Tune-up general information	See Chapter 1
Voltage regulator – replacement	15

5

Specifications

Ignition coil resistance

Distributor with contact breaker points

Primary	1.7 to 2.1 ohms
Secondary	7000 to 12000 ohms

Electronic ignition distributor

Primary

All except PL and 9A	0.52 to 0.76 ohms
PL and 9A	0.60 to 0.80 ohms

Secondary

GX, MZ, HT, RD, RV and PF	2400 to 3500 ohms
PL and 9A	6500 to 8500 ohms

Resistance wire

0.85 to 0.95 ohms

Alternator brush minimum length

3/16-inch (5 mm)

Knock sensor resistance

Type I	about 300 K-ohms
Type II	Infinite ohms

Torque specifications

Knock sensor

Type I	84 to 108 in-lbs
Type II	5-18 ft-lbs

1   General information

The engine electrical systems include all ignition, charging and starting components. Because of their engine-related functions, these components are discussed separately from chassis electrical devices such as the lights, the instruments, etc. (which are included in Chapter 12).

Always observe the following precautions when working on the electrical systems:

a) Be extremely careful when servicing engine electrical components. They are easily damaged if checked, connected or handled improperly.

b) Never leave the ignition switch on for long periods of time with the engine off.

c) Don't disconnect the battery cables while the engine is running.

d) Maintain correct polarity when connecting a battery cable from another vehicle during jump starting.

e) Always disconnect the negative cable first and hook it up last or the battery may be shorted by the tool being used to loosen the cable clamps.

It's also a good idea to review the safety-related information regarding the engine electrical systems located in the Safety first! section near the front of this manual before beginning any operation included in this Chapter.

2   Battery – emergency jump starting

Refer to the *Booster battery (jump) starting* procedure at the front of this manual.

3   Battery – removal and installation

Refer to illustrations 3.1 and 3.2

1   **Caution:** *Always disconnect the negative cable first and hook it up last or the battery may be shorted by the tool being used to loosen the cable clamps.* Disconnect both cables from the battery terminals **(see illustration)**.

2   Remove the battery hold-down clamp or strap **(see illustration)**.

3   Lift out the battery. Be careful – it's heavy.

4   While the battery is out, inspect the carrier (tray) for corrosion (see Chapter 1).

5   If you're replacing the battery, be sure to purchase one that's identical (same dimensions, amperage rating, cold cranking rating, etc.).

6   Installation is the reverse of removal.

4   Battery cables – check and replacement

1   Periodically inspect the entire length of each battery cable for damage, cracked or burned insulation and corrosion. Poor battery cable connections can cause starting problems and decreased engine performance.

2   Check the cable-to-terminal connections at the ends of the cables for cracks, loose wire strands and corrosion. The presence of white, fluffy deposits under the insulation at the cable terminal connection is a sign the cable is corroded and should be replaced. Check the terminals for distortion, missing mounting nuts/bolts and corrosion.

3   When removing the cables, always disconnect the negative cable first and hook it up last or the battery may be shorted by the tool used to loosen the cable clamps. Even if only the positive cable is being replaced, be sure to disconnect the negative cable from the battery first (see Chapter 1 for further information regarding battery cable removal).

4   Disconnect the old cables from the battery, then trace each of them to their opposite ends and detach them from the starter solenoid and ground terminals. Note the routing of each cable to ensure correct installation.

5   If you're replacing either or both cables, take the old ones with you when buying the new ones – the replacements must be identical. Cables have characteristics that make them easy to identify: Positive cables are normally red, larger in diameter and have a larger diameter battery post and clamp; ground cables are normally black, smaller in diameter and have a slightly smaller battery post and clamp.

6   Clean the threads of the solenoid or ground connection with a wire brush to remove rust and corrosion. Apply a light coat of petroleum jelly to the threads to prevent future corrosion.

7   Attach the cable to the solenoid or ground connection and tighten the mounting nut/bolt securely.

8   Before connecting a new cable to the battery, make sure it reaches the battery post without having to be stretched.

9   Connect the positive cable first, followed by the negative cable.

5   Ignition systems – general information

The ignition system includes the ignition switch, the battery, the coil, the primary (low voltage) and secondary (high voltage) wires/circuits, the distributor and the spark plugs. The ignition system on carburetor equipped vehicles is controlled by contact breaker points; the ignition system on fuel-injected vehicles is controlled by the electronic control unit (except 1980 Rabbits and Sciroccos sold outside California with fuel-injected engines). Electronic ignition systems are known as transistorized coil ignition with Hall sender (TCI-h). Some versions of TCI-h use a knock sensor

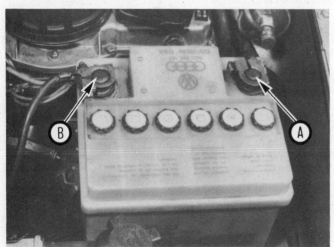

3.1   Always detach the cable from the negative terminal (A – smaller diameter post) first, then detach the positive cable (B – larger diameter post)

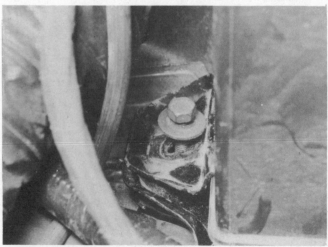

3.2   To remove the battery, unscrew the bolt and detach the hold-down clamp

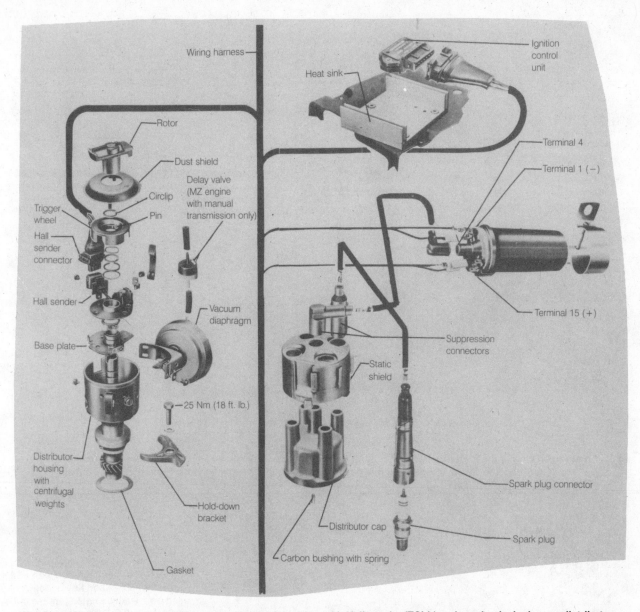

5.2   An exploded view of the basic transistorized coil ignition with Hall sender (TCI-h) and mechanical advance distributor used on Golf and Jetta models with engine codes GX and MZ

to detect knock or ping (see Section 11).

The 12-volt primary current for the special ignition coil on the electronic ignition system is switched on and off electronically by the switching transistor in the ignition control unit. Because the primary current is switched electronically instead of mechanically, there are no points to adjust or maintain.

Transistorized Ignition Coil with Hall sender (TCI-h)
Refer to illustrations 5.2, 5.3 and 5.5

The electronic ignition systems used on the vehicles covered in this manual, generally known as Transistorized Coil Ignition with Hall sender (TCI-h), have an electronic control unit which, depending on the type of fuel-injection system used, controls parameters such as ignition timing and fuel management.

On engines equipped with early TCI-h distributors, ignition timing is adjusted in response to engine load and speed by centrifugal and vacuum advance mechanisms **(see illustration)**.

Later TCI-h ignition systems on engines equipped with CIS-E fuel in-

jection (engine codes HT, RD and PL) use a knock sensor to detect pre-ignition or detonation (known as knock or ping). On these systems, there's no centrifugal or vacuum advance; all adjustments to ignition timing are done electronically by a knock sensor control unit **(see illustration)**.

Engines equipped with the Digifant II fuel-injection system (engine codes RV and PF) also use TCI-h with knock sensor, but combine all ignition functions (including the knock sensor system itself) and fuel-injection functions into a single electronic control unit. In Digifant II systems, ignition timing is based on engine load, engine speed, ignition quality (knock) and coolant temperature.

A third version of TCI-h with knock sensor is used on CIS-E Motronic systems (engine code 9A). This version is similar to that used with Digifant II, but two knock sensors – and a knock control reference sensor – are used **(see illustration)**. The reference sensor allows tells the control unit which pair of cylinders is knocking. CIS-E Motronic systems don't have an ignition control unit; the Hall sender signal is monitored by the Motronic control unit. The control unit sends a signal to the ignition coil power stage, which switches power to the coil.

5

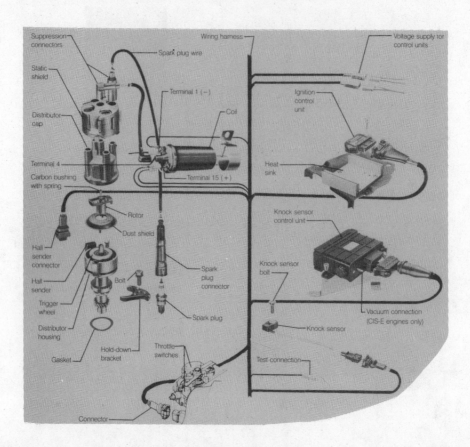

5.3   An exploded view of the transistorized coil ignition with Hall sender (TCI-h) and knock control (system shown is used on HT and RD engine codes; 16-valve (engine code PL) and Digifant II (engine codes RV and PF) are similar

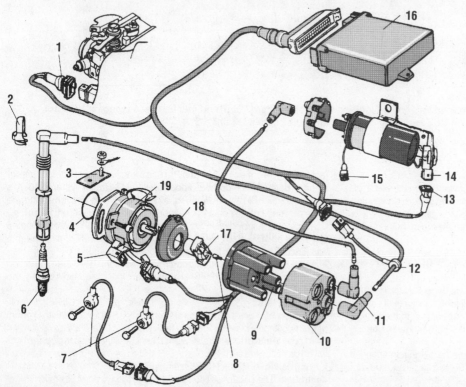

5.5   An exploded view of the transistorized coil ignition with Hall sender (TCI-h) and knock control used on 16-valve engine (engine code 9A) with CIS-E Motronic engine management system

1   Electrical connector
2   Bracket clamp
3   Ground connection on cylinder head
4   O-ring
5   Hall Effect switch
6   Spark plug
7   Knock sensors
8   Carbon brush and spring
9   Distributor cap
10 Radio interference suppression cap
11 Suppression connectors
12 Knock control sensor on number 4 cylinder plug wire
13 Harness connector
14 Power stage
15 Connector
16 Motronic system engine control unit
17 Ignition rotor
18 Dust shield
19 Distributor

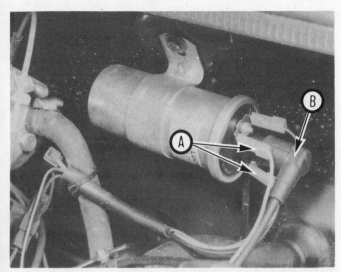

7.1   Coil terminals – primary (A); secondary (B)

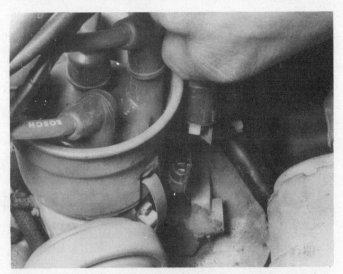

8.3   The first step in distributor removal is to unplug the primary wire electrical connector on the side of the distributor

Identifying an ignition system

The basic TCI-h ignition system has a vacuum diaphragm mounted on the side of the distributor. Ignition systems with knock control have a knock sensor located on the front of the engine block between cylinders 1 and 2 (see Chapter 6). CIS-E Motronic systems have a second knock sensor located between cylinders 3 and 4. TCI-h systems with knock control have a separate knock sensor control unit located on the right (passenger) side of the cowl area above the firewall. Digifant II and CIS-E Motronic systems don't have a separate control unit. For more information on the knock sensor and control unit, refer to Chapter 6.

6   Ignition system – check

1   Attach an inductive timing light to each plug wire, one at a time, and crank the engine.
   a) If the light flashes, voltage is reaching the plug.
   b) If the light doesn't flash, proceed to the next Step.
2   Inspect the spark plug wire(s), distributor cap, rotor and spark plug(s) (see Chapter 1). Fix minor problems and replace defective parts as necessary.
3   If the engine still won't start, check the ignition points, if equipped, (see Chapter 1), then check the ignition coil (see Section 7). On vehicles with an electronic ignition system, check the Hall sender and ignition control unit (see Section 10).

7   Ignition coil and resistance wire – check and replacement

Ignition coil

Refer to illustration 7.1

1   Mark the wires and terminals with pieces of numbered tape, then remove the primary wires and the high-tension lead from the coil **(see illustration)**.
2   Remove the coil from the mount, clean the outer case and check it for cracks and other damage.
3   Clean the coil primary terminals and check the coil tower terminal for corrosion. Clean it with a wire brush if any corrosion is found.
4   Check the coil primary resistance by attaching the leads of an ohmmeter to the positive and negative terminals. Compare the readings to the primary resistance listed in this Chapter's Specifications.
5   Check the coil secondary resistance by hooking one of the ohmmeter leads to one of the primary terminals and the other ohmmeter lead to the

large center terminal. Compare the readings to the secondary resistance listed in this Chapter's Specifications.
6   If the measured resistances are not as specified, the coil is probably defective and should be replaced with a new one.
7   For proper ignition system operation, all coil terminals and wire leads must be kept clean and dry.
8   Install the coil in the vehicle and hook up the wires.

Resistance wire

9   To check the resistance wire that connects terminal 15 of the coil to terminal C15 of the fuse box, disconnect multiple connector C from the back of the fuse box relay plate.
10   Detach the wire from terminal 15 of the ignition coil (it should be marked on the coil). Connect an ohmmeter to terminal pin C15 of the multiple connector and to the wire disconnected from terminal 15 of the coil. The resistance should be as listed in this Chapter's Specifications. If the reading is incorrect, replace the wire.
11   Cut the replacement wire to a length of 50-3/8 inches. Install the replacement resistance wire in the multiple connector and at the ignition coil.
Note: *The correct VW resistance wire has clear insulation with violet stripes and a conductor diameter of 0.030-inch.*

8   Distributor – removal and installation

Refer to illustrations 8.3, 8.6, 8.7 and 8.9

Removal

1   Disconnect the cable from the negative terminal of the battery.
2   Detach the primary lead from the coil. Remove the static shield from the distributor cap.
3   Unplug the electrical connector located on the side of the distributor **(see illustration)**. If the connector isn't right at the distributor, follow the wires as they exit the distributor to find the connector.
4   Look for a raised "1" on the distributor cap. This marks the location for the number one cylinder spark plug wire terminal. If the cap doesn't have a mark for the number one terminal, locate the number one spark plug and trace the wire back to the terminal on the cap.
5   Remove the distributor cap and suppression shield (see Chapter 1) and turn the engine over until the rotor is pointing toward the number one spark plug wire terminal (see locating TDC procedure in Chapter 2 if necessary).
6   Make a mark on the edge of the distributor base directly below the rotor tip and in line with it. Also, mark the distributor base and the engine block (cylinder head on the DOHC engine) to make sure the distributor will

8.6   Using white paint, chalk or a permanent felt-tip marker, mark the relationship of the rotor to the distributor body and the position of the distributor body in relation to the block (SOHC engine) or cylinder head (DOHC engine)

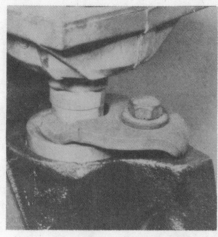

8.7   Typical distributor hold-down clamp and bolt

8.9   When installing the distributor on a SOHC engine, make sure the helical gear meshes with the gear on the intermediate shaft and the slot in the distributor shaft mates with the tang on the tip of the oil pump drive shaft (turn the oil pump shaft with needle-nose pliers if necessary)

be reinstalled correctly **(see illustration)**.

7   Remove the distributor hold down-bolt and clamp **(see illustration)**, then pull the distributor straight out to remove it. **Caution:** *DO NOT turn the crankshaft while the distributor is out of the engine, or the alignment marks will be useless.*

Installation

Note: *If the crankshaft has been moved while the distributor is out, the number one piston must be repositioned at TDC. This can be done by feeling for compression pressure at the number one plug hole as the crankshaft is turned. Once compression is felt, align the ignition timing zero mark with the pointer.*

8   Insert the distributor into the engine positioned exactly as it was before removal.

9   To mesh the helical gears on the intermediate shaft and the distributor (SOHC engine only), it may be necessary to turn the rotor slightly. Also, make sure the slot in the bottom of the distributor shaft **(see illustration)** fits over the tang on the upper end of the oil pump shaft. If it doesn't, the distributor won't seat completely – the oil pump shaft can be turned with needle-nose pliers to line things up if necessary. Recheck the alignment marks between the distributor base and block or head to verify the distributor is in the same position it was before removal. Also check the rotor to see if it's aligned with the mark on the edge of the distributor base.

10   Place the hold-down clamp in position and loosely install the bolt.

11   Install the distributor cap.

12   Plug in the electrical connector at the side of the distributor.

13   Reattach the spark plug wires to the plugs (if removed).

14   Connect the cable to the negative terminal of the battery.

15   Check the ignition timing (see Chapter 1) and tighten the distributor hold-down bolt securely.

9   Distributor – overhaul

Breaker-point ignition

Refer to illustrations 9.2 and 9.5

1   Remove the distributor as described in Section 8, then pull the rotor off the distributor shaft and remove the dust shield.

2   Remove the vacuum advance unit **(see illustration)**.

3   Remove the screws that retain the base plate to the distributor body and lift out the base plate/ignition point assembly.

4   Mark the location of the drive gear on the distributor shaft so it can be installed in the same position during reassembly.

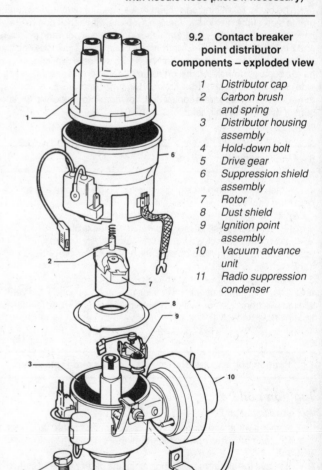

9.2   Contact breaker point distributor components – exploded view

1   Distributor cap
2   Carbon brush and spring
3   Distributor housing assembly
4   Hold-down bolt
5   Drive gear
6   Suppression shield assembly
7   Rotor
8   Dust shield
9   Ignition point assembly
10   Vacuum advance unit
11   Radio suppression condenser

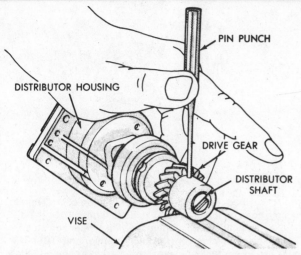

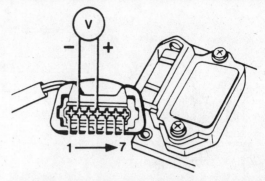

9.5   Use a pin punch to drive out the roll pin that secures the drive gear to the shaft

10.5   To check voltage supply and the ground for the ignition control unit, unplug the electrical connector from the ignition control unit and check for voltage between terminals 2 (-) and 4 (+) – when you turn on the ignition, there should be voltage present (CIS, CIS-E and Digifant II systems)

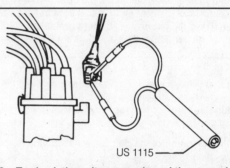

10.8   To check the voltage supply and the ground for the Hall sender, unplug the electrical connector from the Hall sender at the distributor and check for voltage between the outer terminals of the connector – when you turn on the ignition, there should be voltage present (CIS, CIS-E and Digifant II systems)

5   Using a pin punch, drive out the roll pin securing the gear to the shaft **(see illustration)**.

6   Remove the gear and withdraw the distributor shaft from the housing.

7   Remove the nylon spacer (if used) from the distributor shaft.

8   Clean all the parts and inspect them for wear and damage (especially the shaft, the shaft bushings in the housing, the base plate and the points and cam).

9   Check the distributor cap and rotor as described in Chapter 1.

10   Check the fit of the distributor shaft in the housing. If there's excessive side movement, try to obtain replacement bushings or a new housing. Make sure the base plate turns freely.

11   Reassembly is the reverse of disassembly, with the following notes:
   a) Lubricate the distributor shaft with a light film of engine oil. Don't use too much oil.
   b) When installing the distributor shaft, make sure the nylon spacer (if used) contacts the housing bushing.
   c) Use a new roll pin when installing the drive gear on the distributor shaft.
   d) Install new points as described in Chapter 1.
   e) Check the operation of the vacuum and centrifugal advance mechanisms.

Electronic ignition

Although the Hall sender, the trigger wheel, the vacuum advance unit and the dust shield are available separately, they don't have to be routinely replaced and the installation of new ones doesn't constitute a distributor overhaul. The parts that would be required for an overhaul (the housing, centrifugal advance components, base plate, shaft and shaft bushings) aren't available separately, so an overhaul, in the traditional sense, isn't possible. If the major distributor components are damaged or worn out, buy a new or rebuilt distributor or a complete housing assembly. If you need to replace the Hall sender unit, see Section 10.

10   Hall sender and ignition control unit – check and replacement

1   The Hall sender (called a Hall effect switch by some manufacturers), which is located inside the electronic ignition distributor housing, supplies the basic ignition timing signal to the computer.

2   If there's no spark at the spark plugs, but the plugs and the ignition coil are in good working order, the problem is either in the Hall sender or the ignition control unit. The Hall sender is located inside the distributor; the connector for the Hall sender is located on the side of the distributor. The ignition control unit is located in the driver's side cowling, above and behind the firewall, beneath the plastic drip tray.

3   To perform the following tests, you'll need to use a high-impedance voltmeter or low-current LED test light. The sequence of the following tests is important. You'll need to stick with the sequence as it's presented to isolate the faulty component.

Check

All systems except CIS-E Motronic

Checking the voltage supply and the ground for the ignition control unit

Refer to illustration 10.5

4   Make sure the ignition is turned off, then detach the electrical connector from the ignition control unit.

5   Check for voltage between connector terminals 2 (-) and 4 (+) **(see illustration)**. Turn on the ignition. There should be battery voltage.

6   If there's no voltage, look for defects in the wiring harness. Check the continuity of the wire from terminal 2 to ground and from terminal 4 of the connector to terminal 15 of the coil. Make any necessary repairs.

Checking the voltage supply and the ground for the Hall sender

Refer to illustration 10.8

7   The Hall sender used with each of the three ignition systems covered by this manual gets its power a different way. The basic TCI-h system powers the Hall sender through the ignition control unit. On the TCI-h system with knock sensor, the Hall sender gets power from the knock sensor control unit. On Digifant II systems, the Hall sender gets power from the Digifant II control unit.

8   With the ignition off and the ignition control unit connected, unplug the electrical connector from the Hall sender at the distributor. Check for voltage between the outer terminals of the connector **(see illustration)**. Turn on the ignition. There should be voltage present.

5

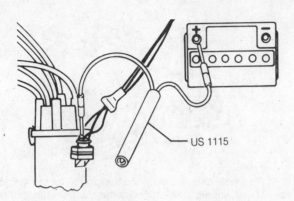

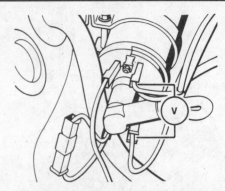

10.10　To check the operation of the switching function of the Hall sender, detach the coil wire from the distributor and ground it with a jumper wire, peel back the boot on the Hall sender connector and connect an LED test light between the center terminal and the positive (+) batter terminal – the LED should flicker (CIS, CIS-E and Digifant II systems)

10.12　To check the voltage from the ignition control unit to the coil, hook up the meter test leads to terminals 1 (-) and 15 (+) on the ignition coil, unplug the Hall sender connector (TCI-h), the connector from the knock sensor unit (TCI-h with knock sensor) or the connector from the control unit (Digifant II), then turn on the ignition – the meter should indicate at least 2 volts for 1 to 2 seconds, then drop back to 0 volts (CIS, CIS-E and Digifant II systems)

9　If there's no voltage, check the wire harness between the electrical connector for the Hall sender and the control unit, and between the control unit and ground. If all of these wires have continuity, but there's still no voltage reaching the Hall sender, the control unit is faulty. Replace it.

Checking the operation of the Hall sender switching function
Refer to illustration 10.10

10　To check the operation of the Hall sender, you need to verify its ability to switch the primary circuit. Detach the coil wire from the center of the distributor and ground it with a jumper wire. With the Hall sender connected, carefully peel back the rubber connector boot to get at the wires from the back side of the connector. Connect an LED test light between the center terminal and the positive (+) battery terminal **(see illustration)**. Now actuate the starter. The LED should flicker.

11　If the LED doesn't flicker, the Hall sender is bad. Replace it (see below).

12　Turn off the ignition, select a 20 volt DC scale on your multimeter and hook up the multimeter test leads to terminals 1 (-) and 15 (+) on the ignition coil **(see illustration)**. Don't disconnect any of the coil wires. On models with the basic TCI-h system, unplug the Hall sender connector from the

distributor. On models with TCI-h and knock sensor, unplug the electrical connector from the knock sensor unit. On Digifant II models, unplug the electrical connector from the Digifant II control unit.

Checking the voltage from the ignition control unit to the coil
Refer to illustration 10.12

13　Turn on the ignition. The meter should indicate the presence of at least 2 volts for about 1 to 2 seconds, then should drop back to 0 volts.

14　If no voltage is indicated, either the ignition coil or the ignition control unit is defective. Check the coil (see Section 7).

15　If the coil is okay, the ignition control unit is bad. Replace it.

Checking the response of the ignition control unit to the Hall sender unit
Refer to illustrations 10.17, 10.18 and 10.19

16　With a voltmeter or multimeter hooked up as described above, you can check the operation of the ignition control unit by sending it a simulated signal from the Hall sender.

17　To check a basic TCI-h system, unplug the electrical connector for the Hall sender. Turn on the ignition and, using a jumper wire, momentarily

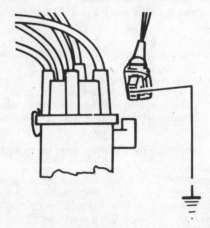

10.17　To check the response of the ignition control unit to the Hall sender on a basic TCI-h system, turn on the ignition and momentarily ground the center terminal of the Hall sender connector with a jumper wire – the voltage should briefly jump to at least 2 volts momentarily (CIS systems)

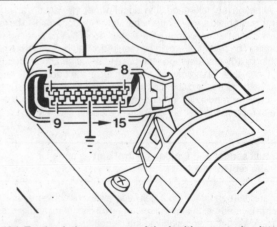

10.18　To check the response of the ignition control unit to the Hall sender on a TCI-h system with knock sensor, unplug the electrical connector of the knock sensor control unit, turn on the ignition and momentarily ground terminal 12 of the control unit connector – the voltage should briefly jump to at least 2 volts (CIS-E systems)

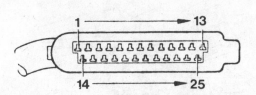

10.19   To check the response of the ignition control unit to the Hall sender on a Digifant II system, unplug the electrical connector for the control unit and momentarily ground the terminal 25 of the connector with a jumper wire – the voltage should briefly jump to at least 2 volts (Digifant II systems)

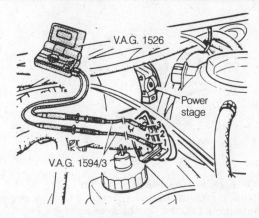

10.22   To check the voltage supply and the ground for the power stage, unplug the electrical connector, hook up a voltmeter to terminals 1 and 3 and turn on the ignition – there should be battery voltage present (CIS-E Motronic systems)

ground the center terminal of the Hall sender connector **(see illustration)**. The voltage should briefly jump to at least 2 volts.

18   To check a TCI-h system with knock sensor, unplug the electrical connector for the knock sensor control unit harness. Turn on the ignition and, using a jumper wire, momentarily ground terminal 12 of the knock sensor control unit connector **(see illustration)**. The voltage should briefly jump to at least 2 volts.

19   To check a Digifant II system, unplug the electrical connector for the Digifant control unit harness. Turn on the ignition and, using a jumper wire, momentarily ground terminal 25 **(see illustration)** of the Digifant control unit connector. The voltage should briefly jump to at least 2 volts.

20   If the control unit for any of the above systems fails to respond as indicated, it's bad. Replace it.

CIS-E Motronic systems

Testing the Hall sender and the coil power stage

21   If there's no spark at the spark plugs, test the Hall sender and the coil power stage. The following tests also verify that the Motronic control unit is responding to the signal from the Hall sender. First, make sure the spark plugs (see Chapter 1) and the ignition coil (see Section 7) are in good condition. The electrical connector for the Hall sender is on the side of the distributor. The coil power stage is located next to the coil.

Checking the voltage supply and the ground for the power stage
Refer to illustration 10.22

22   With the ignition off, unplug the electrical connector for the power stage and hook up a voltmeter to terminals 1 and 3 **(see illustration)**.

23   Turn on the ignition. There should be battery voltage present. Turn off the ignition.

24   If there's no voltage present, either there's a break in the wiring between terminal 1 and the fuse relay panel, or between terminal 3 and

ground. Check both wires for continuity. Make repairs as necessary, then reattach the connector.

Checking the voltage supply and the ground for the Hall sender
Refer to illustration 10.25

25   With the ignition off, unplug the electrical connector for the Hall sender. Using a voltmeter or multimeter, check for voltage between the outer terminals **(see illustration)**. When the ignition is turned on, there should be at least 9 volts present. Turn off the ignition.

26   If there's no voltage, check for continuity in the wiring between terminal 3 of the connector for the Hall sender and terminal 30 of the connector for the Motronic control unit, and between terminal 1 of the connector for the Hall sender and ground. Make repairs as necessary, then reattach the connector.

Checking the switching function of the Hall sender
Refer to illustration 10.27

27   Peel back the protective boot from the electrical connector for the Hall sender and connect an LED test light between the center terminal and the positive terminal of the battery **(see illustration)**. Disconnect the coil wire from the center of the distributor and ground it with a jumper wire. When the starter is actuated, the LED should flicker.

28   If the LED doesn't flicker, the Hall sender is bad. Replace it (see below).

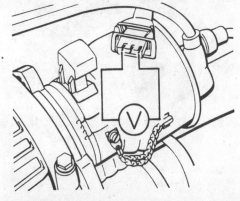

10.25   To check the voltage supply and the ground for the Hall sender, unplug the electrical connector to the Hall sender, hook up a voltmeter or multimeter as shown and check for voltage between the outer terminals – when you turn on the ignition, there should be at least 9 volts present (CIS-E Motronic systems)

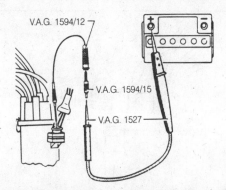

10.27   To check the switching function of the Hall sender, peel back the boot from the electrical connector for the Hall sender, hook up an LED test light between the center terminal and the positive terminal of the battery, detach the coil wire from the distributor and ground it with a jumper wire – when you turn on the starter, the LED should flicker (CIS-E Motronic systems)

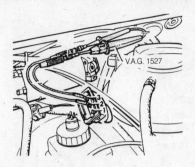

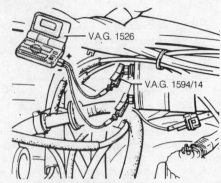

10.29   To check the response of the control unit to the Hall sender signal, unplug the electrical connector from the power stage, hook up an LED test light between terminals 2 and 3, ground the Hall sender and the coil wire and actuate the starter – the test light should flicker (CIS-E Motronic systems)

10.31   To check the response of the power stage to the Motronic control unit signal, plug in the power stage connector, unplug the Hall sender connector and hook up a voltmeter to terminals 1 and 15 of the coil

Checking the response of the control unit to the Hall sender signal

Refer to illustration 10.29

29   Disconnect the electrical connector from the power stage and hook up an LED test light between terminals 2 and 3 of the connector **(see illustration)**. With the Hall sender connector and the coil wire grounded, actuate the starter. The test light should flicker.

30   If the test light doesn't flicker, either the wiring between terminal 2 of the power stage connector and terminal 11 of the control unit is bad, or the Motronic control unit is bad.

Checking the response of the power stage to the Motronic control unit signal

Refer to illustrations 10.31 and 10.32

31   Plug in the power stage connector, then unplug the Hall sender connector and hook up a voltmeter to terminals 1 and 15 of the coil **(see illustration)**.

32   Turn on the ignition and briefly ground the center terminal of the Hall sender connector with a jumper wire **(see illustration)**. The voltage should momentarily jump to at least 2 volts, then drop back to zero.

33   If the voltage doesn't jump to 2 volts, then drop back to zero, either the power stage or the Motronic control unit is bad.

Replacement

Note: *Some disassembly of the distributor is required to replace the Hall sender. You'll need a pair of snap-ring pliers and, on 16-valve engines, a thin drift or punch.*

8-valve engines

Refer to illustrations 10.35 and 10.36

34   Remove the distributor cap and suppression shield, the rotor and the dust shield (see Chapter 1).

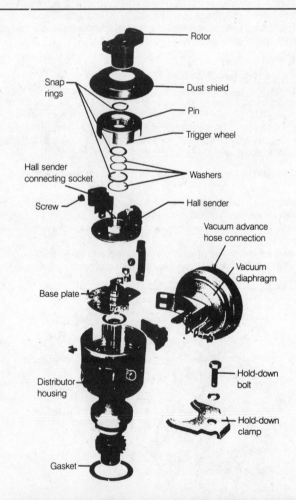

10.35   An exploded view of a typical electronic distributor assembly used on eight-valve engines (basic TCI-h type distributor shown; TCI-h with knock sensor distributor housing has no vacuum diaphragm)

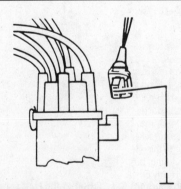

10.32   Then turn on the ignition and briefly ground the center terminal of the Hall sender connector with a jumper wire – the voltage should temporarily jump to at least 2 volts, then drop back to zero (CIS-E Motronic systems)

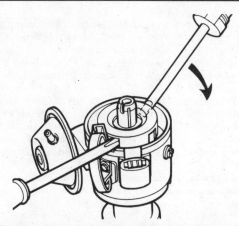

10.36   To remove the trigger wheel, use a pair of screwdrivers wedged under the trigger wheel as shown and *carefully* pry up on the trigger wheel to free it from the distributor shaft – make sure you don't lose the small key that locks the trigger wheel in place and make even more sure you don't bend the trigger wheel (eight-valve engines)

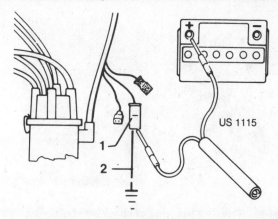

US 1115

11.3   To access the fault code(s) stored in the knock sensor system memory, hook up an LED test light as shown, between the test connector (1) and the battery positive (+) terminal, start the engine, ground the test connector (2) and maintain this ground for at least three seconds – the test light should flash in coded intervals

35   Use a pair of snap-ring pliers to remove the snap-ring which retains the trigger wheel (see illustration).

36   To remove the trigger wheel, use a pair of screwdriver positioned on opposite sides of the wheel and carefully pry it off the distributor shaft (see illustration). Make sure you don't lose the small pin which keys the trigger wheel to the distributor shaft. Caution: *Push the screwdrivers in as far as possible and pry up only on the strongest, center portion of the trigger wheel. If you bend the trigger wheel, you'll have to replace it.*

37   Remove the Hall sender retaining screws and remove the sender unit.

38   Installation is the reverse of removal.

16-valve engines

39   Remove the distributor (see Section 8).

40   Using a thin drift or punch, drive out the retaining pin in the distributor drive clutch and pull the distributor shaft, the rotor, the dust shield and the trigger wheel out from the top as a unit.

41   Remove the Hall sender retaining screws and remove the sender unit.

42   Installation is the reverse of removal.

11   Knock sensor system – description, check and component replacement

Description

1   The knock sensor detects abnormal engine vibrations caused by detonation (also referred to as "knock" or "ping"). This knock causes the sensor to generate a low-voltage signal which is monitored by the knock sensor control unit (CIS-E systems), the Digifant control unit or the Motronic control unit. The control unit then retards the ignition timing in tiny increments until the knocking stops. If the ignition timing advance is incorrect, or if the engine seems to be losing power, the knock sensor is the first component you should check.

Diagnosing the knock sensor system
CIS-E systems
Refer to illustration 11.3

2   The knock sensor control system on vehicles with CIS-E fuel injection (engine codes HT, RD and PL) has a fault memory which uses a computer chip to receive, store and communicate fault codes. This information can be outputted at the test connector located in the wiring harness near the

ignition coil. The test connector is a single blue, or blue and brown, wire which leads to pin 4 of the knock sensor control unit.

3   To display the fault code(s), hook up an LED test between the test connector and the battery positive (+) terminal (see illustration). Turn on the ignition. The LED should light, indicating the control unit is responding.

4   If the LED doesn't light, check the connectors and check for continuity of the wire from the test connector to terminal 4 of the knock sensor control unit connector. If there's continuity, the knock sensor control unit may be bad.

5   Start the engine and briefly rev the engine speed up to at least 3000 rpm. If the LED test light goes out, there's no fault code information stored, and the system is operating correctly. If the LED test light doesn't go out, or if it goes out then comes back on, there is a fault somewhere in the system.

6   Allow the engine speed to return to idle, and leave the test light hooked up. Hook up a jumper wire from the test connector to ground (see illustration 11.3). Maintain this ground connection for at least three seconds. The test light should flash in coded intervals. If the light doesn't flash, the control unit is faulty and should be replaced. Don't turn off the ignition during this procedure – doing so will permanently erase the fault memory.

7   Two flashes per interval indicates a problem in either the circuit wiring, the knock sensor or the knock sensor control unit (see below). Three flashes per interval indicates a problem at the vacuum connection to the knock sensor control unit. Check the vacuum hose for breaks and replace it if necessary. If there's nothing wrong with the vacuum connection, the control unit is faulty. Replace it.

CIS-E Motronic systems

8   Electronic fault diagnosis of the ignition system during normal operation is an integral part of the CIS-E engine management system. When activated, the control unit displays faults as a number code corresponding to a component or function of the system which needs to be checked.

9   Your VW dealer service department is equipped with an analyzer which plugs into a special test connection in the wiring harness. This analyzer retrieves and interprets fault codes and performs an electronic check of the Hall sender, the knock sensors and the knock control reference sensor. VW recommends this electronic check as the first step in any CIS-E Motronic troubleshooting, particularly on those vehicles still protected by VW's extended warranty coverage. The cost of this service is usually offset by the savings in time and effort resulting from immediate identification of the problem.

Checking and replacing the knock sensor
Refer to illustration 11.10

10   Two types of knock sensors are used on the engines covered by this

5

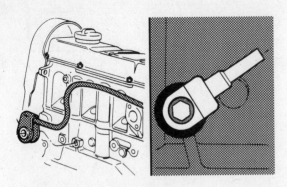

11.10   There are two types of knock sensors used on the engines covered in this manual: The Type I sensor (left) and the Type II sensor (right)

manual **(see illustration)**. The mounting bolt for each type of sensor has a different torque specification. Using the correct torque specification for this mounting bolt is critical to proper operation of the knock sensor. If you overtighten the bolt, it will crush the sensor crystal; if you undertighten it, the sensor might not react to knocking vibrations. In either case, the knock sensor system will go into its "default" mode and radically retard ignition timing to prevent damage to the engine. The symptom is an obvious and significant loss of power.

11   You must perform two simple tests to check the knock sensor: First, check the tightening torque listed in this Chapter's Specifications for the knock sensor(s) used on your engine. If the tightening torque is too loose,

retighten it; if it's too tight, loosen it and retorque it (of course, the next test may indicate that the sensor has been damaged from overtightening).

12   Unplug the electrical connector from the knock sensor and use an ohmmeter to measure the resistance across the terminals of the sensor and compare your reading(s) to the correct resistance listed in this Chapter's Specifications.

13   If the knock sensor fails the resistance test, replace it. To prevent accidental shorting of the alternator wiring, disconnect the cable from the negative battery terminal before you loosen or tighten the knock sensor. Don't use any washers when installing the new sensor. Finally, make sure you tighten the knock sensor to the *exact* torque listed in this Chapter's Specifications.

14   If the knock sensor resistance and mounting bolt torque are correct, the problem is somewhere in the knock sensor system. Proceed to the next step.

Troubleshooting the knock sensor system
Refer to illustrations 11.17a, 11.17b, 11.18a and 11.18b

15   If the resistance of the knock sensor and the torque of its mounting bolt are correct, you'll need to troubleshoot the knock sensor system. The sequence of the following tests if designed to logically isolate the faulty wire or component, so don't deviate from this sequence.

16   With the ignition off, unplug the electrical connector from the knock sensor control unit, Digifant control unit or Motronic control unit. The knock sensor control unit is located in the cowl behind the firewall on right (passenger's side) of the vehicle. The Digifant or Motronic control unit is mounted in the cowl behind the firewall on the left (driver's) side of the vehicle.

17   Using a multimeter, test for resistance or voltage at the terminals of the control unit connector in accordance with the steps outlined in the ac-

CIS-E (HT, RD, PL) engines			
Terminals	**Additional test conditions**	**Results**	**If results not as specified**
3 and 5	Ignition on	Approx. 12 volts	Wire from terminal 3 to ground open, or bad ground connection Wire from terminal 5 to ignition switch open
3 and 8	Ignition on, full-throttle switch on throttle valve closed	Approx. 12 volts	Middle wire to throttle switches open Full-throttle switch defective
3 and 6	Ignition on, idle switch closed	Approx. 12 volts	Middle wire to throttle switches open Idle switch misadjusted or defective (see Chapter 4)
3 and 2		90,000 to 100,000 ohms	Check oxygen sensor control unit (see Chapter 6)
3 and 13		At least 1,000,000 ohms	Knock sensor or wiring to knock sensor faulty
13 and 14	Disconnect knock sensor harness connector, bridge terminals 1 and 2 of harness connector	0 ohms	Wiring to knock sensor faulty
Digifant II (RV and PF) engines			
6 and 11		0 Ohms with throttle closed or fully opened infinite ohms at part-throttle	Replace idle and full-throttle switches
5 and 4	Disconnect knock sensor harness connector, bridge terminals 1 and 2 of harness connector	0 ohms	Wiring to knock sensor faulty

11.17a Knock sensor system wiring/component test table

CIS-E Motronic (9A) engines			
Terminals	Additional test conditions	Results	If results not as specified
26 and 23	Air flow sensor plate at rest	Approx. 5000 ohms	Break in wiring from control unit connector to air flow sensor potentiometer. Potentiometer misadjusted or faulty (see Chapter 4)
26 and 35	Air flow sensor plate at rest	Approx 4000 ohms	Break in wiring from terminal 3 of air flow sensor potentiometer harness connector to ground
27 and 29		1.5 ohms	Wiring break to knock control reference sensor, or reference sensor defective

11.17b Knock sensor system wiring/component test table

companying table (see illustrations). To prevent damage to sensitive electronic components, make your connections with the ignition turned off, and leave it off unless directed to do otherwise. The following tests usually check both the component and its wiring at the same time. If the readings you get deviate from the specified resistance or voltage values, the table provides likely causes and further checks or repairs you can make to fix the problem.

18   The first of the two accompanying terminal guides identifies the terminals of the knock sensor control unit (see illustration) for HT, RD and PL engine codes; the other guide (see illustration) identifies the terminals of the Digifant control unit connector for RV and PF engine codes.

19   If all the wiring and component checks are within the specified values, inspect the wiring to the Hall sender, the ignition control unit and the coil power stage (if equipped) for intermittent wiring opens (see Section 10). If you can't find anything wrong with those components, the control unit is probably bad.

12   Charging system – general information, precautions and check

General information

The charging system includes the alternator, either an internal or external voltage regulator, a charge indicator, the battery, a fusible link and the wiring between all the components. The charging system supplies electrical power for the ignition system, the lights, the radio, etc. The alternator is driven by a drivebelt at the front of the engine.

The purpose of the voltage regulator is to limit the alternator's voltage to a preset value. This prevents power surges, circuit overloads, etc., during peak voltage output.

The fusible link is a short length of insulated wire integral with the engine compartment wiring harness. The link is four wire gauges smaller in diameter than the circuit it protects. Production fusible links and their identification flags are identified by the flag color. See Chapter 12 for additional information regarding fusible links.

The charging system doesn't ordinarily require periodic maintenance. However, the drivebelt, battery and wires and connections should be inspected at the intervals outlined in Chapter 1.

The dashboard warning light should come on when the ignition key is turned to Start, then go off immediately. If it remains on, there is a malfunction in the charging system (see Section 12). Some vehicles are also equipped with a voltmeter. If the voltmeter indicates abnormally high or low voltage, check the charging system (see Section 12).

Precautions

Be very careful when making electrical circuit connections to a vehicle equipped with an alternator and note the following:

a) When reconnecting wires to the alternator from the battery, be sure to note the polarity.

b) Before using arc welding equipment to repair any part of the vehicle, disconnect the wires from the alternator and the battery terminals.

c) Never start the engine with a battery charger connected.

d) Always disconnect both battery leads before using a battery charger.

e) The alternator is turned by an engine drivebelt which could cause serious injury if your hands, hair or clothes become entangled in it with the engine running.

f) Because the alternator is connected directly to the battery, it could arc or cause a fire if overloaded or shorted out.

g) Wrap a plastic bag over the alternator and secure it with rubber bands before steam cleaning the engine.

Checking the charging system

1   If a malfunction occurs in the charging circuit, don't automatically assume the alternator is causing the problem. First check the following items:

a) Check the drivebelt tension and condition (Chapter 1). Replace it if it's worn or deteriorated.

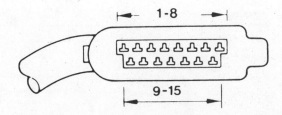

11.18a   Terminal guide for knock sensor control unit connector
(engine codes HT, RD and PL)

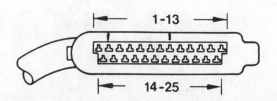

11.18b   Terminal guide for Digifant control unit connector
(engine codes RV and PF)

13.2   Typical alternator wiring connections

b) Make sure the alternator mounting and adjustment bolts are tight.
c) Inspect the alternator wiring harness and the connectors at the alternator and voltage regulator. They must be in good condition and tight.
d) Check the fusible link (if equipped) located between the starter solenoid and the alternator. If it's burned, determine the cause, repair the circuit and replace the link (the vehicle won't start and/or the accessories won't work if the fusible link blows). Sometimes a fusible link may look good, but still be bad. If in doubt, remove it and check it for continuity.
e) Start the engine and check the alternator for abnormal noises (a shrieking or squealing sound indicates a bad bearing).
f) Check the specific gravity of the battery electrolyte. If it's low, charge the battery (doesn't apply to maintenance free batteries).

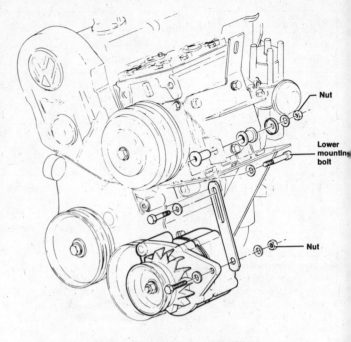

13.3a   Typical alternator and mounting brackets on engines with air conditioning

g) Make sure the battery is fully charged (one bad cell in a battery can cause overcharging by the alternator).
h) Disconnect the battery cables (negative first, then positive). Inspect the battery posts and the cable clamps for corrosion. Clean them thoroughly if necessary (see Chapter 1). Reconnect the cable to the positive terminal.

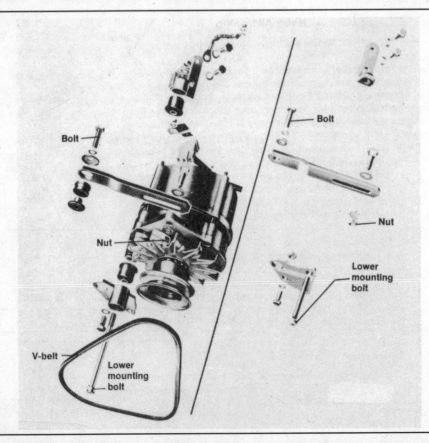

13.3b   Typical alternator and mounting brackets on engines without air conditioning

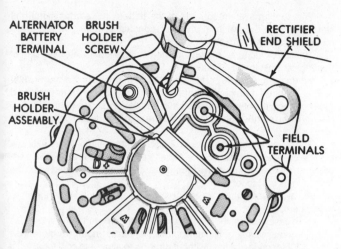

ALTERNATOR BATTERY TERMINAL

BRUSH HOLDER SCREW

RECTIFIER END SHIELD

BRUSH HOLDER ASSEMBLY

FIELD TERMINALS

14.2   On Bosch alternators, loosen the screws in small increments, moving from screw-to-screw, so the holder won't be damaged, . . .

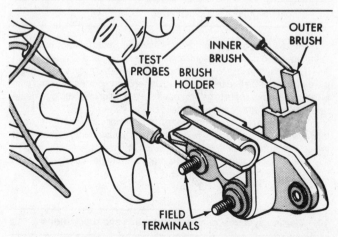

14.3 . . . then rotate the brush holder out of the alternator housing and check the brush length

i)   With the key off, connect a test light between the negative battery post and the disconnected negative cable clamp.

　1)　If the test light doesn't come on, reattach the clamp and proceed to the next Step.

　2)　If the test light comes on, there's a short (drain) in the electrical system of the vehicle. The short must be repaired before the charging system can be checked.

　3)　Disconnect the alternator wiring harness.

　　(a)　If the light goes out, the alternator is bad.
　　(b)　If the light stays on, pull each fuse until the light goes out (this will tell you which component is shorted).

2   Using a voltmeter, check the battery voltage with the engine off. It should be approximately 12-volts.

3   Start the engine and check the battery voltage again. It should now be approximately 14-to-15 volts.

4   Turn on the headlights. The voltage should drop, and then come back up, if the charging system is working properly.

5   If the voltage reading is more than the specified charging voltage, replace the voltage regulator (see Section 14). If the voltage is less, the alternator diode(s), stator or rectifier may be bad or the voltage regulator may be malfunctioning.

13   Alternator – removal and installation

Refer to illustrations 13.2, 13.3a and 13.3b

1   Detach the cable from the negative terminal of the battery.

2   Detach the electrical connectors from the alternator **(see illustration)**.

3   Loosen the alternator adjustment and pivot bolts and detach the drivebelt **(see illustrations)**.

4   Remove the adjustment and pivot bolts and separate the alternator from the engine.

5   If you're replacing the alternator, take the old one with you when purchasing a replacement unit. Make sure the new/rebuilt unit looks identical to the old alternator. Look at the terminals – they should be the same in number, size and location as the terminals on the old alternator. Finally, look at the identification numbers – they'll be stamped into the housing or printed on a tag attached to the housing. Make sure the numbers are the same on both alternators.

6   Many new/rebuilt alternators DO NOT have a pulley installed, so you may have to switch the pulley from the old unit to the new/rebuilt one. When buying an alternator, find out the shop's policy regarding pulleys – some shops will perform this service free of charge.

7   Installation is the reverse of removal.

8   After the alternator is installed, adjust the drivebelt tension (see Chapter 1).

9   Check the charging voltage to verify proper operation of the alternator (see Section 12).

14   Alternator brushes – replacement

1   Disconnect the negative cable from the battery. Label the wires and detach them from the alternator terminals.

Bosch alternator

Refer to illustrations 14.2, 14.3, 14.5 and 14.6

2   Loosen the brush holder mounting screws a little at a time to prevent distortion of the holder, then remove them **(see illustration)**.

3   Rotate the brush holder and separate it from the rear of the alternator **(see illustration)**.

4   If the brushes appear to be significantly worn, or if they don't move smoothly in the brush holder, replace the brush holder assembly with a new one.

5   Before installing the brush holder assembly, check for continuity between each brush and the appropriate field terminal **(see illustration)**.

OUTER BRUSH

INNER BRUSH

TEST PROBES

BRUSH HOLDER

FIELD TERMINALS

14.5   Using an ohmmeter, check for continuity between each brush and the appropriate field terminal (Bosch alternator shown)

5

14.6   Push the brush holder into place, making sure the brushes (which are spring loaded) seat properly (Bosch alternator shown)

6   Insert the holder into position, making sure the brushes seat correctly **(see illustration)**.
7   Hold the brush holder securely in place and install the screws. Tighten them evenly, a little at a time, so the holder isn't distorted. Once the screws are snug, tighten them securely.
8   Reconnect the negative battery cable.

Motorola alternator

Refer to illustration 14.10
9   Remove the alternator.
10   The brushes are mounted under the regulator on the rear of the alternator **(see illustration)**.
11   Remove the mounting screws and insulating washers and separate the regulator and brush holder from the brush end housing.
12   If the brushes appear to be significantly worn or are oil soaked or damaged, replace them with new ones.
13   Make sure the brushes move smoothly in the holder.
14   Reinstall the brush holder/regulator. Tighten the screws securely. Make sure the brushes aren't grounded.
15   Install the alternator.

15   Voltage regulator – replacement

1   The voltage regulator controls the charging system voltage by limiting the alternator output. The regulator is a sealed unit and isn't adjustable.
2   If the ammeter fails to register a charge rate or the red warning light on the dash comes on and the alternator, battery, drivebelt tension and electrical connections seem to be fine, have the regulator checked by a dealer service department or a repair shop.
3   The voltage regulator is located on the exterior of the alternator housing **(see illustration 14.10)**. To replace the regulator, remove the mounting screws and detach it. Installation is the reverse of removal.
4   Some Bosch alternators incorporate an integral voltage regulator which is part of the brush assembly.

16   Starting system – general information and precautions

The sole function of the starting system is to turn over the engine quickly enough to allow it to start.

The starting system consists of the battery, the starter motor, the starter solenoid, the switch and the wires connecting them. The solenoid is mounted directly on the starter motor.
The solenoid/starter motor assembly is installed on the lower part of the engine, next to the transaxle.
When the ignition key is turned to the Start position, the starter solenoid is actuated through the starter control circuit. The starter solenoid then connects the battery to the starter. The battery supplies the electrical energy to the starter motor, which does the actual work of cranking the engine.
The starter motor on a vehicle equipped with a manual transaxle can only be operated when the clutch pedal is depressed; the starter on a vehicle equipped with an automatic transaxle can only be operated when the shift lever is in Park or Neutral.
Always observe the following precautions when working on the starting system:
a) Excessive cranking of the starter motor can overheat it and cause serious damage. Never operate the starter motor for more than 30-seconds at a time without pausing to allow it to cool for at least two minutes.
b) The starter is connected directly to the battery and could arc or cause a fire if mishandled, overloaded or shorted out.
c) Always detach the cable from the negative terminal of the battery before working on the starting system.

17   Starter motor – in-vehicle check

Note: *Before diagnosing starter problems, make sure the battery is fully charged.*

1   If the starter motor doesn't turn at all when the switch is operated, make sure the shift lever is in Neutral or Park (automatic transaxle) or the clutch pedal is depressed (manual transaxle).
2   Make sure the battery is charged and all cable and wire connections, both at the battery and starter solenoid terminals, are clean and tight.
3   If the starter motor spins but the engine isn't cranking, the overrunning clutch in the starter motor is slipping and the starter motor must be replaced.
4   If, when the switch is actuated, the starter motor doesn't operate at all but the solenoid clicks, then the problem lies with either the battery, the main solenoid contacts or the starter motor itself (or the engine is seized).
5   If the solenoid plunger can't be heard when the switch is actuated, the battery is bad, the fusible link is burned (the circuit is open) or the solenoid itself is defective.
6   To check the solenoid, connect a jumper lead between the battery (+) and the ignition switch wire terminal (the small terminal) on the solenoid. If the starter motor now operates, the solenoid is okay and the problem is in the ignition switch, neutral start switch or wire harness.
7   If the starter motor still doesn't operate, remove the starter/solenoid assembly for disassembly, testing and repair.
8   If the starter motor cranks the engine at an abnormally slow speed, first make sure the battery is fully charged and all terminal connections are tight. If the engine is partially seized, or has the wrong viscosity oil in it, it'll crank slowly.
9   Run the engine until normal operating temperature is reached, then disconnect the coil wire from the distributor cap and ground it on the engine.
10   Connect a voltmeter positive lead to the positive battery post and connect the negative lead to the negative post.
11   Crank the engine and take the voltmeter readings as soon as a steady figure is indicated. Don't allow the starter motor to turn for more than 30-seconds at a time. A reading of 9-volts or more, with the starter motor turning at normal cranking speed, is normal. If the reading is 9-volts or more but the cranking speed is slow, the motor is faulty. If the reading is less than 9-volts and the cranking speed is slow, the solenoid contacts are probably burned, the starter motor is bad, the battery is discharged or there's a bad connection.

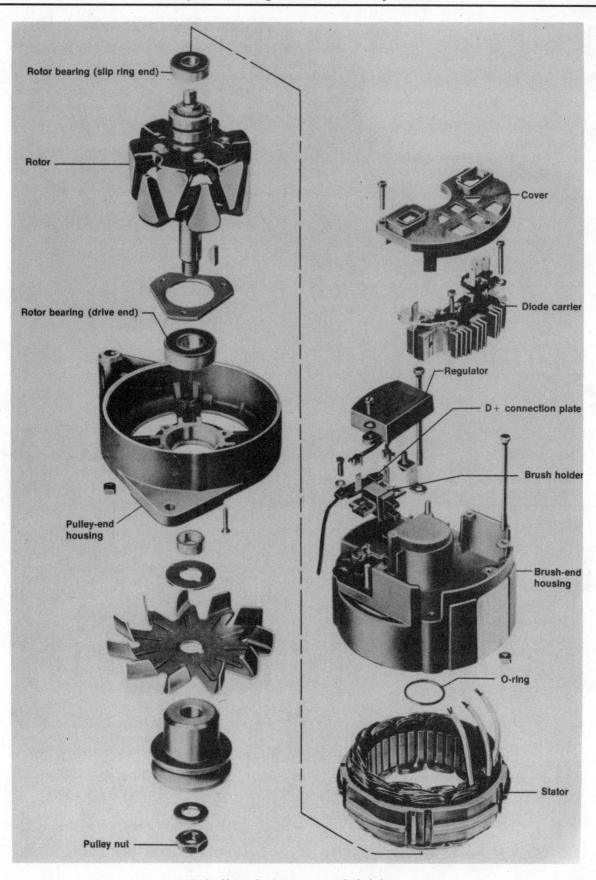

14.10   Motorola alternator – exploded view

18.4   Disconnect the starter motor wires (arrows) and remove the mounting bolts (note that the mounting bolt visible here has a socket [Allen] head – be sure to use the right tool to remove it)

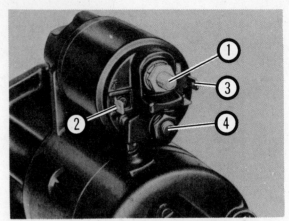

19.3   Remove the nut (4) securing the field coil strap to the solenoid, then detach the strap

1   *Positive battery cable terminal*
2   *Terminal 15a for wire to ignition coil terminal 15*
3   *Terminal 50 for start wire from ignition switch*
4   *Field coil connecting strap terminal*

18   Starter motor – removal and installation

Refer to illustration 18.4

1   Detach the cable from the negative terminal of the battery.
2   Raise the vehicle and support it securely on jackstands.
3   If the starter motor is equipped with a cover plate, loosen the clamp and remove the plate.
4   Clearly label, then disconnect the wires from the terminals on the starter motor and solenoid **(see illustration)**.
5   Remove the mounting fasteners and detach the starter. A large Allen wrench or socket drive tool may be needed for some bolts.
6   Installation is the reverse of removal.

19   Starter solenoid – removal and installation

Refer to illustrations 19.3, 19.5a and 19.5b

1   Disconnect the cable from the negative terminal of the battery.
2   Remove the starter motor (see Section 18).
3   Disconnect the field coil strap from the solenoid terminal **(see illustration)**.
4   Remove the screws that secure the solenoid to the starter motor.
5   If the starter motor is a Bosch unit on a vehicle with a manual transaxle, carefully work the solenoid off the shift fork to detach it **(see illustration)**. If it's a Bosch on a vehicle with an automatic transaxle, slide the solenoid off the plunger to detach it **(see illustration)**.
6   Installation is the reverse of removal.

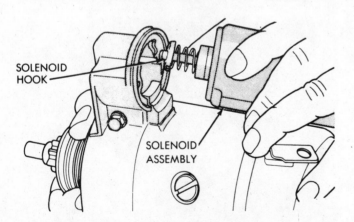

19.5a   If the starter motor is a Bosch unit on a vehicle with a manual transaxle, carefully work the solenoid off the shift fork to detach it

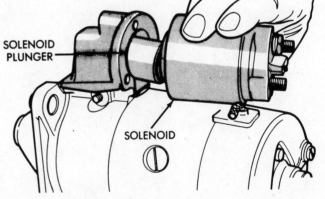

19.5b   If the starter motor is a Bosch unit on a vehicle with an automatic transaxle, slide the solenoid off the plunger to detach it

Chapter 6   Emissions control systems

Contents

Air injection system/air suction system
  (carburetor-equipped models) 6
Catalytic converter 10
Decel valve (1975 through 1979 fuel-injected models) 8
Evaporative emissions control system check
  and canister replacement .... See Chapter 1
Evaporative emissions control (EVAP) system 3
Exhaust Gas Recirculation (EGR) system 5
Exhaust Gas Recirculation (EGR) system check
  and service light resetting .... See Chapter 1

General information 1
Oxygen sensor 9
Positive Crankcase Ventilation (PCV) system 2
Positive Crankcase Ventilation (PCV)
  system check .... See Chapter 1
Temperature-controlled vacuum advance system 7
Thermostatically controlled air cleaner 4

1   General information

Refer to illustrations 1.1a, 1.1b, 1.1c, 1.1d, 1.1e, 1.1f and 1.6

To prevent pollution of the atmosphere from incompletely burned and evaporating gases, and to maintain good driveability and fuel economy, a number of emission control systems are incorporated. The principal systems are **(see illustrations):**

Positive Crankcase Ventilation (PCV) system
Fuel evaporative emission control system
Heated inlet air system (thermostatically controlled
   air cleaner)

Exhaust Gas Recirculation (EGR) system
Air injection system
Carburetor mounted emission control devices
Automatic choke system
Oxygen sensor
Catalytic converter
Computerized control unit

The Sections in this Chapter include general descriptions, checking procedures within the scope of the home mechanic and component replacement procedures (when possible) for each of the systems listed above.

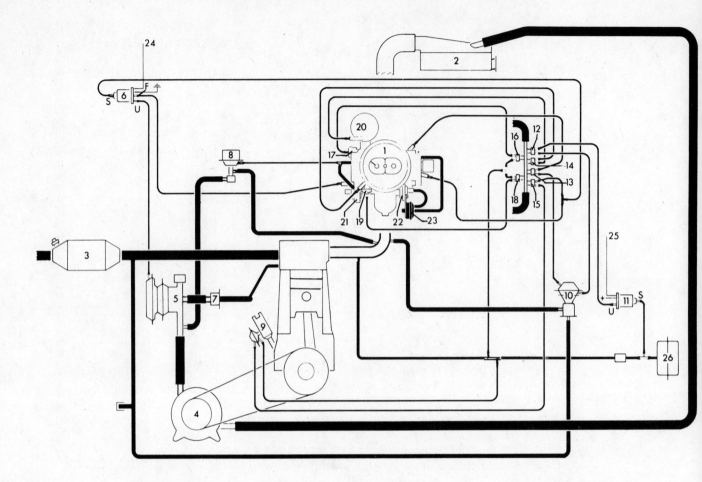

1.1a   Schematic layout of emission control components and vacuum hose routing – 1976 carburetor-equipped vehicles sold in the USA

1	Carburetor	15	Temperature valve for vacuum advance cutoff
2	Air cleaner	16	Temperature valve for acceleration pump
3	Catalytic converter	17	Check valve for temperature-controlled acceleration pump system
4	Air pump		
5	Diverter valve	18	Temperature valve for cold idle valve
6	Two-way valve for air injection system	19	Cold idle valve
7	Check valve for air injection system	20	Vacuum unit for carburetor secondary throttle valve
8	Anti-backfire valve for air injection system		
9	Distributor	21	Vacuum unit for choke pull-down first stage
10	EGR valve	22	Vacuum unit for choke pull-down second stage
11	Two-way valve for EGR second stage (California only)		
		23	Thermo-time vacuum valve for choke pull-down second stage
12	Temperature valve for EGR second stage (California only)		
		24	Electrical wire to relay in two-way valve
13	Temperature valve for EGR first stage	25	Electrical wire to microswitch
14	Temperature valve for carburetor secondary throttle valve vacuum unit	26	Vacuum powered brake servo

Before assuming an emissions control system is malfunctioning, check the fuel and ignition systems carefully. The diagnosis of some emission control devices requires specialized tools, equipment and training. If checking and servicing become too difficult or if a procedure is beyond your ability, consult a dealer service department. Remember, the most frequent cause of emissions problems is simply a loose or broken vacuum hose or wire, so always check the hose and wiring connections first.

This doesn't mean, however, that emission control systems are partic-

ularly difficult to maintain and repair. You can quickly and easily perform many checks and do most of the regular maintenance at home with common tune-up and hand tools. **Note:** *Because of a Federally-mandated extended warranty which covers the emission control system components, check with your dealer about warranty coverage before working on any emissions-related systems. Once the warranty has expired, you may wish to perform some of the component checks and/or replacement procedures in this Chapter to save money.*

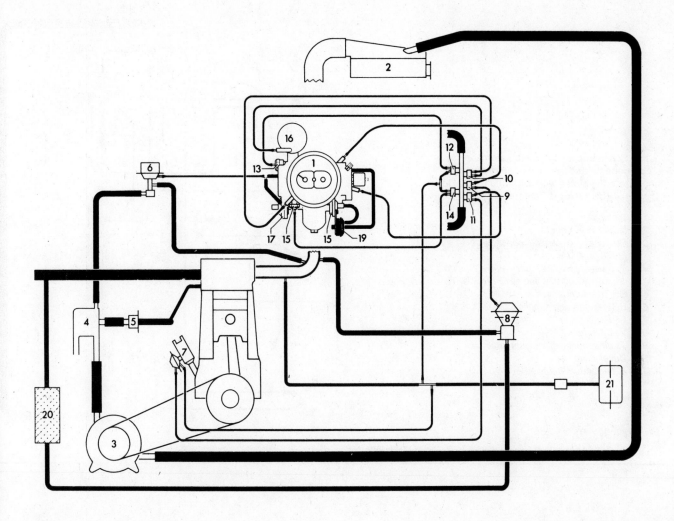

1.1b   Schematic layout of emission control components and vacuum hose routing – 1976 carburetor-equipped vehicles sold in Canada

1	Carburetor	13	Check valve for temperature-controlled
2	Air cleaner		acceleration pump system
3	Air pump for air injection system	14	Temperature valve for cold idle valve
4	Diverter valve for air injection system	15	Cold idle valve
5	Check valve for air injection system	16	Vacuum unit for carburetor secondary
6	Anti-backfire valve for air injection system		throttle valve
7	Distributor	17	Vacuum unit for choke pull-down first
8	EGR valve		stage
9	Temperature valve for EGR first stage	18	Vacuum unit for choke pull-down
10	Temperature valve for carburetor		second stage
	secondary throttle valve vacuum unit	19	Thermo-time vacuum valve for choke
11	Temperature valve for vacuum advance cutoff		pull-down second stage
12	Temperature valve for acceleration	20	EGR filter
	pump	21	Vacuum powered brake servo

Pay close attention to any special precautions outlined in this Chapter. It should be noted that the illustrations of the various systems may not exactly match the system installed on a particular vehicle because of changes made by the manufacturer during production or from year-to-year.

A Vehicle Emissions Control Information label is located in the engine compartment **(see illustration)**. This label contains important emissions specifications and adjustment information. When servicing the engine or emissions systems, the VECI label in the vehicle should always be checked for up-to-date information.

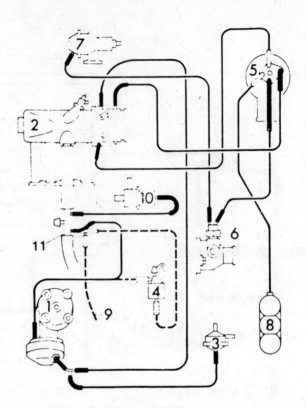

1.1c   Schematic layout of emission control components and vacuum hose routing – fuel-injected vehicles with a manual transaxle (USA except California)

1   Distributor
2   Intake air distributor
3   Charcoal filter canister check valve (1978 only)
4   Two-way valve (A/C only – valve shaped differently on 1976 and 1977 models)
5   EGR vacuum amplifier
6   EGR temperature valve
7   EGR valve
8   Vacuum tank
9   To air conditioner vacuum tank
10 Decel valve
11 Main vacuum manifold

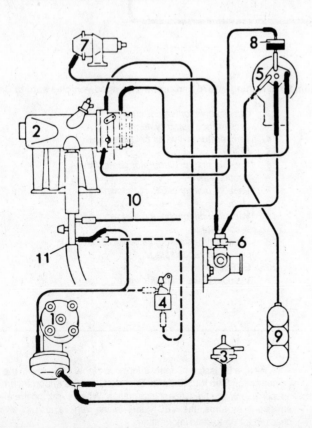

1.1d   Schematic layout of emission control components and vacuum hose routing – fuel-injected vehicles with an automatic transaxle (USA including California)

1   Distributor
2   Intake air distributor
3   Charcoal filter canister check valve (1978 only)
4   Two-way valve (A/C only – valve shaped differently on 1976 and 1977 models)
5   EGR vacuum amplifier
6   EGR temperature valve
7   EGR valve
8   Vacuum check valve
9   Vacuum tank
10 To air conditioner vacuum tank
11 Main vacuum manifold

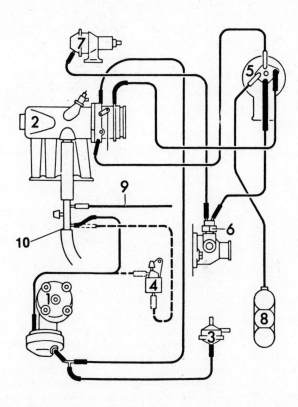

1.1e   Schematic layout of emission control components and vacuum hose routing – fuel-injected Canadian models with an automatic transaxle and California models with a manual transaxle

1   Distributor
2   Intake air distributor
3   Charcoal filter canister check valve (1978 only)
4   Two-way valve (A/C only – valve shaped differently on 1976 models)
5   EGR vacuum amplifier
6   EGR temperature valve
7   EGR valve
8   Vacuum tank
9   To air conditioner vacuum tank
10 Main vacuum manifold

1.1f   Schematic layout of emission control components and vacuum hose routing – fuel-injected Canadian models with a manual transaxle

1   Distributor
2   Intake air distributor
3   Charcoal filter canister check valve
4   Two-way valve (A/C only – valve shaped differently on 1976 and 1977 models)
5   To air conditioner vacuum tank
6   Decel valve (eliminated from 1979 cars)
7   Main vacuum manifold

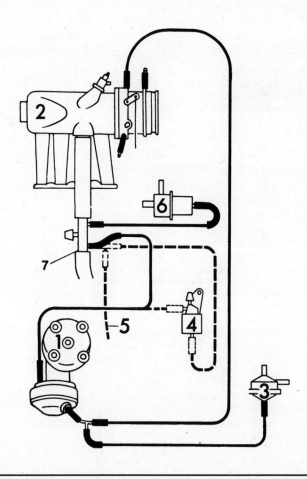

6

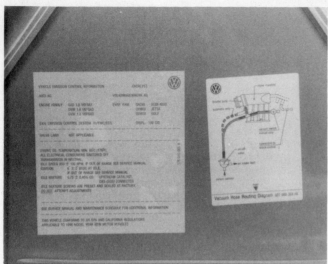

1.6   The Vehicle Emissions Control Information Label (VECI) is located on the underside of the hood

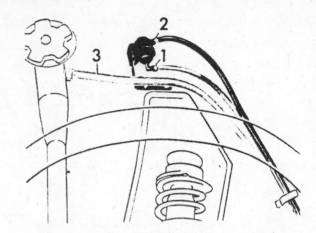

3.5   Correct installation of the fuel tank breather gravity valve

1 To fuel tank	3 Vent hose with coil
2 To expansion tank	spring insert

2   Positive Crankcase Ventilation (PCV) system

1   The Positive Crankcase Ventilation (PCV) system reduces hydrocarbon emissions by scavenging crankcase vapors. It does this by circulating fresh air from the air cleaner through the crankcase, where it mixes with blow-by gases and is then rerouted through a PCV valve to the intake manifold.

2   The main components of the PCV system are the PCV valve, a fresh air filtered inlet and the vacuum hoses connecting these components with the engine.

3   To maintain idle quality, the PCV valve restricts the flow when the intake manifold vacuum is high. If abnormal operating conditions (such as piston ring problems) arise, the system is designed to allow excessive amounts of blow-by gases to flow back through the crankcase vent tube into the air cleaner to be consumed by normal combustion.

4   Checking of the system and replacement of the PCV valve is covered in Chapter 1.

3   Evaporative emissions control (EVAP) system

General description

Refer to illustration 3.5

1   This system is designed to trap and store fuel that evaporates from the fuel system that would normally enter the atmosphere in the form of hydrocarbon (HC) emissions.

2   The system is very simple and consists of a activated charcoal-filled canister, an expansion tank, connecting lines and fuel tank ventilating hoses. Later models may also have a valve (evaporative emission control valve) in the fuel tank vent line which retains vapor until it can be drawn into the canister when the engine is running.

3   When the engine is off and pressure begins to build up in the fuel tank (caused by fuel evaporation), the charcoal in the canister absorbs the fuel vapor. When the engine is started (cold), the charcoal continues to absorb and store fuel vapor. As the engine warms up, the stored fuel vapors are routed to the intake manifold or air cleaner and combustion chambers where they are burned during normal engine operation.

4   The canister is purged using air from the fuel tank gravity valve or the evaporative emission control valve which is controlled by vacuum from the ignition distributor vacuum advance.

5   The fuel tank gravity valve is located on the vehicle body to the right and above the fuel tank (On pick-up trucks, the valve is between the right

rear fender panel and the truck bed's inside panel, close to the fuel filler neck). The valve allows fuel tank fumes into the expansion tank and charcoal canister depending on the angle of the vehicle (**see illustration**). If the vehicle is inverted during an accident, the valve closes to prevent vapors from escaping.

6   All 1978 and later models are equipped with a cutoff valve between the charcoal canister and the engine's air cleaner. When the engine is not running, the cutoff valve is closed so that the vapors from the charcoal canister do not enter the engine. The valve helps to prevent evaporating fuel from entering the air and it also allows the engine to be timed without disconnecting the evaporative emission control hose from the air cleaner.

Checking

Canister, lines, hoses and fuel filler cap

Refer to illustrations 3.7a, 3.7b and 3.7c

7   Check the canister, hoses and lines for cracks and other damage (**see illustrations**).

8   To check the filler cap, look for a damaged or deformed gasket as described in Chapter 1.

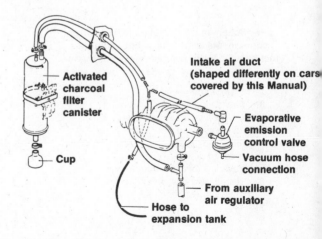

3.7a   Evaporative emission devices used on 1982 and later models

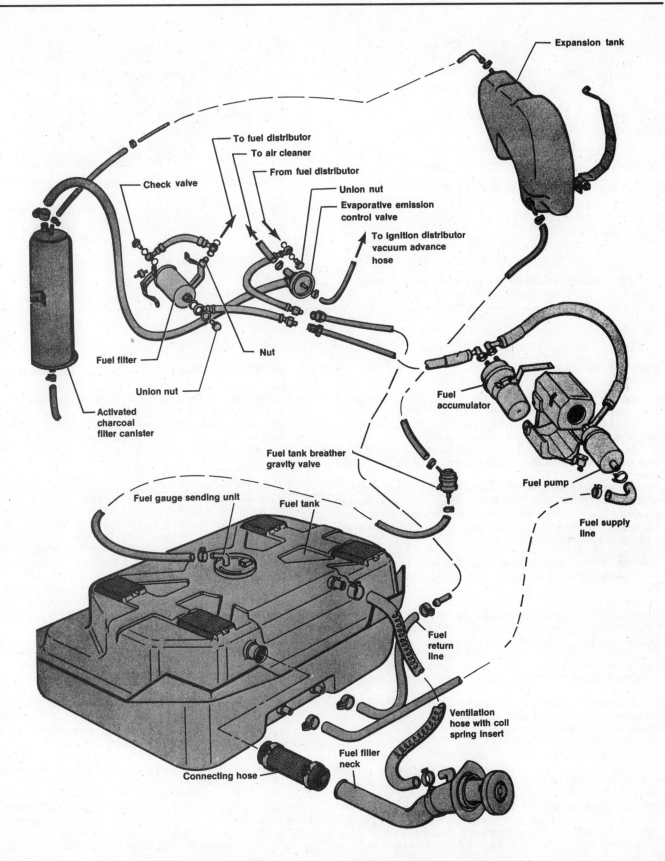

Expansion tank

To fuel distributor

To air cleaner

From fuel distributor

Check valve

Union nut

Evaporative emission control valve

To ignition distributor vacuum advance hose

Fuel filter

Nut

Union nut

Activated charcoal filter canister

Fuel accumulator

Fuel pump

Fuel supply line

Fuel tank breather gravity valve

Fuel gauge sending unit

Fuel tank

Fuel return line

Ventilation hose with coil spring insert

Connecting hose

Fuel filler neck

3.7b   Fuel tank and evaporative emissions devices – exploded view (pick-ups only)

6

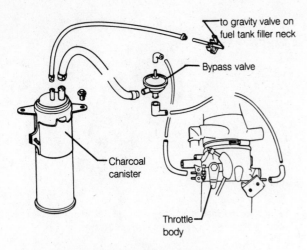

3.7c   Charcoal canister and bypass valve used with the Digifant II fuel-injection system

3.9 Gravity valve port locations

A   To expansion tank   C   To fuel separator
B   Blocked off

Fuel tank gravity valve

Refer to illustration 3.9

9   Remove the gravity valve and attach a hose to port A **(see illustration)**. Immerse the other end of the hose in a cup of water.
10   With the valve held vertically, blow into port C. If air bubbles do not appear in the water, then the valve is defective.
11   Continue to blow into port C and slowly tilt the valve. If bubbles do not stop when the valve is at a 45-degree angle, then the valve is defective and should be replaced.
12   Attach a hose to port C and immerse the other end of the hose in a cup of water. With the valve held vertically, blow into port A. If no bubbles appear in the water, then the valve is faulty. **Note:** *When installing the gravity valve, be sure to check the hoses for breaks, soft spots or deformed areas that might cause leaks.*

Carbon canister solenoid valves (CIS-E Motronic system)

13   The solenoid valves are on a bracket mounted on the airflow sensor housing.
14   The solenoid valve closest to the canister operates as a frequency valve: It pulses open and closed. It should hum or buzz as the Motronic unit varies the valve's "duty cycle" – the ratio of open time to closed time. This duty cycle ratio varies in accordance with the position of the airflow sensor plate and engine rpm.
15   Solenoid valve II has an on/off function: It opens when engine speed rises above 300 rpm and closes to seal the system when the engine isn't running.
16   To check either solenoid valve, unplug the electrical connector and the hoses and blow into the valve. With the ignition off, valve I (the gray one) should be open, and air should pass through. Valve II should be closed, and air shouldn't pass through.
17   If either valve fails to perform as described, it's faulty. Replace it
18   To check the control system, disconnect the hose from the solenoid valve closest to the canister. The engine must be cold (coolant temperature below 140 degrees F.) for this first part of the test. Check for vacuum at the valve connection. With the engine running at idle, the valve shouldn't be cycling and there shouldn't be any vacuum present. As the engine coolant temperature warms above 140 degrees F., there should be strong vacuum present at the valve connection for about 30 seconds, then the solenoid valve should begin cycling, reducing the apparent vacuum to little or zero.
19   If the control system doesn't appear to be operating properly, have the Motronic system checked by VW's special diagnostic test equipment at a dealer.

Component replacement
Canister

20   The canister is located in the engine compartment on later vehicles and behind the fuel tank on early models.
21   To replace the canister, disconnect the vacuum hoses, remove the mounting nuts and separate the canister from the bracket.
22   Installation is the reverse of removal.

Canister bypass valve – Digifant II system

Refer to illustrations 3.23 and 3.24

23   The canister bypass valve is located in the engine compartment near the charcoal canister. To test the bypass valve, disconnect the gravity vent valve line from the bypass valve line **(see illustration)**. Blow into the open port of the valve. It should be closed and not allow air into it.
24   Use a vacuum pump and apply vacuum to the small hose connection on the bypass valve **(see illustration)**. When vacuum is applied, the valve should be open and allow air to pass through.
25   The charcoal canister and bypass valve hose routing is different on vehicles with Digifant II **(see illustration 3.7c)**. The valve can be tested as described above.
26   Install all the hoses and brackets.

---

4   Thermostatically controlled air cleaner

Refer to illustrations 4.1 and 4.8

General description

1   The thermostatically controlled air cleaner system **(see illustration)** provides heated intake air during warm-up, then maintains the inlet air temperature within a 70 to 105-degree F operating range by mixing warm and cool air. This allows leaner fuel/air mixtures, which reduces emissions and improves driveability.
2   Two fresh air inlets – one warm and one cold – are used. The balance between the two is controlled by a thermostat. This bi-metallic element expands and contracts according to the temperature of the incoming air. In turn, the flap will open and close with a cold or warm engine temperature.
3   When the underhood temperature is cold, warm air radiating off the exhaust manifold is routed by a shroud which fits over the manifold up through a hot air inlet tube and into the air cleaner. This provides warm air for the carburetor or fuel-injection, resulting in better driveability and faster warm-up. As the temperature inside the air cleaner rises, the heat duct valve is gradually closed by the bi-metal temperature sensor inside the air

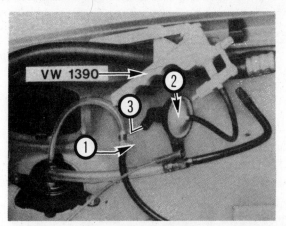

3.23   Typical EVAP system components

Charcoal canister
Canister mounting bolts
Line to gravity/vent valve

4   Line to intake manifold
5   Vacuum line to throttle body
6   Bypass valve

3.24   Detach the connector (1) from the charcoal canister bypass valve (2) and the testing port (3)

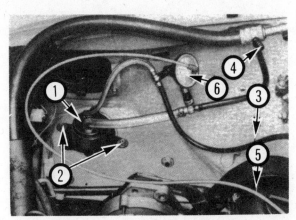

4.1   Thermostatically controlled air box – fuel-injected models

cleaner and the air cleaner draws air through a cold air duct instead. The result is a consistent intake air temperature.

Checking

Note: *Refer to Chapter 1 for the initial system check. If the system doesn't operate as described in Chapter 1, proceed as described below.*

Carbureted engines

4   Remove the top part of the air cleaner and remove the air filter element. Check and make sure the air flap is not loose or damaged.
5   The flap should seal the cold air opening when the temperature inside the air cleaner housing is below 86-degrees F. If the flap is sealing the warm air opening when the engine is cold, then replace the thermostat.

Fuel-injected engines

6   Loosen the clamps that hold the two air duct hoses to the connections on the control box **(see illustration 4.1)**.
7   Remove the screw that holds the control box to the body of the vehicle and remove the control box.
8   Be careful not to break the thermostat's mounting bracket inside the control box and press the thermostat toward the side of the control box **(see illustration)**. Remove the thermostat.
9   Place the thermostat in a pan of water with a thermometer and gradually heat the water. The thermostat should remain open at temperatures up to 68-degrees F. Above 93-degrees F the thermostat should close.
10   Installation of the thermostat and control box is the reverse of removal.

Component replacement

11   The thermostat inside the air cleaner (carbureted engines) or inside the control box (fuel-injected engines) can be replaced by first removing the housing.

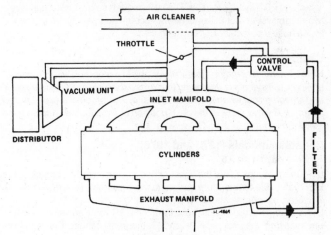

4.8   Remove the thermostat by pressing it toward the side of the control box (arrow)

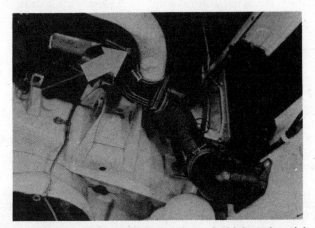

5.2   Typical EGR system components

12   Carefully remove the thermostat and replace it with a new unit.

5   Exhaust Gas Recirculation (EGR) system

General description

Refer to illustration 5.2

1   The EGR system reduces nitrogen oxide (NOx) emissions by recirculating exhaust gases into the incoming fuel/air mixture in the intake manifold.
2   The EGR system **(see illustration)** consists of an EGR valve, an EGR vacuum amplifier and an EGR temperature valve.

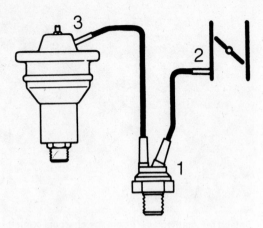

5.6   Single-stage EGR system (1975 and 1976 Canadian models)

1   *Temperature valve*   3   *EGR valve*
2   *Carburetor*

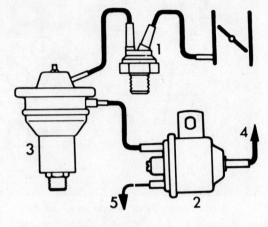

5.13   Two-stage EGR system used on 1975 US models

1   *Temperature valve*   4   *Vacuum line to brake*
2   *Two-way valve*   *servo vacuum*
3   *EGR valve*   5   *Electrical connection*

3   The vacuum operated exhaust gas recirculation valve operates to direct exhaust gas back into the intake manifold. The exhaust gas displaces a small volume of fuel/air mixture which results in lower combustion chamber temperatures and the reduction of certain harmful emissions.

4   The EGR temperature valve permits system operation only when the engine coolant temperature is above 142-degrees F. When the engine temperature is below normal operating temperature, the temperature valve prevents vacuum from reaching the EGR valve. This permits better driveability during the warm-up period.

5   Early carbureted engines are equipped with three different types of EGR systems. A single-stage system is used on 1975 and 1976 vehicles sold in Canada. On 1975 models sold in the USA (including California), a two-stage EGR system is used. The 1976 models sold in California have a two-stage system but utilize different vacuum sources. fuel-injected vehicles have a particular EGR system also.

Checking

Note: *The most common driveability problem associated with a malfunctioning EGR system is an engine that runs extremely rough at idle speed and smoothes out when speed is increased. This problem can be caused by an EGR valve stuck in the open position or a misrouted vacuum hose (allowing vacuum to the EGR valve at idle).*

Canadian models (1975 and 1976)

Refer to illustration 5.6

6   Check to make sure the vacuum hoses are correctly attached to the EGR valve, the temperature valve and the carburetor **(see illustration)**.

7   Start the engine and allow it to idle.

8   Disconnect the vacuum hose from the EGR valve and also the vacuum hose from the anti-backfire valve. Temporarily connect the hose from the anti-backfire valve to the EGR valve. The idle speed should drop, indicating the exhaust gases are being circulated.

9   If the idle speed does not drop during the test, check for: 1) a clogged EGR filter; 2) EGR line or fitting clogged in the exhaust manifold; 3) a faulty EGR valve. **Note:** *Clogged EGR valves can be cleaned out. Replace clogged EGR filters or lines.*

10   If the idle speed drops during the the test but the engine continues to run rough, test the temperature valve.

11   Remove the temperature valve and place it in a pan of water. Gradually heat the water and observe the valve. Below 110 to 120-degrees F the valve should be closed. Above these temperatures you should be able to blow through the open valve.

12   Replace any faulty valves

US models (1975)

Refer to illustrations 5.13, 5.15 and 5.19

13   Check to make sure the vacuum hoses are correctly attached to the EGR valve, the temperature valve, the two-way valve and the carburetor **(see illustration)**.

14   Start the engine and allow it to idle.

15   To check the EGR first stage, disconnect the hose from the top section **(see illustration)** of the EGR valve. Disconnect the hose from the anti-backfire valve and temporarily connect it to the EGR valve. The idle speed should drop, indicating the exhaust gases are recirculating.

16   If the idle speed does not drop, check for the following possible conditions: 1) EGR filter clogged; 2) EGR line or fitting in the exhaust manifold clogged; 3) faulty EGR valve.

17   If the idle speed drops during the test but the engine continues to run roughly, check the temperature valve as described in Step 11.

18   Replace a faulty temperature valve.

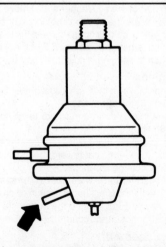

5.15   Connect the anti-backfire valve to the top section of the EGR valve (arrow)

5.19 Push the roller up (arrow) to activate the microswitch

19   To test the EGR second stage, operate the microswitch by pushing the roller up while the engine is idling **(see illustration)**. The idle speed should decrease considerably or the engine should stall.

20   If the engine does not idle down or stall and the EGR first stage is working correctly, then check the voltage at the microswitch and two-way valve. The two-way valve should click when battery voltage is applied. Replace a faulty switch.

US models (1976)
Refer to illustrations 5.21a and 5.21b

21   Check to make sure the hoses are correctly attached to the EGR system components **(see illustrations)**.

22   Start the engine and allow it to idle.

23   To check the EGR valve first stage, disconnect it from the top section **(see illustration 5.15)** and temporarily connect the vacuum hose from the anti-backfire valve directly to the EGR valve. The idle speed should drop, indicating exhaust gases are recirculating.

24   If the idle speed does not drop during the test, check for the following possible conditions: 1) EGR line or fitting in the exhaust manifold clogged; 2) EGR valve faulty or clogged.

25   If the idle speed drops but the engine continues to run roughly, test the temperature valve as described in Step 11. Replace a faulty temperature valve.

26   To test the EGR valve second stage, warm the engine up until the coolant temperature is above 120-degrees F and then operate the microswitch by raising the roller **(see illustration 5.19)**. Perform the procedure described in Step 19.

27   If the engine does not slow down or stall, the EGR first stage is working correctly and the temperature valve is not faulty, then check the microswitch voltage as described in Step 20.

Fuel-injected models except Digifant II
Refer to illustration 5.32

28   Make sure the vacuum connections and hoses are in good condition and tight.

29   Start the engine and warm it up until the temperature is 140-degrees F or higher. With the engine idling, make sure there are no leaks in the EGR feed line (the line that connects the exhaust manifold to the EGR valve).

30   Disconnect the vacuum hose from the EGR valve. Disconnect the vacuum retard hose from the distributor and temporarily connect it to the EGR valve. **Note:** *In order to obtain accurate readings, install a T-fitting in the vacuum hose to allow simultaneous vacuum to both the EGR valve and the distributor retard side.*

31   The engine idle speed should drop or the engine should stall with the test hoses properly routed. If the engine idle speed does not drop, then check for the following possible conditions: 1) EGR valve is clogged; 2) EGR feed line is clogged; 3) EGR valve is faulty.

32   If the idle speed drops during the test but the engine still runs roughly, test the temperature valve by installing a vacuum gauge between the EGR valve and the hose that goes to the EGR temperature control valve **(see illustration)**. With the engine at operating temperature, the gauge should read 2 to 4 in-Hg of vacuum. If not, replace the temperature valve.

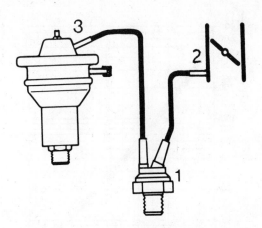

5.21a   Typical EGR system – US models except California

| 1 | Temperature valve | 3 | EGR valve (second |
| 2 | Carburetor | | stage is capped) |

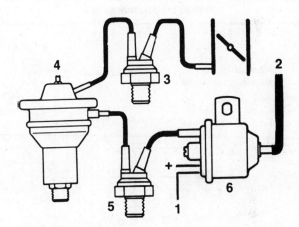

5.21b   Two-stage EGR system – California models

1   *Electrical connection to microswitch*
2   *Vacuum line to brake servo*
3   *First stage temperature valve*
4   *EGR valve*
5   *Second stage temperature valve*
6   *Two-way valve*

6

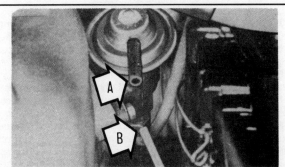

5.32   Connect a vacuum gauge between the EGR valve (A) and the vacuum line to the EGR temperature control valve (B)

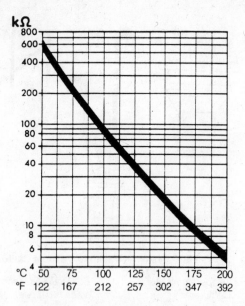

5.39   This graph shows the relationship between the resistance (expressed in ohms, on the vertical scale) and the temperature (expressed in degrees F. and C., on the horizontal scale) of the intake temperature sensor

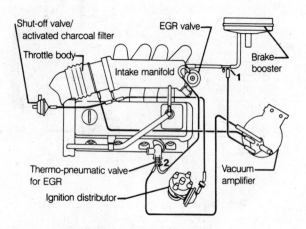

5.47   Remove the vacuum line port from the brake booster line (1) and connect the hose end directly to the thermo-pneumatic valve (2)

33   If the vacuum readings are correct, test the vacuum amplifier. Using a T-fitting, connect a vacuum gauge to the vacuum hose that extends from the amplifier to the throttle valve port. **Note:** *Be sure to use a T-fitting in the vacuum line to allow vacuum to flow to both the amplifier and the throttle valve.*

34   Start the engine and allow it to idle. The vacuum gauge should read 5 to 8 in-Hg. If it doesn't, clean the passage in the throttle valve port, which is most likely clogged.

35   If the vacuum is reaching the amplifier from the throttle port, connect the gauge between the amplifier and the temperature valve. Be sure to use a T-fitting with the vacuum gauge to allow vacuum to flow to both components. At idle, the gauge should read 2 to 4 in-Hg.

36   If the readings are incorrect, replace the vacuum amplifier with a new one.

5.38   Pinch off the idle speed boost valve vacuum line with a pair of locking pliers

California fuel-injected models

Refer to illustration 5.39

37   The EGR valve should open only under part-throttle vacuum. A rough idle may indicate that the valve is also opening at idle. On California models with 2.0L 16-valve engines (engine code 9A), the EGR system is monitored by the CIS-E Motronic control unit. The temperature in the intake manifold is measured by the intake temperature sensor as an indicator of EGR function. Problems with the temperature sensor or the EGR system are stored in the fault memory of the CIS-E Motronic control unit. Always begin troubleshooting by reading out the fault codes (see Section 11). These codes will help you determine which components in the Motronic system must be fixed or replaced.

38   If a Code 2411 is indicated, there's a problem with the temperature sensor, the EGR valve, the thermo-pneumatic valve or the vacuum amplifier.

39   Start the engine, check the resistance of the intake temperature sensor as the engine warms up and compare your readings with the accompanying graph **(see illustration)**.

40   If the indicated resistance doesn't fall within specification, first check the continuity of the wiring between the Motronic control unit and the sensor. If there's nothing wrong with the wiring, replace the sensor.

41   Test the EGR valve with the engine oil temperature above 122 degrees F. Make sure there are no leaks at the vacuum line connections and none of the lines are kinked or plugged. To check the valve, start the engine and let it idle. Detach the vacuum line between the EGR valve and the thermo-pneumatic valve at the thermo-pneumatic valve.

42   When vacuum is applied to the disconnected end of the line, the idle speed should become erratic. If it doesn't, remove the EGR valve and check for blockages in the holes in the exhaust and intake manifolds and in the EGR pipe itself. Clean out any buildup. If there aren't any blockages, replace the EGR valve (see Step 48).

43   To test the thermo-pneumatic valve, locate the two vacuum lines which connect it to the EGR valve and the vacuum amplifier. Detach both lines at the EGR valve and vacuum amplifier, respectively, and blow through one of them. If the engine coolant temperature is below 120 degrees F., air should flow through the valve. If it doesn't, try to determine if the vacuum line is blocked or damaged. If the lines are clear, replace the thermo-pneumatic valve (see Step 51).

44   To test the vacuum amplifier, hook up a hand vacuum gauge inline between the throttle body and the vacuum amplifier (the red line in illustration 5.41). Start the engine and let it idle. The vacuum gauge should indicate 1.945 to 3.590 in Hg. If it doesn't, check for damaged or plugged vacuum lines. If the lines are clear, replace the vacuum amplifier.

Digifant II models

Refer to illustrations 5.38 and 5.39

Caution: *Allow the engine to cool down before performing any work on the EGR system.*

45   The EGR valve should only open under part throttle vacuum. A rough idle may indicate the EGR valve is incorrectly opening at idle. Test the sys-

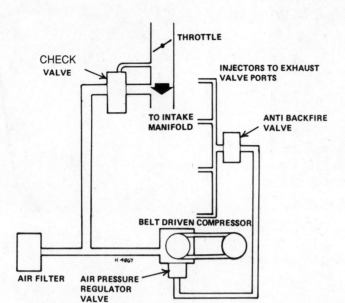

6.2   Typical air injection system components

tem by disconnecting the EGR line to the exhaust manifold at the bottom of the EGR valve and plug both ends to prevent any exhaust gases from leaking. If the idle smooths out, then the EGR valve is leaking and should be replaced.

46   Test the part throttle operation of the EGR valve for proper operation. Pinch off the hose leading from the idle speed boost valve to the throttle body with a pair of locking pliers **(see illustration)**.

47   Remove the vacuum line from the thermo-pneumatic valve **(see illustration)** and temporarily connect it directly to a vacuum port on the brake booster line. At normal operating temperature, the engine should idle roughly or stall. If not, disconnect the EGR line from the bottom of the EGR valve. If the engine idles roughly, then the line from the exhaust manifold to the EGR valve is clogged and the EGR valve is not faulty. If the engine still idles smoothly, then the EGR valve is defective and should be replaced with a new unit.

Component replacement

48   To replace the EGR valve, allow the engine to cool down. Disconnect the vacuum line and the EGR line to the exhaust manifold (if equipped). Remove the two mounting bolts and detach the EGR valve.

49   Install the new part with new gaskets and lubricate the threads with high-temperature anti-seize lubricant.

50   Install the EGR valve and reconnect the vacuum lines.

51   If you'r replacing the Thermo-Pneumatic valve, use a new sealing washer and coat the threads with sealant or Teflon tape. If any coolant leaks out when you remove the old valve, check the coolant level and refill as needed (see Chapter 1)

6   Air injection system/air suctionsystem (carburetor-equipped models)

Air injection system (1975 through 1979 models)
General description
Refer to illustration 6.2

1   This system supplies air under pressure to the exhaust ports to promote the combustion of unburned hydrocarbons and carbon monoxide before they're allowed to exit the exhaust. Air is directly injected into the exhaust ports by the air pump.

2   The air injection system consists of an air pump (driven by a belt from the crankshaft pulley), an anti-backfire valve and associated hoses and

6.6   Remove the hose from the anti-backfire valve and place your hand over the open connection (arrow)

check valves, which protect the system from hot exhaust gases **(see illustration)**.
General

3   Visually check the hoses, tubes and connections for cracks, loose fittings and separated parts. Use soapy water to locate a suspected leak.

4   Check the drivebelt condition and tension (Chapter 1).

Checking
Air pump

5   The air pump can only be checked using special equipment. Noise from the pump can be due to improper drivebelt tension, faulty relief or check valves, loose mounting bolts and leaking hoses or connections. If these conditions have been corrected and the pump still makes excessive noise, there's a good chance that it's faulty.

Anti-backfire valve
Refer to illustration 6.6

6   To check the anti-backfire valve, disconnect the air hose from the valve **(see illustration)**. Start the engine and allow it to establish full oil pressure.

7   Place your hand over the open connection on the valve. Run the engine at high RPM for a few seconds and then release the throttle quickly. You should feel vacuum at the anti-backfire valve for one to three seconds. If there is no vacuum and the hoses connected to the anti-backfire valve are neither clogged nor kinked, then the valve is faulty and must be replaced.

6

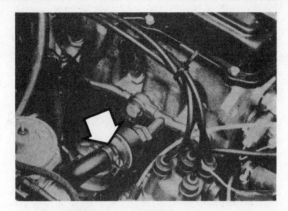

6.9   Remove the hose from the check valve

Check valve

8   Remove the hose from the inlet tube. If exhaust gas escapes past the inlet tube, the check valve is faulty and must be replaced.

Component replacement
Air pump

Refer to illustration 6.9

Caution: *Disconnect the cable from the negative terminal of the battery before removing the pump.*

9   Remove the air hoses from the pump, check valve **(see illustration)** and anti-backfire valve.

10   Loosen the pump pivot and adjustment bolts and remove the drivebelt.

11   Remove the bolts and detach the pump from the engine.

12   Compare the old pump to the new unit. Make sure they have the same part number on the ID label. Transfer the pulley from the old pump to the new one.

13   With the drivebelt over the air pump and crankshaft pulley, place the pump in position and loosely install the bolts.

14   Adjust the air pump drivebelt (see Chapter 1). Tighten the locking bolt, followed by the pivot bolt.

15   Tighten the air pump bracket bolts securely. Reconnect the hoses to the pump, anti-backfire valve and relief valve.

Anti-backfire valve

16   Disconnect the hoses from the anti-backfire valve, remove the two bolts and detach the valve from the housing.

17   Install the new valve. Tighten the bolts securely and reconnect the hoses.

Check valve

18   Disconnect the hose from the valve inlet and remove the nut securing the valve to the air injection tubes.

19   Attach the new valve to the air injection tubes and tighten the nut on the check valve. Connect the air hose.

Air suction system (1980 models)

General description

Refer to illustration 6.20

20   The air suction system draws air from the air cleaner to the exhaust system in order to reduce exhaust emissions. The air travels through a silencer past check valves into the cylinder head **(see illustration)**.

Checking

21   Faulty check valves will increase the exhaust emissions. Check the air suction system by inspecting the check valves for discolorization. If the valves blue, they are overheating because of backflowing exhaust gases and they should be replaced.

Component replacement

22   Make sure the engine is completely cool before removing any air suction system components. Apply penetrating oil to the fittings before trying to loosen them.

6.20   Air suction system

A   *Silencer*   B   *Check valves*

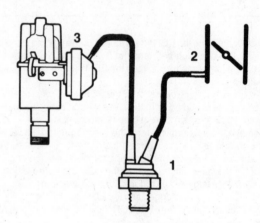

7.1   Schematic diagram of temperature-controlled vacuum advance system

2   *Carburetor*   1   *Temperature*
3   *Distributor*   *valve*

---

7   Temperature-controlled vacuum advance system

General description

Refer to illustration 7.1

1   This system is used on all carburetor-equipped vehicles except Canadian models with an automatic transaxle **(see illustration)**.

2   The temperature valve shuts off vacuum to the distributor if the coolant temperature is below 113-degrees F. At temperatures above 142-degrees F the valve is fully open, allowing vacuum to reach the vacuum advance unit on the distributor.

3   If the idle speed is too high during the warm-up phase, the temperature valve may not be closing properly at cold temperatures. If the valve fails to open at higher temperatures, the vehicle will experience hesitation and poor transition while trying to accelerate. Check the temperature valve if these conditions exist.

Checking

4   Remove the temperature valve and place the threaded end in a pan of water with a thermometer.

8.2   Disconnect the hose from the decel valve (arrow) and put your finger on the port

8.7 Loosen the decel valve locknut (arrow) and turn the fitting to make the adjustment

5   Heat the water and attach a piece of hose to the inlet side of the temperature valve. Blow through the valve and note the temperature of the water. The valve should not open until the water reaches a temperature between 131 and 141-degrees F.

6   If the valve opens at a lower or higher temperature, then it's faulty. Replace the temperature valve.

8   Decel valve (1975 through 1979 fuel-injected models)

General description

1   The decel (deceleration) valve (not used on Canadian vehicles with a manual transaxle), prevents a high vacuum from forming in the engine's intake air distributor during deceleration or when the throttle is closed. By limiting the vacuum, lower exhaust emissions are achieved. The decel valve is adjustable on Canadian and 49-state US models.

Checking

Refer to illustration 8.2

2   Disconnect the hose from the decel valve **(see illustration)**.

3   Start the engine and allow it to idle until full oil pressure has been established.

4   Increase the engine speed to approximately 3000 RPM for a few seconds and then allow the throttle to snap back to idle. Simultaneously, you should feel suction on the open connection of the decel valve **(see illustration 8.2)**.

5   If there isn't any suction during the test, then disconnect the main vacuum hose from the decel valve. Repeat the test. If there is vacuum pres-

ent, then adjust the decel valve (except California models) or replace it with a new unit specific with the state's requirements.

6   If you feel suction from the decel valve (Step 4), disconnect the vacuum hose from the T-fitting and cap the T-fitting. With the engine running at about 3000 RPM, there should not be any suction from the hose disconnected from the decel valve. If there is suction, adjust the valve or replace it with a new unit.

Decel valve adjustment (except California models)

Refer to illustration 8.7

7   Disconnect the vacuum line from the decel valve and loosen the locknut on the vacuum line connection **(see illustration)**.

8   From the factory set position, turn the vacuum line connection 1-1/2 to 2-turns clockwise (into the valve). Tighten the locknut and connect the vacuum hose. **Note:** *This adjustment is for reducing the delay for the engine returning to idle. If the adjustment has been tampered with, check the valve as described above.*

9   Oxygen sensor

1   The oxygen sensor works together with the catalytic converter to reduce the amount of exhaust gas pollution. The oxygen sensor emission control system (Lambda sensor) was installed in all 1981 and later US models (except pick-up trucks sold outside California) and all 1980 and later vehicles sold in California. This system requires a precise proportion of oxygen in the exhaust gases in order to function correctly, consequently reducing not only the amount of carbon monoxide and hydrocarbons in the exhaust but also the oxides of nitrogen. The system also improves fuel economy and eliminates obsolete emission controls that previously robbed power from the engine.

2   The oxygen sensor system, which relies on low-voltage signals, is sensitive to contamination and poor connections. Make sure all electrical contacts are clean and dry before making the decision to plunge into the following tests.

Replacement

3   Replacement of the oxygen sensor is a regularly scheduled maintenance item. The specified interval varies with the model and year (see the maintenance schedule in Chapter 1). On 1985 through 1987 models, which have a 30,000-mile service interval, a service reminder light on the instrument panel indicates that it's time to replace the sensor; after replacing the sensor, be sure to reset the mileage counter on the firewall to deactivate the light (see Section 44 in Chapter 1). There's no service reminder light on 1988 and later models, which have a 60,000 mile interval.

Testing oxygen sensor systems

Note: *Each type of fuel injection system has a different oxygen sensor system, so the following information is organized by fuel-injection type.*

CIS oxygen sensor system

4   The system has four main components: the oxygen sensor, the sensor control unit, the frequency valve and the thermoswitch. The oxygen sensor is located in the exhaust manifold, near the connection to the front exhaust pipe. The control unit, located on the firewall, monitors the signal from the oxygen sensor and controls the frequency valve. The frequency valve (or duty cycle valve), is mounted in a fuel line near the airflow sensor, just to the left (driver's side) of the mixture control unit. It opens and closes at a variable rate to fine tune fuel pressure and, therefore, the air/fuel mixture ratio. The thermoswitch, which is mounted on the coolant outlet of the cylinder head, interrupts the circuit and places the system in a stand-by mode when the engine coolant temperature is less than 82 degrees F.

5   The on-off action of the frequency valve, referred to as its "duty cycle," is the most direct indication of whether the system is operating correctly. To quick-check the system's function, listen for the hum of the frequency valve as it cycles on and off while the engine is running. At the dealer, duty cycle is measured with an expensive tool known as a duty cycle meter; at home, you can check the duty cycle with a dwell meter.

6

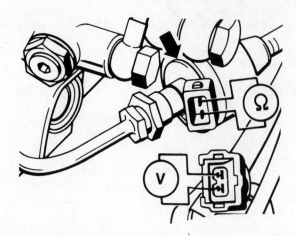

9.19   To check the frequency valve's windings, unplug the electrical connector and measure their resistance at the connector terminals with an ohmmeter – it should be 2 to 3 ohms; to verify that voltage is getting to the valve, check the voltage across the terminals while the fuel pump is operating (CIS systems)

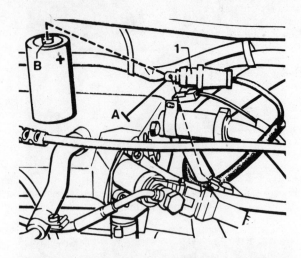

9.26   To check the control unit's mixture regulating function during its normal running mode, unplug the wires from the thermoswitch (don't jumper them), unplug the green wire from the oxygen sensor (1), ground it at (A), hook up a 1.5-volt "D" cell flashlight battery (B) and ground the negative end of the battery (CIS systems)

6   Before testing a CIS oxygen sensor system, make sure the idle speed and ignition timing are correct (see Chapter 1). Once you begin the following tests, don't alter the sequence in which they're presented below. Although it's possible to test individual components out of sequence, the results will be inconclusive if you don't know the status of the other components.

7   Besides the aforementioned dwell meter, the only other tools you'll need to perform the following tests are a multimeter and a set of jumper wires and, for the control unit, a 1.5-volt "D" size battery.
Note: *To test the frequency valve, you'll have to run the fuel pump without running the engine. See "Fuel pump relay check" in Section 2 of Chapter 4.*

Measuring the frequency valve duty cycle

8   The duty cycle, which is expressed as a percentage of time that the frequency valve is open, is the measurement of frequency valve function. The 90-degree scale of the dwell meter corresponds to the 100 percent scale of the professional duty cycle meter used by a dealer service department. For example, a duty cycle of 50 percent would be read as 45 degrees on a dwell meter. To connect the dwell meter, attach the positive lead to the duty cycle test connector in the engine compartment. Volkswagen sells a special adapter (VW special tool no. US1112, order no. TU1 112 000 00 HRN) to make these connections easier and more positive, but you don't have to use it. Connect the negative lead to ground. Set the meter to the four-cylinder scale.

Quick-checking the oxygen sensor system

9   Hook up a dwell meter as described above, start the engine and let it run for at least two minutes to warm up the oxygen sensor.

10   Remove the crankcase ventilation hose from the intake manifold and plug the manifold.

11   The duty cycle reading should drop and then fluctuate within a range of 25 to 65 percent (23 to 59 degrees on a dwell meter).

12   If the reading doesn't fluctuate, rev the engine several times. Now the reading should fluctuate.

13   Stop the engine and reattach the hose. If the reading is correct, test the system in the following sequence:

Checking the thermoswitch

14   The thermoswitch, which is mounted on the cylinder head coolant outlet, inhibits the oxygen sensor system when the engine is cold and the sensor signal is unstable. A faulty thermoswitch can also prevent proper operation at normal operating temperatures.

15   To check the thermoswitch, remove the wiring connectors and test for continuity between the two terminals on the switch. While coolant temperature is still 63 degrees F., there should be continuity (the switch should be closed); by the time the coolant reaches its normal operating temperature, there should be no continuity (the switch is open).

16   If the thermoswitch fails either test, replace it. If it passes both tests, proceed to the next test.

17   Let the engine cool off before you replace the thermoswitch. Use sealing compound and a new sealing washer on the new thermoswitch. If you lose any coolant when you remove the old switch, be sure to top up coolant reservoir.

Checking the frequency valve
Refer to illustration 9.19

18   To check the frequency valve, jump the fuel pump relay (see "Fuel pump relay check" in Section 2 of Chapter 4). On Golf models, you'll also have to turn on the ignition to operate the fuel pump. With the pump running, the frequency valve should make a repeated clicking or buzzing sound. If it does, remove the jumper wire, reinstall the relay and proceed to the next test.

19   If the frequency valve doesn't make a clicking or buzzing sound, unplug the electrical connector and measure the resistance of the valve's windings with an ohmmeter **(see illustration)**. The indicated resistance should be between 2 and 3 ohms. If it isn't, replace the frequency valve (see Step 21).

20   Verify that the valve is getting voltage by testing for voltage at the electrical connector **(see illustration 9.19)**. Again, operate the fuel pump by jumping the relay terminals. There should be voltage at one of the two connector terminals. If there isn't, the system wiring or the power supply relay or the control unit is faulty. Proceed to the next test.

21   To replace the frequency valve, clean and disconnect the fuel line banjo bolts, loosen the mounting clamp bolt and press the valve out of its rubber bushing in the clamp. Installation is the reverse of removal. Be sure to use new sealing washers when you reinstall the fuel line banjo bolts.
Warning: *Gasoline is extremely flammable, so take extra precautions when you work on any part of the fuel system.* Don't smoke or allow open flames or bare light bulbs near the work area and don't work in a garage

where a natural gas-type appliance (such as a water heater or clothes dryer) with a pilot light is present. If you spill any fuel on your skin, rinse it off immediately with soap and water. When you perform any kind of work on the fuel system, wear safety glasses and have a Class B-type fire extinguisher on hand.

Checking the oxygen sensor system control unit

Refer to illustration 9.26

22   The functionality and regulation of the control unit system is checked by measuring the duty cycle of the frequency valve with the fuel pump relay jumpered while simulating the thermoswitch and oxygen sensor signals to the control unit.

23   To check the cold start enrichment function of the control unit, unplug the electrical connector from the thermoswitch and bridge the terminals of the connector with a jumper wire.

24   With the fuel pump running and the ignition turned on, the duty cycle should be a constant 80 percent $\pm$ 2 percent (72 degrees $\pm$ 2 degrees on a dwell meter).

25   To check the control unit's stand-by or limp-home mode, remove the wires from the thermoswitch, but don't bridge them. Run the fuel pump and turn on the ignition. The duty cycle should be a constant 50 percent $\pm$ 2 percent (45 degrees $\pm$ 2 degrees on the dwell meter).

26   To check the control unit's mixture regulating function during its normal running mode, detach the wires from the thermoswitch, but don't bridge them. Unplug the green wire from the oxygen sensor and ground the green wire **(see illustration)**.

27   Run the fuel pump and turn on the ignition. The duty cycle should be over 87 percent (78 degrees on the dwell meter). Stop the fuel pump and turn off the ignition.

28   Finally, connect the green oxygen sensor wire to a 1.5 volt "D" cell flashlight battery with the negative end of the battery touching ground. Run the fuel pump and turn on the ignition. The duty cycle should be under 20 percent (18 degrees on the dwell meter).

29   If any of the above duty cycle readings are incorrect, either some part of the oxygen sensor system wiring is faulty, or the oxygen sensor control unit has failed. For help in troubleshooting the system wiring, refer to "Troubleshooting the oxygen sensor circuits" below.

30   After you've made any necessary repairs, repeat the above tests. If the indicated duty cycle readings are still incorrect, replace the control unit (refer to your owner's manual for information on the coverage provided by the extended emissions warranty – you may not have to pay for a new control unit).

31   Reattach the green oxygen sensor wire and the other wires to the thermoswitch and reinstall the fuel pump relay.

Checking the oxygen sensor

32   The functionality of the oxygen sensor can also be verified by measuring the duty cycle as described in the above tests. Before you can diagnose the oxygen sensor, the rest of the oxygen sensor system must first be checked in the sequence above.

33   Start the engine and let it run until it reaches its normal operating temperature. If it's already warm, run it for at least two minutes. Then, with the engine still running, remove the crankcase ventilation hose from its connection at the intake manifold. When the open port on the intake manifold is plugged, the duty cycle reading should drop. If it doesn't, the sensor is faulty. Replace it.

Replacing the oxygen sensor

See Chapter 1.

Troubleshooting the oxygen sensor circuits

34   If there's no obvious problem indicated by the above tests, check the system wiring and the power supply relay.

35   If there's no voltage reaching the electrical connector for the frequency valve, remove the fuel injection power supply (or Lambda) relay from the fuse panel under the left side of the dash and check for voltage from the battery to the relay when the fuel pump operates. Then check for continuity between the relay and the frequency valve. If there's voltage and continuity, the relay is bad. Replace it.

36   The control unit also receives voltage through the fuel injection power (or Lambda) relay. Unplug the electrical connector to the control unit and verify that voltage is reaching the connector from the relay when the fuel pump is running. There must also be continuity in the wires coming from the frequency valve, the thermoswitch, the control unit ground and the green oxygen sensor wire to the control unit connector. If any of the wiring is faulty, repair it and retest.

CIS – Electronic (CIS-E) oxygen sensor system

37   On the CIS-E fuel injection system, the oxygen sensor control unit operates not only the oxygen sensor system, but also numerous other systems. The signal from the oxygen sensor is but one of many inputs the control unit receives and processes to control the air/fuel mixture. For more information on the CIS-E fuel injection system, see Chapter 4.

Testing the oxygen sensor

38   Because of the way it's integrated with the fuel injection system and the oxygen sensor system, the basic measurement of fuel injection function – the differential pressure regulator current – is also used to evaluate oxygen sensor performance. See Chapter 4 for the procedure for measuring differential pressure regulator current.

39   Before beginning this test, make sure the engine is warmed up, the exhaust system is leak free and all electrical loads – fan, air conditioning, lights, etc. – are turned off. The following measurement is affected by these types of current draws.

40   Unplug the electrical connector from the differential pressure regulator. Hook up a multimeter or ammeter in accordance with the procedure in Chapter 4.

41   Detach the crankcase ventilation hose from the intake manifold and leave it unplugged. Remove the "T" connector from the intake air boot, turn it 90 degrees and insert the blank side (the side with the 1.5 mm restrictor hole) into the hole in the boot.

42   Start the engine and let it idle. After a couple of minutes, the meter reading should be fluctuating. If it isn't, raise the engine speed to about 3000 rpm and look again.

43   A fluctuating current reading indicates the oxygen sensor is operating correctly.

44   No fluctuation in the meter reading (differential pressure regulator current) indicates a problem. Either the control unit, the oxygen sensor or the wiring is faulty. Proceed to the next test.

45   Stop the engine. Reattach the hoses. Remove the test apparatus and plug in the electrical connector.

Checking control unit response

46   If the multimeter shows little or no fluctuation, check the control unit's response to a dramatic change in signal from the oxygen sensor: With the ignition off and the test apparatus for measuring differential pressure regulator current hooked up in accordance with the procedure in Chapter 4, unplug the electrical connector from the coolant temperature sensor and bridge the connector terminals.

47   Unplug the oxygen sensor lead, then turn on the ignition. The differential pressure regulator current should be 9 to 11 mA. Ground the connector for the oxygen sensor at the end of the green wire. After about 20 seconds, the current should increase to 19 to 20 mA.

48   If the indicated values are correct, the control unit is operating properly; if the differential pressure regulator current still doesn't fluctuate when tested as described above, either the oxygen sensor or its wire is faulty. Replace it.

49   If the indicated current doesn't increase to 19 or 20 mA when the oxygen sensor is grounded, turn off the ignition and check for continuity between the green oxygen sensor wire and terminal 8 of the connector for the control unit.

50   If there's no continuity the wiring between the oxygen sensor and the control unit is faulty. Repair it as necessary and test it again.

51   If there's continuity, but the control unit still isn't responding even when the oxygen sensor wire is grounded, the control unit itself is faulty. Replace it.

6

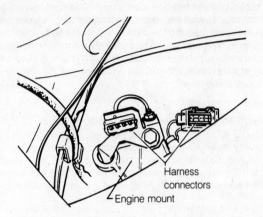

9.57   Unplug the oxygen sensor electrical connector (located on right engine mount) (CIS-E Motronic systems)

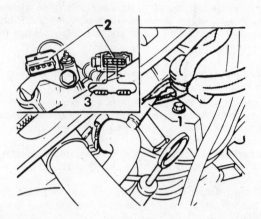

9.61   When you pinch off the crankcase breather hose (1) to test the oxygen sensor system, the indicated current should increase, which indicates the oxygen sensor is responding correctly to a rich condition – if the current doesn't increase, unplug the electrical connector (2) for the oxygen sensor, bridge terminals 2 and 4 for 20 seconds and note the indicated current again (CIS-E Motronic systems)

Replacing the oxygen sensor

See Chapter 1. **Note:** *On vehicles with engine codes HT, RD or PL, the oxygen sensor is located in front of the catalytic converter housing. On vehicles with engine code GX, the oxygen sensor is located in the exhaust manifold, just above the front exhaust pipe connection.*

CIS-E Motronic oxygen sensor system

52   On the CIS-E Motronic fuel injection system, the control unit operates the oxygen sensor system and all other functions. The signal from the oxygen sensor is one of many inputs the control unit uses to control the air/fuel mixture.

53   The CIS-E Motronic engine management system has electronic fault diagnosis for finding faults in the system during normal operation. Problems with the oxygen sensor or the control unit's response to the oxygen sensor signal are stored in the fault memory of the control unit. Always begin troubleshooting by reading out the fault codes (see Section 11). These codes will help you determine which component or function of the system needs to be checked.

Checking the oxygen sensor and control unit response

Refer to illustration 9.57

54   Because of the way it's integrated with the fuel injection system and the oxygen sensor system, the basic measurement of fuel injection function – the differential pressure regulator current – is also used to evaluate oxygen sensor performance. See Chapter 4 for the procedure for measuring differential pressure regulator current.

55   Because the operation of the fuel injection system and the oxygen sensor system are integrated, the basic tool for evaluating the functionality of the fuel injection system – differential pressure regulator current – is also used to determine whether the oxygen sensor system is performing correctly. See Chapter 4 for the procedure on measuring differential pressure regulator current.

56   Before beginning this test, make sure the engine is warmed up, the exhaust system is leak free and all electrical loads – fan, air conditioning, lights, etc. – are off. The following test is affected by these types of loads.

57   Oxygen sensor performance is affected by the operation of the heating element in the sensor. The heater ensures that the sensor is hot enough to generate voltage over a wide range of conditions. An oxygen sensor with a faulty heater might work well during normal driving conditions, while hot exhaust gases are flowing rapidly past it. But that same sensor might not operate as well at idle, when it can cool off. So before you test the response of the control unit, check the oxygen sensor heating function. Unplug the oxygen sensor electrical connector **(see illustration)**. Refer to the Wiring Diagrams at the end of Chapter 12 if you need help identifying the terminals. Check the voltage at the connector and check the resistance of the oxygen sensor heater. **Caution:** *Don't connect the oxygen sensor terminal to the heater terminal when you're doing these tests – this could damage the control unit.*

58   With the ignition turned on, there should be about 12 to 14 volts at the heater power terminal. If there isn't, turn off the ignition and check for continuity between the electrical connector terminal for heater power. If there isn't, turn off the ignition and check for continuity between the electrical connector and the ignition switch. Repair any breaks in the wiring. Heater resistance, checked between the correct terminal and ground, should be 3 to 15 ohms. If it isn't, replace the oxygen sensor.

59   To test the response of the control unit, unplug the electrical connector from the differential pressure regulator and hook up a multimeter or ammeter in accordance with the procedure for checking differential pressure regulator current outlined in Chapter 4.

60   Start the engine and let it idle for at least two minutes. Note the indicated current on the meter.

61   Clamp off the crankcase breather hose. The indicated current should decrease, indicating the oxygen sensor and oxygen sensor system are responding correctly to the rich condition.

62   If the indicated current doesn't increase, unplug the oxygen sensor electrical connector, bridge terminals 2 and 4 on the connector for about 20 seconds and note the indicated current again.

63   If the current now changes, replace the oxygen sensor.

64   If the current doesn't change, look for a break in the wiring between the oxygen sensor electrical connector and the Motronic control unit connector and fix it.

65   If the wiring is okay, replace the Motronic control unit. Refer to the provisions of the extended emissions warranty in your owner's manual before buying a control unit.

Replacing the oxygen sensor

See Chapter 1. **Note:** *On these models, the oxygen sensor is located in the front of the catalytic converter housing.*

Digifant II oxygen sensor system

66   On the Digifant II engine management system, the oxygen sensor provides one of the many inputs to the Digifant control unit. There's no way to actually measure the injector opening time – the basic adjustment for air/fuel mixture – at home, so you can't really verify or measure the operation of the oxygen sensor. In order to even indirectly evaluate sensor function, you would need a carbon monoxide (CO) meter. This equipment is far too expensive to make its purchase worthwhile for this procedure. We suggest you take a Digifant-equipped model to an authorized VW dealer for diagnosing the oxygen sensor system. But you can – and should, at regular scheduled intervals – replace the sensor yourself.

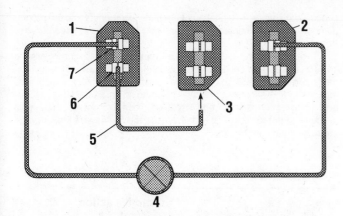

11.5   Here's how to bridge the terminals of the diagnostic connector with a jumper wire and an LED test light to output the fault codes on a CIS-E Motronic system (the connector is located under the shifter boot)

1	Black connector	5	Jumper wire
2	Blue connector	6	Negative terminal
3	White connector	7	Positive terminal
4	LED test light		

Replacing the oxygen sensor

See Chapter 1. **Note:** *On models with engine code PF, the oxygen sensor is located in front of the catalytic converter housing; on models with engine code RV, the sensor is located in the exhaust manifold, just above the front exhaust pipe connection.*

10   Catalytic converter

Note: *Because of a Federally-mandated extended warranty which covers emissions-related components such as the catalytic converter, check with a dealer service department before replacing the converter at your own expense.*

General description

1   The catalytic converter is an emission control device added to the exhaust system to reduce pollutants in the exhaust gas stream. There are two types of converters. The conventional oxidation catalyst reduces the levels of hydrocarbon (HC) and carbon monoxide (CO). The three-way catalyst lowers the levels of oxides of nitrogen (NOx) as well as hydrocarbons (HC) and carbon monoxide (CO).

Checking

2   The test equipment for a catalytic converter is expensive and highly sophisticated. If you suspect the converter is malfunctioning, take the vehicle to a dealer service department or authorized emissions inspection facility for diagnosis and repair.
3   Whenever the vehicle is raised for servicing of underbody components, check the converter for leaks, corrosion, dents and other damage. Check the welds/flange bolts that attach the front and rear ends of the converter to the exhaust system. If damage is discovered, the converter should be replaced.
4   Although catalytic converters don't break too often, they can become plugged. The easiest way to check for a restricted converter is to use a vacuum gauge to diagnose the effect of a blocked exhaust on intake vacuum.

    a) Open the throttle until the engine speed is about 2000 rpm.
    b) Release the throttle quickly.
    c) If there's no restriction, the gauge will quickly drop to not more than 2 in-Hg or more above its normal reading.

    d) If the gauge doesn't show 5 in-Hg or more above its normal reading, or seems to momentarily hover around its highest reading for a moment before it returns, the exhaust system, or the converter, is plugged (or an exhaust pipe is bent or dented, or the core inside the muffler has shifted).
5   Refer to the exhaust system servicing procedures in Chapter 4.

11   CIS-E Motronic engine management system – description and fault diagnosis

Description

The CIS-E Motronic engine management system is used on vehicles equipped with the 2.0L 16-valve engine (engine code 9A). The Motronic system combines the fuel control of the CIS-E fuel injection system with the control of ignition timing, idle speed and emissions into one control unit.

The fuel injection and idle speed control functions of CIS-E Motronic are similar to those used on the CIS-E system. But the Motronic system uses "adaptive circuitry" in its oxygen sensor system. Adaptive circuitry enables the oxygen sensor system to adjust the operating range of fuel metering in accordance with subtle changes in operating conditions caused by such things as normal engine wear, vacuum leaks, changes in altitude, etc.

CIS-E Motronic also has a fault diagnosis capability. The control unit constantly monitors all incoming voltage signals and compares them to the correct values stored in its "map." When a system component malfunctions, it sends the control unit an incorrect signal (higher or lower than its normal operating range), which triggers the automatic storage of a trouble code in the control unit's memory. This code can be outputted from the control unit as a series of electrical pulses on an LED test light. Always begin your diagnosis of a CIS-E Motronic system with these trouble codes (see Section 14). They'll tell you exactly where to look for problems.

Fault diagnosis

Refer to illustrations 11.5, 11.7a and 11.17b

The CIS-E Motronic engine management system can detect faults, store these faults in coded form in its memory and, when activated, display the codes. Each code corresponds to a specific component or function of the Motronic system which should be checked, repaired and/or replaced. When a code is stored on a California vehicle, the "Check" light on the dashboard is illuminated.

One way to access any stored trouble codes is to simply have your local VW dealer do it. The service department has an analyzer which plugs into a special diagnostic connector in the engine wiring harness, retrieves any code(s) stored in memory and displays it/them. The analyzer also checks the differential pressure regulator, the evaporative emission control system, the idle stabilizer valve and the cold-start valve.

Even if you're an avid do-it-yourselfer, Volkswagen strongly recommends that you always start with this electronic check at the dealership before attempting to troubleshoot a CIS-E Motronic system. And if your vehicle is still protected by the Federally-mandated extended warranty which covers all emissions-related components, you could void the warranty if you damage anything while trying to fix it yourself.

However, once the vehicle is no longer protected by the extended emissions warranty, you may wish to get at those codes yourself at home. You can do this by using the diagnostic connectors (located under the shifter boot) to activate the memory of the control unit, which displays any stored code(s) on an LED test light. Here's how to read the trouble codes on a CIS-E Motronic system

1   Make sure the air conditioning is switched off. Verify that fuses 15 (engine electronics), 18 (fuel pump, oxygen sensor) and 21 (interior lights) are good. Inspect the engine ground strap (located near the distributor). Make sure it's in good shape and making a good connection.
2   Test drive the car for at least five minutes. Make sure the engine speed exceeds 3000 rpm at least once, the accelerator is pressed all the way to the floor at least once and the engine reaches its normal operating temperature.

6

3   After the test drive, keep the engine running for at least two minutes before shutting it off.

4   Switch off the ignition.

5   Connect an LED test light to the diagnostic connectors **(see illustration)**.

6   Switch on the ignition.

7   Any stored fault codes are displayed by the LED as a sequence of flashes and pauses. For example, two flashes, a pause, one flash, a pause, two flashes, a pause and one flash indicates a code 2121, which means there's a problem in the idle switch circuit. A complete guide to the codes, their causes, the location of the faulty component and the recommended repair are contained in the accompanying table **(see illustrations)**.

8   To display the first code, connect a jumper wire as shown in illustration 14.5) for at least four seconds, then disconnect it. The LED will flash, indicating a four-digit code. To display the next code, connect the jumper wire for another four seconds, then detach it, and so on. Repeat this process until all stored codes have been displayed. Then connect the jumper wire for more than four seconds – this erases the permanent fault storage memory of the control unit.

Code	Location or description of fault	Probable cause	Corrective action
2141	Knock sensor I	a) Engine knock b) Fuel of incorrect octane c) Incorrect ignition timing damaged shield on knock sensor wiring d) damaged shield on knock sensor wiring	a) Check engine compression pressure (see Chapter 2) b) Confirm use of recommended fuel c) Check and correct ignition timing (see Chapter 1) d) Check wiring
2142	Knock sensor I	a) Open or short circuit in knock sensor wiring b) Faulty knock sensor c) Faulty control unit	a) Check wiring between knock sensor and control unit b) Check knock sensor (see Chapter 6) c) Replace control unit (see Chapter 6)
2144	Knock sensor II	a) Open or short circuit in knock sensor wiring b) Faulty knock sensor c) Faulty control unit	a) Check wiring between knock sensor and control unit b) Check knock sensor (See Chapter 6) c) Replace control unit (see Chapter 6)
2231	Idle speed stabilizer system has exceeded adaptive range	a) Throttle valve basic adjustment incorrect b) Incorrect ignition c) Evaporative emission control system faulty d) Intake air leaks	a) Correct throttle valve basic adjustment (see Section 26) b) Check and adjust ignition timing (see Chapter 1) c) Check carbon canister solenoid valves (see Chapter 6) d) Check and correct intake air leaks
2232	Air flow sensor potentiometer	a) Open circuit or short to ground b) Potentiometer faulty	a) Check wiring b) Check air flow sensor potentiometer (see Section 16)
2312	Coolant temperature sensor	a) Faulty sensor b) Open circuit or short to ground	a) Check sensor and replace if necessary (see Section 28) b) Check wiring
2341	Oxygen sensor control range exceeded	a) Idle mixture (%CO) incorrectly adjusted b) Faulty oxygen sensor wiring c) Leaking cold-start valve d) Evaporative emission control system faulty e) Intake air leaks	a) Check idle speed (see Chapter 1) check; idle b) Check wiring; check oxygen sensor control (See Chapter 6) check mixture (see your dealer c) Check cold-start valve (See Section 21) d) Check carbon canister solenoid valves (See Chapter 6) e) Check and correct intake air leaks
2342	Oxygen sensor system (faulty signal or exceeding adjustment range)	a) Open circuit b) Faulty oxygen sensor c) Incorrect idle speed d) Intake air leakse) Leaking cold-start valve	a) Check wiring b) Check oxygen sensor and control function (see Chapter 6)c) Check idle speed (see Chapter 1) idle speed stabilizer *(see Section 23) d) Check and correct intake air leaks e) Check cold-start valve (See Section 21)

11.7a   CIS-E Motronic fault diagnosis code table

2411	Exhaust Gas Recirculation (EGR) system (California cars only)	a) Intake air temperature sensor faulty b) Open circuit or short circuit to ground c) EGR system faulty or plugged	a) Check intake air temperature sensor (see Chapter 6) b) Check wiring c) Check EGR components (see Chapter 6)
4431	Idle stabilizer valve	a) Open circuit or short circuit to ground b) Control unit faulty	a) Check wiring; check idle stabilizer valve (See Section 23) b) Replace control unit (see Chapter 6)
Code	**Location or description of fault**	**Probable cause**	**Corrective action**
4444	No faults stored in memory		
1111	Control unit	a) Defective control unit	a) Replace control unit
1231	Speed sender	a) Open circuit b) Faulty sender	a) Check wiring b) Check speed sender
2112	Ignition reference sensor	a) Open circuit b) Faulty sensor	a) Check wiring b) Check ingnition reference sensor
2113	Hall sender	a) No signal or faulty signal from Hall sender	a) Check Hall sender (see your dealer)
2121	Idle switch	a) Open circuit or short to ground b) Switch faulty or misadjusted	a) Check wiring b) Check, and adjust idle switch (see Section 26)

11.7b   CIS-E Motronic fault diagnosis code table

12   Digifant II engine management system (California models only) – description and fault diagnosis

Description

1   Some vehicles equipped with the Digifant II engine management system and sold in California have control units with a fault diagnosis capability. This system indicates faults in the engine management system through a combination rocker switch/indicator light located to the right of the instrument cluster. **Note:** *Not all California models are equipped with a fault diagnosis system. Also, there are several variations among those so equipped. We recommend consulting with a VW dealer service department if you have any questions about the specific system used on your model.*

2   If it's operating properly, the light comes on briefly when you turn on the ignition. After a short period of driving, it also comes on to report any fault codes that might be stored in memory.

Fault diagnosis
Refer to illustration 12.3

3   To display any stored fault codes, turn on the ignition – but don't start the engine – and depress the rocker switch for at least four seconds. The indicator will display any stored fault codes in a series of flashes. For example, two flashes, followed by one flash, followed by four flashes, followed by two flashes, indicates the code 2-1-4-2, which means there's a problem with the knock sensor. The accompanying table **(see illustration)** lists all codes.

Flash code	Fault location	Probable causes
2142	Knock sensor	Bad knock sensor (see Chapter 5); knock sensor wiring (see Chapter 12)
2232	Air flow sensor potentiometer	Bad air flow sensor potentiometer (see Chapter 4); potentiometer wiring (see Chapter 12)
2312	Coolant temperature sensor	Bad coolant temperature sensor (see Chapter 4); temperature sensor wiring (see Chapter 12)
2322	Intake air temperature sensor	Bad intake air temperature sensor (see Chapter 4); sensor wiring (see Chapter 12)
2342	Oxygen sensor	Bad oxygen sensor (see Chapter 6); sensor wiring (see Chapter 12)
4444	No faults recorded	
0000	End of fault code sequence (2-1/2 second flashes at 2-1/2 second intervals)	

12.3   Digifant II diagnostic code table (California models)

6

4   To erase the fault code memory, make sure the ignition switch is turned off, unplug the coolant temperature sensor harness connector, depress and hold the rocker switch and, with the switch depressed, turn on the ignition. Keep t he switch depressed for at least five seconds, then turn off the ignition. Reconnect the coolant temperature sensor. Finally, test drive the vehicle for at least 10 minutes.

Chapter 7 Part A   Manual transaxle

Contents

Lubricant level check .... See Chapter 1
Lubricant change .... See Chapter 1
General information 1
Manual transaxle overhaul (four-speed) 6
Manual transaxle overhaul (five-speed) 7

Manual transaxle shift linkage – adjustment 3
Manual transaxle – removal and installation 5
Oil seal replacement 2
Transaxle mount – check and replacement 4

7A

Specifications

General

Lubricant type .... See Chapter 1

Shift linkage

Early 1975 models
  Shift rod length .... 6.41 to 6.5 in (163 to 165 mm)
  Bearing rod length .... 1.18 to 1.26 in (30 to 32 mm)
Late 1975 through 1984 models (shift finger-to-gate clearance)
  Four-speed .... 51/64 in (20 mm)
  Five-speed .... 19/32 in (15 mm)

Torque specifications   **Ft-lbs**

Inner driveaxle flange bolt 32
Front wheel hub nut .... See Chapter 8
Transaxle-to-engine bolt/nut
  1975 through 1984 59
  1985 on
    10 mm bolt 44
    12 mm bolt 55

Torque specifications

Ft-lbs

Four-speed transaxle only

End cover bolt	11
Housing bolt	18
Flywheel cover plate-to-bellhousing bolt	11
Mainshaft bearing retainer bolt	15
Selector shaft detent plunger locknut	15
Reverse shaft screw	14
Back-up light switch	22
Drain/fill plugs	15

Five-speed transaxle only

End cover bolt	11
Fifth gear retaining nut	108
Fifth gear lockout plunger locknut	15
Fifth gear clutch gear-to-mainshaft	111
Mainshaft bearing retainer bolt	11
Reverse shaft retaining screw	22
Pinion shaft retaining bolt	29

1   General information

The vehicles covered by this manual are equipped with either a four or five-speed manual transaxle or a three-speed automatic transaxle. Information on the manual transaxle is included in this Part of Chapter 7. Service procedures for the automatic transaxle are contained in Chapter 7, Part B.

The manual transaxle is a compact, two piece, lightweight aluminum-alloy housing containing both the transmission and differential assemblies.

2   Oil seal replacement

Refer to illustrations 2.4a, 2.4b, 2.7 and 2.11

Note: *A special tool is required to press the driveaxle flange into place.*

1   Oil leaks frequently occur due to deterioration of the driveaxle oil seals and the speedometer drive gear O-ring. Replacement of these seals is relatively easy, since the repairs can usually be performed without removing the transaxle from the vehicle.

2   The driveaxle oil seals are located at the sides of the transaxle, where the driveaxles are attached. If leakage at the seal is suspected, raise the vehicle and support it securely on jackstands. If the seal is leaking, lubricant will be found on the sides of the transaxle.

3   Refer to Chapter 8 and remove the driveaxles.

4   Pry the plastic dust cap out of the center of the driveaxle flange, then remove the circlip and washer **(see illustration)**. Use a puller to draw the driveaxle flange off the sidegear shaft **(see illustration)**. Carefully pry the oil seal out of the transaxle bore with a large screwdriver or a hooked pry bar.

5   If the oil seal cannot be removed with a screwdriver or pry bar, a special oil seal removal tool (available at auto parts stores) will be required.

6   Pack the open side of the new seal with multi-purpose grease and install it, using a large section of pipe or a large deep socket as a drift. Drive it into the bore squarely and make sure it's completely seated.

2.4a   Pry off the plastic cover for access to the circlip (arrow) that retains the flange

2.4b   A puller is required to draw the driveaxle flange off the sidegear shaft splines

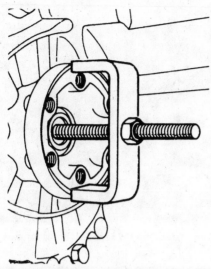

2.7 A special tool is also required to install and seat the driveaxle flanges

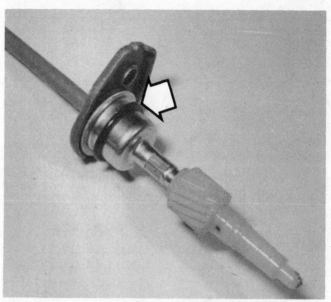

2.11 Insert a small screwdriver under the O-ring (arrow) to pry it out of the groove in the speedometer cable housing

7   If a groove is worn where it contacts the seal, the drive flange must be replaced with a new one. Install the drive flange, using the special tool threaded into the sidegear, then secure it with a new circlip and install the plastic cap **(see illustration)**.

8   Install the driveaxle(s).

9   The speedometer cable and driven gear housing is located on top of the transaxle housing. Look for lubricant around the cable housing to determine if the O-ring is leaking.

10   Remove the bolt and lift the speedometer cable out of the transaxle.

11   Use a small screwdriver to remove the O-ring seal **(see illustration)**.

12   Install a new O-ring on the driven gear housing and reinstall the speedometer cable assembly.

---

3   Manual transaxle shift linkage – adjustment

1   Several shift linkage adjustments are possible, depending on year and model. In addition, the selector shaft detent plunger and fifth gear lockout plunger can be adjusted.

Linkage adjustment

1975 models
Refer to illustrations 3.2a, 3.2b and 3.3

2   On early 1975 models with adjustable linkage, adjust the selector shift rod located over the left driveaxle to the specified length **(see illustration)**. Adjust the bearing rod to the specified length **(see illustration)**.

3   On all models, place the shift lever in Neutral and make sure the lower part of the lever is vertical **(see illustration)**. If it isn't, pull the shift boot up, loosen the nuts and bolts and adjust it until it is vertical.

1976 through 1984 models
(Rabbit from chassis number 175 3108 888, Scirocco from chassis number 536 2 000 001 and all Jetta models)
Refer to illustrations 3.4, 3.5, 3.6 and 3.7

4   Remove the shift boot and shift lever retaining bolts. With the shift lever in Neutral, make sure the holes in the lever bearing assembly line up with the threaded holes in the shift mechanism. The bolt holes must be

7A

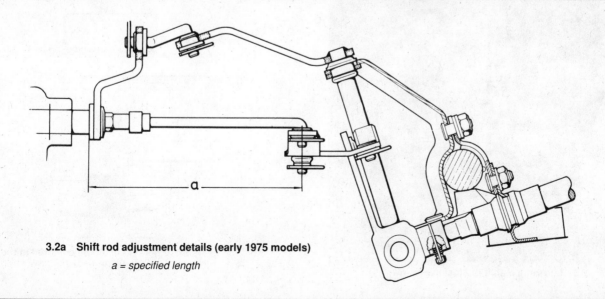

3.2a   Shift rod adjustment details (early 1975 models)

a = specified length

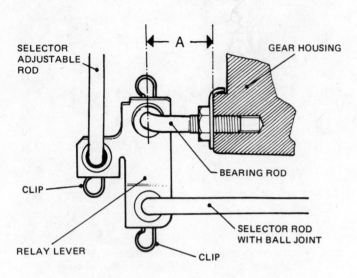

3.2b   Bearing rod adjustment details (early 1975 models)

3.3   The lower part of the 1975 model shift lever must be vertical

3.4   The shift lever lower assembly bolt holes (A) must line up with the corresponding holes and be centered in the slotted holes (B) of the bearing assembly

aligned with the round holes and be centered in the slotted holes **(see illustration)**. If the holes don't line up, turn the bearing assembly 180-degrees. Install the bolts and tighten them securely.

5   Raise the vehicle and support it securely on jackstands. Working under the vehicle, loosen the shift rod clamp locknut so the selector shift finger can move easily **(see illustration)**. On some four-speed models it will be necessary to pull the selector rod boot back out of the way for access.

6   Make sure the transaxle is in Neutral and slide the shift finger back-and-forth as necessary until it's centered in the stop plate **(see illustration)**.

7   Adjust the position of the shift finger to achieve the specified clear-

3.5   Loosen the shift rod locknut (arrow)

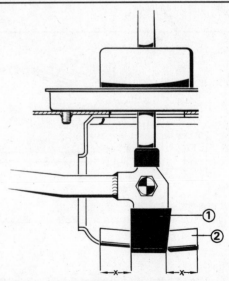

3.6   The gearshift finger (1) should be centered in the stop plate (2)

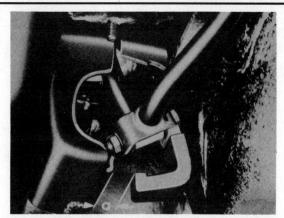

3.7 Adjust the shift lever finger to achieve the specified clearance to the gate (a)

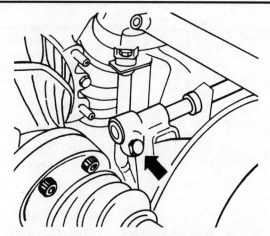

3.10 Shift linkage locknut (1985 and later models)

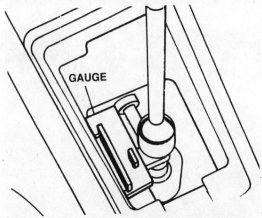

3.12 Insert an alignment gauge at the base of the shift lever to adjust the linkage

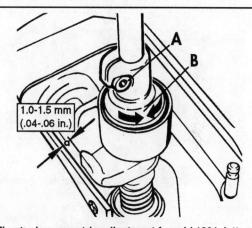

3.13 Fine tuning eccentric adjustment for mid 1991 Jetta and 1992 Golf and Jetta models

1.0-1.5 mm (.04-.06 in.)

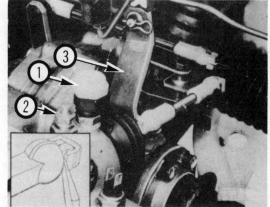

3.14 The selector shaft detent plunger (1) and the fifth gear lockout plunger (2) are located next to the shift lever (3) – the inset shows disconnecting the shift rod with a screwdriver

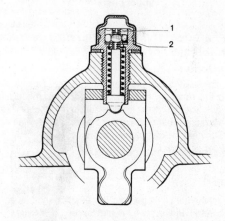

3.16 Turn the selector shaft detent plunger (1) until the nut (2) begins to move (1975 models)

ance between the end of the finger and the shift gate, then tighten the clamp nut securely **(see illustration)**.

1985 and later models

Refer to illustrations 3.10, 3.12 and 3.13

8   Place the shift lever in Neutral.

9   Unscrew the shift knob, detach the shift boot from the base, then pull the boot up and remove it from the lever.

10   Raise the vehicle and support it securely on jackstands. Working Under the vehicle, loosen the shift rod clamp bolt **(see illustration)**.

11   Insert an alignment gauge (VW tool number 3104) at the base of the shift lever.

12   On 1985 through 1991 models, tighten the shift rod clamp bolt securely **(see illustration)**.

13   On mid 1991 Jetta and 1992 Golf and Jetta models, shift the transmission into 1st gear. Push the lever to the left lightly and check the shift lever clearance **(see illustration)**. If necessary loosen the clamping screw (A) and rotate the eccentric (B) in either direction until correct adjustment if obtained. Tighten the screw securely.

7A

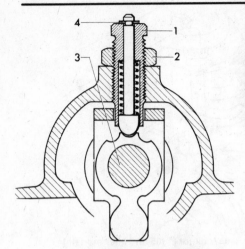

3.20   1976 and later model selector shaft detent plunger adjustment details – loosen the locknut and turn the adjusting sleeve

1   *Adjusting sleeve*
2   *Locknut*
3   *Selector shaft*
4   *Lockring*

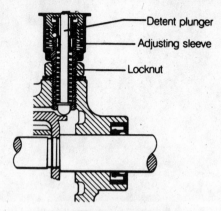

- Detent plunger
- Adjusting sleeve
- Locknut

3.25   Fifth gear lockout plunger adjustment details – loosen the locknut and tighten the adjusting sleeve until the detent plunger begins to move, then loosen the sleeve 1/3-turn

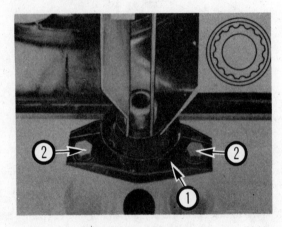

4.4a   Loosen the bolts (2) and move the mount (1) to position the rubber cushion

4.4b   The left side transaxle mount must be equidistant from the sides of the bracket

Selector shaft detent plunger and fifth gear lockout plunger adjustment

Refer to illustration 3.14

14   The selector shaft detent plunger and fifth gear lockout plunger, located on top of the transaxle, can be adjusted on most models if shift linkage adjustment doesn't cure spongy or binding shift action **(see illustration)**. On some later models the selector shaft is retained by a bolt and only the fifth gear lockout plunger is adjustable.

Selector shaft detent plunger adjustment

1975 models

Refer to illustration 3.16

15   Disconnect the shift linkage from the selector shaft lever, place the shift lever in Neutral and remove the plastic cap.
16   Rotate the slotted plunger until the plunger bottoms and the nut starts to move out **(see illustration)**.
17   Turn the plunger back 1/4-turn.
18   Install the plastic cap and connect the shift linkage.

1976 and later models

Refer to illustration 3.20

19   Disconnect the shift linkage and place the shift lever in Neutral.
20   Remove the cap and loosen the lockring. Rotate the adjusting sleeve (counterclockwise on four-speed transaxles; clockwise on five-speed transaxles) until the lockring lifts off the sleeve **(see illustration)**.
21   Turn the adjusting sleeve back until the lockring just contacts the sleeve, then tighten the locknut.
22   Turn the shaft slightly to make sure the lockring lifts as soon as the shaft moves.

23   Connect the shift linkage and install the cap.

Fifth gear lockout plunger adjustment

Refer to illustration 3.25

24   Place the shift lever in Neutral and remove the plastic cap.
25   Loosen the locknut and tighten the adjusting sleeve until the detent plunger in the center of the sleeve just begins to move up **(see illustration)**.
26   Loosen the adjusting sleeve 1/3-turn and tighten the locknut.
27   Check the operation of the shifter to make sure it shifts in and out of fifth gear smoothly and replace the plastic cap.

---

4   Transaxle mount – check and replacement

Refer to illustrations 4.4a, and 4.4b

1   Insert a large screwdriver or pry bar between the mount and the transaxle and pry up-and-down or back-and-forth.
2   The transaxle should not move very far away from the mount. If it does, replace the mount.
3   To replace a mount, support the transaxle with a jack, remove the through-bolt/nut and the mounting bolts and detach the mount. It may be necessary to lower the transaxle slightly to provide enough clearance to remove the mount.
4   Installation is the reverse of removal. The mounts must be installed so there is no binding or twisting of the rubber cushions, otherwise the shift linkage could be misaligned. Loosen the bolts and adjust the mount positions as necessary to center them **(see illustrations)**.

5.7   The lug or cutout on the flywheel must be aligned with the pointer on the bellhousing to allow separation of the engine from the transaxle

5   Manual transaxle – removal and installation

Refer to illustrations 5.7, 5.12 and 5.18

Removal

1   Disconnect the negative cable from the battery.
2   Raise the vehicle and support it securely on jackstands.
3   Drain the transaxle lubricant (Chapter 1).
4   Disconnect the shift and clutch linkage from the transaxle.
5   Detach the speedometer cable and wire harness connectors from the transaxle.
6   Remove the starter motor (see Chapter 5).
7   On some 1975 through 1978 four-speed models, you'll have to turn the crankshaft until the lug or depression on the flywheel lines up with the TDC mark **(see illustration)** so the flywheel cutout will be positioned properly to allow separation of the transaxle.
8   Remove the exhaust system components as necessary for clearance.
9   Support the engine. This can be done from above with an engine hoist, or by placing a jack (with a block of wood as an insulator) under the engine oil pan. The engine must remain supported at all times while the transaxle is out of the vehicle!
10   Remove any chassis or suspension components that will interfere with transaxle removal (Chapter 10).
11   Disconnect the driveaxles from the transaxle (Chapter 8).
12   Support the transaxle with a jack, then remove the bolts securing the transaxle to the engine. Remove the clutch cover plate bolts and the bolts from the small cover plate hidden behind the left driveaxle flange **(see illustration)**.
13   Remove the transaxle mount nuts and bolts. **Note:** *On 1985 and later models, remove the three top (hex head) bolts from the right rear engine mount. Remove the left rear transaxle mount center bolt, then detach the mount support from the transaxle by removing the two through-bolts and nuts.*
14   Make a final check that all wires and hoses have been disconnected from the transaxle, then carefully pull the transaxle and jack away from the engine.
15   Once the input shaft is clear, lower the transaxle and remove it from under the vehicle.
16   With the transaxle removed, the clutch components are now accessible and can be inspected. In most cases, new clutch components should be routinely installed when the transaxle is removed.

Installation

17   If removed, install the clutch components (Chapter 8.)
18   With the transaxle secured to the jack with a chain, raise it into position behind the engine, then carefully slide it forward, engaging the input shaft with the clutch plate hub splines. Make sure the flywheel is properly positioned to clear the driveaxle flange **(see illustration)**. Do not use excessive force to install the transaxle – if the input shaft does not slide into place, readjust the angle of the transaxle so it is level and/or turn the input shaft so the splines engage properly with the clutch plate hub.

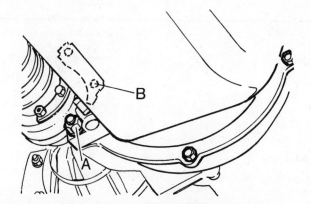

5.12   Remove the nuts from the the clutch cover (A) and the bolts from the cover plate (B), which is hidden

5.18   Make sure the cutout in the flywheel (arrow) is positioned so it will clear the driveaxle flange

19   Install the transaxle-to-engine bolts. Tighten the bolts securely.
20   Install the transaxle mount nuts or bolts. **Note:** *On 1985 and later models, loosen the engine mount through (center) bolts and leave the transaxle mount center bolt loose. Also, loosen the mount-to-chassis bolts. With the vehicle on the ground and the supports removed, shake the engine/transaxle assembly so it centers itself. Tighten the center bolts first, followed by the other mount bolts.*
21   Install the chassis and suspension components which were removed. Tighten all nuts and bolts securely.
22   Remove the jacks supporting the transaxle and engine.
23   Install the various items removed previously, referring to Chapter 8 for installation of the driveaxles and Chapter 4 for information regarding the exhaust system components.
24   Install the starter motor.
25   Make a final check that all wires, hoses, linkages and the speedometer cable have been connected and that the transaxle has been filled with lubricant to the proper level (Chapter 1).
26   Connect the negative battery cable. Road test the vehicle. Check for proper transaxle operation and look for leaks.

7A

6   Manual transaxle overhaul (four-speed)

Housing separation

Refer to illustrations 6.1, 6.4a, 6.4b, 6.4c, 6.4d, 6.5a, 6.5b, 6.6, 6.7a, 6.7b, 6.9a and 6.9b

1   Remove the clutch pushrod. Remove the four bolts securing the transaxle end cover plate and detach the cover plate **(see illustration)**.

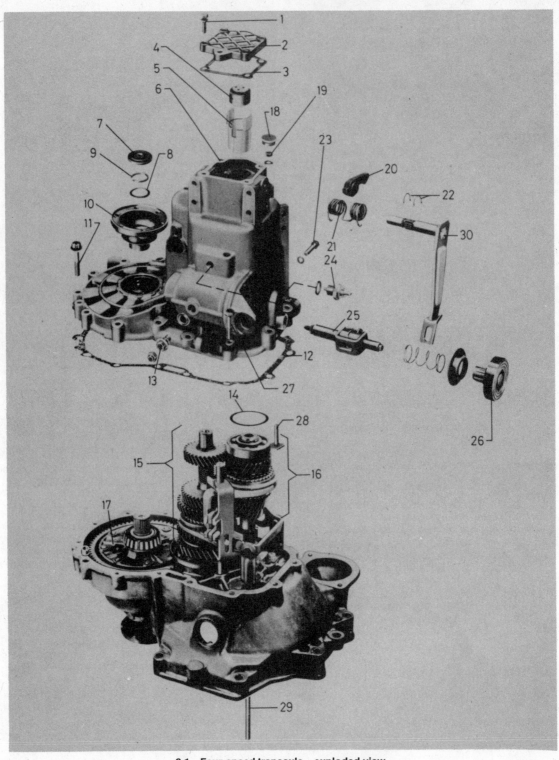

6.1   Four-speed transaxle – exploded view

1	Bolt	9	Circlip	16	Mainshaft	23	Bolt
2	Cover	10	Drive flange	17	Differential	24	Back-up light switch
3	Gasket	11	Bolt	18	Cap	25	Selector shaft
4	Clutch release bearing	12	Gasket	19	Nut	26	Selector shaft cover
5	Guide sleeve	13	Detent plunger	20	Clutch lever	27	Bolts
6	Main housing	14	Shim	21	Return spring	28	Clamp screw
7	Cap	15	Pinion shaft	22	Circlips	29	Clutch pushrod
8	Washer					30	Clutch release shaft

6.4a   Selector shaft detent plunger

6.4b   Unscrew the detent plunger, . . .

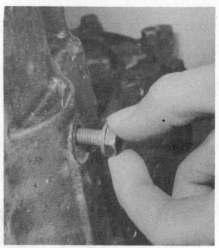
6.4c   . . . the gearshift lever lockbolt . . .

6.4d   . . . and the back-up light switch

6.5a   Use a spark plug socket (arrow) to remove the selector shaft cover

7A

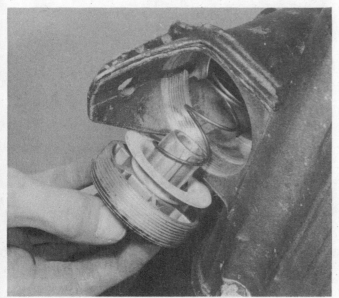
6.5b   Detent plug and spring

This will provide access to the clutch release mechanism. Lift out the clutch release bearing and sleeve.

2   There are two circlips; one on each side of the clutch release lever. Later models may have only one circlip. Remove them and slide the operating shaft out of the main housing, collecting the return spring and release lever as the shaft is withdrawn. Note that there is a master spline on the shaft and the release lever will fit on the shaft one way only.

3   Pry out the plastic cap from the center of the left-hand side drive flange and remove the circlip and spring washer. Withdraw the flange with a puller (see Section 2). There is no need to remove the opposite driveshaft flange.

4   Remove the selector shaft detent plunger or peg bolt and the lockbolt for the reverse gear shaft (see illustrations). Remove the back-up light switch (see illustration) or fuel consumption indicator switch.

5   Use a spark plug socket to remove the clutch selector shaft cover and lift off the spring seat, then remove the two detent springs (see illustration). Later transaxles have only one spring (see illustration).

6   Withdraw the selector shaft from the main housing (see illustration).

7   On the end of the main housing (where the clutch withdrawal mechanism is located) are two plastic caps. Pry them out and remove the nuts underneath them (see illustration). There is a third nut inside the hous-

6.6   Withdraw the selector shaft from the housing

6.7a   Pry the plastic caps out for access to the mainshaft bearing nuts

6.7b   The three mainshaft bearing clamp nuts

6.9a   Removing the main housing with VW tool no. 391

ing, from which the clutch release mechanism was removed, which must also be removed **(see illustration)**. These nuts must be removed in order for the mainshaft bearing to be pulled out of the housing without damage.

8   Remove the bolts securing the two housings together. On most models, twelve bolts are 8 x 50 millimeters long and two are 8 x 36 millimeters long – note where the shorter bolts are installed.

9   The housings are now ready for separation. Secure a puller such as VW tool 391 in the holes for the cover plate with two 7 mm bolts, then screw the center bolt down on the mainshaft until it just touches **(see illustration)**. Fasten a bar or piece of angle iron across the bellhousing to support the end of the mainshaft and then continue to tighten the center bolt of the puller until the housing is pulled away, leaving the mainshaft bearing complete on the mainshaft. Lift away the main housing **(see illustration)**. On top of the bearing there may be one or more shims; collect them and label them to ensure they will be reinstalled in the correct order. The needle bearing for the pinion shaft will remain in the main housing. It can be removed, if necessary, with a puller.

10   Extract the three clamp screws which retain the mainshaft bearing – otherwise they will drop into the transaxle as the housing is being removed. Remove the magnet from the gear carrier housing.

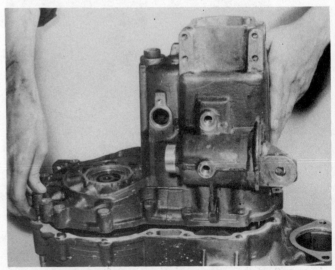

6.9b   After releasing the main housing from the gear carrier housing with the tool, separate the housings

6.11 Gear housing and gear assembly – exploded view

1	Stop bolt	10	Shift fork set
2	Circlip	11	Bearing plate
3	4th gear	12	Pinion shaft
4	Circlip	13	Differential
5	3rd gear	14	Circlips
6	Needle bearing and	15	Reverse selector
	2nd gear inner race		assembly
7	2nd gear	16	Reverse gear and
8	Bolt		shaft
9	Mainshaft	17	Housing

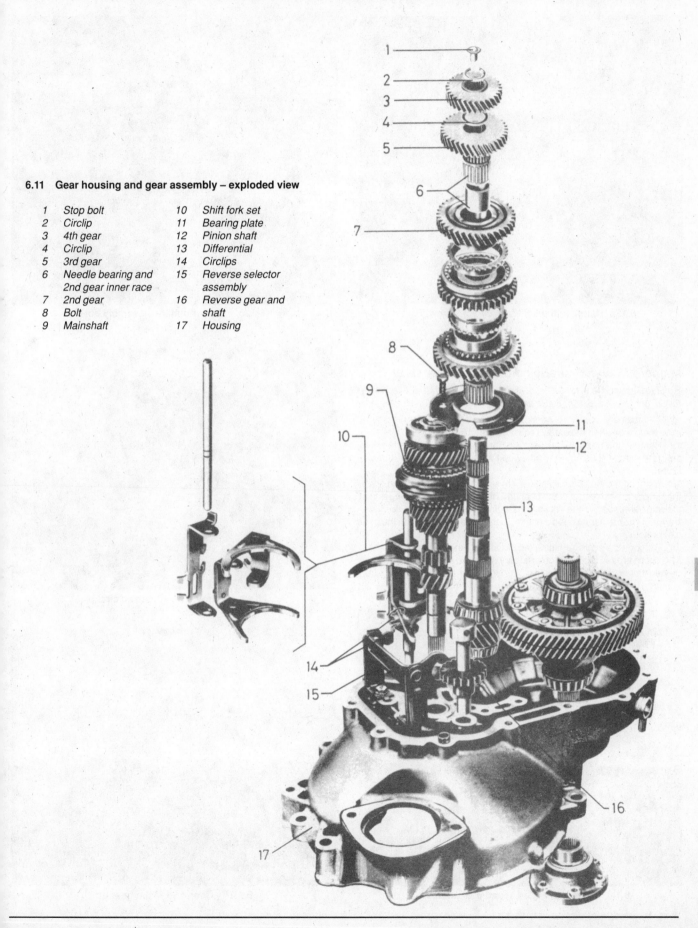

6.12a   Remove the shift fork circlip (arrow) . . .

6.12b   . . . and pull the assembly out

Mainshaft, pinion shaft and differential removal

Refer to illustrations 6.11, 6.12a, 6.12b, 6.13, 6.14a, 6.14b, 6.14c, 6.15a, 6.15b, 6.16, 6.18a, 6.18b, 6.19a and 6.19b

11   The mainshaft assembly can be removed after partially disassembling the pinion shaft assembly **(see illustration)**.

12   Remove the two shift fork shaft circlips and withdraw the shaft from the gear carrier housing, then lift away the shift fork set **(see illustrations)**.

13   Remove the circlip retaining the 4th speed gear on the pinion shaft, then lift the mainshaft out of the bearing in the gear carrier housing and at the same time remove the 4th speed gear from the pinion shaft **(see illustration)**. The mainshaft needle bearing and oil seal will remain in the gear carrier housing.

14   Remove the circlip retaining the 3rd speed gear on the pinion shaft. This circlip is used to adjust the axial play of the 3rd speed gear and must be reinstalled in the same position, so label it for identification at reassembly. Remove the 3rd speed gear **(see illustrations)**.

6.13   Remove the 4th speed circlip

6.14a   Remove the 3rd speed gear circlip . . .

6.14b   . . . and slide the gear off

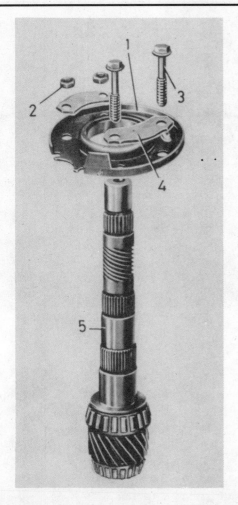

6.14c   Pinion shaft bearing plate details (1975 through early 1977 models)

1 *Bearing plate*	3 *Bolts (later models)*
2 *Nuts (early models)*	4 *Reinforcement plate*

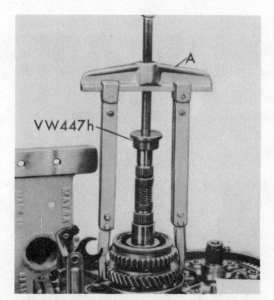

6.16   Use a puller (A) to remove the 1st gear from the pinion shaft

6.15a   2nd speed gear removal

6.15b   2nd gear needle bearing

7A

15   Remove the 2nd speed gear and then the needle bearing from the inner sleeve **(see illustrations)**.

16   Removal of the remaining gears requires a long puller **(see illustration)**. Before pulling off the synchro hub/sleeve and 1st speed gear, remove the reverse gear by tapping the reverse gear shaft out of its seat, then lift the shaft and gear away.

17   Remove the plastic stop button from the end of the pinion shaft and install the puller under the 1st speed gear. Note that the pinion shaft bearing retainer has two notches to accommodate the puller legs. Pull the gear and synchro hub off the shaft. Tape the synchro unit together to prevent it from coming apart.

18   Remove the needle bearing and thrust washer. Note that the flat side of the washer is facing the 1st speed gear **(see illustrations)**.

19   Remove the four nuts or bolts securing the pinion bearing retainer and lift of the retainer. Note that the retainer incorporates the reverse gear stop

6.18a   1st gear needle bearing location

6.18b   1st speed gear thrust washer

6.19a   Remove the bearing
retainer bolts . . .

6.19b   . . . and lift the retainer off

6.21   Driveaxle oil seal

on models manufactured from June 1975 on – previous to this the reverse
gear shaft incorporated a stop bushing. The pinion shaft is seated in a tapered roller bearing and can now be removed from the gear carrier housing **(see illustrations)**.

20   Remove the second drive flange as described in Section 2, then lift
the differential unit out of the gear carrier housing. Differential unit overhaul is not recommended.

Gear carrier housing overhaul

Refer to illustrations 6.21, 6.22 and 6.23

21   Clean the housing with solvent to remove all oil and sludge. Replace
both the oil seals **(see illustration)**. Fill the space between the lips of the
seals with multi-purpose grease before installation. The drive flange oil
seal must be driven in as far as it will go. The special VW tool (no. 194) can
be used, but a piece of pipe can also be used.

22   The mainshaft needle bearing may be removed, if necessary, with a
bearing extractor. Do not remove the bearing unless it is defective as it is
likely to be damaged during removal **(see illustration)**.

6.22   Mainshaft needle bearing

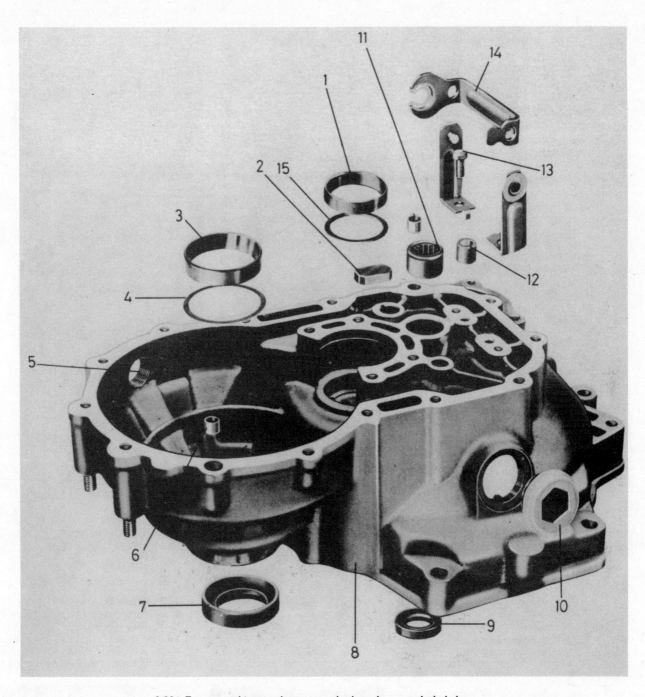

6.23 Four-speed transaxle gear carrier housing – exploded view

1	Pinion outer bearing	6	Dowel pin	11	Mainshaft needle bearing
2	Magnet	7	Drive flange oil seal	12	Starter bushing
3	Differential bearing outer race	8	Bearing housing	13	Bolt
4	Shim	9	Mainshaft oil seal	14	Reverse shift fork
5	Drain plug	10	TDC sender unit (early models)	15	Shim

23   If the outer races of the differential bearings **(see illustration)** are defective, take the housings and differential unit to a dealer service department or repair shop for replacement.

24   Check the starter motor shaft for movement in the starter bushing. If there is excessive movement, remove the bushing with a puller and install a new one.

Main housing overhaul

Refer to illustrations 6.25a, 6.25b, 6.25c, 6.25d, 6.26a, 6.26b and 6.26c

25   Three seals must be replaced: One for the clutch operating lever, one for the selector shaft and a large one for the drive flange **(see illustration)**. Pry out the old seals, noting which way they're installed. Fill the seal lips

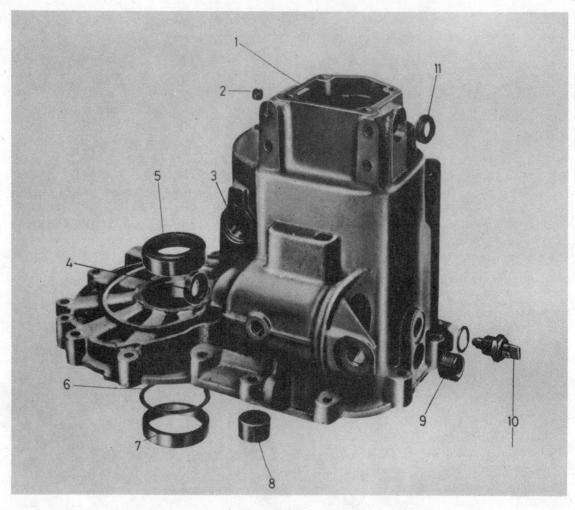

6.25a   Four-speed transaxle gear main housing – exploded view

1	Housing	5	Drive flange oil seal	8	Pinion shaft needle bearing
2	Oil level plug	6	Shim	9	Oil filler plug
3	Speedometer gear opening	7	Differential bearing outer race	10	Back-up light switch
4	Selector shaft oil seal			11	Clutch lever oil seal

6.25b   Clutch lever oil seal

6.25c   Selector shaft oil seal

6.25d   Drive flange oil seal

6.26a   Removing the pinion shaft needle bearing with an extractor tool (early model)

6.26b   Pinion shaft needle bearing

with multi-purpose grease and drive the new seals squarely into the housings with a large socket or piece of pipe and a hammer **(see illustrations)**.
26   On early models, the needle bearing for the pinion shaft is difficult to extract unless the correct tool is used **(see illustration)**. However, the shaft can be checked for fit in the bearing without having to remove the bearing **(see illustration)**. On later models, the bearing is retained with a self-tapping screw **(see illustration)**.
27   If the outer race of the final drive bearing is replaced, the complete unit must be taken to a dealer service department shop for setting up with the correct shims.

Pinion shaft bearing replacement

28   The large and small bearings accurately locate the pinion shaft gear with the ring gear of the differential. If either bearing is defective, then both of them must be replaced because in the removal process the bearings are destroyed. New ones have to be shrunk on and the shim under the smaller bearing changed for one of the correct size.
29   This operation is quite complicated and requires special equipment for preloading of the shaft and measurement of the torque required to rotate the new bearings. In addition, the shim at the top of the mainshaft and the axial play at the circlip of the 3rd speed gear on the pinion shaft will be affected. This will require selection of a new shim and circlip. There are six different circlip thicknesses. If the bearings require replacement, the unit should be taken to a dealer service department or a repair shop to have the job done.

Mainshaft disassembly and reassembly

Refer to illustrations 6.30, 6.31a, 6.31b, 6.33, 6.34a, 6.34b, 6.38a, 6.38b, 6.38c, 6.38d, 6.40a and 6.40b

30   Remove the ball-bearing retaining circlip and then, supporting the bearing under the inner race, press the shaft out of the inner race **(see illustration)**. VW tool no. 402 can be used to remove the bearing but a tool can be made from a piece of steel. During assembly, the bearing is pressed into the gear carrier housing and the shaft pressed into the race.
31   Remove the 4th speed gear and the needle bearing, together with the synchro ring **(see illustrations)**. On early models, a thrust washer is also installed, and the 4th gear and washer must be pressed off the shaft.
32   Remove the circlip, then support the 3rd speed gear and press the

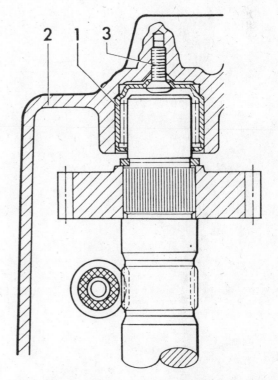

6.26c   Later model pinion shaft needle bearing details

1	*Needle bearing*	*3 Self-tapping screw*
2	*Main housing*	

mainshaft through the 3rd-4th synchro hub. Tape the synchro unit together to prevent it from coming apart.
33   Remove the needle bearing to complete the disassembly of the shaft **(see illustration)**.
34   If the clutch pushrod is loose in the mainshaft, the bushing can be driven out of the end of the shaft and a new bushing and oil seal installed.

7A

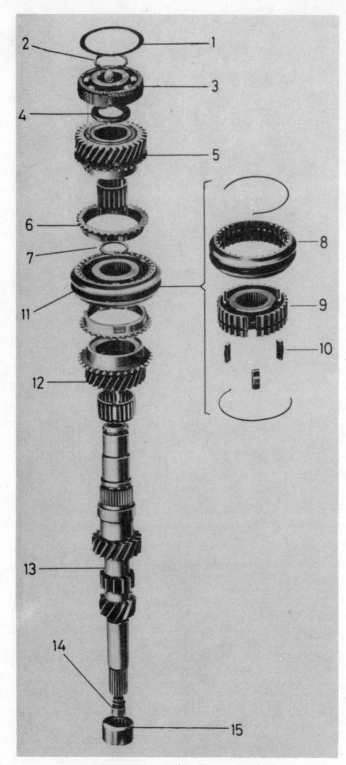

6.30   Mainshaft components – exploded view

1	Shim	8	Sleeve
2	Circlip	9	Hub
3	Ball bearing	10	Sliding key
4	Thrust washer (early model)	11	3rd-4th synchronizer
5	4th speed gear	12	3rd speed gear
6	4th speed gear baulk ring	13	Mainshaft
7	Circlip	14	Clutch pushrod bushing and seal
		15	Needle bearing

6.31a   Removing the 4th speed gear from the shaft

6.31b   4th speed gear needle bearing

6.33   3rd speed gear needle bearing

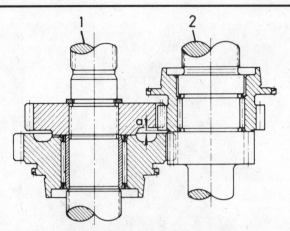

6.34a   Later model modified type clutch pushrod seal (A)
and bushing (B)

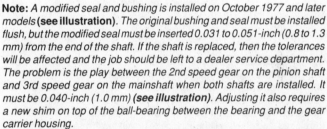

6.34b   2nd and 3rd gear clearance

1   Pinion shaft   a = 0.040-inch (1.0 mm)
2   Mainshaft

6.38a   3rd gear installation details

Note: *A modified seal and bushing is installed on October 1977 and later models* **(see illustration).** *The original bushing and seal must be installed flush, but the modified seal must be inserted 0.031 to 0.051-inch (0.8 to 1.3 mm) from the end of the shaft. If the shaft is replaced, then the tolerances will be affected and the job should be left to a dealer service department. The problem is the play between the 2nd speed gear on the pinion shaft and 3rd speed gear on the mainshaft when both shafts are installed. It must be 0.040-inch (1.0 mm)* **(see illustration).** *Adjusting it also requires a new shim on top of the ball-bearing between the bearing and the gear carrier housing.*

35   If gears on either shaft are to be replaced, then the mating gear on the other shaft must be replaced as well. They are supplied in pairs only.

36   The inspection of the synchro units is dealt with in Steps 41 through 45.

37   When reassembling the mainshaft, lightly oil all the parts.

38   Install the 3rd gear needle bearing and the 3rd speed gear **(see illustrations)**. Press on the 3rd-4th gear synchro hub and install the retaining circlip. When pressing on the synchro hub and sleeve, turn the rings so the keys and grooves line up. The chamfer on the inner splines of the hub must face 3rd gear **(see illustrations)**.

7A

6.38b   3rd gear baulk ring installation details

6.38c   Installing the 3rd-4th gear synchro assembly on
the mainshaft

6.38d   Make sure the 3rd-4th gear synchro hub circlip is securely installed

6.40a   Install the mainshaft bearing . . .

39 On early transaxles, install the thrust washer and 4th speed gear. Later transaxles have a ball-bearing with a wider inner race and the thrust washer is not used. If the old type bearing is being replaced with a new type, the 4th gear thrust washer must be left out.

40 The mainshaft ball-bearing should now be pressed into the main housing. Make sure the same shim(s) removed at disassembly are reinstalled between the bearing and the housing. The bearing is installed with the closed side of the ball-bearing cage facing the 4th speed gear. Insert the retainer bolts and tighten the retainer bolt nuts to the specified torque **(see illustrations)**. **Note:** *The endplay will have to be adjusted if either of the bearings, the thrust washer or mainshaft have been replaced, so the unit must be taken to a dealer service department.*

Synchronizer inspection

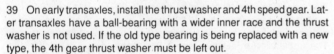

Refer to illustrations 6.41 and 6.44

41 The synchronizer unit hubs and sleeves are supplied as a matched set and must not be interchanged. Before disassembling them, mark the sleeve and hub in relation to each other **(see illustration)**.

42 When replacing the synchro baulk rings, also install new sliding keys and retaining springs.

43 When examining the synchros for wear, there are two important features to check:

  a) The fit of the splines. With the keys removed, the hub and sleeve should slide easily with minimum backlash or axial lock. The degree of permissible wear is difficult to specify – no movement at all is exceptional, yet excessive movement will affect operation and result in jumping out of gear. If in doubt consult a dealer service department.

  b) Selector fork grooves and selector forks should not exceed the maximum permissible clearance of 0.012-inch (0.3 mm). The wear can be either on the fork or in the groove, so try a new fork in the existing sleeve groove first to see if the clearance is reduced enough. If not, then a new synchro assembly is needed.

6.40b   . . . and the retainers, bolts and nuts

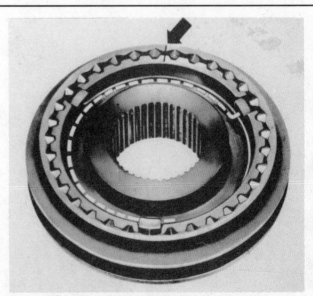

6.41   Mark the synchro hub and sleeve relationship before disassembling them

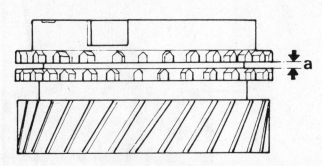

6.44   Check the synchro ring-to-gear gap ("a" must not be less than 0.020-inch [0.5 mm])

6.49   Install the pinion shaft in the housing with the gear meshed with the differential ring gear

Differential unit inspection

46   The major symptom of a faulty differential will be noise while the vehicle is moving. If the differential was extremely noisy prior to disassembling the transaxle or if inspection reveals excessive wear or damage, it should be replaced as a unit.

Differential, pinion shaft and mainshaft reassembly

Refer to illustrations 6.49, 6.50, 6.51a, 6.51b, 6.51c, 6.51d, 6.51e, 6.53a, 6.53b, 6.57a, 6.57b, 6.57c, 6.57d, 6.57e, 6.57f and 6.59

47   Remove the differential unit in the gear carrier housing. Using VW tool no. 391, install the drive flange in the gear carrier housing and install the spring washer, retaining circlip and cap.

48   Make sure the mainshaft ball-bearing is correctly installed in the main housing, plastic cage towards the housing, and the bearing retainer nuts are tightened securely.

49   Install the pinion shaft complete with the tapered bearings in the gear carrier housing so the pinion gear meshes with the differential ring gear **(see illustration)**.

6.50   Install the pinion shaft bearing retainer and bolts

44   The installation of the synchro ring on the gear is also important. Press the ring onto the gear and check the gap with feeler gauges **(see illustration)**.

45   When installing the springs, they must be curved in opposite directions and inserted in different sliding keys.

7A

6.51a   Install 1st gear, . . .

6.51b   . . . followed by the baulk ring, . . .

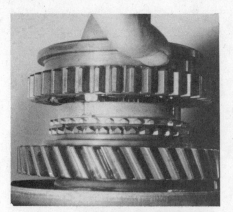

6.51c   . . . then line up the baulk ring slots with the sliding keys in the synchro assembly

6.51d   Install the 1st-2nd synchro

6.51e   Use a piece of pipe and a hammer to drive the assembly onto the pinion shaft

6.53a   The reverse idler gear and shaft alignment details – distance X must be equal

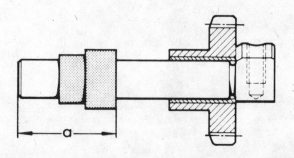

6.53b   Early model reverse idler ("a" = 1.61-inch [41 mm])

6.57a   Lower the mainshaft into position in the housing

50   Install the bearing retaining plate and the four bolts **(see illustration)**. Install the 1st speed gear thrust washer with the flat side up (facing the 1st gear). Install the needle roller cage.

51   Slide the 1st speed gear over the needle bearing. Heat the synchro hub a little and press it into position. The hub will slide on if heated to 250-degrees F (120-degrees C) and it can then be tapped into position. Make sure the cut-outs are in line with the shift keys in the 1st-2nd synchro to avoid damage to the baulk ring during reassembly. The shift fork groove in the operating sleeve should be nearer 2nd gear and the groove on the hub nearer 1st gear **(see illustrations)**. Install the 2nd gear synchro baulk ring.

52   The inner race for the 2nd speed gear needle bearing must be installed next and pressed down as far as it will go.

53   Install the reverse idler gear and shaft with the shaft aligned as shown in the accompanying illustration. Use a soft-face hammer to drive the shaft into the housing. Make sure the stop bush is positioned correctly on early models **(see illustration)**.

54   Install the 2nd speed gear needle bearing on the pinion shaft and the 2nd gear with the shoulder down.

55   Heat the 3rd speed gear and press it down over the splines with the collar thrust face towards the 2nd gear.

56   Install the 3rd gear retaining circlip and measure the play between the gear and the circlip with feeler gauges. It must be less than 0.008-inch 0.20 mm). If it's more, a thicker circlip must be installed. The following table gives the sizes available:

Part no.	Thickness (mm)	Thickness (inches)	Color
020 311 381	2.5	0.098	brown
020 311 381 A	2.6	0.102	black
020 311 381 B	2.7	0.106	bright
020 311 381 C	2.8	0.110	copper
020 311 381 D	2.9	0.114	brass
020 311 381 E	3.0	0.118	blue

57   At this stage the mainshaft must be installed in position on the gear carrier housing **(see illustration)**. Slide it into the needle bearing in the

6.57b   Install the shift fork assembly, . . .

6.57c   . . . then slide the shift fork shaft into place

6.57d   Reverse shift fork pivot post
installation details

6.57e   Reverse shift fork assembly
installation details

6.57f   Reverse shift fork located on the
reverse idler gear

7A

6.59   Gear carrier housing and shafts ready for installation of the
main housing (note the new gasket in position)

housing and install the shift forks in the operating sleeves **(see illustra-tions)**. Insert the retaining circlips. Install the reverse gear shift fork **(see illustration)**.

58   Install the 4th speed gear and the retaining circlip on the pinion shaft. Finally, inspect the stop button (where installed) for the pinion shaft needle bearing in the end of the pinion shaft.

59   The gear carrier housing and shafts are now ready for the assembly of the main housing **(see illustration)**.

Housing reassembly

Refer to illustrations 6.63a and 6.63b

60   Make sure the reverse gear shaft is in the correct position (see illus-tration 6.53a) and set the gears in Neutral. Install a new gasket on the gear carrier housing flange.

61   Lower the main housing over the gears, checking that the pinion shaft is aligned with the pinion shaft needle bearing in the housing. Drive the mainshaft into the bearing, using a piece of pipe on the inner race. Make sure the mainshaft is supported on a block of wood when driving it into the bearing.

62   Insert the 14 bolts which secure the two housings together and tighten them to the specified torque in a criss-cross pattern.

63   Install the circlip over the end of the mainshaft, working through the release bearing hole. Insert the clutch pushrod into the mainshaft. Make sure the circlip is properly seated, then install the clutch release bearing and sleeve assembly **(see illustrations)**.

6.63a   Make sure the circlip (arrow) is seated

6.63b   Insert the clutch pushrod into the mainshaft

64   Install the clutch release shaft and lever. Make sure the spring is hooked over the lever in the center and the angled ends rest against the housing. The shaft can be inserted into the lever in one position only. Install the two circlips, one on each side of the lever.
65   Install the clutch release sleeve and bearing.
66   Position a new gasket on the end of the housing and install the end cover plate and bolts. Tighten the bolts to the specified torque.
67   Lubricate the selector shaft and insert it into the housing. When it's in position, install the spring(s) and screw in the shaft cover with a spark plug wrench. Tighten it to the specified torque.
68   Install the selector shaft detent plunger (or peg bolt). This has a plastic cap. If the housing, selector shaft or plunger were replaced, adjust the plunger (Section 3).

7   Manual transaxle overhaul (five-speed)

Housing separation

Refer to illustrations 7.2 and 7.14

1   Remove the clutch pushrod from the mainshaft.
2   Unbolt and remove the end cover from the main housing. Remove the gasket **(see illustration on next page)**.
3   Remove the selector shaft detent plug or peg bolt, the 5th gear retaining screw and the back-up light switch or fuel consumption indicator switch.
4   Using a spark plug socket, unscrew the selector shaft and cap and remove the spring.
5   Engage neutral and withdraw the selector shaft. If difficulty is experienced, extract the circlip and drive out the shaft. However, this may cause damage to the shaft components.
6   Unscrew the reverse gear shaft lockbolt.
7   Pry the plastic cap out of the center of the left-hand side drive flange, remove the circlip and washer and withdraw the flange with a puller (Section 2).
8   Engage 5th and reverse gears by removing the selector forks, then unscrew the 5th gear synchronizer retaining nut using a 12 mm Allen wrench. The bolt is very tight and an assistant will be required to hold the main housing.
9   Engage neutral, then unscrew the sleeve or pry out the locking plate from the end of the shift fork rod.
10   Unscrew the selector tube counterclockwise from the 5th gear selector fork, but don't remove the selector rod.
11   Withdraw the 5th gear, together with the synchronizer and selector fork, from the mainshaft.

12   Extract the circlip from the end of the pinion shaft, then remove the 5th gear with a puller.
13   Using a 5 mm Allen wrench, unscrew the bolts securing the mainshaft bearing retaining plate.
14   Unscrew the bolts attaching the main housing to the gear carrier housing, then use a puller to draw the main housing off the mainshaft bearing **(see illustration)**. Refer to Section 6, Step 9 for alternative methods of separating the housings. Recover the shim located against the bearing outer race. Remove the gasket and the magnet from the gear carrier housing.

Mainshaft, pinion shaft and differential removal

Refer to illustration 7.16

15   Pull the selector fork rod out of the gear carrier housing and withdraw the fork set to the side.
16   Extract the circlip from the end of the pinion shaft, then remove the mainshaft assembly from the gear carrier housing while removing the 4th gear from the pinion shaft **(see illustration on page 217)**.

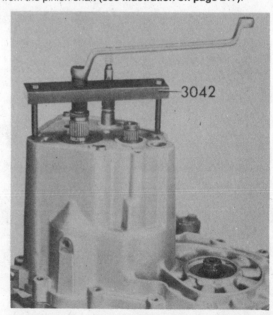

7.14   Separating the main housing from the gear carrier housing

7.2 Five-speed transaxle – exploded view

1   Cover
2   Gasket
3   Screw
4   5th gear shift fork
5   5th gear synchronizer
6   Spacer sleeve (early models)
7   Baulk ring
8   Lock plate (later models)
9   5th speed gear
10 Circlip
11 Needle bearing
12 Thrust washer
13 5th speed gear
14 Cap
15 Circlip
16 Dished washer
17 Main housing
18 Selector shaft
19 Spring
20 End cap
21 Drive flange
22 Bolt
23 Back-up light switch
24 5th gear retaining screw
25 Selector shaft retaining screw
26 Shim
27 Gasket
28 Gear assemblies
29 Clutch pushrod

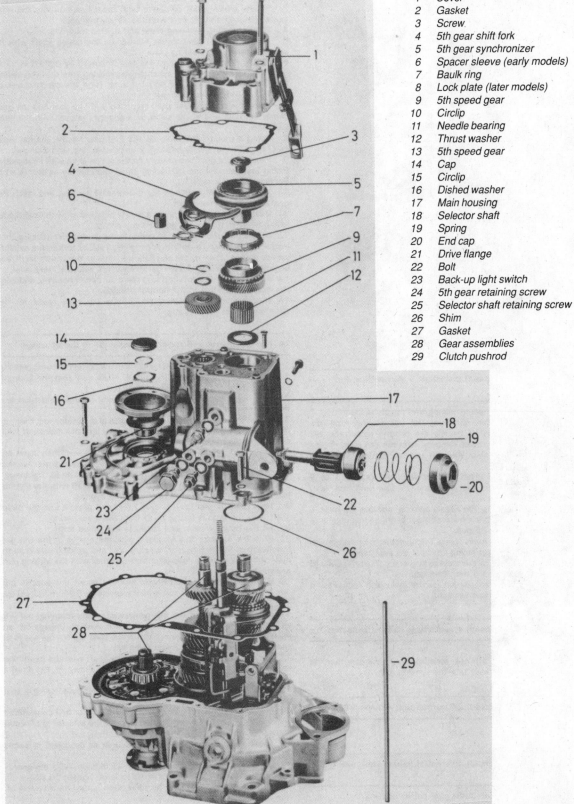

7A

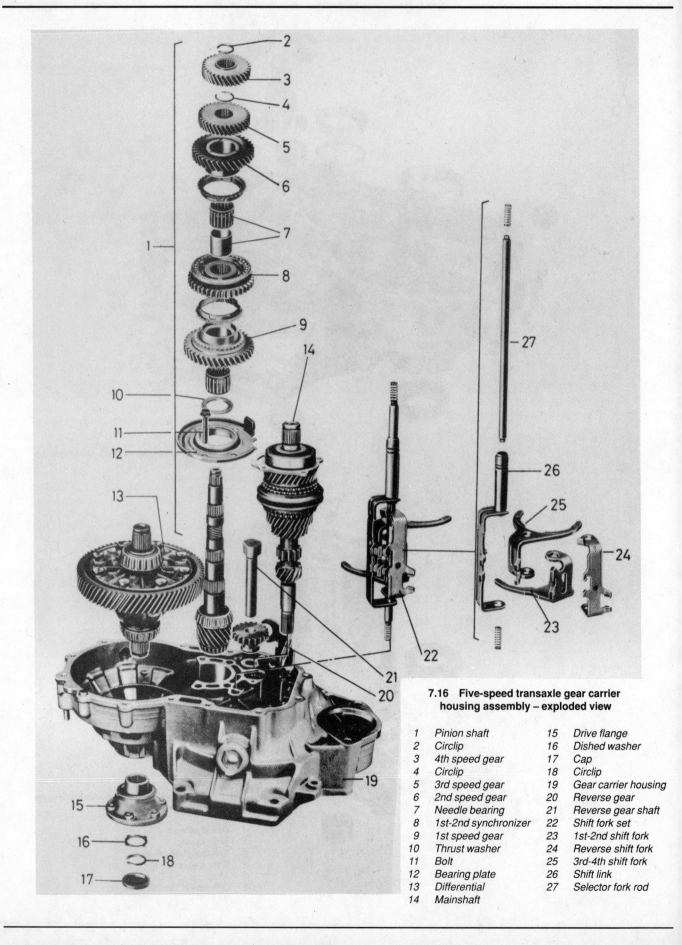

7.16   Five-speed transaxle gear carrier housing assembly – exploded view

1	Pinion shaft	15	Drive flange
2	Circlip	16	Dished washer
3	4th speed gear	17	Cap
4	Circlip	18	Circlip
5	3rd speed gear	19	Gear carrier housing
6	2nd speed gear	20	Reverse gear
7	Needle bearing	21	Reverse gear shaft
8	1st-2nd synchronizer	22	Shift fork set
9	1st speed gear	23	1st-2nd shift fork
10	Thrust washer	24	Reverse shift fork
11	Bolt	25	3rd-4th shift fork
12	Bearing plate	26	Shift link
13	Differential	27	Selector fork rod
14	Mainshaft		

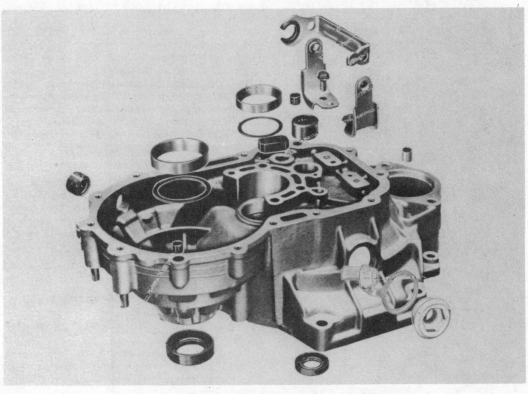

7.22a   Five-speed transaxle gear cover housing – exploded view

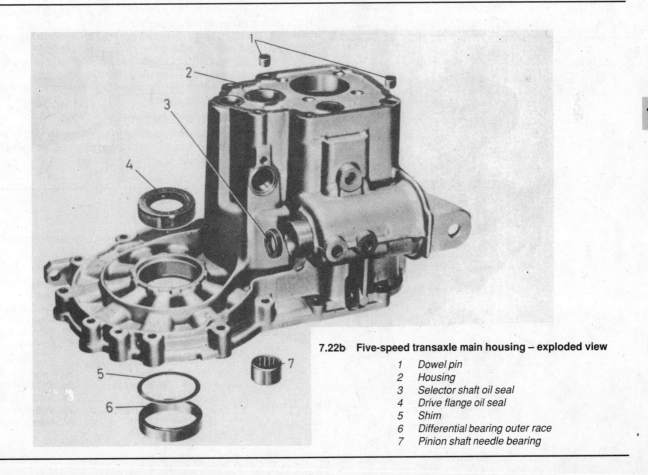

7.22b   Five-speed transaxle main housing – exploded view

1   Dowel pin
2   Housing
3   Selector shaft oil seal
4   Drive flange oil seal
5   Shim
6   Differential bearing outer race
7   Pinion shaft needle bearing

7A

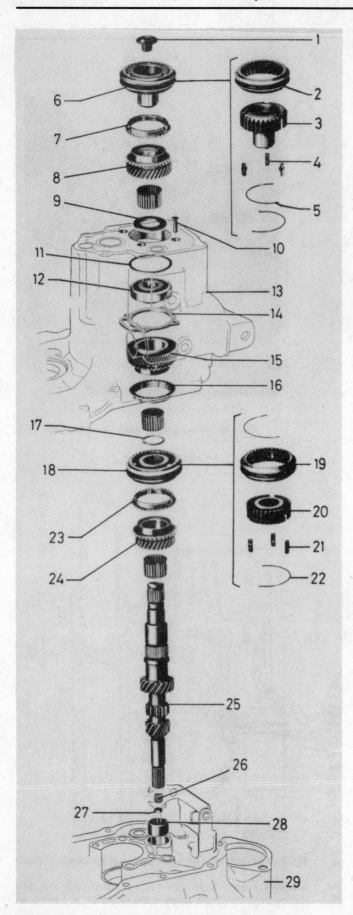

17   Extract the remaining circlip from the pinion shaft and remove 3rd gear, 2nd gear, the 2nd synchro ring and the needle bearing with a puller, if necessary.

18   Remove the reverse gear and shaft from the gear carrier housing.

19   Using a puller, remove the 1st gear and 1st-2nd synchronizer from the pinion shaft, together with the 2nd gear needle bearing inner race. Remove the 1st gear needle bearing and thrust washer.

20   Unbolt the bearing retaining plate and remove the pinion shaft from the gear carrier housing. Note that the retaining plate incorporates the reverse gear stop, which is located under the reverse gear.

21   Remove the remaining drive flange as described in Section 2, then lift out the differential unit. Overhaul of the differential unit should be left to a dealer service department or a repair shop.

Housing overhaul

Refer to illustrations 7.22a and 7.22b

22   The procedure is identical to the one described in Section 6, except the end cover retaining the clutch release components is separate from the main housing **(see illustrations)**. To remove the clutch release components, refer to Chapter 8.

Pinion shaft bearing replacement

23   Refer to Section 6, Step 19 for the pinion shaft bearing replacement procedure.

Mainshaft disassembly and reassembly

Refer to illustration 7.24

24   Remove the 5th gear needle bearing and thrust washer **(see illustration)**.

25   Using a puller, withdraw the ball-bearing from the mainshaft. On pre-May 1979 models, the bearing inner race will remain.

26   Remove the clamping plate, 4th gear and needle bearing and the 4th synchro ring.

27   Follow the procedure in Section 6, Steps 32 to 38 inclusive, but disregard the reference to 2nd and 3rd gear clearance.

28   Install the 4th synchro ring, the needle bearing and the 4th gear.

29   On pre-1979 models, press the mainshaft bearing inner race onto the mainshaft next to the 4th gear.

30   Locate the shim in the main housing, then press in the bearing with the inner race wide shoulder facing 4th gear (as applicable).

31   Attach the retainer to the main housing and tighten the bolts to the specified torque with a 5 mm Allen-head socket driver.

32   Note that there is no adjustment for the mainshaft endplay and the bearing shim remains constant.

Synchroniser unit inspection

33   Refer to Section 6, Steps 41 through 45, for this procedure.

34   When reassembling the 5th gear synchronizer, make sure the longer ends of the sliding keys face the synchro ring.

7.24 Five-speed transaxle mainshaft assembly – exploded view

1	Screw	16	Baulk ring
2	Sleeve	17	Circlip
3	Hub	18	3rd-4th synchronizer
4	Locking key	19	Sleeve
5	Spring	20	Hub
6	5th gear synchronizer	21	Locking key
7	Baulk ring	22	Spring
8	5th speed gear	23	Baulk ring
9	Thrust washer	24	3rd speed gear
10	Screw	25	Mainshaft
11	Shim	26	Bushing
12	Ball-bearing	27	Seal
13	Main housing	28	Needle bearing
14	Clamp plate	29	Gear carrier housing
15	4th speed gear		

7.58   Screw the selector tube in and then back it out to achieve the specified distance ("X" = 0.20-inch [5.0 mm])

Differential unit inspection

Refer to Section 6, Step 46.

Differential, pinion shaft and mainshaft reassembly

35   Remove the differential unit in the gear carrier housing.

36   Install the right-hand drive flange, followed by the spring washer, retaining circlip and cap.

37   Install the pinion shaft, complete with tapered bearings in the gear carrier housing and mesh it with the differential gear.

38   Install the bearing retaining plate and tighten the bolts.

39   Locate the 1st gear thrust washer on the pinion shaft with the shoulder facing the bearing plate.

40   Install the needle bearing and 1st gear, followed by the 1st synchro ring. Press on the 1st-2nd synchronizer, making sure the sliding keys locate in the synchro ring cut-outs. Heat the synchronizer to 250-degrees F (120-degrees C) before installing it.

41   Insert the reverse gear shaft, complete with the gear, into the gear carrier housing. At the same time, engage the gear with the relay lever jaw.

42   Using a piece of pipe, drive on the 2nd gear needle bearing inner race, then install the needle bearing, 2nd synchro ring and 2nd gear.

43   Heat the 3rd gear and press it onto the pinion shaft with the shoulder facing 2nd gear. Install the circlip and check the endplay as described in Section 6, Step 56.

44   Insert the mainshaft into the gear carrier housing and mesh the gears with the pinion shaft.

45   Heat the 4th gear and press it onto the pinion shaft with the shoulder facing away from the 3rd gear. Install the circlip.

46   Locate the selector fork rod spring in the gear carrier housing, then install the fork set. To do this, engage the 1st-2nd fork in the synchro sleeve groove, then rotate the fork set around the pinion shaft and engage the 3rd-4th fork and the reverse fork with the relay lever.

47   Push the selector fork rod into the gear carrier housing and align the slots in the forks in the neutral position.

48   The gear carrier housing and shafts are now ready for the assembly of the main housing.

Housing reassembly

Refer to illustrations 7.58, 7.60, 7.65 and 7.66

49   Make sure the reverse gear shaft is in the correct position (see illustration 6.53a) and set the gears in neutral. Make sure the spring is located on the end of the selector fork rod.

50   Install a new gasket on the gear carrier housing flange and make sure the magnet is in position.

51   Lower the main housing over the shafts and selector rod, then use a piece of pipe to drive the bearing inner race onto the mainshaft while supporting the mainshaft on a block of wood.

52   Insert and tighten the reverse gear shaft lockbolt, then insert and tighten the bolts attaching the main housing to the gear carrier housing.

7.60   Insert the selector shaft using a piece of thick wire (A) to keep the mechanism from turning

53   Check the mainshaft bearing retaining plate bolts for tightness.

54   Install the 5th gear thrust washer on the mainshaft with the chamfer facing the bearing, followed by the needle bearing.

55   Heat the 5th gear to 212-degrees F (100-degrees C) and press it onto the pinion shaft with the groove facing away from the main housing.

56   Install the thrust washer and circlip on the pinion shaft.

57   With the selector fork engaged with the groove in the 5th gear synchronizer, install the 5th gear, synchro ring and synchronizer on the mainshaft and selector fork extension, together with the locking plate or sleeve.

58   Without displacing the selector fork rod, screw the selector tube into the fork, then screw it out until it projects 0.20-inch (5.0 mm) **(see illustration)**.

59   Coat the threads of the 5th gear synchronizer retaining nut with locking compound, then screw it onto the mainshaft. Engage 5th and reverse gears by moving the selector forks, then tighten the nut to the specified torque using a 12 mm Allen-head socket driver.

60   Engage neutral and insert the selector shaft with the transaxle on its side; insert a length of thick wire to prevent the mechanism from turning **(see illustration)**.

7A

7.65   Use large pliers to clamp the locking plate in position

61   Install the spring and tighten the selector shaft cover using a spark plug socket.

62   Insert and tighten the back-up light switch or fuel consumption indicator, the 5th gear retaining screw and the selector shaft detent plunger or peg bolt.

63   If the selector shaft and/or fifth gear detent plunger were replaced, adjust the plungers as described in Section 3.

64   Lubricate the clutch pushrod and insert it into the mainshaft.

65   If a locking plate is installed, clamp it in position without tilting it **(see illustration)**.

66   If a fifth gear spacer sleeve is installed, lock it in place by peening it in two places with a blunt chisel **(see illustration)**. Make sure the selector rod moves freely in the tube.

67   Install the end cover on the main housing, using a new gasket. Tighten the bolts securely.

68   Install the left-hand drive flange, followed by the spring washer, retaining circlip and cap.

7.66   Peen the 5th gear spacer sleeve in place ("a" = 0.75-inch [19 mm])

Chapter 7 Part B Automatic transaxle

Contents

Automatic transaxle differential lubricant change .... See Chapter 1
Automatic transaxle differential lubricant level check . See Chapter 1
Automatic transaxle fluid and filter change .... See Chapter 1
Automatic transaxle fluid level check .... See Chapter 1
Automatic transaxle – removal and installation 7
Band adjustment 6
Diagnosis – general 2

General information 1
Neutral safety/back-up light switch – check and replacement 5
Oil seal replacement .... See Chapter 7A
Shift cable – removal, installation and adjustment 3
Throttle valve (TV) cable – check and adjustment 4
Transaxle mount – check and replacement .... See Chapter 7A

7B

Specifications

General

Fluid type .... See Chapter 1
Band adjustment (2nd gear band)
  Initial torque .... 8 ft-lbs
  Final torque .... 3.5 ft-lbs
Locknut .... 15 ft-lbs

Torque specifications   **Ft-lbs**

Transaxle-to-engine bolt/nut
  1975 through 1984 40
  1985 on
    10 mm bolt 33
    12 mm bolt 55
Torque converter bolt 22
Chassis subframe-to-body bolt (1985 on) 96

1   General information

All vehicles covered in this manual come equipped with either a four or five-speed manual transmission or an automatic transmission. All information on the automatic transmission is included in this Part of Chapter 7. Information on the manual transmissions can be found in Part A of this Chapter.

Due to the complexity of the automatic transmission and the need for special equipment to perform most service operations, this Chapter contains only general diagnosis, routine maintenance, adjustments and removal and installation procedures.

If the transmission requires major repair work, it should be left to a dealer service department or an automotive or transmission repair shop. You can, however, remove and install the transmission yourself and save the expense, even if the repair work is done by a transmission shop.

2   Diagnosis – general

Note: *Automatic transaxle malfunctions may be caused by four general conditions: Poor engine performance, improper adjustments, hydraulic malfunctions or mechanical malfunctions. Diagnosis of these problems should always begin with a check of the easily repaired items: Fluid level and condition (Chapter 1), shift linkage adjustment and throttle linkage adjustment. Next, perform a road test to determine if the problem has been corrected or if more diagnosis is necessary. If the problem persists after the preliminary tests and corrections are completed, additional diagnosis should be done by a dealer service department or transmission repair shop. Refer to the Troubleshooting section at the front of this manual for transaxle problem diagnosis.*

Preliminary checks

1   Drive the vehicle to warm the transaxle fluid to normal operating temperature.
2   Check the fluid level as described in Chapter 1:
   a) If the fluid level is unusually low, add enough fluid to bring the level within the designated area on the dipstick, then check for external leaks.
   b) If the fluid level is abnormally high, drain off the excess, then check the drained fluid for contamination by coolant. The presence of engine coolant in the automatic transaxle fluid indicates that a failure has occurred in the internal radiator walls that separate the coolant from the transmission fluid (see Chapter 3).
   c) If the fluid is foaming, drain it and refill the transaxle, then check for coolant in the fluid or a high fluid level.
3   Check the engine idle speed. **Note:** *If the engine is malfunctioning, do not proceed with the preliminary checks until it has been repaired and runs normally.*
4   Check the throttle valve cable for freedom of movement. Adjust it if necessary (Section 4). **Note:** *The throttle valve cable may function properly when the engine is shut off and cold, but it may malfunction once the engine is hot. Check it cold and at normal engine operating temperature.*
5   Inspect the shift cable (Section 3). Make sure it's properly adjusted and that the linkage operates smoothly.

Fluid leak diagnosis

6   Most fluid leaks are easy to locate visually. Repair usually consists of replacing a seal or gasket. If a leak is difficult to find, the following procedure may help.
7   Identify the fluid. Make sure it's transmission fluid and not engine oil or brake fluid (automatic transmission fluid is a deep red color).
8   Try to pinpoint the source of the leak. Drive the vehicle several miles, then park it over a large sheet of cardboard. After a minute or two, you should be able to locate the leak by determining the source of the fluid dripping onto the cardboard.
9   Make a careful visual inspection of the suspected component and the area immediately around it. Pay particular attention to gasket mating surfaces. A mirror is often helpful for finding leaks in areas that are hard to see.
10   If the leak still cannot be found, clean the suspected area thoroughly with a degreaser or solvent, then dry it.
11   Drive the vehicle for several miles at normal operating temperature and varying speeds. After driving the vehicle, visually inspect the suspected component again.
12   Once the leak has been located, the cause must be determined before it can be properly repaired. If a gasket is replaced but the sealing flange is bent, the new gasket will not stop the leak. The bent flange must be straightened.
13   Before attempting to repair a leak, check to make sure the following conditions are corrected or they may cause another leak.

Note: *Some of the following conditions cannot be fixed without highly specialized tools and expertise. Such problems must be referred to a transmission shop or a dealer service department.*

Gasket leaks

14   Check the pan periodically. Make sure the bolts are tight, no bolts are missing, the gasket is in good condition and the pan is flat (dents in the pan may indicate damage to the valve body inside).
15   If the pan gasket is leaking, the fluid level or the fluid pressure may be too high, the vent may be plugged, the pan bolts may be too tight, the pan sealing flange may be warped, the sealing surface of the transaxle housing may be damaged, the gasket may be damaged or the transaxle casting may be cracked or porous. If sealant instead of gasket material has been used to form a seal between the pan and the transaxle housing, it may be the wrong sealant.

Seal leaks

16   If a transaxle seal is leaking, the fluid level or pressure may be too high, the vent may be plugged, the seal bore may be damaged, the seal itself may be damaged or improperly installed, the surface of the shaft protruding through the seal may be damaged or a loose bearing may be causing excessive shaft movement.
17   Make sure the dipstick tube seal is in good condition and the tube is properly seated. Periodically check the area around the speedometer gear or sensor for leakage. If transmission fluid is evident, check the O-ring for damage. Also inspect the side gear shaft oil seals for leakage.

Case leaks

18   If the case itself appears to be leaking, the casting is porous and will have to be repaired or replaced.
19   Make sure the oil cooler hose fittings are tight and in good condition.

Fluid comes out vent pipe or fill tube

20   If this condition occurs, the transaxle is overfilled, there is coolant in the fluid, the case is porous, the dipstick is incorrect, the vent is plugged or the drain back holes are plugged.

3   Shift cable – removal, installation and adjustment

Refer to illustrations 3.4a, 3.4b, 3.6 and 3.7

Removal

1   Disconnect the negative cable from the battery.
2   Place the selector lever in Park. If the cable is broken, move the shift lever on the transaxle all the way to the left to the Park position.
3   Remove the set screw and detach the shift knob. Carefully pry the indicator plate up and remove it. Remove the shift console for access to the cable.
4   Pry off the E-clip and detach the selector lever (shift cable) assembly from the selector lever (**see illustrations on next page and page 225**).
5   On 1985 and later models, raise the vehicle and support it securely on jackstands. Disconnect the cable assembly from the bottom of the shift selector support under the vehicle. Remove the screws and lower the selector support, pull back the rubber boot, then remove the cable conduit nut and disengage the cable conduit from the support.

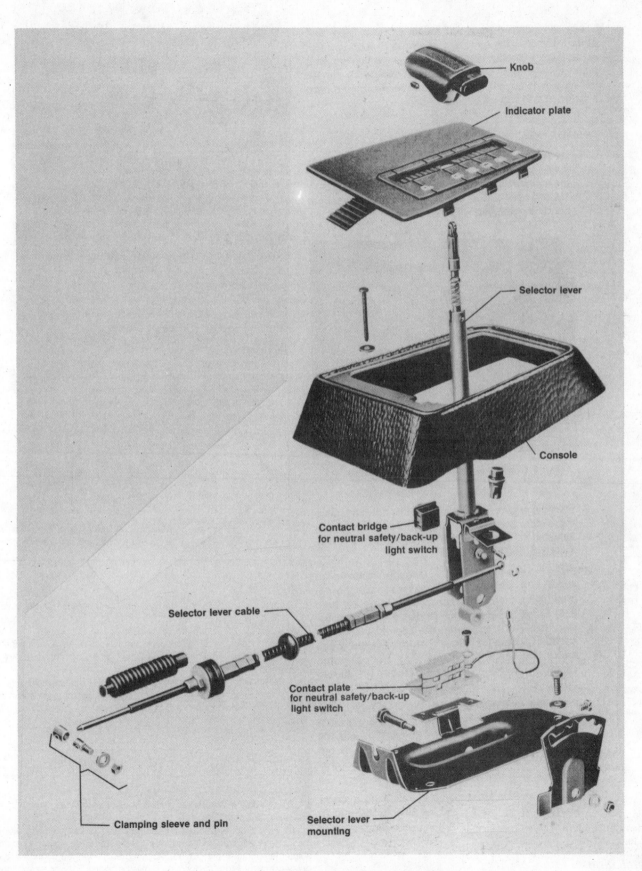

Knob

Indicator plate

Selector lever

Console

Contact bridge
for neutral safety/back-up
light switch

Selector lever cable

Contact plate
for neutral safety/back-up
light switch

Clamping sleeve and pin

Selector lever
mounting

3.4a   Shift lever and cable – 1975 through 1984 models

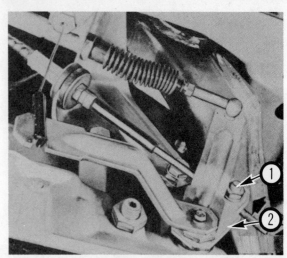

3.6   The clamp nut (1) secures the shift cable to the transaxle shift lever (2)

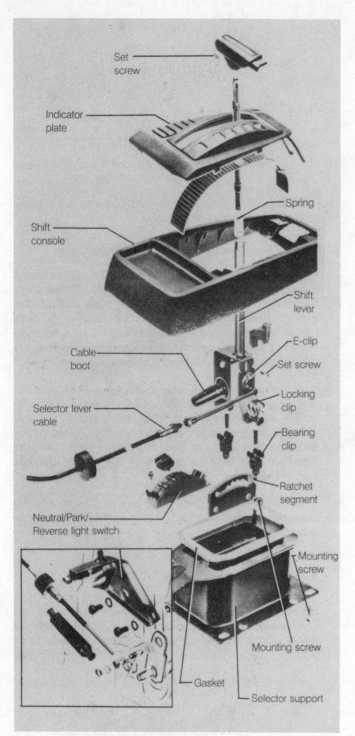

3.4b   Shift lever and cable – 1985 and later models

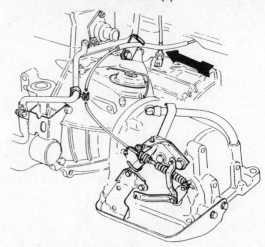

3.7   Make sure the speedometer cable doesn't interfere with the shift cable – it must be routed to the outside (arrow)

Adjustment

8   With the selector lever in Park, make sure the transaxle shift lever is also in Park (lever all the way to the left). Make sure the parking pawl is engaged by trying to push the vehicle forward and backward.

9   Loosen the cable clamp nut on the transaxle shift lever, verify the selector and transaxle levers are in Park, then tighten the nut securely **(see illustration 3.6)**.

10   Check the operation of the transaxle in each selector lever position (try to start the engine in each gear – the starter should operate in Park and Neutral only). Adjust the neutral safety/back-up light switch if necessary (Section 5).

4   Throttle valve (TV) cable – check and adjustment

Refer to illustration 4.4

1   The throttle valve (TV) cable adjustment is very important to proper transaxle operation. The cable positions a valve inside the transaxle which controls shift speed, shift quality and part throttle downshift sensitivity. If the cable is adjusted so it's too short, early shifts and slippage between shifts may occur. If the cable is adjusted so it's too long, shifts may be delayed and part-throttle downshifts may be erratic. The accelerator pedal cable must be adjusted at the same time so they will work together in the proper relationship.

6   Working in the engine compartment, loosen the shift cable-to-transaxle lever clamp nut and disengage the cable from the transaxle shift lever **(see illustration)**. Pull the cable through into the engine compartment and remove it from the vehicle.

Installation

7   Installation is the reverse of removal. Make sure the speedometer cable is routed so it won't interfere with the shift cable **(see illustration)**.

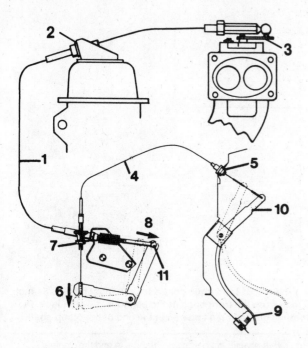

4.4   Throttle valve (TV) cable routing/adjustment details

1	TV cable
2	Adjusting locknuts (camshaft cover)
3	TV cable carburetor or fuel-injection connection
4	Accelerator pedal cable
5	Firewall ferrule
6	Accelerator pedal cable connection at transaxle TV lever (arrow indicates closed throttle position)
7	Accelerator pedal cable locknut
8	TV cable connection at TV lever (arrow indicates lever kickdown direction)
9	Accelerator pedal
10	Accelerator pedal kickdown position
11	Cable end

2   On carburetor-equipped models, make sure the choke is off. On fuel-injected models, the primary throttle must be closed.

TV cable

3   Loosen the TV cable housing locknuts on the camshaft cover or carburetor.
4   Have an assistant move the TV lever on the transaxle all the way counterclockwise to the closed throttle position and hold it there. Alternatively, the cable can be disconnected from the transaxle lever. Adjust the

6.3   Loosen the band locknut with a box-end wrench and tighten the adjusting screw with a torque wrench

cable position at the camshaft cover or carburetor until there is no play, using the locknuts, then tighten the locknuts **(see illustration)**. The cable is properly adjusted when the cable end (11 in illustration 4.4) can be attached to the lever when it's in the closed throttle position without moving the lever.

Throttle cable

5   Have an assistant push the accelerator pedal down to the kickdown position and hold it there.
6   Loosen the locknut (7 in illustration 4.4) and remove any freeplay in the cable by turning the knurled adjusting nut. Tighten the locknut.
7   Check the operation of the TV cable – readjust as necessary.

---

5   Neutral safety/back-up light switch – check and replacement

Check

1   Try to start the engine in each gear – the starter should operate in Park and Neutral only. If the engine does not start, or starts in any gear other than Park or Neutral and the shift cable is properly adjusted (Section 3), check the neutral safety/back-up light switch.
2   Remove the center console.
3   The neutral safety/back-up light switch is actuated by the selector lever **(see illustrations 3.4a and 3.4b)**. If the lever isn't contacting the switch or doesn't fully actuate it, change the position of the switch on the mount as necessary to adjust it. If adjusting the switch position has no effect, replace it with a new one.

Replacement

4   Unplug the electrical connector, remove the screws and detach the switch from the mount.
5   Installation is the reverse of removal.
6   Check the operation of the transaxle in each shift lever position, readjusting the switch position as necessary.

---

6   Band adjustment

Refer to illustration 6.3

1   The transaxle 2nd gear band should be adjusted whenever there is no drive in 2nd gear (D or 2) or when gear engagement is delayed in all forward gears. The adjusting screw is located on the transaxle housing, next to the shift lever.
2   The transaxle must be level or the band could jam during the adjustment procedure.
3   Loosen the band locknut, then center the band by temporarily tightening the adjusting screw to the initial torque listed in this Chapter's specifications **(see illustration)**.
4   Loosen the adjusting screw and then tighten it to the specified torque.
5   Back the screw off exactly 2-1/2 turns, carefully hold it from moving and tighten the locknut to the specified torque.

---

7   Automatic transaxle – removal and installation

Refer to illustration 7.20

Removal

1   Disconnect the negative cable from the battery.
2   Raise the vehicle and support it securely on jackstands.
3   Drain the transaxle fluid (Chapter 1).
4   Remove the transaxle protection plate and torque converter cover.
5   Remove the three torque converter-to-driveplate bolts. Turn the crankshaft pulley bolt clockwise for access to each bolt.
6   Remove the starter motor (Chapter 5).
7   Disconnect the driveaxles from the transaxle (Chapter 8).
8   Disconnect the speedometer cable.
9   Disconnect the wire harness from the transaxle (if equipped).

7B

10 Remove any exhaust components which will interfere with transaxle removal (chapter 4).

11 Disconnect the TV cable.

12 Disconnect the shift cable.

13 Support the engine with a hoist from above or a jack from below (position a block of wood between the jack and oil pan to spread the load).

14 Support the transaxle with a jack – preferably a special jack made for this purpose. Safety chains will help steady the transaxle on the jack.

15 Remove any chassis or suspension components which will interfere with transaxle removal.

16 Remove the bolts securing the transaxle to the engine.

17 Remove the transaxle mount nuts and bolts. Remove the front and side mounts from the transaxle if necessary to facilitate removal.

18 Lower the transaxle slightly and disconnect and plug the transaxle cooler lines.

19 Move the transaxle back to disengage it from the engine block dowel pins and make sure the torque converter is detached from the driveplate. Secure the torque converter to the transaxle so it won't fall out during removal. Lower the transaxle from the vehicle.

Installation

20 Prior to installation, make sure the torque converter hub is securely engaged in the pump. The distance from the end of the torque converter hub to the edge of the bellhousing must be 1-13/64-inch (30 mm) **(see illustration)**.

21 With the transaxle secured to the jack, raise it into position. Be sure to keep it level so the torque converter doesn't slide out. Connect the fluid cooler lines.

22 Turn the torque converter to line up the bolt holes with the holes in the driveplate.

23 Move the transaxle forward carefully until the dowel pins and the torque converter are engaged.

24 Install the transaxle housing-to-engine bolts. Tighten them securely.

25 Install the torque converter-to-driveplate bolts. Tighten the bolts to the specified torque.

26 Install the transaxle and any suspension and chassis components which were removed. Tighten the bolts and nuts to the specified torque.

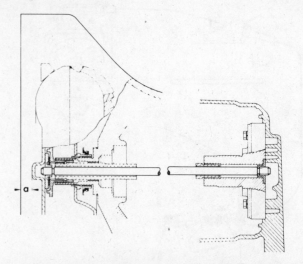

7.20 The end of the torque converter hub must be 1-13/64-inch (30 mm) from the front edge of the bellhousing – if it isn't, the torque converter isn't seated in the end of the pump shaft

27 Remove the jacks supporting the transaxle and the engine.

28 Install the starter motor (Chapter 5).

29 Connect the shift and TV cables.

30 Plug in the transaxle electrical connector (where applicable).

31 Install the torque converter cover.

32 Connect the driveaxles (Chapter 8).

33 Connect the speedometer cable.

34 Adjust the shift cable (Section 3).

35 Install any exhaust system components that were removed or disconnected.

36 Lower the vehicle.

37 Fill the transaxle (Chapter 1), run the vehicle and check for fluid leaks.

Chapter 8   Clutch and driveaxles

Contents

Clutch cable – removal, installation and adjustment 5
Clutch components – removal, inspection and installation 3
Clutch – description and check 2
Clutch freeplay check and adjustment .... See Chapter 1
Clutch release bearing and related
  components – removal and installation 4
Constant velocity (CV) joint boots – replacement 9
Constant velocity (CV) joints – disassembly, inspection
  and reassembly 8
Driveaxle boot check .... See Chapter 1
Driveaxle oil seal replacement .... See Chapter 7
Driveaxle vibration damper – removal and installation 10
Driveaxles – general information and inspection 6
Driveaxles – removal and installation 7
Flywheel – removal and installation .... See Chapter 2A
General information 1

Specifications

Clutch pedal freeplay .... See Chapter 1

Driveaxle damper-to-collar clearance ("a") .... 0.157 in (4mm)

8

Torque specifications   Ft-lbs

	Ft-lbs
Pressure plate-to-crankshaft bolts	55
Flywheel-to-pressure plate bolts	15
Driveaxle hub nut	170
Inner driveaxle CV joint-to-transaxle flange bolts	33
Steering knuckle-to-balljoint clamp bolt nut	
1975 through 1979 models	22
1980 on	37
Wheel lug bolts	See Chapter 1

---

1   General information

The information in this Chapter deals with the components from the rear of the engine to the front (drive) wheels (except for the transaxle, which is covered in the previous Chapter). In this Chapter, the compo-nents are grouped into two categories; clutch and driveaxles. Separate Sections within this Chapter offer general information, checks and repair procedures for components in each of the two groups.

Warning: *Since nearly all the procedures included in this Chapter involve working under the vehicle, make sure it's securely supported on sturdy jackstands or on a hoist where it can be easily raised and lowered.*

2   Clutch – description and check

1   All vehicles with a manual transaxle have a single dry plate, dia-phragm spring-type clutch. The clutch disc has a splined hub which allows it to slide along the splines of the transaxle input shaft or mainshaft. The clutch disc is held in place against the flywheel by the pressure plate springs.

2   The clutch cable on early models requires periodic adjustment (see Chapter 1). The clutch cable used on later models incorporates a self-ad-justing device which compensates for clutch disc wear. A spring incorpo-rated into the cable maintains tension on the cable when the pedal is depressed and the clutch is released. Consequently, the slack is always taken up in the cable, making adjustment unnecessary.

3   When pressure is applied to the pedal to release the clutch, the cable pulls against the end of the clutch operating lever. The operating lever mo-tion is transferred to the release bearing, which contacts a long pushrod. The pushrod, which runs through the hollow transaxle mainshaft, pushes on the release plate, disengaging the clutch.

4   Terminology can be a problem when discussing the clutch compo-nents because common names are in some cases different from those used by the manufacturer. For example, the clutch disc is also called the clutch plate or driven plate, the clutch release bearing is sometimes called a throwout bearing and the release fork is sometimes called the release lever.

5   Other than to replace components with obvious damage, some pre-liminary checks should be performed to diagnose clutch problems.

a) The first check should be of the clutch cable adjustment (if applica-ble). If there's too much slack in the cable, the clutch won't release completely, making gear engagement difficult or impossible. Refer to Chapter 1 for the adjustment procedure.

b) To check "clutch spin down time," run the engine at normal idle speed with the transaxle in Neutral (clutch pedal up – engaged). Disengage the clutch (pedal down), wait several seconds and shift the transaxle into Reverse. No grinding noise should be heard. A grinding noise would most likely indicate a problem in the pressure plate or the clutch disc.

c) To check for complete clutch release, run the engine (with the park-ing brake applied to prevent vehicle movement) and hold the clutch pedal approximately 1/2-inch from the floor. Shift the transaxle be-tween First and Reverse gear several times. If the shift is rough, component failure is indicated, or as stated above, the cable is out of adjustment.

d) Visually inspect the pivot bushing at the top of the clutch pedal to make sure there's no binding or excessive play.

e) A clutch pedal that's difficult to operate is most likely caused by a faulty clutch cable. Check the cable at the clutch lever for frayed wires, rust and other signs of corrosion. If it looks good, lubricate the cable with penetrating oil. If pedal operation improves, the cable is worn out and should be replaced.

3   Clutch components – removal, inspection and installation

Refer to illustration 3.3

Removal

1   Access to the clutch components is normally accomplished by re-moving the transaxle, leaving the engine in the vehicle. Of course, if the engine is being removed for major overhaul, then check the clutch for wear and replace worn components as necessary. However, the relatively low cost of the clutch components, compared to the time and trouble spent gaining access to them, warrants their replacement anytime the engine or transaxle is removed (unless they're new or in near perfect condition). The following procedures are based on the assumption the engine will stay in place.

2   Referring to Chapter 7, Part A, remove the transaxle from the vehicle. Support the engine while the transaxle is out. Preferably, an engine hoist should be used to support it from above. However, if a jack is used under-neath the engine, make sure a piece of wood is positioned between the jack and oil pan to spread the load. **Caution:** *The pick-up for the oil pump is very close to the bottom of the oil pan. If the pan is bent or distorted in any way, engine oil starvation could occur.*

3   On these models, the clutch cover/pressure plate assembly is bolted directly to the crankshaft and the flywheel is bolted to the clutch cover/pressure plate **(see illustration)**. Loosen the flywheel-to-clutch cover bolts 1/4-turn at a time in a criss-cross sequence to avoid warping any-thing, then remove the flywheel and clutch disc.

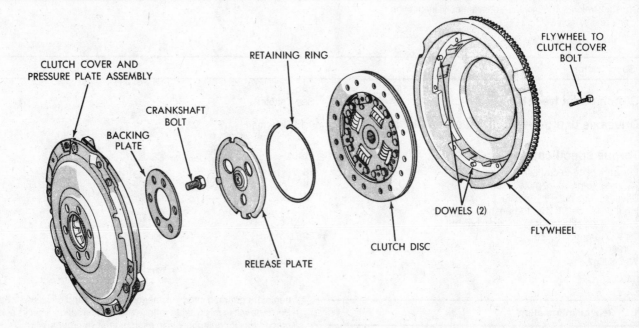

3.3   An exploded view of the clutch components used on these models – the clutch cover/pressure plate assembly is bolted to the crankshaft and the flywheel mounts on the clutch cover

CLUTCH COVER AND PRESSURE PLATE ASSEMBLY

BACKING PLATE

CRANKSHAFT BOLT

RETAINING RING

RELEASE PLATE

CLUTCH DISC

DOWELS (2)

FLYWHEEL

FLYWHEEL TO CLUTCH COVER BOLT

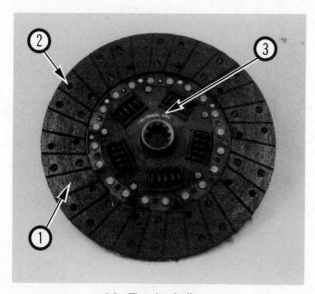

3.8 The clutch disc

1 **Lining** – will wear down in use
2 **Rivets** – secure the lining and will damage the pressure plate or flywheel surface if allowed to contact it
3 **Marks** – "flywheel side" or something similar

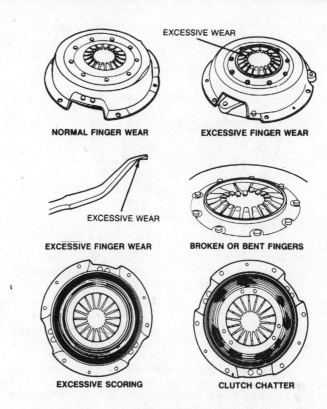

3.10a Replace the pressure plate if excessive wear or damage is noted

3.10b Also examine the pressure plate friction surfaces for score marks, cracks and evidence of overheating (blue discolored areas)

4 Note where the ends of the retaining ring are positioned (make marks on the release plate if necessary), then use a screwdriver to detach the retaining ring **(see illustration 3.3)**. Remove the release plate from the clutch assembly.

5 Mark the relationship of the clutch cover and pressure plate assembly to the crankshaft. Following a criss-cross pattern, loosen the bolts in 1/4-turn increments until they can be removed by hand. Remove the bolts and detach the clutch cover and pressure plate assembly, as well as the backing plate.

Inspection

Refer to illustrations 3.8, 3.10a and 3.10b

6 Ordinarily, when a problem occurs in the clutch, it can be attributed to wear of the clutch disc. However, all components should be inspected at this time. **Note:** *If the clutch components are contaminated with oil, there will be shiny, black, glazed spots on the clutch disc lining, which will cause the clutch to slip. Replacing clutch components won't completely solve the*

problem – *be sure to check the rear crankshaft oil seal and the transaxle input shaft/mainshaft seal for leaks. If it looks like a seal is leaking, be sure to install a new one to avoid the same problem with a new clutch.*

7 Inspect the flywheel for cracks, heat checking, grooves and other obvious defects. If the imperfections are slight, a machine shop can machine the surface flat and smooth, which is highly recommended regardless of the surface appearance. Refer to Chapter 2, Part A, for the flywheel removal and installation procedure.

8 Inspect the lining on the clutch disc. There should be at least 1/16-inch of lining above the rivet heads. Check for loose rivets, distortion, cracks, broken springs and other obvious damage **(see illustration)**. As mentioned above, ordinarily the clutch disc is routinely replaced, so if in doubt about its condition, replace it with a new one.

9 The release bearing is easier to replace with the transaxle in the vehicle, so it isn't as critical. However, be sure to check the release plate for distortion and for wear at the point where the pushrod touches it (wear greater than 0.010-inch is unacceptable). Also, check the pushrod seal inside the transaxle mainshaft to make sure it's in good condition.

10 Check the machined surfaces and the diaphragm spring fingers of the pressure plate **(see illustrations)**. If the surface is scored or otherwise damaged, replace the pressure plate. Also check for obvious damage, distortion, cracks, etc. Light glazing can be removed with emery cloth. If the pressure plate must be replaced, new and factory-rebuilt units are available.

Installation

Refer to illustrations 3.14a and 3.14b

11 Before installation, clean the flywheel and pressure plate machined surfaces with lacquer thinner or acetone. It's important to keep these surfaces, and the clutch disc lining, clean and free of oil or grease. Handle the parts only with clean hands.

12 Prior to installation, apply thread locking compound to the pressure plate bolts. Align the marks made during removal, place the clutch cover/

8

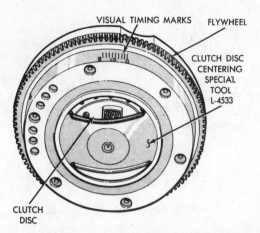

3.14a   Center the clutch disc with the special tool and install the flywheel and clutch disc – line up the radial V-groove hole on the outer flange of the clutch cover with the dowel in the flywheel located near the visual timing marks

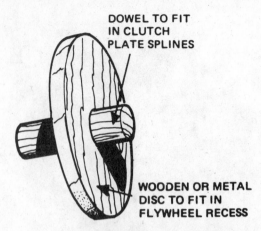

3.14b   A substitute clutch centering tool can be fabricated if the factory tool isn't available

pressure plate and backing plate in position on the crankshaft and install the bolts **(see illustration 3.3)**. Tighten the bolts to the torque listed in this Chapter's specifications.

13   Install the release plate and secure it with the retaining ring. Make sure the ends of the ring are positioned correctly.

14   Note the location of the dowel hole in the outer flange of the clutch cover. It's marked with a radial V-groove. Align the flywheel dowel near the visual timing marks with the dowel hole in the clutch cover. Using a centering tool (Volkswagen tool no. 545 or a home-made substitute), install the new clutch disc and flywheel on the pressure plate **(see illustrations)**. **Note:** *Make sure the clutch disc is installed correctly – it should be marked to indicate which side faces the flywheel or pressure plate.*

15   Install the flywheel-to-pressure plate bolts finger tight, then tighten them in 1/4-turn increments, in a criss-cross pattern, to the torque listed in this Chapter's specifications.

16   Remove the centering tool, install the transaxle and adjust the clutch freeplay (see Chapter 1).

17   Install the transaxle and all components removed previously. Tighten all fasteners to the proper torque specifications.

4   Clutch release bearing and related components – removal and installation

Refer to illustrations 4.3, 4.4, 4.5 and 4.6

Warning: *Dust produced by clutch wear and deposited on clutch components may contain asbestos, which is a health hazard. DO NOT blow it out with compressed air or inhale any of it. DO NOT use gasoline or petroleum-based solvents to clean off the dust. Brake system cleaner should be used to flush the dust into a drain pan. After the clutch components are wiped clean with rags, dispose of the contaminated rags and cleaner in a sealed, marked container.*

1   Raise the vehicle and support it securely on jackstands.

2   Detach the clutch cable from the operating lever (see Section 5).

3   Remove the bolts and detach the clutch release bearing end cover from the transaxle **(see illustration)**. **Note:** *You may be able to move the operating lever enough to position the release lever (the lever inside the housing) out of the way far enough to withdraw the release bearing at this point. However, if the release lever is in the way, or if the shaft seal must be replaced, proceed to Step 4.*

4   Pry out the circlips (one on each side of the release lever) **(see illustration)**.

4.3   The clutch release bearing is accessible after removing the end cover from the transaxle (the cover is held in place with four bolts as shown here)

4.4   Remove the circlips (arrow), . . .

4.5   . . . then support the release lever while pulling out the operating lever and shaft

4.6   The release bearing can now be pulled out of the bore in the transaxle housing

5   Note how the spring is positioned, then pull out the operating lever shaft **(see illustration)**. Remove the release lever and return spring from the housing.
6   Lift out the release bearing and guide sleeve **(see illustration)**.
7   Hold the center of the bearing and turn the outer portion while applying pressure. If it doesn't turn smoothly or if it's noisy, install a new one.
8   Check the shaft seal in the transaxle housing. If it's worn or deteriorated, pry it out and drive a new one into place with a socket and hammer. Lubricate the seal lips with grease.
9   Installation is the reverse of removal. Note that the release lever will only slide onto the shaft in one position. The return spring must be installed with the center engaged with the release lever and the ends bearing against the housing.
10   If the shaft bushings are worn, they should be replaced.
11   Lubricate the release shaft bushings with high-temperature grease, slide the shaft part way into the housing and hold the fork in position. Continue to slide the shaft into place, through the fork, until it seats in the inner bushing.
12   Install the E-clip in the shaft groove. Make sure it's seated correctly.

13   Lubricate the release fork ends with a small amount of high-temperature grease (don't overdo it). Lubricate the release bearing bore with the same grease.
14   Install the release bearing on the fork. Make sure the wire retainer is properly engaged.
15   Install the transaxle.

---

5   Clutch cable – removal, installation and adjustment

Refer to illustrations 5.2, 5.3 and 5.5

1   Raise the front of the vehicle and support it securely on jackstands. Apply the parking brake and block the rear wheels so the vehicle can't roll off the stands.

Non-self adjusting clutch cable

2   Loosen the locknut and back off the adjuster until the cable is loose **(see illustration)**.

5.2   Loosen the locknut (A) and back off the adjuster (B) until clutch cable is loose

5.3   With the clutch cable loose, detach the clip (arrow) from the end

8

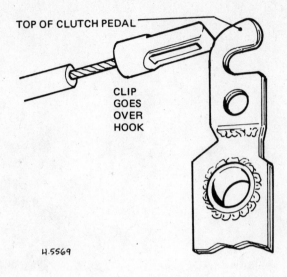

TOP OF CLUTCH PEDAL

CLIP
GOES
OVER
HOOK

H.5569

5.5   Clutch cable connection to clutch pedal details

3   Lift up on the transaxle operating lever to release the cable tension, then remove the clutch cable clip, pad and retainer and disengage the cable end from the lever **(see illustration)**.

Self-adjusting clutch cable

4   Depress the clutch several times. Compress the self adjuster spring located under the rubber boot at the cable bracket to provide enough slack in the cable so an assistant can detach the cable from the transaxle operating lever.

All models

5   Working inside the vehicle, disengage the cable end from the clutch pedal **(see illustration)**.
6   Pull the cable through the firewall.
7   Lubricate both ends of the new cable, then insert it through the firewall opening and connect the cable end to the pedal.
8   Engage the lower end of the cable in the transaxle mount and connect the cable end to the operating lever. Don't forget to install the cable clip or retainer.
9   Refer to Chapter 1 and adjust the clutch pedal freeplay. On self-adjusting clutch cables, relieve the spring tension and operate the clutch pedal several times to adjust the freeplay.

---

6   Driveaxles – general information and inspection

General information

Refer to illustration 6.1

Power from the engine passes through the clutch and transaxle to the front wheels via two driveaxles **(see illustration)**. Because the driveaxles are unequal in length, one shaft is hollow so that it weighs the same as the other, solid, shaft. Each driveaxle consists of three sections: An inner end which bolts to the differential flange, two constant velocity (CV) joints and an outer splined end which is held in the hub by a nut. The CV joints are internally splined and contain ball bearings which allow them to operate at various lengths and angles as the driveaxles move through their full range of travel. The CV joints are lubricated with special grease and protected by rubber boots which must be inspected periodically for damage and deterioration that could lead to contamination of the joints and failure of the driveaxle.

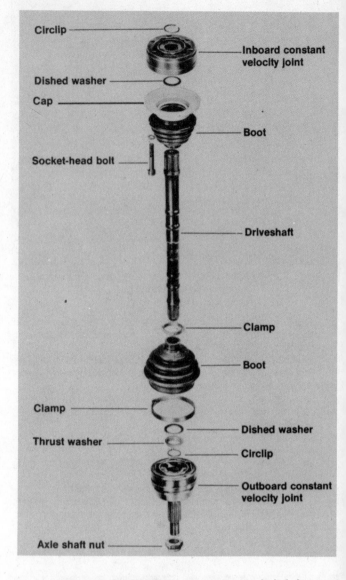

Circlip
Inboard constant velocity joint
Dished washer
Cap
Boot
Socket-head bolt
Driveshaft
Clamp
Boot
Clamp
Dished washer
Thrust washer
Circlip
Outboard constant velocity joint
Axle shaft nut

6.1   Driveaxle and CV joint components – exploded view

Inspection

The boots should be periodically inspected for leaks, damage and deterioration (see Chapter 1). Damaged CV joint boots must be replaced immediately or the joints can be damaged. Boot replacement involves removal of the driveaxle. **Note:** *Some auto parts stores carry "split" type replacement boots, which can be installed without removing the driveaxle from the vehicle – a convenient alternative. However, the driveaxle should be removed and the CV joint disassembled and cleaned to make sure the joint is free from contaminants such as moisture and dirt, which will accelerate CV joint wear.*

The most common symptom of worn or damaged CV joints, besides lubricant leaks, is a clicking noise in turns, a clunk when accelerating from a coasting condition or vibration at highway speeds.

To check for wear in the CV joints and driveaxle shafts, grasp each axle (one at a time) and rotate it in both directions while holding the CV joint housings. Watch for movement, indicating worn splines or sloppy CV joints. Also, check the driveaxle shafts for cracks and distortion.

7.5a   Lower the inner end of the driveaxle, . . .

7.5b   . . . then pull the outer joint out of the hub – be sure to support both CV joints as the driveaxle is lowered from the vehicle

7   Driveaxles – removal and installation

Removal

Refer to illustrations 7.5a, 7.5b, 7.7 and 7.9

1   Remove the front hub dust cap. With the weight of the vehicle on the wheels and an assistant applying the brakes, loosen the hub nut.

2   Raise the front of the vehicle, support it securely on jackstands, apply the parking brake and block the rear wheels. Remove the front wheel, hub nut and washer.

3   Remove the six socket head bolts retaining the inner CV joint to the transaxle flange.

1975 through 1984 models (except left driveaxle on 1978 through 1984 models with an automatic transaxle)

4   On these models both driveaxles on manual models and the right driveaxle on automatic transaxle models can be removed or installed without disconnecting the balljoint from the steering knuckle.

5   Grasp the CV joints securely, lower the inner end of the driveaxle and pull the outer CV joint from the hub **(see illustrations)**. Lower the driveaxle from the vehicle.

1985 and later models and left driveaxle on 1978 through 1984 models with an automatic transaxle

6   On these models, the balljoint must be disconnected from the steering knuckle to provide sufficient clearance for driveaxle removal.

7   Remove the steering knuckle-to-balljoint clamp bolt **(see illustration)**.

8   Pry the lower balljoint stud out of the steering knuckle. **Note:** *The sway bar (if equipped) may have to be disconnected from the suspension arm to allow enough movement to separate the balljoint (see Chapter 10).*

9   Grasp the inner and outer CV joints securely while an assistant pulls the steering knuckle out to separate the driveaxle from the hub **(see illustration)**. Be careful not to damage the CV joint boot. Lower the driveaxle from the vehicle.

10   The driveaxles, when in place, secure the hub bearing assemblies. If the vehicle must be supported or moved on the front wheels while the driveaxles are out, install bolts through the hubs and thread nuts onto them to keep the bearings from loosening.

8

7.7   Remove the nut from the balljoint clamp bolt (arrow)

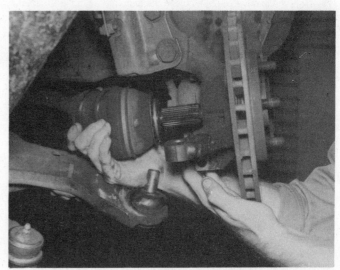

7.9   Grasp the outer CV joint and pull the steering knuckle out to separate it from the driveaxle splines

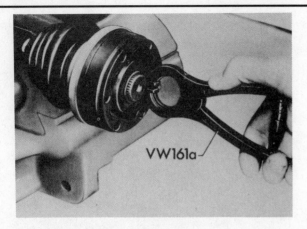

8.4   Use a special tool or snap-ring pliers to remove the circlip from the driveaxle groove

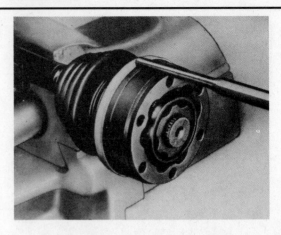

8.5   Use a hammer and punch to dislodge the inner joint cap

Installation

11   Prior to installation, install a new adhesive gasket on the inner CV joint.

12   Apply a small amount of multi-purpose grease to the outer CV joint splines.

1975 through 1984 models (except left driveaxle on 1978 through 1984 models with an automatic transaxle)

13   Raise the driveaxle into place and carefully insert the outer CV joint splines into the hub and position the inner CV joint flange on the transaxle flange.

1985 and later models and left driveaxle on 1978 through 1984 models with an automatic transaxle

14   Push the steering knuckle out and insert the outer splined shaft of the CV joint into the hub and position the inner CV joint flange on the transaxle flange.

15   Rejoin the balljoint stud to the steering knuckle, install the clamp bolt and tighten it to the torque listed in this Chapter's specifications.

All models

16   Install the six socket head bolts that retain the inner CV joint to the flange, then tighten them to the torque listed in this Chapter's specifications.

17   Install the sway bar ends, if removed (see Chapter 10).

18   Install the wheels, washers and axle hub nuts.

19   Tighten the driveaxle hub nuts to the torque listed in this Chapter's specifications.

---

8   Constant velocity (CV) joints – disassembly, inspection and reassembly

---

1   Obtain a CV joint rebuild or replacement kit.

2   Remove the driveaxles (see Section 7).

3   Place one of the driveaxles in a vise, using wood blocks to protect it from the vise jaws. If the CV joint has been operating properly with no noise or vibration, replace the boot as described in Section 9. If the CV joint is badly worn or has run for some time with no lubricant due to a damaged boot, it should be disassembled and inspected.

Inner CV joint

Refer to illustrations 8.4, 8.5, 8.7, 8.9, 8.12, 8.13, 8.14, 8.15 and 8.19

4   Use circlip pliers to remove the circlip from the end of the driveaxle shaft **(see illustration)**.

5   Use a hammer and punch to drive the boot cap off, then peel the boot back over the joint **(see illustration)**. The driveaxle will now have to be taken to a machine shop to have the joint pressed off the shaft.

6   Clean the grease from the joint assembly. Mark the relatiave position of the cage, cross and outer housing.

7   Rotate the cage and cross 90-degrees and push it out of the housing **(see illustration)**.

8   Remove the ball bearings one at a time, keeping track of their position so they can be reinstalled in the same relationship.

9   Rotate the cross so the ball bearing groove is lined up with the edge of the cage, then rotate the cross out of the cage **(see illustration)**.

8.7   Rotate the cage and cross assembly 90-degrees and push it out of the housing

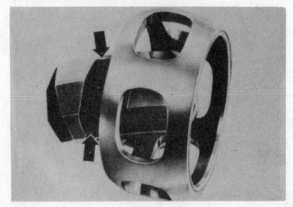

8.9   Line up the bearing groove with the edge (arrows), then lift it out of the cage

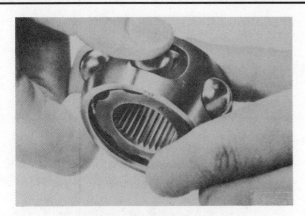

8.12   Press each ball bearing into place

8.13   The wide (a) and narrow (b) grooves must line up to allow installation

8.14   Rotate the assembly to line up the ball bearings with the grooves

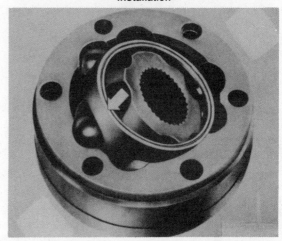

8.15   Engage the ball bearings in the housing grooves – use only hand pressure, don't force them

8.19   The concave surface of the dished washer must be flush with the axle collar

10   Clean all of the components and inspect for worn or damaged splines, ball bearings, cage, cross and housing. Replace the joint with a new one if any of the components are not servicable.

11   Coat the components with moly-base grease and install the race in the cage.

12   Install the ball bearings in the cage and cross assembly **(see illustration)**.

13   Insert the cage, bearings and cross assembly into the housing with the chamferred side of the splines facing the larger diameter side of the housing. When the components are rotated into place, the wide-spaced grooves in the cage should be lined up with the wide-space grooves in the housing **(see illustration)**.

14   Pivot the assembly in the housing until the ball bearings and grooves line up **(see illustration)**.

15   Press the cage into the housing **(see illustration)**.

16   Check the joint for smooth operation.

17   Pack the joint with 3 oz (90 grams) of moly-base grease: 2/3 of the grease goes on the joint outer side and 1/3 on the inner side.

18   Install the new boot on the axle.

19   Install a new dished washer in the groove in the driveaxle shaft with the convex side flush against the shoulder of the axleshaft **(see illustration)**.

20   Take the driveaxle and CV joint to a machine shop and have the joint pressed onto the driveaxle. The press must keep pressure on the joint while the new circlip is installed.

21   Install the boot to the joint and secure it with a new cap.

Outer CV joint

Refer to illustrations 8.24, 8.25, 8.29, 8.30, 8.31, 8.32, 8.41 and 8.42

22   Remove the boot clamps and push the boot back. Wipe the grease out of the joint.

8

8.24   On early model outer CV joints, release the circlip (A), grasp the end of the shaft (B) and pull the joint off

8.25   The outer joint housing can be dislodged from the shaft circlip by tapping around the outer circumference with a soft-face hammer

8.29   Mark the bearing cage, cross and housing relationship after removing the grease

8.30   With the cage and cross tilted, the balls can be removed one at a time

8.31   With the inner race and cage vertical, align the windows in the cage (arrow) with the lands and rotate the inner race up and out of the outer race

8.32   Turn the cross 90-degrees, align the cross land with the cage elongated window (arrow) and rotate the cross out of the cage

23   Two types circlips are used on these models to secure the CV joint to the driveaxle which affect the removal procedure. On early models the circlip can be removed from the back of the joint. On later models the circlip is internal.

24   On early models, open the circlip with snap ring pliers, grasp the axleshaft end of the CV joint and pull the joint off the driveaxle **(see illustration)**.

25   On later models, use a soft-face hammer to drive the housing off the axle **(see illustration)**. Support the CV joint as this is done and rap the housing sharply on the outer edge to dislodge it from the internal circlip installed on the shaft.

26   Slide the boot off the driveaxle. If the CV joint was operating properly and the grease doesn't appear to be contaminated, just replace the boot (see Section 9). Bypass the following disassembly procedure. If the CV joint was noisy or the grease was contaminated, proceed with the disassembly procedure to determine if it should be replaced with a new one.

27   Remove the circlip (if equipped) from the driveaxle groove and discard it (the rebuild kit will include a new circlip).

28   Clean the axle spline area and check the splines for wear, damage and corrosion.

29   Clean the outer CV joint bearing assembly with a clean cloth to remove excess grease. Mark the relative position of the bearing cage, cross and housing **(see illustration)**.

30   Grip the housing shaft securely in the wood blocks in the vise. Push down one side of the cage and remove the ball bearing from the opposite side. Repeat the procedure in a criss-cross pattern until all of the balls are

removed **(see illustration)**. If the joint is tight, tap on the cross (not the cage) with a hammer and brass punch.

31   Remove the bearing cage assembly from the housing by tilting it vertically and aligning two opposing elongated cage windows in the area between the ball grooves **(see illustration)**.

32   Turn the cross 90-degrees to the cage and align one of the spherical lands with an elongated cage window. Raise the land into the window and swivel the cross out of the cage **(see illustration)**.

33   Clean all of the parts with solvent and dry them with compressed air (if available).

34   Inspect the housing, splines, balls and races for damage, corrosion, wear and cracks. Check the bearing cross for wear and scoring in the races. If any of the components are not serviceable, the entire CV joint assembly must be replaced with a new one.

35   Coat all of CV joint components with moly-base grease before beginning reassembly.

36   Align the marks and install the cross in the cage so one of the cross lands fits into the elongated window **(see illustration 8.32)**.

37   Rotate the cross into position in the cage and install the assembly in the CV joint housing, again using the elongated window for clearance.

38   Rotate the cage into position in the housing. The marks made during disassembly should face out and be aligned.

39   Install the balls into the elongated holes, one at a time, until they're all in position.

40   Pack the lubricant from the kit into the ball races and grooves. Use 2/3 of the grease in the joint itself and the remaining 1/3 in the open side.

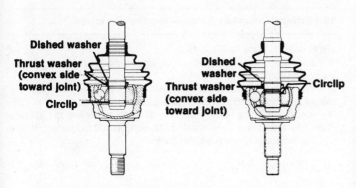

8.41 Early (right) and late model outer CV joint circlip and washer arrangements

41   Place the driveaxle in the vise and slide the boot over it. Install new circlip in the axle groove and (if equipped) thrust washer **(see illustration)**.
42   Place the CV joint housing in position on the axle and align the splines. On early models, expand the circlip using snapring pliers as the joint is started on the axle. On all models, rap the end of the joint sharply with a soft-face hammer **(see illustration)**. Make sure it's seated on the circlip by attempting to pull it off the shaft.
43   Install the boot (see Section 9).
44   Install the driveaxle (see Section 7).

9   Constant velocity (CV) joint boots – replacement

Note: *If the instructions supplied with the replacement boot kit differ from the instructions here, follow the ones with the new boots. A special tool is required to install the factory-supplied boot clamps, so it may be a good idea to leave the entire procedure to a dealer service department. Do-it-yourself kits which offer greatly simplified installation may be available for your vehicle. Consult an auto parts store or dealer parts department for more information on these kits.*

1   If the boot is cut, torn or leaking, it must be replaced and the CV joint inspected as soon as possible. Even a small amount of dirt in the joint can cause premature wear and failure. Obtain a replacement boot kit before beginning this procedure.
2   Remove the driveaxle (see Section 7).
3   Disassemble the CV joint and remove the boot as described in Section 8.
4   Inspect the CV joint to determine if its been damaged by contamination or running with too little lubricant. If you have any doubts about the condition of the joint components, perform the inspection procedures described in Section 8.
5   Clean the old grease out of the CV joint and repack it with the grease supplied with the kit.
6   Pack the interior of the new boot with the remaining grease.
7   Install the boot and clamps as follows.

Inner boot

8   Slide the boot in position on the joint and seat the small end in the groove in driveaxle shaft (make sure the boot is not twisted).
9   Place the cap in place on the inner housing, making sure the holes line up with the bolt holes in the housing. Use a hammer and punch to seat the cap securely into position.

Outer boot

Refer to illustration 9.13

10   Make sure the small end of the boot is properly located in the groove in the axleshaft (make sure it isn't twisted) and install the clamp. Tighten the clamp securely with the tool.

11   Locate the large end of the boot over the shoulder or in the groove in the housing (make sure the boot isn't twisted).
12   Install the ladder-type clamp, then locate the metal clamp tangs in the slots, making the clamp as tight as possible by hand.
13   Squeeze the clamp bridge with the tool to complete the tightening procedure **(see illustration)**. Don't cut through the clamp bridge or damage the rubber boot.

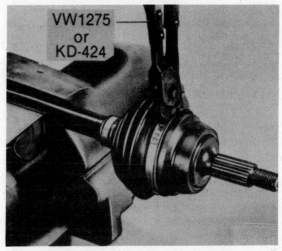

8.42   Strike the end of the CV joint with a soft-faced hammer to engage it with the axle circlip

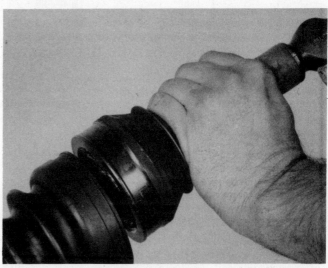

9.13   Boot clamp installation details

8

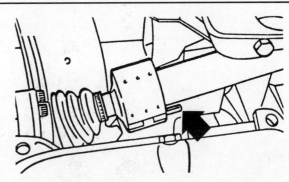

10.2   Drive out the roll pin and separate the vibration damper halves

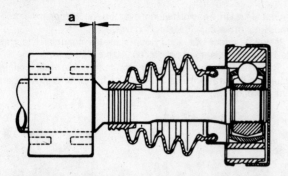

10.3   Make sure the damper is mounted the specified distance (a) from the driveaxle collar

10   Driveaxle vibration damper – removal and installation

Refer to illustrations 10.2 and 10.3

1   Some later model right (passenger) side driveaxles are equipped with a vibration damper.

2   The damper can be removed by marking it's position, driving out the roll pin and separating the halves **(see illustration)**.

3   Installation is the reverse of removal. Before installing the roll pin, make sure the damper-to-driveaxle collar clearance is as specified in this Chapter's Specifications **(see illustration)**.

Chapter 9   Brakes

Contents

Brake disc – inspection, removal and installation 6
Brake fluid level check . . . . See Chapter 1
Brake light switch – removal, installation and adjustment 14
Brake lines and hoses – inspection and replacement 10
Brake system check . . . . See Chapter 1
Brake system bleeding 11
Drum brake adjustment (1975 through
    1978 models only) . . . . See Chapter 1
Drum brake shoes – replacement 7
Front disc brake caliper – removal, overhaul and installation 3

Front disc brake pads – replacement 2
General information 1
Master cylinder – removal, overhaul and installation 9
Parking brake handle and cable – removal, installation
    and adjustment 13
Power brake booster – check, removal and installation 12
Rear disc brake pads – replacement 4
Rear disc brake caliper – removal and installation 5
Wheel cylinder – removal, overhaul and installation 8

Specifications

General

Brake fluid type . . . .   See Chapter 1
Brake light switch-to-brake pedal arm **(see illustration 14.9)** . . . .   7/32 to 1/4 in (5 to 6 mm)
Brake disc runout limit . . . .   0.004 in (0.10 mm)

Brake pedal dimensions
1975 through 1979 models **(see illustration 12.7a)**
   Dimension a
      1975 . . . .   1-27/32 in (47 mm)
      1976 and 1977 . . . .   1-5/8 in (41 mm)
      1978 and 1979 (pedal arm lower hole) . . . .   2 in (51 mm)
   Dimension b
      1975 . . . .   4-23/32 in (120 mm)
      1976 through 1979 . . . .   3-15/16 in (100 mm)
   Dimension c
      1975 . . . .   8-29/32 in (226 mm)
      1976 through 1979 . . . .   8-7/64 in (206 mm)

9

Dimension d
     1975 ....   7-23/64 in (187 mm)
       1976 through 1979 ....   6-47/64 in (171 mm)
1980 through 1984 models **(see illustration 12.7b)**
     Dimension a ....   8-7/64 in (206 mm)

Torque specifications

	Ft-lbs
Brake light switch-to-master cylinder nut	15
Master cylinder-to-brake booster nut	15
Power brake booster-to-bracket nut	15
Front caliper mounting bolts	
1975 through 1984	
Standard	43
Self-locking	52
1985 on	18
U-shaped pad retainer bolt (Girling)	15
Caliper guide pins (Kelsey-Hayes)	30
Rear caliper mounting bolts	26
Rear disc brake pad carrier-to-axle bolt	48
Wheel-cylinder-to-backing plate bolt	8
Brake backing plate-to-axle bolt	44
Wheel lug bolts	See Chapter 1

1   General information

The vehicles covered by this manual are equipped with hydraulically operated front and rear brake systems. 1975 through 1978 models are equipped with drum brakes on all four wheels. These brakes require periodic adjustment to compensate for shoe wear (see Chapter 1).

On 1979 and later models, the front brakes are disc type and the rear brakes are drum type with both the front and rear brakes being self adjusting. Some later models are equipped with rear disc brakes. Disc brakes automatically compensate for pad wear, while the rear drum brakes incorporate an adjusting wedge mechanism which is activated as the brakes are applied. The front disc brakes are from three different manufacturers: Kelsey-Hayes, Teves (ATE) and Girling. Although similar in design, these brakes vary considerably in detail.

Hydraulic system

The hydraulic system consists of two separate circuits. The master cylinder has separate reservoirs for the two circuits and in the event of a leak or failure in one hydraulic circuit, the other circuit will remain operative. A visual warning of circuit failure or air in the system is given by a warning light activated by displacement of the piston in the pressure differential switch portion of the combination valve from its normal "in balance" position.

Proportioning valve, rear residual pressure valve and pressure regulator

To prevent rear wheel lockup, these vehicles are equipped with a proportioning valve located in the engine compartment at the master cylinder and a brake pressure regulator which is bolted to the chassis and connected to the rear axle by a spring-loaded lever. On pickup models, a residual pressure valve in the rear brake lines is used in place of a brake pressure regulator.

Power brake booster

The optional power brake booster, utilizing engine manifold vacuum and atmospheric pressure to provide assistance to the hydraulically operated brakes, is mounted on the firewall in the engine compartment.

Parking brake

The parking brake operates the rear brakes only, through cable actuation. It's activated by a lever mounted between the seats.

Service precautions

After completing any operation involving disassembly of any part of the brake system, always test drive the vehicle to check for proper braking performance before resuming normal driving. When testing the brakes, perform the tests on a clean, dry flat surface. Conditions other than these can lead to inaccurate test results.

Test the brakes at various speeds with both light and heavy pedal pressure. The vehicle should stop evenly without pulling to one side or the other. Avoid locking the brakes because this slides the tires and diminishes braking efficiency and control of the vehicle.

Tires, vehicle load and front-end alignment are factors which also affect braking performance.

2   Front disc brake pads – replacement

Warning: *Disc brake pads must be replaced on both front wheels at the same time – never replace the pads on only one wheel. Also, the dust created by the brake system may contain asbestos, which is harmful to your health. Never blow it out with compressed air and don't inhale any of it. An approved filtering mask should be worn when working on the brakes. Do not, under any circumstances, use petroleum based solvents to clean brake parts. Use brake cleaner or denatured alcohol only!*

Note: *When servicing the disc brakes, use only high quality, nationally recognized name brand pads.*

1   Remove the cover from the brake fluid reservoir.

2   Loosen the wheel lug bolts, raise the front of the vehicle and support it securely on jackstands. Apply the parking brake and block the rear wheels.

3   Remove the front wheels. Work on one brake assembly at a time, using the assembled brake for reference if necessary.

4   Inspect the brake disc carefully as outlined in Section 6. If machining is necessary, follow the information in that Section to remove the disc, at which time the pads can be removed from the calipers as well.

Teves (ATE) caliper

Refer to illustrations 2.5, 2.6, 2.7, 2.8, 2.9 and 2.12

5   Detach the clips from the ends of the pad retaining pins **(see illustration)**.

6   Use a hammer and small punch to dislodge the pins, then withdraw them from the caliper using pliers **(see illustration)**.

7   Detach the spreader spring and lift it out of the caliper **(see illustration)**.

2.5   Detach the ends of the clips (arrows) so the pad retaining pins can be removed (Teves/ATE)

2.6   Withdraw the two retaining pins (Teves/ATE)

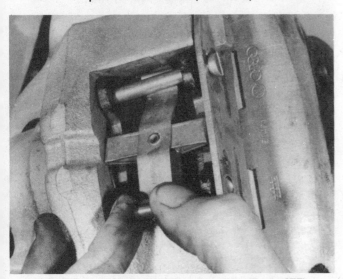

2.7   Rotate the spreader out of the caliper (Teves/ATE)

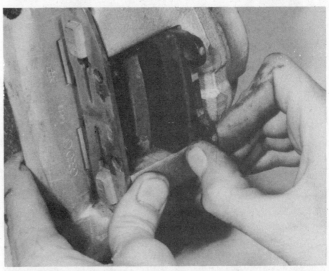

2.8   Grasp the ear of the inner pad and pull it out (Teves/ATE)

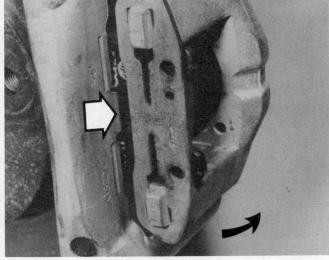

2.9   Push the caliper in the direction of the arrows to detach the inner pad (arrow) (Teves/ATE)

2.12   The recess in the piston face must be at a 20-degree angle from the face of the caliper – a cardboard gauge makes it easier to check this (Teves/ATE)

9

2.16   Use a screwdriver to detach the spreader spring (Girling)

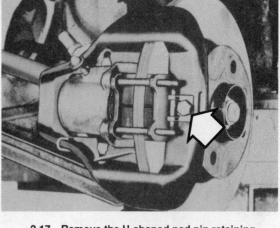

2.17   Remove the U-shaped pad pin retaining
bolt (arrow) (Girling)

2.18   Use pliers to pull the pad retaining pins out (Girling)

2.25   Detach the retaining clip seated in the ends of the pads (not
all models) (Kelsey-Hayes)

8   Grasp the ear of the inner pad and silencer shim (if equipped) and pull them out of the caliper **(see illustration)**.
9   The outer pad is held in position in the caliper mount by a metal finger which extends into a notch in the back of the pad. Push the caliper in (toward the vehicle) to detach the pad from the frame, then lift it from the caliper **(see illustration)**. Remove the silencer shim and wear indicator (if equipped) from the pad.
10   Clean the pad mounting and caliper and mount sliding surfaces and inspect the piston boot for cracks or leaks. Replace or overhaul the caliper if it is damaged or leaking. Inspect the brake disc (Section 6). Check the spreader spring and mounting pins for cracks, distortion and corrosion, replacing as necessary.
11   Push the piston back into the bore to provide room for the new brake pads. A C-clamp can be used to accomplish this. As the piston is depressed to the bottom of the caliper bore, the fluid in the master cylinder will rise. Make sure it doesn't overflow. If necessary, siphon off some of the fluid.
12   Before installing the pads, make sure the recess in the piston face is at a 20-degree angle to the caliper face **(see illustration)**. If necessary, rotate the piston carefully to achieve the proper angle.
13   Install the wear indicator on the outer pad.
14   Install the inner and outer pads and silencer shims in the caliper.
15   Install the spreader spring, then insert one of the pins through one end, press the other end of the spring into place and secure it with the remaining pin. Install the clips at the ends of the pins.

Girling caliper

Refer to illustrations 2.16, 2.17 and 2.18
16   Pry off the spreader spring with a screwdriver **(see illustration)**.

17   Remove the bolt from the U-shaped retainer which holds the brake pad pins in place **(see illustration)**.
18   Use pliers to pull the two pad retaining pins out of the caliper **(see illustration)**.
19   Lift the two pads out of the caliper, noting the location the shims (if equipped).
20   Clean the pad mounting and caliper and mount sliding surfaces and inspect the piston boot for cracks or leaks. Replace or overhaul the caliper if it is damaged or leaking. Inspect the brake disc (Section 6). Check the spreader spring and mounting pins for cracks, distortion and corrosion, replacing as necessary.
21   Prior to installation, make sure both pistons are pushed back into their bores to allow room for the new pads. As the pistons are depressed to the bottom of the caliper bores, the fluid in the master cylinder will rise. Make sure it doesn't overflow. If necessary, siphon off some of the fluid. Lubricate the contact surfaces of the retaining pins and the holes in the pads where the pins extend through them with high temperature grease.
22   Place the brake pads and shims in the caliper and insert the pad retaining pins.
23   Install the U-shaped retainer and bolt. Tighten the bolt securely.
24   Install the spreader spring, making sure the arrow faces down.

Kelsey-Hayes caliper

Refer to illustrations 2.25, 2.26, 2.27, 2.32, 2.33 and 2.34
25   Use needle-nose pliers to detach the pad retaining clip **(see illustration)**.

2.26   Use an Allen wrench to remove the caliper bolts (Kelsey-Hayes)

2.27   Rotate the caliper down and away from the mounting bracket (Kelsey-Hayes)

2.32   The inner brake pad chamfer (arrow) must face up (Kelsey-Hayes)

2.33   The slots in the ends of the pads must seat in the bracket (Kelsey-Hayes)

26   Unscrew the two caliper retaining bolts with an Allen wrench **(see illustration)**.

27   Rotate the lower end of the caliper away from the mounting bracket, lift the caliper off and hang it out of the way on a piece of wire **(see illustration)**. Residual brake system pressure could push the piston out of the caliper so it is a good idea to use a large rubber band around the piston and caliper to secure the piston

28   Detach the outer pad from the brake mount and remove it.

29   Slide the inner pad and anti-rattle springs (if equipped) out from between the bracket and disc and lift them from the vehicle.

30   Clean the pad mounting and caliper and mounting bracket sliding surfaces. Inspect the piston boot for cracks or leaks. Replace or overhaul the caliper if it is damaged or leaking. Inspect the brake disc (Section 6). Check the mounting bolts for damaged threads, distortion and corrosion, replacing as necessary.

31   Push the piston back into the bore to provide room for the new brake pads. As the piston is depressed to the bottom of the caliper bore, the fluid in the master cylinder will rise. Make sure it doesn't overflow. If necessary, siphon off some of the fluid.

32   Place the inner pad in position, with the chamfered end facing up **(see illustration)**.

33   Place the slots in the ends of the outer pads in the mounting bracket **(see illustration)**.

34   Engage the top of the caliper in the bracket and rotate the bottom of the caliper into place **(see illustration)**.

35   Install the caliper bolts. Tighten the bolts securely.

All models

36   Firmly depress the brake pedal a few times to bring the pads into contact with the disc.

9

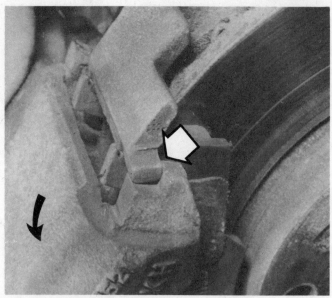

2.34   Engage the top of the caliper with the bracket, then rotate it down into place (Kelsey-Hayes)

37   Check for fluid leakage and make sure the brakes operate normally before driving in traffic.

---

3   Front disc brake caliper – removal, overhaul and installation

Warning: *Dust created by the brake system may contain asbestos, which is harmful to your health. Never blow it out with compressed air and don't inhale any of it. An approved filtering mask should be worn when working on the brakes. Do not, under any circumstances, use petroleum-based solvents to clean brake parts. Use brake cleaner or denatured alcohol only!*

Note: *If an overhaul is indicated (usually because of fluid leakage) explore all options before beginning the job. New and factory rebuilt calipers are available on an exchange basis, which makes this job quite easy. If it's decided to rebuild the calipers, make sure a rebuild kit is available before proceeding. Always rebuild the calipers in pairs – never rebuild just one of them.*

Removal

1   Remove the cover from the brake fluid reservoir, siphon off two thirds of the fluid into a container and discard it.
2   Loosen the wheel lug bolts, raise the front of the vehicle and support it securely on jackstands. Apply the parking brake and block the rear wheels. Remove the front wheels.
3   Refer to Section 2 and remove the brake pads from the caliper.
4   **Note:** *Do not remove the brake hose from the caliper if you are only removing the caliper.* Use a proper size wrench to unscrew the brake hose inlet fitting so that fitting is not rounded off (a flare nut wrench is best) and detach the hose. On some later model Girling calipers, the inlet fitting has a left-hand thread. Have a rag handy to catch spilled fluid and wrap a plastic bag tightly around the end of the hose to prevent fluid loss and contamination.
5   Remove the two mounting bolts and detach the caliper from the vehicle (refer to Section 2 if necessary).

Overhaul

Refer to illustrations 3.9, 3.12a, 3.12b and 3.12c

6   Clean the exterior of the caliper with brake cleaner or denatured alcohol. Never use gasoline, kerosene or petroleum-based cleaning solvents. Place the caliper on a clean workbench.

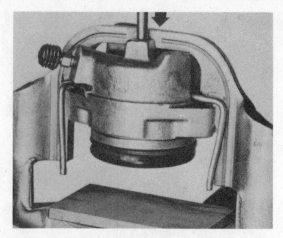

3.9   Press the cylinder down out of the floating frame (Teves/ATE)

Teves (ATE) caliper

7   Push the cylinder sideways until the closed end is against the floating frame.
8   Lift the mounting frame out of the floating frame.
9   Place a wood block in the floating frame and press the cylinder out of the floating frame **(see illustration)**. Remove the guide spring.

Girling caliper

10   Press the cylinder assembly out of the frame.

Teves (ATE) and Girling calipers

11   Remove the dust seal retaining rings (if equipped), then remove the dust seals.

All models

12   Position a wooden block or several shop rags in the caliper as a cushion, then use compressed air to remove the piston(s) from the caliper **(see illustrations)**. Girling calipers have two pistons, so it will be necessary to place the caliper in a padded vise to keep both pistons from flying out as air pressure is applied. Use only enough air pressure to ease the piston out of the bore. If the piston is blown out, even with the cushion in place, it may be damaged. **Warning:** *Never place your fingers in front of the piston in an attempt to catch or protect it when applying compressed air, as serious injury could occur.*

Kelsey Hayes caliper

13   If it was not detached by the piston removal procedure, remove the dust seal.

All models

14   Using a wood or plastic tool, remove the piston seal from the groove in the caliper bore. Metal tools may cause bore damage.
15   Remove the caliper bleeder screw.

Kelsey Hayes caliper

16   Remove and discard the guide pin sleeves and bushings from the caliper ears. Use the longer of the two guide pins to push the bushings out.

All models

17   Discard all rubber parts.
18   Clean the remaining parts with brake system cleaner or denatured alcohol then blow them dry with compressed air.
19   Carefully examine the piston for nicks and burrs and loss of plating. If surface defects are present, the parts must be replaced.
20   Check the caliper bore in a similar way. Light polishing with crocus cloth is permissible to remove light corrosion and stains. Discard the mounting bolts if they're corroded or damaged.

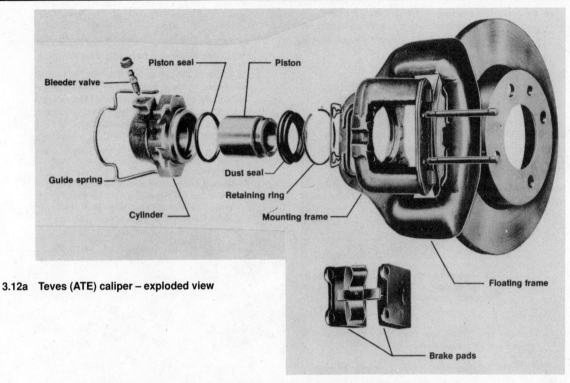

3.12a   Teves (ATE) caliper – exploded view

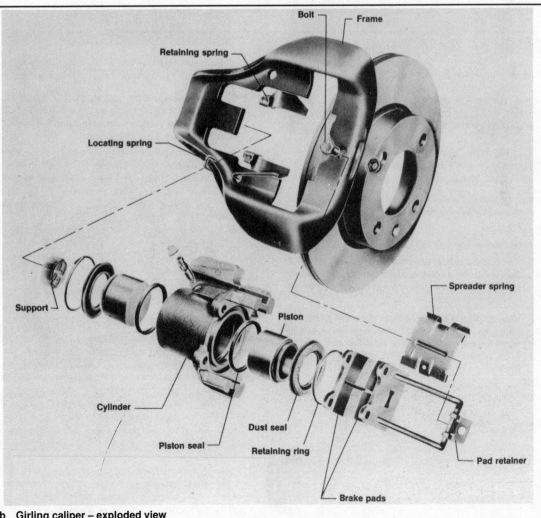

3.12b   Girling caliper – exploded view

9

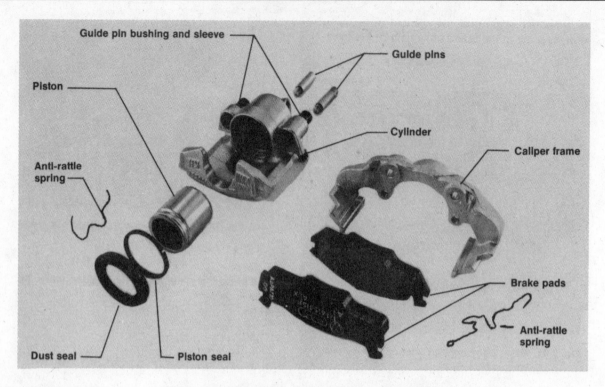

3.12c   Early model Kelsey-Hayes caliper – exploded view

21 When assembling, lubricate the piston bores and seal with clean brake fluid. Position the seal in the caliper bore groove.

22 Lubricate the piston with clean brake fluid, then install a new dust seal in the piston groove **(see illustrations 3.12a, 3.12b and 3.12c)**.

23 Insert the piston squarely into the caliper bore, then apply force to bottom it. On Girling calipers, use a vise to push the pistons evenly into the the bores.

24 Position the dust seal in the caliper counterbore, then press it securely into position. Make sure the seal is recessed evenly. On Teves and Girling calipers, secure the dust seals with the retaining rings.

25 Install the bleeder screw.

Kelsey Hayes caliper

26 Install new bushings in the mounting bolt holes. Push the sleeves into the mounting bolt holes.

Teves (ATE) caliper

27 Install the guide spring on the cylinder, place the assembly in position in the floating frame and then use a punch and hammer drive it evenly into position, alternating on each side of the cylinder.

28 Place the mounting frame in the guide spring, then push the frame onto the floating frame. The two grooves in the mounting frame must fit over the ribs on the floating frame.

Girling caliper

29 Lubricate the sliding surfaces of the cylinder and frame with silicone grease.

30 Install the support in the hollow of the piston which presses against the caliper frame and slide the cylinder into the frame. Make sure the retaining springs are between the sliding surfaces of both the frame and cylinder. The locating spring must exert pressure against the upper edge of the cylinder.

Installation

31 Inspect the mounting bolts for excessive corrosion.

32 Place the caliper in position over the rotor and mounting bracket, install the bolts and tighten them to the specified torque.

33 On Teves calipers, make sure the piston is positioned at a 20-degree angle to the caliper face (Section 2, Step 12), rotating the piston as necessary.

34 Install the brake pads (Section 2).

35 Install the brake hose inlet fitting, making sure not to cross thread it, using new copper washers, then tighten the fitting securely.

36 If the line was disconnected, be sure to bleed the brakes (Section 11).

37 Install the wheels and lower the vehicle.

38 After the job has been completed, firmly depress the brake pedal a few times to bring the pads into contact with the disc.

39 Check brake operation before driving the vehicle in traffic.

---

4   Rear disc brake pads – replacement

Refer to illustrations 4.6, 4.7, 4.8, 4.9 and 4.15

Warning: *Disc brake pads must be replaced on both rear wheels at the same time – never replace the pads on only one wheel. Also, the dust created by the brake system may contain asbestos, which is harmful to your health. Never blow it out with compressed air and don't inhale any of it. An approved filtering mask should be worn when working on the brakes. Do not, under any circumstances, use petroleum based solvents to clean brake parts. Use brake cleaner or denatured alcohol only!*

Note: *When servicing the disc brakes, use only high quality, nationally recognized name brand pads.*

1 Remove the cover from the brake fluid reservoir.

2 Loosen the wheel lug bolts, raise the rear of the vehicle and support it securely on jackstands. Apply the parking brake and block the rear wheels.

3 Remove the rear wheels. Work on one brake assembly at a time, using the assembled brake for reference if necessary.

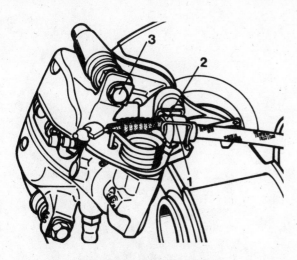

4.6   Rear disc brake details

1   Parking brake cable end   3   Caliper guide pin
2   Retaining clip

4   Before removing anything, wash the brake assembly with aerosol brake cleaner and allow it to dry. Remember – NEVER blow off the brake dust with compressed air – asbestos is a health hazard!

5   Inspect the brake disc carefully as outlined in Section 6. If machining is necessary, follow the information in that Section to remove the disc, at which time the pads can be removed from the calipers as well.

6   Remove the retaining clip, detach the parking brake cable and slide it out of the cable guide **(see illustration)**.

7   Use a hex head wrench to unscrew the upper self-locking caliper mounting bolt **(see illustration)**. Grasp the head of the upper guide pin with pliers to steady the assembly and remove the mounting bolt.

8   Rotate the caliper down for access to the brake pads **(see illustration)**. Lift the pads out of the brake pad carrier.

9   Before the new, thicker pads can be installed, it will be necessary to adjust the piston back into the bore by turning the socket in the back of the piston all the way clockwise to provide room for the new brake pads. Use an Allen wrench to accomplish this **(see illustration)**. As the piston is depressed to the bottom of the caliper bore, the fluid in the master cylinder will rise. Make sure it doesn't overflow. If necessary, siphon off some of the fluid.

10   Place the new brake pads in position.

11   Rotate the caliper into place and install a new mounting bolt. Hold the guide pin with pliers and tighten the mounting bolt to the specified torque.

12   Connect the parking brake cable and secure it with the clip.

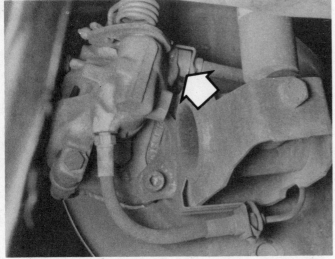

4.7   Upper self-locking caliper retaining bolt location (arrow)

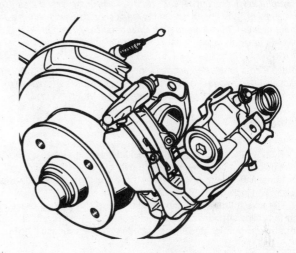

4.8   With the upper bolt removed, rotate the caliper back for access to the pads

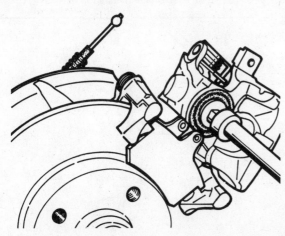

4.9   Use an Allen wrench to rotate the piston adjusting screw fully clockwise to make room for the new pads

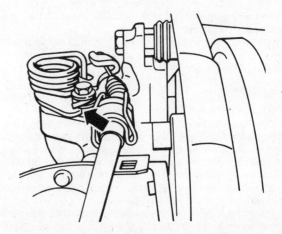

4.15   The parking brake lever (arrow) must be against the stop as shown on both rear brakes when adjusting the cables

13   Pump the brake pedal at least 40 times to reset the parking brake automatic adjuster.

14   Make sure the parking brake is not applied and adjust the parking brake as follows.

15   Loosen the locknuts under the parking brake lever and turn the adjusting nuts until the cable tension is just relieved. The parking brake levers at the calipers must be against their stops **(see illustration)**.

16   Set and release the parking brake three times to stretch the cables, then turn the adjusting nuts until the discs can just be turned with the brake applied one click. After two clicks the discs should turn only with considerable effort and they should be locked after three clicks.

17   Check to make sure there is little or no clearance between the parking brake levers and the stops at the calipers, adjusting as necessary.

18   Tighten the locknuts.

19   After the job has been completed, firmly depress the brake pedal a few times to bring the pads into contact with the disc.

20   Check for fluid leakage and make sure the brakes operate normally before driving in traffic.

---

5   Rear disc brake caliper – removal and installation

Warning: *Dust created by the brake system may contain asbestos, which is harmful to your health. Never blow it out with compressed air and don't inhale any of it. An approved filtering mask should be worn when working on the brakes. Do not, under any circumstances, use petroleum-based solvents to clean brake parts. Use brake cleaner or denatured alcohol only!*

Note: *The manufacturer recommends replacement of a faulty or leaking caliper with a new one. New and factory rebuilt calipers are available on an exchange basis, which makes this job quite easy.*

Removal

Refer to illustration 5.5

1   Remove the cover from the brake fluid reservoir, siphon off two thirds of the fluid into a container and discard it.

2   Loosen the wheel lug bolts, raise the rear of the vehicle and support it securely on jackstands. Remove the rear wheels.

3   Remove the retaining clip and disconnect the parking brake cable from the caliper. If necessary to provide sufficient slack in the cable, loosen the cable locknuts located under the parking brake lever and then back off the adjusting nuts.

4   **Note:** *Do not remove the brake hose from the caliper if you are merely removing the caliper to provide access for some other related task – this will prevent having to bleed the system later.* Unscrew the brake hose inlet fitting using the proper size wrench so the fitting is not rounded off (a flare nut wrench is best) and detach the hose. Have a rag handy to catch spilled fluid and wrap a plastic bag tightly around the end of the hose to prevent fluid loss and contamination.

5   Hold each adjacent guide pin to steady the assembly and remove the two self-locking mounting bolts, then detach the caliper from the vehicle **(see illustration)**.

Installation

Refer to illustration 5.6

6   If the brake hose was disconnected, the brake bleeding procedure can be speeded up by pre-bleeding the caliper. Loosen the bleeder valve screw, lay the caliper on its side with the piston facing down and fill it with new, clean brake fluid through the bleeder screw valve until bubble-free fluid comes out of the inlet hose opening **(see illustration)**. Tighten the bleeder screw and connect the fluid inlet hose. Tighten the inlet hose fitting securely.

7   Prior to installation, it may be necessary to adjust the piston of the new caliper back in its bore so the caliper will fit over the brake pads as described in Section 3, Step 9. Place the caliper in position over the rotor and brake pad carrier, install new self-locking mounting bolts and tighten them to the specified torque.

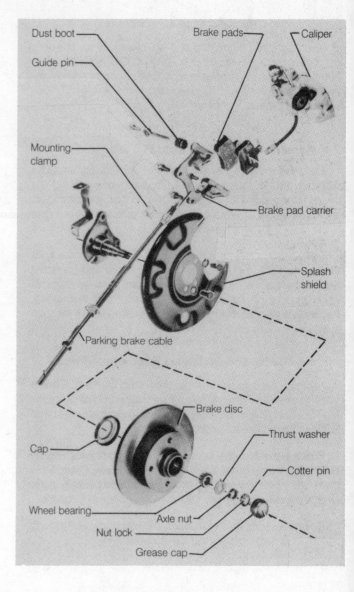

Dust boot — Brake pads — Caliper
Guide pin
Mounting clamp
Brake pad carrier
Splash shield
Parking brake cable
Brake disc
Cap
Thrust washer
Cotter pin
Wheel bearing
Axle nut
Nut lock
Grease cap

5.5   Rear disc brake installation details

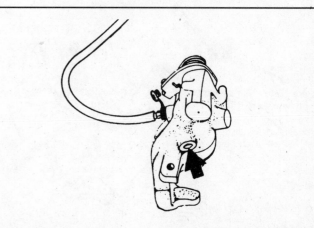

5.6   With the piston facing down, add fluid through the bleeder valve until bubble-free fluid comes out of the inlet opening (arrow)

6.4a   Check the disc runout with a dial indicator – if the reading exceeds the maximum allowable runout limit, the disc will have to be machined or replaced

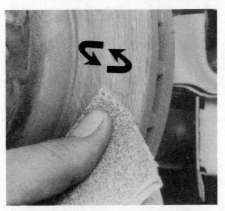

6.4b   Using a swirling motion, remove the glaze from the disc with emery cloth or sandpaper

6.5   Check the thickness of the disc with a micrometer at several points around the outer edge

8   Connect the parking brake cable and adjust the parking brake as described in Section 3, Steps 12 through 20.
9   If the line was disconnected, bleed the brakes (Section 11).
10   Install the wheels and lower the vehicle.
11   After the job has been completed, firmly depress the brake pedal a few times to bring the pads into contact with the disc.
12   Check brake operation before driving the vehicle in traffic.

6   Brake disc – inspection, removal and installation

Inspection

Refer to illustrations 6.4a, 6.4b and 6.5
1   Loosen the wheel lug bolts, raise the vehicle and support it securely on jackstands. Remove the wheel.
2   Remove the brake caliper as outlined in Sections 3 and 5. It's not necessary to disconnect the brake hose. After removing the caliper bolts, suspend the caliper out of the way with a piece of wire. Don't let the caliper hang by the hose and don't stretch or twist the hose.
3   Visually check the disc surface for score marks and other damage. Light scratches and shallow grooves are normal after use and may not always be detrimental to brake operation, but deep score marks – over 0.015-inch (0.38 mm) – require disc removal and refinishing by an automotive machine shop. Be sure to check both sides of the disc. If pulsating has been noticed during application of the brakes, suspect disc runout. Be sure to check the wheel bearings to make sure they're properly adjusted.
4   To check disc runout, place a dial indicator at a point about 1/2-inch from the outer edge of the disc **(see illustration)**. Set the indicator to zero and turn the disc. The indicator reading should not exceed the specified allowable runout limit. If it does, the disc should be refinished by an automotive machine shop. **Note:** *Professionals recommend resurfacing of brake discs regardless of the dial indicator reading (to produce a smooth, flat surface that will eliminate brake pedal pulsations and other undesirable symptoms related to questionable discs). At the very least, if you elect not to have the discs resurfaced, de-glaze them with sandpaper or emery cloth (use a swirling motion to ensure a nondirectional finish)* **(see illustration)**.
5   The disc must not be machined to a thickness less than the specified minimum refinish thickness. The minimum wear (or discard) thickness is cast into the inside of the disc. The disc thickness can be checked with a micrometer **(see illustration)**.

Removal

Front disc
6   Remove the countersunk retaining screw and detach the disc from the hub. If the disc is stuck, use a soft face mallet to free it.

Rear disc
7   Refer to Chapter 1, Rear wheel bearing check, repack and adjustment for the hub/disc removal procedure.

Installation

Front disc
8   Place the disc in position and install the countersunk screw. Tighten the screw securely.

Rear disc
9   Install the disc and hub assembly and adjust the wheel bearing (Chapter 1).

All models
10   Install the caliper and brake pad assembly (refer to appropriate Sections for the caliper installation procedure, if necessary). Tighten the caliper bolts to the specified torque.
11   Install the wheel, then lower the vehicle to the ground. Depress the brake pedal a few times to bring the brake pads into contact with the disc. Bleeding of the system will not be necessary unless the brake hose was disconnected from the caliper. Check the operation of the brakes carefully before placing the vehicle into normal service.

7   Drum brake shoes – replacement

Warning: *Drum brake shoes must be replaced on both wheels at the same time – never replace the shoes on only one wheel. Also, the dust created by the brake system may contain asbestos, which is harmful to your health. Never blow it out with compressed air and don't inhale any of it. An approved filtering mask should be worn when working on the brakes. Do not, under any circumstances, use petroleum based solvents to clean brake parts. Use brake cleaner or denatured alcohol only!*

Caution: *Whenever the brake shoes are replaced, the retractor and hold-down springs should also be replaced. Due to the continuous heating/ cooling cycle that the springs are subjected to, they lose their tension over a period of time and may allow the shoes to drag on the drum and wear at a much faster rate than normal. When replacing the rear brake shoes, use only high quality nationally recognized brand-name parts.*

Note: *All four brake shoes must be replaced at the same time, but to avoid mixing up parts, work on only one brake assembly at a time.*

1   Loosen the wheel lug bolts, raise the vehicle and support it securely on jackstands.
2   Remove the wheel.

9

1975 through 1978 models

Front brake

Refer to illustrations 7.6 and 7.9

3   Remove the countersunk retaining screw and pull the drum off. If the drum does not come off easily, remove the rubber plug in the backing plate, insert a screwdriver and turn the starwheel to adjust the shoes away from the drum.

4   Use pliers to remove the lower return springs.

5   Remove the spring clips and pins retaining the brake shoes.

6   Pull the lower ends of the shoes out over the hub, then unhook the upper return springs and remove the shoe assembly from the vehicle **(see illustration)**.

7   Carefully unhook the adjuster locating spring and remove the adjuster.

7.6   Front drum brake – exploded view

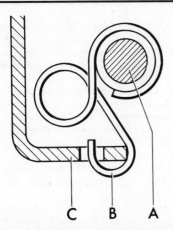

7.9   Front brake adjusting strut retaining spring installation details

A   Adjuster
B   Locating spring

C   Backing plate bracket

8   Disassemble the adjuster assembly, clean the threads, lubricate them with moly-base grease, then reassemble it in the fully backed-off position.

9   Hook the upper return spring onto the backing plate bracket. Install the brake adjuster and locating spring **(see illustration)**.

10   Hook the upper return springs to the shoes, engage the shoes in the wheel cylinder and parking brake, then swing the lower ends of the shoes over the hub and engage them in the lower support. Use pliers to install the lower return springs.

11   Install the retaining pins and secure the shoes with the spring clips.

12   Inspect the brake drum as described in Step 41. Install the drum and adjust the front brake (Chapter 1).

Rear brake

Refer to illustrations 7.15a, 7.15b, 7.16, 7.17 and 7.22

13   Release the parking brake.

14   Remove the brake drum/hub by referring to the Chapter 1 Rear wheel bearing check, repack and adjustment procedure. If the brake drum cannot be easily pulled off the axle and shoe assembly the brake shoes will have to be retracted. Remove the rubber plug in the backing plate, insert a screwdriver and back off the adjuster until the drum/hub can be pulled off. If the right rear hub is difficult to remove, push on the pressure regulator to relieve the residual pressure.

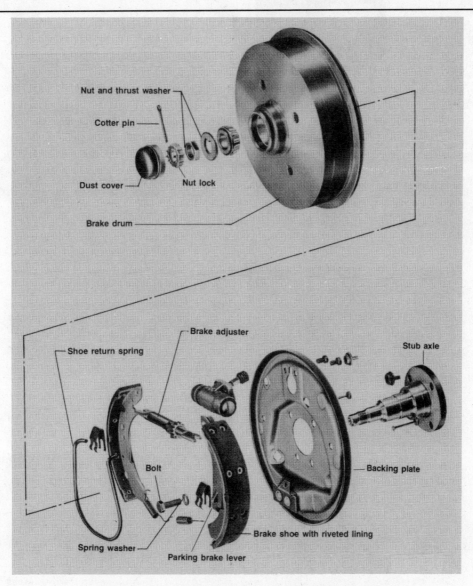

7.15a   1975 through 1978 rear drum brake component layout

15   Use pliers to detach the U-shaped return spring from both shoes **(see illustrations)**. **Warning:** *The U-shaped return spring is under considerable pressure and if not handled carefully, could fly off during removal, causing personal injury.*

16   Compress the shoe retaining springs, slide them off the pins, then remove the springs and pins **(see illustration)**.

17   Use pliers to unhook the lower return springs from the backing plate **(see illustration)**.

18   Pull the parking brake lever (attached to the rear shoe) forward and detach the end of the cable.

19   Pull the shoes out and remove the adjuster. Disengage the shoes from the lower support and remove the shoe assembly.

20   Disassemble the adjuster, clean the threads and lubricate the assem- bly with moly-base grease. Reassemble the adjuster in the fully backed-off position.

21   Connect the lower return springs to the shoes, then attach the shoes and springs to the lower support on the backing plate. Make sure the parking brake lever is installed on the rear shoe.

22   With the shoes loosely installed, move one of the shoes out at the top, install the adjuster and seat the shoes in the piston **(see illustration)**.

23   Install the shoe retaining pins and secure them with the springs.

24   Connect the parking brake cable to the lever on the rear shoe.

25   Use pliers to install the U-shaped upper return spring.

26   Inspect the brake drum as described in Step 41. Install the drum/hub and adjust the brake shoes as described in the appropriate Sections of Chapter 1.

7.15b   Detach the ends (arrows) of the U-shaped return spring from the holes in the shoes – be very careful because the spring is under considerable pressure

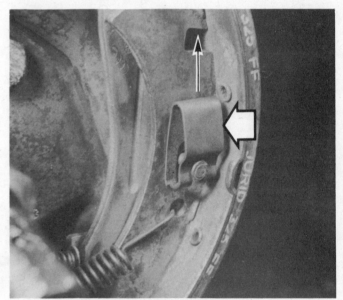

7.16   Compress the retainer and slide it up to remove it from the pin

7.17   Unhook the lower retaining springs (arrows) from the backing plate

7.22   With the adjuster in the fully backed off position, install the ends securely in the shoes

7.28 Insert the screwdriver through the lug bolt hole and push the adjusting wedge up

7.29 Push the retainer in and rotate it 90-degrees to detach it from the pin

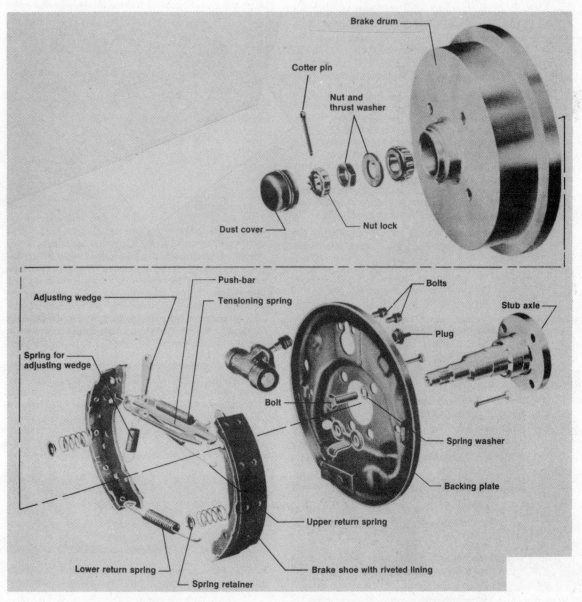

7.31 1979 and later model self-adjusting brake assembly – exploded view

9

1979 and later models

Refer to illustrations 7.28, 7.29, 7.31, 7.37, 7.39, 7.40 and 7.41

27   Release the parking brake.

28   Remove the rear brake drum/hub by referring to the Chapter 1 Rear wheel bearing check, repack and adjustment procedure. If the brake drum cannot be easily pulled off the brake shoe assembly the shoes will have to be retracted. Insert a screwdriver through the lug bolt hole in the brake drum and push the wedge adjuster up until the drum/hub can be pulled off **(see illustration)**.

29   Reach behind the backing plate and support the shoe retaining pin, then use pliers to push the spring retain in and rotate it 90-degrees to release the spring tension **(see illustration)**.

30   Remove the retainers, springs and pins from both shoes.

31   Detach the lower ends of the shoes from the lower backing plate support, then use pliers to remove the lower return spring from the shoes **(see illustration)**.

32   Detach the parking brake cable from the lever on the rear brake shoe.

33   Unhook the spring from the bottom of the adjusting wedge, remove the upper return spring and lift the brake shoe assembly off.

34   Clamp the adjuster push-bar in a vise and use pliers to remove the tensioning spring.

35   Lubricate the contact surfaces of the backing plate, front shoe, adjuster push-bar, tensioning spring and adjusting wedge with moly-base brake grease.

36   Install the adjuster push-bar, secure it with the tensioning spring, then install the adjusting wedge with the lug facing the backing plate.

37   Attach the rear brake shoe and parking brake lever and hook them together with the upper return spring **(see illustration)**.

38   Hold the assembly together, place it in position near the backing plate and connect the parking brake cable.

39   Place the upper ends of the brake shoes in the wheel cylinder, install the lower return spring, engage the shoe bottom ends in the support and secure the assembly with the retainer, pins and springs **(see illustration)**.

40   Connect the adjusting wedge spring, then push the wedge up to retract the shoes so the drum can be installed **(see illustration)**.

41   Before reinstalling the drum it should be checked for cracks, score marks, deep scratches and hard spots, which will appear as small discolored areas. If the hard spots cannot be removed with fine emery cloth or if any of the other conditions listed above exist, the drum must be taken to an automotive machine shop to have it turned. **Note:** *Professionals recommend resurfacing the drums whenever a brake job is done. Resurfacing will eliminate the possibility of out-of-round drums. If the drums are worn so much that they can't be resurfaced without exceeding the maximum allowable diameter (stamped into the drum)* **(see illustration)***,*

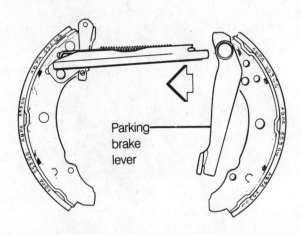

7.37   Attach the rear shoe (complete with parking brake lever) to the front shoe, using the return spring

7.39   Make sure the lower ends of the shoes (A) are secure in the support and the lower return spring (B) is hooked in the holes, then install the shoe retaining pins, springs and retainers (C)

7.40   Hook the spring to the adjusting wedge, then push the wedge up

7.41   The maximum wear limit is cast into the drum

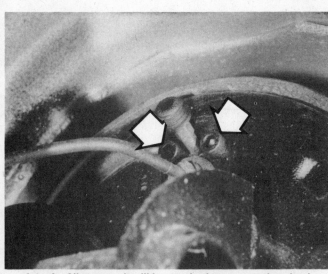

8.4   An Allen wrench will be required to remove the wheel cylinder bolts (arrows) on most models

then new ones will be required. At the very least, if you elect not to have the drums resurfaced, remove the glazing from the surface with medium-grit emery cloth using a swirling motion.

42   Install the brake hub/drum and adjust the wheel bearings as described in Chapter 1.

43   Mount the wheel, install the lug bolts, then lower the vehicle.

44   Apply the brakes firmly to set the adjusting wedge.

45   Check brake operation before driving the vehicle in traffic.

---

8   Wheel cylinder – removal, overhaul and installation

Note: *If an overhaul is indicated (usually because of fluid leakage or sticky operation) explore all options before beginning the job. New wheel cylinders are available, which makes this job quite easy. If it's decided to rebuild the wheel cylinder, make sure that a rebuild kit is available before proceed-*

ing. Never overhaul only one wheel cylinder – always rebuild both of them at the same time.

Removal

Refer to illustration 8.4

1   Raise the vehicle and support it securely on jackstands.

2   Remove the brake shoe assembly (Section 7).

3   Remove all dirt and foreign material from around the wheel cylinder.

4   Unscrew the brake line fitting **(see illustration)**. Don't pull the brake line away from the wheel cylinder.

5   Remove the wheel cylinder mounting bolts.

6   Detach the wheel cylinder from the brake backing plate and place it on a clean workbench. Immediately plug the brake line to prevent fluid loss and contamination. **Note:** *If the brake shoe linings are contaminated with brake fluid, install new brake shoes.*

Overhaul

Refer to illustration 8.7

7   Remove the bleeder screw, cups, pistons, boots and spring assembly from the wheel cylinder body **(see illustration)**.

8   Clean the wheel cylinder with brake fluid, denatured alcohol or brake system cleaner. **Warning:** *Do not, under any circumstances, use petroleum based solvents to clean brake parts!*

9   Use compressed air to remove excess fluid from the wheel cylinder and to blow out the passages.

10   Check the cylinder bore for corrosion and score marks. Crocus cloth can be used to remove light corrosion and stains, but the cylinder must be replaced with a new one if the defects cannot be removed easily, or if the bore is scored.

11   Lubricate the new cups with brake fluid.

12   Assemble the wheel cylinder components. Make sure the cup lips face in.

Installation

13   Place the wheel cylinder in position and install the bolts.

14   Connect the brake line and tighten the fitting. Install the brake shoe assembly.

15   Bleed the brakes (Section 11).

16   Check brake operation before driving the vehicle in traffic.

9

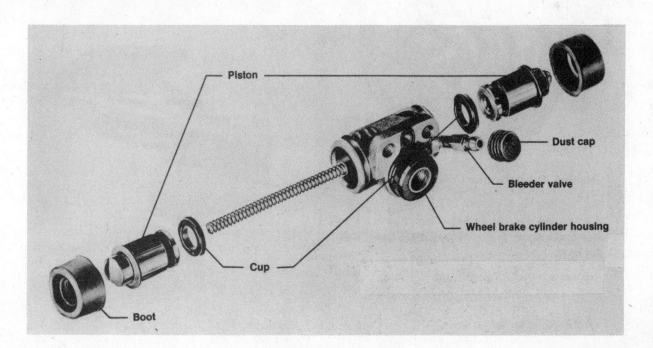

8.7   Wheel cylinder – exploded view

9   Master cylinder – removal, overhaul and installation

Refer to illustrations 9.10, 9.11a, 9.11b and 9.11c

Note: *Before deciding to overhaul the master cylinder on 1975 through 1978 models, check on the availability and cost of a new or rebuilt unit and also the availability of a rebuild kit. The manufacturer does not recommend overhaul for 1985 and later models, so a new or rebuilt unit is the only option.*

Removal

1   The master cylinder is located in the engine compartment, mounted to the firewall or power brake booster.

2   Remove as much fluid as you can from the reservoir with a syringe.

3   Place rags under the fluid fittings and prepare caps or plastic bags to cover the ends of the lines once they are disconnected. **Caution:** *Brake fluid will damage paint. Cover all body parts and be careful not to spill fluid during this procedure.*

4   Loosen the tube nuts at the ends of the brake lines where they enter the master cylinder. To prevent rounding off the flats on these nuts, the use of a flare nut wrench, which wraps around the nut is preferred.

5   Pull the brake lines slightly away from the master cylinder and plug the ends to prevent contamination.

6   Disconnect the electrical connector at the master cylinder, then remove the two nuts attaching the master cylinder to the firewall or power booster. Pull the master cylinder off the studs and out of the engine compartment. Again, be careful not to spill the fluid as this is done. Keep track of the gaskets or sealing rings used on some models.

Overhaul

7   Before attempting the overhaul of the master cylinder, obtain the proper rebuild kit, which will contain the necessary replacement parts and also any instructions which may be specific to your model.

8   Inspect the rubber plugs for indications of leakage near the base of the reservoir. Remove the reservoir.

9   Place the cylinder in a vise and use a punch or Philips screwdriver to depress the pistons until they bottom against the other end of the master cylinder. On all but Bendix master cylinders, hold the pistons in this position and remove the stop screw on the top of the master cylinder.

10   Carefully remove the snap-ring at the end of the master cylinder **(see illustration)**.

11   The internal components can now be now be removed from the cylinder bore **(see illustrations)**.

9.10   Remove the snap-ring with pliers

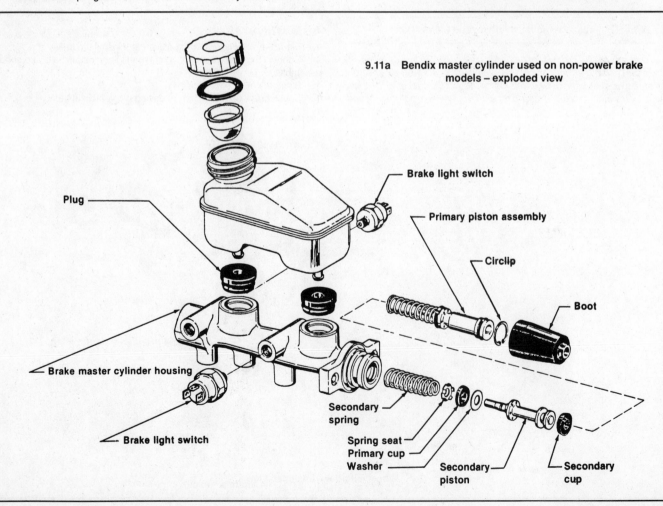

9.11a   Bendix master cylinder used on non-power brake models – exploded view

Plug

Brake light switch

Primary piston assembly

Circlip

Boot

Brake master cylinder housing

Secondary spring

Spring seat
Primary cup
Washer

Secondary piston

Secondary cup

Brake light switch

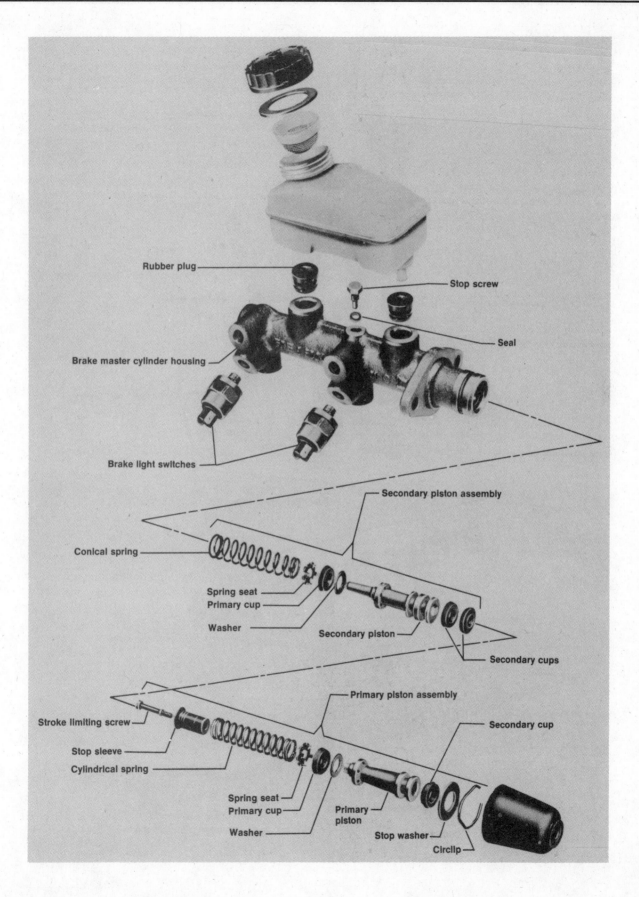

Rubber plug

Stop screw

Seal

Brake master cylinder housing

Brake light switches

Secondary piston assembly

Conical spring

Spring seat
Primary cup
Washer

Secondary piston

Secondary cups

Primary piston assembly

Stroke limiting screw

Secondary cup

Stop sleeve
Cylindrical spring

Spring seat
Primary cup

Primary piston

Washer

Stop washer

Circlip

9

9.11b   ATE master cylinder used on non-power brake models – exploded view

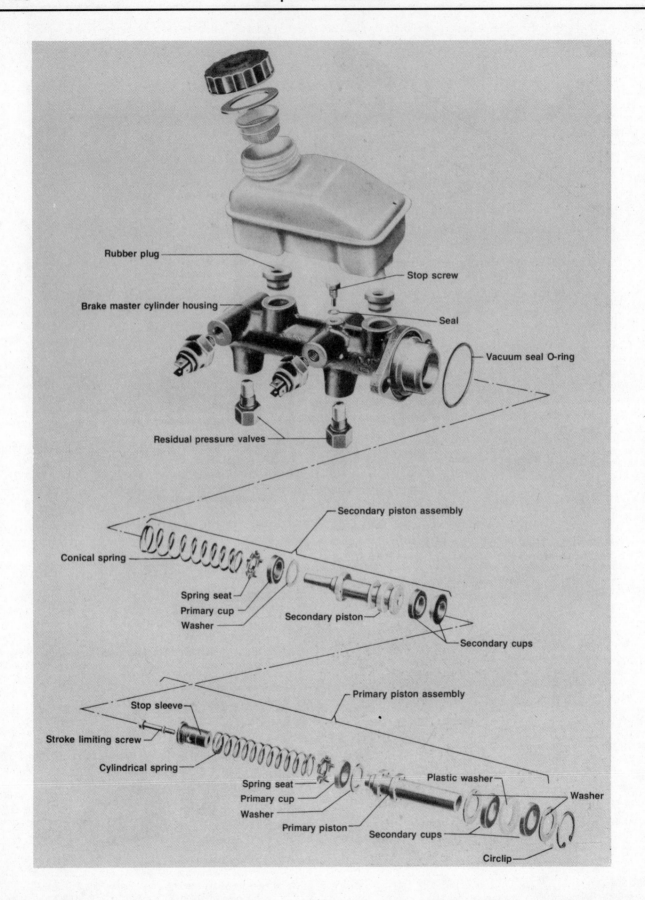

Rubber plug

Stop screw

Brake master cylinder housing

Seal

Vacuum seal O-ring

Residual pressure valves

Secondary piston assembly

Conical spring

Spring seat
Primary cup
Washer

Secondary piston

Secondary cups

Primary piston assembly

Stop sleeve

Stroke limiting screw

Cylindrical spring

Spring seat
Primary cup
Washer

Plastic washer

Washer

Primary piston

Secondary cups

Circlip

9.11c   Master cylinder used on power brake models – exploded view

12   Carefully inspect the bore of the master cylinder. Any deep scoring or other damage will mean a new master cylinder is required.

13   Replace all parts included in the rebuild kit, following any instructions in the kit. Clean all reused parts with clean brake fluid or denatured alcohol. Do not use any petroleum-based cleaners. During reassembly, lubricate all parts liberally with clean brake fluid.

14   Push the assembled components into the bore, bottoming them against the end of the of the master cylinder, then install the stop screw (except Bendix).

15   Install the new snap-ring, making sure it is seated properly in the groove.

16   Before installing the master cylinder it should be bench bled. Because it will be necessary to apply pressure to the master cylinder piston and, at the same time, control flow from the brake line outlets, it is recommended that the master cylinder be mounted in a vise, with the jaws of the vise clamping on the mounting flange. Be careful not to damage it.

17   Insert threaded plugs into the brake line outlet holes and snug them down so that there will be no air leakage past them, but not so tight that they cannot be easily loosened.

18   Fill the reservoir with brake fluid of the recommended type (see Chapter 1).

19   Remove one plug and push the piston assembly into the master cylinder bore to expel the air from the master cylinder. A large Philips screwdriver can be used to push on the piston assembly.

20   To prevent air from being drawn back into the master cylinder the plug must be replaced and snugged down before releasing the pressure on the piston assembly.

21   Repeat the procedure until only brake fluid is expelled from the brake line outlet hole. When only brake fluid is expelled, repeat the procedure with the other outlet hole and plug. Be sure to keep the master cylinder reservoir filled with brake fluid to prevent the introduction of air into the system.

22   Since high pressure is not involved in the bench bleeding procedure, an alternative to the removal and replacement of the plugs with each stroke of the piston assembly is available. Before pushing in on the piston assembly, remove the plug as described in Step 19. Before releasing the piston, however, instead of replacing the plug, simply put your finger tightly over the hole to keep air from being drawn back into the master cylinder. Wait several seconds for brake fluid to be drawn from the reservoir into the piston bore, then depress the piston again, removing your finger as brake fluid is expelled. Be sure to put your finger back over the hole each time before releasing the piston, and when the bleeding procedure is complete for that outlet, replace the plug and snug it before going on to the other port.

Installation

23   Install the master cylinder over the studs on the firewall or power brake booster (don't forget to first install any gaskets or sealing rings which were removed) and tighten the attaching nuts only finger tight at this time.

24   Thread the brake line fittings into the master cylinder. Since the master cylinder is still a bit loose, it can be moved slightly for the fitting to thread in easily. Do not strip the threads as the fittings are tightened.

25   Fully tighten the mounting nuts and the brake fittings.

26   Fill the master cylinder reservoir with fluid, then bleed the master cylinder (only if the cylinder has not been bench bled) and the brake system as described in Section 11. To bleed the cylinder on the vehicle, have an assistant pump the brake pedal several times and then hold the pedal to the floor. Loosen the fitting nut to allow air and fluid to escape. Repeat this procedure on both fittings until the fluid is clear of air bubbles. Test the operation of the brake system carefully before placing the vehicle in normal service.

---

10   Brake lines and hoses – inspection and replacement

Inspection

1   About every six months, with the vehicle raised and supported securely on jackstands, the rubber hoses which connect the steel brake lines with the front and rear brake assemblies should be inspected for cracks, chafing of the outer cover, leaks, blisters and other damage. These are important and vulnerable parts of the brake system and inspection should be complete. A light and mirror will be helpful for a thorough check. If a hose exhibits any of the above conditions, replace it with a new one.

Replacement

Front brake hose

2   Using a back-up wrench, disconnect the brake line from the hose fitting, being careful not to bend the frame bracket or brake line.

3   Use a pair of pliers to remove the U-clip from the female fitting at the bracket, then detach the hose from the bracket.

4   Unscrew the brake hose from the caliper.

5   To install the hose, first thread it into the caliper, tightening it securely.

6   Without twisting the hose, install the female fitting in the hose bracket. It will fit the bracket in only one position.

7   Install the U-clip retaining the female fitting to the frame bracket.

8   Using a back-up wrench, attach the brake line to the hose fitting.

9   When the brake hose installation is complete, there should be no kinks in the hose. Make sure the hose doesn't contact any part of the suspension. Check this by turning the wheels to the extreme left and right positions. If the hose makes contact, remove it and correct the installation as necessary. Bleed the system (Section 11).

Rear brake hose

10   Using a back-up wrench, disconnect the hose at the frame bracket, being careful not to bend the bracket or steel lines.

11   Remove the U-clip with a pair of pliers and separate the female fitting from the bracket.

12   Unscrew the brake hose from the wheel cylinder or caliper.

13   To install the hose, first thread it into the wheel cylinder or caliper, tightening it securely.

14   Without twisting the hose, install the female fitting in the hose bracket. It will fit the bracket in only one position.

15   Install the U-clip retaining the female fitting to the frame bracket.

16   Using a back-up wrench, attach the brake line to the hose fitting.

---

11   Brake system bleeding

Refer to illustration 11.8

Warning: *Wear eye protection when bleeding the brake system. If the fluid comes in contact with your eyes, immediately rinse them with water and seek medical attention.*

Note: *Bleeding the hydraulic system is necessary to remove any air that manages to find its way into the system when it's been opened during removal and installation of a hose, line, caliper or master cylinder.*

1   It will probably be necessary to bleed the system at all four brakes if air has entered the system due to low fluid level, or if the brake lines have been disconnected at the master cylinder.

2   If a brake line was disconnected only at a wheel, then only that caliper or wheel cylinder must be bled.

3   If a brake line is disconnected at a fitting located between the master cylinder and any of the brakes, that part of the system served by the disconnected line must be bled.

4   Remove any residual vacuum from the brake power booster by applying the brake several times with the engine off.

5   Remove the master cylinder reservoir cover and fill the reservoir with brake fluid. Reinstall the cover. **Note:** *Check the fluid level often during the bleeding operation and add fluid as necessary to prevent the fluid level from falling low enough to allow air bubbles into the master cylinder.*

6   Have an assistant on hand, as well as a supply of new brake fluid, a clear container partially filled with clean brake fluid, a length of 5/32-inch plastic, rubber or vinyl tubing to fit over the bleeder valve and a wrench to open and close the bleeder valve.

9

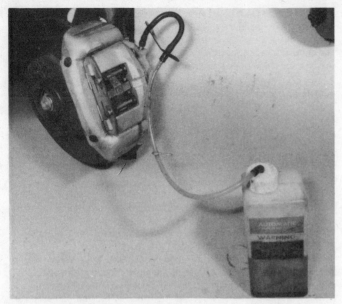

11.8   When bleeding the brakes, a hose is connected to the bleeder screw at the caliper or wheel cylinder and then submerged in brake fluid. Air will be seen as bubbles in the tube and container. All air must be expelled before moving on to the next wheel.

7   Beginning at the right rear wheel, loosen the bleeder valve slightly, then tighten it to a point where it is snug but can still be loosened quickly and easily.

8   Place one end of the tubing over the bleeder valve and submerge the other end in brake fluid in the container **(see illustration)**.

9   Have the assistant pump the brakes slowly a few times to get pressure in the system, then hold the pedal firmly depressed.

10   While the pedal is held depressed, open the bleeder valve just enough to allow a flow of fluid to leave the valve. Watch for air bubbles to exit the submerged end of the tube. When the fluid flow slows after a couple of seconds, close the valve and have your assistant release the pedal.

11   Repeat Steps 9 and 10 until no more air is seen leaving the tube, then tighten the bleeder valve and proceed to the left rear wheel, the right front wheel and the left front wheel, in that order, and perform the same procedure. Be sure to check the fluid in the master cylinder reservoir frequently.

12   Never use old brake fluid. It contains moisture which will deteriorate the brake system components.

13   Refill the master cylinder with fluid at the end of the operation.

14   Check the operation of the brakes. The pedal should feel solid when depressed, with no sponginess. If necessary, repeat the entire process.

Warning: *Do not operate the vehicle if you are in doubt about the effectiveness of the brake system.*

---

12   Power brake booster – check, removal and installation

Refer to illustrations 12.7a, 12.7b and 12.7c

Operating check

1   Depress the brake pedal several times with the engine off and make sure that there is no change in the pedal reserve distance.

2   Depress the pedal and start the engine. If the pedal goes down slightly, operation is normal.

Air tightness check

3   Start the engine and turn it off after one or two minutes. Depress the brake pedal several times slowly. If the pedal goes down farther the first time but gradually rises after the second or third depression, the booster is air tight.

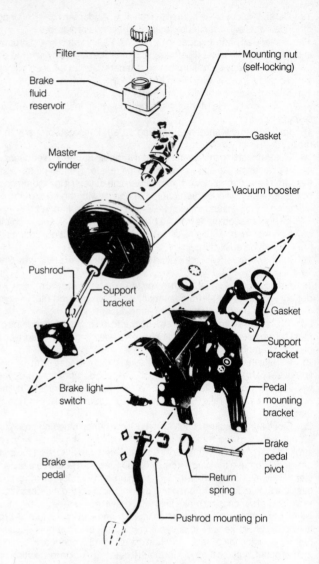

12.7a   1985 and later model brake pedal and power brake booster details

4   Depress the brake pedal while the engine is running, then stop the engine with the pedal depressed. If there is no change in the pedal reserve travel after holding the pedal for 30 seconds, the booster is air tight.

Removal

5   Power brake booster units should not be disassembled. They require special tools not normally found in most service stations or shops. They are fairly complex and because of their critical relationship to brake performance it is best to replace a defective booster unit with a new or rebuilt one.

6   To remove the booster, first remove the brake master cylinder as described in Section 9.

7   On 1975 through 1980 automatic transaxle models, measure and record the distance between the brake pedal foot pad and the steering wheel. Locate the pushrod clevis connecting the booster to the brake pedal **(see illustrations)**. This is accessible from the interior in front of the driver's seat after removing the left hand under dash cover.

8   Remove the clevis pin retaining clip with pliers and pull out the pin.

11   Remove the four nuts and washers holding the brake booster to the firewall. You may need a light to see these, as they are up under the dash area **(see illustrations 12.7a, 12.7b and 12.7c)**.

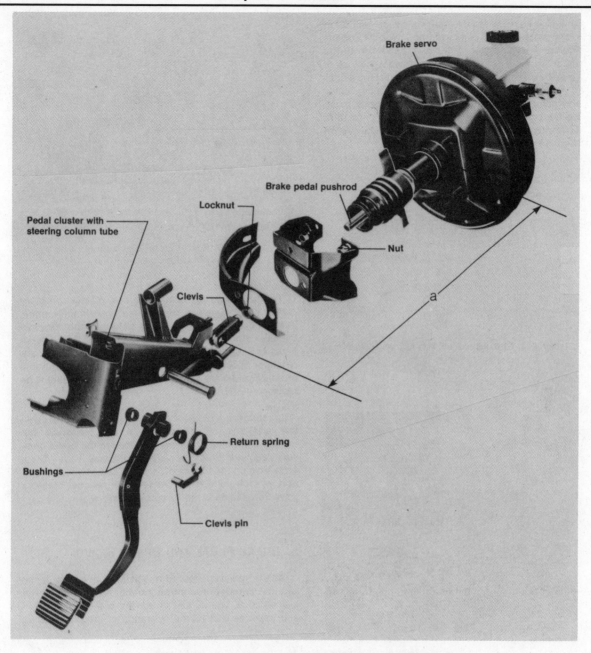

12.7b   1980 through 1984 brake pedal and power brake booster details

9   Holding the clevis with pliers, disconnect the clevis locknut with a wrench. The clevis is now loose.

10   Disconnect the hose leading from the engine to the booster. Be careful not to damage the hose when removing it from the booster fitting.

12   Slide the booster straight out from the firewall until the studs clear the holes and pull the booster, brackets and gaskets from the engine compartment area.

Installation

13   Installation procedures are basically the reverse of those for removal. Tighten the clevis locknut and booster mounting nuts to the specified torque figures. On 1975 through 1979 automatic transaxle models, adjust the brake pedal height if necessary to achieve the pedal-to-steering wheel measurement taken in Step 7.

14   If the power booster unit is being replaced on 1975 through 1984 models, the distance between the brake rod clevis and the face of the vacuum booster must be measured (see illustrations 12.7a and 12.7b and this Chapter's Specifications). Loosen the locknut on the clevis and turn the brake pedal pushrod to adjust this distance.

15   After the final installation of the master cylinder and brake hoses and lines, the brake pedal height and free play may have to be adjusted on 1975 through 1984 models (see illustrations 12.7a and 12.7b and this Chapter's Specifications). Loosen the locknut on the clevis and turn the brake pedal pushrod to adjust this distance. On all models the system must be bled (Section 11).

13   Parking brake handle and cable – removal, installation and adjustment

1   Remove the parking brake handle cover.

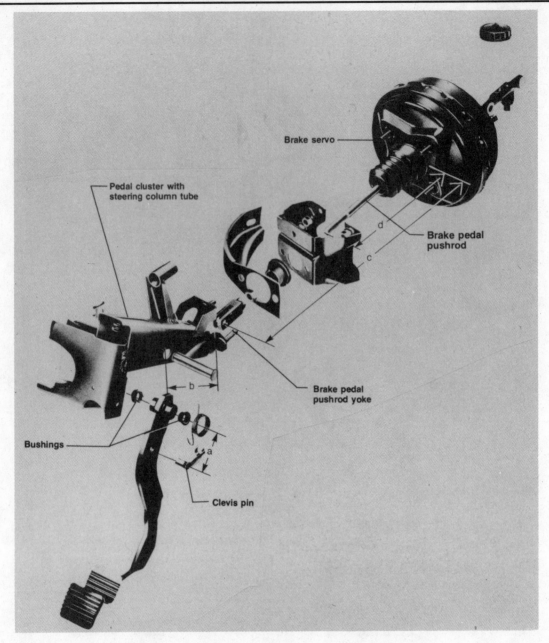

12.7c   1975 through 1979 brake pedal and power brake booster details

Handle

Refer to illustration 13.3

2   Loosen the cable locknuts and adjusting nuts and detach the assembly from the handle **(see illustration)**.
3   Pry the clip from the end of the pivot pin with a screwdriver. Withdraw the pin and detach the handle.
4   Installation is the reverse of removal, taking care to lubricate the pivot pin with lithium base grease.

Cable

5   In the passenger compartment, remove the locknuts and adjusting nuts and detach the cable from the handle.
6   Raise the rear of the vehicle and support it securely on jackstands. Block the front wheels.

Rear drum brakes

7   Remove the brake drums and detach the parking brake cables from the levers on the rear shoes (Section 7). Pull the cables out of the backing plates.

Rear disc brakes

8   Pry off the clips and disengage the parking brake cables from the parking brake levers on the rear calipers.

All models

9   Detach the cables from the clips and remove it from under the vehicle.
10   Installation is the reverse of removal.

Adjustment

Rear drum brakes

11   On 1975 through 1978 models, adjust the brake shoes (Chapter 1) prior to adjusting the parking brake.

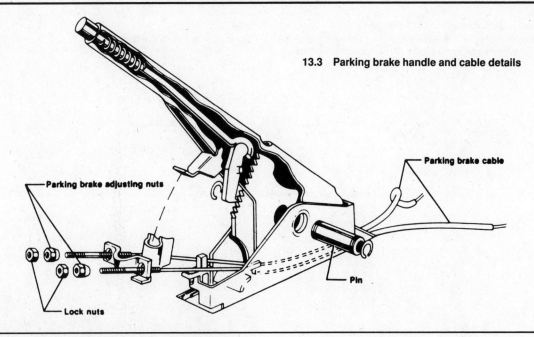

13.3   Parking brake handle and cable details

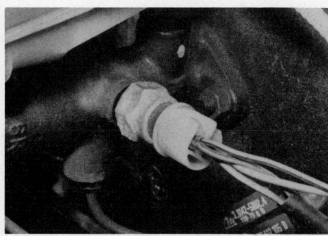

14.1   On earlier models, the brake light switch screws into the master cylinder

12   On 1979 and later models, press the brake pedal one time to seat the shoes.

13   Pull the parking brake lever up one (1975 through 1978 models) or two (1979 on) clicks.

14   With the locknuts at the brake handle loose, turn the adjusting nuts alternately so that both cables are adjusted evenly until the rear wheels won't turn. Release the parking brake lever and make sure the wheels will now turn easily.

15   Tighten the locknuts securely and install the parking brake cable handle cover.

Rear disc brakes

16   Refer to Section 4, Step 15 for the rear disc parking brake adjustment procedure.

---

14   Brake light switch – removal, installation and adjustment

1975 through 1980 models

Refer to illustration 14.1

1   The brake light switches on these models are threaded into the master cylinder **(see illustration)**.

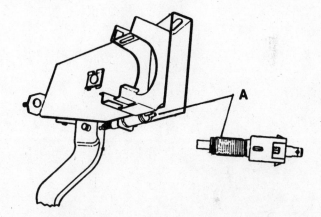

14.9   1981 and later model brake light switch (A) details – the switch must be adjusted so the face is the specified distance from the brake pedal arm (arrow) (refer to this Chapter's Specifications)

2   Unplug the electrical connector.

3   Unscrew the old switch from the master cylinder and transfer the sealing ring to the new switch.

4   Screw the new switch into the master cylinder, tighten it to the specified torque and plug in the connector. These switches require no adjustment.

1981 and later models

Refer to illustration 14.9

5   On these models the brake light switch is mounted in the brake pedal bracket.

6   Unplug the electrical connector.

7   Unscrew the switch from the pedal bracket.

9

8   Screw the new switch into position in the bracket.

9   Screw the switch in or out as necessary to achieve the specified clearance between the brake pedal arm and the switch contact **(see illustration)**.

10 Plug in the electrical connector.

Chapter 10
Suspension and steering systems

Contents

Balljoints – check and replacement 6
Control arm – removal, inspection and installation 5
Front axle hub and bearing – replacement 8
Front end alignment – general information 25
Front strut/shock absorber and coil spring
   assembly – removal, inspection and installation 3
Front shock absorber – replacement 4
General information 1
Intermediate shaft – removal and installation 19
Power steering fluid level check .... See Chapter 1
Power steering pump – removal and installation 22
Power steering system – bleeding 23
Rear axle assembly (hatchback and sedan models) – removal
   and installation 12
Rear axle assembly (pick-up models) – removal and installation . 15
Rear shock absorber (pick-up models) – replacement 13
Rear shock absorber and coil spring (1985 and later
   hatchback and sedan models) – removal and installation 11

Rear strut/shock absorber and coil spring (1975 through 1984
   hatchback and sedan models) – removal and installation 9
Rear shock absorbers (1975 through 1984 hatchback
   and sedan models) – replacement 10
Rear spring assembly (pick-up models) – removal
   and installation 14
Stabilizer bars – removal and installation 2
Rear wheel bearing check, repack and adjustment ... See Chapter 1
Steering and suspension checks .... See Chapter 1
Steering gear boots – replacement 21
Steering gear – removal and installation 19
Steering knuckle and hub assembly – removal and installation ... 7
Steering system – general information 16
Steering wheel – removal and installation 17
Tie-rod ends – removal and installation 20
Tire and tire pressure checks .... See Chapter 1
Tire rotation .... See Chapter 1
Wheels and tires – general information 24

10

Specifications

Torque specifications   Ft-lbs

Front suspension

Front strut/shock absorber upper mounting nuts
   1975 through 1984 15
   1985 on 44
Tie-rod-to-steering arm nut
   1975 through 1984 22
   1985 on 26

Front suspension (continued)

Control arm balljoint stud-to-steering knuckle clamp bolt/nut	37
Balljoint-to-control arm bolt/nut	18
Steering knuckle-to-strut bolt/nut	59
Control arm front pivot bolt	
1975 through 1984	52
1985 on	96
Control arm rear bolt/nut	
1975 through 1984	33
1985 on	96
Stabilizer bar mounting nuts	18

Rear suspension

1975 through 1984

Sedan	
Shock strut-to-axle bolt/nut	33
Shock strut-to-body nut	26
Coil spring retainer-to-strut slotted nut	15
Rear axle beam-to-mount bolt/nut	44
Rear shock absorber mount-to-body nut	33
Pick-up truck	
Shock absorber bolt/nut	30
Axle-to-spring U-bolt nut	30
Shackle bolt/nut	44
Spring-to-front mount bolt/nut	70

1985 on

Rear shock absorber lower bolt/nut	52
Shock strut-to-body nut	11
Coil spring retainer-to-rear shock nut	11
Rear axle beam pivot bolt	44
Rear axle mounting bracket-to-body bolt	33
Rear control arm-to-subframe bolt	96
Subframe-to-body bolt	96

Steering

Tie-rod end-to-steering knuckle nut	22 to 26
Power steering pump-to-bracket bolt	11 to 15
Steering wheel nut	30
Steering gear-to-crossmember nuts	22
Intermediate shaft pinch bolts	22
Wheel lug bolts	See Chapter 1

---

1   General information

The front suspension is a MacPherson strut design. The steering knuckle is located by a triangulated lower arm. A stabilizer bar, mounted to the front crossmember and connecting the lower arms, minimizes body lean.

The rear suspension on sedan and hatchback models consists of trailing arms connected to an axle with integral spindles, coil springs and telescopic shock absorbers. Pick-up models have a solid beam rear axle suspended by leaf springs and tubular shock absorbers.

The rack-and-pinion steering gear is located behind the engine/transaxle assembly on the firewall and actuates the steering arms, which are integral with the steering knuckles. The steering column is designed to collapse in the event of an accident.

Frequently, when working on the suspension or steering system components, you may come across fasteners which seem impossible to loosen. These fasteners on the underside of the vehicle are continually subjected to water, road grime, mud, etc., and can become rusted or "frozen," making them extremely difficult to remove. In order to unscrew these stubborn fasteners without damaging them (or other components), be sure to use lots of penetrating oil and allow it to soak in for a while. Using a wire brush to clean exposed threads will also ease removal of the nut or bolt and prevent damage to the threads. Sometimes a sharp blow with a hammer and punch is effective in breaking the bond between a nut and bolt threads, but care must be taken to prevent the punch from slipping off the fastener and ruining the threads. Heating the stuck fastener and surrounding area with a torch sometimes helps too, but isn't recommended because of the obvious fire hazard. Long breaker bars and extension, or "cheater," pipes will increase leverage, but never use an extension pipe on a ratchet – the ratcheting mechanism could be damaged. Sometimes, turning the nut or bolt in the tightening (clockwise) direction first will help to break it loose. Fasteners that require drastic measures to unscrew should always be replaced with new ones.

Since most of the procedures in this Chapter involve jacking up the vehicle and working underneath it, a good pair of jackstands will be needed. A hydraulic floor jack is the preferred type of jack to lift the vehicle, and it can also be used to support certain components during various operations. **Warning:** *Never, under any circumstances, rely on a jack to support the vehicle while working on it. Whenever any of the suspension or steering fasteners are loosened or removed, they must be inspected and, if necessary, replaced with new ones of the same part number or of original equipment quality and design. Torque specifications must be followed for proper reassembly and component retention. Never attempt to heat or straighten any suspension or steering components. Instead, replace bent or damaged parts with new ones.*

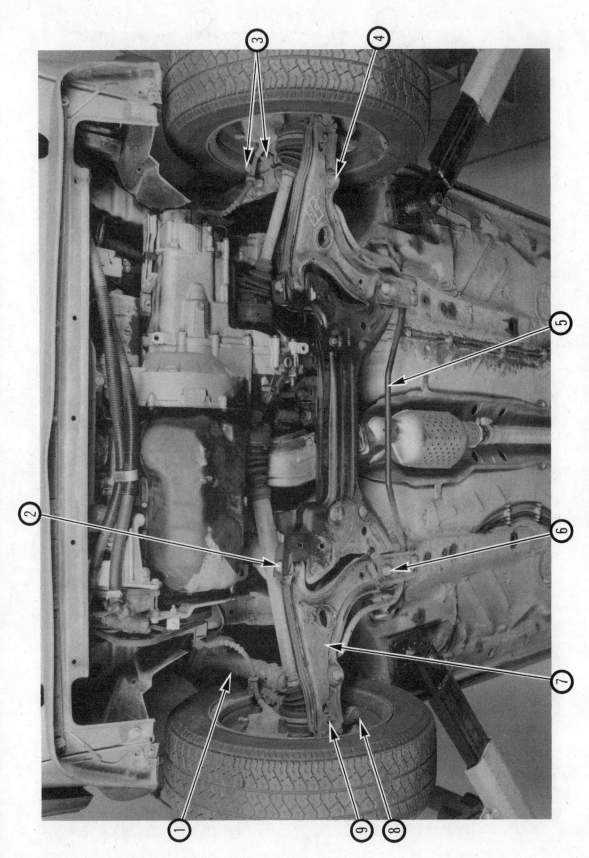

Front suspension and steering components

1 Strut/shock absorber and
   coil spring assembly
2 Control arm pivot bolt
3 Strut-to-steering knuckle bolts
4 Stabilizer bar stud and nut
5 Stabilizer bar
6 Control arm bushing bolt (1985 and on)
7 Control arm
8 Tie-rod end
9 Balljoint

10

Rear suspension components

1   Shock absorber and
    coil spring
2   Trailing arm
3   Rear axle beam

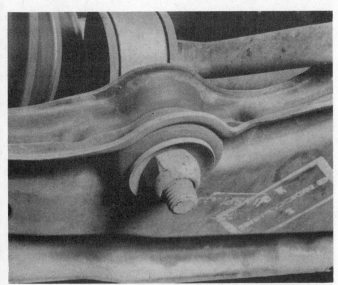

2.2 Remove the stabilizer bar-to-control arm nuts, washers and rubber bushings to separate the bar from the control arms

2.3 Remove the nut and rotate the bracket back and down so the rear stabilizer bar can be detached (1975 through 1984 models)

2 Stabilizer bars – removal and installation

Refer to illustrations 2.2 and 2.3

Warning: *Whenever any of the suspension or steering fasteners are loosened or removed, they must be inspected and, if necessary, replaced with new ones of the same part number or of original equipment quality and design. Torque specifications must be followed for proper reassembly and component retention.*

Removal

1   Raise the vehicle and support it securely on jackstands.
2   Remove the front stabilizer bar-to-control arm nuts, noting how the mount bushings and washers are positioned **(see illustration)**. The stabilizer bar is also attached to the rear control arm mounts.
3   Remove the rear stabilizer bar bracket nuts and detach the bar from the vehicle **(see illustration)**.
4   Pull the brackets off the stabilizer bar and inspect the bushings for cracks, hardness and other signs of deterioration. If the bushings are damaged, replace them.

Installation

5   To install the rear bar, position the bushings on the bar.
6   Insert the lower ends of the brackets into the slots, push the brackets over the bushings and raise the bar up to the frame. Install the bracket nuts but don't tighten them completely at this time.
7   To install the front bar, install the stabilizer bar-to-control arm rubber bushings, washers and nuts. Tighten the nuts finger tight.
8   Lower the vehicle and tighten the rear bar bracket nuts. Tighten the front bar-to-control arm nuts.

3 Front strut/shock absorber and coil spring assembly – removal, inspection and installation

Refer to illustrations 3.3, 3.5a, 3.5b and 3.5c

Warning: *Whenever any of the suspension or steering fasteners are loosened or removed, they must be inspected and, if necessary, replaced with new ones of the same part number or of original equipment quality and de-*

sign. Torque specifications must be followed for proper reassembly and component retention.

Removal

1   Loosen the wheel lug bolts, raise the front of the vehicle and support it securely on jackstands. Apply the parking brake and position blocks behind the rear wheels. Remove the front wheel.
2   Disconnect the brake hose bracket from the strut.
3   Mark the relative position of the strut to the knuckle so it can be installed in the same position, otherwise the camber setting will be affected **(see illustration)**. Remove the strut-to-knuckle nuts and knock the bolts out with a hammer and punch.
4   Separate the strut from the steering knuckle. Be careful not to overextend the inner CV joint. It's a good idea to wire the top of the steering knuckle to the body to prevent this from happening.

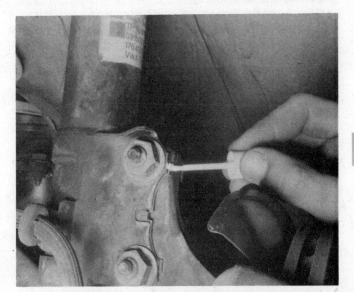

3.3 Mark the strut-to-steering knuckle relationship at the eccentric (upper) bolt before loosening it

3.5a   On 1975 through 1984 models, the upper end of the front strut is held in place by two nuts (arrows)

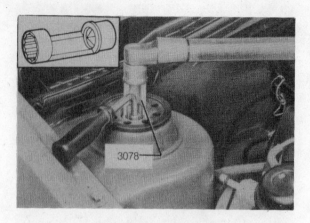

3.3b   On 1985 and later models, a special cutaway tool is required to hold the strut shaft while the hex head flange nut is removed

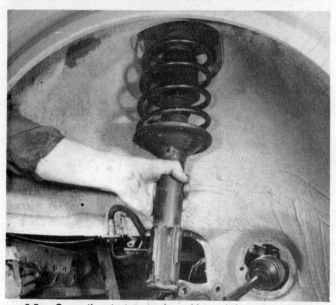

3.5c   Grasp the strut securely and lower it from the vehicle

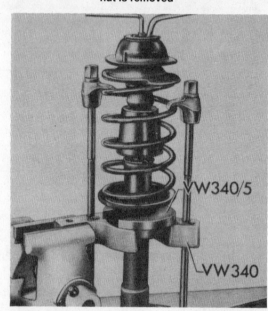

4.4   Hold the piston rod with an Allen wrench while loosening the piston rod nut with a box-end wrench

5   Support the strut and spring assembly with one hand and remove the strut-to-body nuts (1975 through 1984 models) or nut and flange (1985 on) **(see illustrations)**. Remove the assembly out through the fender well **(see illustration)**.

Inspection

6   Check the strut body for leaking fluid, dents, cracks and other obvious damage which would warrant repair or replacement.

7   Check the coil spring for chips or cracks in the spring coating (this will cause premature spring failure due to corrosion).

8   If any undesirable conditions exist, proceed to Section 4 for the strut disassembly procedure.

Installation

9   Guide the strut assembly up into the fender well and insert the upper mounting studs or shock strut end through the hole(s) in the body. Once the studs or shock strut end protrude through the body, install the nuts or nut and flange so the strut won't fall back out. This may require an assistant, as the strut is quite heavy and awkward.

10   Slide the steering knuckle into the strut flange and insert the two bolts. Install the nuts and, after aligning the marks made during removal, tighten them to the specified torque.

11   Connect the brake hose bracket to the strut.

12   Install the wheel, lower the vehicle and tighten the lug bolts to the specified torque.

13   Tighten the upper mounting nuts to the specified torque.

---

4   Front shock absorber – replacement

Refer to illustrations 4.4, 4.5a and 4.5b

1   If the struts exhibit the telltale signs of wear (leaking fluid, loss of dampening capability, knocking sounds when going over bumps) explore all options before beginning any work. The strut cartridges cannot be replaced. However, rebuilt strut assemblies (some complete with springs) are available on an exchange basis, which can eliminate much time and work. Considerable savings can be realized by removing the spring yourself and installing it on a new shock absorber strut unit. Whichever route you choose to take, check on the cost and availability of parts before disassembling the vehicle. **Warning:** *Disassembling a strut is a dangerous job. Be very careful and follow the instructions to the letter or serious injury may result. Use only a high quality spring compressor and carefully follow the*

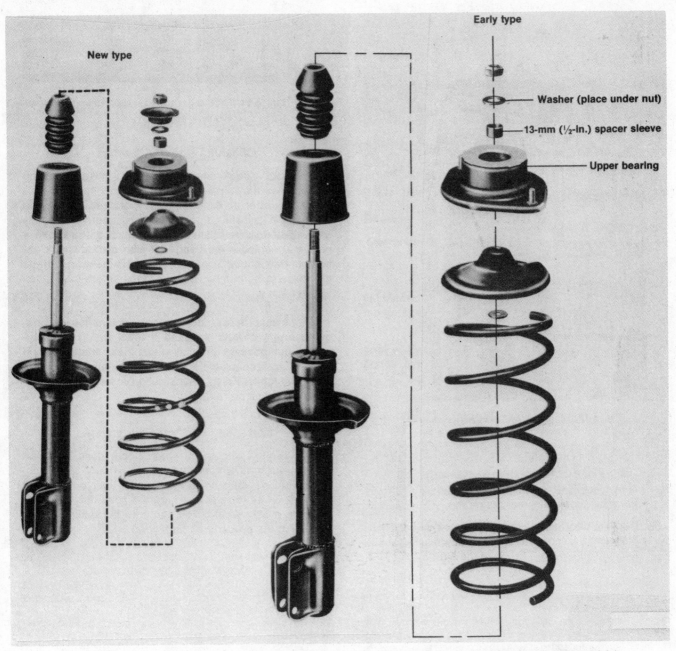

4.5a   Exploded view of the strut/shock absorber and coil spring assembly components (1975 through 1984 models)

manufacturer's instructions furnished with the tool. After removing the coil spring from the strut assembly, set it aside in a safe, isolated area (a steel cabinet is preferred).

2   Remove the strut and spring assembly following the procedure described in Section 3. Mount the strut assembly in a vise with the jaws of the vise cushioned with rags or blocks of wood.

3   Following the tool manufacturer's instructions, install the spring compressor (which can be rented at most auto parts stores or equipment yards on a daily basis) on the spring and compress it enough to relieve all pressure from the spring seat. This can be verified by wiggling the spring seat.

4   Unscrew the piston rod nut with a box-end wrench while using an Allen wrench on the rod to prevent it from turning **(see illustration)**.

5   Lift the washer, spacer sleeve, upper bearing and upper spring retainer off the shock absorber shaft, keeping track of the order in which they were removed **(see illustrations)**. Inspect the strut bearing for smooth operation and replace it if necessary.

6   Carefully remove the compressed spring assembly and set it in a safe place, such as inside a steel cabinet. **Warning:** *Never place your head near the end of the spring! Slide the bump rubber up off the piston rod.*

7   Place the new shock absorber assembly securely in the cushioned vise.

8   Stroke the shock absorber shaft up and down a few times to verify proper operation.

9   Fully extend the shock absorber shaft. Assemble the strut, making

10

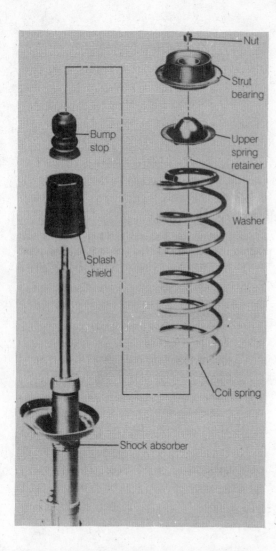

4.5b   Exploded view of the strut/shock absorber and coil spring assembly components (1985 and later models)

5.2   Control arm pivot bolt

5.3a   On 1975 through 1984 models, a clamp and bushing holds the rear of the control arm in place

sure the spring is properly positioned in the lower and upper seats **(see illustrations 4.5a and 4.5b).**

10   Install the spring retainer upper bearing and a new piston rod nut, tightening it to the specified torque. Remove the spring compressor.

11   Install the strut and spring assembly on the vehicle as outlined in Section 3.

---

5   Control arm – removal, inspection and installation

Refer to illustrations 5.2, 5.3a, 5.3b, 5.4, 5.5, 5.6a, 5.6b and 5.7

Warning: *Whenever any of the suspension or steering fasteners are loosened or removed, they must be inspected and, if necessary, replaced with new ones of the same part number or of original equipment quality and design. Torque specifications must be followed for proper reassembly and component retention.*

Removal

1   Loosen the wheel lug bolts on the side to be dismantled, raise the front of the vehicle, support it securely on jackstands, apply the parking brake and place blocks behind the rear wheels. Remove the wheel.

2   Remove the front control arm-to-chassis pivot bolt **(see illustration).** Pry the arm from the crossmember if it is stuck.

3   Remove the rear control arm clamp and nuts or bushing bolt **(see illustrations).**

4   On models with bolt-on balljoints, remove the balljoint bolts **(see illustration).**

5   On models with riveted balljoints, remove the clamp bolt and separate the balljoint from the steering knuckle **(see illustration).**

6   Lower the control arm from the vehicle **(see illustrations).**

Inspection

7   Use a straight-edge to determine if the control arm is bent or distorted **(see illustration).** Check the bushings for wear, damage and deterioration. Replace a damaged or bent control arm with a new one. If the bushings are worn, take the control arm to a dealer service department or a repair shop, as special tools are required to replace them.

Installation

8   Place the control arm in position. Install the front pivot bolt and the rear clamp and nuts or bushing bolt, but don't tighten them completely yet.

9   On models with bolt-on balljoints, connect the outer end of the arm to the balljoint, install the bolts and tighten them to the specified torque.

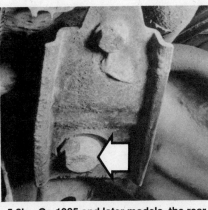

5.3b   On 1985 and later models, the rear corner of the lower control arm is attached by the bushing bolt (arrow)

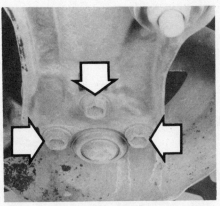

5.4   Control arm balljoint bolt locations (arrows)

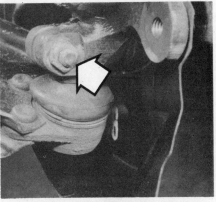

5.5   Balljoint clamp nut (arrow)

5.6a   1975 through 1984 model control arm details

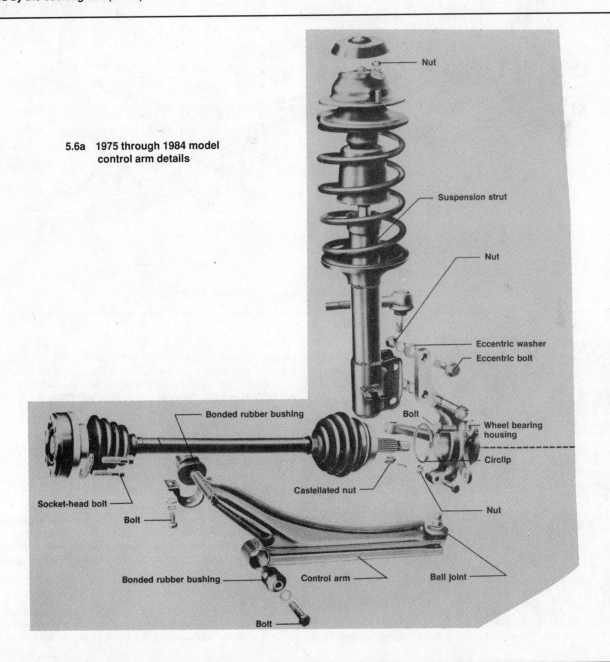

Nut

Suspension strut

Nut

Eccentric washer

Eccentric bolt

Bolt

Wheel bearing housing

Circlip

Nut

Castellated nut

Ball joint

Control arm

Bonded rubber bushing

Socket-head bolt

Bolt

Bonded rubber bushing

Bolt

10

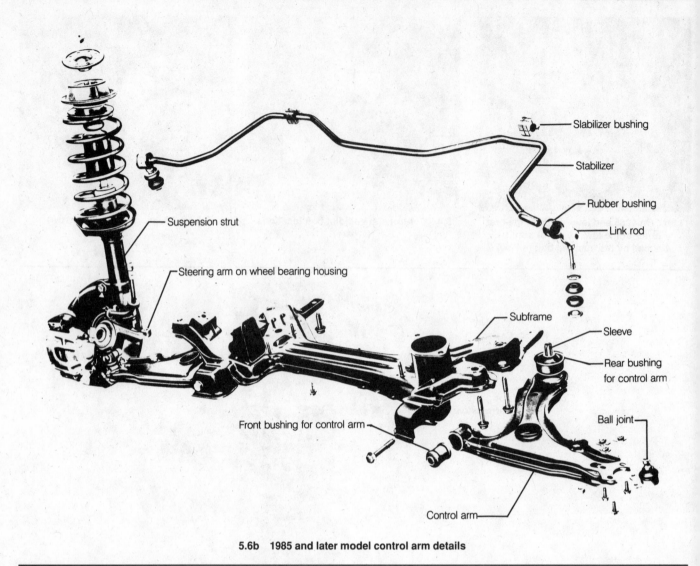

Suspension strut

Steering arm on wheel bearing housing

Slabilizer bushing

Stabilizer

Rubber bushing

Link rod

Subframe

Sleeve

Rear bushing
for control arm

Ball joint

Front bushing for control arm

Control arm

5.6b   1985 and later model control arm details

5.7   Use a straightedge to check the control arm for distortion

10   On models with riveted balljoints, connect the balljoint to the steering knuckle, install the clamp bolt and tighten it to the specified torque.
11   Place a jack under the balljoint, with a block of wood on the jack head as a cushion. Raise the control arm to simulate normal ride height, then tighten the pivot and rear clamp or bushing bolts to the specified torque.
12   Install the wheel and lug bolts, lower the vehicle and tighten the lug bolts to the specified torque.
13   Have the front end alignment checked.

6   Balljoints – check and replacement

Refer to illustrations 6.7 and 6.10

Warning: *Whenever any of the suspension or steering fasteners are loosened or removed, they must be inspected and, if necessary, replaced with new ones of the same part number or of original equipment quality and design. Torque specifications must be followed for proper reassembly and component retention.*

Check

1   Raise the vehicle and support it securely on jackstands.
2   Visually inspect the rubber boot for cuts, tears or leaking grease. If any of these conditions are noticed, the balljoint should be replaced.

6.7   Use a "pickle-fork" type balljoint separator to break the balljoint loose from the steering knuckle – boot damage can be minimized by applying grease to the boot first

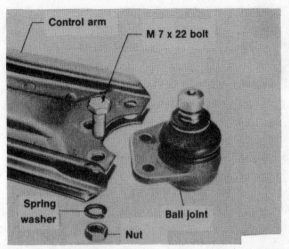

6.10   After drilling out the rivets, the new balljoint can be installed using bolts, nuts and washers

3   Place a large pry bar under the balljoint and attempt to push the ball-joint up. Next, position the pry bar between the steering knuckle and the control arm and apply downward pressure. If any movement is seen or felt during either of these checks, a worn out balljoint is indicated.

4   Have an assistant grasp the tire at the top and bottom and shake the top of the tire in an in-and-out motion. Touch the balljoint stud nut. If any looseness is felt, suspect a worn out balljoint stud or a widened hole in the steering knuckle boss. If the latter problem exists, the steering knuckle should be replaced as well as the balljoint.

Replacement

5   Loosen the wheel lug bolts, raise the vehicle and support it securely on jackstands. Remove the wheel.

6   On bolt-on balljoints, break the balljoint-to-control arm bolts loose, but don't remove them yet.

7   Loosen the balljoint stud nut a couple of turns. Separate the balljoint from the steering knuckle with a balljoint separator **(see illustration)**, then remove the nut.

8   On bolt-on balljoints, unscrew the three balljoint-to-control arm bolts and remove the balljoint.

9   On riveted balljoints, drill out the rivets using a 1/4-inch bit on two rivet models or a 7/32-inch bit on three rivet models and remove the balljoint. On two rivet models, drill out the holes with a 21/64-inch bit. Obtain 8 mm bolts and nuts for two rivet models. Three rivet balljoints require 7 mm bolts and nuts.

10   To install the balljoint, position it on the control arm and install the bolts and nuts or lockplate, but don't tighten them yet **(see illustration)**.

11   Insert the balljoint stud into the steering knuckle and install the nut, tightening it to the specified torque.

12   Tighten the balljoint-to-control arm bolts to the specified torque.

13   Install the wheel and lug bolts. Lower the vehicle and tighten the lug bolts to the specified torque.

---

7   Steering knuckle and hub assembly – removal and installation

---

Warning: *Whenever any of the suspension or steering fasteners are loosened or removed they must be inspected and, if necessary, replaced with new ones of the same part number or of original equipment quality and design. Torque specifications must be followed for proper reassembly and component retention. Dust created by the brake system may contain asbestos, which is harmful to your health. Never blow it out with compressed air and don't inhale any of it. Do not, under any circumstances, use petro-* leum-based solvents to clean brake parts. Use brake cleaner or denatured alcohol only.

Removal

1   Remove the wheel cover and unscrew the hub nut (see Chapter 8).

2   Loosen the wheel lug bolts, raise the vehicle and support it securely on jackstands. Remove the wheel. Remove the brake caliper and support it with a piece of wire as described in Chapter 9.

3   Mark the relative position of the strut on the knuckle then loosen, but do not remove the strut-to-steering knuckle bolts/nuts **(see illustration 3.3)**.

4   Separate the tie-rod from the steering knuckle arm as outlined in Section 20.

5   Separate the balljoint from the steering knuckle (Section 6). The strut-to-knuckle bolts can now be removed.

6   Remove the steering knuckle and hub assembly from the strut, ball-joint and driveaxle. If the driveaxle sticks in the hub splines, push it from the hub. Support the end of the driveaxle with a piece of wire.

Installation

7   Guide the knuckle and hub assembly into position, inserting the dri-veaxle into the hub.

8   Push the knuckle into the strut flange, line up the marks made in Step 3 and install the bolts, but don't tighten them yet.

9   Insert the balljoint stud into the steering knuckle hole and install the nut, but don't tighten it yet.

10   Attach the tie-rod to the steering knuckle arm as described in Section 20. Tighten the strut bolt nuts, the balljoint nut and the tie-rod nut to the specified torque.

11   Install the caliper as outlined in Chapter 9.

12   Install the hub nut and tighten it securely (Chapter 9).

13   Install the wheel and lug bolts.

14   Lower the vehicle and tighten the lug bolts to the specified torque.

15   Tighten the hub nut to the specified torque (see Chapter 8).

---

8   Front axle hub and bearing – replacement

Due to the need for special tools to replace the hub and bearing assembly in the steering knuckle and to properly adjust the hub bearing preload, the steering knuckle and hub assembly must be taken to a Volkswagen dealer service department or a repair shop equipped with the necessary tools for this procedure. Refer to Section 7 for the steering knuckle removal procedure.

10

9.3   Remove the plastic cap for access to the upper shock strut nut

9.5   Lower shock absorber mounting details (1975 through 1984 models)

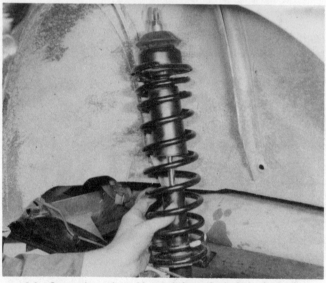

9.6   Grasp the unit and lower it from the hole in the body (1975 through 1984 models)

10.2   With the spring held securely in a vise, unscrew the slotted nut with the special tool (1975 through 1984 models)

4   Slowly lower the jack until the end of the strut starts to pull away from the body.
5   Working under the vehicle, remove the shock absorber-to-rear axle nut and bolt **(see illustration)**.
6   Lower the axle until it is possible to detach the strut/shock unit from the body and axle, then remove it from the vehicle **(see illustration)**.
7   Installation is the reverse of the removal procedure.

9   Rear strut/shock absorber and coil spring (1975 through 1984 hatchback and sedan models) – removal and installation

Refer to illustrations 9.3, 9.5 and 9.6

Warning: *Whenever any of the suspension or steering fasteners are loosened or removed, they must be inspected and, if necessary, replaced with new ones of the same part number or of original equipment quality and design. Torque specifications must be followed for proper reassembly and component retention.*

1   Loosen the rear wheel lug bolts, raise the rear of the vehicle and support it securely on jackstands. The jackstands must be placed under the vehicle at the lifting points, not under the rear axle assembly. Remove the wheel.
2   Position a floor jack under the suspension trailing arm, next to the lower shock mount. Raise it just enough to feel resistance from the spring.
3   Working inside the vehicle, remove the plastic cap for access to the rear shock absorber nut **(see illustration)**. Remove the nut and washer from the strut.

10   Rear shock absorbers (1975 through 1984 hatchback and sedan models) – replacement

Refer to illustrations 10.2 and 10.3

Warning: *Whenever any of the suspension or steering fasteners are loosened or removed, they must be inspected and, if necessary, replaced with new ones of the same part number or of original equipment quality and design. Torque specifications must be followed for proper reassembly and component retention.*

1   Remove the rear strut\shock absorber and spring unit from the vehicle (Section 9).
2   It isn't necessary to use a spring compressor tool to remove the shock absorber on rear units. Place the unit in a vise and remove the special slotted nut, using Volkswagen tool 50-200 **(see illustration)**.
3   Separate the spring, protective cap and related mounting components from the shock absorber **(see illustration)**.
4   Installation is the reverse of removal.

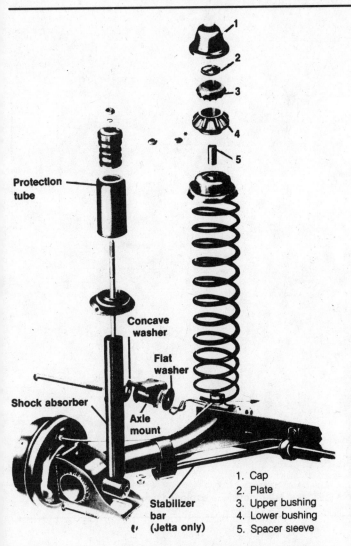

Protection tube

Concave washer

Flat washer

Shock absorber

Axle mount

Stabilizer bar (Jetta only)

1. Cap
2. Plate
3. Upper bushing
4. Lower bushing
5. Spacer sleeve

10.3   Rear strut/shock absorber and spring unit – exploded view (1975 through 1984 models)

11   Rear shock absorber and coil spring (1985 and later hatchback and sedan models) – removal and installation

Refer to illustrations 11.3, 11.5 and 11.6

Warning: *Whenever any of the suspension or steering fasteners are loosened or removed, they must be inspected and, if necessary, replaced with new ones of the same part number or of original equipment quality and design. Torque specifications must be followed for proper reassembly and component retention.*

1   On these models the spring and shock absorber separate from one another when removed from the vehicle so replacement of either the spring or shock absorber is a straightforward procedure. Loosen the rear wheel lug bolts, raise the rear of the vehicle and support it securely on jackstands. The jackstands must be placed under the vehicle at the lifting points, not under the rear axle assembly. Remove the wheel.
2   Position a floor jack under the suspension trailing arm, next to the lower shock mount. Raise it just enough to feel resistance from the spring.
3   Working inside the vehicle, remove the plastic cap for access to the rear shock absorber nut. Remove the nut and washer from the strut. On some models, Volkswagen tool 3079 will be required to remove the nut because of the limited access **(see illustration)**.
4   Slowly lower the jack until the spring is loose and the end of the strut starts to pull away from the body.

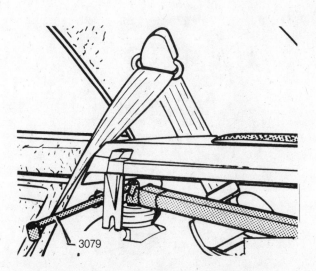

11.3   A special tool may be required to remove the strut upper nut because access is tight (1985 and later models)

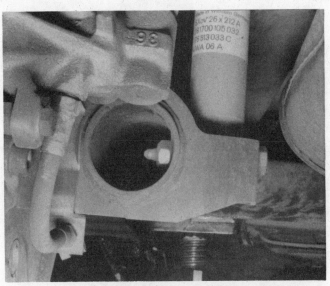

11.5   Lower shock absorber through-bolt and nut location (1985 and later models)

5   Working under the vehicle, remove the shock absorber-to-rear axle nut and bolt **(see illustration)**.
6   Lower the axle until it is possible to detach the spring and shock absorber from the body and axle, then remove them from the vehicle **(see illustration)**.
7   Installation is the reverse of the removal procedure.

12   Rear axle assembly (hatchback and sedan models) – removal and installation

Warning: *Whenever any of the suspension or steering fasteners are loosened or removed, they must be inspected and, if necessary, replaced with new ones of the same part number or of original equipment quality and design. Torque specifications must be followed for proper reassembly and component retention.*

10

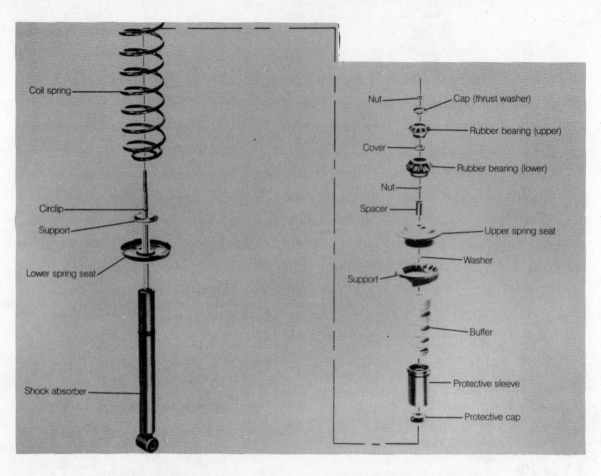

11.6   Shock absorber and spring components (1985 and later models) – exploded view

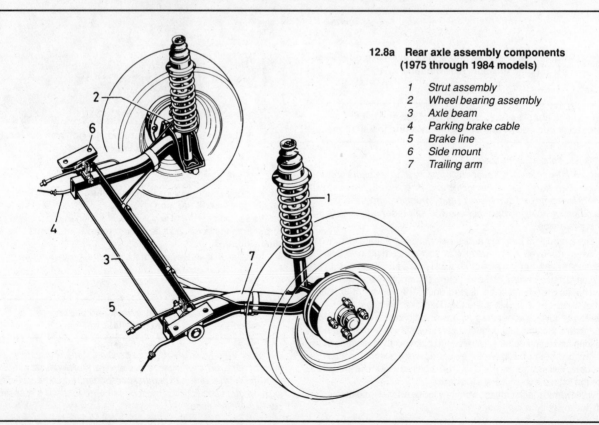

12.8a   Rear axle assembly components (1975 through 1984 models)

1   *Strut assembly*
2   *Wheel bearing assembly*
3   *Axle beam*
4   *Parking brake cable*
5   *Brake line*
6   *Side mount*
7   *Trailing arm*

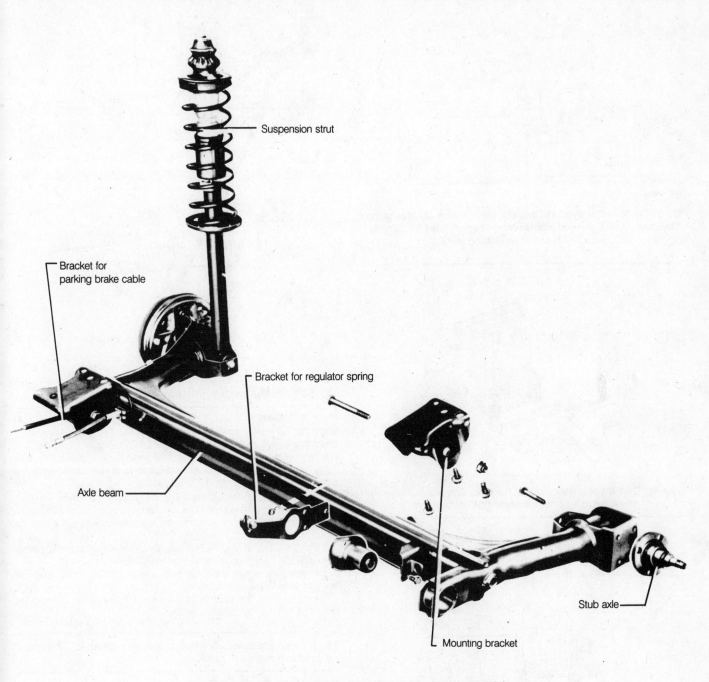

Suspension strut

Bracket for
parking brake cable

Bracket for regulator spring

Axle beam

Stub axle

Mounting bracket

12.8b   Rear axle assembly components (1985 and later models)

10

Removal

Refer to illustrations 12.8a and 12.8b

1   Loosen the rear wheel lug nuts (both wheels), raise the rear of the vehicle and support it securely on jackstands placed underneath the lifting points, not under the axle assembly. Position blocks in front of the front wheels.

2   Disconnect the parking brake cable at the parking brake handle.

3   Disconnect and plug the brake hydraulic lines at the rear wheel cylinders. Refer to Chapter 9 if necessary.

4   On 1975 through 1984 models, remove the upper strut nuts and washers (Section 9).

5   On 1985 and later models, remove the rear shock absorbers and springs.

6   On models so equipped, disconnect the brake pressure regulator from the bracket on the axle, nothing the location of the spring.

7   Support the axle with one or more floor jacks so that it can't fall during removal.

8   Remove the mounting nuts and bolts **(see illustrations)**. Slowly lower the axle assembly, making sure nothing is left connected.

Installation

Refer to illustrations 12.9, 12.10a and 12.10b

9   Install the axle assembly by reversing the removal steps. Be sure to tighten the nuts and bolts to the specified torque. On 1975 through 1984 models, the axle beam mounting pivot bolts must be tightened in the sequence shown in the accompanying illustration.

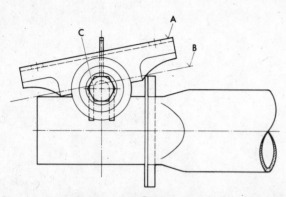

12.9   On 1975 through 1984 models, the rear axle pivot bushing bolts must be tightened in this order – edge A must be parallel with line B before tightening nut C

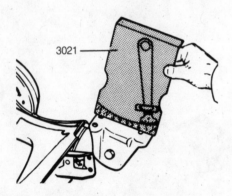

12.10a   On 1985 and later models, the mounting bracket must be installed at a 12-degree angle (VW tool shown)

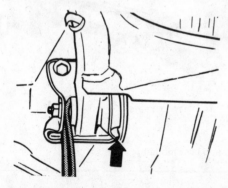

12.10b   Use pry bars to position the left side of the axle beam so there's a slight gap (arrow) (1985 and later models)

10   On 1985 and later models, if the axle beam mounting bracket has been removed from the axle or the pivot bolts loosened, the bracket surface must be aligned at 12-degrees to the face of the beam, before tightening the bolts to the specified torque **(see illustration)**. Place the axle assembly in position. With the bolts loosely and centered in the elongated passenger side bolt holes, tighten them to the specified torque. Use two prybars to push the driver's side mounting bracket to the left, leaving a slight gap between the bushing and the mounting bracket, then tighten the bolts to the specified torque **(see illustration)**.
11   Bleed the brake system (Chapter 9).

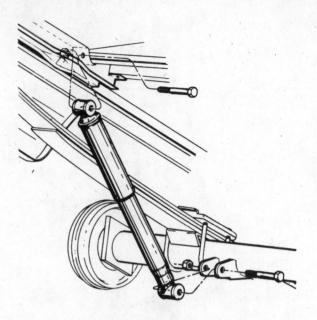

13.3   Pick-up truck rear shock absorber

13   Rear shock absorber (pick-up models) – replacement

Refer to illustration 13.3
Warning: *Whenever any of the suspension or steering fasteners are loosened or removed, they must be inspected and, if necessary, replaced with new ones of the same part number or of original equipment quality and design. Torque specifications must be followed for proper reassembly and component retention.*
1   Loosen the rear wheel lug bolts, raise the rear of the vehicle and support it securely on jackstands. The jackstands must be placed under the vehicle at the lifting points, not under the rear axle assembly. Remove the wheel.
2   Position a floor jack under the axle, next to the lower shock absorber mount. Raise it just enough to feel resistance from the spring.
3   Remove the upper and lower bolts and detach the shock absorber from the vehicle **(see illustration)**.
4   Installation is the reverse of the removal procedure. Tighten the mounting bolts to the specified torque

14   Rear spring assembly (pick-up models) – removal and installation

Refer to illustration 14.6
Warning: *Whenever any of the suspension or steering fasteners are loosened or removed, they must be inspected and, if necessary, replaced with new ones of the same part number or of original equipment quality and design. Torque specifications must be followed for proper reassembly and component retention.*
1   Loosen the rear wheel lug bolts, raise the rear of the vehicle and support it securely on jackstands. The jackstands must be placed under the vehicle at the lifting points, not under the rear axle assembly. Remove the wheel.
2   Position a floor jack under the axle, next to the spring being removed. Raise it just until the shock absorber begins to compress.
3   Detach the parking brake cable and cut the strap.
4   Remove the lower shock absorber bolt and swing the shock absorber up out of the way.
5   If the left spring is being removed, remove the three bolts attaching the exhaust pipe to the manifold. Detach the exhaust pipe, unhook the hanger and remove the assembly from the vehicle.

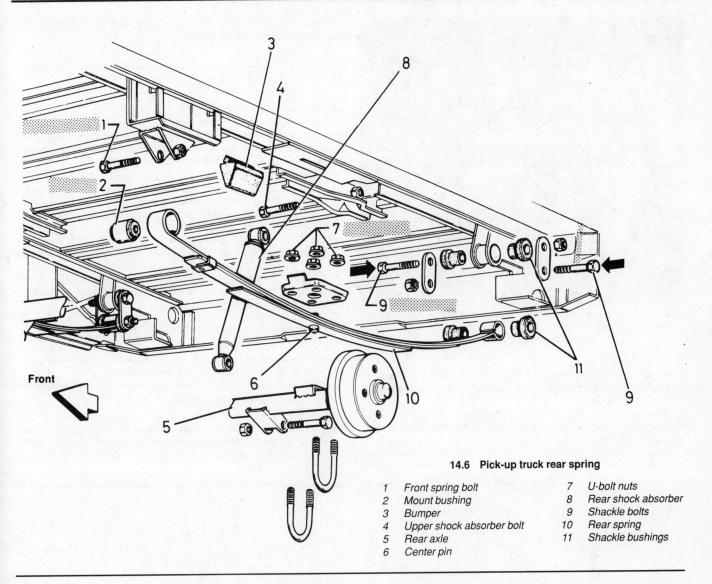

14.6   Pick-up truck rear spring

1	Front spring bolt	7	U-bolt nuts
2	Mount bushing	8	Rear shock absorber
3	Bumper	9	Shackle bolts
4	Upper shock absorber bolt	10	Rear spring
5	Rear axle	11	Shackle bushings
6	Center pin		

6   Remove the U-bolt nuts, then detach the mounting plate **(see illustration)**.

7   Loosen the upper spring shackle nut. Remove the lower shackle nut and withdraw the bolt.

8   Remove the front spring mounting bolt and lower the spring from the vehicle.

9   Installation is the reverse of the removal procedure, making sure the spring locater pin seats securely in the hole in the axle bracket. Tighten the bolts to the specified torque after the vehicle weight has been lowered onto the suspension.

15   Rear axle assembly (pick-up models) – removal and installation

Warning: *Whenever any of the suspension or steering fasteners are loosened or removed, they must be inspected and, if necessary, replaced with new ones of the same part number or of original equipment quality and design. Torque specifications must be followed for proper reassembly and component retention.*

1   Loosen the rear wheel lug bolts, raise the rear of the vehicle and support it securely on jackstands. The jackstands must be placed under the vehicle at the lifting points, not under the rear axle assembly. Remove the wheels.

2   Detach the parking brake cables by unbolting the brackets from the tops of the clamps and cut the tie strap.

3   Raise the rear axle evenly with two floor jacks until the shock absorbers begin to compress. Support the axle with the jacks during the remainder of this procedure.

4   Noting the positions of the ends, unhook the brake pressure regulator coil spring.

5   Disconnect and plug the brake hose connections at the top of the axle.

6   Remove the brake pressure regulator spring's bolt on the top of the axle and detach the brake hose attachment plate.

7   Remove the lower shock absorber bolts and swing the shock absorbers up out of the way.

8   Remove the spring mounting plate nuts, then remove the U-bolts and plate.

9   Lower the axle with the jacks and remove it from under the vehicle.

10   Installation is the reverse of the removal procedure. When tightening the U-bolt nuts, work alternately on the two nuts on each U-bolt until the specified torque is reached.

16   Steering system – general information

All models are equipped with rack-and-pinion steering. The steering gear is bolted to the crossmember at the firewall and operates the steering

10

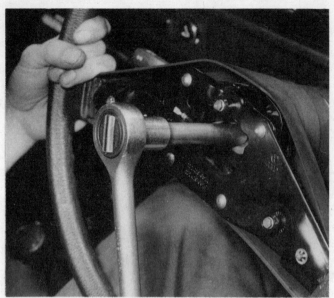

17.3   Remove the steering wheel nut, then make alignment marks on the shaft and hub – this will ensure correct steering wheel alignment during installation

arms via tie-rods. The inner ends of the tie-rods are protected by rubber boots which should be inspected periodically for secure attachment, tears and leaking lubricant.

The power assist system consists of a belt-driven pump and associated lines and hoses. The power steering pump reservoir fluid level should be checked periodically (Chapter 1).

The steering wheel operates the steering shaft, which actuates the steering gear through universal joints. Looseness in the steering can be caused by wear in the steering shaft universal joints, the steering gear, the tie-rod ends and loose retaining bolts.

17   Steering wheel – removal and installation

Refer to illustration 17.3
Warning: *Whenever any of the suspension or steering fasteners are loosened or removed, they must be inspected and, if necessary, replaced with new ones of the same part number or of original equipment quality and design. Torque specifications must be followed for proper reassembly and component retention.*

1   Disconnect the cable from the negative terminal of the battery.
2   Pry the horn pad from the steering wheel.
3   Remove the steering wheel retaining nut then mark the relationship of the steering shaft to the hub to simplify installation and ensure steering wheel alignment **(see illustration)**.
4   Use a steering wheel puller to detach the steering wheel from the shaft.
5   To install the wheel, align the mark on the steering wheel hub with the mark on the shaft and slip the wheel onto the shaft. Install the hub nut and tighten it to the specified torque.
6   Install the horn pad.
7   Connect the negative battery cable.

18   Steering gear – removal and installation

Refer to illustrations 18.5a and 18.5b
Warning: *Whenever any of the suspension or steering fasteners are loosened or removed, they must be inspected and, if necessary, replaced with new ones of the same part number or of original equipment quality and design. Torque specifications must be followed for proper reassembly and component retention.*

18.5a   Typical manual steering gear mounting details

1	Steering gear (rack-and-pinion)	5	Clamp
2	Bushing	6	Washer
3	Bushing	7	Washer
4	Clamp	8	Nuts

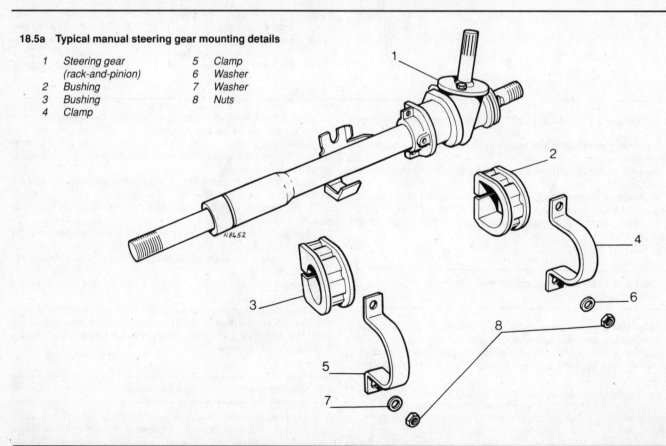

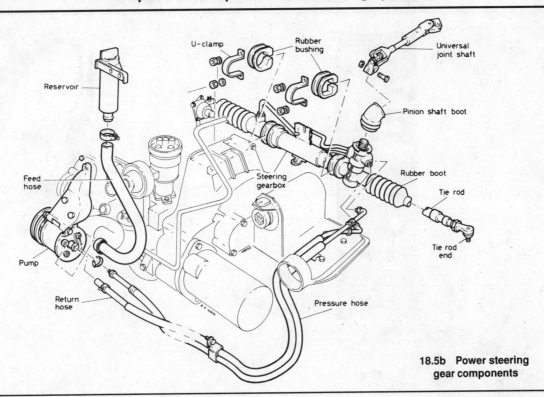

Reservoir

U-clamp

Rubber bushing

Universal joint shaft

Pinion shaft boot

Feed hose

Steering gearbox

Rubber boot

Tie rod

Tie rod end

Pump

Return hose

Pressure hose

18.5b   Power steering gear components

Note: *This procedure applies to both power and manual steering gear assemblies. When working on a vehicle equipped with a manual steering gear, simply ignore any references made to the power steering system.*

Removal

1   Raise the front of the vehicle and support it securely on jackstands. Apply the parking brake.

2   Place a drain pan under the steering gear (power steering only). Remove the power steering pressure and return lines and cap the ends to prevent excessive fluid loss and contamination.

3   Mark the relationship of the lower intermediate shaft universal joint to the steering gear input shaft (see Section 19). Remove the lower intermediate shaft pinch bolt.

4   Separate the tie-rod ends from the steering knuckle arms (see Section 20).

5   Support the steering gear and remove the steering gear housing clamp nuts **(see illustrations)**. Lower the unit, separate the intermediate shaft from the steering gear input shaft and remove the steering gear from the vehicle.

Installation

6   Raise the steering gear into position and connect the intermediate shaft, aligning the marks.

7   Install the gear housing clamps and nuts and tighten the nuts to the specified torque.

8   Connect the tie-rod ends to the steering knuckle arms (Section 20).

9   Install the intermediate shaft lower pinch bolt and tighten it to the specified torque.

10   Connect the power steering pressure and return hoses to the steering gear and fill the power steering pump reservoir with the recommended fluid (Chapter 1).

11   Lower the vehicle and bleed the steering system as outlined in Section 23.

19   Intermediate shaft – removal and installation

Refer to illustrations 19.2 and 19.3

Warning: *Whenever any of the suspension or steering fasteners are loos-*

ened or removed, they must be inspected and, if necessary, replaced with new ones of the same part number or of original equipment quality and design. Torque specifications must be followed for proper reassembly and component retention.

1   Turn the front wheels to the straight ahead position. Raise the vehicle and support it securely on jackstands.

2   Using white paint, place alignment marks on the upper universal joint, the steering shaft, the lower universal joint and the steering gear input shaft **(see illustration)**.

3   Remove the upper and lower universal joint pinch bolts **(see illustration)**.

4   Pry the intermediate shaft universal joint off the steering gear input shaft. Separate the shaft from the steering column and pull the assembly into the driver's compartment.

5   Installation is the reverse of the removal procedure. Be sure to align the marks and tighten the pinch bolts to the specified torque.

10

19.2   Pull the rubber boot up for access to the intermediate shaft-to-steering gear connection

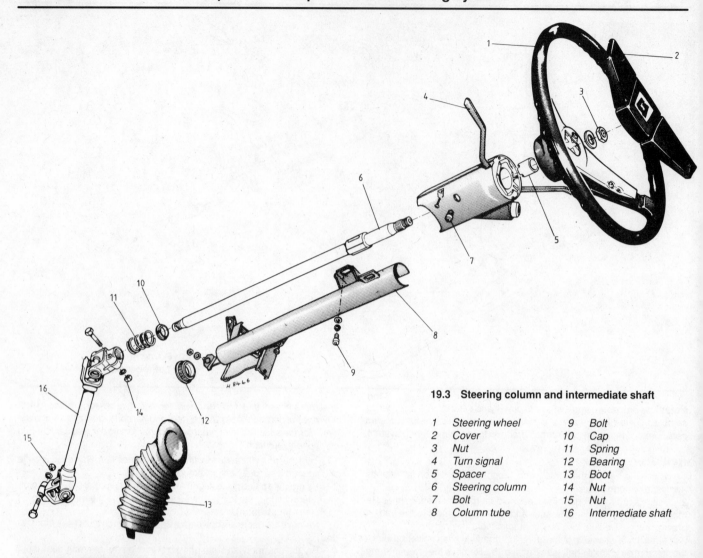

19.3   Steering column and intermediate shaft

1	Steering wheel	9	Bolt
2	Cover	10	Cap
3	Nut	11	Spring
4	Turn signal	12	Bearing
5	Spacer	13	Boot
6	Steering column	14	Nut
7	Bolt	15	Nut
8	Column tube	16	Intermediate shaft

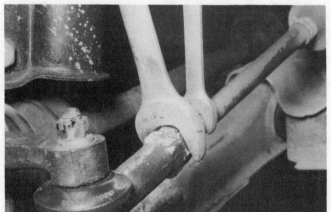

20.2a   Loosen the jam nut while holding the tie-rod with a wrench (or a pair of locking pliers) on the flat portion of the rod to prevent it from turning

20.2b   The relationship of the tie-rod end to the tie-rod can be marked with white paint

20   Tie-rod ends – removal and installation

Refer to illustrations 20.2a, 20.2b and 20.4

Warning: *Whenever any of the suspension or steering fasteners are loosened or removed, they must be inspected and, if necessary, replaced with new ones of the same part number or of original equipment quality and de-*sign. Torque specifications must be followed for proper reassembly and component retention.

Removal

1   Loosen the wheel lug bolts. Raise the front of the vehicle, support it securely, block the rear wheels and apply the parking brake. Remove the front wheel(s).

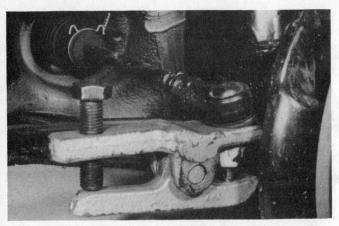

20.4   Use a tie-rod separator to detach the tie-rod end from the steering knuckle arm

2   Hold the tie-rod with a pair of locking pliers or a wrench and loosen the jam nut enough to mark the position of the tie-rod end in relation to the threads **(see illustrations)**.
3   Remove the cotter pin and loosen the nut on the tie-rod end stud.
4   Disconnect the tie-rod from the steering knuckle arm with a puller **(see illustration)**. Remove the nut and separate the tie-rod.
5   Unscrew the tie-rod end from the tie-rod.

Installation

6   Thread the tie-rod end on to the marked position and insert the tie-rod stud into the steering knuckle arm. Tighten the jam nut securely.
7   Install the castellated nut on the stud and tighten it to the specified torque. Install a new cotter pin.
8   Install the wheel and lug bolts. Lower the vehicle and tighten the lug bolts to the specified torque.
9   Have the alignment checked by a dealer service department or an alignment shop.

21   Steering gear boots – replacement

1   Loosen the lug bolts, raise the front of the vehicle and support it securely on jackstands. Apply the parking brake and block the rear wheels. Remove the front wheel(s).
2   Refer to Section 20 and remove the tie-rod end and jam nut.
3   Remove the steering gear boot clamps and slide the boot off.
4   Before installing the new boot, wrap the threads and serrations on the end of the steering rod with a layer of tape so the small end of the new boot isn't damaged.
5   Slide the new boot into position on the steering gear until it seats in the groove in the steering rod and install new clamps.
6   Remove the tape and install the tie-rod end (Section 20).
7   Install the wheel and lug bolts. Lower the vehicle and tighten the lug bolts to the specified torque.

22   Power steering pump – removal and installation

Refer to illustrations 22.5a and 22.5b
Warning: *Whenever any of the suspension or steering fasteners are loosened or removed, they must be inspected and, if necessary, replaced with new ones of the same part number or of original equipment quality and design. Torque specifications must be followed for proper reassembly and component retention.*

1   Disconnect the cable from the negative battery terminal.
2   Loosen the tension on the pump drivebelt (Chapter 1) and remove the belt.

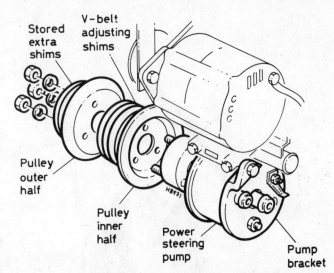

22.5a   Typical early model power steering pump

3   Using a suction gun, suck out as much fluid from the power steering fluid reservoir as possible. Place a drain pan under the vehicle to catch any fluid that may spill out when the hoses are disconnected.
4   Disconnect the pressure and return lines from the pump. Unbolt the high pressure line bracket from the pump.
5   Remove the adjuster bolt and pivot bolt from the pump and detach the pump from the vehicle **(see illustrations)**.
6   Installation is the reverse of the removal procedure. Be sure to adjust the power steering pump drivebelt tension and top up the power steering fluid reservoir (Chapter 1).
7   Bleed the power steering system as described in Section 23.

23   Power steering system – bleeding

1   Following any operation in which the power steering lines have been disconnected, the power steering system must be bled to remove all air and obtain proper steering performance.
2   With the front wheels in the straight ahead position, check the power steering fluid level and, if low, add fluid (see Chapter 1).
3   Start the engine and allow it to run at fast idle. Recheck the fluid level and add more if necessary.
4   Bleed the system by turning the steering wheel from side-to-side, without hitting the stops. This will work the air out of the system. Keep the reservoir full of fluid as this is done.
5   When the air is out of the system, return the wheels to the straight ahead position and leave the vehicle running for several more minutes before shutting it off.
6   Road test the vehicle to be sure the steering system is functioning normally and noise free.
7   Recheck the fluid level to be sure it's correct. Add fluid if necessary (see Chapter 1).

24   Wheels and tires – general information

Refer to illustration 24.1
All vehicles covered by this manual are equipped with metric-sized fiberglass or steel belted radial tires **(see illustration)**. Use of other size or type of tires may affect the ride and handling of the vehicle. Don't mix different types of tires, such as radials and bias belted, on the same vehicle as handling may be seriously affected. It's recommended that tires be replaced in pairs on the same axle, but if only one tire is being replaced, be sure it's the same size, structure and tread design as the other.

Because tire pressure has a substantial effect on handling and wear, the pressure on all tires should be checked at least once a month or before any extended trips (see Chapter 1).

10

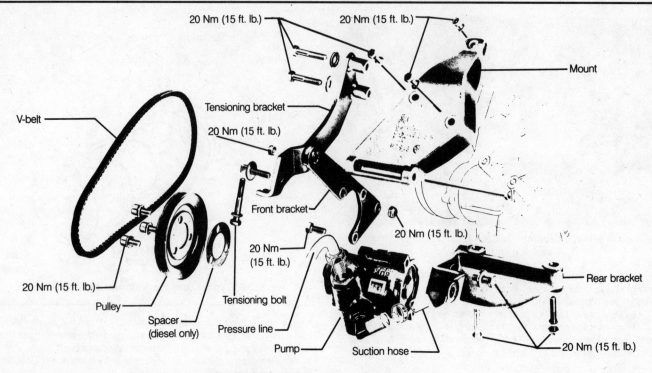

20 Nm (15 ft. lb.)

20 Nm (15 ft. lb.)

Mount

V-belt

Tensioning bracket

20 Nm (15 ft. lb.)

Front bracket

20 Nm (15 ft. lb.)

20 Nm (15 ft. lb.)

Rear bracket

20 Nm (15 ft. lb.)

Pulley

Tensioning bolt

Spacer (diesel only)

Pressure line

Pump

Suction hose

20 Nm (15 ft. lb.)

22.5b   1985 and later model power steering pump

Wheels must be replaced if they are bent, dented, leak air, have elongated bolt holes, are heavily rusted, out of vertical symmetry or if the lug nuts won't stay tight. Wheel repairs that use welding or peening are not recommended.

Tire and wheel balance is important in the overall handling, braking and performance of the vehicle. Unbalanced wheels can adversely affect handling and ride characteristics as well as tire life. Whenever a tire is installed on a wheel, the tire and wheel should be balanced by a shop with the proper equipment.

A front end alignment refers to the adjustments made to the front wheels so they are in proper angular relationship to the suspension and the ground. Front wheels that are out of proper alignment not only affect steering control, but also increase tire wear. The only front end adjustment normally required on this vehicle is toe-in. Caster angle is slightly adjustable.

Getting the proper front wheel alignment is a very exacting process, one in which complicated and expensive machines are necessary to perform the job properly. Because of this, you should have a technician with the proper equipment perform these tasks. We will, however, use this space to give you a basic idea of what is involved with front end alignment so you can better understand the process and deal intelligently with the shop that does the work.

25   Front end alignment – general information

Toe-in is the turning in of the front wheels. The purpose of a toe specification is to ensure parallel rolling of the front wheels. In a vehicle with zero toe-in, the distance between the front edges of the wheels will be the same as the distance between the rear edges of the wheels. The actual amount of toe-in is normally only a fraction of an inch. Toe-in adjustment is controlled by the tie-rod end position on the tie-rod. Incorrect toe-in will cause the tires to wear improperly by making them scrub against the road surface.

Caster is the tilting of the front steering axis from the vertical. A tilt toward the rear is positive caster and a tilt toward the front is negative caster. Caster is adjusted by changing the position of the adjusting nuts on the strut bar.

Camber is the angle the wheel tilts from the vertical when viewed from the front of the vehicle. If the top of the wheel tilts in toward the vehicle, this is negative camber. The camber is positive when the bottom of the wheel is closer to the vehicle. Camber angle is adjusted on this vehicle by turning the eccentric bolt which is the top bolt connecting the front strut to the steering knuckle.

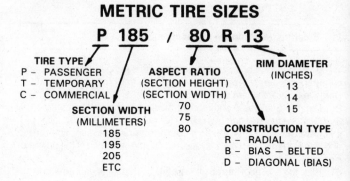

METRIC TIRE SIZES

P 185 / 80 R 13

TIRE TYPE
P – PASSENGER
T – TEMPORARY
C – COMMERCIAL

SECTION WIDTH
(MILLIMETERS)
185
195
205
ETC

ASPECT RATIO
(SECTION HEIGHT)
(SECTION WIDTH)
70
75
80

RIM DIAMETER
(INCHES)
13
14
15

CONSTRUCTION TYPE
R – RADIAL
B – BIAS – BELTED
D – DIAGONAL (BIAS)

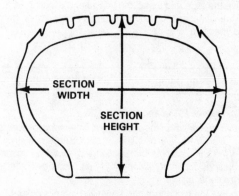

SECTION WIDTH

SECTION HEIGHT

24.1   Metric tire size code

Chapter 11   Body

Contents

Body – maintenance   2
Body repair – major damage   6
Body repair – minor damage   5
Bumpers – removal and installation   12
Center console – removal and installation   14
Door lock, handle and lock cylinder – removal and installation . . .   19
Door – removal, installation and adjustment   15
Door trim panel – removal and installation   13
Door window glass – removal and installation   20
Fixed glass – replacement   8
Front fender – removal and installation   11
Front wheelhouse liner – removal and installation   22
General information   1
Hood – removal, installation and adjustment   9
Hinges and locks – maintenance   7
Liftgate – removal, installation and adjustment   17
Outside mirror – removal and installation   21
Pick-up tailgate handle and latch – removal and installation   18
Radiator grille – removal and installation   10
Seat belt check   23
Trunk lid – removal, installation and adjustment   16
Upholstery and carpets – maintenance   4
Vinyl trim – maintenance   3

1   General information

These models feature a "unibody" layout, using a floor pan with front and rear frame side rails which support the body components, front and rear suspension systems and other mechanical components.

Certain components are particularly vulnerable to accident damage and can be unbolted and repaired or replaced. Among these parts are the body moldings, bumpers, the hood and trunk lids and all glass.

Only general body maintenance practices and body panel repair procedures within the scope of the do-it-yourselfer are included in this Chapter.

2   Body – maintenance

1   The condition of your vehicle's body is very important, because the resale value depends a great deal on it. It's much more difficult to repair a neglected or damaged body than it is to repair mechanical components. The hidden areas of the body, such as the wheel wells, the frame and the engine compartment, are equally important, although they don't require as frequent attention as the rest of the body.

2   Once a year, or every 12,000 miles, it's a good idea to have the underside of the body steam cleaned. All traces of dirt and oil will be removed and the area can then be inspected carefully for rust, damaged brake lines, frayed electrical wires, damaged cables and other problems.

3   At the same time, clean the engine and the engine compartment with a steam cleaner or water soluble degreaser.

4   The wheel wells should be given close attention, since undercoating can peel away and stones and dirt thrown up by the tires can cause the paint to chip and flake, allowing rust to set in. If rust is found, clean down to the bare metal and apply an anti-rust paint.

5   The body should be washed about once a week. Wet the vehicle thoroughly to soften the dirt, then wash it down with a soft sponge and plenty of clean soapy water. If the surplus dirt is not washed off very carefully, it can wear down the paint.

6   Spots of tar or asphalt thrown up from the road should be removed with a cloth soaked in solvent.

7   Once every six months, wax the body and chrome trim. If a chrome cleaner is used to remove rust from any of the vehicle's plated parts, remember that the cleaner also removes part of the chrome, so use it sparingly.

11

3   Vinyl trim – maintenance

Don't clean vinyl trim with detergents, caustic soap or petroleum based cleaners. Plain soap and water works just fine, with a soft brush to clean dirt that may be ingrained. Wash the vinyl as frequently as the rest of the vehicle.

After cleaning, application of a high quality rubber and vinyl protectant will help prevent oxidation and cracks. The protectant can also be applied to weatherstripping, vacuum lines and rubber hoses, which often fail as a result of chemical degradation, and to the tires.

4   Upholstery and carpets – maintenance

1   Every three months remove the carpets or mats and clean the interior of the vehicle (more frequently if necessary). Vacuum the upholstery and carpets to remove loose dirt and dust.

2   Leather upholstery requires special care. Stains should be removed with warm water and a very mild soap solution. Use a clean, damp cloth to remove the soap, then wipe again with a dry cloth. Never use alcohol, gasoline, nail polish remover or thinner to clean leather upholstery.

3   After cleaning, regularly treat leather upholstery with a leather wax. Never use car wax on leather upholstery.

4   In areas where the interior of the vehicle is subject to bright sunlight, cover leather seats with a sheet if the vehicle is to be left out for any length of time.

5   Body repair – minor damage

See photo sequence

Repair of scratches

1   If the scratch is superficial and does not penetrate to the metal of the body, repair is very simple. Lightly rub the scratched area with a fine rubbing compound to remove loose paint and built up wax. Rinse the area with clean water.

2   Apply touch-up paint to the scratch, using a small brush. Continue to apply thin layers of paint until the surface of the paint in the scratch is level with the surrounding paint. Allow the new paint at least two weeks to harden, then blend it into the surrounding paint by rubbing with a very fine rubbing compound. Finally, apply a coat of wax to the scratch area.

3   If the scratch has penetrated the paint and exposed the metal of the body, causing the metal to rust, a different repair technique is required. Remove all loose rust from the bottom of the scratch with a pocket knife, then apply rust inhibiting paint to prevent the formation of rust in the future. Using a rubber or nylon applicator, coat the scratched area with glaze-type filler. If required, the filler can be mixed with thinner to provide a very thin paste, which is ideal for filling narrow scratches. Before the glaze filler in the scratch hardens, wrap a piece of smooth cotton cloth around the tip of a finger. Dip the cloth in thinner and then quickly wipe it along the surface of the scratch. This will ensure that the surface of the filler is slightly hollow. The scratch can now be painted over as described earlier in this section.

Repair of dents

4   When repairing dents, the first job is to pull the dent out until the affected area is as close as possible to its original shape. There is no point in trying to restore the original shape completely as the metal in the damaged area will have stretched on impact and cannot be restored to its original contours. It is better to bring the level of the dent up to a point which is about 1/8-inch below the level of the surrounding metal. In cases where the dent is very shallow, it is not worth trying to pull it out at all.

5   If the back side of the dent is accessible, it can be hammered out gently from behind using a soft-face hammer. While doing this, hold a block of wood firmly against the opposite side of the metal to absorb the hammer blows and prevent the metal from being stretched.

6   If the dent is in a section of the body which has double layers, or some other factor makes it inaccessible from behind, a different technique is required. Drill several small holes through the metal inside the damaged area, particularly in the deeper sections. Screw long, self tapping screws into the holes just enough for them to get a good grip in the metal. Now the dent can be pulled out by pulling on the protruding heads of the screws with locking pliers.

7   The next stage of repair is the removal of paint from the damaged area and from an inch or so of the surrounding metal. This is easily done with a wire brush or sanding disk in a drill motor, although it can be done just as effectively by hand with sandpaper. To complete the preparation for filling, score the surface of the bare metal with a screwdriver or the tang of a file or drill small holes in the affected area. This will provide a good grip for the filler material. To complete the repair, see the Section on filling and painting.

Repair of rust holes or gashes

8   Remove all paint from the affected area and from an inch or so of the surrounding metal using a sanding disk or wire brush mounted in a drill motor. If these are not available, a few sheets of sandpaper will do the job just as effectively.

9   With the paint removed, you will be able to determine the severity of the corrosion and decide whether to replace the whole panel, if possible, or repair the affected area. New body panels are not as expensive as most people think and it is often quicker to install a new panel than to repair large areas of rust.

10   Remove all trim pieces from the affected area except those which will act as a guide to the original shape of the damaged body, such as headlight shells, etc. Using metal snips or a hacksaw blade, remove all loose metal and any other metal that is badly affected by rust. Hammer the edges of the hole inward to create a slight depression for the filler material.

11   Wire brush the affected area to remove the powdery rust from the surface of the metal. If the back of the rusted area is accessible, treat it with rust inhibiting paint.

12   Before filling is done, block the hole in some way. This can be done with sheet metal riveted or screwed into place, or by stuffing the hole with wire mesh.

13   Once the hole is blocked off, the affected area can be filled and painted. See the following subsection on filling and painting.

Filling and painting

14   Many types of body fillers are available, but generally speaking, body repair kits which contain filler paste and a tube of resin hardener are best for this type of repair work. A wide, flexible plastic or nylon applicator will be necessary for imparting a smooth and contoured finish to the surface of the filler material. Mix up a small amount of filler on a clean piece of wood or cardboard (use the hardener sparingly). Follow the manufacturer's instructions on the package, otherwise the filler will set incorrectly.

15   Using the applicator, apply the filler paste to the prepared area. Draw the applicator across the surface of the filler to achieve the desired contour and to level the filler surface. As soon as a contour that approximates the original one is achieved, stop working the paste. If you continue, the paste will begin to stick to the applicator. Continue to add thin layers of paste at 20-minute intervals until the level of the filler is just above the surrounding metal.

16   Once the filler has hardened, the excess can be removed with a body file. From then on, progressively finer grades of sandpaper should be used, starting with a 180-grit paper and finishing with 600-grit wet or dry paper. Always wrap the sandpaper around a flat rubber or wooden block, otherwise the surface of the filler will not be completely flat. During the sanding of the filler surface, the wet-or-dry paper should be periodically rinsed in water. This will ensure that a very smooth finish is produced in the final stage.

17   At this point, the repair area should be surrounded by a ring of bare metal, which in turn should be encircled by the finely feathered edge of good paint. Rinse the repair area with clean water until all of the dust produced by the sanding operation is gone.

18   Spray the entire area with a light coat of primer. This will reveal any imperfections in the surface of the filler. Repair the imperfections with fresh filler paste or glaze filler and once more smooth the surface with sandpaper. Repeat this spray-and-repair procedure until you are satisfied that the surface of the filler and the feathered edge of the paint are perfect. Rinse the area with clean water and allow it to dry completely.

19   The repair area is now ready for painting. Spray painting must be carried out in a warm, dry, windless and dust free atmosphere. These conditions can be created if you have access to a large indoor work area, but if you are forced to work in the open, you will have to pick the day very carefully. If you are working indoors, dousing the floor in the work area with water will help settle the dust which would otherwise be in the air. If the repair area is confined to one body panel, mask off the surrounding panels. This will help minimize the effects of a slight mismatch in paint color. Trim pieces such as chrome strips, door handles, etc., will also need to be masked off or removed. Use masking tape and several thicknesses of newspaper for the masking operations.

20   Before spraying, shake the paint can thoroughly, then spray a test area until the spray painting technique is mastered. Cover the repair area with a thick coat of primer. The thickness should be built up using several thin layers of primer rather than one thick one. Using 600-grit wet-or-dry sandpaper, rub down the surface of the primer until it is very smooth. While doing this, the work area should be thoroughly rinsed with water and the wet-or-dry sandpaper periodically rinsed as well. Allow the primer to dry before spraying additional coats.

21   Spray on the top coat, again building up the thickness by using several thin layers of paint. Begin spraying in the center of the repair area and then, using a circular motion, work out until the whole repair area and about two inches of the surrounding original paint is covered. Remove all masking material 10 to 15 minutes after spraying on the final coat of paint. Allow the new paint at least two weeks to harden, then use a very fine rubbing compound to blend the edges of the new paint into the existing paint. Finally, apply a coat of wax.

6   Body repair – major damage

1   Major damage must be repaired by an auto body shop specifically equipped to perform unibody repairs. These shops have the specialized equipment required to do the job properly.

2   If the damage is extensive, the body must be checked for proper alignment or the vehicle's handling characteristics may be adversely affected and other components may wear at an accelerated rate.

3   Due to the fact that all of the major body components (hood, fenders, etc.) are separate and replaceable units, any seriously damaged components should be replaced rather than repaired. Sometimes the compo-

nents can be found in a wrecking yard that specializes in used vehicle components, often at considerable savings over the cost of new parts.

7   Hinges and locks – maintenance

Once every 3000 miles, or every three months, the hinges and latch assemblies on the doors, hood and trunk should be given a few drops of light oil or lock lubricant. The door latch strikers should also be lubricated with a thin coat of grease to reduce wear and ensure free movement. Lubricate the door and trunk locks with spray-on graphite lubricant.

8   Fixed glass – replacement

Replacement of the windshield and fixed glass requires the use of special fast-setting adhesive/caulk materials and some specialized tools and techniques. These operations should be left to a dealer service department or a shop specializing in glass work.

9   Hood – removal, installation and adjustment

Refer to illustrations 9.2, 9.10 and 9.11
Note: *The hood is heavy and somewhat awkward to remove and install – at least two people should perform this procedure.*

Removal and installation

1   Use blankets or pads to cover the cowl area of the body and the fenders. This will protect the body and paint as the hood is lifted off.

2   Scribe or paint alignment marks around the bolt heads to insure proper alignment during installation **(see illustration)**.

3   Disconnect any cables or wire harnesses which will interfere with removal.

4   Have an assistant support the weight of the hood. Remove the hinge-to-hood nuts or bolts.

5   Lift off the hood.

6   Installation is the reverse of removal.

Adjustment

7   Fore-and-aft and side-to-side adjustment of the hood is done by moving the hood in relation to the hinge plate after loosening the bolts or nuts.

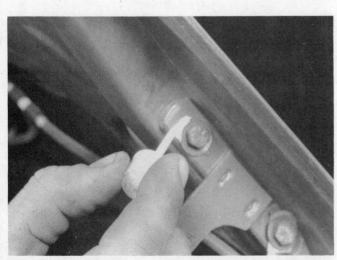

9.2   Use white paint or a marker to mark the hood bolt locations

9.10   The hood can be adjusted by loosening the latch bolts and moving the latch – the lock pin (in the middle of the spring) can be screwed in or out to adjust the closing position

11

9.11   Screw the rubber bumpers in or out to adjust for a flush fit of the hood with the fenders

8   Scribe a line around the entire hinge plate so you can judge the amount of movement **(see illustration 9.2)**.

9   Loosen the bolts or nuts and move the hood into correct alignment. Move it only a little at a time. Tighten the hinge bolts or nuts and carefully lower the hood to check the alignment.

10   If necessary after installation, the entire hood latch assembly can be adjusted up-and-down as well as from side-to-side on the hood so the hood closes securely and is flush with the fenders. To do this, scribe a line around the hood latch mounting bolts to provide a reference point. Then loosen the bolts and reposition the latch assembly as necessary. Following adjustment, retighten the mounting bolts, then if necessary use a screwdriver to screw the lockpin in or out to adjust for a flush fit **(see illustration)**.

11   Finally, adjust the hood bumpers on the radiator support or hood so the hood, when closed, is flush with the fenders **(see illustration)**.

12   The hood latch assembly, as well as the hinges, should be periodically lubricated with white lithium-base grease to prevent sticking and wear.

---

10   Radiator grille – removal and installation

Early models

Refer to illustration 10.1

1   Remove the mounting screws and detach the grille from the vehicle

(see illustration).

2   Installation is the reverse of the removal procedure.

Later models

Refer to illustrations 10.3 and 10.4

3   Disengage the grille retaining clips along the top of the grille with a small screwdriver **(see illustration)**.

4   Once all of the retaining clips are disengaged, detach the grille and remove it **(see illustration)**. On some models it may be necessary to also remove the headlight bezels and some screws along the bottom of the grille before it can be removed.

5   To install the grille, press it into place until the clips lock it into position.

---

11   Front fender – removal and installation

Refer to illustrations 11.3a and 11.3b

1   Raise the vehicle, support it securely on jackstands and remove the front wheel.

2   Disconnect the antenna and all light bulb wiring harness connectors and other components that would interfere with fender removal.

3   Referring to the accompanying illustrations, remove the fender mounting bolts.

4   Detach the fender. It is a good idea to have an assistant support the fender while it's being moved away from the vehicle to prevent damage to the surrounding body panels.

5   Installation is the reverse of removal.

6   Tighten all nuts, bolts and screws securely.

---

12   Bumpers – removal and installation

Refer to illustrations 12.4a and 12.4b

1   Detach the bumper cover (if equipped).

2   Disconnect any wiring or other components that would interfere with bumper removal.

3   Support the bumper with a jack or jackstand. Alternatively, have an assistant support the bumper as the bolts are removed.

4   Remove the retaining bolts and detach the bumper **(see illustrations)**.

5   Installation is the reverse of removal.

6   Tighten the retaining bolts securely.

7   Install the bumper cover and any other components that were removed.

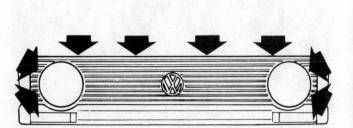

10.1   Early model radiator grille retaining screw locations (arrows)

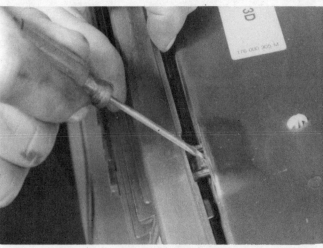

10.3   Use a small screwdriver to disengage the radiator grille clips (later models)

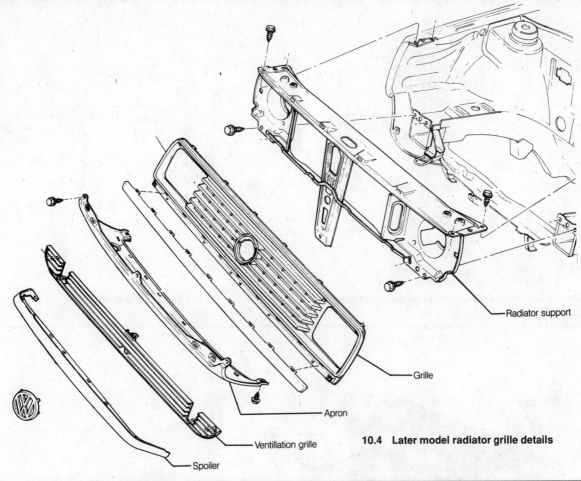

10.4   Later model radiator grille details

11.3a   Typical 1975 through 1984 model front fender details

A1	Two screws	B	Guides
A	Eight screws along the top, front and rear	C	Bumper mount location

11

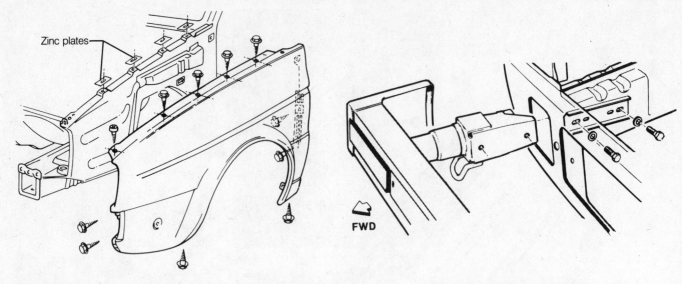

11.3b   1984 and later model front fender installation details

12.4a   Typical bumper details

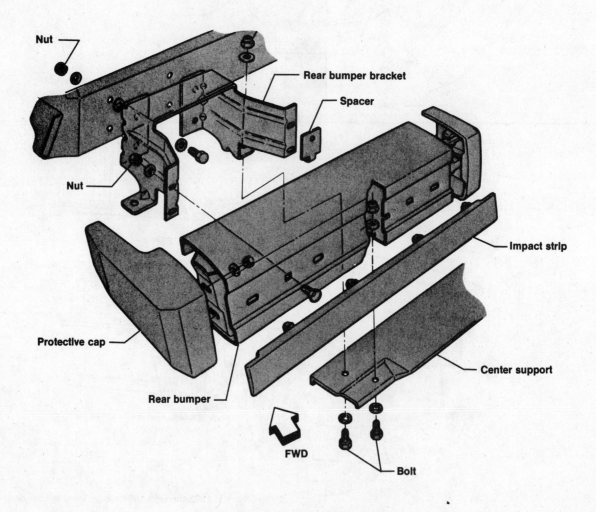

12.4b   Pick-up truck rear bumper details

13.2a   Remove the armrest screws

13.2b   Pull the end covers off for access to the screws

13.2c   Pull the door handle out, pry the cover off with a screwdriver and . . .

13.2d   . . . remove the screw

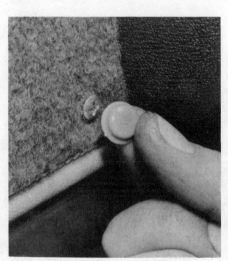

13.2e   Pry the screw cover off

13.3   Pry the cover off and remove the window crank screw

13.4   Pull the door panel out sharply to disengage the clips

13   Door trim panel – removal and installation

Refer to illustrations 13.2a, 13.2b, 13.2c, 13.2d, 13.2e, 13.3 and 13.4

Removal

1   Disconnect the negative cable from the battery.
2   Remove all door trim panel retaining screws and door pull/armrest assemblies **(see illustrations)**.
3   Remove the window crank **(see illustration)**.
4   Insert a putty knife between the trim panel and the door and disengage the retaining clips **(see illustration)**. Work around the outer edge until the panel is free.
5   Once all of the clips are disengaged, detach the trim panel, unplug any wire harness connectors and remove the trim panel from the vehicle.
6   For access to the inner door, carefully peel back the plastic watershield.
7   Prior to installation of the door panel, be sure to reinstall any clips in the panel which may have come out during the removal procedure and remain in the door itself.

11

These photos illustrate a method of repairing simple dents. They are intended to supplement *Body repair - minor damage* in this Chapter and should not be used as the sole instructions for body repair on these vehicles.

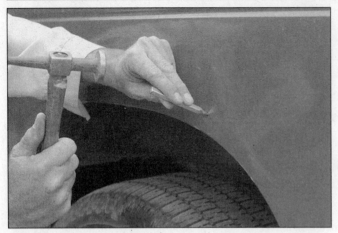

1   If you can't access the backside of the body panel to hammer out the dent, pull it out with a slide-hammer-type dent puller. In the deepest portion of the dent or along the crease line, drill or punch hole(s) at least one inch apart . . .

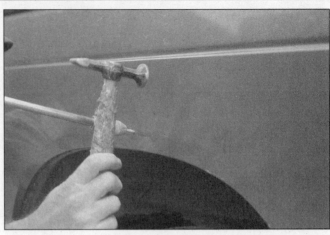

2   . . . then screw the slide-hammer into the hole and operate it. Tap with a hammer near the edge of the dent to help 'pop' the metal back to its original shape. When you're finished, the dent area should be close to its original contour and about 1/8-inch below the surface of the surrounding metal

3   Using coarse-grit sandpaper, remove the paint down to the bare metal. Hand sanding works fine, but the disc sander shown here makes the job faster. Use finer (about 320-grit) sandpaper to feather-edge the paint at least one inch around the dent area

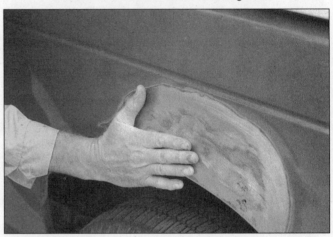

4   When the paint is removed, touch will probably be more helpful than sight for telling if the metal is straight. Hammer down the high spots or raise the low spots as necessary. Clean the repair area with wax/silicone remover

5   Following label instructions, mix up a batch of plastic filler and hardener. The ratio of filler to hardener is critical, and, if you mix it incorrectly, it will either not cure properly or cure too quickly (you won't have time to file and sand it into shape)

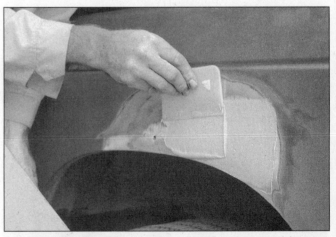

6   Working quickly so the filler doesn't harden, use a plastic applicator to press the body filler firmly into the metal, assuring it bonds completely. Work the filler until it matches the original contour and is slightly above the surrounding metal

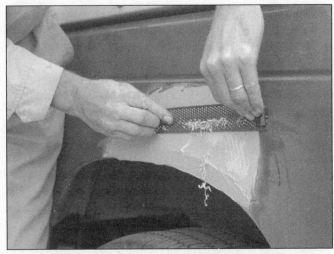

7   Let the filler harden until you can just dent it with your fingernail. Use a body file or Surform tool (shown here) to rough-shape the filler

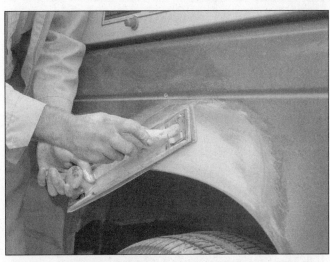

8   Use coarse-grit sandpaper and a sanding board or block to work the filler down until it's smooth and even. Work down to finer grits of sandpaper - always using a board or block - ending up with 360 or 400 grit

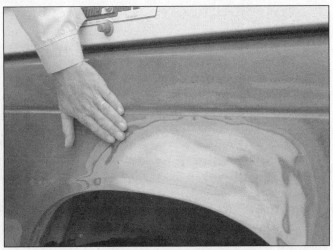

9   You shouldn't be able to feel any ridge at the transition from the filler to the bare metal or from the bare metal to the old paint. As soon as the repair is flat and uniform, remove the dust and mask off the adjacent panels or trim pieces

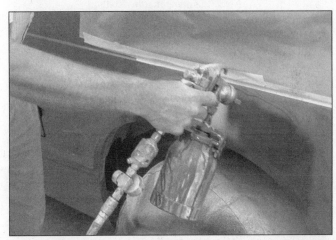

10   Apply several layers of primer to the area. Don't spray the primer on too heavy, so it sags or runs, and make sure each coat is dry before you spray on the next one. A professional-type spray gun is being used here, but aerosol spray primer is available inexpensively from auto parts stores

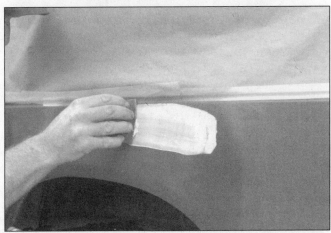

11   The primer will help reveal imperfections or scratches. Fill these with glazing compound. Follow the label instructions and sand it with 360 or 400-grit sandpaper until it's smooth. Repeat the glazing, sanding and respraying until the primer reveals a perfectly smooth surface

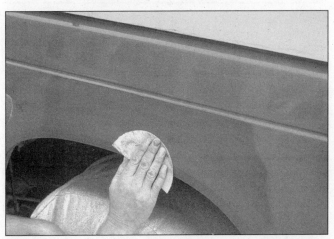

12   Finish sand the primer with very fine sandpaper (400 or 600-grit) to remove the primer overspray. Clean the area with water and allow it to dry. Use a tack rag to remove any dust, then apply the finish coat. Don't attempt to rub out or wax the repair area until the paint has dried completely (at least two weeks)

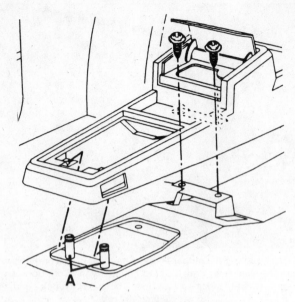

14.2   Center console details

15.4   Remove the check strap pin (arrow) and remove the bolt (an impact tool will probably be necessary – the bolts are very tight)

Installation

8   Plug in the wire harness connectors and place the panel in position on the door. Press the door panel into place until the clips are seated and install the armrest/door pulls. Install the window crank.

14   Center console – removal and installation

Refer to illustration 14.2

1   On manual transaxle models, remove the knob, pry the shift boot loose and remove the assembly. On automatic transaxle models, pry the selector plate up.
2   Remove the screws, detach the center console and lift it out **(see illustration)**.
3   Installation is a reversal of the removal procedure.

15   Door – removal, installation and adjustment

Refer to illustration 15.4

1   Remove the door trim panel. Disconnect any wire harness connectors and push them through the door opening so they won't interfere with door removal.
2   Place a jack or jackstand under the door or have an assistant on hand to support it when the hinge bolts are removed. **Note:** *If a jack or jackstand is used, place a rag between it and the door to protect the door's painted surfaces.*
3   Scribe around the door hinges.
4   Remove the pin from the door check strap **(see illustration)**. Remove the hinge-to-door bolts using an impact wrench and carefully lift off the door.
5   Installation is the reverse of removal.
6   Following installation of the door, check the alignment and adjust it if necessary as follows:
   a) Up-and-down and forward-and-backward adjustments are made by loosening the hinge-to-body bolts and moving the door as necessary.
   b) The door lock striker can also be adjusted both up-and-down and sideways to provide positive engagement with the lock mechanism. This is done by loosening and moving the striker as necessary.

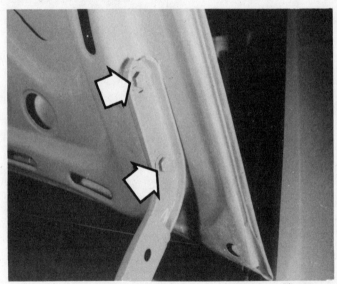

16.3   Scribe or paint around the trunk lid bolts (arrows)

16   Trunk lid – removal, installation and adjustment

Refer to illustrations 16.3, 16.7a and 16.7b

1   Open the trunk lid and cover the edges of the trunk compartment with pads or cloths to protect the painted surfaces when the lid is removed.
2   Disconnect any cables or wire harness connectors attached to the trunk lid that would interfere with removal.
3   Scribe or paint alignment marks around the hinge bolt mounting flanges **(see illustration)**.
4   While an assistant supports the trunk lid, remove the hinge bolts from both sides and lift it off.
5   Installation is the reverse of removal. **Note:** *When reinstalling the trunk lid, align the hinge bolt flanges with the marks made during removal.*
6   After installation, close the lid and see if it's in proper alignment with the surrounding panels. Fore-and-aft and side-to-side adjustments of the lid are controlled by the position of the hinge bolts in the slots. To adjust, loosen the hinge bolts, reposition the lid and retighten the bolts.

16.7a   Loosen the screws before adjusting the trunk latch striker

16.7b   Trunk lid striker location

7   The height of the lid in relation to the surrounding body panels when closed can be adjusted by loosening the lock latch screws or striker, repositioning the latch or striker and retightening them **(see illustrations)**.

the position of the hinge bolts in the slots. To adjust it, loosen the hinge bolts and reposition the hinges either side-to-side or fore-and-aft the desired amount and retighten the bolts.

17   Liftgate – removal, installation and adjustment

1   Open the liftgate and cover the upper body area around the opening with pads or cloths to protect the painted surfaces when the liftgate is removed.
2   Disconnect all cables and wire harness connectors that would interfere with removal of the liftgate.
3   Paint or scribe around the hinge flanges.
4   While an assistant supports the liftgate, detach the support struts.
5   Pull back the headliner for access and remove the hinge bolts or screws using an impact wrench or screwdriver and detach the liftgate from the vehicle.
6   Installation is the reverse of removal.
7   After installation, close the liftgate and make sure it's in proper alignment with the surrounding body panels. Adjustments are made by moving

18   Pick-up tailgate handle and latch – removal and installation

Refer to illustration 18.2
1   Open the tailgate and remove the three bolts from the latch.
2   Remove the latch screws, disconnect the latch rod and withdraw the latch, complete with rod assemblies from the tailgate **(see illustration)**.
3   Installation is the reverse of removal but the procedure can be made easier by removing the tailgate. Release the holding straps, lift the tailgate out of the left side hinge and pull it out of the right side hinge. Stand the tailgate on end and insert the latch rod assembly.

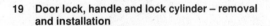

19   Door lock, handle and lock cylinder – removal and installation

Refer to illustrations 19.2, 19.7 and 19.9

Lock

Early models
1   Remove the door trim panel and plastic watershield (Section 13).
2   Detach the control, remove the two screws and withdraw the lock from the inside of the door **(see illustration)**.
3   Installation is the reverse of removal.

Later models
4   On most later models the lock can be removed without removing the door trim panel.
5   Open the door and set the lock in the locked position with the key or knob.
6   Remove the two hex head retaining screws, pull the lock away from the door about 1/2 inch and use a screwdriver inserted in the hole in the bottom of the lock to hold the operating lever in the extended position.
7   Unhook the remote control rod from the operating lever, pull the upper lever from the sleeve and withdraw the lock from the door **(see illustration)**.

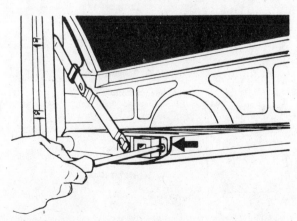

18.2   Use a Phillips screwdriver to remove the pick-up tailgate latch screws

11

19.2   Early model door lock installation details

8   Installation is the reverse of removal, however make sure a screwdriver is inserted so the lock is in the locked position before beginning.

Handle

9   Pry off the trim strip, remove the screws, then push the handle forward to release it, pulling it slightly out and to the rear to remove it from the door **(see illustration)**.
10   Installation is the reverse of removal.

Lock cylinder

11   Remove the door handle.
12   Insert the key in the lock cylinder; otherwise the tumbler and springs will fall out when the cylinder is withdrawn.

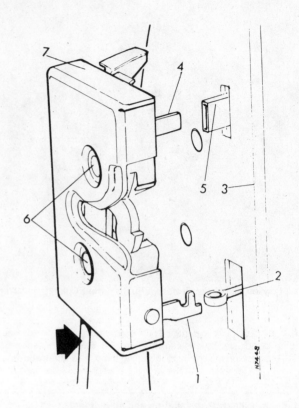

19.7   Later model door lock removal details

1	Remote control lever in the pulled out position	4	Upper control lever
2	Remote control rod	5	Control lever sleeve
3	Door face	6	Screw holes
		7	Lock assembly

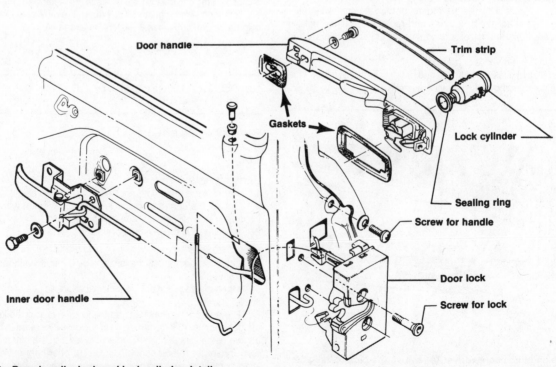

19.9   Door handle, lock and lock cylinder details

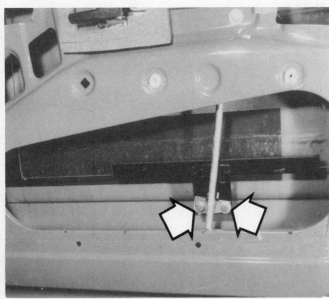

20.3   Door glass-to-regulator bolts (arrows)

13   Pull the lock cylinder out of the handle.
14   Install the hairpin spring located under the lock operating cam so that it is under tension, then insert the lock cylinder into the handle.

20   Door window glass – removal and installation

Refer to illustration 20.3
1   Lower the window glass.
2   Remove the door trim panel and plastic watershield (Section 13).
3   Remove the bolts securing the regulator to the door and the lifting plate to the window glass channel **(see illustration)**.
4   Detach the window regulator and withdraw it through the inner door panel.
5   Remove the glass channel adjacent to the window opening. On some models it will be necessary to drill out the lower rivet holding this assembly in place.
6   Unclip the window seals and remove the corner window.
7   Lift the window glass up through the opening, angle it, then remove it from the door.
8   Installation is the reverse of removal. Be sure to lubricate the regulator cable with multi-purpose grease and install a new rivet (if equipped) when securing the window channel.

21   Outside mirror – removal and installation

Refer to illustration 21.2
1   Remove the mirror control knob, then remove the door trim panel and plastic watershield.
2   Remove the nut securing the cable to the door **(see illustration)**.
3   Remove the two screws, detach the mirror and lift it away from the door, guiding the cable through the opening.
4   Installation is the reverse of removal.

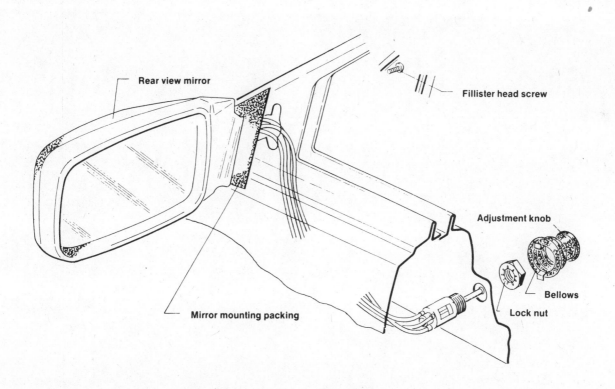

21.2   Outside mirror details

11

22   Front wheelhouse liner – removal and installation

Refer to illustration 22.2

1   Raise the vehicle, support it on jackstands and remove the front wheel(s).

2   Remove the mounting screws/bolts and lower the liner from the fender well **(see illustration)**.

3   Installation is the reverse of removal.

23   Seat belt check

1   Check the seat belts, buckles, latch plates and guide loops for obvious damage and signs of wear.

2   Check that the seat belt reminder light comes on when the key is turned to the Run or Start positions. A chime should also sound.

3   The seat belts are designed to lock up during a sudden stop or impact, yet allow free movement during normal driving. Check that the retractors return the belt against your chest while driving and rewind the belt fully when the buckle is unlatched.

4   If any of the above checks reveal problems with the seat belt system, replace parts as necessary.

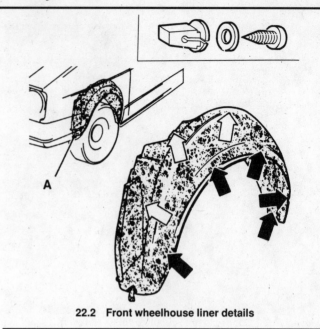

22.2   Front wheelhouse liner details

Chapter 12   Chassis electrical system

Contents

Battery check and maintenance . . . . See Chapter 1	Headlights – adjustment 10
Battery – removal and installation . . . . See Chapter 5	Headlights – replacement 9
Brake light switch – removal, installation	Ignition switch and lock cylinder – removal and installation 7
and adjustment . . . . See Chapter 9	Instrument cluster – removal and installation 13
Bulb replacement 11	Instrument panel – removal and installation 14
Central locking system – description and check 16	Neutral safety/back-up light switch – check
Combination switch – removal and installation 8	and replacement . . . . See Chapter 7B
Cruise control system – description and check 15	Relays – general information 5
Electrical troubleshooting – general information 2	Speedometer cable – replacement 17
Fuses – general information 3	Turn signal and hazard flashers – check and replacement 6
Fusible links – general information 4	Wiper motors – removal and installation 12
General information 1	Wiring diagrams – general information 18

1   General information

The electrical system is a 12-volt, negative ground type. Power for the lights and all electrical accessories is supplied by a lead/acid-type battery which is charged by the alternator.

This Chapter covers repair and service procedures for the various electrical components not associated with the engine. Information on the battery, alternator, distributor and starter motor can be found in Chapter 5.

It should be noted that when portions of the electrical system are serviced, the negative battery cable should be disconnected from the battery to prevent electrical shorts and/or fires.

2   Electrical troubleshooting – general information

A typical electrical circuit consists of an electrical component, any switches, relays, motors, fuses, fusible links or circuit breakers related to that component and the wiring and connectors that link the component to both the battery and the chassis. To help you pinpoint an electrical circuit problem, wiring diagrams are included at the end of this book.

Before tackling any troublesome electrical circuit, first study the appropriate wiring diagrams to get a complete understanding of what makes up that individual circuit. Trouble spots, for instance, can often be narrowed down by noting if other components related to the circuit are operating properly. If several components or circuits fail at one time, chances are the

12

problem is in a fuse or ground connection, because several circuits are often routed through the same fuse and ground connections.

Electrical problems usually stem from simple causes, such as loose or corroded connections, a blown fuse, a melted fusible link or a bad relay. Visually inspect the condition of all fuses, wires and connections in a problem circuit before troubleshooting it.

If testing instruments are going to be utilized, use the diagrams to plan ahead of time where you will make the necessary connections in order to accurately pinpoint the trouble spot.

The basic tools needed for electrical troubleshooting include a circuit tester or voltmeter (a 12-volt bulb with a set of test leads can also be used), a continuity tester, which includes a bulb, battery and set of test leads, and a jumper wire, preferably with a circuit breaker incorporated, which can be used to bypass electrical components. Before attempting to locate a problem with test instruments, use the wiring diagram(s) to decide where to make the connections.

Voltage checks

Voltage checks should be performed if a circuit is not functioning properly. Connect one lead of a circuit tester to either the negative battery terminal or a known good ground. Connect the other lead to a connector in the circuit being tested, preferably nearest to the battery or fuse. If the bulb of the tester lights, voltage is present, which means that the part of the circuit between the connector and the battery is problem free. Continue checking the rest of the circuit in the same fashion. When you reach a point at which no voltage is present, the problem lies between that point and the last test point with voltage. Most of the time the problem can be traced to a loose connection. **Note:** *Keep in mind that some circuits receive voltage only when the ignition key is in the Accessory or Run position.*

Finding a short

One method of finding shorts in a circuit is to remove the fuse and connect a test light or voltmeter in its place to the fuse terminals. There should be no voltage present in the circuit. Move the wiring harness from side-to-side while watching the test light. If the bulb goes on, there is a short to ground somewhere in that area, probably where the insulation has rubbed through. The same test can be performed on each component in the circuit, even a switch.

Ground check

Perform a ground test to check whether a component is properly grounded. Disconnect the battery and connect one lead of a selfpowered

test light, known as a continuity tester, to a known good ground. Connect the other lead to the wire or ground connection being tested. If the bulb goes on, the ground is good. If the bulb does not go on, the ground is not good.

Continuity check

A continuity check is done to determine if there are any breaks in a circuit – if it is passing electricity properly. With the circuit off (no power in the circuit), a self-powered continuity tester can be used to check the circuit. Connect the test leads to both ends of the circuit (or to the "power" end and a good ground), and if the test light comes on the circuit is passing current properly. If the light doesn't come on, there is a break somewhere in the circuit. The same procedure can be used to test a switch, by connecting the continuity tester to the switch terminals. With the switch turned On, the test light should come on.

Finding an open circuit

When diagnosing for possible open circuits, it is often difficult to locate them by sight because oxidation or terminal misalignment are hidden by the connectors. Merely wiggling a connector on a sensor or in the wiring harness may correct the open circuit condition. Remember this when an open circuit is indicated when troubleshooting a circuit. Intermittent problems may also be caused by oxidized or loose connections.

Electrical troubleshooting is simple if you keep in mind that all electrical circuits are basically electricity running from the battery, through the wires, switches, relays, fuses and fusible links to each electrical component (light bulb, motor, etc.) and to ground, from which it is passed back to the battery. Any electrical problem is an interruption in the flow of electricity to and from the battery.

---

3   Fuses – general information

Refer to illustrations 3.1a, 3.1b and 3.3

The electrical circuits of the vehicle are protected by a combination of fuses and fusible links. The fuse block is located under the instrument panel on the left side of the dashboard **(see illustrations)**.

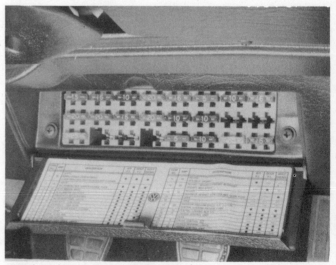

3.1a   On early models the fuse block is located under the dash to the left of the driver

| A | Dimmer switch relay | C | Wiper relay |
| B | Rear window heater relay | D | Hazard/turn signal relay |

3.1b   On later models the fuse block is located under a panel to the left of the driver

GOOD

BLOWN

3.3   On later models the fuse can be easily checked visually to determine if it is blown

Each of the fuses is designed to protect a specific circuit, and the various circuits are identified on the fuse panel itself.

Miniaturized fuses are employed in the fuse block on later models. These compact fuses, with blade terminal design, allow fingertip removal and replacement. If an electrical component fails, always check the fuse first. A blown fuse is easily identified through the clear plastic body. Visually inspect the element for evidence of damage (see illustration). If a continuity check is called for, the blade terminal tips are exposed in the fuse body.

Be sure to replace blown fuses with the correct type. Fuses of different ratings are physically interchangeable, but only fuses of the proper rating should be used. Replacing a fuse with one of a higher or lower value than specified is not recommended. Each electrical circuit needs a specific amount of protection. The amperage value of each fuse is molded into the fuse body.

If the replacement fuse immediately fails, don't replace it again until the cause of the problem is isolated and corrected. In most cases, the cause will be a short circuit in the wiring caused by a broken or deteriorated wire.

4   Fusible links – general information

Some circuits are protected by fusible links. The links are used in circuits which are not ordinarily fused, such as the ignition circuit.

Although the fusible links appear to be a heavier gauge than the wire they are protecting, the appearance is due to the thick insulation. All fusible links are four wire gauges smaller than the wire they are designed to protect.

Fusible links cannot be repaired, but a new link of the same size wire can be put in its place. The procedure is as follows:
a) Disconnect the negative cable from the battery.
b) Disconnect the fusible link from the wiring harness.
c) Cut the damaged fusible link out of the wiring just behind the connector.
d) Strip the insulation back approximately 1/2-inch.
e) Position the connector on the new fusible link and crimp it into place.
f) Use rosin core solder at each end of the new link to obtain a good solder joint.
g) Use plenty of electrical tape around the soldered joint. No wires should be exposed.
h) Connect the battery ground cable. Test the circuit for proper operation.

5   Relays – general information

Refer to illustration 5.2

Several electrical accessories in the vehicle use relays to transmit the electrical signal to the component. If the relay is defective, that component will not operate properly.

The various relays are grouped together in several locations (see illustration). If a faulty relay is suspected, it can be removed and tested by

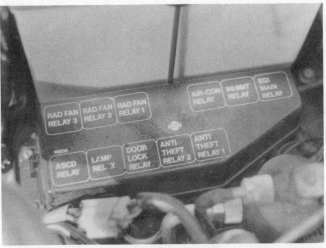

5.2   On most models, the relays are located on a panel next to the battery

a dealer service department or a repair shop. Defective relays must be replaced as a unit.

6   Turn signal and hazard flashers – check and replacement

1   The turn signal and hazard flasher are operated by the same relay, but have separate fuses. The small canister-shaped relay is located in the fuse block or wiring harness and flashes the turn signals.
2   When the flasher unit is functioning properly, an audible click can be heard during its operation. If the turn signals fail on one side or the other and the flasher unit does not make its characteristic clicking sound, a faulty turn signal bulb is indicated.
3   If both turn signals fail to blink, the problem may be due to a blown fuse, a faulty flasher relay, a broken turn signal switch or a loose or open connection. Because both systems use the same relay, if either the turn signal or emergency flasher systems are inoperative, check the fuse for that system. If a quick check of the fuse box indicates that the turn signal fuse has blown, check the wiring for a short before installing a new fuse. If both the turn signal and emergency flasher systems don't work, either the relay or associated switch is faulty.
4   To replace the flasher relay, simply pull it out of the fuse block or wiring harness.
5   Make sure that the replacement unit is identical to the original. Compare the old one to the new one before installing it.
6   Installation is the reverse of removal.

7   Ignition switch and lock cylinder – removal and installation

Refer to illustrations 7.3, 7.5 and 7.8
1   Disconnect the negative battery cable.
2   Remove the steering column switches (Section 8).

Lock cylinder

1975 and 1976
3   Use pliers to pull out the locking plate, then insert the ignition key, turn it clockwise a distance of about one thickness of the key and withdraw the lock cylinder from the steering column (see illustration).
4   Installation is the reverse of removal. After installation use a hammer and small punch to peen the edge of the opening to secure the locking plate.

1977 on
5   Drill a 0.11-inch (3 mm) hole on the lock housing for access to the cylinder as shown in the accompanying illustration. Drill only through the housing, not into the lock cylinder.

12

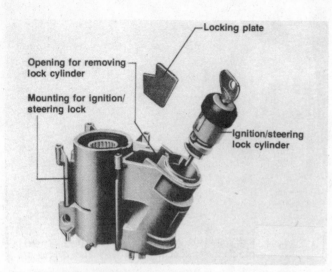

7.3   On 1975 and 1976 models, use pliers to pull out the locking plate and release the lock cylinder

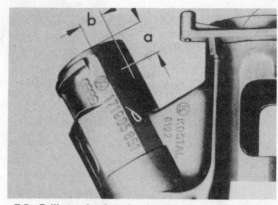

7.5   Drill at point A to the depth indicated at point B

A   15/32 in (12 mm)   B   3/8 in (10 mm)

6   Insert a small drill or piece of thick wire into the access hole and depress the release spring, insert the key and pull the lock cylinder out.
7   To install, insert the new lock cylinder into the housing until it clicks in place.

Ignition switch

8   Remove the retaining screw and lower the switch from the steering column **(see illustration)**.
9   Installation is the reverse of removal.

8   Combination switch – removal and installation

Refer to illustrations 8.2, 8.4, 8.5, 8.6 and 8.7
1   Disconnect the negative battery cable.
2   Pull or pry the horn pad off and unplug the electrical connector **(see illustration)**.
3   Remove the steering wheel (Chapter 10).
4   Remove the screws and lower the lower steering column cover **(see illustration)**.
5   Unplug the wiring harness from the switches **(see illustration)**.

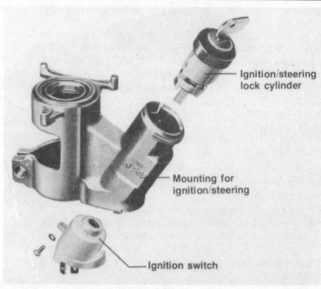

7.8   Ignition switch details

8.2   Detach the horn switch connector from the pad

8.4   Remove the screws and detach the lower column cover

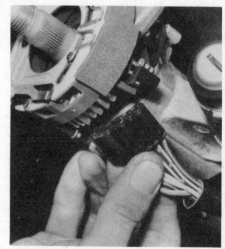

8.5   Unplug the connectors from the switches

8.6   Remove the switch screws

8.7   Slide the switch assembly off the steering shaft

6   Remove the switch retaining screws **(see illustration)**.
7   Slide the switch assembly off the steering shaft and remove it from the vehicle**(see illustration)**.
8   Installation is the reverse of removal.

9   Headlights – replacement

1   Disconnect the negative cable from the battery.

Sealed-beam type
Refer to illustration 9.3
2   Remove the retaining screws and detach the headlight bezel. On some models, the grille will also have to be removed (Chapter 11).
3   Remove the headlight retainer screws, taking care not to disturb the adjustment screws **(see illustration)**.
4   Remove the retainer and pull the headlight out far enough to allow the connector to be unplugged.
5   Remove the headlight.

6   Plug the connector in, place the headlight in position and install the retainer and screws. Tighten the screws securely.
7   Place the headlight bezel in position and install the retaining screws.

Halogen bulb-type
Refer to illustrations 9.9 and 9.10
Warning: *Halogen gas filled bulbs are under pressure and may shatter if the surface is scratched or the bulb is dropped. Wear eye protection and handle the bulbs carefully, grasping only the base whenever possible. Do not touch the surface of the bulb with your fingers because the oil from your skin could cause it to overheat and fail prematurely. If you do touch the bulb surface, clean it with rubbing alcohol.*
8   Open the hood.
9   Reach behind the headlight assembly, lift up the clip and pull the bulb holder back **(see illustration)**. Lift the holder assembly out for access to the bulb.
10   Use a small screwdriver to release the clip and remove the bulb from the holder **(see illustration)**.
11   Insert the new bulb into the holder until the clip snaps in place to seat it in the holder.
12   Install the bulb holder in the headlight assembly.

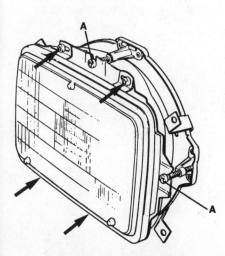

9.3   Typical sealed beam headlight retaining screws (arrows) and adjustment screws (A)

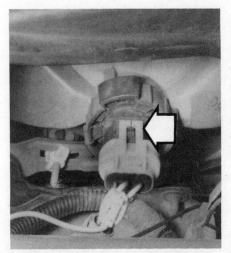

9.9   Lift the clip (arrow) to release the bulb holder from the housing

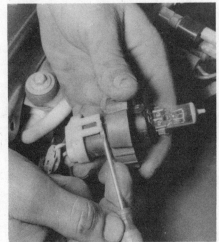

9.10   Pry the clip up with a small screwdriver and detach the bulb

10.1   Bulb-type headlight housing adjustment screws (arrows)

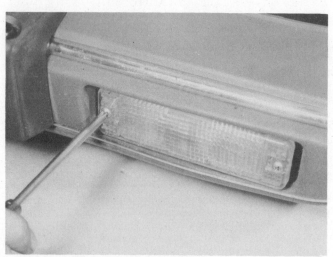

11.1a   Remove the turn signal/parking light screws and detach the lens

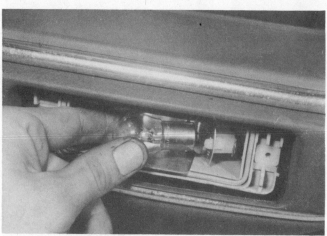

11.1b   Push the bulb in and turn it counterclockwise to remove it

10   Headlights – adjustment

Refer to illustration 10.1

Note: *The headlights must be aimed correctly. If adjusted incorrectly they could blind the driver of an oncoming vehicle and cause a serious accident or seriously reduce your ability to see the road. The headlights should be checked for proper aim every 12 months and any time a new headlight is installed or front end body work is performed. It should be emphasized that the following procedure is only an interim step which will provide temporary adjustment until the headlights can be adjusted by a properly equipped shop.*

1   Headlights have two spring loaded adjusting screws, one on the top controlling up-and-down movement and one on the side controlling left-and-right movement **(see illustration 9.3 and the accompanying illustration)**.

2   There are several methods of adjusting the headlights. The simplest method requires a blank wall 25 feet in front of the vehicle and a level floor.

3   Position masking tape vertically on the wall in reference to the vehicle centerline and the centerlines of both headlights.

4   Position a horizontal tape line in reference to the centerline of all the headlights. **Note:** *It may be easier to position the tape on the wall with the vehicle parked only a few inches away.*

5   Adjustment should be made with the vehicle sitting level, the gas tank half-full and no unusually heavy load in the vehicle.

6   Starting with the low beam adjustment, position the high intensity zone so it is two inches below the horizontal line and two inches to the right of the headlight vertical line. Adjustment is made by turning the top adjusting screw clockwise to raise the beam and counterclockwise to lower the beam. The adjusting screw on the side should be used in the same manner to move the beam left or right.

7   With the high beams on, the high intensity zone should be vertically centered with the exact center just below the horizontal line. **Note:** *It may not be possible to position the headlight aim exactly for both high and low beams. If a compromise must be made, keep in mind that the low beams are the most used and have the greatest effect on driver safety.*

8   Have the headlights adjusted by a dealer service department or service station at the earliest opportunity.

11   Bulb replacement

Refer to illustrations 11.1a, 11.1b, 11.2, 11.3a, 11.3b and 11.4

1   The lenses of many lights are held in place by screws, which makes it a simple procedure to gain access to the bulbs **(see illustrations)**.

2   On some lights the lenses are held in place by clips. The lenses can be removed either by unsnapping them or by using a small screwdriver to pry them off **(see illustration)**.

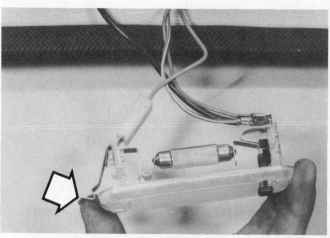

11.2   Pry out the dome light retaining spring (arrow) with a screwdriver and lower the housing for access to the bulb

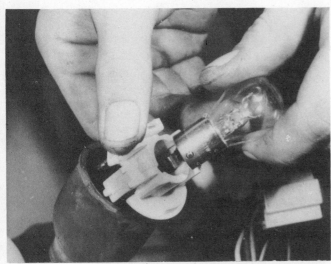

11.3a   Push the bulb in and turn it counterclockwise to detach it from the holder

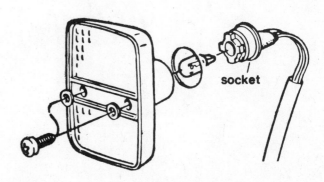

11.3b   After removing the side marker light lens, the bulb can be pulled straight out of the socket

3   Several types of bulbs are used. Some are removed by pushing in and turning them counterclockwise (**see illustration**). Others can simply be unclipped from the terminals or pulled straight out of the socket (**see illustration**).

4   To gain access to the instrument panel lights, the instrument cluster will have to be removed first (**see illustration**).

11.4   After removing the instrument cluster, the bulbs can be removed from the back of the housing

12   Wiper motors – removal and installation

1   Disconnect the negative cable at the battery.

Windshield wiper
Refer to illustrations 12.2, 12.4, 12.6a, 12.6b and 12.6c

2   Remove the wiper arm assemblies (**see illustration**).

3   Pry off the wiper motor cover (if equipped).

4   On 1982 and later Scirocco models, remove the ring nut, detach the motor drive spindle from the body, remove the bolts and lift the motor and wiper frame from the vehicle as an assembly (**see illustration**). Remove the bolts and detach the motor from the frame.

5   On all other models, disconnect the wiper arm spindle link from the motor.

6   Remove the attaching screws from the wiper motor mounting plate (**see illustrations**). Unplug the electrical connector and remove the assembly from the vehicle.

7   Installation is the reverse of removal, however make sure to adjust the crank arm angle if necessary, as described below.

Crank arm angle adjustment

8   The crank arm angle position must be adjusted on 1975 through 1984 models if the crank arm has been removed or a new motor is being installed and on all 1985 and later models.

1975 through 1984 models (except 1982 and later Scirocco)
Refer to illustration 12.9

9   Connect the negative battery cable. Plug in the electrical connector, run the motor for about three minutes, then turn it off. The motor shaft will stop in the parked position and the crank arm can be installed (**see illustration**).

1985 and later models and 1982 and later Scirocco
Refer to illustrations 12.10a and 12.10b

10   Install the motor, run it for one minute (all except Scirocco) or three minutes (1982 and later Scirocco), then shut if off and connect the crank arm (**see illustrations**).

12.2   Pry the wiper arm cover up for access to the retaining nut

12

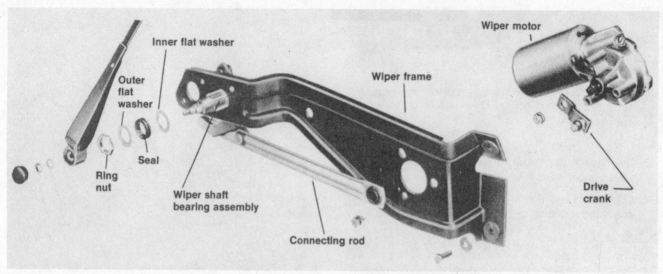

12.4   1982 and later Scirocco windshield wiper details

12.6a   Scirocco wiper motor retaining bolt locations (arrows)

12.6b   1975 through 1984 Rabbit and Jetta wiper motor retaining bolt locations (arrows)

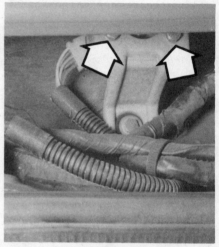

12.6c   1985 and later model wiper motor retaining bolt locations (arrows)

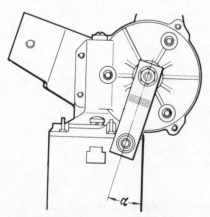

12.9   1975 through 1984 model windshield wiper motor arm parked position (a = 20-degrees)

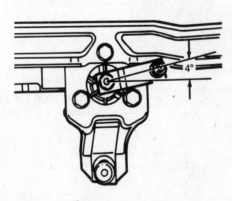

12.10a   1985 and later model windshield wiper motor arm parked position

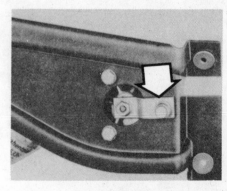

12.10b   1982 and later Scirocco model windshield wiper motor arm parked position

12.11   1982 and later Scirocco rear wiper details

1   Wiper arm
2   Blade assembly
3   Jet
4   Hose
5   Nut
6   Ring nut
7   Washer
8   Seal
9   Housing
10   Wiper motor
11   Mounting bracket
12   Cover
13   Washer pump
14   Washer fluid reservoir
15   Cap

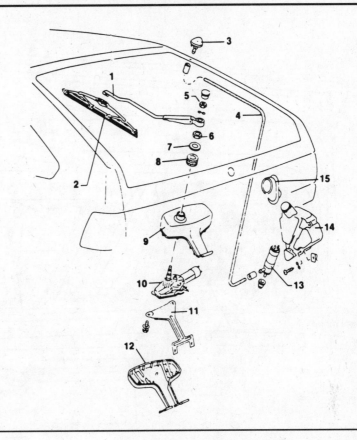

12.15a   1975 through 1984 model rear wiper details

1   Wiring grommet
2   Blade assembly
3   Hose grommet
4   Wiper arm
5   Jet
6   Spindle and frame
7   Wiper motor
8   Crank
9   Washer pump
10   Hose
11   Reservoir

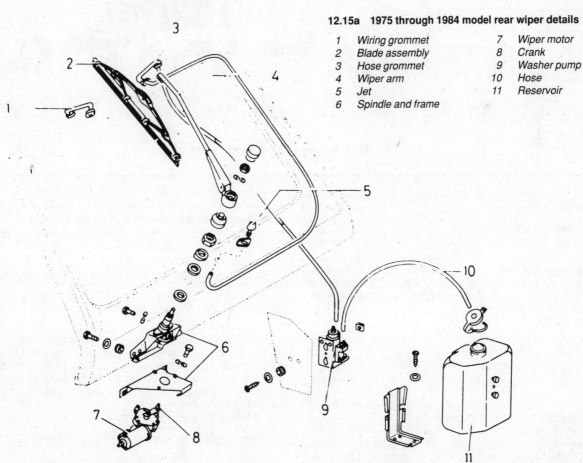

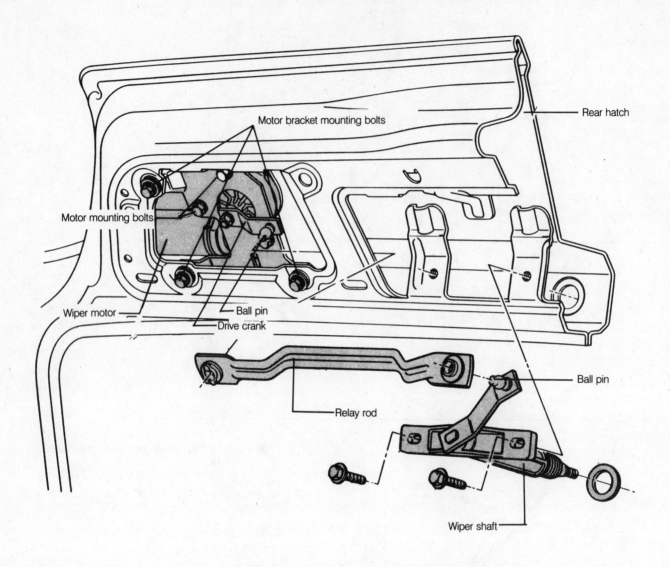

12.15b   1985 and later Golf rear wiper details

Rear window wiper

1982 and later Scirocco

Refer to illustration 12.11

11   Remove the wiper arm, spindle nut and washers. Note the order in which the wiper spindle washers are arranged for ease of installation (**see illustration**). Remove the cover, unbolt the wiper mounting bracket and remove the wiper and bracket as an assembly. Remove the bolts and detach the motor from the bracket.

12   Installation is the reverse of removal.

All others

Refer to illustrations 12.15a and 12.15b

13   Open the liftgate and remove the trim panel.

14   Use a screwdriver to detach the wiper drive crank from the wiper mechanism.

15   Unplug the electrical connector, detach the attaching screws and lower the motor from the tailgate (**see illustrations**).

16   Installation is the reverse of removal. Before connecting the crank arm, run the wiper motor (three minutes for 1975 through 1984 models or one minute for 1985 and later models) and then switch it off so the crank arm will be in the correct parked position.

13   Instrument cluster – removal and installation

1   Disconnect the negative cable from the battery.

2   Remove the steering wheel.

3   Pull off the heater control knobs and pry off the trim panel, if applicable.

1975 through 1980 models

Refer to illustration 13.4

4   Pull off the radio knobs, use a screwdriver to detach the spring clips and slide the radio out (**see illustration**). Unplug the connectors and remove the radio, then reach through the opening, unscrew the collar and detach the speedometer cable. Remove the dashboard-to-cluster screw.

5   Pull the cluster out of the dashboard, unplug the electrical connectors and remove the cluster.

6   Installation is the reverse of removal.

1981 through 1984 American-built models

Refer to illustrations 13.8, 13.10 and 13.11

7   Remove the left radio speaker.

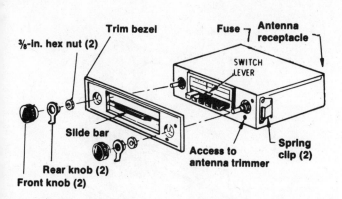

13.4   On most models the radio is held in place by a spring clip

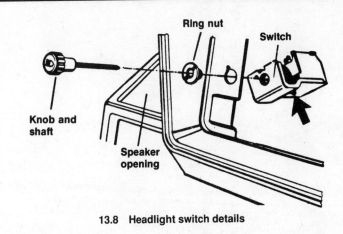

13.8   Headlight switch details

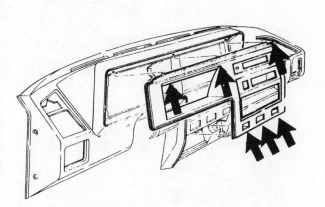

13.10   Instrument cluster bezel screw locations (arrows) (1981 through 1984 US models)

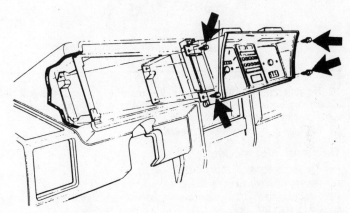

13.11   Cluster screw locations (1981 through 1984 US models)

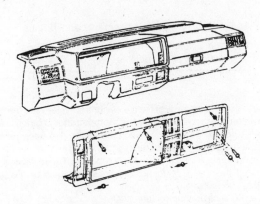

13.21   1985 and later Jetta instrument cluster bezel screw locations

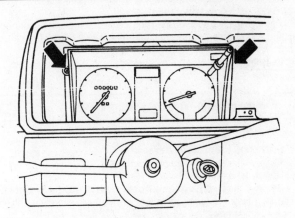

13.22   1985 and later cluster screw locations

8   Pull the headlight switch knob out, reach through the speaker opening and press the release button, then pull the knob and shaft from the switch (**see illustration**).

9   Remove the radio (**see illustration 13.4**).

10   Remove the screws and detach the cluster bezel (**see illustration**).

11   Remove the retaining screws, pull the cluster out and disconnect the speedometer cable, then unplug the electrical connectors and remove the cluster (**see illustration**).

12   Installation is the reverse of removal.

1981 through 1984 Jetta and German-built models

13   Tilt the fuse block/relay cover back down and away from the dashboard, remove the three screws and remove the shelf under the steering column and the cover.

14   Remove the three screws and clips holding the lower cover to the dashboard and remove the cover.

15   Remove the two screws and remove the insert cover from the cluster bezel.

12

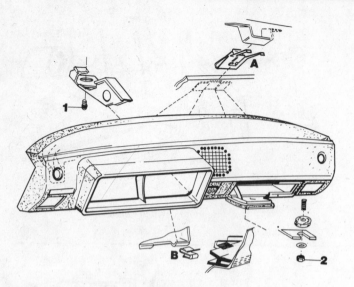

14.5a   1975 through 1980 instrument panel details

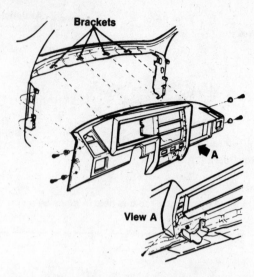

14.5b   1981 through 1984 instrument panel details

16   Remove the screw from the top of the cluster, tilt the top the cluster away from the dashboard, squeeze the tabs to disconnect the speedometer, unplug the electrical connectors and remove the cluster.
17   Installation is the reverse of removal.

1985 and later models

Refer to illustrations 13.21 and 13.22
18   Remove the center console and left side instrument panel tray.
19   Reach up behind the cluster, squeeze the speedometer cable clips and disconnect the cable.
20   Remove the headlight switch, if applicable (Golf and GTI models).
21   Remove the cluster bezel. On Golf and GTI models this is accomplished by detaching the ten spring clips, working around the outer circumference of the bezel, then detaching it. On Jetta models, remove the retaining screws **(see illustration)**.
22   Remove the two screws, then pull the cluster out and disconnect the vacuum and electrical connectors and remove the cluster **(see illustration)**.
23   Installation is the reverse of removal.

14.5c   1985 and later instrument panel details

A	Nuts (in engine compartment air plenum)	B Bolts C Bolts

---

14   Instrument panel – removal and installation

Refer to illustrations 14.5a, 14.5b and 14.5c
1   Disconnect the negative cable from the battery.
2   Remove the steering wheel (Chapter 10).
3   Remove the instrument cluster (Section 13).
4   Remove the fuse block, dashboard lower support, glove compartment, ashtray, radio, heater controls and any other components which will interfere with removal.
5   Remove the retaining bolts, nuts and screws, unplug any electrical connectors and pull the instrument panel out to remove it **(see illustrations)**.
6   Installation is the reverse of removal.

---

15   Cruise control system – description and check

The cruise control system maintains vehicle speed with a vacuum actuated servo motor located in the engine compartment, which is connected to the throttle linkage by a cable. The system consists of the servo motor, clutch switch, brake switch, control switches, a relay and associated vacuum hoses.

Because of the complexity of the cruise control system and the special tools and techniques required for diagnosis, repair should be left to a dealer service department or a repair shop. However, it is possible for the home mechanic to make simple checks of the wiring and vacuum connections for minor faults which can be easily repaired. These include:
 a) Inspect the cruise control actuating switches for broken wires and loose connections.
 b) Check the cruise control fuse.
 c) The cruise control system is operated by vacuum so it's critical that all vacuum switches, hoses and connections are secure.Check the hoses in the engine compartment for tight connections,cracks and obvious vacuum leaks.

---

16   Central locking system – description and check

The central locking system operates the door lock actuators mounted in each door, at the trunk lid and the gas cap door. The system consists of a vacuum pump located in the trunk, actuators and associated wiring and hoses. Since special tools and techniques are required to diagnose

17.2   On most models, removing the bolt will allow the speedometer cable to be pulled out of the transaxle

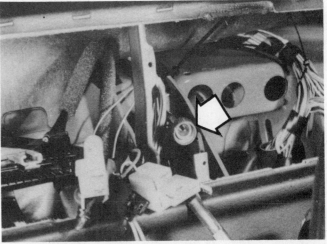

17.5a   On some models, the collar on the end of the speedometer cable (arrow) is unscrewed to detach the cable

17.5b   On other models, squeeze the clips (arrows) to detach the cable

the system, it should be left to a dealer service department or a repair shop. However, it is possible for the home mechanic to make simple checks of the hoses, wiring connections and actuators for minor faults which can be easily repaired. These include:

   a) Check the system fuse and/or circuit breaker.
   b) Check the actuator hoses for damage and loose connections. Check the switches for continuity.
   c) Remove the door panel(s) and check the actuator hoses to see if they're loose or damaged. Inspect the actuator rods to make sure they aren't bent or damaged.

17   Speedometer cable – replacement

Refer to illustrations 17.2, 17.5a and 17.5b

1   Disconnect the negative cable from the battery.
2   Disconnect the speedometer cable from the transaxle **(see illustration)**.
3   Detach the cable from its mountings in the engine compartment and pull it up to provide enough slack to allow disconnection from the speedometer.
4   On models equipped with an oxygen sensor counter, unscrew the collars and detach the cables at the counter.
5   Remove the instrument cluster screws, pull the cluster out and disconnect the speedometer cable from the back of the cluster **(see illustrations)**. On some models the cable is accessible after removing the radio (Section 13).
6   Remove the cable(s) from the vehicle.
7   Prior to installation, lubricate the speedometer end of the cable with spray-on speedometer cable lubricant (available at auto parts stores).
8   Installation is the reverse of removal.

18   Wiring diagrams – general information

    Since it isn't possible to include all wiring diagrams for every year covered by this manual, the following diagrams are those that are typical and most commonly needed.
    Prior to troubleshooting any circuits, check the fuse and circuit breakers (if equipped) to make sure they're in good condition. Make sure the battery is properly charged and check the cable connections (Chapter 1).
    When checking a circuit, make sure that all connectors are clean, with no broken or loose terminals. When unplugging a connector, do not pull on the wires. Pull only on the connector housings themselves.
    Refer to the accompanying table for the wire color codes applicable to your vehicle.

12

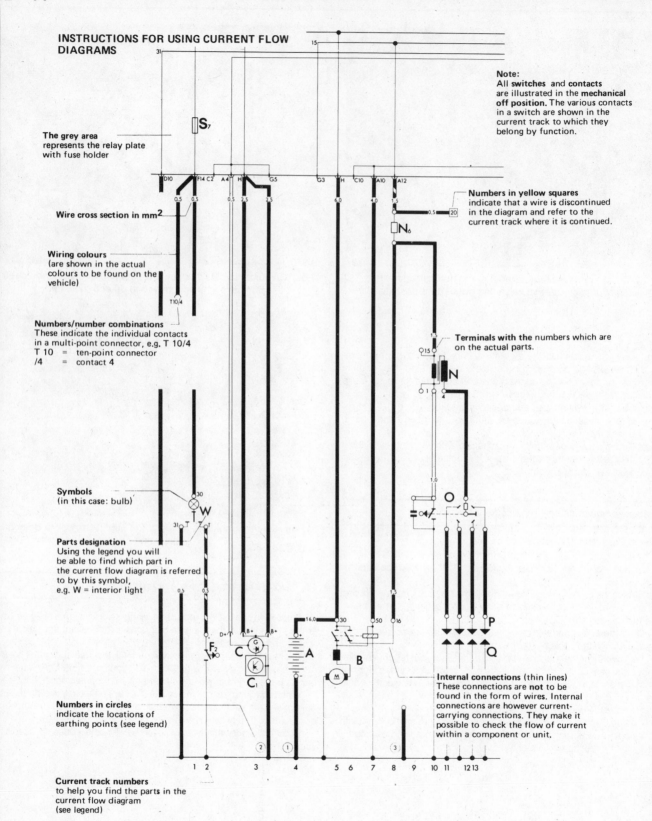

INSTRUCTIONS FOR USING CURRENT FLOW DIAGRAMS

Note:
All **switches** and **contacts** are illustrated in the **mechanical off position.** The various contacts in a switch are shown in the current track to which they belong by function.

The grey area represents the relay plate with fuse holder

Numbers in yellow squares indicate that a wire is discontinued in the diagram and refer to the current track where it is continued.

Wire cross section in mm²

Wiring colours (are shown in the actual colours to be found on the vehicle)

Terminals with the numbers which are on the actual parts.

Numbers/number combinations These indicate the individual contacts in a multi-point connector, e.g. T 10/4
T 10 = ten-point connector
/4   = contact 4

Symbols (in this case: bulb)

Parts designation Using the legend you will be able to find which part in the current flow diagram is referred to by this symbol, e.g. W = interior light

Internal connections (thin lines) These connections are **not** to be found in the form of wires. Internal connections are however current-carrying connections. They make it possible to check the flow of current within a component or unit.

Numbers in circles indicate the locations of earthing points (see legend)

Current track numbers to help you find the parts in the current flow diagram (see legend)

Instructions for using wiring diagrams

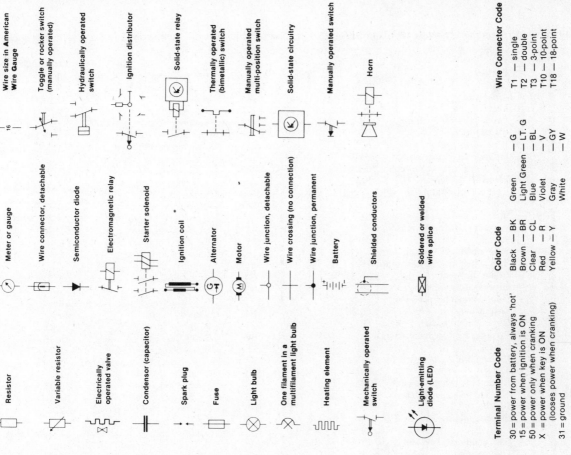

Key to symbols used in wiring diagrams

Wire size in American Wire Gauge

Toggle or rocker switch (manually operated)

Hydraulically operated switch

Ignition distributor

Solid-state relay

Thermally operated (bimetallic) switch

Manually operated multi-position switch

Solid-state circuitry

Manually operated switch

Horn

Meter or gauge

Wire connector, detachable

Semiconductor diode

Electromagnetic relay

Starter solenoid

Ignition coil

Alternator

Motor

Wire junction, detachable

Wire crossing (no connection)

Wire junction, permanent

Battery

Shielded conductors

Soldered or welded wire splice

Resistor

Variable resistor

Electrically operated valve

Condensor (capacitor)

Spark plug

Fuse

Light bulb

One filament in a multifilament light bulb

Heating element

Mechanically operated switch

Light-emitting diode (LED)

Terminal Number Code

30 = power from battery, always 'hot'
15 = power when ignition is ON
50 = power only when cranking
X = power when key is ON (looses power when cranking)
31 = ground

Color Code

Black — BK		Green — G	
Brown — BR		Light Green — LT. G	
Clear — CL		Blue — BL	
Red — R		Violet — V	
Yellow — Y		Gray — GY	
		White — W	

Wire Connector Code

T1 — single
T2 — double
T3 — 3-point
T10 — 10-point
T18 — 18-point

INSTRUCTIONS FOR USING WIRING DIAGRAMS

Specimen legend

The same part designations are used in all current flow diagrams.

eg: A is always used for the battery or N for the ignition coil.

Designation

			in current track
A	—	Battery	4
B	—	Starter	5,6,7,8
C	—	Alternator	3
C1	—	Voltage regulator	3
F2	—	Door contact switch	2
N	—	Ignition coil	10,11
N6	—	Series resistance (for coil)	8
O	—	Distributor	10,11,12,13
P	—	Spark plug connector	11,12,13
Q	—	Spark plugs	11,12,13
S7	—	Fuse in fusebox	
T10	—	Connector, ten-point, on instrument panel insert	
W	—	Interior light	1

① — Earthing strap, battery/body

② — Earthing strap, alternator/engine

③ — Earthing strap, gearbox/chassis

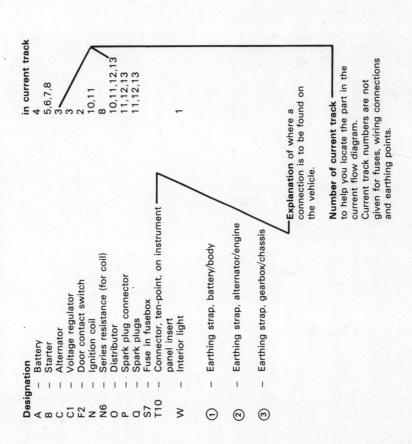

Explanation of where a connection is to be found on the vehicle.

Number of current track to help you locate the part in the current flow diagram. Current track numbers are not given for fuses, wiring connections and earthing points.

Instructions for using wiring diagrams

12

Key for wiring diagrams on pages 12-17 through 12-20 - numbers in triangles are connections to diagnostic test socket

Description		Current track
A	– Battery	3
B	– Starter	4-6
C	– Alternator	1,2
C1	– Regulator	2
D	– Ignition/starter switch	17-20
E1	– light switch	65-67
E2	– Turn signal switch	55
E3	– Emergency flasher switch	51-59
E4	– Headlight dimmer switch	93
E9	– Fresh air fan switch	8,9
E15	– Rear window defogger switch	83
E20	– Instrum. panel light switch	68
E22	– Windshield wiper intermittent switch	88-91
E24	– Safety belt lock contact, left	18
E25	– Safety belt lock contact, right	18
F	– Brake light switch	36,37
F1	– Oil pressure switch	46
F2	– Door contact buzzer switch, switch, left	16,17
F3	– Door contact switch, right	15
F4	– Back-up light switch warning light	40
F9	– Parking brake warning light switch	28
F18	– Radiator fan thermoswitch	99
F24	– Elapsed mileage switch CAT light	30
F27	– Elapsed mileage switch/EGR light	29
G	– Fuel gauge sending unit	48
G1	– Fuel gauge	21
G2	– Coolant temperature sending unit	47
G3	– Coolant temperature gauge	22
G7	– TDC marker unit	24
G20	– Temperature sensor for catalytic converter	33
H	– Horn button	39
H1	– Horn	38
J	– Headlight dimmer relay	93-95
J2	– Emergency flasher relay	53-55
J9	– Rear window defogger relay	81,82
J34	– Safety belt warning system relay	16-20
J42	– Relay for catalytic converter (behind dash)	32,33
K1	– Headlight high beam warning light	98
K2	– Alternator warning light	25
K3	– Oil pressure warning light	24
K5	– Turn signal warning light	26
K6	– Emergency flasher warning light	58
K7	– Dual circuit brake/parking brake/safety belt warning light	27-29
K10	– Rear window defogger warning light	84
K21	– Catalytic converter warning light	31
K22	– EGR warning light	30
L1	– Left headlight, high/low beam	94,96
L2	– Right headlight, high/low beam	95,97
L10	– Instrument panel light	68-70
L15	– Ashtray light	11

Description		Current track
L16	– Heater lever light	60
L28	– Cigarette lighter bulb	12
M1	– Parking light, left front	74
M2	– Tail light, right	79
M3	– Parking light, right front	77
M4	– Tail light, left	76
M5	– Turn signal, left front	61
M6	– Turn signal, left rear	62
M7	– Turn signal, right front	63
M8	– Turn signal, right rear	64
M9	– Brake light, left	44
M10	– Brake light, right	45
M11	– Side marker, front	73,78
M12	– Side marker, rear	75,80
M16	– Back-up light, left	42
M17	– Back-up light, rear	43
N	– Ignition coil	34
N1	– Automatic choke	85
N3	– Electromagnetic cut-off valve	84
N6	– Ballast resistor	34
O	– Ignition distributor	34,35
P	– Spark plug connectors	35,36
Q	– Spark plugs	42,43
S1 to S14	– Fuses on fuse/relay panel	
U1	– Cigarette lighter	13
V	– Windshield wiper motor	86,87
V2	– Fresh air fan	9
V5	– Windshield washer pump	92
V7	– Radiator fan	99
W	– Interior light	14
W6	– Glove compartment light	10
X	– License plate light	71,72
Y	– Clock	66
Z1	– Rear window defogger heat, element	81

Wire connectors

T	– Behind dashboard	
T1a	– Single, behind dashboard	
T1b	– Single, behind dashboard	
T1c	– Single, in engine compartment	
T1d	– Single, engine compartment, front left	
T1e	– Single, engine compartment, front right	
T1f	– Single, trunk	
T1g	– Single, trunk, right rear	
T1h	– Single, trunk, left rear	
T2a	– Double, engine compartment	
T2b	– Double, behind dashboard	
T2c	– Double, behind dashboard	
T2d	– Double, behind dashboard	
T3a	– 3-point, engine compartment, left front	
T3b	– 3-point, engine compartment, right front	
T12	– 12 point, on dashboard cluster	
T20	– Test socket	

Ground connectors

①	– Battery to body	
②	– Alternator to engine	
⑩	– Instrument cluster	
⑪	– Body	
⑮	– Engine compartment, front left	
⑯	– Engine compartment, front right	

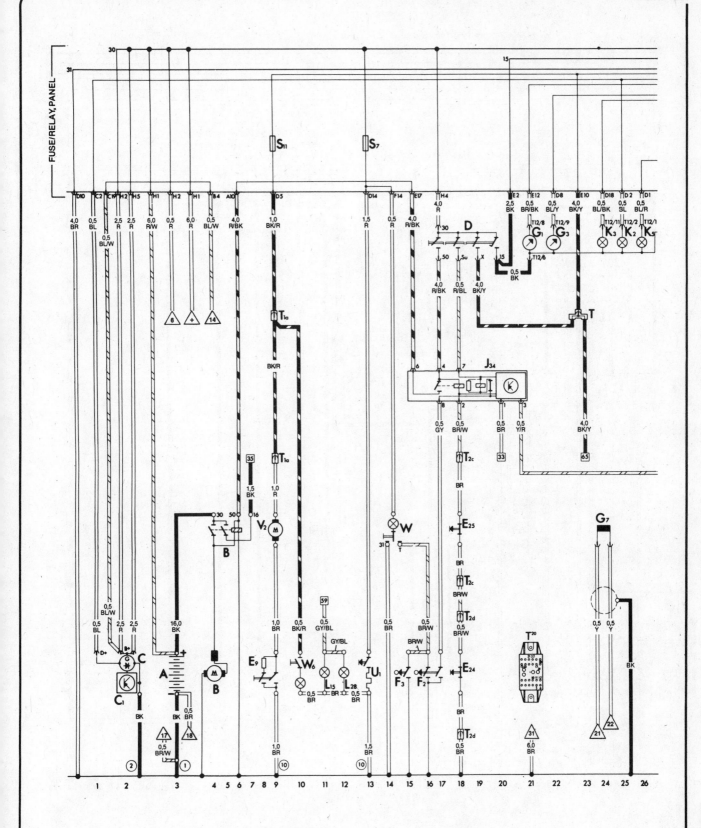

Wiring diagram (typical) for pre-1977 Rabbit models

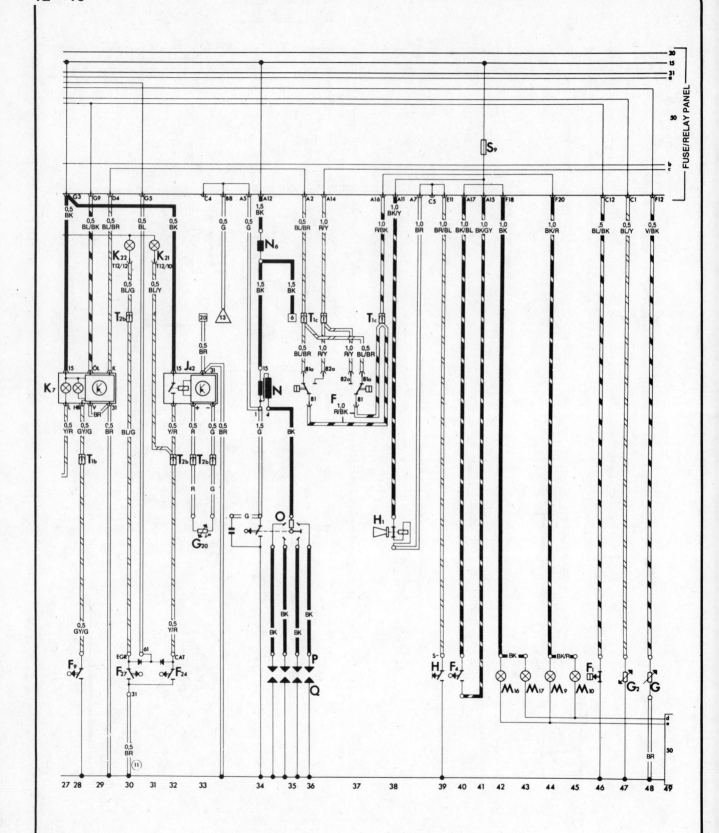

Wiring diagram (typical) for pre-1977 Rabbit models

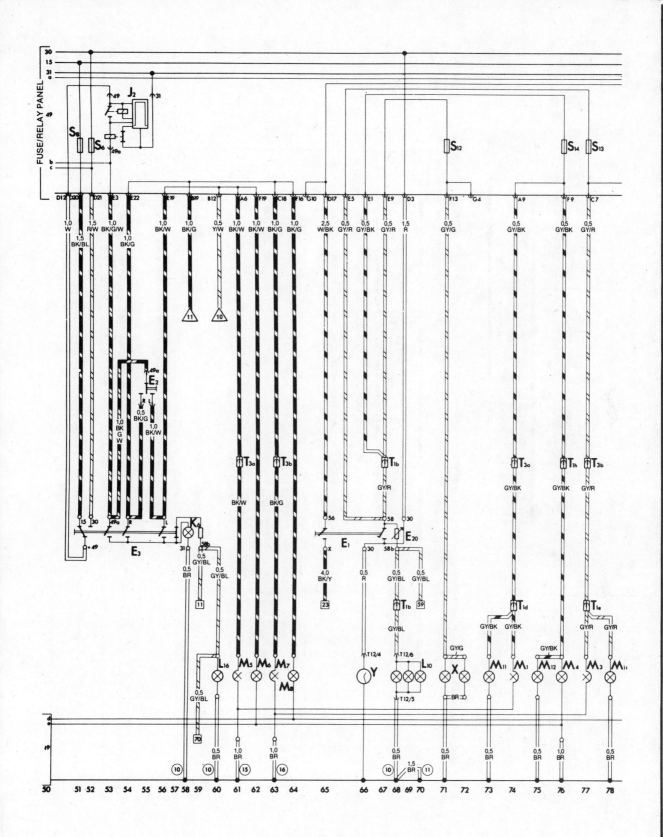

Wiring diagram (typical) for pre-1977 Rabbit models

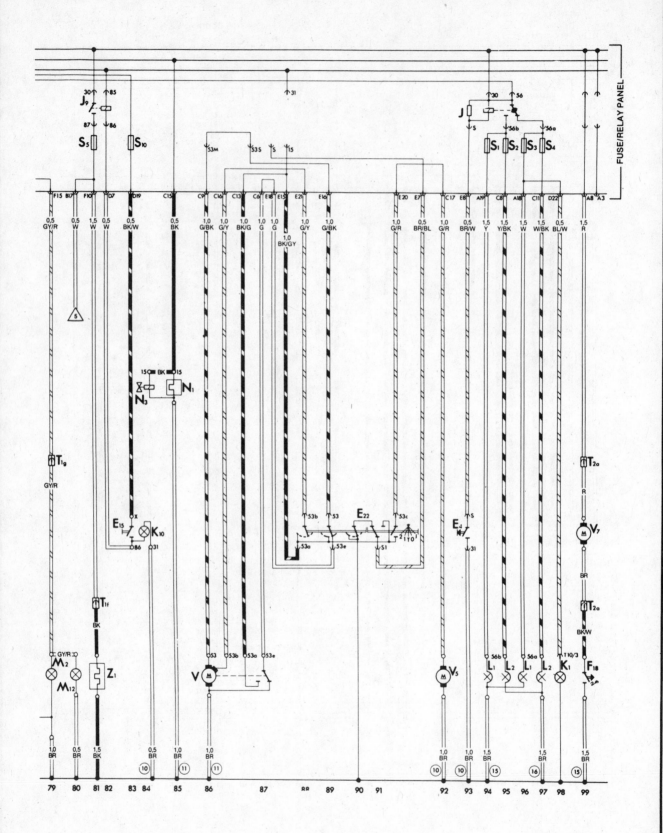

Wiring diagram (typical) for pre-1977 Rabbit models

Key for wiring diagrams on pages 12-22 through 12-25 - numbers in triangles are connections to diagnostic test socket

Description		Current track
A	– Battery	2
B	– Starter motor	3.4
C	– Alternator	1
C1	– Regulator	1
D	– Ignition/starter switch	10-14
E1	– Light switch	58,60
E2	– Turn signal switch	46
E3	– Emergency flasher switch	42-48
E4	– Headlight dimmer switch	93
E9	– Fresh air fan switch	78,79
E15	– Rear window defogger switch	91
E20	– Instrument panel light switch	61
E22	– Windshield wash/wipe intermittent switch	84-88
E24	– Safety belt lock contact, left	11
F	– Brake light switch	36,37
F1	– Engine oil pressure switch	39
F2	– Door switch/buzzer, left	107,108
F3	– Door switch/buzzer, right	106
F4	– Back-up light switch	31
F9	– Parking brake warning light switch	22
F18	– Radiator fan thermoswitch	102
F24	– Elapsed mileage switch/ CAT light	25
F25	– Throttle valve micro switch	9
F26	– Thermotime switch for cold start	30
F27	– Elapsed mileage switch/ EGR light	23
F37	– Thermoswitch for secondary stage	31
G	– Fuel gauge sending unit	41
G1	– Fuel gauge	15
G2	– Coolant temperature. sending unit	40
G3	– Coolant temperature gauge	16
G5	– Tachometer	18
G7	– to TDC sensor	18
G14	– Voltmeter	77
G20	– Temp. sensor for CAT converter	26
H	– Horn button	36
H1	– Horn	33,34
J	– Headlight dimmer switch	93-95
J2	– Emergency flasher relay	44-46
J4	– Horn relay	35,36
J6	– Voltage stabilizer	15
J9	– Rear window defogger relay	90
J31	– Wiper intermittent relay	82-84
J34	– Safety belt warning relay	11-15
J42	– Relay for CAT converter (behind dash)	25-28
K1	– Headlight high beam warning light	101
K2	– Alternator charging warning light	19
K3	– Oil pressure warning light	18
K5	– Turn signal warning light	20
K6	– Emergency flasher warning light	49
K7	– Dual circuit brake/parking brake/safety belt warning light	21,22
K10	– Rear window defogger light	92
K21	– CAT converter warning light	24
K22	– EGR warning light	23
L1	– Left headlight, high/low beam	94, 96
L2	– Right headlight, high/low beam	95,100
L8	– Clock light	65
L10	– Instrument panel light	61-63
L15	– Ashtray light	52
L16	– Fresh air lever light	50
L17	– Left headlight, high beam	98
L18	– Right headlight, high beam	99
L25	– Voltmeter light	64
L28	– Cigarette lighter light	53
M1	– Parking light, front left	70
M2	– Tail light, right	75
M3	– Parking light, front right	73

Description		Current track
M4	– Tail light, left	72
M5	– Turn signal, front left	54
M6	– Turn signal, rear left	55
M7	– Turn signal, front right	56
M8	– Turn signal, rear right	57
M9	– Brake light, left	38
M10	– Brake light, right	37
M11	– Side marker lights, front	69,74
M12	– Side marker lights, rear	71,76
M16	– Back-up light, left	32
M17	– Back-up light, right	33
N	– Ignition coil	6
N1	– Automatic choke	30
N3	– Electro-magnetic cut-off valve	29
N6	– Ballast resistor	6
N18	– EGR valve	9
N38	– Diverter valve for air injection	28
O	– Ignition distributor	6,8
P	– Spark plug connectors	8
Q	– Spark plugs	8
S1 to S15	– Fuses on fuse/relay panel	
U1	– Cigarette lighter	104
V	– Windshield wiper motor	81,82
V2	– Fresh air fan	79
V5	– Windshield wiper pump	89
V7	– Radiator cooling fan	102
W	– Interior light	105
W3	– Trunk light	66
W6	– Glove compartment light	80
X	– License plate light	67,68
Y	– Clock	59
Z1	– Rear window defogger light	90

Wire connectors

T	– Single, behind dashboard	
T1a	– Single, in engine compartment front left	
T1b	– Single, in engine compartment front right	
T1c	– Single, behind dashboard	
T1d	– Single, in engine compartment	
T1e	– Single, in engine compartment	
T1f	– Single, in engine compartment	
T1g	– Single, behind dashboard	
T1h	– Single, behind dashboard	
T1i	– Single, behind dashboard	
T1k	– Single, behind dashboard	
T1l	– Single, behind dashboard	
T1m	– Single, behind dashboard	
T1n	– Single, in trunk	
T1o	– Single, behind dashboard	
T1p	– Single, behind dashboard	
T1q	– Single, behind dashboard	
T1f	– Single, behind dashboard	
T1s	– Single, in trunk	
T1t	– Single, in trunk, left	
T1v	– Single, in trunk, right	
T2a	– Double, in engine compartment front	
T2b	– Double, in engine compartment on firewall	
T2c	– Double, behind dashboard	
T2d	– Double, behind dashboard	
T2e	– Double, in engine compartment	
T2f	– Double, on frame, left	
T3	– 3-point, behind dashboard	
T12	– 12-point, instrument cluster	
T20	– Diagnosis socket	

Ground connectors

①	– Battery to body	
②	– Alternator to engine	
⑩	– Instrument cluster	
⑪	– Dashboard	
⑮	– Engine compartment front left	
⑯	– Engine compartment front right	

12

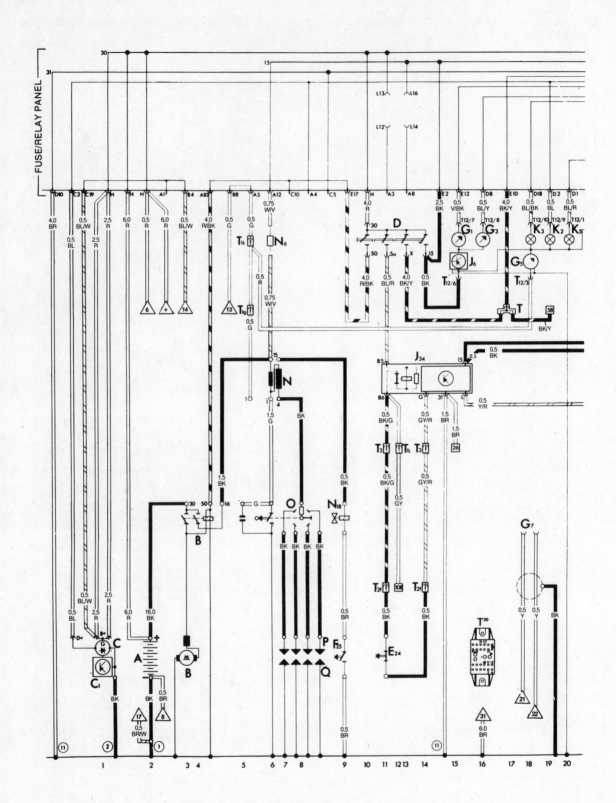

Wiring diagram (typical) for pre-1977 Scirocco models

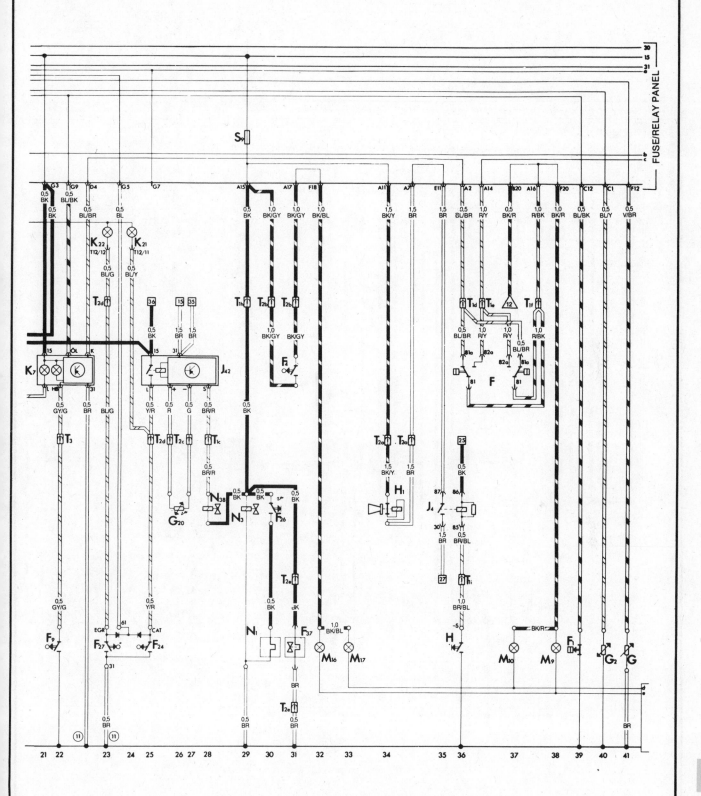

FUSE/RELAY PANEL

Wiring diagram (typical) for pre-1977 Scirocco models

12

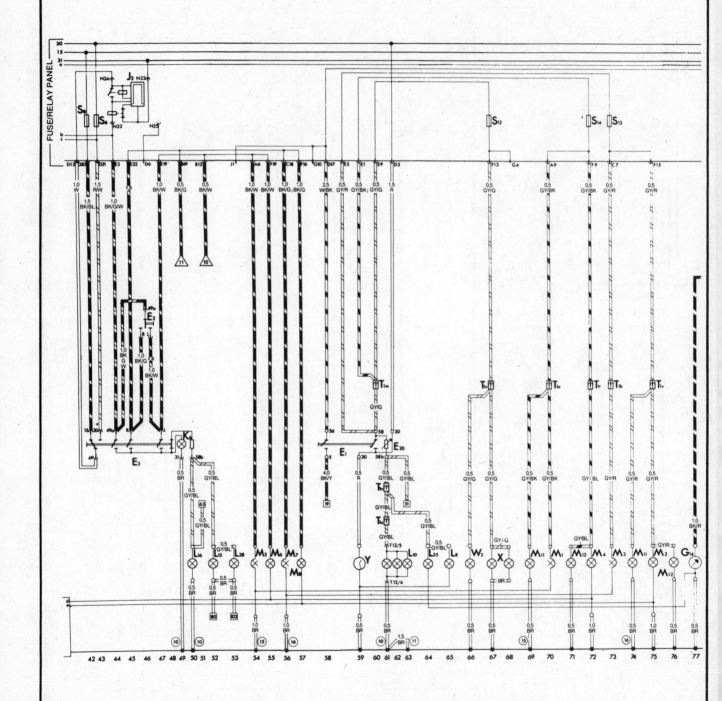

Wiring diagram (typical) for pre-1977 Scirocco models

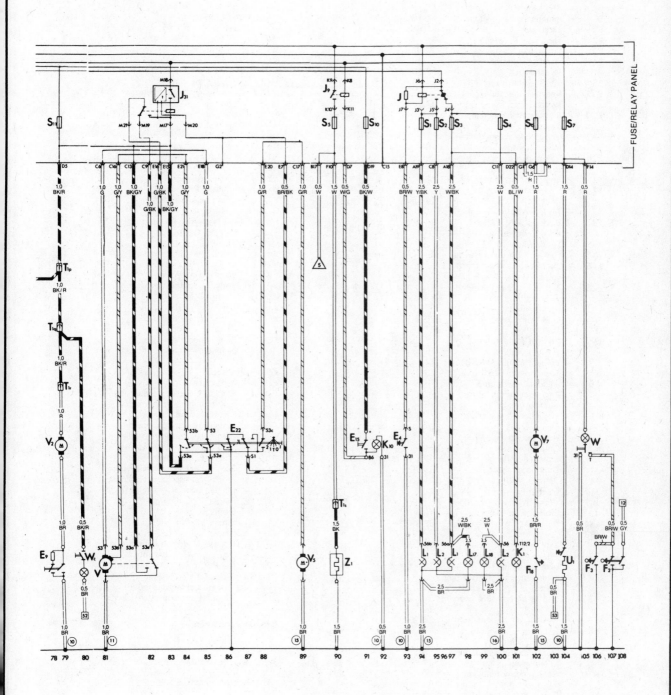

Wiring diagram (typical) for pre-1977 Scirocco models

Key for wiring diagrams on pages 12-27 through 12-30

Description		Current track
A	– Battery	2
B	– Starter motor	10-12
C	– Alternator	1
C1	– Regulator	1
D	– Ignition/starter switch	17-20
E1	– Light switch	81-84
E2	– Turn signal switch	61
E3	– Emergency flasher switch	57-65
E4	– Headlight dimmer/flasher switch	79,80
E5	– Fresh air fan switch	94,95
E15	– Rear window defogger switch	97,98
E20	– Instrument panel lights switch	83
E22	– Windshield washer/wiper intermittent switch	101-105
E24	– Safety belt switch, left	38
F	– Brake light switch	43,44
F1	– Engine oil pressure switch	28
F2	– Door switch/buzzer, front left	54,55
F3	– Door switch, front right	53
F4	– Back-up light switch	32
F9	– Parking brake warning light switch	42
F18	– Radiator fan thermoswitch	107
F26	– Thermoswitch/cold start valve	8
F29	– Elapsed mileage switch/ EGR light (not for Canada)	27
G	– Fuel gauge sending unit	30
G1	– Fuel gauge	21
G2	– Coolant temperature sending unit	29
G3	– Coolant temperature gauge	22
G5	– Tachometer	23
G6	– electrical fuel pump	7
G8	– Engine oil temperature sending unit	37
G9	– Engine oil temperature gauge	37
H	– Horn button	36
H1	– Dual horn	34,35
J2	– Emergency flasher relay	59-61
J4	– Dual horn relay	35,36
J6	– Voltage stabilizer	21·
J17	– Electric fuel pump relay	4-10
J31	– Windscreen washer/wiper intermittent relay	100-103
J34	– Safety belt warning relay	38,39
J59	– Load reducing relay – X terminal	15,16
K1	– Headlight high beam warning light	78
K2	– Alternator charging warning light	25
K3	– Engine oil pressure warning light	24
K5	– Turn signal warning light	26
K6	– Emergency flasher warning light	64
K7	– Dual circuit brake/parking brake warning light	41
K10	– Rear window defogger warning light	98
K19	– Safety belt warning light	40
K22	– EGR warning light (not for Canada)	27
L1	– Left headlight, low/ high beam	72,74
L2	– Right headlight, low/ high beam	73,77
L8	– clock light	51
L10	– instrument panel light	65-67
L15	– Ashtray light	48
L17	– Left headlight, high beam	75
L18	– Right headlight, high beam	76
L24	– Engine oil temperature gauge light	50

Description		Current track
L28	– Cigarette lighter light	47
M1	– Left parking light	88
M2	– Right tail light	92
M3	– Right front parking light	91
M4	– Left tail light	90
M5	– Left front turn signal	68
M6	– Left rear turn signal	69
M7	– Right front turn signal	70
M8	– Right rear turn signal	71
M9	– Brake light, left	45
M10	– Brake light, right	44
M12	– Rear side marker lights	89,93
M16	– Back-up light, left	33
M17	– Back-up light, right	34
N	– Ignition coil	14,15
N6	– Ballast resistor wire	14
N9	– Control pressure regulator	3
N17	– Cold start valve	8
N21	– Auxiliary air regulator	3
N23	– Fresh air ballast resistor	94
O	– Ignition distributor	16
P	– Spark plug connectors	16
Q	– Spark plugs	16
S1 to S14	– fuses in fuse box	
S20	– fuse for fuel pump	
U1	– Cigarette lighter	46
V	– Windshield wiper motor	99,100
V2	– Fresh air fan	95
V5	– Windshield washer pump	106
V7	– Radiator cooling fan	107
W	– Interior light	52,53
W3	– Trunk light	87
X	– License plate light	85,86
Y	– Clock	56
Z	– Rear window defogger element	96

Wire connectors

T	–	Next to relay panel
T1a	–	Single, in engine compartment
T1b	–	Single, behind dashboard
T1c	–	Single, behind dashboard
T1d	–	Single, behind dashboard
T1e	–	Single, behind dashboard
T1f	–	Single, behind dashboard
T1g	–	Single, behind dashboard
T1h	–	Single, next to fuse/relay panel
T1i	–	Single, next to fuse/relay panel
T1j	–	Single, next to fuse/relay panel
T1l	–	Single, in trunk, right
T1m	–	Single, in trunk, left
T1n	–	Single, in trunk, left
T1k	–	Single, behind dashboard
T2	–	Double, in engine compartment
T2b	–	Double, behind dashboard
T2c	–	Double, in engine compartment
T3	–	3-point, behind dashboard
T4a	–	4-point, behind dashboard
T12	–	12-point, on instrument cluster

Ground connectors

①	–	Battery/body/engine
②	–	Alternator/engine
⑩	–	Instrument cluster
⑪	–	Steering column bracket
⑭	–	Footwell, right
⑩	–	Instrument cluster
⑪	–	Steering column bracket
⑮	–	Engine compartment front left
⑯	–	Engine compartment front right
⑰	–	Trunk
⑳	–	Steering gear

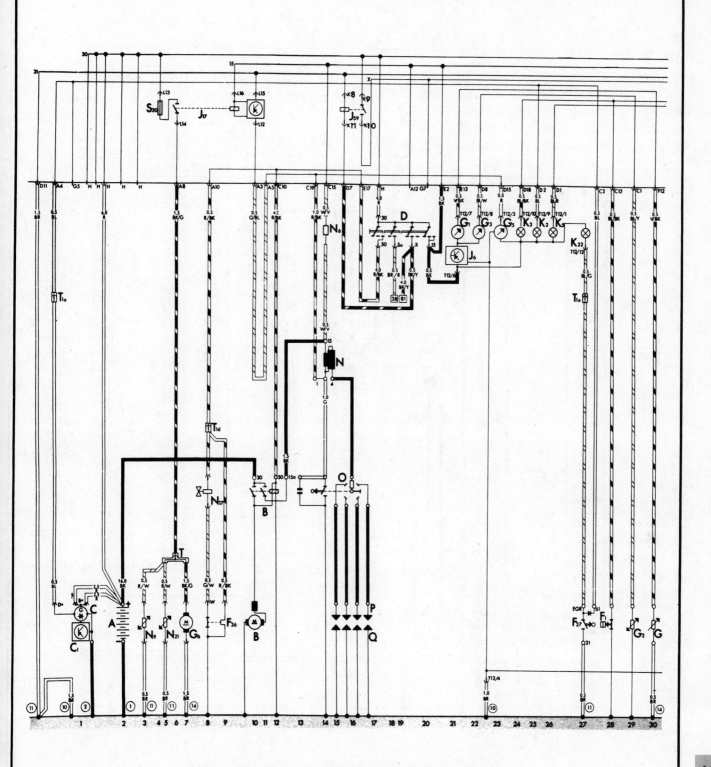

Wiring diagram (typical) for 1977/78 Rabbit and Scirocco models

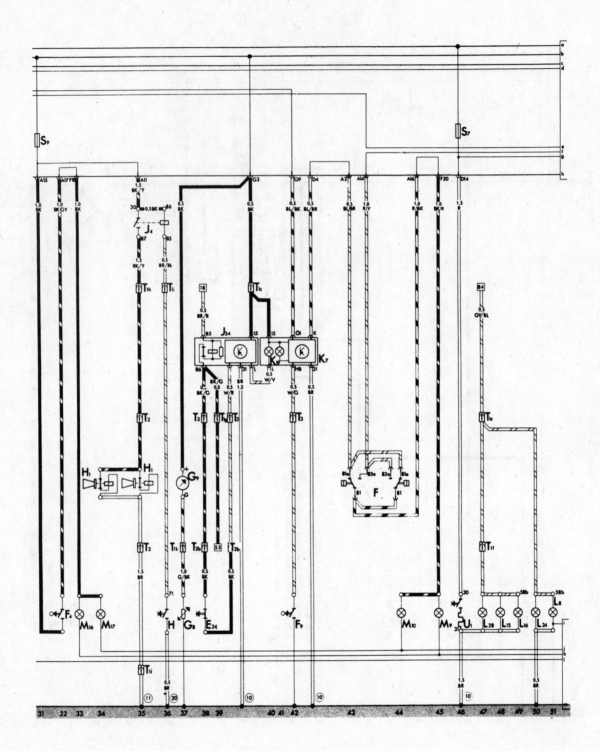

Wiring diagram (typical) for 1977/78 Rabbit and Scirocco models

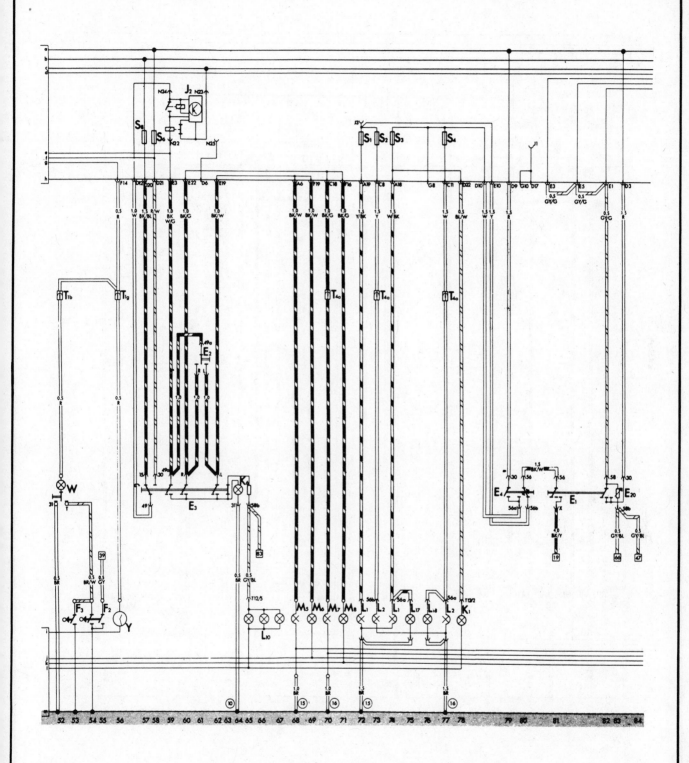

Wiring diagram (typical) for 1977/78 Rabbit and Scirocco models

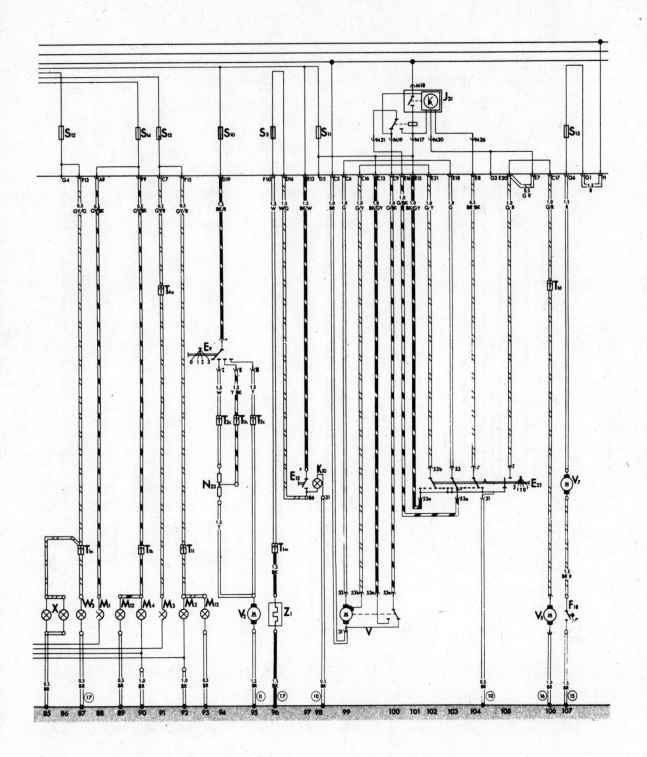

Wiring diagram (typical) for 1977/78 Rabbit and Scirocco models

Key for wiring diagrams on pages 12-32 through 12-36

Description	Current track
Alternator	3
Alternator charging light	24
Ashtray light	53
Auxiliary air regulator	6
Back-up lights	35-36
Back-up light switch	34
Ballast resistance wire	11
Battery	4
Cigarette lighter	48
Cigarette lighter light	52
Cold start valve	14
Control pressure regulator	5
Coolant temperature light	29
Coolant temperature switch	32
Door switch (right)	44
Door switch/buzzer (left)	45-46
EGR elapsed mileage switch (inoperative in Canada)	29-30
EGR light (inoperative in Canada)	29
Emergency flasher relay	51-53
Emergency flasher switch	49-56
Emergency flasher indicator light	55
Fresh air fan	86
Fresh air fan speed control resistors	84
Fresh air fan switch	84-86
Fuel gauge	20
Fuel level sensor	33
Fuel pump	7
Fuel pump relay	5-10
Fuses S1-S15, on fuse/relay panel (under dash) S20 (on fuel pump relay)	
Headlights	63-66
Headlight dimmer/flasher switch	68-69
Heater lever light	54
High beam indicator light	67
Horn	36
Horn button	37
Ignition coil	11
Ignition/starter switch	15-19
Ignition distributor	12-13
Instrument panel lights	56-58
Instrument panel light switch/dimmer	72
Interior lights	43-44
License plate lights	74-75
Light switch	70-73
Load reduction relay	70-71
Oil pressure switch	31
Oil pressure warning light	23
Parking brake indicator light	24-28
Parking brake indicator light switch	27
Parking light, left	77
Parking light, right	80
Radiator fan	42
Radiator fan thermal switch	42
Radio	100
Rear window defogger	87
Rear window defogger indicator light	89
Rear window defogger switch	88-89
Seat belt/relay	15-20
Seat belt warning light	25
Shift console light (auto.trans)	29
Side marker lights, front	76-81
Side marker lights, rear	78-83
Spark plug suppressors	12-13
Spark plugs	12-13
Starter	8-10
Stop-lights	40-41
Stop-light switch	38-39
Tail light, left	79
Tail light, right	82
Thermal time switch	14-15
Turn signal lights	59-62

Description	Current track
Turn signal switch	53
Turn signal indicator light	25
Voltage regulator	3
Voltage stabilizer	20
Windshield washer pump	99
Windshield wiper motor	90-93
Windshield wiper switch	94-98

Wire connectors		Current track
T	– Cable adaptor, engine compartment	6-7
T1a	– In engine compartment	2
T1b	– In engine compartment, front left	77
T1c	– In engine compartment, front right	80
T1d	– Behind instrument panel	99
T1e	– Behind instrument panel	29
T1f	– Behind instrument panel	15
T1g	– Behind instrument panel	47
T1h	– Behind instrument panel	85
T1i	– Behind instrument panel	27
T1j	– Behind instrument panel	15
T1k	– In luggage compartment, left rear	79
T1l	– In luggage compartment, right rear	82
T1m	– In luggage compartment, left rear	87
T1p	– Behind instrument panel	97
T2a	– In engine compartment, front left	59,77
T2b	– In engine compartment, front right	61,80
T2c	– Behind instrument panel	84,86
T2d	– Behind instrument panel	16
T2e	– Behind instrument panel	16
T2f	– Behind instrument panel	15
T2g	– Behind instrument panel, right of steering column	49
T3	– Behind instrument panel, right of steering column	48,52
T4	– In engine compartment	61,64,66,80
T14	– On rear of instrument panel	20,21,23,24,25 29,47,56,67

Ground connectors

①	– From battery to body	
②	– From alternator to engine	
⑩	– On steering column support	
⑪	– On steering column support	
⑫	– In luggage compartment, rear	
⑬	– On dome light	
⑭	– Middle body member, rear	
⑮	– In engine compartment, front left	
⑯	– In engine compartment, front right	
⑰	– On steering column	
⑱	– On tail light cover, left	
⑲	– On tail light cover, right	

12

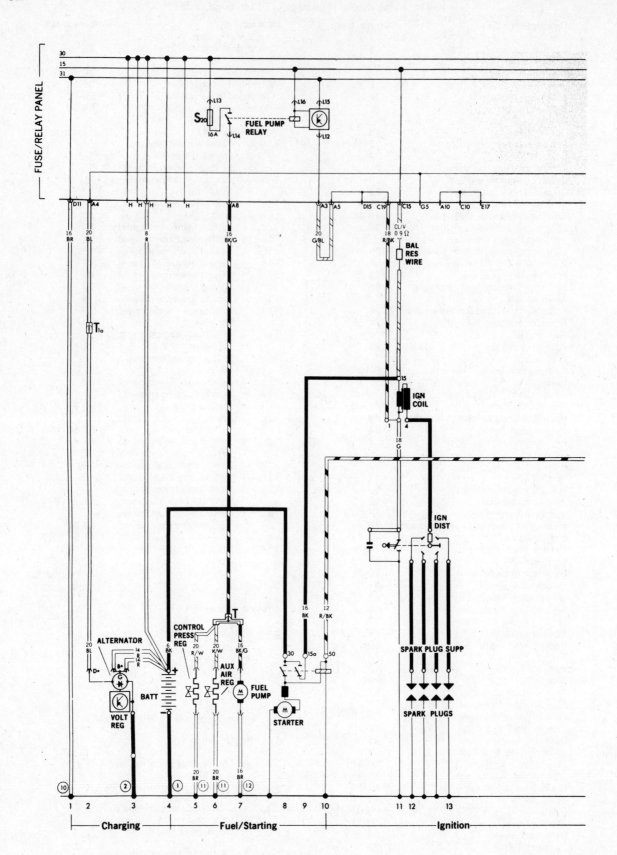

Wiring diagram for 1979 Rabbit Custom and Basic models

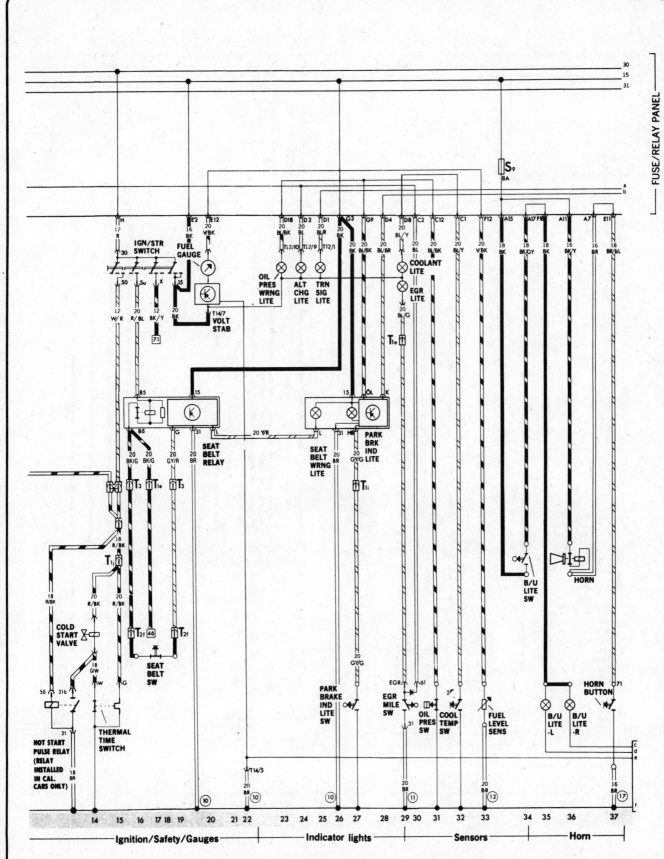

Wiring diagram for 1979 Rabbit Custom and Basic models

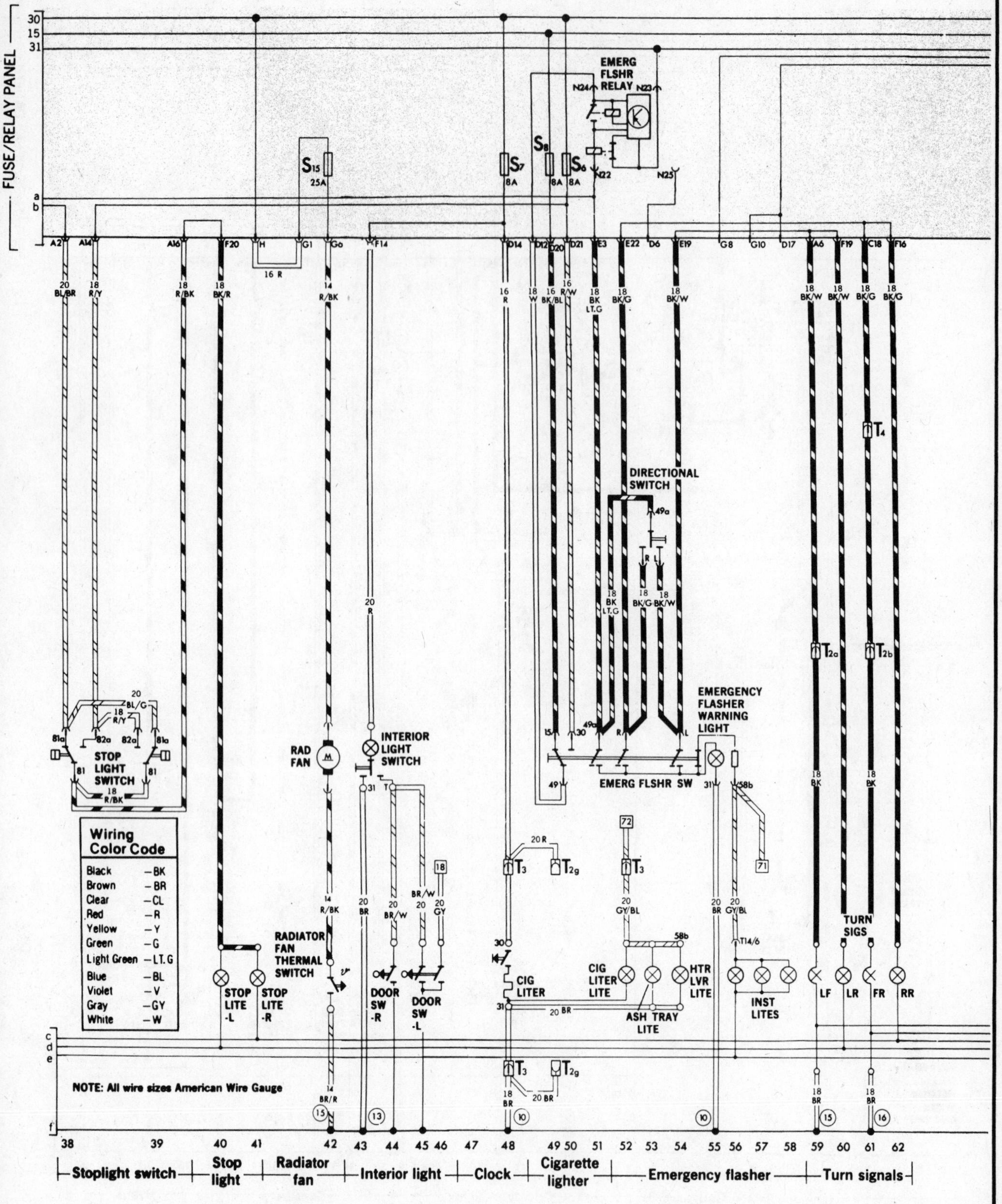

FUSE/RELAY PANEL

30
15
31

EMERG FLSHR RELAY

N24   K   N23

S15   25A
S7   8A
S8   8A   S6   8A
N22   N25

a
b

A2   A14   A16   F20   H   G1   G0   F14   D14   D12 D20   D21   E3   E22   D6   E19   G8   G10   D17   A6   F19   C18   F16

20 BL/BR   18 R/Y   18 R/BK   18 BK/R   16 R   14 R/BK   16 R   18 W   16 BK/BL   16 R/W   18 BK LT.G   18 BK/G   18 BK/W   18 BK/W   18 BK/W   18 BK/G   18 BK/G

T4

DIRECTIONAL SWITCH
49a
R   L

T2a   T2b

EMERGENCY FLASHER WARNING LIGHT

20 R

20 BL/G
18 R/Y
81a   82a   82a   81a
STOP LIGHT SWITCH
81   81
18 R/BK

RAD FAN   M

INTERIOR LIGHT SWITCH
31   T

15   49b   R   L
49   EMERG FLSHR SW
30
31   58b

BK LT.G   BK/G BK/W

72
T3   T2g   T3   71

Wiring Color Code

Black	— BK
Brown	— BR
Clear	— CL
Red	— R
Yellow	— Y
Green	— G
Light Green	— LT. G
Blue	— BL
Violet	— V
Gray	— GY
White	— W

14 R/BK   20 BR   20 BR/W   20 GY   18

20 GY/BL   20 BR   20 GY/BL

RADIATOR FAN THERMAL SWITCH

STOP LITE -L   STOP LITE -R

DOOR SW -R   DOOR SW -L

30   CIG LITER   31   20 BR

CIG LITER LITE   ASH TRAY LITE   HTR LVR LITE   INST LITES

TURN SIGS
LF   LR   FR   RR

18 BK   18 BK

NOTE: All wire sizes American Wire Gauge

14 BR/R   T3   T2g   18 BR   20 BR   18 BR   18 BR

c
d
e
f

15   13   10   10   15   16

38   39   40   41   42   43   44   45   46   47   48   49 50   51   52   53   54   55   56   57   58   59   60   61   62

Stoplight switch ─ Stop light ─ Radiator fan ─ Interior light ─ Clock ─ Cigarette lighter ─ Emergency flasher ─ Turn signals

Wiring diagram for 1979 Rabbit Custom and Basic models

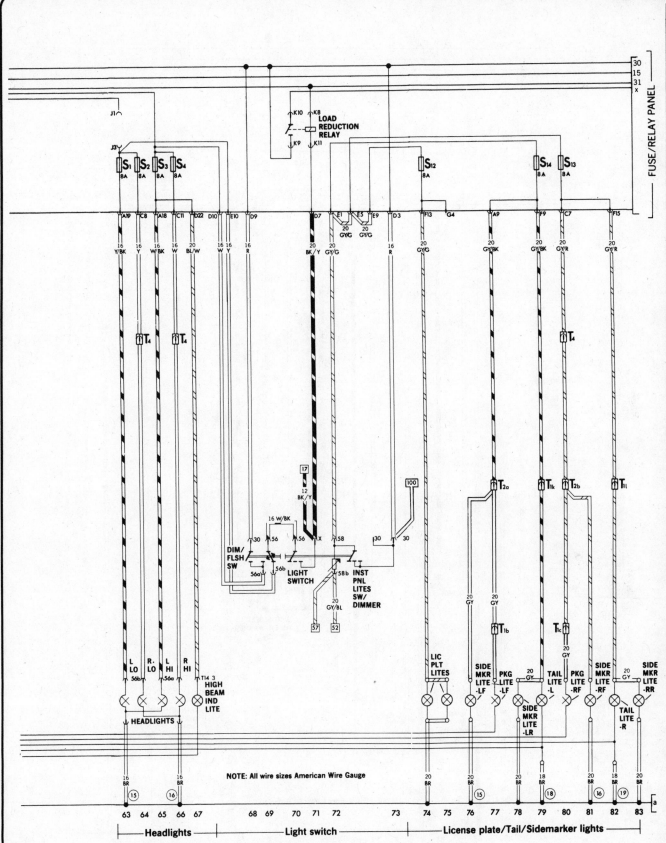

NOTE: All wire sizes American Wire Gauge

| 63 | 64 | 65 | 66 | 67 | | 68 | 69 | 70 | 71 | 72 | | 73 | 74 | 75 | 76 | 77 | 78 | 79 | 80 | 81 | 82 | 83 |

Headlights — Light switch — License plate/Tail/Sidemarker lights

Wiring diagram for 1979 Rabbit Custom and Basic models

12

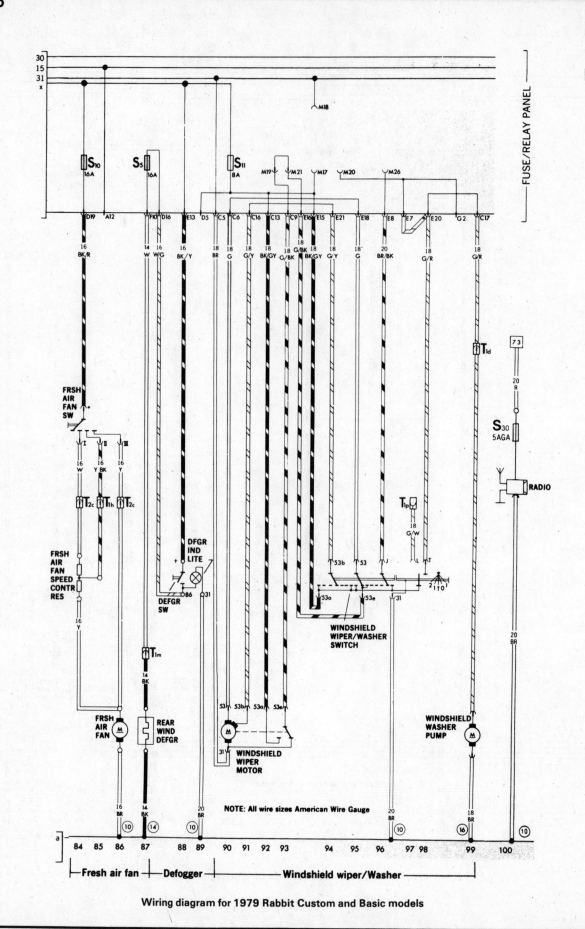

NOTE: All wire sizes American Wire Gauge

Wiring diagram for 1979 Rabbit Custom and Basic models

Key for wiring diagrams on pages 12-38 through 12-42

Description	Current track
Alternator	3
Alternator charging light	24
Ashtray light	53
Auxiliary air regulator	6
Back-up lights	35-36
Back-up light switch	34
Ballast resistance wire	11
Battery	4
Cigarette lighter	48
Cigarette lighter light	52
Clock	47
Cold start valve	14
Control pressure regulator	5
Coolant temperature gauge	21
Coolant temperature sensor	32
Door switch (right)	44
Door switch/buzzer (left)	45-46
EGR elapsed mileage switch (inoperative in Canada)	29-30
EGR light (inoperative in Canada)	29
Emergency flasher relay	51-53
Emergency flasher switch	49-56
Emergency flasher indicator light	55
Fresh air fan	86
Fresh air fan speed control resistors	84
Fresh air fan switch	84-86
Fuel gauge	20
Fuel level sensor	33
Fuel pump	7
Fuel pump relay	5-10
Fuses S1-S15, on fuse/relay panel (under dash) S20 (on fuel pump relay)	
Headlights	63-66
Headlight dimmer/flasher switch	68-69
Heater lever light	54
High beam indicator light	67
Horn	36
Horn button	37
Ignition coil	11
Ignition/starter switch	15-19
Ignition distributor	12-13
Instrument panel lights	56-58
Instrument panel light switch/dimmer	72
Interior lights	43-44
License plate lights	74-75
Light switch	70-73
Load reduction relay	70-71
Oil pressure switch	31
Oil pressure warning light	23
Parking brake indicator light	24-28
Parking brake indicator light switch	27
Parking light, left	77
Parking light, right	80
Radiator fan	42
Radiator fan thermal switch	42
Radio	100
Rear window defogger	87
Rear window defogger indicator light	89
Rear window defogger switch	88-89
Seat belt/starter lock-out relay	15-20
Seat belt switch, left	16
Seat belt switch, right	16
Seat belt warning light	25
Shift console light (auto.trans)	29
Side marker lights, front	76-81
Side marker lights, rear	78-83
Spark plug suppressors	12-13
Spark plugs	12-13
Starter	8-10
Stop-lights	40-41
Stop-light switch	38-39
Tail light, left	79
Tail light, right	82

Description	Current track
Thermal time switch	14-15
Turn signal lights	59-62
Turn signal switch	53
Turn signal indicator light	25
Voltage regulator	3
Voltage stabilizer	20
Windshield washer pump	99
Windshield wiper motor	90-93
Windshield wiper switch	94-98

Wire connectors		Current track
T	Cable adaptor, engine compartment	6-7
T1a	In engine compartment	2
T1b	In engine compartment, front left	77
T1c	In engine compartment, front right	80
T1d	Behind instrument panel	99
T1e	Behind instrument panel	29
T1f	Behind instrument panel	15
T1g	Behind instrument panel	47
T1h	Behind instrument panel	85
T1i	Behind instrument panel	27
T1j	Behind instrument panel	15
T1k	In luggage compartment, left rear	79
T1l	In luggage compartment, right rear	82
T1m	In luggage compartment, left rear	87
T1p	Behind instrument panel	97
T2a	In engine compartment, front left	59,77
T2b	In engine compartment, front right	61,80
T2c	Behind instrument panel	84,86
T2d	Behind instrument panel	16
T2e	Behind instrument panel	16
T2f	Behind instrument panel	15
T2g	Behind instrument panel, right of steering column	49
T3	Behind instrument panel, right of steering column	48,52
T4	In engine compartment	61,64,66,80
T14	On rear of instrument panel	20,21,23,24,25 29,47,56,67

Ground connectors

①	From battery to body	
②	From alternator to engine	
⑩	On steering column support	
⑪	On steering column support	
⑫	In luggage compartment, rear	
⑬	On dome light	
⑭	Middle body member, rear	
⑮	In engine compartment, front left	
⑯	In engine compartment, front right	
⑰	On steering column	
⑱	On tail light cover, left	
⑲	On tail light cover, right	

12

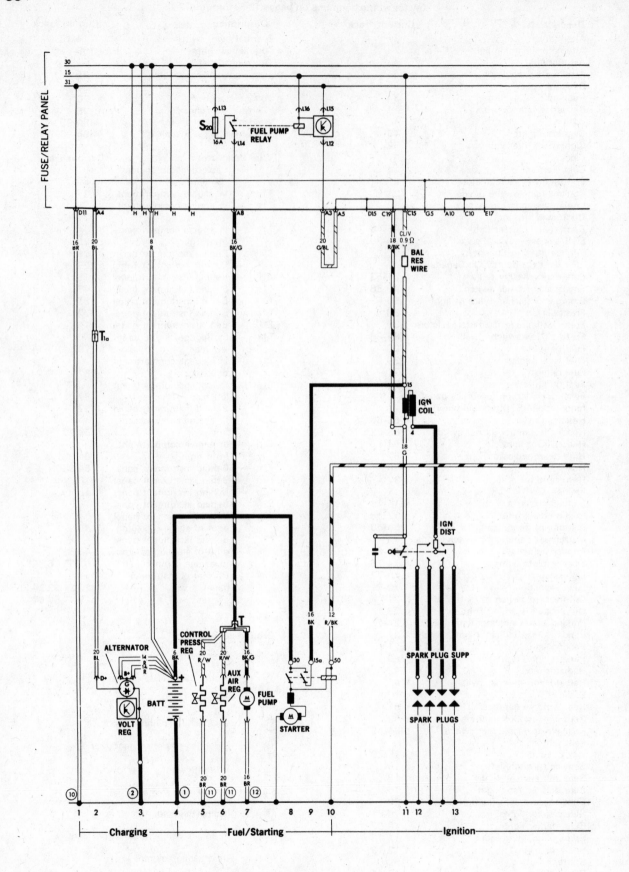

Wiring diagram for 1979 Rabbit Deluxe

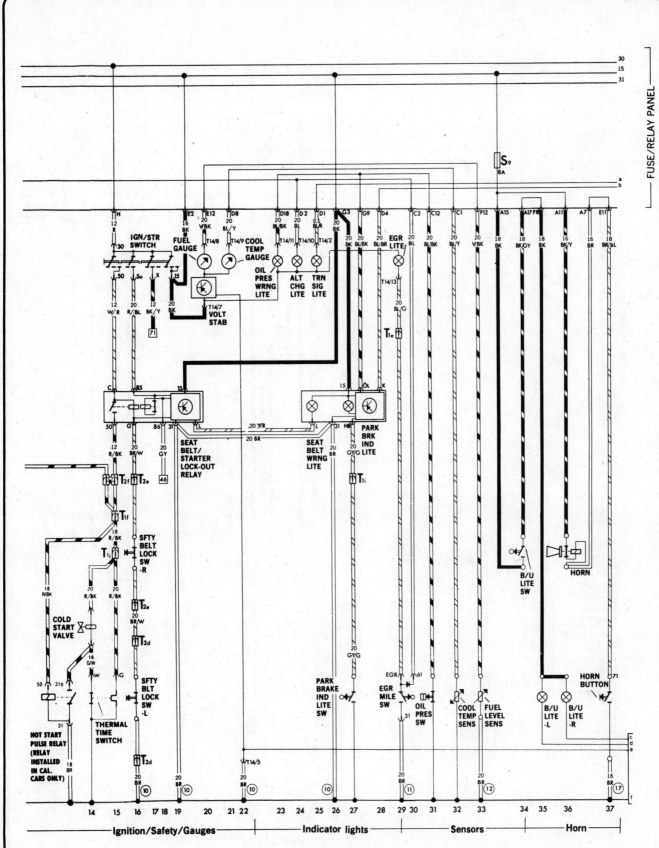

Wiring diagram for 1979 Rabbit Deluxe

Wiring diagram for 1979 Rabbit Deluxe

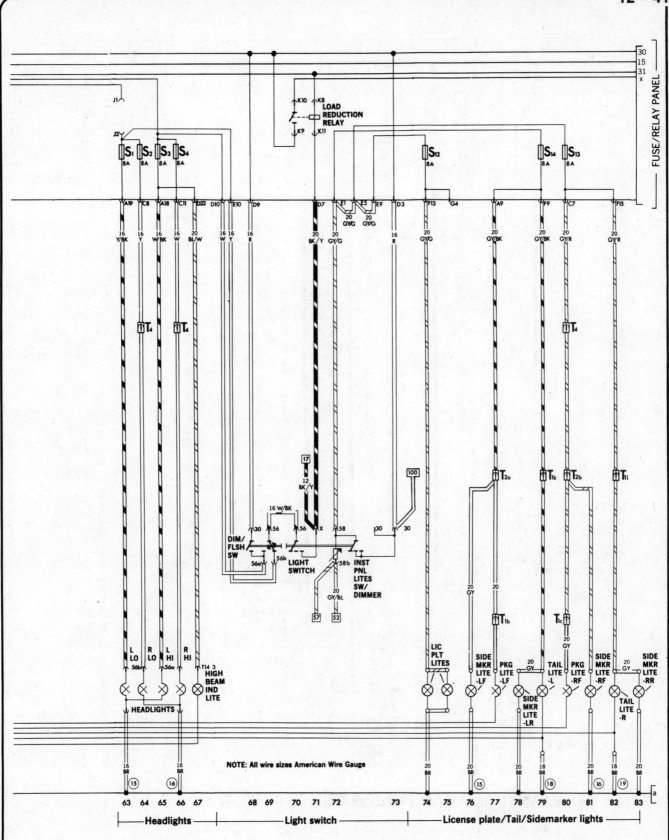

Wiring diagram for 1979 Rabbit Deluxe

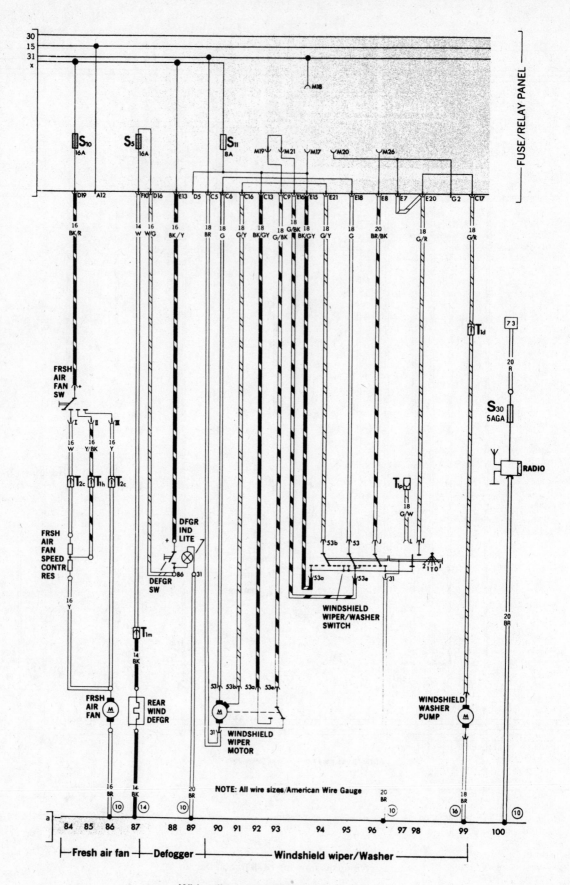

Wiring diagram for 1979 Rabbit Deluxe

Key for wiring diagrams on pages 12-44 through 12-48

Description	Current track
Alternator	3
Alternator charging light	24
Ashtray light	53
Auxiliary air regulator	6
Back-up lights	35-36
Back-up light switch	34
Ballast resistance wire	11
Battery	4
Cigarette lighter	48
Cigarette lighter light	52
Clock	47
Cold start valve	14
Control pressure regulator	5
Coolant temperature light	29
Coolant temperature switch 32	
Door switch (right)	44
Door switch/buzzer (left)	45-46
EGR elapsed mileage switch (inoperative in Canada)	29-30
EGR light (inoperative in Canada)	29
Emergency flasher relay	51-53
Emergency flasher switch	49-56
Emergency flasher indicator light	55
Fresh air fan	86
Fresh air fan speed control resistors	84
Fresh air fan switch	84-86
Fuel gauge	20
Fuel level sensor	33
Fuel pump	7
Fuel pump relay	5-10
Fuses S1-S15, on fuse/relay panel (under dash) S20 (on fuel pump relay)	
Headlights	63-64
Headlight dimmer/flasher switch	68-69
Heater lever light	54
High beam indicator light	67
Horn	36
Horn button	37
Ignition coil	11
Ignition/starter switch	15-19
Ignition distributor	12-13
Instrument panel lights	56-58
Instrument panel light switch/dimmer	72
Interior lights	43-44
Intermittent wiper relay	93
License plate lights	74-75
Light switch	70-73
Load reduction relay	70-71
Oil pressure switch	31
Oil pressure warning light	23
Oil temperature gauge	23
Parking brake indicator light	24-28
Parking brake indicator light switch	27
Parking light, left	77
Parking light, right	80
Radiator fan	42
Radiator fan thermal switch	42
Rear window defogger	87
Rear window defogger indicator light	89
Rear window defogger switch	88-89
Seat belt/starter lock-out relay	15-20
Seat belt switch, left	16
Seat belt switch, right	16
Seat belt warning light	25
Shift console light (auto.trans)	29
Side marker lights, rear	78-83
Spark plug suppressors	12-13
Spark plugs	12-13
Starter	8-10
Stop-lights	40-41
Stop-light switch	38-39
Tachometer	23
Tail light, left	79
Tail light, right	82

Description	Current track
Thermal time switch	14-15
Turn signal lights	59-62
Turn signal switch	53
Turn signal indicator light	25
Trunk signal indicator light	25
Trunk light	73
Voltage regulator	3
Voltage stabilizer	20
Windshield washer pump	99
Windshield wiper motor	90-93
Windshield wiper switch	94-98

Wire connectors		Current track
T	– Cable adaptor, engine compartment	6-7
T1a	– In engine compartment	2
T1b	– In engine compartment, front left	77
T1c	– In engine compartment, front right	80
T1d	– Behind instrument panel	99
T1e	– Behind instrument panel	29
T1f	– Behind instrument panel	15
T1g	– Behind instrument panel	47
T1h	– Behind instrument panel	85
T1i	– Behind instrument panel	27
T1j	– Behind instrument panel	15
T1k	– In luggage compartment, left rear	79
T1l	– In luggage compartment, right rear	82
T1m	– In luggage compartment, left rear	87
T1p	– Behind instrument panel	97
T2a	– In engine compartment, front left	59,77
T2b	– In engine compartment, front right	61,80
T2c	– Behind instrument panel	84,86
T2d	– Behind instrument panel	16
T2e	– Behind instrument panel	16
T2f	– Behind instrument panel	15
T2g	– Behind instrument panel, right of steering column	49
T3	– Behind instrument panel, right of steering column	48,52
T4	– In engine compartment	61,64,66,80
T14	– On rear of instrument panel	20,21,23,24,25 29,47,56,67

Ground connectors

①	– From battery to body	
②	– From alternator to engine	
⑩	– On steering column support	
⑪	– On steering column support	
⑫	– In luggage compartment, rear	
⑬	– On dome light	
⑭	– Middle body member, rear	
⑮	– In engine compartment, front left	
⑯	– In engine compartment, front right	
⑰	– On steering column	
⑱	– On tail light cover, left	
⑲	– On tail light cover, right	

12

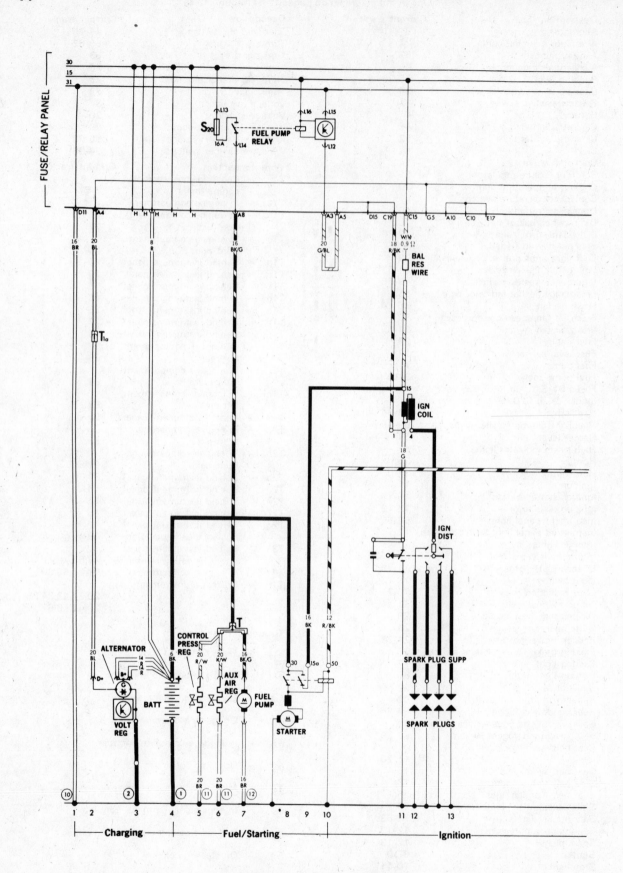

Wiring diagram for 1979 Scirocco models

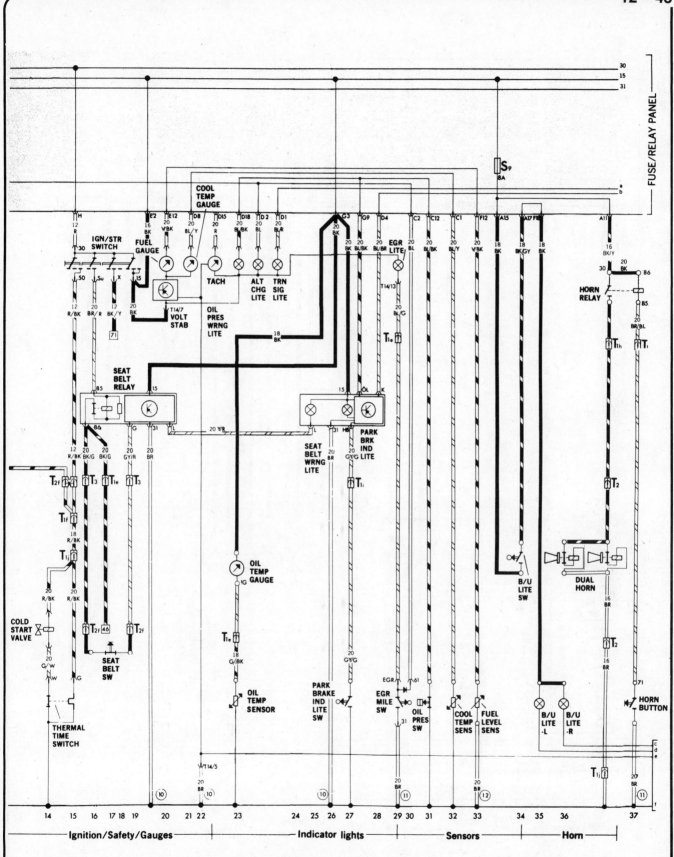

Wiring diagram for 1979 Scirocco models

Wiring diagram for 1979 Scirocco models

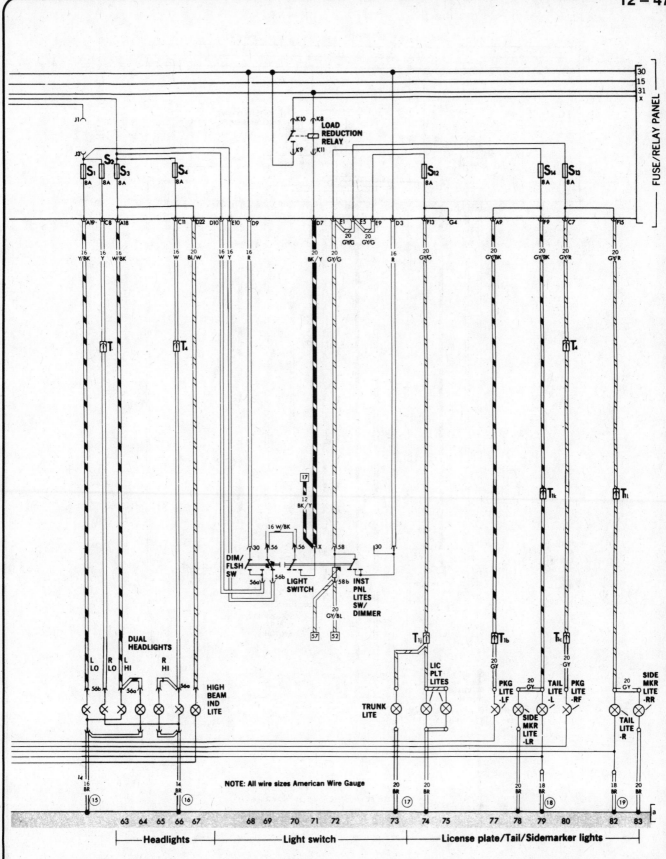

Wiring diagram for 1979 Scirocco models

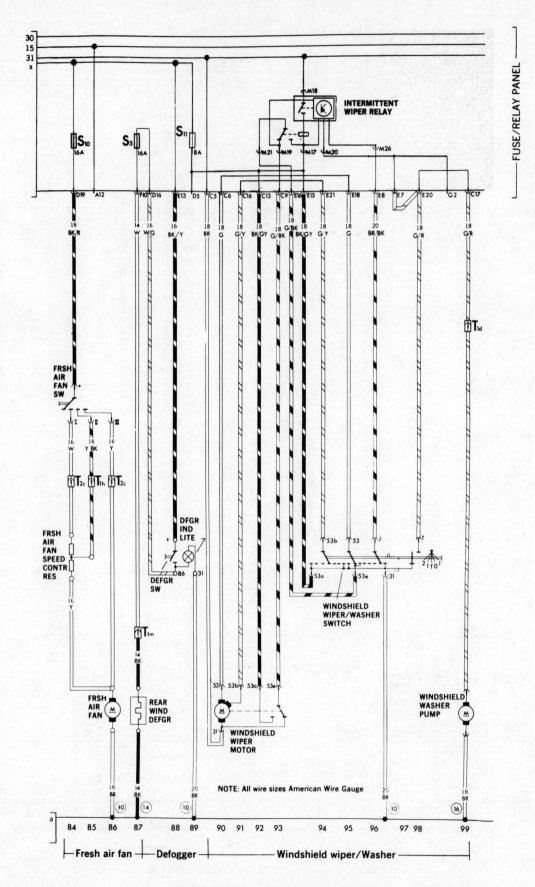

NOTE: All wire sizes American Wire Gauge

Fresh air fan — Defogger — Windshield wiper/Washer

Wiring diagram for 1979 Scirocco models

Key for wiring diagrams on pages 12-50 through 12-54

Description	Current track
Alternator	3
Alternator charging light	24
Ashtray light	53
Auxiliary air regulator	6
Back-up lights	35–36
Back-up light switch	34
Ballast resistance wire	11
Battery	4
Cigarette lighter	48
Cigarette lighter light	52
Cold start valve	14
Control pressure regulator	5
Coolant temperature light	29
Coolant temperature switch	32
Door switch (right)	44
Door switch/buzzer (left)	45–46
EGR elapsed mileage switch	29–30
(inoperative in Canada)	
EGR light (inoperative in Canada)	29
Emergency flasher relay	51–53
Emergency flasher switch	49–56
Emergency flasher indicator light	55
Fresh air fan	86
Fresh air fan speed control resistors	84
Fresh air fan switch	84–86
Fuel gauge	20
Fuel level sensor	33
Fuel pump	7
Fuel pump relay	5–10
Fuses S-S15, on fuse/relay panel	
(under dash) S20 (on fuel/pump relay)	
Headlights	63–66
Headlight dimmer/flasher switch	68–69
Heater lever light	54
High beam indicator light	67
Horn	36
Horn button	37
Ignition coil	11
Ignition/starter switch	15–19
Ignition distributor	12–13
Instrument panel lights	56–58
Instrument panel light switch/dimmer	72
Interior lights	43–44
License plate lights	74–75
Light switch	70–73
Load reduction relay	70–71
Oil pressure switch	31
Oil pressure warning light	23
Parking brake indicator light	24–28
Parking brake indicator light switch	27
Parking light, left	77
Parking light, right	80
Radiator fan	42
Radiator fan thermal switch	42
Radio	100
Rear window defogger	87
Rear window defogger indicator light	89
Rear window defogger switch	88–89
Seat belt/relay	15–20
Seat belt warning light	25
Shift console light (auto. trans.)	29
Side marker lights, front	76–81
Side marker lights, rear	78–83
Spark plug suppressors	12–13
Spark plugs	12–13
Starter	8–10
Stop-lights	40–41
Stop-light switch	38–39
Tail light, left	79
Tail light, right	82
Thermal time switch	14–15
Turn signal lights	59–62

Description	Current track
Turn signal switch	53
Turn signal indicator light	25
Voltage regulator	3
Voltage stabilizer	20
Windshield washer pump	99
Windshield wiper motor	90–93
Windshield wiper switch	94–98

Wire connectors		Current track
T	Cable adaptor, engine compartment	6–7
T1a	In engine compartment	2
T1b	In engine compartment, front left	77
T1c	In engine compartment, front right	80
T1d	Behind instrument panel	99
T1e	Behind instrument panel	29
T1f	Behind fuse/relay panel	15
T1g	Behind instrument panel	47
T1h	Behind instrument panel	85
T1i	Behind instrument panel	27
T1j	Behind instrument panel	15
T1k	In luggage compartment, left rear	79
T1l	In luggage compartment, right rear	82
T1m	In luggage compartment, left rear	87
T1p	Behind instrument panel	97
T2a	In engine compartment, front left	59,77
T2b	In engine compartment, front right	61,80
T2c	Behind instrument panel	84,86
T2d	Behind instrument panel	16
T2e	Behind instrument panel	16
T2f	Behind instrument panel	15
T2g	Behind instrument panel, right of steering column	49
T3	Behind instrument panel, right of steering column	48,52
T4	In engine compartment	61,64 66,80
T14	On rear of instrument panel	20,21,23, 24,25,29, 47,56,67

Ground connectors

①	From battery to body	
②	From alternator to engine	
⑩	On steering column support	
⑪	On steering column support	
⑫	In luggage compartment, rear	
⑬	On dome light	
⑭	Middle body member, rear	
⑮	In engine compartment, front left	
⑯	In engine compartment, front right	
⑰	On steering column	
⑱	On tail light cover, left	
⑲	On tail light cover, right	

12

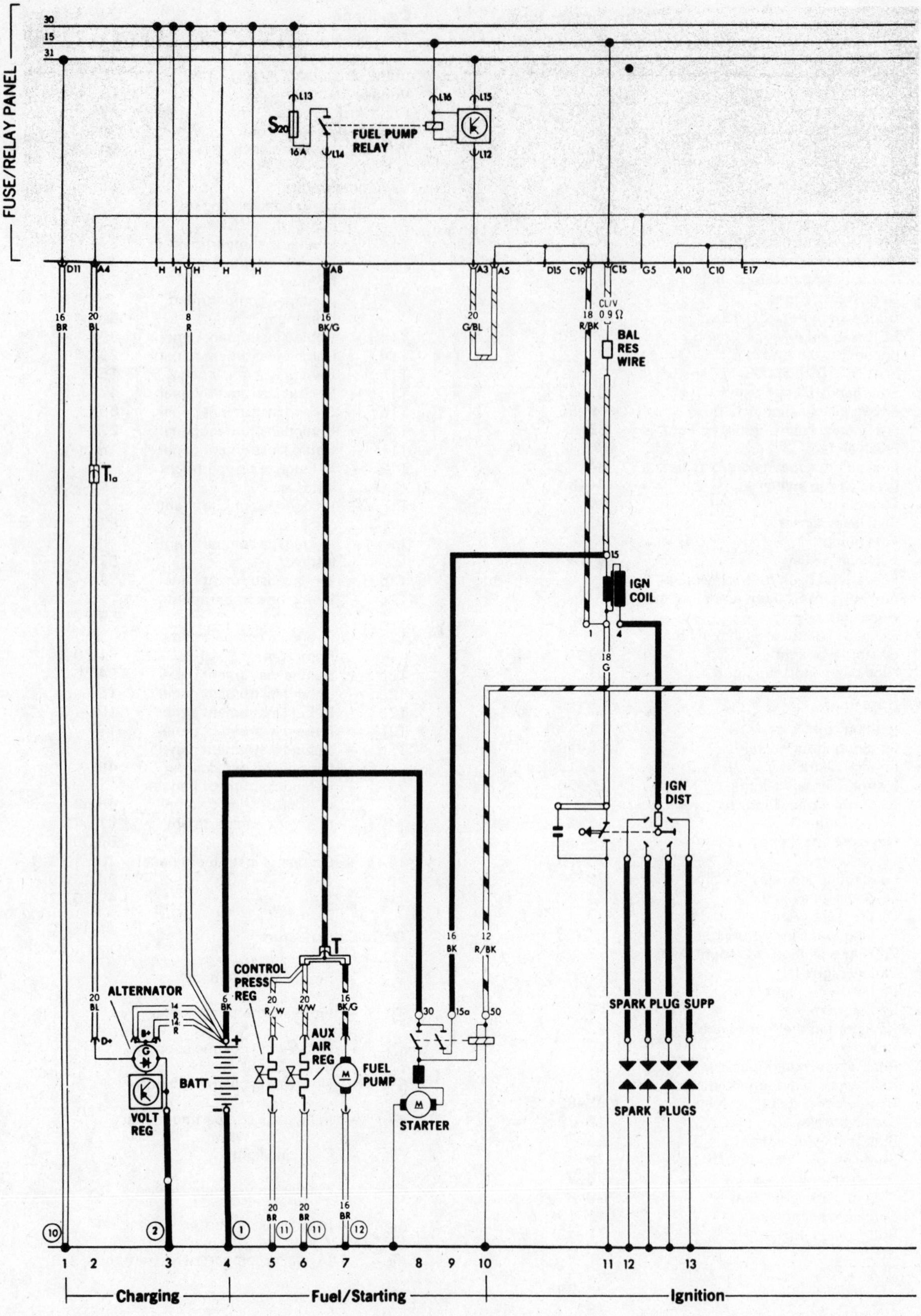

FUSE/RELAY PANEL

30
15
31

L13
S20
16A
L14
FUEL PUMP RELAY
L16
L15
K
L12

D11 A4 H H H H H A8 A3 A5 D15 C19 C15 G5 A10 C10 E17

16
BR
20
BL
8
R
16
BK/G
20
G/BL
18
R/BK
CL/V
0.9 Ω
BAL
RES
WIRE

T1a

15

IGN
COIL

1 4

18
G

IGN
DIST

SPARK PLUG SUPP

SPARK PLUGS

16
BK
12
R/BK

ALTERNATOR
20
BL
D+
G
B+
14
14
R
CONTROL
PRESS
REG
6
BK
20
R/W
20
K/W
16
BK/G
T

AUX
AIR
REG
FUEL
PUMP
M

BATT

VOLT
REG
K

30 15a 50
M
STARTER

20
BR
20
BR
16
BR

⑩ ② ① ⑪ ⑪ ⑫

1 2 3 4 5 6 7 8 9 10 11 12 13

— Charging —   — Fuel/Starting —   — Ignition —

Wiring diagram for 1980 Rabbit Basic and Custom, and Pick-up Truck

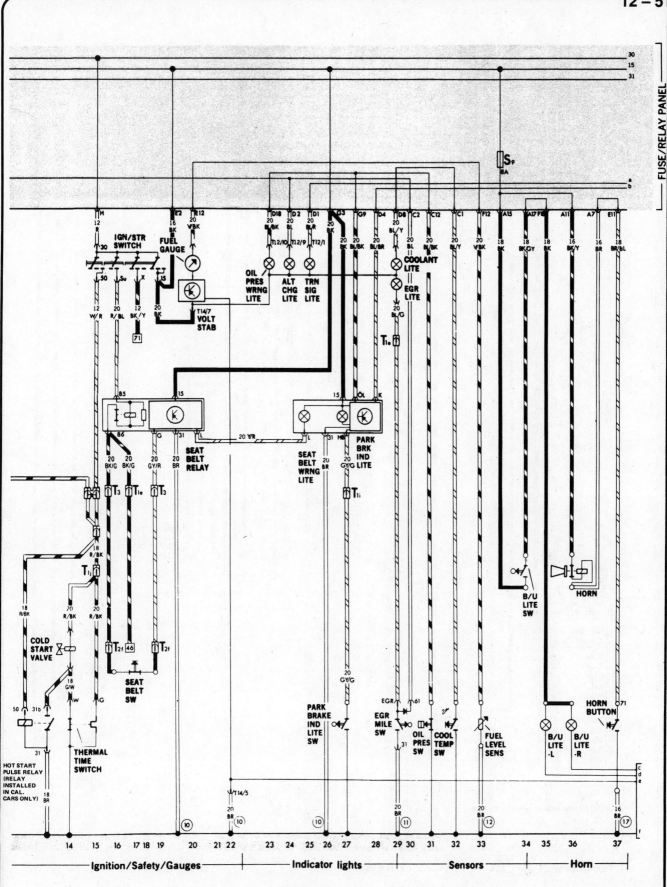

Wiring diagram for 1980 Rabbit Basic and Custom, and Pick-up Truck

Wiring diagram for 1980 Rabbit Basic and Custom, and Pick-up Truck

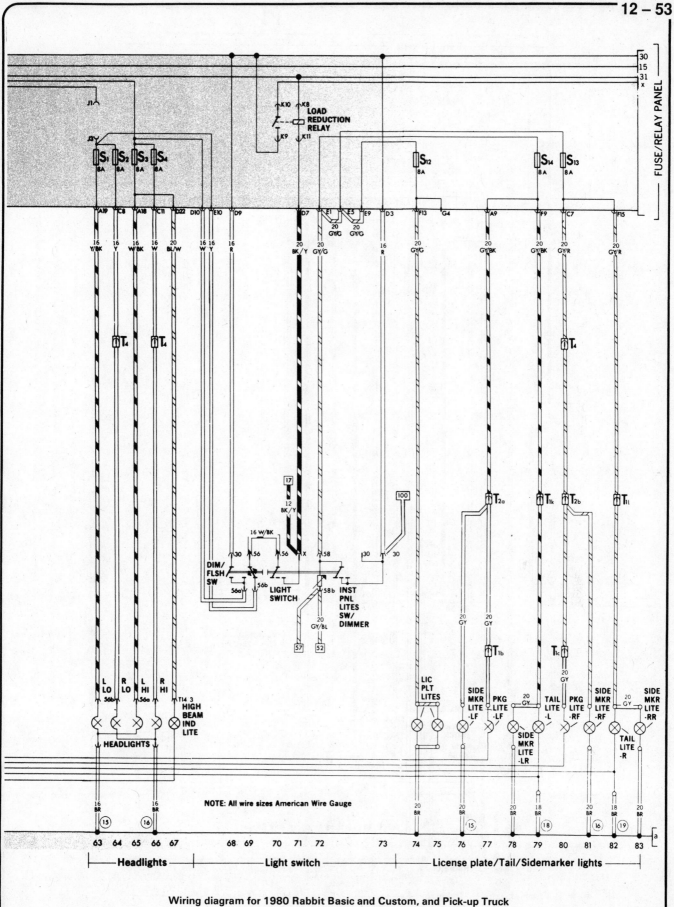

Wiring diagram for 1980 Rabbit Basic and Custom, and Pick-up Truck

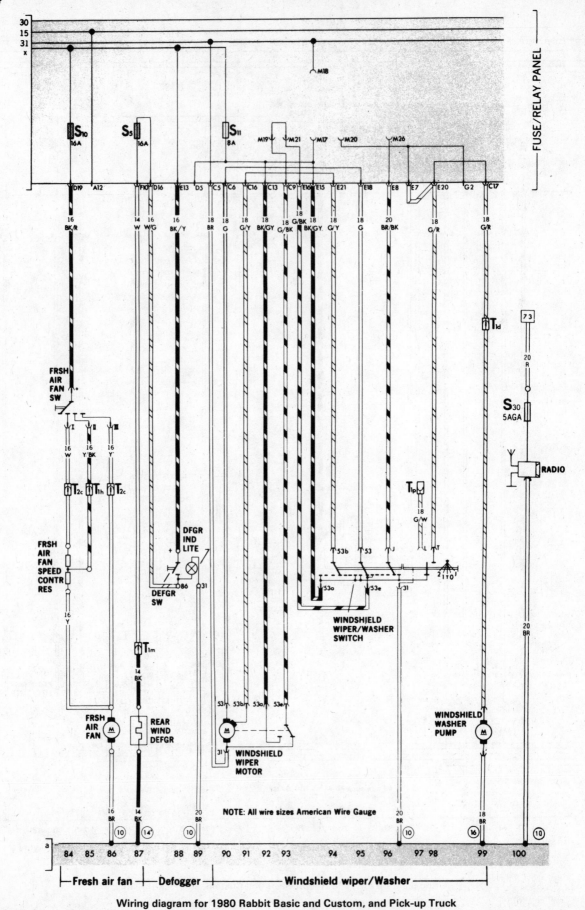

NOTE: All wire sizes American Wire Gauge

Wiring diagram for 1980 Rabbit Basic and Custom, and Pick-up Truck

Key for wiring diagrams on pages 12-56 through 12-60

Description	Current track
Alternator	3
Alternator charging light	24
Ashtray light	53
Auxiliary air regulator	6
Back-up lights	35–36
Back-up light switch	34
Ballast resistance wire	11
Battery	4
Cigarette lighter	48
Cigarette lighter light	52
Clock	47
Cold start valve	14
Control pressure regulator	5
Coolant temperature light	21
Coolant temperature sensor	32
Door switch (right)	44
Door switch/buzzer (left)	45–46
EGR elapsed mileage switch (inoperative in Canada)	29–30
EGR light (inoperative in Canada)	29
Emergency flasher relay	51–53
Emergency flasher switch	49–56
Emergency flasher indicator light	55
Fresh air fan	86
Fresh air fan speed control resistors	84
Fresh air fan switch	84–86
Fuel gauge	20
Fuel level sensor	33
Fuel pump	7
Fuel pump relay	5–10
Fuses S1-S15, on fuse/relay panel (under dash) S20 (on fuel/pump relay)	
Headlights	63–66
Headlight dimmer/flasher switch	68–69
Heater lever light	54
High beam indicator light	67
Horn	36
Horn button	37
Ignition coil	11
Ignition/starter switch	15–19
Ignition distributor	12–13
Instrument panel lights	56–58
Instrument panel light switch/dimmer	72
Interior lights	43–44
License plate lights	74–75
Light switch	70–73
Load reduction relay	70–71
Oil pressure switch	31
Oil pressure warning light	23
Parking brake indicator light	24–28
Parking brake indicator light switch	27
Parking light, left	77
Parking light, right	80
Radiator fan	42
Radiator fan thermal switch	42
Radio	100
Rear window defogger	87
Rear window defogger indicator light	89
Rear window defogger switch	88–89
Seat belt/starter lock-out relay	15–20
Seat belt switch, left	16
Seat belt switch, right	16
Seat belt warning light	25
Shift console light (auto. trans.)	29
Side marker lights, front	76–81
Side marker lights, rear	78–83
Spark plug suppressors	12–13
Spark plugs	12–13
Starter	8–10
Stop-lights	40–41
Stop-light switch	38–39
Tail light, left	79
Tail light, right	82

Description	Current track
Thermal time switch	14–15
Turn signal lights	59–62
Turn signal switch	53
Turn signal indicator light	25
Voltage regulator	3
Voltage stabilizer	20
Windshield washer pump	99
Windshield wiper motor	90–93
Windshield wiper switch	94–98

Wire connectors		Current track
T	– Cable adaptor, engine compartment	6–7
T1a	– In engine compartment	2
T1b	– In engine compartment, front left	77
T1c	– In engine compartment, front right	80
T1d	– Behind instrument panel	99
T1e	– Behind instrument panel	29
T1f	– Behind fuse/relay panel	15
T1g	– Behind instrument panel	47
T1h	– Behind instrument panel	85
T1i	– Behind instrument panel	27
T1j	– Behind instrument panel	15
T1k	– In luggage compartment, left rear	79
T1l	– In luggage compartment, right rear	82
T1m	– In luggage compartment, left rear	87
T1p	– Behind instrument panel	97
T2a	– In engine compartment, front right	59,77
T2b	– In engine compartment, front right	61,80
T2c	– Behind instrument panel	84,86
T2d	– Behind instrument panel	16
T2e	– Behind instrument panel	16
T2f	– Behind instrument panel	15
T2g	– Behind instrument panel, right of steering column	49
T3	– Behind instrument panel, right of steering column	48,52
T4	– In engine compartment	61,64 66,80
T14	– On rear of instrument panel	20,21,23, 24,25,29, 47,56,67

Ground connectors

①	–	From battery to body
②	–	From alternator to engine
⑩	–	On steering column support
⑪	–	On steering column support
⑫	–	In luggage compartment, rear
⑬	–	On dome light
⑭	–	Middle body member, rear
⑮	–	In engine compartment, front left
⑯	–	In engine compartment, front right
⑰	–	On steering column
⑱	–	On tail light cover, left
⑲	–	On tail light cover, right

12

Wiring diagram for 1980 Rabbit Deluxe and Pick-up Truck LX models

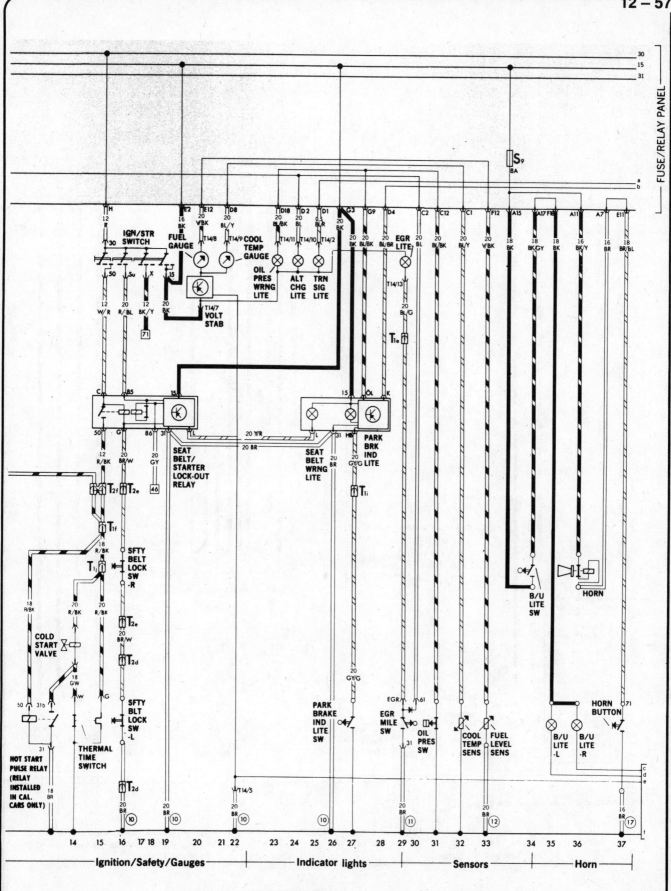

Wiring diagram for 1980 Rabbit Deluxe and Pick-up Truck LX models

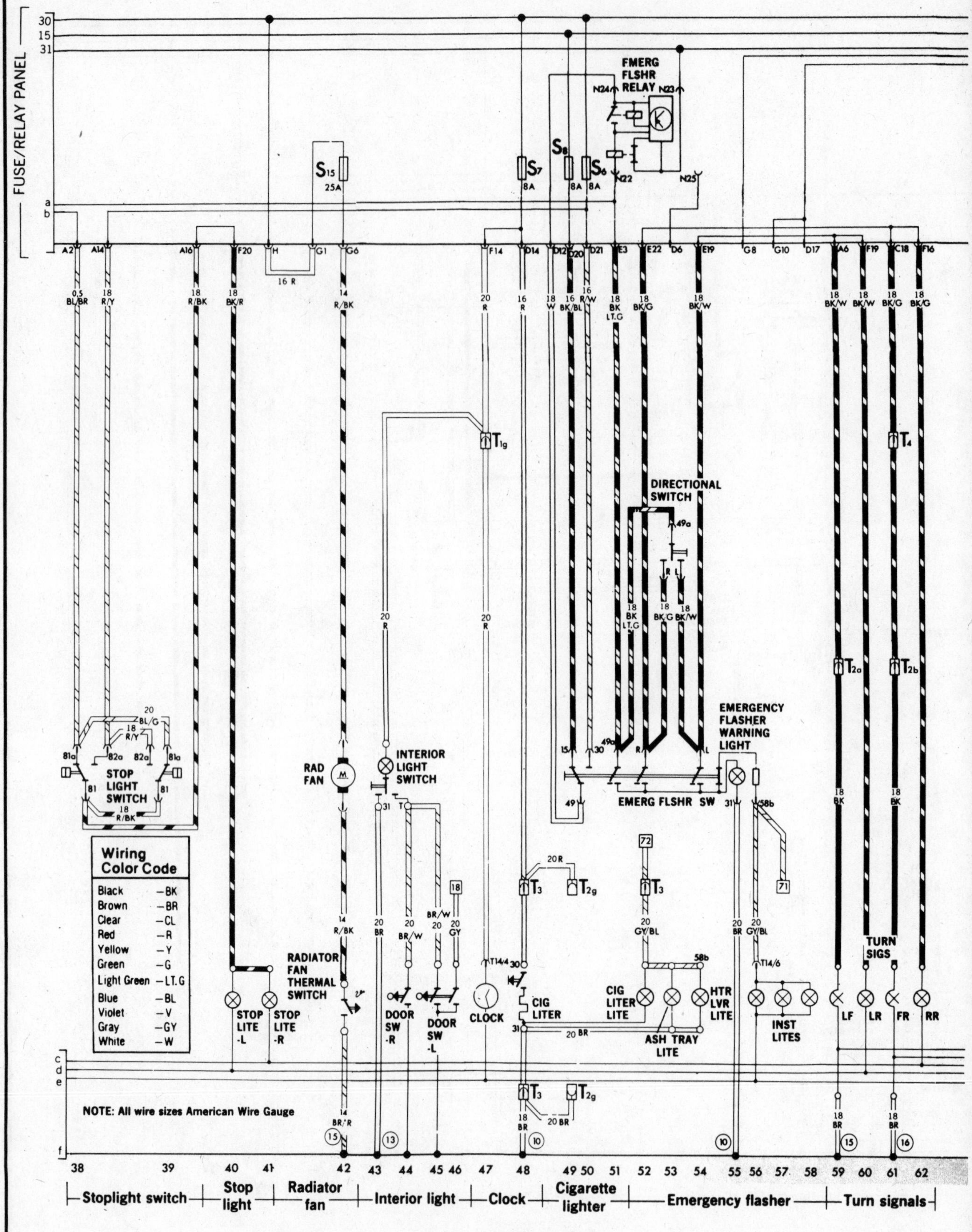

FUSE/RELAY PANEL

30
15
31

EMERG
FLSHR
RELAY

N24
N23

S15
25A

S7
8A

S8

S6
8A
8A

N22

N25

A2
A14
A16
F20
H
G1
G6
F14
D14
D12
D20
D21
E3
E22
D6
E19
G8
G10
D17
A6
F19
C18
F16

0.5
BL/BR

18
R/Y

18
R/BK

18
BK/R

16 R

14
R/BK

20
R

16
R

18
W

16
BK/BL

16
R/W

18
BK
LT.G

18
BK/G

18
BK/W

18
BK/W

18
BK/W

18
BK/G

18
BK/G

T1g

T4

DIRECTIONAL
SWITCH

49a

R
L

18
BK
LT.G

18
BK/G

18
BK/W

EMERGENCY
FLASHER
WARNING
LIGHT

20
BL/G

18
R/Y

82a
82a

8la

81a

STOP
LIGHT
SWITCH

81

81

18
R/BK

RAD
FAN

INTERIOR
LIGHT
SWITCH

31

T

15
30
49a
R
L

49

EMERG FLSHR SW

31

58b

20
R

20
R

18
BK

18
BK

T2a

T2b

T3

T2g

72

T3

71

20R

20
GY/BL

20
BR

20
GY/BL

T14/6

Wiring
Color Code

Black	– BK
Brown	– BR
Clear	– CL
Red	– R
Yellow	– Y
Green	– G
Light Green	– LT. G
Blue	– BL
Violet	– V
Gray	– GY
White	– W

RADIATOR
FAN
THERMAL
SWITCH

STOP
LITE
-L

STOP
LITE
-R

20
BR

20
BR/W

20
BR/W

20
GY

BR/W

18

14
R/BK

T14/4
30

CLOCK

CIG
LITER

31

20 BR

CIG
LITER LITE

ASH TRAY
LITE

58b

HTR
LVR
LITE

INST
LITES

LF

LR

FR

RR

TURN
SIGS

DOOR
SW
-R

DOOR
SW
-L

NOTE: All wire sizes American Wire Gauge

14
BR/R

T3

T2g

18
BR

20 BR

18
BR

18
BR

c
d
e
f

15

13

10

10

15

16

38   39   40   41   42   43   44   45   46   47   48   49 50   51   52   53   54   55   56   57   58   59   60   61   62

|Stoplight switch| Stop light | Radiator fan | Interior light | Clock | Cigarette lighter | Emergency flasher | Turn signals |

Wiring diagram for 1980 Rabbit Deluxe and Pick-up Truck LX models

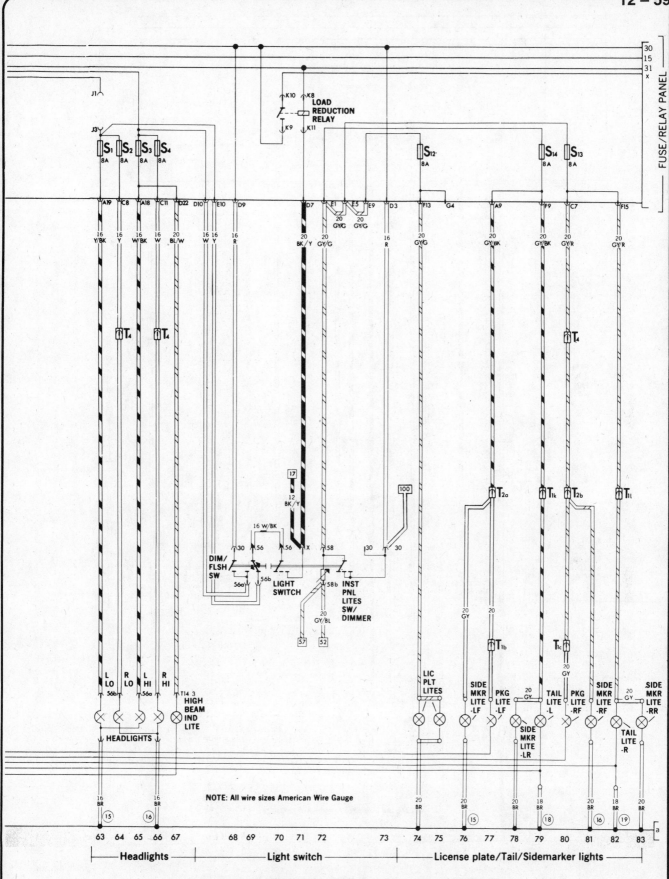

NOTE: All wire sizes American Wire Gauge

Wiring diagram for 1980 Rabbit Deluxe and Pick-up Truck LX models

12

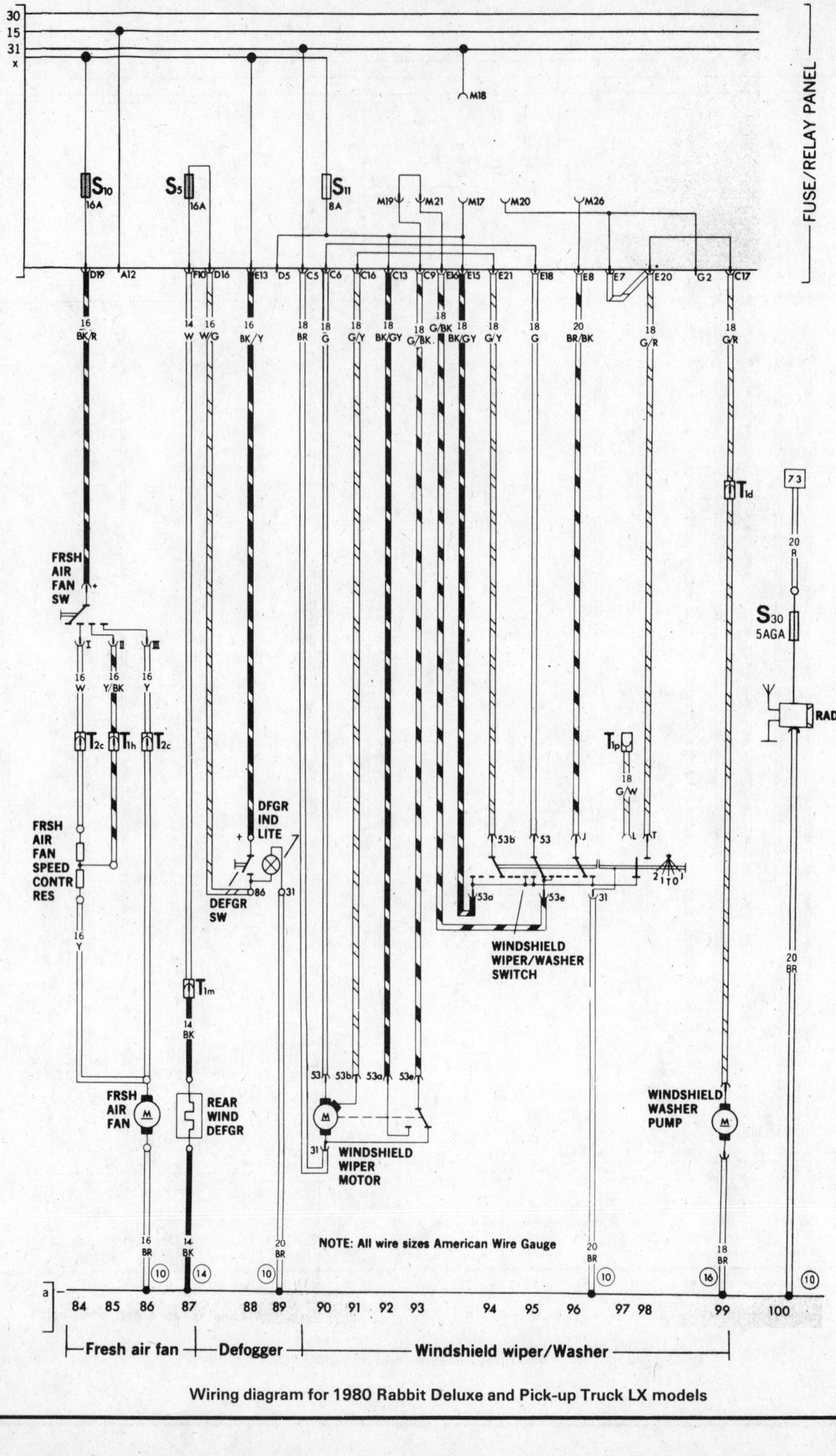

FUSE/RELAY PANEL

30
15
31
x

M18

S10 16A

S5 16A

S11 8A

M19 M21 M17 M20 M26

D19 A12 F10 D16 E13 D5 C5 C6 C16 C13 C9 E16 E15 E21 E18 E8 E7 E20 G2 C17

16 BK/R   14 W   16 W/G   16 BK/Y   18 BR   18 G   18 G/Y   18 BK/GY   18 G/BK   18 BK/GY   18 G/Y   18 G   20 BR/BK   18 G/R   18 G/R

FRSH AIR FAN SW

I   II   III

16 W   16 Y/BK   16 Y

T2c   T1h   T2c

FRSH AIR FAN SPEED CONTR RES

16 Y

DFGR IND LITE

DEFGR SW

D86   31

T1m

14 BK

FRSH AIR FAN

REAR WIND DEFGR

53   53b   53a   53e

WINDSHIELD WIPER MOTOR

31

T1p

18 G/W

53b   53   J   L   T

53a   53e   31

0

WINDSHIELD WIPER/WASHER SWITCH

T1d

73

20 R

S30 5AGA

RADIO

20 BR

WINDSHIELD WASHER PUMP

NOTE: All wire sizes American Wire Gauge

a

16 BR   14 BK   20 BR   20 BR   18 BR

10   14   10   10   16   10

84 85 86 87 88 89 90 91 92 93 94 95 96 97 98 99 100

Fresh air fan — Defogger — Windshield wiper/Washer

Wiring diagram for 1980 Rabbit Deluxe and Pick-up Truck LX models

Key for wiring diagrams on pages 12-62 through 12-67

Description	Current track	Description	Current track
Alternator	2–3	Stop-light, right	94
Alternator charging light	31	Stop-light, left	68
Air conditioner control lever light	60	Stop-light, right	67
Ashtray light	61	Stop-light switch	64
Auxiliary air regulator	17	Tachometer	26
Back-up light, left	40	Thermal time switch	13–14
Back-up light, right	41	Turn signal light, front left	72
Back-up light switch	39	Turn signal light, rear left	73
Ballast resistor	9	Turn signal light, front right	74
Ballast resistor, fresh air fan	112	Turn signal light, rear right	75
Battery	4	Turn signal indicator light	32
Cigarette lighter	63	Turn signal switch	78
Cigarette lighter light	62	Voltage regulator	3
Clock	57	Voltage regulator	25
Clock illumination light	58	Warm air regulator	16
Cold start valve	15	Windshield washer motor/pump	111
Coolant over-temperature indicator	29	Windshield washer/wiper intermittent	
Coolant temperature indicator	27	relay	107–108
Coolant temperature sensor	36	Windshield wiper intermittent selector	
Cut-out relay (load reduction)	81–82	switch	108–110
Door switch (right)	55	Windshield wiper motor	106–107
Door switch/buzzer (left)	53–54		
EGR elapsed mileage indicator	34–35	**Wire connectors**	
EGR indicator light	33	T – Cable adaptor behind instrument panel	
Electric fuel pump	19	T1a – Single, behind instrument panel	
Emergency flasher light	80	T1b – Single, behind instrument panel	
Emergency flasher relay	77–79	T1c – Single, engine compartment, left headlight	
Emergency flasher switch	76–81	T1d – Single, near relay panel	
Fog light connector	101	T1e – Single, behind instrument panel	
Fresh air fan	113	T1f – Single, behind instrument panel	
Fresh air fan switch	112–113	T1g – Single, behind instrument panel	
Fuel gauge	25	T1h – Single, luggage compartment, rear left	
Fuel gauge sender unit	38	T1j – Single, behind instrument panel	
Fuel pump relay	18–20	T1k – Single, left engine compartment, near main	
Fuses S1-S15, on fuse/relay panel	–	brake cylinder	
S31 fuel pump fuse on fuel/pump		T1l – Single, behind instrument panel	
relay	–	T1m – Single, luggage compartment, rear left	
Glove compartment light	105	T1n – Single, behind instrument panel	
Headlight, high beam left	102	T1o – Single, behind instrument panel	
Headlight, high beam right	101	T1p – Single, behind instrument panel	
Headlight, low left	97–99	T1r – Single, behind instrument panel	
Headlight, low right	98–100	T1s – Single, near left stop-light	
Headlight dimmer switch	95–96	T1t – Single, near right stop-light	
High beam indicator light	103	T1u – Single, behind instrument panel	
Horn, double tone	41–42	T2a – Double, engine compartment, near double horn	
Horn button	44	T2b – Double, behind instrument panel	
Horn relay, double tone	43–44	T2c – Double, near main brake cylinder	
Ignition coil	9	T2d – Double, engine compartment, near right headlight	
Ignition distributor	8–12	T2e – Double, engine compartment fixed to coolant hose	
Ignition/starter switch	21–24	T2f – Double, behind instrument panel	
Instrument panel lights	81–83	T2g – Double, under drivers seat	
Instrument panel light switch/dimmer	86	T2h – Double, behind instrument panel	
Interior lighting	56	T3a – Three-point, engine compartment, near left headlight	
License plate lights	88–89	T3b – Three-point, behind instrument panel	
Light switch	83–86	T4 – Four-point, behind instrument panel	
Luggage compartment light	87	T14 – Fourteen-point, instrument panel	
Oil pressure switch	37		
Oil pressure warning light	30		
Oil temperature indicator	46		
Oil temperature indicator light	59	**Ground connectors**	
Oil temperature sensor	45		
Parking brake switch	65–66	① – Battery to body	
Parking brake indicator light	48		
Parking brake light switch	47	② – Alternator to engine	
Parking light, left	90		
Parking light, right	93	⑨ – Fuse/relay panel	
Radiator fan	104		
Radiator fan thermoswitch	104	⑩ – Steering column support	
Rear window defogger	69		
Rear window defogger indicator light	71	⑫ – Rear baggage compartment	
Rear window defogger switch	70		
Seat belt buzzer switch, left	52	⑭ – Rear roof middle support	
Seat belt warning light	49		
Seat belt warning relay	50–52	⑮ – From isolated tubing, front harness	
Side marker light, rear	92–95		
Spark plugs	10–12	⑰ – Steering column	
Spark plug connector	10–12		
Starter	5–6	⑱ – Tail light cover, left	
Stop-light, left	91	⑲ – Tail light cover, right	

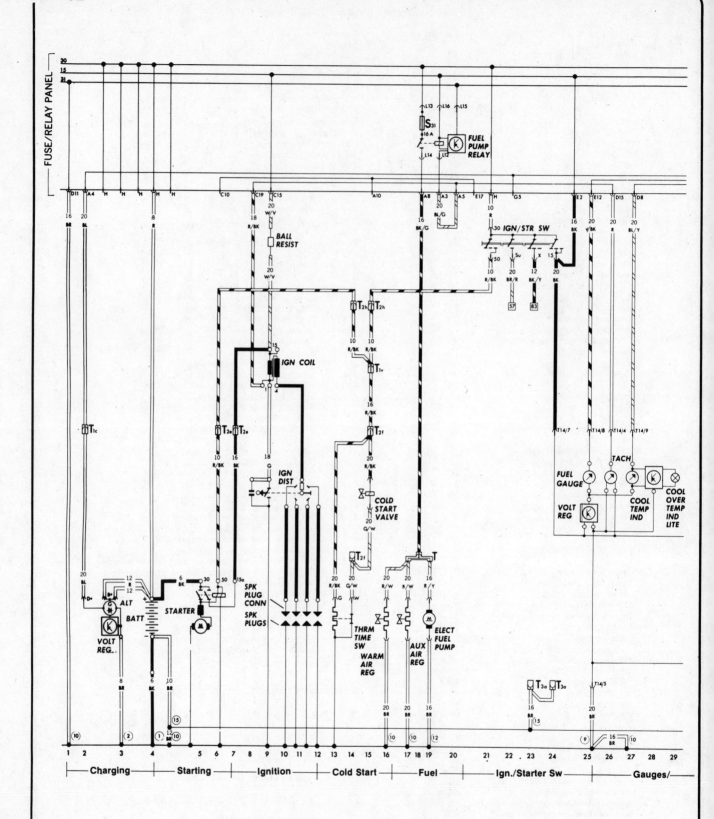

Wiring diagram for 1980/81 Scirocco and 1980 Jetta models (except California)

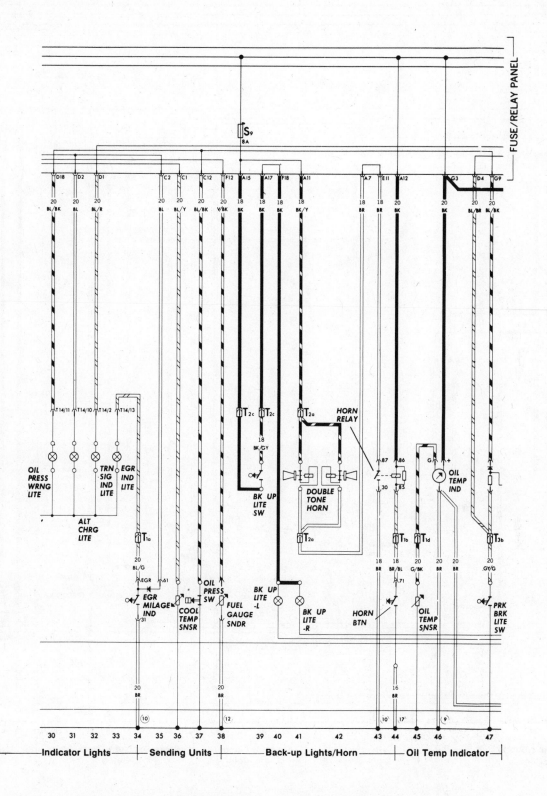

Wiring diagram for 1980/81 Scirocco and 1980 Jetta models (except California)

12

Wiring diagram for 1980/81 Scirocco and 1980 Jetta models (except California)

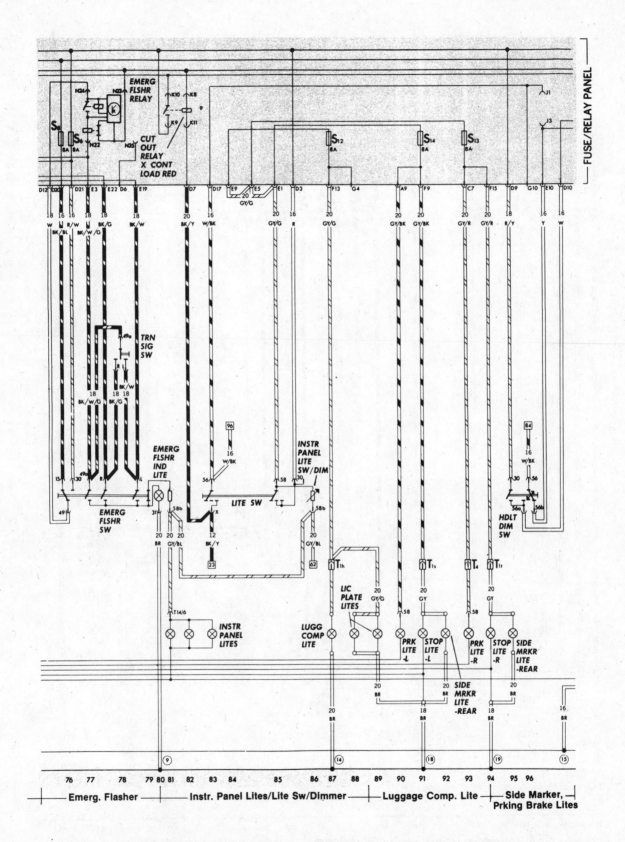

Wiring diagram for 1980/81 Scirocco and 1980 Jetta models (except California)

12

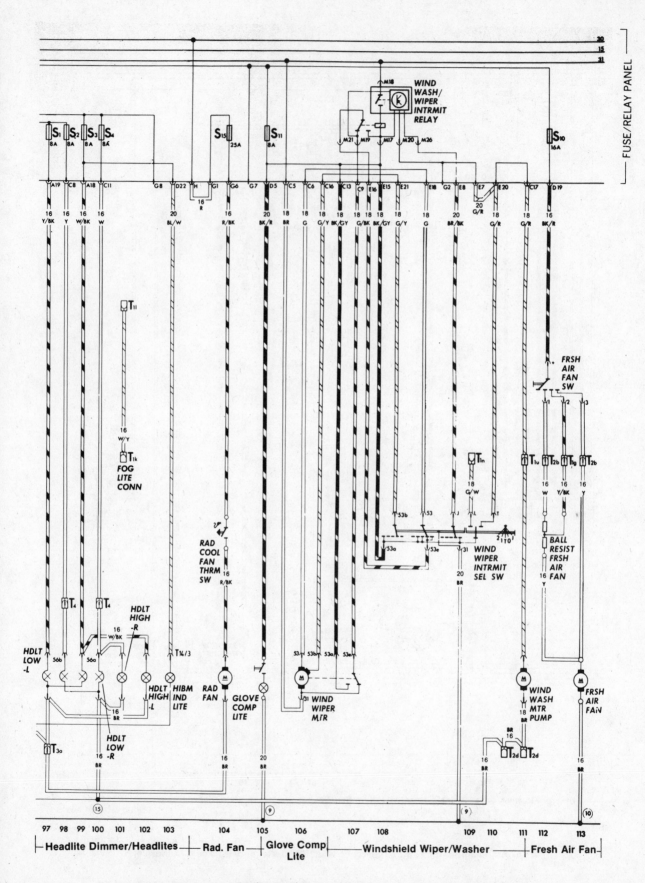

Wiring diagram for 1980/81 Scirocco and 1980 Jetta models (except California)

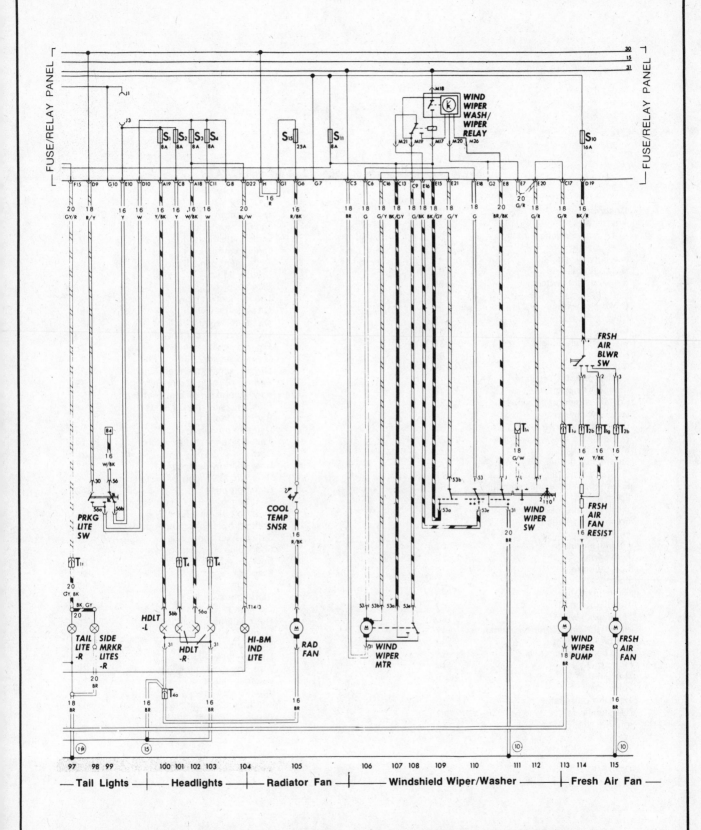

Wiring diagram for 1980 Rabbit Convertible (except California) and 1980 Canadian Rabbit Deluxe models

Key for wiring diagrams on pages 12-69 through 12-74

Description	Current track	Description	Current track
Alternator	2	Ignition/starter switch	32
Alternator charging light	35	Ignition distributor	9
Ashtray light	54	Ignition module	11
Auxiliary air regulator	17	Instrument panel lights	54
Back-up lights	60	Interior light	64
Back-up light switch	60	License plate lights	55
Battery	4	Load reduction relay	33
Brake proportioning valve	36	Oil pressure switch	38
Bulb check relay	39	Oil pressure warning light	38
Cigarette lighter	84	Oxygen sensor control unit	23
Cigarette lighter light	54	Oxygen sensor frequency valve	33
Clock	68	Oxygen sensor relay	21
Cold start valve	29	Oxygen sensor thermal switch	23
Control pressure regulator	16	Parking brake indicator light	35
Coolant temperature gauge	26	Parking brake indicator light switch	35
Coolant temperature sensor	39	Parking – side marker lights	48
Door switch (right)	64	Radiator fan	15
Door switch/buzzer (left)	63	Radiator fan relay	14
EGR elapsed mileage switch	35	Radiator fan thermal switch	14
EGR light	35	Radio	90
Emergency flasher relay	72	Rear window defogger	78
Emergency flasher switch	72	Rear window defogger switch	78
Emergency flasher indicator light	54	Seat belt relay	40
Fresh air fan	77	Seat belt switch	40
Fresh air fan speed control resistors	76	Seat belt warning light	38
Fresh air fan switch	77	Shift console light (auto. trans.)	54
Fuel gauge	27	Side marker lights, rear	50
Fuel level sensor	27	Spark plug suppressors	9
Fuel pump	18	Spark plugs	9
Fuel pump relay	19	Starter	5
Fuse links	2	Stop-lights	57
Glovebox light	66	Stop-light switch	57
Headlights	47	Tail light	52
Headlight switch	50	Thermal time switch	29
Headlight dimmer/flasher switch	47	Trunk light	67
Heater lever light	54	Turn signal lights	72
High beam indicator light	54	Turn signal switch	72
Horn	44	Turn signal indicator light	35
Horn button	45	Voltage regulator	2
Horn relay	44	Voltage stabilizer	27
Hot start pulse relay	28	Windshield washer pump	81
Idle stabilizer	12	Windshield wiper motor	83
Ignition coil	8	Windshield wiper switch	83

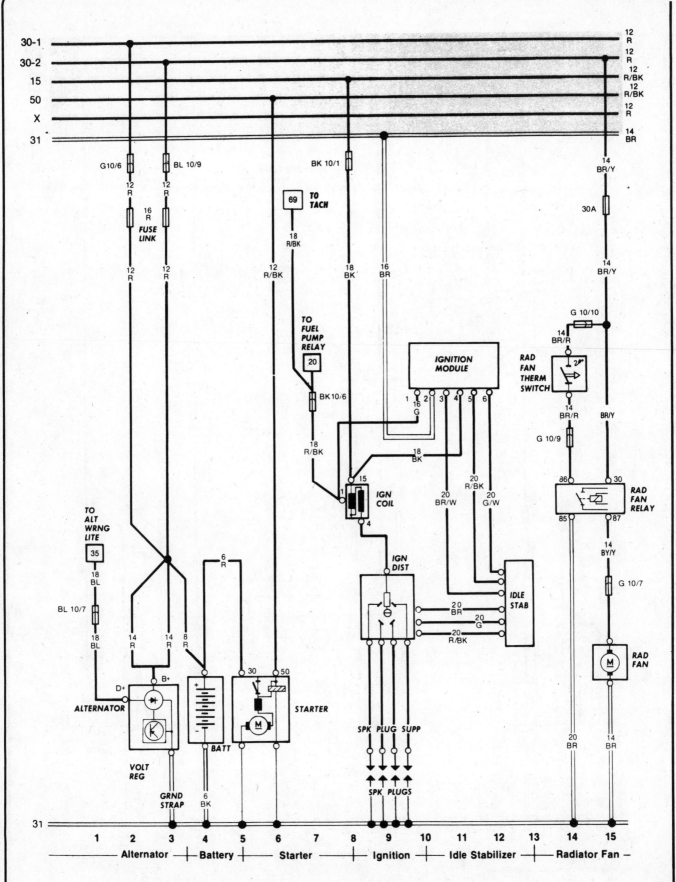

Wiring diagram for 1981 Rabbit (except Convertible) and Pick-up Truck models

Wiring diagram for 1981 Rabbit (except Convertible) and Pick-up Truck models

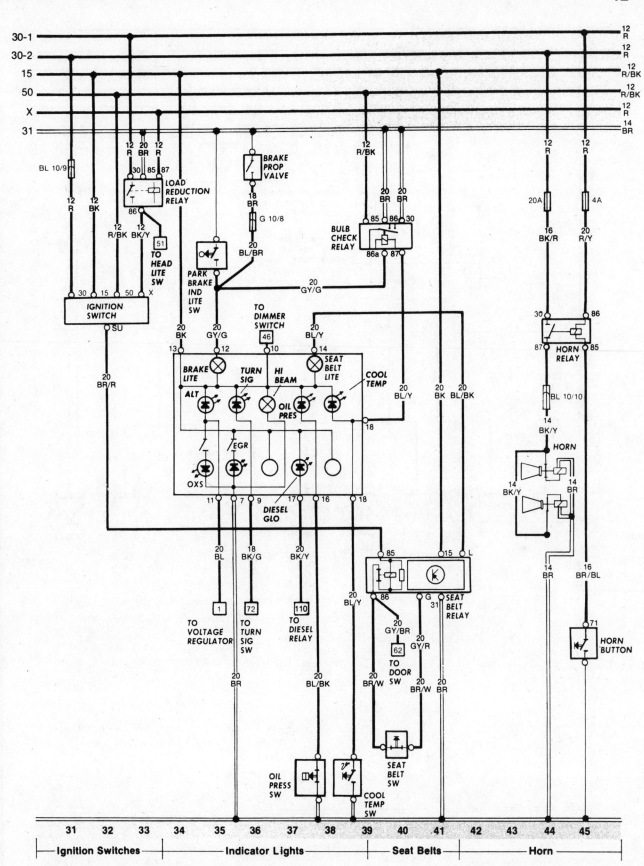

Wiring diagram for 1981 Rabbit (except Convertible) and Pick-up Truck models

All wire sizes American Wire Gauge

31	32	33	34	35	36	37	38	39	40	41	42	43	44	45

— Ignition Switches — Indicator Lights — Seat Belts — Horn —

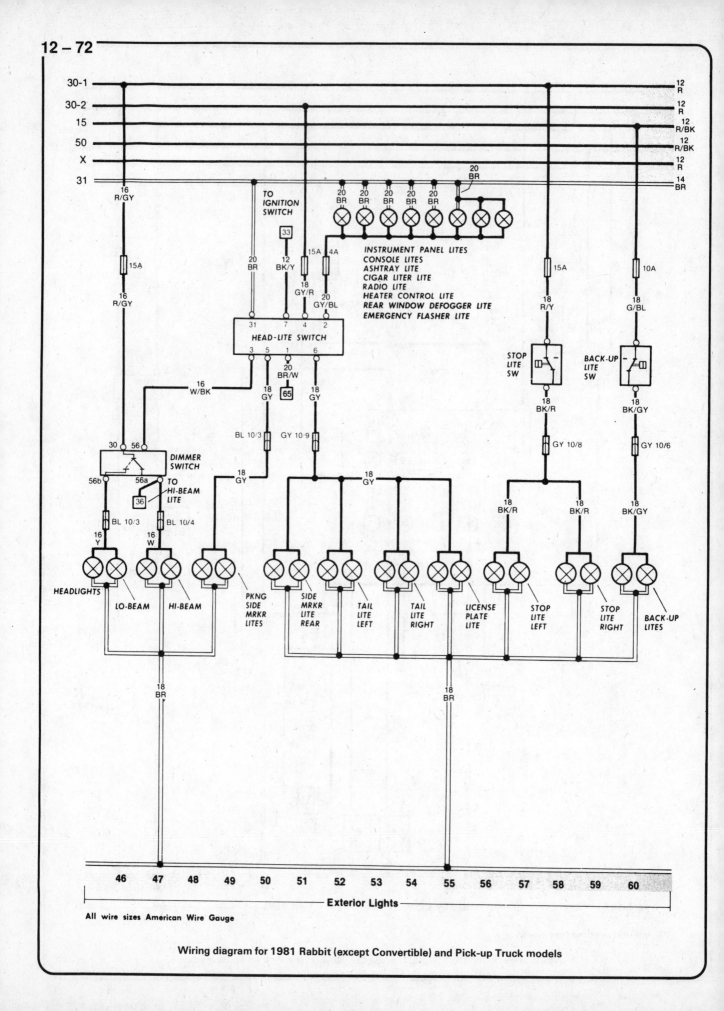

Wiring diagram for 1981 Rabbit (except Convertible) and Pick-up Truck models

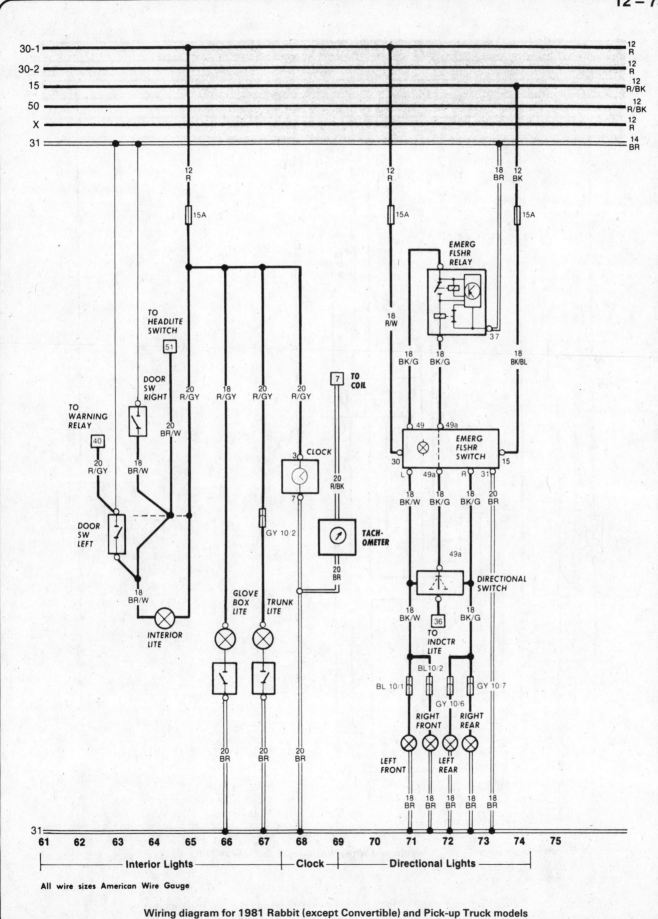

Wiring diagram for 1981 Rabbit (except Convertible) and Pick-up Truck models

All wire sizes American Wire Gauge

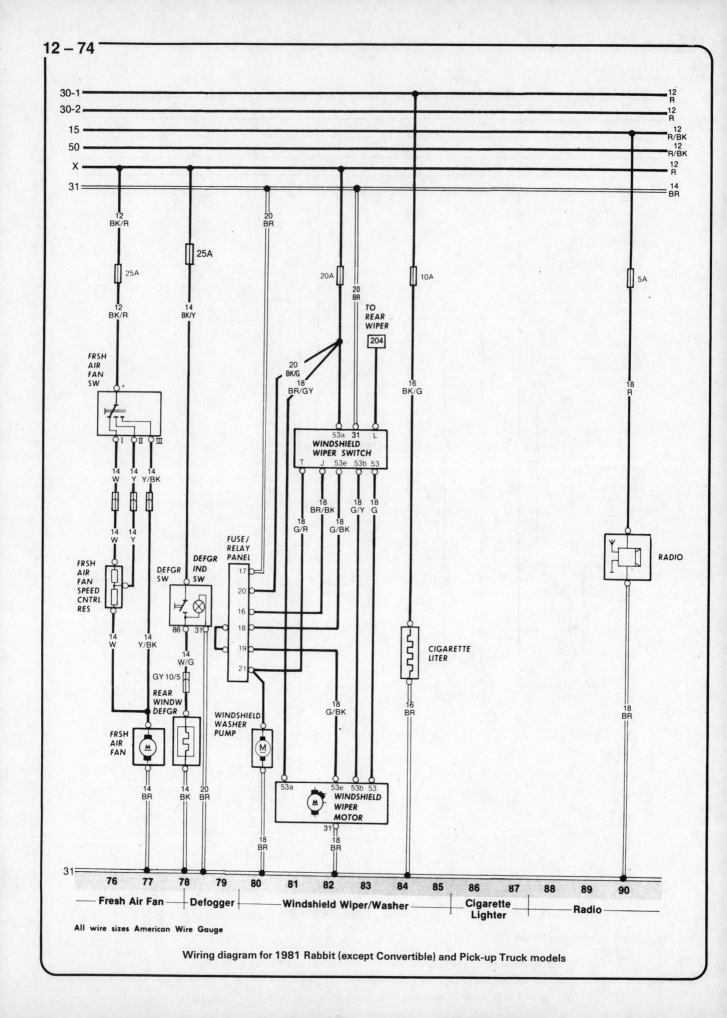

All wire sizes American Wire Gauge

Wiring diagram for 1981 Rabbit (except Convertible) and Pick-up Truck models

Key for wiring diagrams on pages 12-76 through 12-80

Description	Current track
Alternator	2–3
Alternator charging indicator light	33
Auxiliary air regulator	20
Back-up light, left	43
Back-up light, right	45
Back-up light switch	42
Battery	4
Brake fluid level warning switch	61
Brake light, left	64
Brake light, right	63
Brake light switch	62–63
Brake warning light	47
Cigarette lighter	58
Cigarette lighter light	59
Clock	60
Cold start valve	25
Control pressure regulator	19
Coolant overheat warning light	31
Coolant temperature gauge	30
Coolant temperature sender	40
Door switch, left front, with buzzer contact	51–52
Door switch, left rear	53
Door switch, right front	55
Door switch, right rear	54
Electronic ignition control unit	6–10
Emergency flasher indicator light	74
Emergency flasher pilot light	76
Emergency flasher relay	71–72
Emergency flasher switch	69–75
Frequency valve	17
Fresh air fan	114
Fresh air fan series resistor	113
Fresh air fan switch	113–114
Fuel gauge	29
Fuel gauge sender	23
Fuel pump	22
Fuel pump fuse (on fuel pump relay)	–
Fuel pump relay	13–14
Fuse S1-S15 on fuse/relay panel (under dash)	–
Hall generator	8–9
Headlight dimmer switch/flasher	96–97
Headlight, high beam, left inner	104
Headlight, high beam, left outer	101
Headlight, high beam, right inner	103
Headlight, high beam, right outer	102
Headlight, low beam, left outer	99
Headlight, low beam, right outer	100
Heater/fresh air controls light	57
High beam indicator light	36
Horn	44
Horn button	46
Ignition coil	10–11
Ignition distributor	10–12
Ignition/starter switch	25–28
Interior light, front	55–56
Instrument panel lights	83–85
Instrument panel light switch	85
License plate light	87–88
Light switch	82–85
Light switch light	80
Load reduction relay	80–81
Oil pressure light	35
Oil pressure switch	41
OXS control unit (behind dash, on right)	13–17
OXS elapsed mileage switch	38–39
OXS (oxygen) sensor	13
OXS voltage supply relay	16–18
OXS warning light	37
Parking brake indicator light switch	47
Parking light, left	89
Parking light, right	93
Radiator fan motor	105
Radiator fan thermoswitch	105
Radio ground connector	58
Radio power connector	70
Rear window defogger	79
Rear window defogger indicator light	77
Rear window defogger switch	78
Seat belt safety switch, left	50

Description	Current track
Seat belt warning/interlock relay	48–51
Seat belt warning light	47
Side marker light, left front	90
Side marker light, left rear	92
Side marker light, right front	94
Side marker light, right rear	96
Spark plugs	10–12
Spark plug connectors	10–12
Starter	5–6
Tail light, left	91
Tail light, right	95
Thermoswitch for OXS system	14
Thermotime switch	24
Trunk light (convertible only)	86
Trunk light switch (convertible only)	86
Turn signal indicator light	34
Turn signal, left front	65
Turn signal, left rear	66
Turn signal, right front	67
Turn signal, right rear	68
Turn signal switch	72
Voltage regulator	2–3
Voltage stabilizer	29
Windshield washer pump motor	112
Windshield wiper intermittent switch	108–111
Windshield wiper motor	106–107
Windshield wiper/washer intermittent relay	108–110

Wire connectors

T	–	Behind dash, near fuse/relay panel
T1a	–	Behind dash
T1b	–	Behind dash
T1c	–	In engine compartment, left side
T1d	–	Near left headlight
T1e	–	Near left headlight
T1f	–	Near right headlight
T1g	–	Behind dash
T1h	–	In trunk, left rear
T1k	–	Near right headlight
T1m	–	In trunk, left rear
T1n	–	Behind dash
T1p	–	Behind dash
T1u	–	Behind dash
T1v	–	Behind dash
T1y	–	In engine compartment, on fuel line
T2b	–	Behind dash
T2c	–	Behind dash
T2f	–	Behind dash
T2g	–	Behind dash
T2l	–	Under dash, left side
T2m	–	Behind dash
T3a	–	Behind dash
T3b	–	Behind dash
T3c	–	Behind dash
T3d	–	Near right headlight
T4	–	Near right headlight
T4q	–	Near left headlight
T14	–	On instrument cluster

Ground connectors

①	–	Ground cable, battery to transmission
②	–	Ground cable, alternator to engine block
⑦	–	On cold start valve
⑧	–	On cold start valve
⑩	–	On fuse/relay panel mounting
⑬	–	On rear panel, left
⑭	–	On steering column
⑮	–	Insulated ground wire, engine compartment
⑯	–	Insulated ground wire, on instrument cluster
⑱	–	On rear panel, center
⑲	–	On rear roof crossmember, center

12

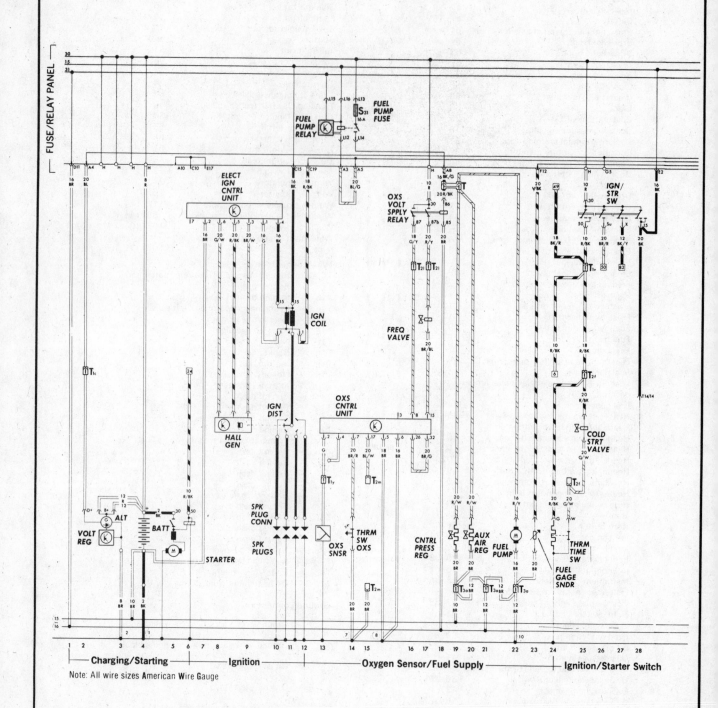

Note: All wire sizes American Wire Gauge

Wiring diagram for 1981 Rabbit Convertible and Jetta models (except California)

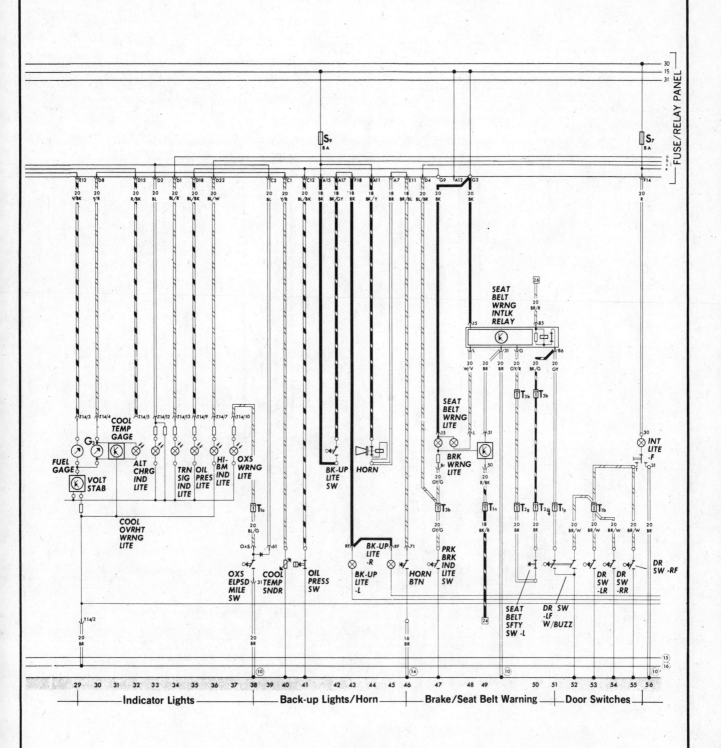

Wiring diagram for 1981 Rabbit Convertible and Jetta models (except California)

12

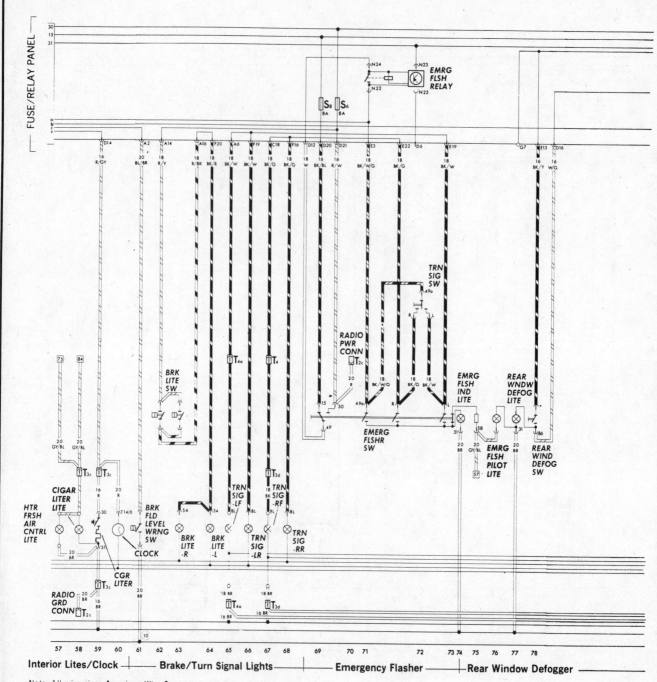

Wiring diagram for 1981 Rabbit Convertible and Jetta models (except California)

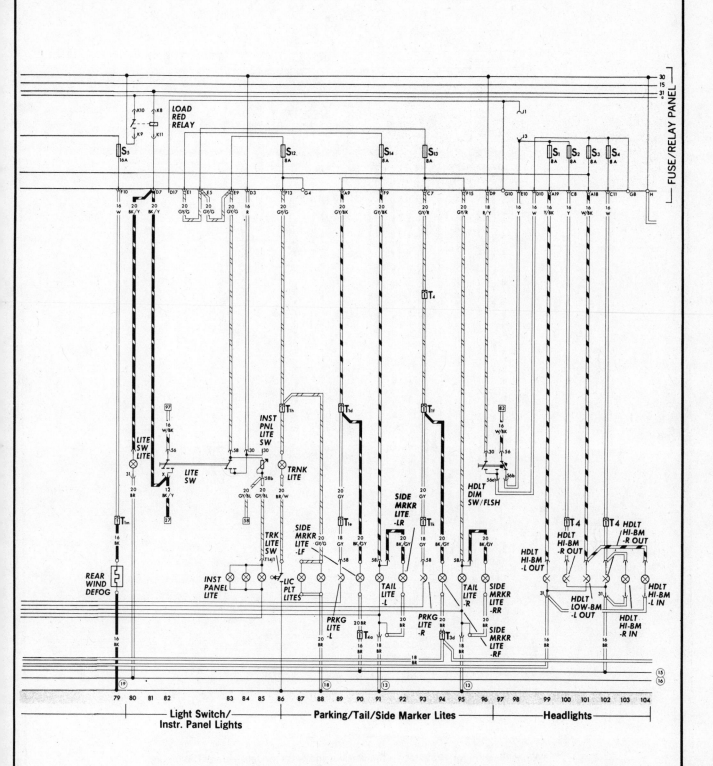

Wiring diagram for 1981 Rabbit Convertible and Jetta models (except California)

12

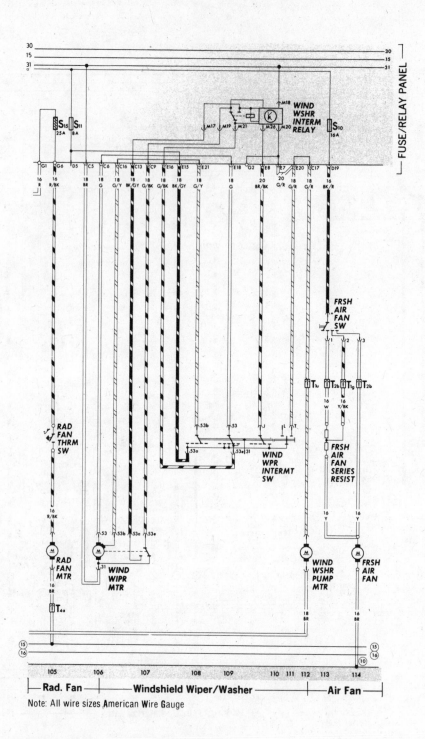

Wiring diagram for 1981 Rabbit Convertible and Jetta models (except California)

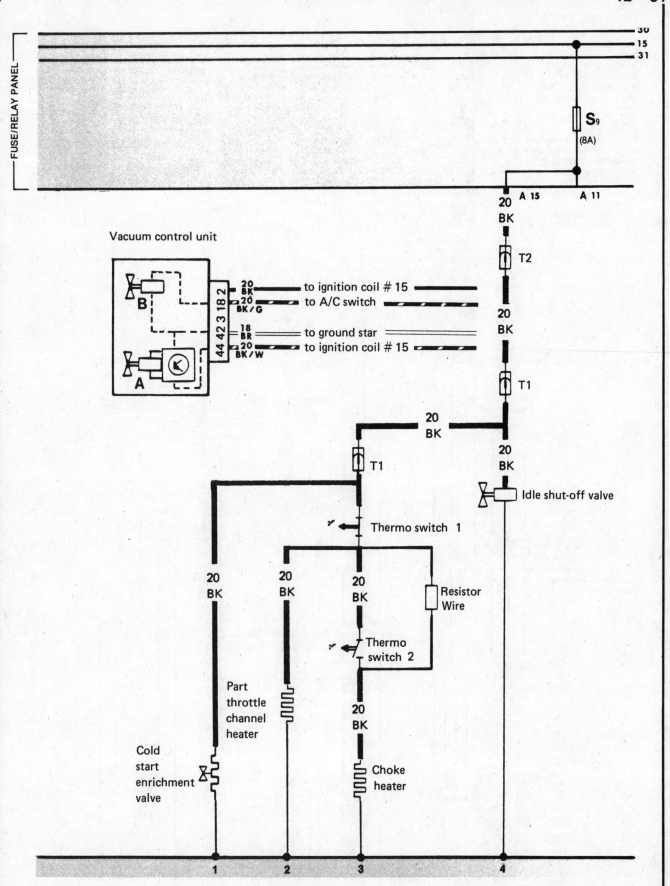

FUSE/RELAY PANEL

30
15
31

S₉
(8A)

A 15   A 11
20
BK

T2

20
BK

T1

20
BK

Idle shut-off valve

Vacuum control unit

B

A

44 42 3 18 2

20
BK   to ignition coil # 15
20
BK/G   to A/C switch
18
BR   to ground star
20
BK/W   to ignition coil # 15

20
BK

T1

Thermo switch 1

20
BK

20
BK

20
BK

Resistor
Wire

Thermo
switch 2

20
BK

Part
throttle
channel
heater

Choke
heater

Cold
start
enrichment
valve

1   2   3   4

12

Description	Current track	Wire connectors		Ground connectors	
Cold start valve	26	T – Cable adaptor behind dashboard	12–14	⑦ – On cold start valve	
Distributor	7–10	T1a – Single, behind dashboard	23	⑧ – On cold start valve	
Hall sender unit	3–5	T1v – Single, behind dashboard	24	⑨ – Near relay/fuse box	
Hot start relay	24–25	T1w – Single, behind dashboard	24	⑩ – Steering column support	
Idle stabilizer (California only)	3–5	T1y – Single, clamped to fuel line in engine compartment	15		
Ignition coil	8–9	T2f – Double, right side in engine compartment	26		
Ignition control unit	1–8	T2h – Double, behind dashboard	24,25		
Oxygen sensor	15	T2l – Double, behind dashboard	15,16		
Oxygen sensor control light	23	T2m – Double, behind dashboard in right side	18		
Oxygen sensor control unit (behind dashboard on right)	15–21	T14 – Fourteen point, on dashboard	23		
Oxygen sensor elapsed mileage switch	22–23				
Oxygen sensor relay	14–16				
Oxygen sensor thermal switch	16				
Spark plugs	7–10				
Spark plug connector	7–10				
Thermal time switch	27–28				

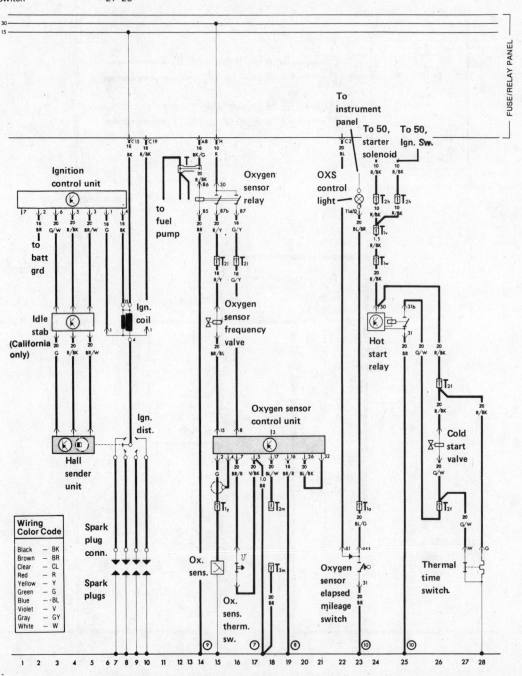

Additional wiring diagram for carburettor (1980 models)

Description	Current track
Brake warning light	23
Cold start valve	37
Door switch, left front, with buzzer contact	26–28
Electronic ignition control unit	1–8
Frequency valve	15
Hall generator	3–5
Hot start pulse relay	31–34
Idle stabilizer	3–5
Ignition coil	8
Ignition distributor	7–10
Ignition/starter switch	29–35
Interior light, front	26
OXS control unit (behind dash, on right)	15–21
OXS elapsed mileage switch	20
OXS (oxygen) sensor	15
OXS voltage supply relay	14–16
OXS warning light	20
Parking brake indicator light switch	23
Seat belt switch, left	30
Seat belt switch, right	30
Seat belt warning/interlock relay	25–31
Seat belt warning light	24
Spark plugs	7–10
Spark plug connectors	7–10
Thermoswitch for OXS systems	16
Thermotime switch	38–39

Wire connectors

T	–	behind dash
T1	–	behind dash
T1a	–	behind dash
T1b	–	behind dash
T1c	–	behind dash
T1d	–	behind dash
T1y	–	in engine compartment, on fuel line
T2a	–	behind dash, right side
T2b	–	behind dash, left side
T2f	–	behind dash
T2l	–	behind dash
T2m	–	behind dash

Ground connectors

7 – On cold start valve
8 – On cold start valve
10 – On fuse/relay panel mounting
10 – Insulated ground wire on instrument cluster

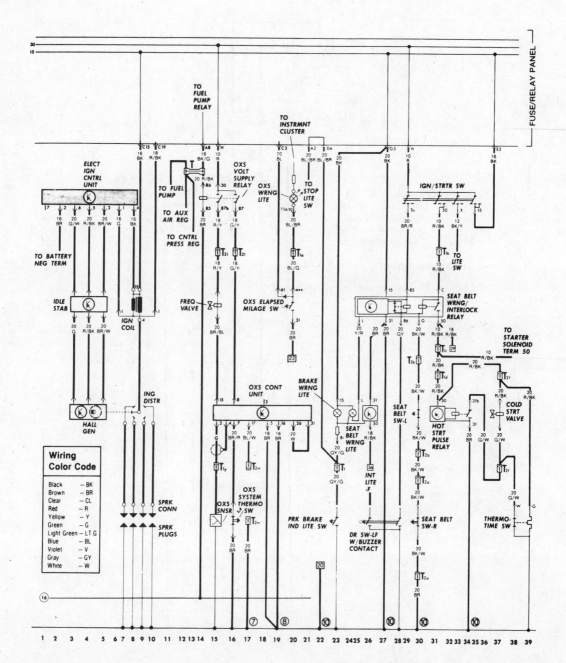

Additional wiring diagram for oxygen sensor system (except 1981 Rabbit Convertible and Jetta, California models)

12

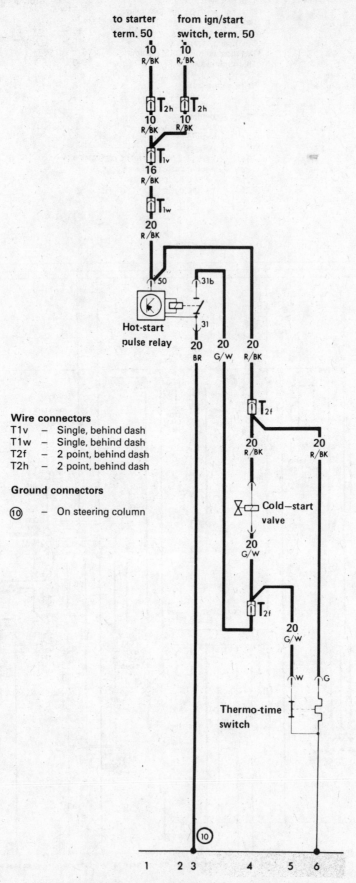

Additional wiring diagram for hot start pulse relay

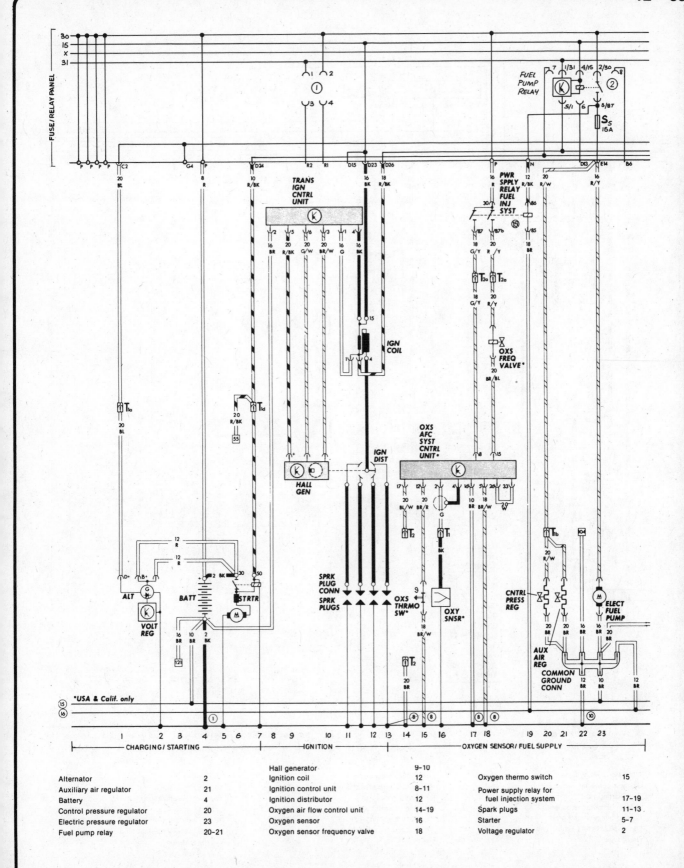

Wiring diagram for 1983 and 1984 Jetta and Rabbit Convertible models

Alternator	2	Hall generator	9–10	
Auxiliary air regulator	21	Ignition coil	12	Oxygen thermo switch	15
Battery	4	Ignition control unit	8–11	Power supply relay for
Control pressure regulator	20	Ignition distributor	12	fuel injection system	17–19
Electric pressure regulator	23	Oxygen air flow control unit	14–19	Spark plugs	11–13
Fuel pump relay	20–21	Oxygen sensor	16	Starter	5–7
		Oxygen sensor frequency valve	18	Voltage regulator	2

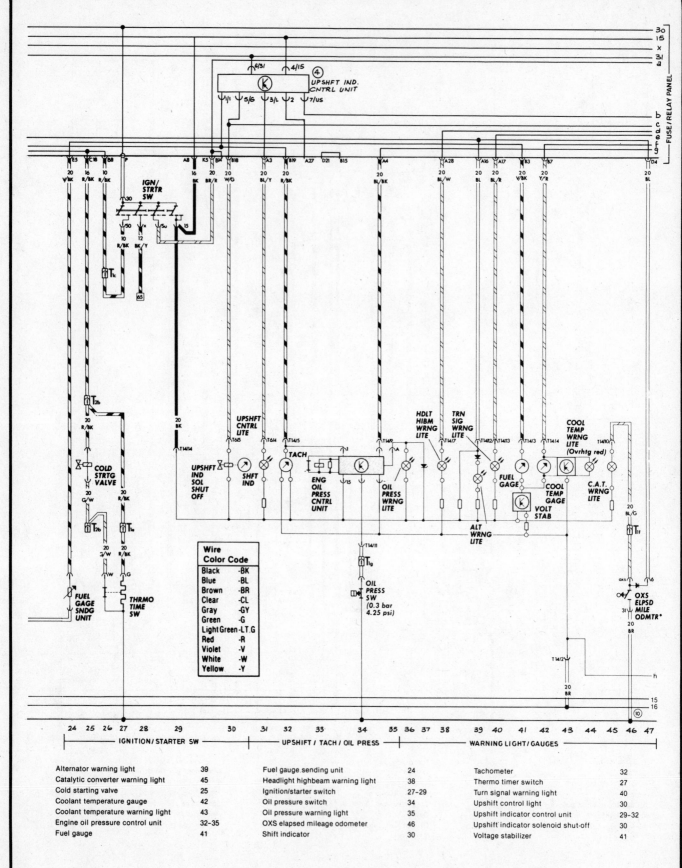

24	25	26	27	28	29	30	31	32	33	34	35	36	37	38	39	40	41	42	43	44	45	46	47

IGNITION/STARTER SW ——— **UPSHIFT / TACH / OIL PRESS** ——— **WARNING LIGHT / GAUGES**

Alternator warning light	39	Fuel gauge sending unit	24	Tachometer	32
Catalytic converter warning light	45	Headlight highbeam warning light	38	Thermo timer switch	27
Cold starting valve	25	Ignition/starter switch	27-29	Turn signal warning light	40
Coolant temperature gauge	42	Oil pressure switch	34	Upshift control light	30
Coolant temperature warning light	43	Oil pressure warning light	35	Upshift indicator control unit	29-32
Engine oil pressure control unit	32-35	OXS elapsed mileage odometer	46	Upshift indicator solenoid shut-off	30
Fuel gauge	41	Shift indicator	30	Voltage stabilizer	41

Wiring diagram for 1983 and 1984 Jetta and Rabbit Convertible models (continued)

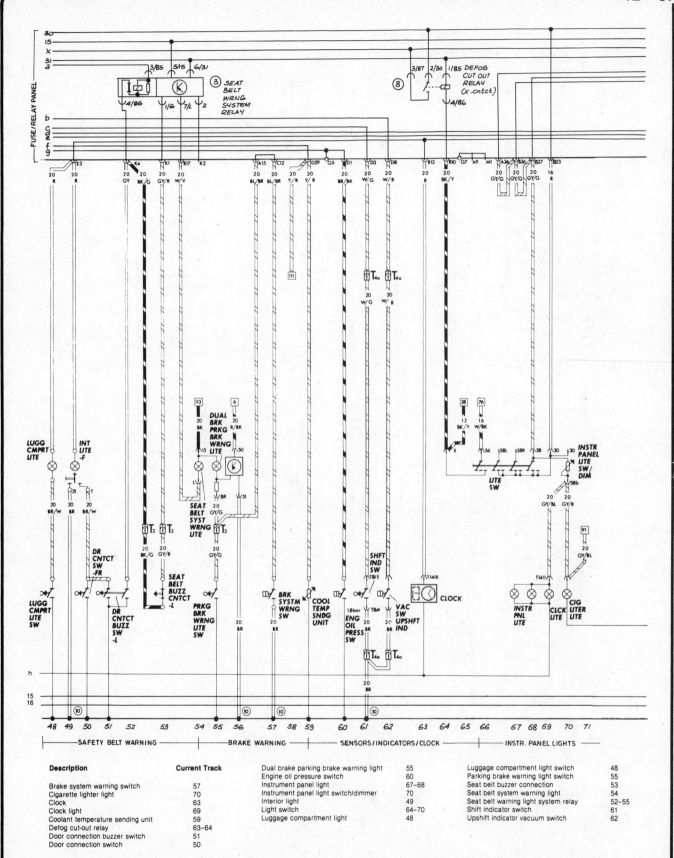

Description	Current Track
Brake system warning switch	57
Cigarette lighter light	70
Clock	63
Clock light	69
Coolant temperature sending unit	59
Defog cut-out relay	63–64
Door connection buzzer switch	51
Door connection switch	50

Dual brake parking brake warning light	55
Engine oil pressure switch	60
Instrument panel light	67–68
Instrument panel light switch/dimmer	70
Interior light	49
Light switch	64–70
Luggage compartment light	48

Luggage compartment light switch	48
Parking brake warning light switch	55
Seat belt buzzer connection	53
Seat belt system warning light	54
Seat belt warning light system relay	52–55
Shift indicator switch	61
Upshift indicator vacuum switch	62

Wiring diagram for 1983 and 1984 Jetta and Rabbit Convertible models (continued)

12

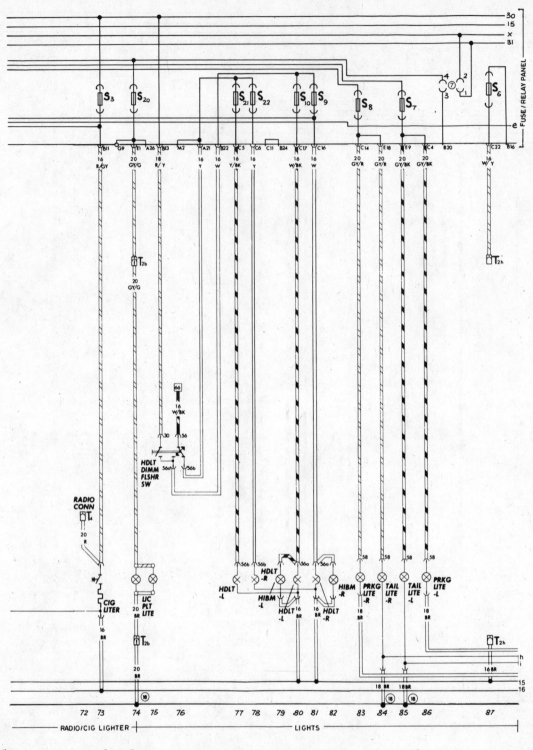

Description	Current Track				
Cigarette lighter	73	Highbeam (right)	82	Radio connection	72
Headlight dimmer/flasher switch	76	License plate light	74	Taillight (left)	85
Headlight (left)	77, 80	Parking light (left)	86	Taillight (right)	84
Headlight (right)	78, 81	Parking light (right)	83		
Highbeam (left)	79				

Wiring diagram for 1983 and 1984 Jetta and Rabbit Convertible models (continued)

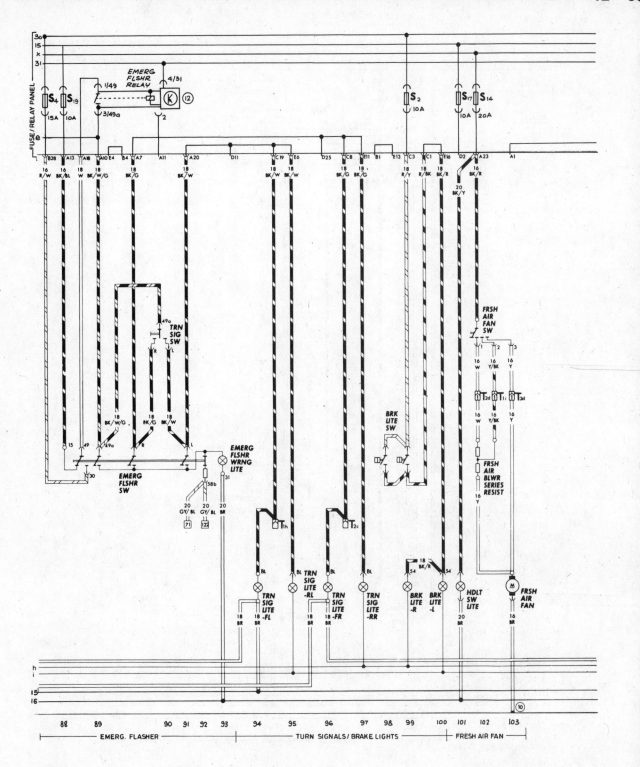

Wiring diagram for 1983 and 1984 Jetta and Rabbit Convertible models (continued)

Description	Current track				
Brake light (left)	100	Emergency flasher warning light	93	Turn signal light (front/left)	94
Brake light (right)	99	Fresh air blower series-resistor	102	Turn signal light (front/right)	96
Brake light switch	98–99	Fresh air fan	103	Turn signal light (rear/left)	95
Emergency flasher relay	89–91	Fresh air fan switch	102	Turn signal light (rear/right)	97
Emergency flasher switch	88–91	Headlight switch light	101	Turn signal switch	90

12

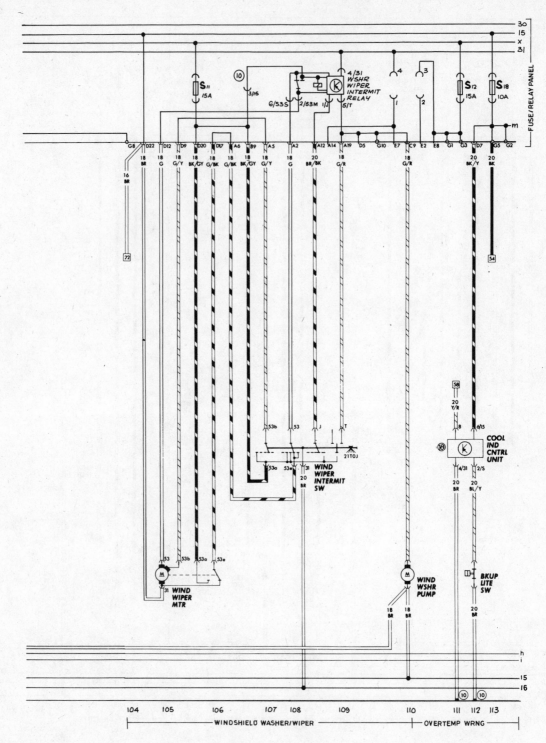

Description	Current Track				
Back-up light switch	112	Windshield washer pump	110	Windshield wiper intermittent switch	108
Coolant indicator control unit	112	Windshield wiper intermittent relay	107–109	Windshield wiper motor	105

Wiring diagram for 1983 and 1984 Jetta and Rabbit Convertible models (continued)

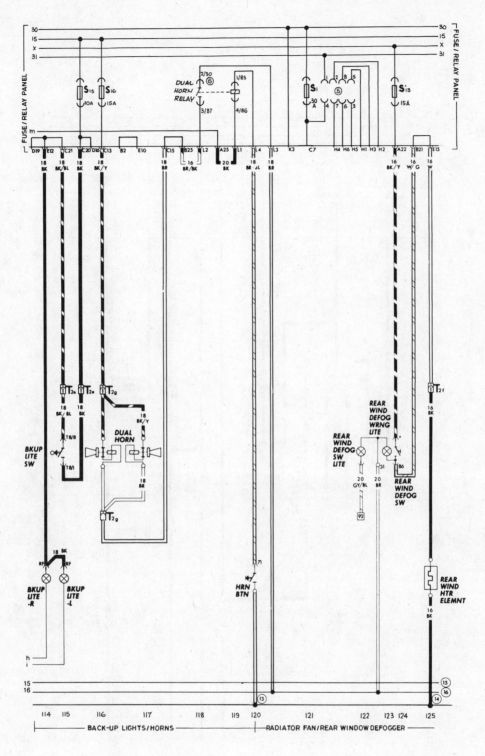

114	115	116	117	118	119	120	121	122	123 124	125

BACK-UP LIGHTS/HORNS — RADIATOR FAN/REAR WINDOW DEFOGGER

Description	Current Track				
Back up light (left)	115	Dual horns	116–117	Rear window defog switch	124
Back up light (right)	114	Horn button	120	Rear window defog switch light	122
Back up light switch	115	Rear window heating element	125	Rear window defog warning light	123
Dual horn relay	118–119				

12

Wiring diagram for 1983 and 1984 Jetta and Rabbit Convertible models (continued)

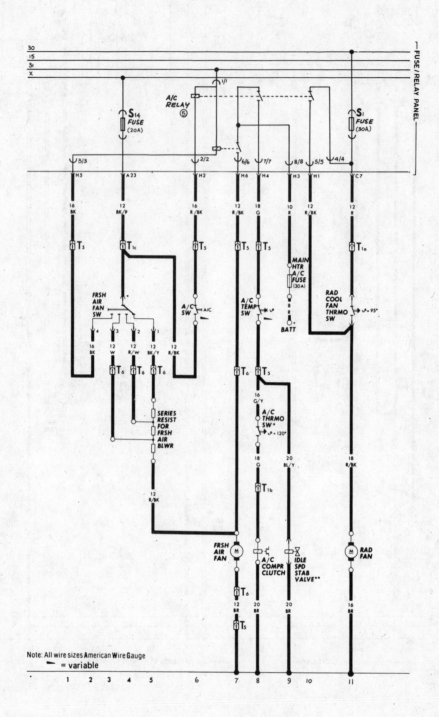

Wiring diagram for 1983 and 1984 Jetta and Rabbit Convertible models (continued)

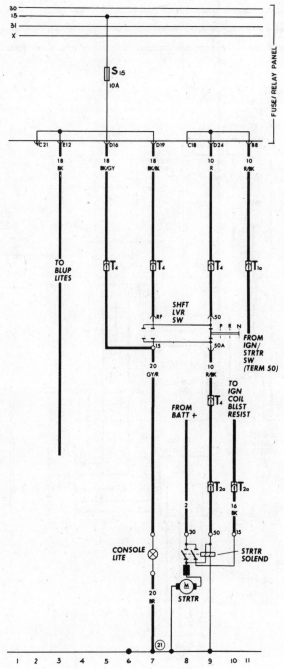

Wire connectors

T1a — single, behind fuse/relay panel
T2a — double, in engine compartment next to
     coolant hose
T4 — 4-point, behind dash

Ground connectors

(21) — next to gear-shift lever

Wiring diagram for 1983 and 1984 Jetta and Rabbit Convertible models (continued)

12

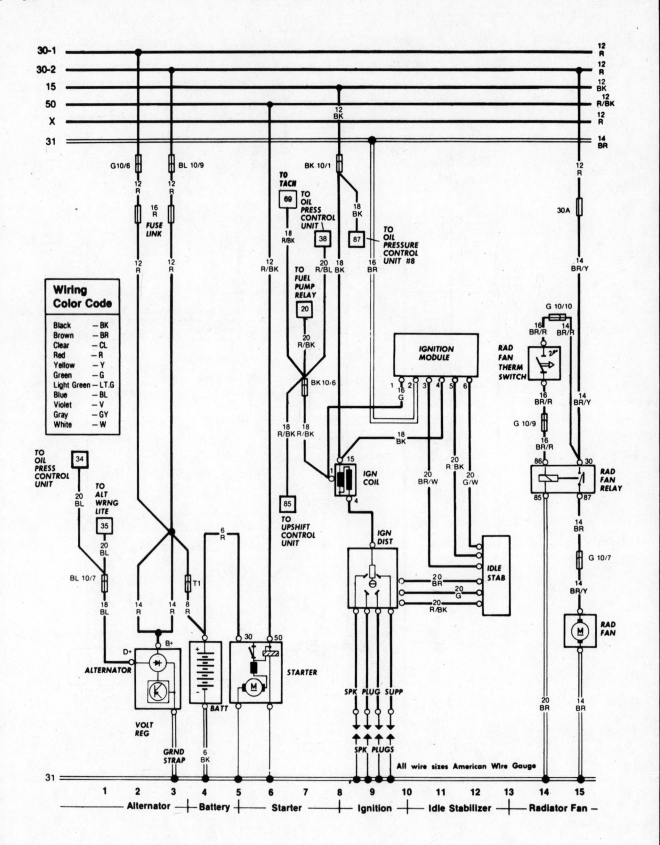

Wiring diagram for 1982, 1983 and 1984 Rabbit and 1982 and 1983 Pick-up models

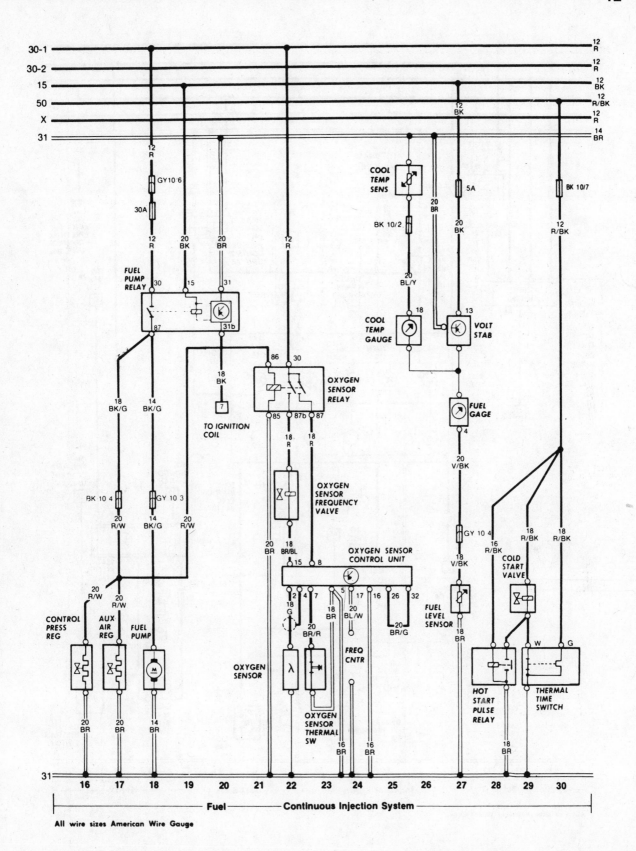

Wiring diagram for 1982, 1983 and 1984 Rabbit and 1982 and 1983 Pick-up models (continued)

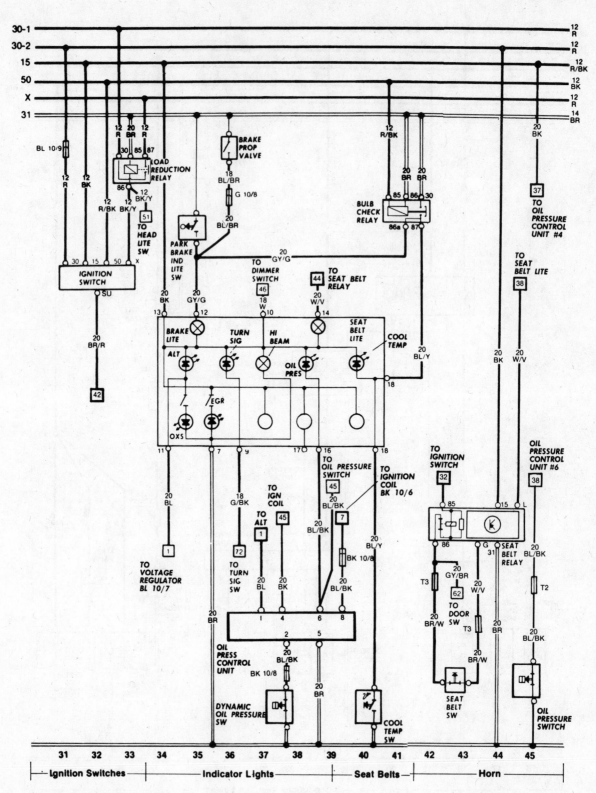

Wiring diagram for 1982, 1983 and 1984 Rabbit and 1982 and 1983 Pick-up models (continued)

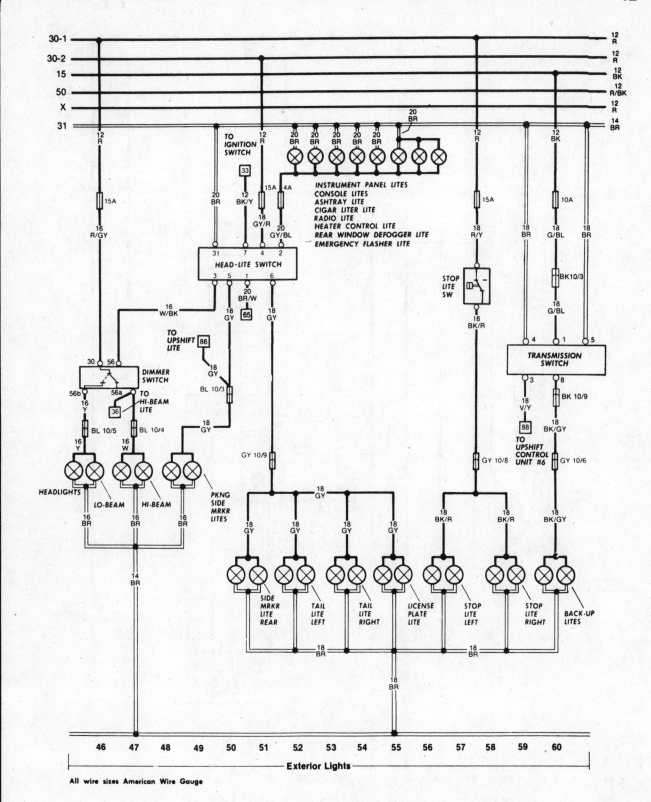

Wiring diagram for 1982, 1983 and 1984 Rabbit and 1982 and 1983 Pick-up models (continued)

12

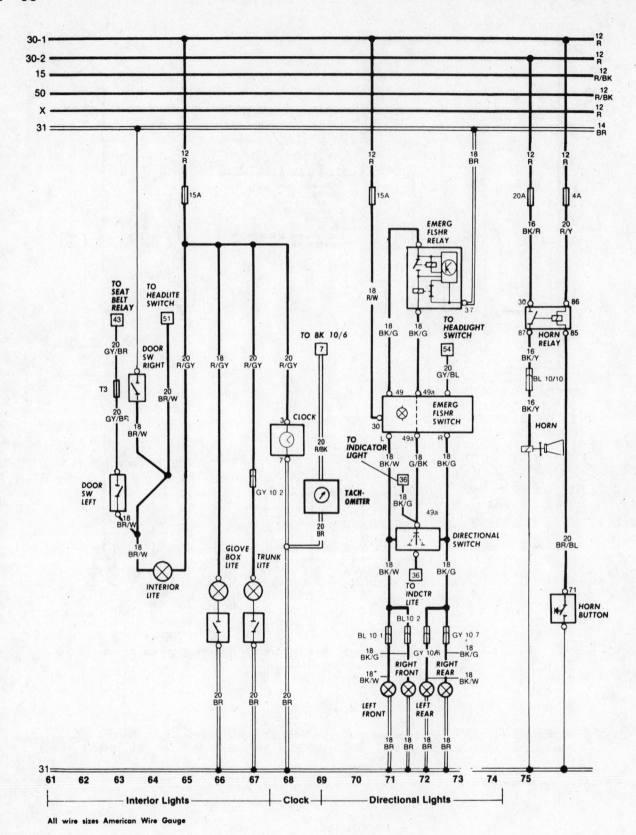

Wiring diagram for 1982, 1983 and 1984 Rabbit and 1982 and 1983 Pick-up models (continued)

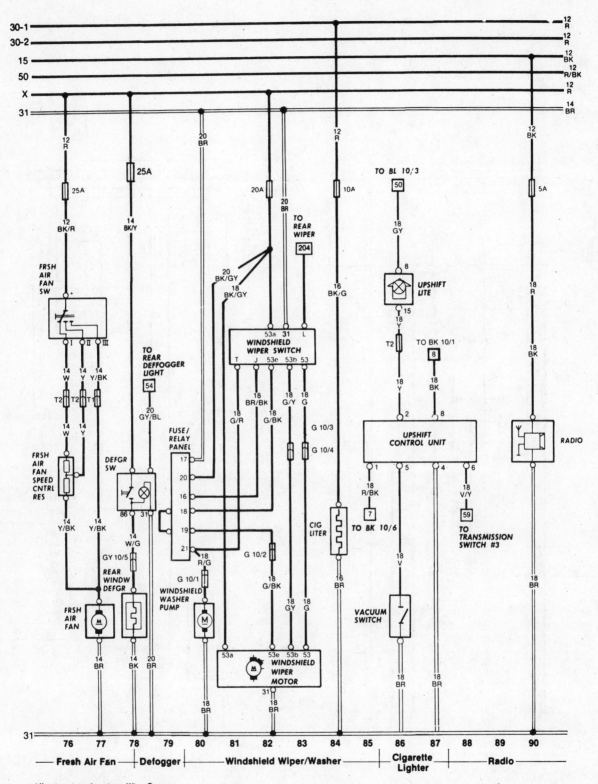

Wiring diagram for 1982, 1983 and 1984 Rabbit and 1982 and 1983 Pick-up models (continued)

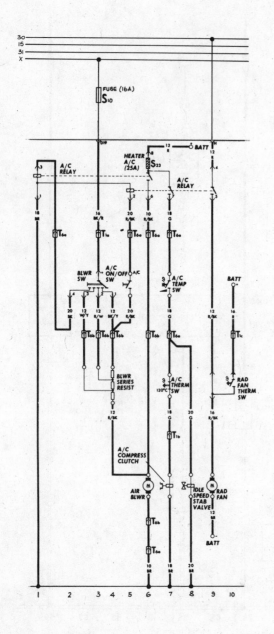

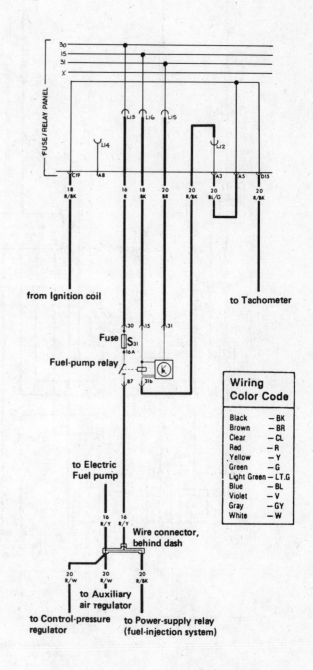

Additional wiring diagram for 1982 Jetta and Rabbit Convertible air conditioning and fuel pump relay

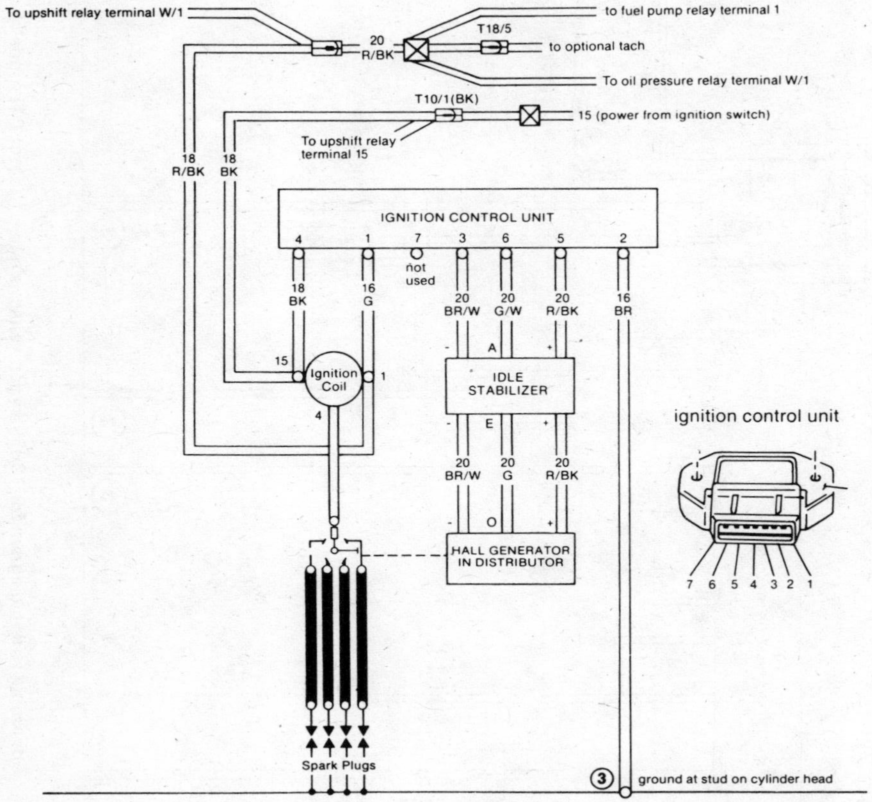

Additional wiring diagram for 1982, 1983 and 1984 fuel injection system

T10/6(BK)

15-power from ignition switch

signal from ignition coil
terminal 1

R/BK
20

31

20 BR

BK
20

④

15

14
BK/G
T10/3
(GY)

14
BK/G

fuel
pump

14 BR

⑥

to oxygen sensor relay
terminal 86

16 R
30

87
18
BK/G
T10/4
(BK)

R/W
20

control
press
reg.

fuel
pump
relay

aux.
air
reg.

18 BR

③

F6-20a

power from battery-30

T10/7(BK)

50- power from
ignition switch

18
R/BK

G
W

thermal
time
switch

hot start
pulse
relay

31b

20
G/W

16
R/BK
50

31

20
BR

cold
start
valve

18
R/BK

Additional wiring diagram for 1982, 1983 and 1984 ignition systems

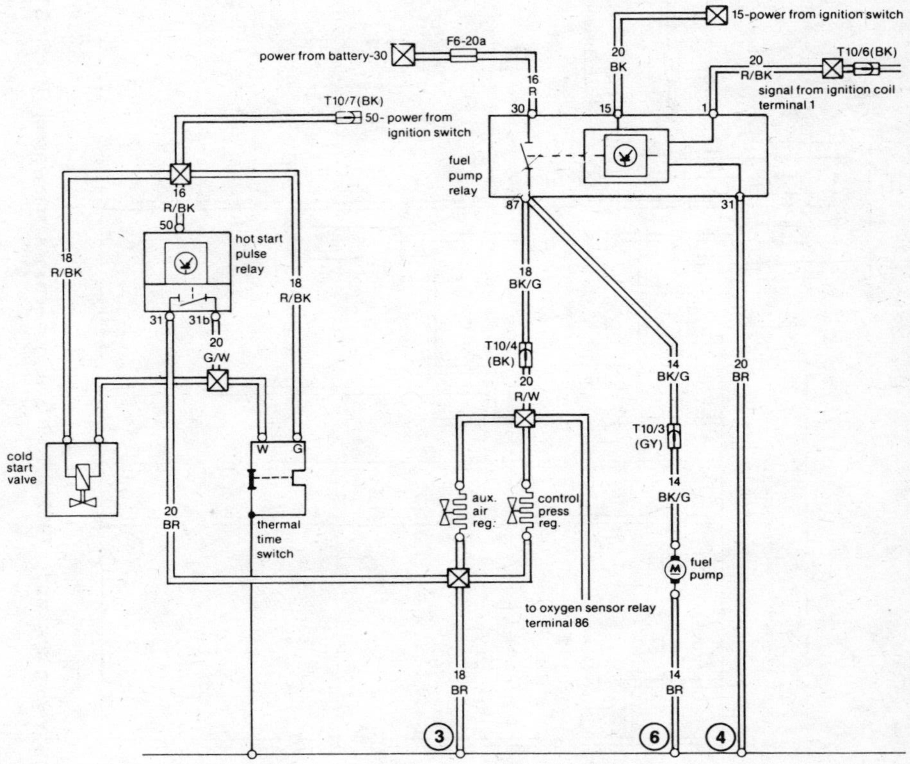

ignition control unit

ground at stud on cylinder head

to fuel pump relay terminal 1

to optional tach

To oil pressure relay terminal W/1

15 (power from ignition switch)

T18/5

T10/11(BK)

20 R/BK

To upshift relay
terminal 15

2
16
BR

③

IGNITION CONTROL UNIT

5
20 R/BK
R/BK 20

IDLE
STABILIZER

A

6
20 G/W
G 20

E

HALL GENERATOR
IN DISTRIBUTOR

3
BR/W
20
BR/W 20

O

not
used

1
16 G

Ignition
Coil

Spark Plugs

4
18 BK

15

To upshift relay terminal W/1

18 BK

18 R/BK

12

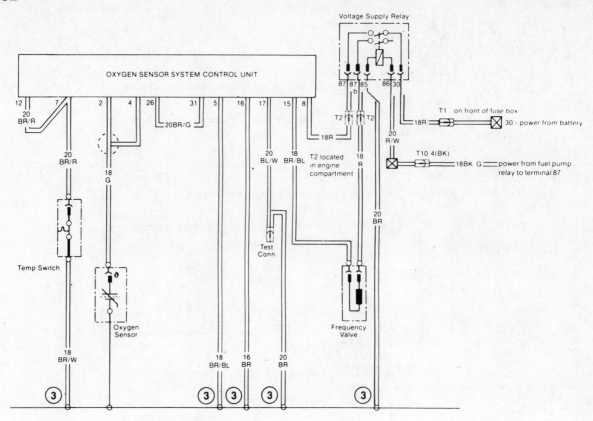

Additional wiring diagram for 1982 and 1983 oxygen sensor system (except Rabbit GTi models)

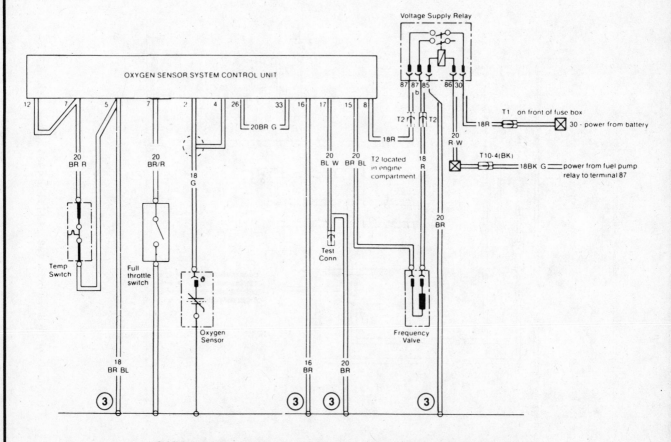

Additional wiring diagram for 1983 oxygen sensor system (Rabbit GTi models)

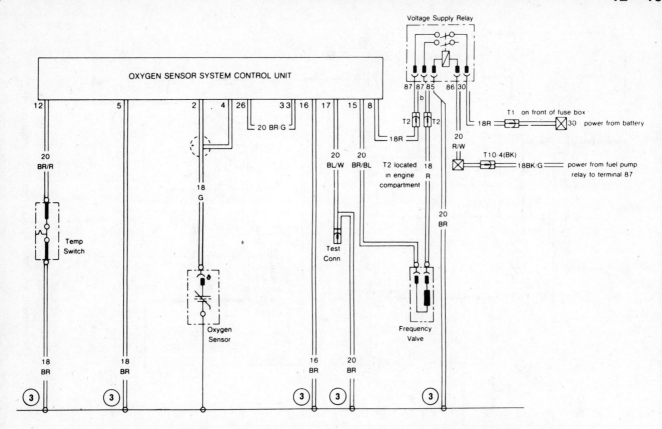

Additional wiring diagram for 1984 oxygen sensor system (except Rabbit GTi and California models)

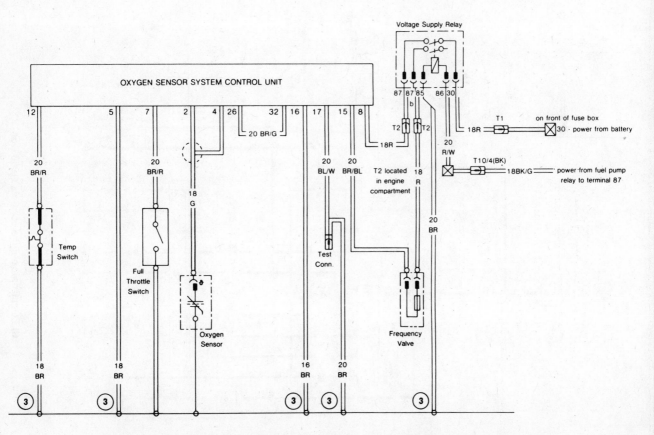

Additional wiring diagram for 1984 oxygen sensor system (Rabbit GTi and California models)

12

CIS electronic engine controls (1986 Golf) (continued)

CIS electronic engine controls (1986 Golf)

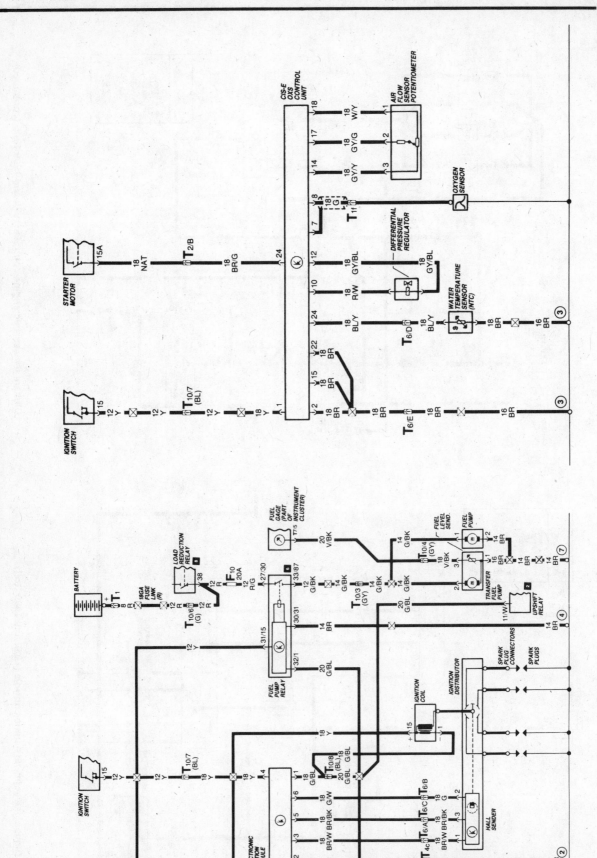

CIS-E electronic engine controls (1986 Golf) (continued)

CIS-E electronic engine controls (1986 Golf)

12

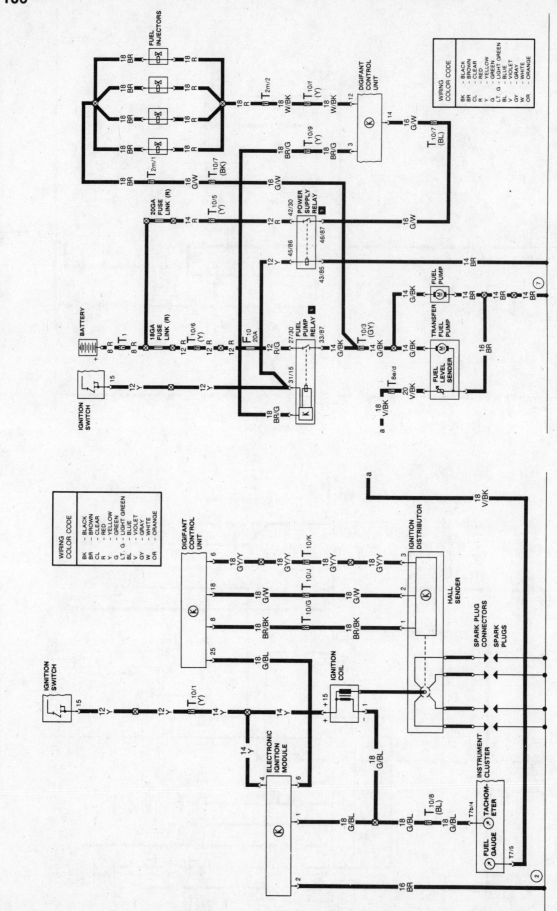

Digifant II electronic engine controls (1988 and 1989 Golf) (continued)

Digifant II electronic engine controls (1988 and 1989 Golf)

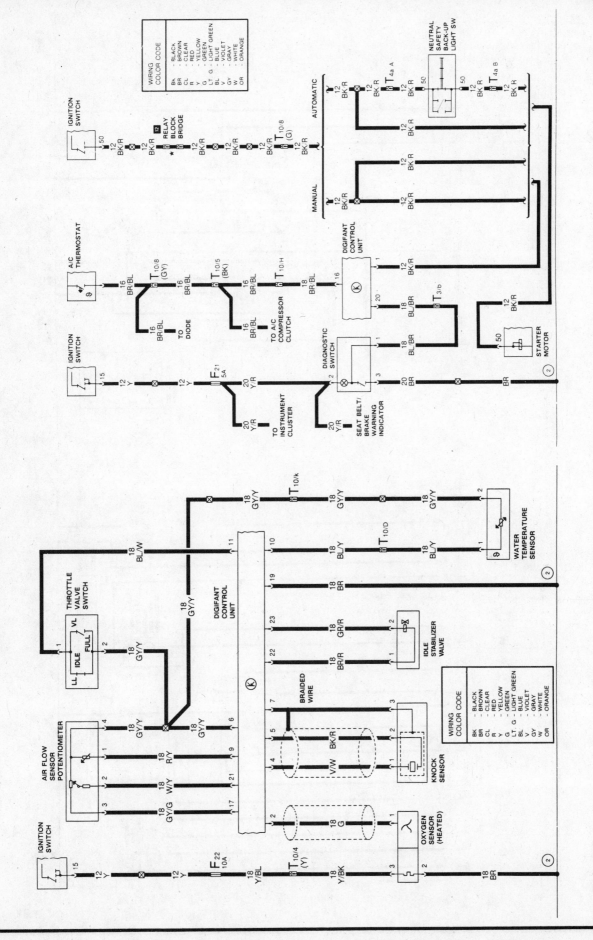

Digifant II electronic engine controls (1988 and 1989 Golf (continued)

Digifant II electronic engine controls (1988 and 1989 Golf) (continued)

12

Main electrical system (1989 and 1990 Golf and GTI) (continued)

Main electrical system (1989 and 1990 Golf and GTI)

WIRING COLOR CODE

BK	— BLACK
BR	— BROWN
CL	— CLEAR
R	— RED
Y	— YELLOW
G	— GREEN
LT G	— LIGHT GREEN
BL	— BLUE
V	— VIOLET
GY	— GRAY
W	— WHITE
OR	— ORANGE

30
15
X
31
S2
10A
C3
C1
E16
P
1.0 R Y
1.0 R BK
1.0 BK R
T2h
BRK LT SW
WIRING COLOR CODE
BK — BLACK
BR — BROWN
CL — CLEAR
R — RED
Y — YELLOW
G — GREEN
LT G — LIGHT GREEN
BL — BLUE
V — VIOLET
GY — GRAY
W — WHITE
OR — ORANGE
B2
B1
1.0 GY BK
1.0 GY R
TAIL LIGHTS, LEFT
TAIL LIGHTS, RIGHT
BRAKE LIGHTS, LEFT
HIGH MOUNTED BRAKE LIGHT
BRAKE LIGHTS, RIGHT
T1h
2.0 BR
1.0 BR
1.0 BK
120
121
122
123
124
125
126
127
128
129

Main electrical system (1989 and 1990 Golf and GTI) (continued)

Description	Current track
2-way idle speed boost valve	16
Alternator	1,2
Auxiliary air regulator	32
Battery	3
Cold start valve	5
Control pressure regulator	34
Fuel gauge sending unit	28
Fuel injection power supply relay	17-19
Fuel pump	30
Fuel pump relay	29-31
Hall generator	9,10
Idle boost control unit	14,15
Ignition coil	11,12
Ignition control unit	8-11
Ignition distributor	11-13
OXS control unit	19-22
OXS frequency valve	18
OXS thermoswitch	21
Oxygen sensor	20
Resistor	18
Spark plug connectors	11-13
Spark plugs	11-13
Starter	4,5
Thermo time switch	6,7
Transfer fuel pump	29
Up-shift indicator control unit	24-27
Upshift switch, transmission	26
Voltage regulator	1,2

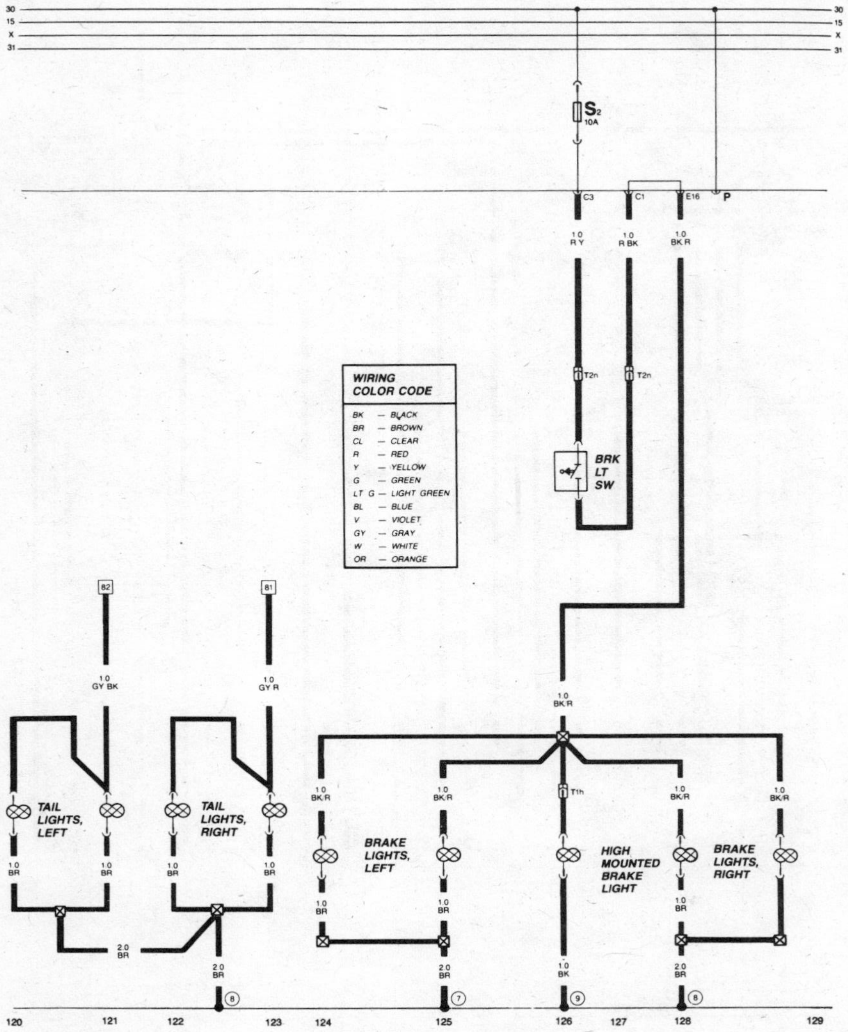

Wire connectors

T — wire distributor, under fuse/relay panel
T1a — single, under fuse/relay panel
T1c — single, under instrument panel
T1d — single, in eng compart, right
T2a — double, in eng compart, near ign. coil
T2b — double, in lugg compart, near fuel gauge sender
T2c — double, in eng compart, near ign coil
T2h — double, under fuse/relay panel
T8/ — eight-point, and transmission

Ground connectors

(1) — battery ground strap
(8) — near cold start valve
(10) — near fuse/relay panel
(15) — in front wiring harness
(16) — in inst panel wiring harness

CIS electronic engine controls (1985 through 1987 Jetta)

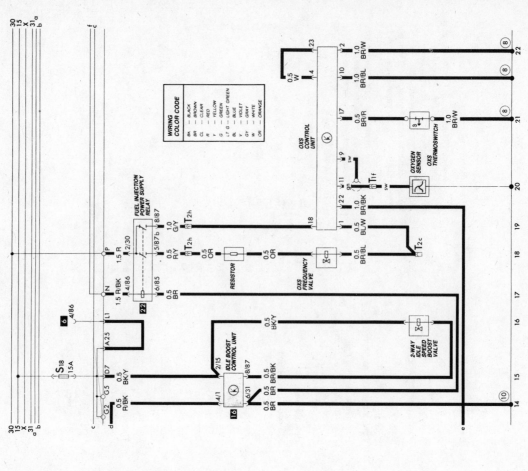

CIS electronic engine controls (1985 through 1987 Jetta) (continued)

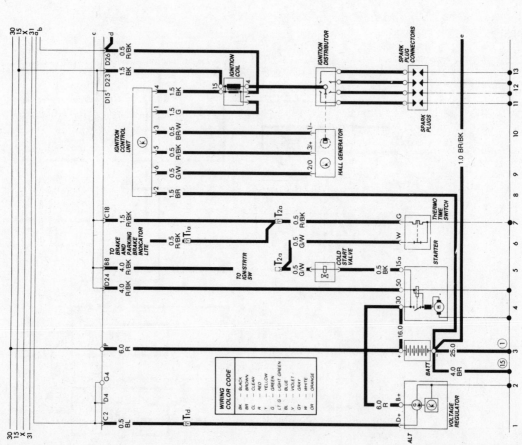

CIS electronic engine controls (1985 through 1987 Jetta) (continued)

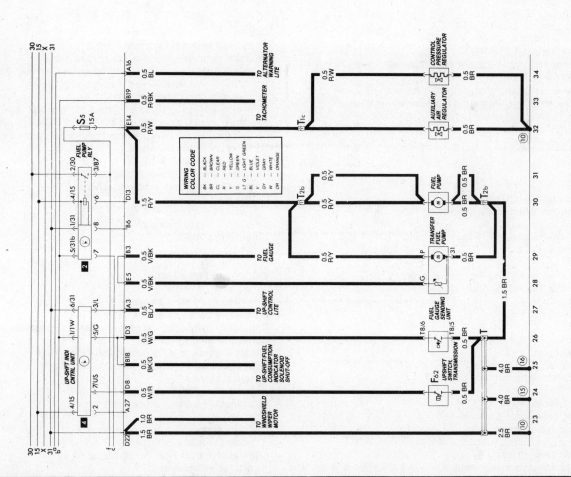

CIS electronic engine controls (1985 through 1987 Jetta) (continued)

12

Index

A

About this manual: 0-6
Accelerator cable, removal, installation and adjustment: 4-7
Air cleaner housing, removal and installation: 4-7
Air conditioning system
    check and maintenance: 3-12
    compressor, removal and installation: 3-15
    condenser, removal and installation: 3-15
    general information: 3-2
    receiver/drier, removal and installation: 3-14
Air filter, replacement: 1-18
Air injection pump, filter replacement: 1-19
Air injection system/air suction system: 6-13
Airflow sensor, check and adjustment: 4-39
Alignment (wheel), general information: 10-22
Alternator, removal and installation: 5-15
Alternator brushes, replacement: 5-15
Antifreeze, general information: 3-2
Automatic transaxle: 7B-1 through 6
    band adjustment: 7B-5
    diagnosis: 7B-2
    differential lubricant change: 1-37
    differential lubricant level check: 1-33
    filter change: 1-36
    fluid change: 1-36
    fluid level check: 1-12
    general information: 7B-2
    removal and installation: 7B-5
    shift cable, removal, installation and adjustment: 7B-2
    specifications: 7B-1
    throttle valve (TV) cable, check and adjustment: 7B-4
Auxiliary air regulator, check and replacement: 4-44

B

Balljoints, check and replacement: 10-10
Band adjustment (automatic transaxle): 7B-5
Battery
    check and maintenance: 1-14
    jump starting: 0-8
    removal and installation: 5-2
Battery cables, check and replacement: 5-2
Blower motor, removal and installation: 3-8
Body: 11-1 through 14
    general information: 11-1
    maintenance: 11-1
Body repair
    major damage: 11-3
    minor damage: 11-2
Booster battery jump starting: 0-8
Boots
    CV joint, replacement: 8-11
    steering gear, replacement: 10-21
Brake, fluid replacement: 1-36
Brake disc, inspection, removal and installation: 9-11
Brake fluid, level check: 1-9
Brake light switch, removal, installation and adjustment: 9-25
Brake lines and hoses, inspection and replacement: 9-21

Brake system, check: 1-30
Brake system bleeding: 9-21
Brakes: 9-1 through 26
    adjustment: 1-30
    bleeding: 9-21
    caliper (front), removal, overhaul and installation: 9-6
    caliper (rear), removal, overhaul and installation: 9-10
    disc, inspection, removal and installation: 9-11
    general information: 9-2
    lines and hoses, inspection and replacement: 9-21
    master cylinder, removal, and installation: 9-18
    pad replacement (front): 9-2
    pad replacement (rear): 9-8
    parking brake handle and cable, removal, installation
      and adjustment: 9-23
    power booster, check, removal and installation: 9-22
    shoes, replacement: 9-11
    specifications: 9-1
    wheel cylinder, removal, overhaul and installation: 9-17
Bulb, replacement: 12-6
Bumpers, removal and installation: 11-4
Buying parts: 0-9

C

Cable
    battery, check and replacement: 5-2
    clutch, removal, installation and adjustment: 8-5
    parking brake, removal, installation and adjustment: 9-23
    shift, removal, installation and adjustment: 7B-2
    speedometer, replacement: 12-13
    throttle, removal, installation and adjustment: 4-7
    throttle valve (TV), check and adjustment: 7B-4
Caliper (brake), removal, overhaul and installation: 9-6, 10
Camshaft and cam followers, removal, inspection
    and installation: 2A-10
Camshaft cover, removal and installation: 2A-4
Camshaft oil seal, replacement: 2A-9
Carburetor
    general information: 4-8
    removal and installation: 4-10
Carburetor (Solex)
    adjustments: 4-17
    overhaul: 4-14
Carburetor (Solex/Zenith)
    adjustments: 4-13
    overhaul and initial adjustments: 4-10
Carburetor choke, check: 1-33
Carburetor diagnosis and repair, general information: 4-9
Catalytic converter: 6-19
Center console, removal and installation: 11-10
Central locking system, description and check: 12-12
Charging system
    alternator, removal and installation: 5-15
    alternator brushes, replacement: 5-15
    check: 5-13
    general information and precautions: 5-13
    voltage regulator, replacement: 5-16
Chassis electrical system: 12-1 through 13
    general information: 12-1
Chemical and lubricants: 0-18

Index

CIS-E Motronic engine management system, description and fault diagnosis: 6-19
Clutch
 description and check: 8-2
 specifications: 8-1
Clutch and driveaxles: 8-1 through 12
 general information: 8-1
Clutch cable, removal, installation and adjustment: 8-5
Clutch components, removal, inspection and installation: 8-2
Clutch freeplay, check and adjustment: 1-20
Clutch release bearing, removal and installation: 8-4
Coil spring (rear), removal and installation: 10-13
Cold start valve, check and replacement: 4-43
Combination switch, removal and installation: 12-4
Compressor, air conditioning system, removal and installation: 3-15
Condenser, removal and installation: 3-15
Connecting rod, installation and rod bearing oil clearance check: 2B-22
Connecting rod bearings, inspection: 2B-18
Connecting rods
 inspection: 2B-16
 removal: 2B-12
Constant velocity (CV) joint boots, replacement: 8-11
Constant velocity (CV) joints, disassembly, inspection and reassembly: 8-8
Control arm, removal, inspection and installation: 10-8
Control pressure regulator, check and replacement: 4-42
Coolant, level check: 1-8
Coolant reservoir, removal and installation: 3-6
Coolant temperature sending unit, check and replacement: 3-7
Coolant temperature sensor, check and replacement: 4-49
Cooling system
 check: 1-18
 general information: 3-1
Cooling system servicing, draining, flushing, refilling: 1-34
Cooling, heating and air conditioning systems: 3-1 through 16
Crankshaft
 inspection: 2B-17
 installation and main bearing oil clearance check: 2B-20
 removal: 2B-13
Crankshaft front oil seal, replacement: 2A-10
Crankshaft rear oil seal, replacement: 2A-16
Cruise control system, description and check: 12-12
Cylinder compression check: 2B-4
Cylinder head
 cleaning and inspection: 2B-10
 disassembly: 2B-9
 reassembly: 2B-11
 removal and installation: 2A-13
Cylinder honing: 2B-15

D

Decel valve: 6-15
Diagnosis: 0-21
Differential pressure regulator, description and replacement: 4-48
Digifant II engine management system, description and fault diagnosis: 6-21
Distributor
 overhaul: 5-6
 removal and installation: 5-5
Distributor cap, check and replacement: 1-27
Door, removal, installation and adjustment: 11-10
Door lock, handle and lock cylinder, removal and installation: 11-11
Door trim panel, removal and installation: 11-9
Door window glass, removal and installation: 11-13

Driveaxle boots, check: 1-32
Driveaxle vibration damper, removal and installation: 8-12
Driveaxles
 general information and inspection: 8-6
 removal and installation: 8-7
 specifications: 8-1
Drivebelt, check, adjustment and replacement: 1-16
Driveplate, removal and installation: 2A-16
Drum brake, adjustment: 1-30
Drum brake shoes, replacement: 9-11

E

EGR (Exhaust Gas Recirculation) system: 6-9
 check and service light resetting: 1-19
Electrical system (chassis): 12-1 through 13
Electrical systems (engine): 5-1 through 18
Electrical troubleshooting, general information: 12-1
Emergency battery jump starting: 0-8
Emissions control systems: 6-1 through 22
 general information: 6-1
Emissions reminder light, resetting: 1-38
Emissions reminder light, resetting: 1-19
Engine: 2A-1 through 18
 block
  cleaning: 2B-13
  inspection: 2B-14
 break-in: 2B-24
 camshaft and cam followers, removal and installation: 2A-10
 crankshaft
  inspection: 2B-17
  installation and main bearing oil clearance check: 2B-20
  removal: 2B-13
 cylinder head, removal and installation: 2A-13
 cylinder honing: 2B-15
 general information: 2A-2
 general overhaul procedures: 2B-1 through 24
 main and connecting rod bearings, inspection: 2B-18
 mounts, check and replacement: 2A-17
 oil pan, removal and installation: 2A-14
 oil pump, removal, inspection and installation: 2A-14
 oil seal replacement
  camshaft: 2A-9
  crankshaft: 2A-10
  intermediate shaft: 2A-9
  rear main: 2A-16; 2B-21
 overhaul: 2B-1 through 24
 overhaul specifications: 2B-1
 piston rings, installation: 2B-19
 piston/connecting rod installation: 2B-22
 pistons/connecting rods
  inspection: 2B-16
  removal: 2B-12
 rebuilding alternatives: 2B-6
 removal, methods and precautions: 2B-4
 removal and installation: 2B-4
 repair operations possible with the engine in the vehicle: 2A-3
 specifications: 2A-1
 timing belt and sprockets, removal, inspection and installation: 2A-6
 tune-up: 1-1 through 38
 valves, servicing: 2B-11
Engine coolant, level check: 1-8
Engine cooling fan and thermoswitch, check and replacement: 3-3
Engine drivebelt, check, adjustment and replacement: 1-16
Engine electrical system
 general information: 5-2
 specifications: 5-1

Index

Engine electrical systems: 5-1 through 18
Engine fuel and exhaust systems: 4-1 through 52
Engine number: 0-8
Engine oil, level check: 1-7
Engine oil and filter, change: 1-12
Engine overhaul
    disassembly sequence: 2B-7
    general information: 2B-3
    reassembly sequence: 2B-18
Engine removal, methods and precautions: 2B-4
Evaporative emissions control (EVAP) system: 6-6
Evaporative emissions control system, check and
    canister replacement: 1-37
Exhaust Gas Recirculation (EGR) system: 6-9
    check and service light resetting: 1-19
Exhaust manifold, removal and installation: 2A-4
Exhaust system, check: 1-32
Exhaust system servicing, general information: 4-52

F

Fan (radiator), check and replacement: 3-3
Fault finding: 0-21
Filter
    air, replacement: 1-18
    air injection pump, replacement: 1-19
    automatic transaxle, change: 1-36
    fuel, replacement: 1-28
    oil, replacement: 1-12
Fixed glass, replacement: 11-3
Fluid level checks: 1-7
Front axle hub and bearing, replacement: 10-11
Front disc brake caliper, removal, overhaul and installation: 9-6
Front disc brake pads, replacement: 9-2
Front end alignment, general information: 10-22
Front fender, removal and installation: 11-4
Front hub, removal, inspection and installation: 10-11
Front shock absorber, replacement: 10-6
Front strut/shock absorber and coil spring assembly, removal,
    inspection and installation: 10-5
Front wheelhouse liner, removal and installation: 11-14
Fuel, specifications: 4-2
Fuel and exhaust systems: 4-1 through 52
Fuel distributor, check and adjustment: 4-42
Fuel filter, replacement: 1-28
Fuel gauge sending unit, removal and installation: 4-50
Fuel injection system
    airflow sensor, description, check and adjustment: 4-39
    auxiliary air regulator, check and replacement: 4-44
    cold start valve, check and replacement: 4-43
    control pressure regulator, check and replacement: 4-42
    coolant temperature sensor, check and replacement: 4-49
    differential pressure regulator (CIS-E), description
        and replacement: 4-48
    fuel distributor, check and adjustment: 4-42
    fuel injectors, check and replacement: 4-46
    fuel pressure regulator, check and replacement: 4-49
    general checks and adjustments: 4-29
    idle air stabilizer, check and replacement: 4-45
    idle speed boost valve, check: 4-46
    thermo-time switch, check and replacement: 4-43
    throttle switches, check and adjustment: 4-47
    throttle valve, check and adjustment: 4-47
Fuel injection system troubleshooting, general information: 4-24
Fuel injection systems, general information: 4-20
Fuel injectors, check and replacement: 4-46
Fuel pressure regulator, check and replacement: 4-49

Fuel pressure relief procedure: 4-29
Fuel pump
    check: 4-4
    replacement: 4-7
Fuel system: 4-1 through 52
    check: 1-28
    general information: 4-4
Fuel tank, removal and installation: 4-50
Fuel tank cleaning and repair, general information: 4-52
Fuses, general information: 12-2
Fusible links, general information: 12-3

G

General information
    antifreeze: 3-2
    body: 11-1
    brakes: 9-2
    chassis electrical system: 12-1
    clutch: 8-1
    driveaxles: 8-1
    emissions control systems: 6-1
    engine: 2A-2
    engine electrical systems: 5-2
    engine overhaul: 2B-3
    fuel system: 4-4
    manual transaxle: 7A-2
    tune-up: 1-7
Generator (alternator)
    brushes, replacement: 5-15
    removal and installation: 5-15
Glass
    door window, removal and installation: 11-13
    fixed, replacement: 11-3
Grille, removal and installation: 11-4

H

Hall sender and ignition control unit, check and replacement: 5-7
Hazard flashers, check and replacement: 12-3
Head (cylinder)
    cleaning and inspection: 2B-10
    disassembly: 2B-9
    reassembly: 2B-11
    removal and installation: 2A-13
Headlights
    adjustment: 12-6
    replacement: 12-5
Heater and air conditioner blower motor, removal
    and installation: 3-8
Heater core, replacement: 3-10
Heater/air conditioner control assembly, removal, installation
    and cable adjustment: 3-11
Heating system, general information: 3-2
Hinges and locks, maintenance: 11-3
Hood, removal, installation and adjustment: 11-3
Hose (underhood), check and replacement: 1-17

I

Identification numbers: 0-7
Idle air stabilizer system, check and replacement: 4-45
Idle speed boost valve, check: 4-46
Idle speed check and adjustment: 1-21

Index

Ignition coil and resistance wire, check and replacement: 5-5
Ignition points, replacement: 1-24
Ignition switch and lock cylinder, removal and installation: 12-3
Ignition system
    check: 5-5
    coil, check and replacement: 5-5
    distributor
        overhaul: 5-6
        removal and installation: 5-5
    general information: 5-2
    hall sender and ignition control unit, check and replacement: 5-7
    knock sensor system, description, check and
        component replacement: 5-11
Ignition timing, check and adjustment: 1-22
Initial start-up and break-in after overhaul: 2B-24
Instrument cluster, removal and installation: 12-10
Instrument panel, removal and installation: 12-12
Intake/exhaust manifold, removal and installation: 2A-4
Intermediate shaft, removal and installation: 10-19
Intermediate shaft oil seal, replacement: 2A-9
Introduction to the VW Rabbit, Golf, Jetta, Scirocco
    and Pick-up: 0-6

J

Jacking the vehicle: 0-8
Jump starting: 0-8

K

Key lock cylinder (ignition), removal and installation: 12-3
Knock sensor system, description, check and
    component replacement: 5-11

L

Liftgate, removal, installation and adjustment: 11-11
Lubricants: 0-18

M

Main and connecting rod bearings, inspection: 2B-18
Main bearings (engine), installation and oil
    clearance check: 2B-20
Maintenance, techniques: 0-9
Maintenance schedule: 1-6
Manifold
    exhaust, removal and installation: 2A-4
    intake, removal and installation: 2A-4
Manual transaxle: 7A-1 through 30
    general information: 7A-2
    lubricant change: 1-37
    lubricant level check: 1-33
    oil seal, replacement: 7A-2
    overhaul
        five-speed: 7A-24
        four-speed: 7A-7
    removal and installation: 7A-7
    specifications: 7A-1
Master cylinder, removal, overhaul and installation: 9-18

Mixture control unit, check and adjustment: 4-42
Mount, transaxle, check and replacement: 7A-6

N

Neutral safety/back-up light switch, check and replacement: 7B-5

O

Oil
    change: 1-12
    level check: 1-7
    seal replacement, manual transaxle: 7A-2
Oil filter, change: 1-12
Oil pan, removal and installation: 2A-14
Oil pump, removal, inspection and installation: 2A-14
Outside mirror, removal and installation: 11-13
Overhaul, engine: 2B-1 through 24
Owner maintenance: 1-1
Oxygen sensor: 6-15
    replacement and service light resetting: 1-38

P

Pads (brake), replacement: 9-2, 8
Parking brake handle and cable, removal, installation
    and adjustment: 9-23
Parts, replacement: 0-9
PCV (Positive Crankcase Ventilation) system, check: 1-38
Pick-up tailgate handle and latch, removal and installation: 11-11
Piston rings, installation: 2B-19
Pistons/connecting rods
    inspection: 2B-16
    installation and rod bearing oil clearance check: 2B-22
    removal: 2B-12
Points, ignition, replacement: 1-24
Positive Crankcase Ventilation (PCV) system: 6-6
    check: 1-38
Power brake booster, check, removal and installation: 9-22
Power door locks, description and check: 12-12
Power steering, fluid level check: 1-11
Power steering pump, removal and installation: 10-21
Power steering system, bleeding: 10-21
Pump
    fuel
        check: 4-4
        replacement: 4-7
    oil, removal, inspection and installation: 2A-14
    power steering, removal and installation: 10-21

R

Rack-and-pinion assembly, removal and installation: 10-18
Radiator, removal and installation: 3-4
Radiator grille, removal and installation: 11-4
Rear axle assembly, removal and installation: 10-13, 17
Rear disc brake caliper, removal and installation: 9-10
Rear disc brake pads, replacement: 9-8
Rear main oil seal, installation: 2B-21
Rear shock absorber, replacement: 10-16
Rear shock absorber and coil spring, removal
    and installation: 10-13
Rear shock absorbers, replacement: 10-12

Index

Rear spring assembly, removal and installation: 10-16
Rear strut/shock absorber and coil spring, removal
  and installation: 10-12
Rear wheel bearings, check, repack and adjustment: 1-34
Receiver/drier, removal and installation: 3-14
Recommended lubricants and fluids: 1-1
Refrigerant, adding: 3-14
Relays, general information: 12-3
Release bearing, removal and installation: 8-4
Repair operation possible with the engine in the vehicle: 2A-3
Rings (piston), installation: 2B-19
Rotor (brake), inspection, removal and installation: 9-11
Rotor (distributor), check and replacement: 1-27
Routine maintenance: 1-1 through 38

S

Safety: 0-19
Seat belt check: 11-14
Shift cable, removal, installation and adjustment: 7B-2
Shift linkage, adjustment: 7A-3
Shock absorbers (rear), replacement: 10-12
Shoes (brake), replacement: 9-11
Spark plug wire, distributor cap and rotor, check
  and replacement: 1-27
Spark plugs, replacement: 1-25
Speedometer cable, replacement: 12-13
Stabilizer bars, removal and installation: 10-5
Starter motor
  in-vehicle check: 5-16
  removal and installation: 5-18
Starter solenoid, removal and installation: 5-18
Starting system
  general information and precautions: 5-16
  starter motor
    check: 5-16
    removal and installation: 5-18
  starter solenoid, removal and installation: 5-18
Steering, general information: 10-2
Steering and suspension, check: 1-31
Steering gear, removal and installation: 10-18
Steering gear boots, replacement: 10-21
Steering knuckle and hub assembly, removal
  and installation: 10-11
Steering system: 10-1 through 22
  general information: 10-17
Steering wheel, removal and installation: 10-18
Strut, replacement: 10-6
Suspension system: 10-1 through 22
  general information: 10-2

T

Temperature sending unit, check and replacement: 3-7
Temperature-controlled vacuum advance system: 6-14
Thermo-time switch, check and replacement: 4-43
Thermostat, check and replacement: 3-2
Thermostatically controlled air cleaner: 6-8
  check: 1-34

Throttle cable, removal, installation and adjustment: 4-7
Throttle switches, check and replacement: 4-47
Throwout bearing, removal and installation: 8-4
Tie-rod ends, removal and installation: 10-20
Timing, ignition, check and adjustment: 1-22
Timing belt and sprockets, removal, inspection
  and installation: 2A-6
Tire, rotation: 1-18
Tire and tire pressure, check: 1-9
Tools: 0-9
Top Dead Center (TDC), locating: 2A-3
Towing the vehicle: 0-9
Transaxle (automatic), removal and installation: 7B-5
Transaxle (manual): 7A-1 through 30
  general information: 7A-2
  overhaul
    five-speed: 7A-24
    four-speed: 7A-7
  removal and installation: 7A-7
Transaxle number: 0-8
Troubleshooting: 0-21
Trunk lid, removal, installation and adjustment: 11-10
Tune-up, general information: 1-7
Tune-up and routine maintenance: 1-1 through 38
  introduction: 1-2
Tune-up specifications: 1-1
Turn signal and hazard flashers, check and replacement: 12-3
Turn signal switch, removal and installation: 12-4

U

Upholstery and carpets, maintenance: 11-2

V

Vacuum advance system: 6-14
Valve clearance, check and adjustment: 1-21
Valve cover, removal and installation: 2A-4
Valves, servicing: 2B-11
Vehicle identification numbers: 0-7
VIN: 0-7
Vinyl trim, maintenance: 11-2
Voltage regulator, replacement: 5-16

W

Water pump
  check: 3-6
  replacement: 3-6
Wheel alignment, general information: 10-22
Wheel bearings (rear), check, repack and adjustment: 1-34
Wheel cylinder, removal, overhaul and installation: 9-17
Wheels and tires, general information: 10-21
Windshield wiper blade, inspection and replacement: 1-14
Wiper motors, removal and installation: 12-7
Wiring diagrams, general information: 12-13
Working facilities: 0-9